Child Psychology

Child Psychology

Gerald R. Levin
Bucknell University

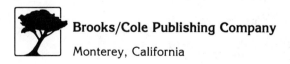

Brooks/Cole Publishing Company
Monterey, California

Brooks/Cole Publishing Company
A Division of Wadsworth, Inc.

Printed in the United States of America

10 9 8 7 6 5 4 3 2 1

Library of Congress Cataloging in Publication Data

Levin, Gerald Richard.
    Child psychology.

    Bibliography: p.
    Includes indexes.
    1. Child psychology. I. Title. [DNLM: 1. Child
psychology.   WS 105 L665c]
BF721.L5214   1982   155.4   82-9691
ISBN 0-534-01229-9

Cover art courtesy of Shirley Holt.

Photo credits appear on p. 496.

Subject Editor: *C. Deborah Laughton*
Production Editor: *Marlene Thom*
Manuscript Editor: *Sylvia Stein*
Interior and Cover Design: *Victoria A. Van Deventer*
Art Coordinator: *Rebecca Ann Tait*
Illustrations: *Alan Arellano*
Typesetting: *Typography Systems International, Dallas, Texas*

To my mother, Rhea R. Levin,
And the memory of my father, George C. Levin

Preface

Child psychology is changing. Along with tremendous growth have come new orientations. Popular terms such as *interaction* reflect more than fashion; heightened interest in memory, temperament, and peer relations is not a fad. Both the cognitive and the biological revolutions are reshaping child psychology. New insights make us look beyond parent-child relations in explaining social development.

The shifts have made the field less isolated than it was. Cross-talk with colleagues in nearly every other part of psychology has become common. Now we exchange ideas with anthropologists, ethologists, and social historians, and these changes were vital influences on this book. I present the field as it is emerging rather than as it was a decade ago, as is apparent in the reference list. Current thinking is also reflected in the structure of chapters and sections. For example, recent thinking about language development made me start the language chapter with pragmatics, how children communicate with language. The concept of temperament is central in the chapter on personality. The chapter on sex differences draws heavily on anthropology and on recent biological research.

My orientation is integrative. I emphasize ideas and findings that add up to a coherent whole and omit isolated bits and pieces. With this approach three theories get the most attention: social-learning theory, cognitive-developmental theory, and ethology, both because they seem to make up the mainstream of child psychology today and because they share Darwinian roots that make them more compatible than often is realized. When attention turns to child-environment relations, I emphasize concepts from ecological psychology and systems thinking, with Bronfenbrenner's multilevel scheme providing a framework to tie the last three chapters together. I am pleased that reviewers have found this a more cohesive text than most and have regarded its synthetic quality as one of its major strengths.

The book is organized topically, making it easier to present current thinking because theories today are process-oriented. The topical approach also makes for more coherence; I could develop and relate ideas without jumping around. The chapters are grouped into six sections that are linked in terms of the kinds of issues and types of lawfulness involved.

The first section is an orientation, an introduction both to the field and to children. I present child psychology as a search for understanding that rests on the interaction of theory and method. Descriptions of the typical child at five reference ages provide a concrete anchor, so useful at the beginning of a course.

The second, third, and fourth parts make up the conceptual heartland. They describe processes of physical development and learning basic to developmental change and sum up regularities in development. Four chapters present the growth of competence; four, social-emotional development.

I treat developmental differences in a coordinated way in the fifth section. I discuss general matters such as methodological issues in correlational research and biological foundations of individuality in context in chapters on sex differences, intellectual differences, and personality.

In the final part the focus shifts from the child to child-environment relations. I develop an ecological framework and use it in examining families and the child's relation to the world outside the family.

The most important pedagogical features of this book were built right in, not added on. I designed chapters to be read as wholes; each tells a unified story, emphasizing key concepts and findings and relating them. I bring abstractions down to earth through concrete examples aimed at making important points easier to remember. Tables and figures illustrate central points.

Boxes and photographs enliven the presentation without breaking the flow of ideas. Boxes sum up new lines of research, illustrate practical applications of new knowledge, and provide descriptions of how real children act. Photographs illustrate key ideas and often remind the reader how varied children are and how childhood is changing.

I have also prepared, with the help of Bruce Henderson, supplementary materials for the text. The student workbook offers self-tests for students and includes observation exercises of children that increase in difficulty as the students' research abilities progress. An instructor's resource manual offers guidelines on planning the course and suggests ways of using the observation exercises in the student workbook in class discussions. Also available are multiple-choice test items that require either a memorized response or conceptual application from the student. These additional resources will, I hope, not only help students get the most out of their reading but also make this a more valuable text.

In writing this book I kept in mind the students who study child psychology with me. They usually start with a sense that there is something important here, a feeling that this is an area with special implications for their lives. Time proves most of them right. They become parents, teachers, nurses, day-care workers, pediatricians, psychologists, and others for whom child psychology is much more than a course passed and a textbook studied.

I have tried to create a book that will make a lasting contribution to the lives of its readers. I give an account of the field that is current and authoritative, yet interesting and digestible; an accurate and balanced picture, but one that students can remember. I present an optimistic picture that highlights the accomplishments and prospects of the field. I have also been honest, avoiding "hype." Above all, I give the reader a sense of what it all means, trying to make it clear why child psychologists think what they think and do what they do.

Acknowledgments

While I wrote, Bucknell University was my intellectual home. It fostered the process. I am particularly grateful for a sabbatical, for countless courtesies from the library staff, and for helpful feedback from colleagues and students.

Early drafts were improved as a result of reactions from Doug Candland, Tom Denne, John Gerdes, Allan Grundstrom, Bruce Henderson, Ernie Keen, Adi Levin, Carole Madle, Ed Marston, David Milne, Elizabeth Nolan, and Roger Tarpy. Discussions with Betsy Comstock, Genie Gerdes, Alan Leshner, Hulda Magelhaes, and Bill Moore helped me in dealing with their areas.

Ruth Craven and Kay Ocker typed the manuscript, combining professional skill with friendly tolerance. Mary Chenoweth, Beth Levin, and Kate Levin assisted with editorial chores. Carole Madle and Adi Levin served as sounding boards.

The official reviewers turned out to be an immensely helpful group. I thank them one and all: Ruth Ault, Davidson College; Audrey Clark, California State University, Northridge; Marvin Daehler, University of Massachusetts; Raymond Dansereau, Hudson Valley Community College; Nancy Eisenberg-Berg, Arizona State University; Jeffrey W. Fagan, Rutgers University; Herbert Ginsburg, University of Rochester; John W. Hagen, University of Michigan; Charles F. Halverson, Jr., University of Georgia; Bruce Henderson, Western Carolina University; Frank Kessel, University of Houston; Richard E. Maslow, San Joaquin Delta College; Joseph M. Pirone, Rockland Community College; Freda Rebelsky, Boston University; Paul Roodin, State University of New York at Oswego; Eleanor Willemsen, University of Santa Clara; Steve Yussen, University of Wisconsin.

The Books/Cole staff provided extensive, friendly, and helpful support. Roger Peterson encouraged me to embark. Todd Lueders guided me for much of the way. C. Deborah Laughton came along toward the end, held up a high standard, and helped me reach it. During production the efforts of Marlene Thom and her staff were valued and appreciated.

Gerald R. Levin

Brief Contents

Detailed Contents

PART I
Orientation

In this part of the book you meet both the child psychologists who construct the field and the children they study. In presenting the psychologists, I emphasize what they are trying to achieve, where they stand, and how they move ahead.

The first chapter is called "The Search" because that is what child psychology is, a journey more than an arrival. A textbook on child psychology is a progress report, not a summary of an enterprise completed. Chapter 1 takes a broad view, explaining what child psychologists seek and summing up where they stand in their quest. In it you are treated as a new arrival, just settling in, not quite ready for prolonged work.

Chapter 2, in contrast, gets down to specifics and demands much more of you. The focus is on theory and method and how child psychology advances as they come together. It is a long chapter, the longest in the book, providing a perspective that should help in reading those that follow. It will help you both in understanding how psychologists go about their business in general and in seeing where particular theories and research methods fit in.

You meet children in Chapter 3, getting a concrete overview of child development by reading descriptions of the typical child at five ages. These portraits are presented as reference points that you can use to put in place details that you'll come across in later chapters. The portrayals also provide you with a basis for seeing general trends and for considering the advantages and disadvantages of approaching child psychology in terms of age.

Taken together, these opening chapters provide you with an orientation that will keep you from getting lost in the chapters that follow. They help you see both what child psychologists do and what child development is like.

CHAPTER 1

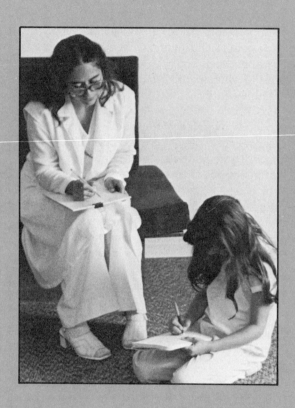

The Search

Millions of babies will be born this year. Their cries will add to the din created by the earth's billions of noisy children. Their smiles will warm the hearts of the adults who care for them. An even larger group of grown-ups will worry about their futures. Child psychology is relevant to all these people, the big ones and the little ones.

This book was written to help you understand the search we call *child psychology*. In this introductory chapter I focus on two questions: What do we seek? Where are we now?

WHAT WE SEEK

The goals of child psychology fall into three main groups: understanding, appreciation, and helping. They link together. The field and this book make more sense when you recognize our aims and see how they connect.

Understanding

At heart child psychology is a search for understanding. Child psychologists look for patterns in what children do in the same spirit that others try to figure out the movements of stars or the growth of starfish. How do children learn to talk? Why do fears of the dark come, go, and sometimes stay? Is a child who masters reading unusually early more likely to read well later? How do parents' actions influence the personalities of their offspring? Dozens of specific questions challenge our curiosity. They all relate to the general questions that define child psychology: How do children's actions change as they grow up, or develop? What determines, or "causes," the pattern of developmental changes we observe?

Understanding and observation

Modern child psychologists follow the scientific tradition in our search for understanding: we test understanding through observation. We look at children and listen to them. If what we observe fits our ideas, we think we understand. This position provides a common viewpoint, even when we disagree, for it involves an attitude about how to deal with disagreement.

Arguments about the importance of early experience illustrate the point. In the United States many think that events in the early years play a special role in determining the later development of the child. The idea turns up in old

3

proverbs—for example, "As the twig is bent, so is the tree inclined"—and in psychologists' theories (Hunt, 1961; Watson, 1928). It has been a basis for efforts at early intervention, as when child-guidance clinics were founded to prevent deliquency and programs were designed to give disadvantaged babies and preschool children a "head start."

But despite the popularity of the early experience idea, not everyone agrees with it. Some argue that heredity is so important in determining personality and intelligence that early experience plays a small part. Others agree that early experience is important but challenge the idea that it is uniquely important. For example, *Early Experience: Myth and Evidence* (Clarke & Clarke, 1976) is filled with dramatic examples of children who got off to a bad start yet turned out normal. They include a study of a group of children who started life in a Nazi concentration camp and failed to form secure attachments to adults at what many think is the critical age for normal development. Another study describes the outcome when older children from impoverished and often pathological homes were taken from unstable environments and adopted into normal families. A third describes the later development of a child who lived for years locked alone in a room with little human contact or stimulation. In all these cases basically normal development took place later, despite early experience of a most negative kind.

How do we resolve our disputes about early experience? One approach is to criticize the evidence of the "other side," to point out weaknesses in the studies and arguments of those who disagree with you. A second is to go out and get more evidence to support your own position. Still another is to formulate a theory that reconciles seemingly conflicting ideas and observations. All three strategies foster the search for understanding. All three reflect agreement on how to find "truth," even though they arise out of disagreement over where it lies.

As you will see in later chapters, the early experience question has helped to foster a broad perspective. Early experience can be important. But just as clearly, heredity and later experience play crucial roles. We try to harmonize the findings by formulating a broader view that helps us understand child development in terms of the interaction of varied factors.

Understanding is not what a child psychologist "thinks" she or he has. The early experience issue is a good example here because these personal beliefs have varied so. There have been "experts" on all sides deeply convinced that they were right and the others wrong. But we don't rely on the expert's feeling of understanding. We look at the evidence instead. Like people in chemistry or biology, we use the "show me" test in our search. What can be demonstrated in observations of children is what decides who "wins" in our arguments.

Prediction

Prediction is our key measure of understanding. How well can we tell what children will do in the future? Can we forecast the details of how newborn Glen will learn to talk? The answer tests our understanding of language development. Which of two approaches to lonely children will produce more new friendships?

Our skill in forecasting helps show which theories of social behavior yield more understanding.

This way the theories that come to be most important are those with the most predictive power (Chapter 2). For example, social-learning theory is impressive because it predicts the impact of the everyday environment, as in forecasting how television shows such as "Batman" and "Mister Rogers" influence children (Chapter 19), and also helps us design ways of treating children that reduce their fears (Chapter 10). Piaget's theory of cognitive development gained prominence as it became clear that his ideas made it possible to predict mental development in diverse cultures and within such varied domains as children's number concepts and their jokes (Chapter 7).

Appreciation

Learning more about children should give more than this predictive kind of understanding. When you study music, astronomy, or American history, you look for a deeper appreciation. You hope to get more of a kick out of going to a concert, looking at the stars, or visiting Washington, D.C., as a result of understanding more. It's the same with child psychology.

Children are fun and fascinating, beautiful and heartwarming, as you probably have noticed already. But a study of child psychology should deepen your appreciation of children. After you finish this book, you should better understand "cute" questions such as "Daddy, when you were little, were you a boy or a girl?" A 6-year-old who offers to share her candy with you should produce a warmer smile then than now. Living with children should be a richer experience after learning more about them.

Helping

Child psychologists want to help children. For most of us this is a central goal. But we look at helping in a special way. We think that helping rests on understanding. Efforts to help children conquer fears or master reading can become more successful only when we understand fear and learning better. Because our understanding in these and other areas still is limited, we take a broad view of what is helpful. We think research on emotional development, learning, and memory in children is at least as "practical," or "helpful," as working with fearful individuals or designing new first-grade readers. As a result, you'll find child psychologists with varied career activities all convinced that what they are doing is aimed at helping.

Because our helping goal is shared by millions of others, including parents, teachers, nurses, social workers, and pediatricians, many of us in child psychology see our search for understanding and our emphasis on the understanding/helping connection as our special contribution to children and to the total picture. Fortunately, there is broad agreement that studying academic child psychology is important for those who want to help children, whether or not they become child psychologists. That's why introductory books on child psychology such as this one are seen as useful for students with varied goals.

WHERE WE ARE

Child psychology is "visible." It's hard to read a magazine or watch television for an evening without meeting it. One reaction is to conclude that with so many "experts" telling people how to run families and schools, child psychology must be an advanced field built on solid knowledge. But a more careful look shows that the "experts" often disagree and sometimes make claims based on obviously weak evidence; so some draw the opposite conclusion: child psychology is a pseudoscience, going around in circles and getting nowhere.

Neither of these extreme views seems valid. I think it's more accurate to say that in child psychology we are near the end of the beginning. A start has been made. By looking back, we can see real progress. But much is still unknown, and we still have far to go. To support this position, we will look first at the roots of modern child psychology (its history) and then at its fruits (the results of what has grown).

Roots

Children have crawled and walked on this planet for at least 30,000 years (Campbell, 1974). For over 1000 generations there has been an unbroken sequence: human parents raised children who grew into adults who were successful enough as parents so that their children in turn became parents and raised children.

So practical knowledge about children has been with us for thousands of years. The child-rearing lore of dozens of societies was good enough to keep us going for hundreds of generations. In this sense, then, child psychology is an ancient field.

But practical wisdom is hardly the same as knowledge put in systematic form and preserved in writing. Cave people kept fires burning without understanding the physics and chemistry of combustion. Their insights about fires were limited in scope and probably were passed on mostly by demonstration. Their knowledge of child psychology most likely was similar.

We must jump over most of human history to about 10,000 years ago when writing was invented before we encounter signs of the kind of understanding that modern child psychologists seek—written statements about children and child rearing.

In the bible of the Israelites, Moses charged his people to teach their children to follow the commandments. In China, Confucius emphasized the vital role of family life to society. The written roots of child psychology are perhaps as diverse as the oldest civilizations that used writing.

But only one root of modern child psychology has gotten attention: Western thought dating back to the Greeks of 2500 years ago and flourishing mostly in the last 200 years. The child psychology we know grew up during a brief part of human history. It reflects the ideas of but one of the dozens of groups that have lived successfully with children.

Modern child psychology developed as part of a more general interest in children. In Europe around 1500, no one seemed to have been concerned with children or with child psychology (Ariès, 1960/1965; Tuchman, 1978). Then the situation changed. The process involved two periods (Kessen, 1965): (1) precursors, writings from 1700 to 1859, and (2) the birth of the field, beginning with the publication of Charles Darwin's *Origin of Species* in 1859.

Precursors of child psychology

After 1700, children gradually became more interesting to major thinkers. This was actually a rebirth of interest; questions such as the nature/nurture issue had surfaced and disappeared repeatedly over the centuries. Now, once again, as thoughts about human nature and how best to cultivate it became central, the child and issues of education and child rearing became important to philosophers (Kessen, 1965). John Locke in England argued the nurture side. He claimed that the mind was a blank slate at birth and emphasized the importance of learning and experience in shaping development. In contrast, Jean Jacques Rousseau in France thought that the child was born good and needed to be protected from the corrupting influence of society. Philosophical disputes like these were to be echoed in the psychological theories to come.

Concrete projects stimulated broader interest (Kessen, 1965). Pestalozzi, a Swiss, wrote a series of books on early education grounded in ideas about the nature of the child. Jean M.G. Itard (1806/1962) translated the revolutionary and scientific spirit of his times in France into a project that excited wide interest. A "wild boy" was found in the woods in 1799. He was dirty, without language, repeatedly swayed back and forth, and apparently had grown up outside human society. Pinel, the expert of the day, pronounced the boy an incurable idiot. But Itard, a 25-year-old physician, saw him as a challenge. He wanted to show that the boy suffered only from a lack of social experiences. Itard worked intensively with him and wrote a report summarizing his partially successful efforts. Itard's student, Séquin, built on those techniques in his pioneer work in educating retarded people. Later, Maria Montessori borrowed from both Itard and Séquin in developing her own famous methods of education (Humphrey, 1962).

As industry grew and rural society was transformed in the 19th century, new problems arose. In London and Paris, babies were abandoned and died by the thousands in foundling homes. Children as young as 5 started work in coal mines and factories, working over 65 hours a week. The new patterns of work and family life suggested that mass education might be necessary as a new alternative.

Concern with these social problems helped set the stage for the beginning of child psychology (Kessen, 1965). Who could tell the best solutions to new problems of child care? In the new era that was dawning, scientific knowledge was coming to be seen as the most solid basis for practice. In child rearing and education, as in medicine and agriculture, the times were ripe for the idea of scientifically sound practices.

Concern for the social problems of the 19th-century industrial society, such as young children working in coal mines, helped set the stage for the rise of child psychology.

Birth of child psychology

The actual birth of child psychology as a separate and systematic field seems to have resulted from two influences: Charles Darwin and his evolutionary theory and a shift from individual concern about children's welfare to more organized social movements and institutions (Kessen, 1965; Sears, 1975).

Darwin's influence.   Darwin's theory that people had gradually evolved from animals made a developmental approach to human nature relevant. It stimulated thinking and observation in child psychology and in a number of fields that later were to influence it: animal behavior, intellectual differences, studies of "primitive" societies, and psychoanalysis. Many separate strands started from Darwin's work. Later they were to be gathered together as part of the complex and varied fabric of modern child psychology.

At first the child was a curiosity to early psychologists, made particularly interesting by Darwin's notion that complex patterns could be understood if you looked at change over time. Early theorists formulated evolutionary views of child development and began to observe children systematically (Figure 1–2).

Darwin also was a pioneer in the observation of children. He kept a "baby diary" in which he recorded descriptions of how his son, Doddy, developed

Figure 1-1 Charles Darwin's theory of evolution was an important influence on the birth of child psychology.

from the first days after birth (see Box 1-1). Years later the publication of some of these descriptions by the now famous Darwin helped foster the growing interest in early development (Darwin, 1877).

Organized concern for children.   By 1900, a new set of organizations and social institutions focused on children had appeared. The first psychological clinic, juvenile courts, and compulsory education were in operation. Child-study organizations had been created and helped popularize the idea that child psychology would contribute to the new institutions for dealing with children (Rhodes & Ensor, 1979; Wolf, 1973).

By 1900, child psychology was here to stay. Important theories had been formulated; systematic research had begun; and organized support for the field had appeared. You might think that these early beginnings were followed by steady growth, but they were not. The years between 1900 and 1960 were marked by surprising ups and downs in activity, gaps and reversals in thinking.

The irregular pattern of development of child psychology seems to make most sense when seen in the light of a historical quirk: child psychology as a scientific field was born and developed largely *outside* of mainstream psychology, the new academic psychology that was born at about the same time as child study and practiced by the first people who called themselves psychologists.

The child's place in academic psychology

When we look at the child's place in the new field of academic psychology, a number of historical peculiarities make more sense. The story can be dramatized by saying that the child's place in the "house" of academic psychology went through four main phases. At first the child was treated as someone who didn't really belong. From 1877 to 1910, the child was a curiosity to some

Specimen box 1–1 Doddy Darwin

Charles Darwin's first child was born in 1839. Darwin observed him carefully throughout his infancy and recorded his observations. He paid special attention to the emergence of emotional reactions because he considered them important and had never seen their development described (Stone, 1980). Never one to rush into print, Darwin finally published these studies in 1877, stimulated by the appearance of a somewhat similar paper by Hippolyte Taine earlier in the year. Thus, 37-year-old William Erasmus Darwin was to become famous in child psychology under the name Doddy, a baby nickname derived from a slang term of the day, Mr. Hoddy-Doddy, a name for a short, stout person (Stone, 1980).

As shown in the quotes that follow, Darwin's observations, like those of many early baby biographers, correspond with those made more recently. Thus, they provide both an interesting historical note and a glimpse of seemingly universal aspects of development.

> During the first seven days various reflex actions, namely sneezing, hiccuping, yawning, stretching, and of course, sucking and screaming, were well performed by my infant. On the seventh day, I touched the naked sole of his foot with a bit of paper, and he jerked it away, curling at the same time his toes, like a much older child when tickled. . . .
>
> The movements of his limbs and body were for a long time vague and purposeless, and usually performed in a jerking manner; but there was one exception to this rule, namely that from a very early period, certainly long before he was 40 days old, he could move his hands to his own mouth. . . .
>
> This infant smiled when 45 days, a second infant when 46 days old; and these were true smiles, indicative of pleasure, for their eyes brightened and eyelids slightly closed. The smiles arose chiefly when looking at their mother. . . . When 110 days old he was exceedingly amused by a pinafore being thrown over his face and then suddenly withdrawn; and so he was when I suddenly uncovered my own face and approached his. He then uttered a little noise which was an incipient laugh. . . .
>
> At exactly the age of a year, he made the great step of inventing a word for food, namely, *mum,* but what led him to it I did not discover. And now instead of beginning to cry when he was hungry, he used this word in a demonstrative manner or as a verb, implying "Give me food." . . . But he also used *mum* as a substantive of wide signification; thus he called sugar *shu-mum,* and a little later after he had learned the word "black," he called liquorice "*black-shu-mum*"—black-sugar food [Darwin, 1877, pp. 286–294].

maverick thinkers such as Baldwin, Binet, and Hall (see Figure 1–2). But as academic psychology became more established, the child was treated more like a stepchild who didn't really belong (about 1911 to 1939). Then the child became an imaginary playmate for academic psychologists. They became interested in children, but invented "pretend" children based on their own

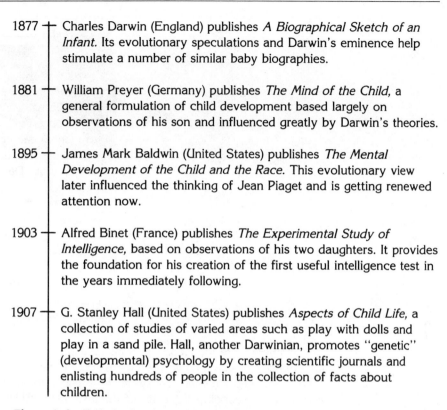

1877 — Charles Darwin (England) publishes *A Biographical Sketch of an Infant*. Its evolutionary speculations and Darwin's eminence help stimulate a number of similar baby biographies.

1881 — William Preyer (Germany) publishes *The Mind of the Child*, a general formulation of child development based largely on observations of his son and influenced greatly by Darwin's theories.

1895 — James Mark Baldwin (United States) publishes *The Mental Development of the Child and the Race*. This evolutionary view later influenced the thinking of Jean Piaget and is getting renewed attention now.

1903 — Alfred Binet (France) publishes *The Experimental Study of Intelligence*, based on observations of his two daughters. It provides the foundation for his creation of the first useful intelligence test in the years immediately following.

1907 — G. Stanley Hall (United States) publishes *Aspects of Child Life*, a collection of studies of varied areas such as play with dolls and play in a sand pile. Hall, another Darwinian, promotes "genetic" (developmental) psychology by creating scientific journals and enlisting hundreds of people in the collection of facts about children.

Figure 1–2 Early landmarks in child psychology

wishes rather than bringing in real ones (about 1939 to 1959). Finally, academic psychologists started to take real children seriously. They started studying them and gave priority to theories based on child study (about 1960). Here's the basis for this oversimplified way of putting it.

Stepchild. Wilhelm Wundt's influence helped to create the child's early status as a stepchild within psychology. Wundt is credited with having founded scientific psychology in 1879. His psychology focused on the workings of the *adult* human mind. Both the questions he asked and the methods he used made the child unimportant and a poor object of study (Kessen, 1965). Wundt wanted to make psychology a pure science, with no immediate, practical use. The main line of psychology, as represented in the prestigious new departments in universities, followed Wundt.

Applied psychology, as represented in psychological testing and in child-guidance clinics, flourished after 1900. But leaders within academic psychology worked to keep it separate from the mainstream (O'Donnell, 1979). For a long period their efforts were largely successful. The fact that applied psychology often focused on work with children also probably helped to keep child psychology outside academic psychology.

In about 1930, child psychology and related fields received a tremendous boost. Several child-study institutes and the Society for Research in Child

How children learned was one of the key questions asked by child psychologists in the 1940s and 1950s.

Development were founded. These interdisciplinary settings provided a base for extensive research on children when such research was not popular within psychology departments. Today it is amusing to learn that when John Anderson was appointed director of the Institute of Child Welfare at the University of Minnesota, he apologized to Edgar Boring at Harvard (O'Donnell, 1979). In the eyes of Boring and "the establishment," Anderson's move from animal psychology to a place where children were to be studied for both scientific and practical purposes was a betrayal. Nevertheless, the research at the institutes led to important advances during the 1930s (Sears, 1975; Senn, 1975).

Imaginary playmate.   An exciting new synthesis dominated psychology in the 1940s and 1950s. By the 1930s, many psychologists (particularly in the United States) had turned from the Wundtian tradition toward *behaviorism,* a new approach that stemmed directly from the Darwinian revolution. About 1939, behaviorism was brought together with two other fields that had been inspired by evolutionary thought: psychoanalysis and cultural anthropology (Dollard, Doob, Miller, Mowrer, & Sears, 1939). The mix showed connections between laboratory and clinic and offered great promise (Dollard & Miller, 1950). More to the point, it put questions of child psychology as central. How children learned and how they were reared in the early years were assumed to be key questions in understanding adult personality and human behavior in general.

But the new mix had a surprising feature. The specific ideas about children came largely from speculation and were not based on studies of children. Freud's ideas about children came mostly from talking to adult patients. The behaviorists' views came largely from experiments on adult rats. Yet these two sources were the main support for theories about child psychology. Much of the relevant pioneer research on children done during the stepchild period was ignored. Despite the child's new status, it seemed as if hypothetical, or imaginary, children were taken more seriously than real ones.

Real child.   Suddenly, about 1959, everything changed. Influential theorists showed how child development was of central importance in resolving arguments about learning, intelligence, and motivation (Harlow, 1949, 1958; Hebb, 1949; Hunt, 1961; White, 1959). Distinguished psychologists from conventional areas started studying children, child rearing, and education (Berko & Brown, 1960; Bruner, 1960; Gibson & Olum, 1960; McClelland, 1958a, 1958b; Skinner, 1954). The concerns with problems such as poverty and education that peaked during the 1960s made it possible to get funds for research on children. Ivy League psychology departments started hiring child psychologists and even training them. In 1969, the American Psychological Association finally established its first journal in the field, *Developmental Psychology*. Today we find a field whose old roots have been fed as never before.

Fruits

Now child psychology looks different. It is more solidly integrated into psychology, but it keeps its practical concerns. We find a few thousand people in the field, and their activities show where the field is.

Child psychologists are busy: doing studies, publishing hundreds of new articles and books each year, meeting together, teaching the field to hundreds of thousands of students, and applying child psychology to varied real-world problems.

The most tangible fruit of all of this "busyness" is the papers, the books, and the articles. No one can read them all. The last major attempt to summarize the entire field resulted in a 2300-page handbook with references to thousands of articles (Mussen, 1970). A look at that handbook or at the article titles in recent journals shows a startling diversity of topics. You can get the flavor of this variety by reading through the reference list in this text or, better, by going to the library and browsing through important journals, such as *Child Development* or *Developmental Psychology.*

What has been gained beyond all the activity and paper? This more important question is hard to answer briefly. (Think of the rest of the book as a detailed answer.) But two points stand out. First, for many questions the activity of the last hundred years has resulted in a big reduction of the room left for reasonable argument. Second, we now have a more solid and promising foundation than ever before for further progress.

Less room for argument

We still lack clear answers to many important questions, but we know a lot and know that many old claims are wrong. We have a detailed picture of how the child develops basic skills such as walking, talking, and thinking. Social accomplishments such as loving, having a conscience, and getting along with peers are better understood. Early ideas that now stand out as myths include the beliefs that newborn babies cannot hear, gifted children face bleak futures, and boys are smarter than girls. Arguments on old questions such as the contributions of heredity and environment continue, but now there are facts that make many positions unreasonable. Informed disagreements are smaller than before. By studying what we now know, we can avoid countless blind alleys.

Foundation for progress

Three elements in the current scene seem likely to foster progress over the next hundred years: our community of scholars, our theories, and our research tools.

International community.   Today child psychologists make up an international community working together. Psychology is being reborn in China (Stevenson, Lee, & Stigler, 1981) and child-development units are being established all over the Third World (Werner, 1979). Ideas and findings travel across oceans and continents in the form of visits and letters, as well as through such formal channels as journals. The importance of this kind of international cross-talk becomes obvious when you trace the roots of current ideas—for example, to Darwin in England, Binet in France, and Baldwin in the United States. With a larger and more varied group working together, the pace of progress should quicken and the scope of the field should broaden.

Theories.   Current knowledge is not a collection of stray facts. Instead, many of our observations tie together around a few theories of central importance. Although present theories undoubtedly will be changed and replaced, their existence makes it easier to move ahead, for even organized error is a better foundation for progress than chaos.

Tools.   The work of the past has given us better tools, or research methods. We have "hardware" such as television cameras and computers that make it possible to study what the tiny baby sees and hears. "Software" such as statistical concepts and techniques make it possible to boil down thousands of observations of children made over 40 years into a few graphs and tables that make patterns clear. All these tools make it easier to do better work.

Relevance

Relevance helped shape child psychology's past and undoubtedly will influence its future. But it is hard to predict what will happen.

The promise of practical value brought public support to a new field. When child psychology was born, when the new institutes of child development were founded, and again in the 1960s, the hope that child psychology would be useful was a key factor in making funds available to support research and training (Sears, 1975).

This concern with practical results has been a mixed blessing. On the positive side it led to a rapid pace of activity that fostered the growth of both basic understanding and helpful applications. For example, recent research on retarded children has enlightened us about children's learning and memory in general, as well as providing concrete leads for helping the retarded. More negatively, concern with quick answers to practical questions fostered impatience. Often the search for immediate applications turned out to be shortsighted and diverted attention from more basic and central questions. Research on child rearing illustrates this problem. Numerous studies of how child-rearing techniques influenced the development of aggression and conscience were conducted before we had basic knowledge of how conscience and aggression developed. Hindsight suggests that the practical concern with child-rearing influences probably slowed progress.

Many child psychologists have become discouraged with the idea of trying to find immediate answers to important practical problems. They think that in the long run it will be more useful to work on central questions, such as how memory and personality develop, first (Sears, 1975).

Meanwhile there are signs that the public is becoming less enthusiastic about supporting child psychology (Sears, 1975). The big spending of the 1960s and 1970s did not result in the quick solutions in education and other areas that some promised and many expected. President Reagan tried to curtail federal spending on psychological research. It is not at all clear how much public support we need or will get (Sears, 1975). Further progress seems inevitable, but its pace is hard to foresee.

Helping today

The rest of this book summarizes our current understandings in detail. Because it says much less about where we stand in relation to our helping goal, a brief summary of that seems appropriate here.

Start with the familiar picture of how child psychologists help: by working with individuals who have problems. The most dramatic gains have come in

Child psychologists have made dramatic gains in the field of mental retardation and are teaching these once-called uneducable children basic skills.

the field of mental retardation. As late as the 1950s, a psychologist's main contribution to the lives of severely retarded children was to test them and advise whether to place them in special classes or residential institutions. Now psychologists can and do teach these children (once called uneducable) basic skills such as dressing and feeding themselves that make a crucial difference in how and where they can live. We also can see progress in such areas as helping children get over fears, learn to read, get along better with peers, and exercise more self-control. All these new techniques can be defined concretely, communicated, and taught to large numbers of people who work with children. We are shifting from an era in which skill in helping children depended mostly on the helper's special talents and experience. Now a broader range of people can use what we know.

George Miller (1969) argued that psychologists must learn how "to give psychology away," to put our knowledge in the hands of nonpsychologists who would apply it to practical problems. Child psychologists are doing it. Fully trained child psychologists (those with doctoral degrees) are spending less time working with individual children now. Instead, we see them in schools, hospitals, and parent groups, spending more time in teaching others and show-ing how to teach the retarded, stimulate language, or handle problems such as fear and aggression. They now are found in toy companies, television production groups, and government policy councils, helping to design products and programs that will influence millions of children. As these new and less direct forms of helping grow, the old image of helping as working with children on a one-to-one basis becomes less and less adequate (Forgays, 1978; Murphy & Frank, 1979).

This shift in how and where child psychologists try to help grows out of new understandings. They will be explained in later chapters, particularly in Part VI. For now the main point is that our emerging definitions of how and where to help probably will turn out to be more important than the more concrete techniques such as behavior modification (used in teaching retarded children and in controlling disruptive behavior) or specific projects such as "Sesame Street" and *Head Start* that have resulted in part from the work of child psychologists.

Applications box 1–2 The researcher as helper

When child psychologists move into new settings to help, they often bring along the "show me" attitude characteristic of the field. An example of this hardheaded attitude, which often distinguishes them from other helpers, occurred in the development of the television program "Sesame Street." Psychologists were involved from the beginning, bringing with them current theories and their own hunches about how these might be useful in novel ventures in which there was little past experience on which to draw. But the psychologists also brought in the "show me" attitude and demonstrated its practicality.

Gerald Lesser served as research director for the Children's Television Workshop, which developed "Sesame Street." He described the early history of the project in a fascinating book (Lesser, 1974). A basic idea was that the "creative" people who actually wrote and filmed the shows would work in harmony with researchers, who would test whether the ideas worked with real children. This kind of cooperation was new and hard to maintain. As you can imagine, artistic types are not pleased when someone uses statistics to shoot down some of their favorite ideas. Researchers, in turn, don't like complaints about their jargon and the pressure for concrete results.

The method worked, however, as shown in the spectacular success of the show (Chapter 19). But the hidden story of bright ideas that did not work and were dropped or changed is an important part of that success story, as was the gradual development of research-based principles that made it easier to generate new program ideas rather than relying on inspiration.

A more recent application of the tradition that Lesser started came after the introduction of Linda Bove to the series in 1976 (Children's Television Workshop, 1979). Linda is a young, deaf actress who was made a regular on the show to demonstrate that a handicap need not stand in the way of a productive life and to teach children to understand the concept of deafness and sign language.

The innovation was largely successful. Children like Linda and say that because of her they think that using sign language is fun. Many have learned some sign language from her. But research indicated that the educational message was not entirely successful.

The findings showed that young children had trouble understanding that Linda signs not for fun, but because she cannot hear. So the producers went back to the drawing board to try to do better. They decided to use more obvious cues in showing why Linda signs, such as "having characters forget to face Linda when signing or talking so that she can't understand them until they turn to her" (Children's Television Workshop, 1979, pp. 1–2).

The research also showed that signing was learned best from simple and straightforward presentations. They thus decided to use more one-word signs and to have central themes that involved repeated signing in clarifying the theme.

Presumably, there will be further research to see how well the improvements work in actual practice. The importance of this researcher-as-helper role becomes clear when you realize that over 8 million children a year watch "Sesame Street."

SUMMARY

Attention in this chapter centered on the goals of child psychology, what we seek, and on where we stand in reaching them. The goal of *understanding* children's actions was emphasized most because it is most basic and central.

Here the idea of *prediction,* the "show me" test of understanding, was underlined. *Appreciating* and *helping* children were presented as aims that rest on understanding. Child psychologists' concern with understanding and with becoming more helpful through better understanding was seen as their special contribution among the millions of others concerned with children's behavior.

A progress report on where child psychology stands today was built around the theme that the field is near the end of its beginnings. Those beginnings, or roots, were summarized in a historical account that focused on the rise of Darwinian thinking and social concern as foundations for the field as it is today. For simplicity the child's place in psychology proper was presented as having gone through four main phases: *curiosity, stepchild, imaginary playmate,* and *real child.*

The full integration of the child into academic psychology was dated at about 1960 and related to the fact that the field had grown in an extraordinary way in the past 20 years. The fruits of past work were summarized in terms of two main achievements: reduction of room for argument and a foundation for progress. A detailed explanation of where we now stand in the search for understanding was reserved for the rest of the book, where it is the central concern. In contrast, progress toward being more helpful was spelled out in a summary that emphasized recent shifts in how and where child psychologists work.

CHAPTER 2

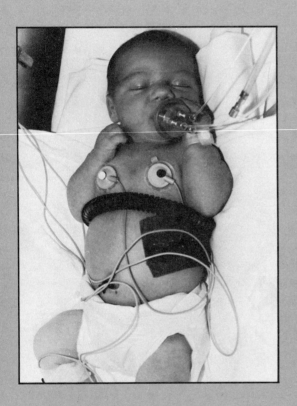

Theory and Method

Our understanding of children's actions moves ahead as we get better evidence and develop better ideas about the meaning of what we observe. In this chapter the emphasis is on how we do it. The problem of getting better evidence takes us to the question of *research method*. The topic of better ideas comes under the heading of *theory*.

Child psychology grows mostly through short articles presented at conventions and published in technical magazines, or journals. Hundreds of these little pieces appear each year; some of them turn out to have been steps ahead. Journal articles, then, are concrete units of progress. They give us a tangible place to start in looking at theory, method, and the two-sided process by which we move ahead.

TECHNICAL ARTICLES

Technical articles illustrate the scientific method in action. They show how the investigator's ideas and the facts of observation fit into a continuing search for understanding. Usually they include four main sections: problem, method, results, and discussion. By looking at these sections in turn and seeing how they link together, you can see how questions of theory and method merge whenever we try to learn more about children.

Problem

A study starts from an idea or question. As in all searches, the direction you take at the beginning influences what follows. Accordingly, a psychologist's preconceptions about what is important and worth studying have a lot to do with what is found. Freudian theory led one generation of researchers to ask questions about how children were weaned and toilet-trained because they thought these matters were central in understanding personality development. Hindsight tells us they were wrong. The evidence they produced showed that how a child was weaned or toilet-trained did *not* make a big difference (Schaffer, 1977). A modern researcher would ask a different question, perhaps looking for a specific connection between how parents respond to the approaches of 1-year-olds and how the children react to their parents six months later. The questions asked today reflect both past evidence and present ways of thinking. The first part of an article tells us about the investigator's ideas and prepares us to look at how these ideas were translated into a process of observing, or gathering evidence.

Method

In the method section we find out how observations were made. All studies involve some concrete way of studying children and/or their environments. Under "method" we get the particulars. What *tools* were used (psychological tests, observations of reactions to peers, interviews with parents, and so on)? What *sample* of children was studied (age, sex, family background)? In what *setting* was the evidence gathered (homes, schools, laboratory)? What *procedure* for making observations was employed (was ongoing activity interrupted to make the study, was activity allowed to go on naturally, was the person who collected observations familiar or strange to the children or informed or uninformed about the purpose of the study)? In the method section we look for a description of how the evidence was gathered, and the description must be specific and concrete enough so that we can decide for ourselves what the evidence might mean or repeat the study if we want to get our own evidence.

Results

The evidence is summarized in the results section. Here the emphasis is on objective facts, findings that all observers could agree on, regardless of their own theories and biases. For example, a study of language development might include lists of sentences uttered by a child at ages 2 and 4. A study of sex differences might include a comparison of the play of girls and boys brought to a standard playroom—how often each group touched each toy, for instance.

Because the meaning of the evidence depends on how it was gathered, the evidence can be interpreted only by looking at the two together. Suppose a study of language development were based entirely on what three children whose parents were graduate students said while playing in front of a stranger with a tape recorder. We would look at graphs showing how sentence length grows with age differently than if some other sample or procedure had been used.

Discussion

The evidence never speaks for itself. It must be interpreted. The interpretation is made by people, even when the facts were gotten by using machines such as television cameras and computers. The discussion section contains the author's efforts to make sense out of the findings. The last section of an article thus gets us back to ideas, or theory. The segregation of the more factual parts of an article (method and results) from the more speculative and theoretical ones (problem and discussion) makes it easier for different readers to look at the same evidence in varied ways.

This look at technical articles illustrates how the search for better evidence (method) and the development of better ideas (theory) link together. We see an exchange in which today's ideas influence the evidence gathered tomorrow. That evidence in turn colors the ideas that follow, and so on. Now we move to a more detailed look at theory and then at method.

THEORY

A theory is a set of statements. Samples of important theoretical statements by Jean Piaget, Sigmund Freud, Lawrence Kohlberg, B. F. Skinner, Albert Bandura, Walter Mischel, John Bowlby, and Erik Erikson follow. They include technical concepts (such as *representation* and *reinforcement*) and often state relations between concepts (Baldwin, 1980).

> . . . the infant lacks the symbolic function, that is, he does not have representations by which he can evoke persons or objects in their absence [Piaget & Inhelder, 1969, p. 3].

> The long period of childhood, during which the growing human being lives in dependence upon his parents, leaves behind it a precipitate, which forms within his ego a special agency in which this parental influence is prolonged. It has received the name of *superego* [Freud, 1940/1963, p. 16].

> The child can internalize the moral values of his parents and culture and make them his own only as he comes to relate these values to a comprehended social order and to his own goals as a social self [Kohlberg, 1968, p. 491].

> The immediate family functions as an educational agency in teaching the child to walk, to talk, to play, to eat in a given way, to dress himself, and so on. It uses the primary reinforcers available to the family: food, drink, and warmth, and such conditioned reinforcers as attention, approval, and affection [Skinner, 1953, p. 403].

> . . . observational learning occurs through symbolic processes during exposure to modeled activity before any responses have been performed and does not necessarily require extrinsic reinforcement [Bandura, 1977, p. 37].

> . . . children's sex-typed patterns and preferences are not merely a child-sized version of those displayed by the same-sex parent. In some areas, such as toys and activity preferences, parental patterns may have virtually no influence on the child [Mischel, 1970, p. 31].

> . . . that the child's tie to his mother is the human version of behaviour seen commonly in many other species of animals now seems indisputable [Bowlby, 1969, p. 183].

> Infantile sexuality and incest taboo, castration complex and superego all unite here to bring about that specifically human crisis during which the child must turn from an exclusive, pregenital attachment to his parents to the slow process of becoming a parent, a carrier of tradition [Erikson, 1963, p. 256].

The role of theory

The main role of theory is to sum up patterns of evidence, to coordinate what we know, and to suggest new findings. Walter Mischel's statement was made in a review of dozens of studies. The concept of sex-typed refers to any action, such as playing with dolls, playing football, wearing dresses, and fighting back when attacked, that society sees as "feminine" or "masculine." By using this concept, making a statement about the relation of children's sex-typed patterns and preferences to those of same-sex parents, Mischel goes from specific past findings to a formulation about children and parents in general. A look at the existing studies would quickly show that many aspects of sex typing and many subgroups of children and parents have not yet been examined. Thus, Mischel's statement points us toward specific, yet new, observations.

Characteristics of a useful theory

A good theory enables us to make predictions, predictions that any qualified person can check through observation and predictions of a kind that can be shown to be false.

Mischel's statement obviously fits these specifications. It predicts that we would not find a close connection between the sex-typed actions of girls and those of their mothers (beyond those common to girls and mothers in general). If we found that there were a close connection, as in the popular notion that "more feminine" mothers have "more feminine" daughters, Mischel would be shown to be wrong.

The fact that Mischel's statement could easily be shown to be wrong makes it more valuable. A theory that cannot be pinned down and shown to be false does not help us in making predictions; so it is not useful.

Operational definitions

The theorists' examples of how terms such as *sex typing* or *representations* can be turned into concrete observations are what we call operational definitions. A definition of aggression as the amount of hitting a child does while in a playroom is an operational one. It tells us what to do to see it. In contrast, when aggression is defined as letting out hostile impulses, we are left up in the air about how and where to look for it. The latter is not an operational definition.

Contemporary theory

Theories of child psychology are abundant. New ones are born each decade; old ones rarely die. We need a reasonable basis for picking out theories that are important today.

A simple operational definition helps. It stems from the idea that good theories are *fertile* — they generate research. An important theory today can be defined as one that influences important new research.

Once we limit our focus to the theories that guide active investigators, it becomes easier to see what ideas are shared and what contrasts divide the field and to examine a few major positions.

Shared ideas among modern theorists

A common core of ideas is agreed on, though different theorists do not emphasize them equally. These ideas stem from the work of Charles Darwin and are part of a broader synthesis that unifies most of the biological sciences

(Simpson, 1949) and some of the social sciences as well (LeVine, 1973). They can be summarized in seven points.

Naturalism.   Child psychologists see children as part of the natural world rather than as creatures apart from it. This idea made Darwin's writing controversial in his time. It contradicted a view deep in the Judeo-Christian tradition that people were a special creation and not to be understood in the same terms as plants and animals.

Action.   Many child psychologists are interested in children's inner thoughts, feelings, and experiences. Others care only about behavior they can observe. But we share the view that actions we can see and hear are what we must study and explain. This agreement about actions, or behavior, as our subject matter follows naturally from our "show me" orientation toward understanding and our shared belief that operational definitions are crucial in testing theories. Ideas about children's thoughts and feelings must be tested by looking at actions: behaviors such as talking or crying, verbal statements of "likes" and "feelings," and physiological reactions such as heart rate changes.

Bodily foundations.   What a child does is always rooted in bodily structure and function. Remembering, feeling angry, and being happy depend on the body, as do seeing or walking. We disagree on the value of trying to explain what a child does or experiences in bodily terms. Some think it useful; others do not. But we agree that injuries to the brain, swallowing a drug, and similar events can have important influences on a child's actions.

Environmental interaction.   A child's actions always interact with some environment. Such simple actions as walking and such complex ones as cooperating always take place in a world that influences them. Space flight and zero-gravity conditions help us see that even an action such as walking is related to the physical environment. Similarly, social actions such as talking, sharing, and hitting are closely tied to the social environment.

History.   According to all theories, what happens as a child walks or shares today reflects some history of interactions in some set of somewhat similar situations. Whether or not the history gets attention depends on the theorist; all agree that it matters.

Adaptation.   All current theories embrace the view that the child's actions tend to result in a better fit between the child and the environment. Darwin's three-element, trial-and-success model turns up in diverse garbs: (1) The child's actions *vary*. (2) Some *selective* principle operates. (3) The actions that "work" are preserved and those that don't work are less likely to be preserved.

Reciprocity.   A newer trend is to emphasize the two-way, or reciprocal, pattern of influence as child and environment interact. Older views more often looked only at the child adapting to the environment. Today theorists emphasize both kinds of influence.

Contrasts among modern theorists

Theorists often argue, despite their common viewpoints. Specific differences of opinion often reflect a few deeper contrasts. Three of these are presented here.

Time scale.   Many theoretical contrasts trace to a difference of opinion on what time scale is most interesting and important when studying children (Waddington, 1957). A hypothetical example illustrates the point.

Suppose that three psychologists, A, B, and C, visit an elementary school together and watch the children at play during recess. They see a familiar pattern (Freedman, 1975). The girls and boys tend to separate so that children (particularly boys) play mostly with others of their own sex. The girls play mostly in groups of two or three, and the boys tend to form larger groups. The girls more often stay in one area and more often engage in such activities

Boys of elementary-school age tend to play mostly with other boys and get involved in rough-and-tumble activities.

as jumping rope, in which there is no winner or loser. The boys more commonly get involved in rough and tumble and competitive activities and tend to cover more ground. The psychologists agree on what they have seen. But when they discuss their observations, revealing contrasts emerge.

Psychologist A says, "Notice how these sex differences parallel those found in varied settings. Similar patterns have been seen in children growing up in the United States and in Bantu tribes in Africa. What's more, some of our monkey relatives show the same kind of sex differences. These sex-typed patterns of play illustrate how thousands of years of evolution have prepared girls and boys to take on distinctive behaviors more easily." These comments illustrate concern with the *evolutionary time scale:* an attempt to understand children's actions in terms of what has happened over a period of thousands of years.

Psychologist B says, "The intriguing point here is how these sex differences usually emerge and peak during the middle years of childhood (about age 6 to 12). Thus, they illustrate how children here and around the world develop according to a universal developmental schedule. Certain sequences of behavior follow each other in a predictable pattern and tend to follow a similar age schedule." Here the interest is in a *life-span developmental time scale:* a concern with what happens over months and years in the lives of individuals.

Psychologist C says, "What's most revealing is to look at the details of how these behavior patterns appear and are maintained. Children are rewarded by peers and teachers for 'appropriate' behavior. The girl who tries to join in with the boys often is rejected. The boy who plays with girls is teased. The new child watches what goes on, quickly learns what pays off here, and quickly learns how to adapt." Psychologist C focuses on the *episodic time scale:* what happens during relatively short periods of minutes and hours.

The three psychologists witness the same actions but interpret them in terms of contrasting time perspectives. A closer look shows that their preferences for varied time scales go along with other contrasts.

Preadaptation and adaptation.   A current way of summarizing a related contrast puts it in terms of *preadaptation* and *adaptation.* Evolutionary theory leads to an emphasis on preadaptation, the idea that every living creature receives a biological inheritance that makes it easier for the individual today to fit in with the kinds of environments in which its ancestors survived. Concern with the evolutionary time scale typically goes with an interest in preadaptation and biological predispositions in explaining what children do.

At the other extreme, psychologists interested mostly in the processes that help individuals make a precise adaptation to minute-by-minute changes in the present environment (and in changing matters) tend to ignore preadaptation. Those who look mostly at brief episodes emphasize learning and factors in the environment that foster adaptation now.

Psychologists who take a life-span view and focus mostly on developmental sequences in individuals also tend to be middle-of-the-roaders on the preadaptation and adaptation issue. When they explain the regularities that take the typical newborn in any natural environment and turn it into a typical

10-year-old, they usually emphasize both hereditary and environmental factors, drawing on both the concepts of preadaptation and adaptation during the life of the individual. Table 2–1 sums up how interest in three contrasting time scales parallels these other concerns.

TABLE 2–1 Time scales and related emphases

Time Scale	Emphasis	Typical Questions
Evolutionary (thousands of years)	mainly on preadaptation	How do features of contemporary child behavior reflect human evolution?
		In what ways is the baby's attachment to its care giver similar to that of other mammal babies?
		In what ways are distinctive aspects of human language acquisition related to the unique features of the human brain?
Life span (months and years)	equally on preadaptation and adaptation	What universal sequences are there in the development of children growing up in diverse environments?
		What universals are there in language and sex-role development?
		What are the contributions of biological and personal experience variables in personality development?
Episodic (minutes and hours)	mainly on adaptation	Through what processes do children learn and remember?
		How are new words learned?
		How do babies come to acquire the language and sex-appropriate actions of their own group?

Contrasting interest in preadaptation or adaptation reflects the modern version of the old nature/nurture argument. Today there is more tendency to see room for varied interest within one broad field, rather than denying the validity of alternative positions.

Root metaphor: machine or organism.   Another theoretical contrast comes from the idea that any theory rests on a *root metaphor,* a central image that unifies other theoretical notions (Pepper, 1942). Some of the oldest arguments in child psychology stem from contrasting root metaphors (Overton & Reese, 1973; Reese & Overton, 1970). One camp takes a *mechanistic* view that starts from the idea that the child is like a machine. The other starts from the image of the child as an *organism,* an integrated living creature. Table 2–2 sums up some of the contrasts. An important implication of the differences in root metaphors is in the possibility of combining ideas. Reese and Overton think it's impossible to integrate parts of mechanistic and organismic theories into one unified position. Instead, they think we must live with alternative models that each sums up part of the truth.

TABLE 2–2 Contrasts between mechanistic and organismic models of the child

Basis of Contrast	Mechanistic Models	Organismic Models
Root metaphor	machine	organism
Source of activity	from outside (reactive child)	from inside (active child)
Direction or purpose	absent	present
Change	reversible	irreversible
Can complex actions be predicted from simple ones?	yes (elementarism)	no (holism)
Can later actions be explained entirely in terms of earlier ones?	yes (continuity)	no (noncontinuity)
Can actions in principle be predicted entirely from outside, situational factors?	yes (one-way causality)	no (two-way causality)

Based primarily on Overton and Reese, 1973.

Specific contemporary theories

Examination of journals, convention programs, and a major handbook (Mussen, 1970) suggests that three theoretical positions now are of primary importance and another three are of somewhat secondary prominence.

Today we find three active theoretical positions reflecting the three main alternatives along the central axis previously described (see Table 2–3). Social-learning theory focuses chiefly on short-term events and carries on the heritage of the nurture position, though with important changes. Cognitive-developmental theory is the most prominent life-span position within child psychology. It incorporates the more balanced view of biological predispositions and social experiences typical of such approaches. The final alternative, ethological theory, takes the ancient nature end of the pole and puts it in the modern perspective. These three mainline positions will be elaborated on and referred to again and again in the chapters that follow. A brief sketch of each is presented here.

Social-learning theory.   Social-learning theory starts from the insight that almost all important human actions reflect the influence of learning. It joins traditional learning concepts from the animal laboratory to ideas and topics from other traditions. In the 1940s and 1950s, problems such as aggression, fear, and child rearing were faced. More recently, the mind has become more

TABLE 2–3   Three important theoretical positions compared

	Social-learning Theory	Cognitive-developmental Theory	Ethological Theory
Time Scale	episodic (minutes & hours)	life span (months & years)	evolutionary (thousands of years)
Emphasis	adaptation	adaptation & preadaptation	preadaptation
Root Metaphor	mechanism	organism	organism
Forerunners	John B. Watson B. F. Skinner	James Mark Baldwin John Dewey	Charles Darwin Arnold Gesell
Recent Advocates	Albert Bandura Walter Mischel Robert Sears	Jean Piaget Lawrence Kohlberg Heinz Werner	Daniel Freedman John Bowlby

important. Today we find in social-learning theory a position that is a major departure from its mechanistic roots (White, 1970, 1976). As found in contributions by such authors as Albert Bandura (1977) and Walter Mischel (1970), old strengths are preserved while ideas more relevant to distinctively human behavior are now prominent.

A continuing feature of the learning-theory tradition is an emphasis on experimental research. This kind of investigation fits in well with an interest in short-term processes, a focus on how the child's environment influences the child, and a concern for practical applications.

In recent years many of the experiments have been on observational learning (learning by imitation). Early work demonstrated that children could learn much just by watching other people or movies or television. This simple fact has broad implications. The finding that a child can learn new words or actions such as hitting without making visible reactions during the learning process challenged the traditional learning-theory emphasis on observable responses as necessary for such learning. The recognition of the importance of learning through observing others made the theory more social.

If a child quietly watches a television program today and then imitates an action from it tomorrow, we must assume that the child has some way of symbolizing, or representing, the action so as to store the memory over time. Thus, concern with observational learning brought in a more mentalistic focus on attention, symbolization, and memory.

Walter Mischel (1974) put children in conflict between taking the less-preferred candy now and waiting for a candy they liked better. The experiments show that self-control varies greatly from situation to situation. For example, when told to think about the candy, 4-year-olds wait only for about 2 minutes. When they are told to think about something else, the average wait moves up to a surprising 17 minutes.

This research shows both the new scope of social-learning theory and some old features. The new problem of self-control comes into the laboratory, but the old idea that manipulable outside factors have a great impact continues. Similarly, the idea that a child's behavior is discriminative, varying with the situation, and reversible, changing when the situation changes, remains.

Cognitive-developmental theory.   Cognitive-developmental theory rests on two key ideas: (1) The nature of the child's mind is reflected in virtually all his or her actions. (2) When a child grows up in any "normal" environment, his or her mind changes dramatically and predictably from birth to maturity. Taken together these ideas result in a position with broad implications. It says that if we are to understand a child's sense of humor, fears, ideas about right and wrong, concept of a "good child," or reaction to varied methods of teaching arithmetic, we must pay attention to where the child stands in terms of cognitive, or mental, development.

Research on cognitive development once could be summed up almost entirely in terms of ideas originating with one person, Jean Piaget (Chapter 7). But now we are entering a new era. The cognitive-developmental position is becoming neo-Piagetian: keeping a basically Piagetian orientation, modifying or dropping many of his specific assertions, and bringing in ideas and evidence from other sources. The trend is perhaps clearest in a book by John Flavell (1977), who helped launch the "Piaget boom" in 1963.

The Piagetian contributions that remain prominent are the overall model of how the child's mind works and the description of the major steps in mental development from birth to maturity.

Flavell retains Piaget's basic picture of the child: actively adapting to the environment, going out to explore and learn rather than waiting for a "push" and simply reacting, and gradually coming to understand reality through a series of small modifications of old understandings. This picture of the child's mind makes learning and mental development inevitable in any of the natural environments in which biologically normal children grow up.

Flavell also keeps Piaget's general description of the path that such mental development takes. The baby is seen as having a practical intelligence that deals only with concrete and here-and-now matters, such as objects and problems of dealing with them. Toward the end of the second year after birth, a new intellectual era dawns. The child becomes capable of symbolizing, or representing reality through images and words. Now the child can deal with absent objects, as in saying "Ball!" in requesting a ball that was played with yesterday. Mental constructions make it possible to treat sand as pretend food and to imitate the way someone else poured milk. At about 6 years the child's symbolic activities become more systematic and organized. The child now becomes able to deal with rules, such as those of arithmetic, checkers, and acting like a "good child." The elementary-school child is able to reason, but on a less abstract level than that of the teenager. Formal reasoning of the kind characteristic of geometry and algebra becomes possible only in the last stage of mental development.

The non-Piagetian features of the cognitive-developmental position favored by Flavell and others include the following:

1. A reduction of the emphasis on Piaget's concepts and terms
2. A replacement of Piaget's concepts with ones from such fields as perception, learning, thinking, and memory
3. A picture of mental development that puts more emphasis on continuous, small changes and less on dramatic, big ones
4. A view that the younger child's failure to perform like the adult often reflects situational factors rather than inability
5. More emphasis on the role of specific learning experiences in influencing the particular lines of intellectual progress

The information-processing orientation has been an important source of non-Piagetian ideas about cognitive development. Theorists from this perspective focus on how people deal with information, emphasizing such processes as attention and memory (Chapter 8). Developmental studies of information processing have become common and now provide an important alternative to a Piagetian view. Flavell (1977) illustrated that current trend by bringing together ideas from Piaget and the information-processing perspective.

An important trend that parallels one in social-learning theory can be seen in the work of Flavell, Lawrence Kohlberg, and other cognitive-developmentalists. The cognitive-developmental approach is being applied more and more to social and emotional development. Kohlberg (1963) first advanced Piaget's work on how the child comes to understand right and wrong (moral development). Later he took the cognitive-developmental approach into new areas, such as how children come to understand society's way of assigning contrasting roles for females and males (sex-role development) and how their understandings influence their feelings and actions (Kohlberg, 1966). Still more recently he has related the position to such areas as the self (Kohlberg, 1969) and to mental health questions (Kohlberg, LaCrosse, & Ricks, 1972). Flavell (1977) and others (Damon, 1977; Selman, 1980) have been pushing forward in similar fashion on questions such as how children understand other people and themselves.

With both social-learning theory and cognitive-developmental theory moving into these social-emotional areas, we find a stimulating situation. Conflicting ideas generate new research. As knowledge grows, a new synthesis may emerge (Baldwin, 1980; Bronfenbrenner, 1963).

Ethological theory. *Ethology* can be used in two ways. In a narrow sense it refers to the specific concepts developed by Konrad Lorenz, Niko Tinbergen, and other biologists who took an evolutionary approach to animal behavior. In a broader sense it refers to an attitude, or orientation, in which behavior is looked at in its natural context and approached in terms of evolution and adaptive function. This broader attitude is more relevant for child psychology (E. H. Hess, 1970) and is the one taken here.

An ethological, or evolutionary, orientation in the broader sense is as old as child psychology. It was taken by Charles Darwin. Herbert Spencer, a 19th-century theorist with an evolutionary viewpoint, promoted ideas about development now identified with Freud and Piaget (Fishbein, 1976). These pioneers and others to follow who emphasized biological determinants, such as Gesell (1954), took what now would be called an ethological approach.

Today we find a renewed interest in the evolutionary approach (Blurton Jones, 1972; Slater, 1980; Wilson, 1975). John Bowlby's (1969) work on attachment is an important illustration. He used evolutionary concepts to explain how human babies become attached to the people who take care of them. He emphasized similarities in the actions of birds, monkeys, and humans. Many child psychologists who take this kind of approach refer to their orientation as ethological, whether or not they agree with the specific ideas of the biologists who popularized the term.

The ethological position is gaining in importance, even though it remains less prominent than the social-learning and cognitive-developmental theories. It deserves attention because it supplements the other views and provides a modern way of thinking about the nature, or biological, position that always has been part of our field.

Three other positions deserve emphasis, even though they do not seem as central as the three just described: Freud's psychoanalytic theory, Erikson's theory, and behaviorism.

Frontiers box 2-1 Rhythmical behavior in infancy

Babies spend lots of their time engaged in rhythmical actions such as bouncing, banging, kicking, waving, and swaying. These common behaviors have rarely been studied carefully, but a recent study by Esther Thelen (1981) was the exception. She thoroughly examined the rhythmical behavior of 20 babies and, in so doing, illustrated the nature and the value of an ethological approach.

Thelen studied rhythmic behavior as a zoologist might study a little-understood behavior in any species, cataloging the behavior in its natural settings and then using her findings to answer the basic questions of interest to ethologists.

The babies were followed longitudinally in their own homes from age 4 weeks to 1 year. Every two weeks an observer visited the baby at home and observed for one hour as the baby went about its regular activities. All bouts of "rhythmical stereotypy" (movements of body parts or the whole body repeated in the same form at least three times at regular short intervals of about a second or less) were recorded.

The babies spent an average of about 5% of their time in rhythmic behavior, with some babies at some times spending as much as 40% of the observation hour doing it. The total of more than 16,000 bouts of rhythmical stereotypy included 47 distinct movements.

In analyzing the behavior Thelen focused on the four classic questions basic to an ethological analysis (Tinbergen, 1951): (1) Why did the animal perform the behavior *now* (*causal*)? (2) How did the animal *grow* to respond in that way (*developmental*)? (3) What *survival value* does the behavior have (*functional*)? (4) How did this group of animals come to solve the problem of survival in this way (*evolutionary origins*)?

When the developmental question was investigated, it became clear that rhythm was a developmental phenomenon, rising to a peak in the middle of the first year and then dropping off. The development of stereotypies was found to relate to motor development generally. The onset of a particular kind of movement was related to a baby's level of motor development. Actually, landmarks such as sitting up or grasping could be predicted by the prior emergence of stereotypy involving the same muscle group. It looked as if the rhythmical behaviors were transitions between uncoordinated behavior and voluntary, coordinated motor control.

Immediate causation was studied by looking at when the behavior occurred. Most often it came when the babies were in nonalert states, particularly during "fussiness." It also was more likely when there was stimulus change, as when a toy was presented or feeding was interrupted. Thelen thought the data indicated that rhythmic behavior came when the situation called on the baby to "do something" and no voluntary behavior was available.

Adaptive function was suggested by the fact that the babies who showed the most stereotypy were those who got the least movement stimulation—were carried, rocked, bounced, and jiggled the least—and by adult responses to videotapes suggesting that they would respond more quickly to a fussy baby who acted rhythmically. Perhaps rhythmic behavior hastens care giving.

The difficult question of evolutionary origins was approached by a microanalysis of one behavior pattern: early kicking. Frame-by-frame examination of videotapes indicated that the timing of stereotyped kicks was remarkably uniform and similar to that of stereotyped movements in other species. Close parallels were found between the movement pattern in early kicking and that seen later in walking. These findings suggested that the kicking reflected an innate program in the nervous system, basic to walking and related to similar programs in other species.

Taken together, the findings suggested that the rhythmic stereotypies reflect old evolutionary patterns used in a special way by humans because human development includes an unusually long period before voluntary movements are fully mature.

Freud's psychoanalytic theory.   Sigmund Freud was trained as a neurologist, a physician who specialized in disorders of the nervous system. He got into psychology because in his era "neurotics" came to neurologists with their problems. As a result of his exposure to the psychological problems of adults, Freud became a psychological theorist starting when he was in his forties. During the remainder of his long and productive life he wrote a shelf full of books rich in concepts and hypotheses about human personality and how it developed. He pointed out important happenings in normal development, such as the baby's attachment to its mother and the development of sex role and conscience in a creature who started with neither of these. Freud formulated a stage theory of development that related adult disorders to what he thought were interruptions in the normal sequence of early development.

The scope and grandeur of Freud's theory caught the imagination of many concerned with social and emotional development, even though Freud's ideas were not based on systematic observation of children. Much pioneer research on problems such as child rearing, personality development, and fear was influenced by both Freud's insights into what were major features of child development and his more specific concepts and hypotheses.

A pattern has emerged. Often we find that Freud's more general ideas about what was important have been confirmed, but his specific concepts and hypotheses have not been. For example, the quotes from Kohlberg and Mischel earlier in this chapter follow Freud in emphasizing moral development and sex typing as important, but in each quote there is a position that negates specific Freudian ideas. Kohlberg's emphasis on the child's understanding and goals as limiting the extent to which a child takes over the parental values contradicts Freud's emphasis and is in line with our current picture. Similarly, Mischel's denial of the special contribution of the same-sex parent in sex typing illustrates how the studies inspired by Freud led us away from his specific claims.

Erikson's stage theory.   Erikson outlined a theory that closely parallels Freud's, but with significant changes and additions that make it more relevant today.

Erikson (1963) formulated a stage theory that sums up development in terms of a series of crises that the child must resolve:

1. *Basic trust versus basic mistrust.* Children must develop confidence in the predictability of the world and in their ability to influence it.
2. *Autonomy versus shame and doubt.* Children must learn to cope with problems resulting from greater ability to move and control muscles. Self-control and willpower must be developed.
3. *Initiative versus guilt.* Children must develop the ability to take initiative in achieving goals without going too far.
4. *Industry versus inferiority.* Children must learn how to win approval through mastering and successfully using culturally approved skills.
5. *Identity versus role confusion.* Puberty and rapid growth confront adolescents with the need to question and search for a new sense of continuity and sameness. Occupational and sex-role identity must be established.

Successful resolution of each crisis is seen as necessary for normal development. Although the early crises depend heavily on Freud's original thinking, Erikson went beyond Freud in dealing with adolescence and adulthood. As a result, Erikson has been of special interest to psychologists whose interest is in personality development after childhood.

Erikson's theory deals with the development of the self, or ego, one of the most central yet ignored problems in child psychology. Developments within both cognitive-developmental (Kohlberg, 1969; Lewis & Brooks, 1975) and social-learning theory (Bandura, 1977; Mischel, 1973) suggest that anecdote and speculation on such questions as the origins of the self and of self-regulation are being replaced by systematic research. Perhaps the growth of such work on problems of self will reduce Erikson's importance; maybe it will increase it. The question is where such work takes us.

Behaviorism.   Behaviorism was created by John B. Watson (1928) and today is most prominently advanced by B. F. Skinner (1953) and his followers. It was inspired by work on animal learning (Pavlov, 1941; Thorndike, 1898) and often is referred to as learning theory. One of its most important contributions was to serve as a basis for social-learning theory. However, in recent years an active group of behaviorists has popularized behavior-modification or conditioning approaches to a variety of children's problems (Chapter 5). It is in practically oriented studies that we can distinguish a more traditional behaviorism from the social-learning theory that is so prominent in theoretically oriented research.

METHODS: GETTING BETTER EVIDENCE

Investigating children's behavior is like doing a good newspaper story. You have to go where the story is (find children and observe them). You focus on the facts and try to keep out opinions and interpretations until the evidence is in.

Collecting observations

There is a variety of ways of collecting the facts (Mussen, 1960), differing most centrally in whether you interrupt the normal stream of events to get them (obtrusive or controlled methods) or try to let life go on naturally (unobtrusive or naturalistic methods).

The normal stream of events is not interrupted in any way while collecting observations using unobtrusive or naturalistic techniques (Irwin & Bushnell, 1980; Wright, 1960):

1. *Case studies.* Everyday observations are recorded and summarized with little or no system for observing or categorizing what is observed. As in the early baby biographies, there are no standard definitions or units.

2. *Specimen records.* A continuous narrative is made of what happens during a relatively short period of time. For example, a full conversation might be recorded so as to include all words and pauses.

3. *Time sampling.* Behavior is recorded during a relatively large number of short periods of time. For example, the investigator might look for aggressive behavior during 600 periods of one minute each, distributed over all recess periods in an elementary school during one month. Children are each observed in turn for one minute. Each instance of aggressive behavior (hitting, teasing, taking toys, and so on) would be tallied during each time period.

4. *Event sampling.* The investigator watches a group of children and waits for a particular kind of behavior, such as helping, to occur. Each time one of these events of interest occurs, the observer records it and when it happened.

5. *Rating scales.* The child is observed for either a short or a long period of time. The child's activity during the time period is then rated according to a standard scale. For example, after watching children in a day-care center for a week, an observer might rate each with respect to activity level, selecting one category out of several for each child—for example, inactive (rarely moves around), average amount of moving around, or active (moves around frequently).

The investigator interrupts normal activity to make observations using obtrusive or controlled techniques. The following examples illustrate these techniques (Achenbach, 1978; Levin, 1973; Mussen, 1960):

1. *Tests.* The investigator presents a standard series of situations, or questions—for example, asking each child to "draw a man, draw me the best man that you can."

2. *Interview.* The researcher holds a conversation in which the general focus and perhaps the particular questions are decided on in advance. Piaget combined the test and interview approach in a clinical method designed to clarify why children responded to test questions as they did. For example, after wrong answers children were asked to explain why they answered as they did or were given related questions designed to see how their minds worked.

3. *Experiments.* In experiments there is a maximum degree of control over the observation situation. In laboratory research all aspects of the situation are set up by the investigator and held constant so that only the variable of interest is manipulated. For example, babies are studied in research cubicles with their mothers seated behind them out of sight. Then a series of pictures is shown at constant time intervals under standard levels of illumination. Videotapes of the children's eyes make it possible to tell how long they looked at each picture.

Major contributions often have come from researchers who used tools no more complicated than those of a newspaper reporter. Jean Piaget watched his own three children grow up and made notes on what he saw. Two landmark books on infancy were based on evidence gathered through this method (Piaget, 1952, 1954). Roger Brown (1973) and his group studied language development through a method almost as simple. They repeatedly visited three children in their homes and made tape recordings of their spontaneous remarks. Later the recordings were transcribed. The evidence revealed more about language development than that from many fancier studies.

New methods of getting evidence can open up whole new fields. Alfred Binet's invention of a convenient intelligence test is perhaps our most dramatic example (Wolf, 1973). Binet's test made it possible to study what had not been studied before. Soon great masses of evidence were collected, and new insights resulted (Chapter 15). Robert Fantz (1961) devised new techniques for investigating what babies look at, with similar results. He showed how you could observe and record what a baby looked at by looking at the baby's eyes or photographing them from behind the target. Others followed his lead and we soon had dozens of studies of infant vision (Chapter 6).

The early progress from good reporting, or using a new tool, often produces a new situation: interpretation becomes more important. We wonder how to make sense out of Piaget's observations or of the thousands of scores from Binet's new test. We wonder how far to trust the early findings.

Psychologists have used tests of drawing as parts of intelligence testing since the earliest days of testing.

Now progress requires *better* evidence, not just more; so complicated and sophisticated methods become crucial. A good way to make sense out of them is to see them as part of a strategy for dealing with the obstacles that face us.

Obstacles and strategies

Unavoidable obstacles stand in the way whenever we try to get better evidence on how children act. Standard strategies for dealing with them have been developed. Four sets of obstacles and corresponding strategies are summarized here.

Particularity and replication

Evidence always results from studying a particular group of children in a particular way at a particular time. Jean Piaget (1952, 1954) studied his children in Switzerland over 40 years ago. He drew conclusions that he hoped would apply to babies in general in any country and any year. Years later Ina Uzgiris and J. McV. Hunt (1975) carried Piaget's work further, testing dozens of babies in Urbana, Illinois. They, too, wanted to use the particulars of their findings to make generalizations that would apply to different babies in other circumstances. But even with a much larger sample of children they could not be sure where their findings would be applicable.

There is no way out of the problem. Findings always are past history. Even if you studied every baby alive today, there would be new ones next year. Even if you used 1000 ways of studying children, there would be additional ways you wondered about. The facts always are tied to the particulars of the method used to get them. We *always* want to go beyond the evidence we gather.

Because individual studies are particularistic, the safest way to make sense out of their findings is to gather additional evidence. Three-year-olds from poverty homes do worse than 3-year-olds from middle-class homes on almost any test we give during their first week in a new preschool. Does this difference tell us anything about the children's ability, or only about their reaction to a strange, new world? We can tell more if we repeat the comparison after the children have had a month to get used to the preschool, to educational materials, and to the person who tests them. By repeating, or replicating, a study with some particulars held constant and others changed, we learn more about how to interpret the original findings.

Imperfect observers and safeguards

Critics of psychology often point out that people have trouble in observing people objectively. Psychologists agree. We know that appearances can fool us, memory can deceive us, and prejudice can blind us. There is no way to make a person entirely objective, but there are safeguards that reduce the room for human error and show where it gets mixed into our findings. Table 2–4 illustrates how many features of sophisticated research are ways of making up for the limitations of people as observers.

Resources and compromises

Child psychologists have fixed amounts of time, energy, and money. This resource limitation makes it harder to deal with other problems. The particularity problem can be reduced by studying in ten countries rather than one or by testing 10,000 children rather than 10, but these extra efforts cost more in time and money.

Because of fixed resources, when research gains in one way, it often suffers in another. A central conflict is between *range* and *rigor*. A study of friendships among boys and among girls at ages 9 and 11 is broader in range than a study of friendships limited to 9-year-old girls. But in taking on the broader topic, you would make compromises in such matters as thoroughness of method and the number of children studied at any one age. The broader the scope of a study (range), the less careful, or rigorous, it can be. The more safeguards that are built in (rigor), the less flexibility and room there is for studying new issues (range).

One way to deal with the conflict is to make different compromises at different stages of inquiry (Achenbach, 1978). In exploring a new area and trying to discover what questions are worth answering, a broader and more flexible method and fewer safeguards seem more appropriate. Much of the pioneer work by major contributors such as Sigmund Freud and Jean Piaget had this quality of broad scope and few safeguards. At the confirmation stage the balance shifts.

TABLE 2–4 Safeguards in observational research that reduce the influence of limitations of the human observer

Limitation	Standard Safeguards
Expectations. People approach any study with biases that can influence what they do and see and how they interpret their findings.	Reduce the room for bias to operate. For example, give observers standard rules for what to record and train them to make notes according to a standard system.
Perceptual Limits. Small movements, actions that occur rapidly or extremely slowly, and soft sounds easily can be missed.	Use video recorders and other automatic recording devices to get permanent records that can be slowed down, speeded up, amplified, and examined repeatedly at leisure.
Attention. People cannot pay attention to a lot at once.	Simplify the situation in which observations are made so that there is less to follow. Four children in a standard playroom are easier to monitor than four children playing in the middle of a busy playground.
	Require systematic attention to defined events. An observation schedule that calls for looking at one child for 15 seconds and recording where he or she is and what he or she touches, then switching to another child for the next 15 seconds, and so on makes it much easier to keep track of several children at once.
Memory. People are poor at remembering a lot of details accurately, particularly if they are busy while the action goes on.	Use automatic recording devices.
	Separate the observing-recording role from action roles. For example, have an observer other than the group leader make notes.
	Require immediate writing down of what was observed and provide a simple code to make recording quicker and easier.
Summarizer-Reporter. When people summarize and report on what they have observed, they often introduce biases and inaccuracies not present in what they recorded in their original records.	Make original observation records available to others to summarize and interpret.
	Present observations in a form that makes it convenient for others to interpret for themselves.
	Use standard statistical techniques in summarizing material.
General. Despite safeguards, errors always enter the evidence from these and other sources.	Measure the amount of error present and use estimates of error in determining how far to trust the findings. For example, compare the records of two observers independently recording what the same children do to find percentage of agreement. By comparing records made by observers told a clothed baby is a girl with those told it is a boy, you can measure how much bias comes in from sex stereotypes.

After an area has been explored, the problem often is how to interpret a striking finding. The question of *replication*, or *confirmation*, becomes central. Now it seems sounder to take a narrower and more rigorous approach. That's what Uzgiris and Hunt (1975) did in following up on Piaget. They developed detailed and standardized procedures for observing children. These carefully defined tests, along with statistical analysis, resulted in a more rigorous study of what Piaget had discovered through less formal methods.

Risks and research ethics

Our goal of understanding children in general can put us in conflict with our concern for treating individuals ethically. Does spanking children for poor reading influence their later interest in reading? A study would pose real risks for the children who got spanked. Less obviously, a study of how children learn concepts might scare, bore, or confuse some of the participants. What right do we have to interrupt a child's reading lesson or enjoyment of a good book just because we want to do a study? These examples illustrate that the problem of *risk* confronts us in any research that interferes with the natural course of events.

Other examples illustrate that even naturalistic research can subject children to risk. A study based on school records threatens children's right to privacy even though it doesn't disturb their day. Publication of a comparison of children from varying social backgrounds can help the arguments of a bigot. The problem of risk is there whenever we do research. We always have to stop and consider what risks are present and how grave they are (Society for Research in Child Development, 1973).

When the risks are big and there is no way around them, they prevent research. That's why our knowledge on many issues is limited. We could clear up many questions through experiments in which children were extensively punished, raised in isolation, or not talked to, but we don't try to get what would be the clearest evidence from a scientific point of view because it would be unethical.

When researchers and review panels of colleagues think the risks of a study are small and the study is worth doing, a second issue arises: *informed consent.* We have no right to decide whether the risk to Juan is worth it if he participates in a study that we hope will help children in general. That's up to Juan and the adults who are responsible for him. The investigator has a responsibility to get permission before enlisting a child in a study. Adults (and children if old enough) are entitled to know what they are getting into. Informed consent means that they agree only after hearing an honest summary of what will be involved and what risks it will entail.

Research designs

The best way to answer a research question depends on the kind of question asked. If you want to know how humor changes between age 6 and age 12, you need children of the right age to find out. There is no need to study parents because your question does not concern their influence. But if you wanted to know how children's humor reflected the way they were raised, you would need to look at parents as well. The problem of fitting the investigation plan to the question asked is known as *research design.*

Several types of research designs are important in child psychology because we are concerned with varied kinds of questions, or types of lawfulness. First we consider the main kinds of questions of interest.

Types of questions

A key distinction is whether we ask how children's behavior relates to *child characteristics,* such as age, sex, or intelligence, or how it relates to *environmental characteristics,* such as past parental actions or influences in the present situation. (Notice that both kinds are questions about children's actions, or behavior, which is the subject matter of child psychology.)

One child characteristic, age, is of special importance in our field, so we can separate it and give it special status (Kessen, 1960; Wohlwill, 1973). Questions about how children's behaviors relate to age are *developmental questions.* They include the following: Do newborns see colors? When does anger first appear? How does the learning of 6-year-olds and of 13-year-olds differ?

The remaining questions about child characteristics can be termed *differential questions.* They refer to any differences among children other than age: Are girls more sociable than boys? Do more active toddlers grow up to be more active fifth-graders? How close is the relation between intelligence-test scores and reading performance?

Questions about how the child's actions relate to environmental variables can be classified as *child-environment questions*—for example: Are certain child-rearing techniques more likely to be associated with antisocial behavior? Do rich and poor children respond in the same way to academic situations? How does reward influence children's learning?

As illustrated in Table 2–5, we can ask all three types of questions about any topic, such as sharing, problem solving, fear, or humor. In the present sense "types of questions" refer to varied forms of lawfulness, *not* to contrasting content areas.

TABLE 2-5 Three important kinds of questions

	Sample Questions About Sharing	Sample Questions About Problem Solving
Questions About What Children Do		
Developmental questions Focus on the typical changes in how children act as they grow older.	When do children usually start to share their toys?	What are the characteristic methods of problem solving shown by 6- and 13-year-olds?
Differential questions Focus on contrasts in the actions of children of the same age.	Are children who share toys more likely also to be more helpful and caring in other ways?	Is a child who is better than average at solving problems at age 6 more likely to be better than average at 13?
Questions About the Relation Between What Children Do and Their Environments		
Child-environment questions Focus on how both the typical developmental changes and the contrasts among same-aged children relate to the kind of world in which children live.	Do children who show more sharing come from particular kinds of homes? Does watching a television program in which actors share influence a child's sharing behavior later?	What kinds of societies produce the children who do best in solving problems on their own? Can problem-solving skills be influenced by systematic training programs?

For each of the three main kinds of questions, there are distinctive research designs. The most basic distinctions among research designs are in what is varied and controlled. The general approach is to vary what you are interested in studying while holding constant, or controlling, other variables (see Table 2–6).

Usually the questions that prompt an investigation make it clear which variables are to be held constant and which varied. But after we decide those questions, another arises that is not so easily answered: *how* are variables to be varied or controlled? At this point the key decisions in research planning, or design, are made. Consider first the child side, then the environment.

TABLE 2–6 Contrasts in what is varied and controlled in three kinds of research

Type of Research	Main Question	Vary	Try to Hold Constant
Developmental Study	How does what children do vary with age?	age	environment nonage child characteristics
Differential Study	How does what children do vary with nonage variables such as sex, intelligence, personality?	sex, intelligence, and so forth	environment age
Child-environment Study	How does what children do vary with environment and experience?	environment	age nonage child characteristics

Child characteristics

Age. Age cannot be manipulated. You deal with it either by selecting or by waiting. You can hold age constant by looking at children of only one age, say 10-year-olds or 10-day-olds. To vary age you have two possibilities: look at the same children at two or more ages—a *longitudinal* study—or look at different children at two or more ages—a *cross-sectional* study. As shown in Table 2–7, we can also mix the two approaches by starting with groups at two or more ages and looking at everyone at least twice.

Table 2–7 emphasizes the most obvious differences among these three kinds of developmental studies: the amount of time they take. Longitudinal studies take the most time because you have to wait for the children to get older. Cross-sectional studies take the least. Not surprisingly, then, the vast majority of developmental studies are cross-sectional.

But the convenience of cross-sectional studies is balanced by advantages of the longitudinal method. For example, only in a longitudinal study can you actually watch developmental changes take place. Actually, each approach has both strengths and weaknesses. That's why *mixed designs* are becoming more popular. Often they combine the advantages of the two (Achenbach, 1978; Wohlwill, 1973).

TABLE 2-7 Three methods for studying how fearful behavior varies with age between 6 and 12 years

Type of Design	What You Might Do	Minimum Time Needed to Complete the Study
Longitudinal Design	Study one group: 6-year-olds. Then look at the same children again when they are 9 and when they are 12.	6 years
Cross-sectional Design	Study three groups: 6-year-olds, 9-year-olds, and 12-year-olds.	1 day
Mixed Design (combines features of longitudinal and cross-sectional designs)	Study two groups: 6-year-olds and 9-year-olds. Then look at the same children again 3 years later when the original 6-year-olds are 9 and the original 9-year-olds are 12.	3 years

Differential.   Variables such as children's sex, intelligence, and personality are varied and controlled through selection. By looking only at girls or only at children with test scores in a certain range, you can control these characteristics so as to make relations between other variables clearer. For example, if you wanted to see if game preferences related to intelligence level, you might first look only at girls to avoid the complications resulting from the fact that game preferences also vary with sex. Then if you wanted to see how game preferences related to sex, you might look at both sexes, but only at children of average intelligence to reduce the complicating role of intellectual differences.

Environmental characteristics

Questions about how the child's actions relate to the child's environment can be approached in either of two ways: naturalistically or experimentally. In naturalistic research we try not to change the everyday, or natural, world. In experimental research, in contrast, the investigator actively manipulates what happens. These two approaches are more fundamentally different than you might suspect. It's important to understand the contrast and see its implications. Research on children and television illustrates the contrast.

In the Rip VanWinkle Study a large group of children in New York was studied in a search for relations between aggressive behavior and TV viewing (Eron, Lefkowitz, Huesmann, & Walder, 1972). Information about the children's regular TV viewing was obtained by interviewing the children and their parents. Information about the children's aggressive actions at school was obtained there. Then the investigators put the two kinds of evidence together to see if the tendency to be mean to other children related to particular patterns of television watching. It did. Children who acted more aggressively at school were more likely to watch television programs with lots of violence in them.

This *naturalistic* study showed that there was a correlation between television exposure and how a child acted with peers. A big advantage of this and other naturalistic studies is that its real-world quality gives us more confidence that similar results would be found in other real-world settings. But notice that this approach leaves us without any clear evidence on the question of how the relationship came about. Perhaps the television violence influenced the children's behavior in school. Perhaps children who already were aggressive in school picked out TV shows with lots of violence. Perhaps some other variable, such as tension in the home, resulted in both aggressive behavior at school and watching violent TV. A naturalistic study leaves us unable to draw strong conclusions about cause-and-effect relationships.

Experimental studies usually are more artificial, but better at illuminating whether a variable such as TV violence can influence what children do. Albert Bandura (Bandura & Walters, 1963) did the classic experiments here. He brought children to a laboratory and randomly assigned them to watch either violent or nonviolent television programs. Then he observed the children in a playroom and compared the levels of violence in the two groups. By randomly assigning children to the two groups, Bandura controlled, or assumed to be constant in the two groups, other variables such as home conditions and prior tendencies toward aggression. Because everything else was constant, the fact that the group that watched violent television showed more aggression in its play afterward was a clear demonstration that the television content had influenced what the children did. The experimental approach involved a contrived, laboratory situation rather than real life, but it provided a clearer answer to the question of whether television violence can promote aggression in children.

Field experiments make it possible to combine advantages of naturalistic research with genuine experimental manipulation of variables. A good example here was a study by Lynette Friedrich and Aletha Stein (1973). They set up a special preschool program in which they could determine what happened and television watching could be made part of a continuing real-world experience. After a baseline period in which the children's activity was observed without any TV viewing at school, children were randomly assigned to one of three groups: aggressive television ("Batman" and "Superman"), prosocial television ("Mister Rogers"), or neutral television. Then the actions of the three groups were compared during and after several weeks of these contrasting treatments. Obeying rules and being tolerant of delays became more common for the children who viewed "Mister Rogers" and less common for those who watched "Batman" and "Superman."

SUMMARY

In this chapter the focus was on how child psychology advances. Technical articles were examined first because they illustrate the scientific process in action. In looking at the basic parts of a technical article (problem, method, results, discussion), the two-sided nature of progress was seen: building better theory and getting better evidence. A more careful examination of theory and of method followed.

General characteristics of theories were discussed first. A theory was defined as a set of statements that summed up and coordinated patterns of evidence. Good theory makes prediction possible and includes operational definitions that translate concepts into concrete ways of observing.

Then contemporary theories were examined. An important theory was defined as one that is generating research now. With this definition it was possible to point first at ideas shared by all important theories (naturalism, action, bodily foundation, environmental interaction, history, adaptation, and reciprocity) and to then look at contrasts (time scale, preadaptation versus adaptation, root metaphor: machine or organism). Specific theories were examined next, looking first at three in center stage (social-learning theory, cognitive-developmental theory, and ethology) and then at three others (Freud's psychoanalytic theory, Erikson's stage theory, and behaviorism).

The question of getting better evidence hinges on how research is done (method). One choice is in how observations are collected. The main alternatives are to gather it without interfering with everyday life (unobtrusive or naturalistic research) or to collect it in a more controlled and obtrusive way. In any area there are unavoidable obstacles that confront investigators once the early stages of research are past, and strategies are used in dealing with these obstacles (particularity and replication, imperfect observers and safeguards, limited resources and compromises, risks to children and research ethics).

The varied plans, or research designs, used in conducting studies relate to the three main kinds of questions of interest: developmental, differential, and child-environment questions. In answering developmental questions three main research designs are used: longitudinal, cross-sectional, and mixed designs, each with its own advantages. Differential questions require a design in which age is held constant. In looking at child-environment relations, there are two main alternatives: correlational and experimental studies. They differ fundamentally in that correlational studies (such as studies of person-child similarities in which only naturally occurring variation is examined) cannot show what causes what, but experimental studies (in which the investigator manipulates environmental variables) can.

CHAPTER 3

Reference Points

This chapter introduces you to children. The development of the typical child at five reference ages is described. Brief summaries of what children are like at conception, birth, 2 years, 6 years, and 13 years are presented. These ages were selected because each marks an important turning point in development and is often thought of as the beginning of a major developmental period. However, some would argue that *all* ages are key ages or present strong arguments for an alternate set. Keep in mind that these ages are a somewhat arbitrary way of dividing the essentially continuous stream of life. In any case the descriptions here can give you a concrete and familiar framework for organizing the details and abstractions that follow.

After the descriptions of the child at each age, more general topics are considered: overall trends, the gains and limitations of an age-bound approach, and the relation of this chapter to those that follow. A quick look at those summary sections now should help you decide how to read the material on the reference ages.

CONCEPTION AND THE ZYGOTE

All children start as *zygotes,* fertilized eggs formed when an ovum from the mother unites with a sperm from the father. Tiny and hidden from sight, the zygote often is ignored. Society measures your age from birth, rather than conception, and thereby ignores the entire nine-month period of life before birth. But in child psychology we start when a new individual is formed.

Each child begins as a single cell smaller than the period at the end of this sentence. Microscopic examination reveals that such cells lack arms, legs, eyes, and brains (see Figure 3–1). The old view that we start as miniature, perfectly formed little people is wrong and misleading. The zygote is more a sack of chemicals, a complex pattern of molecules. Among the chemicals are some comprising a *genetic code* whose details influence the characteristics of the child we will see later. But this code is a plan or "recipe for a child," not a miniscule baby.

The one-celled zygote lacks the basic equipment required for human behavior as we know it. Without muscles, sense organs, nerves, or brain the zygote does not walk, talk, or grasp. Most likely it cannot see, hear, think, or feel either. A survey of psychological functioning in the zygote thus must differ from an examination of behavior in a creature with different equipment.

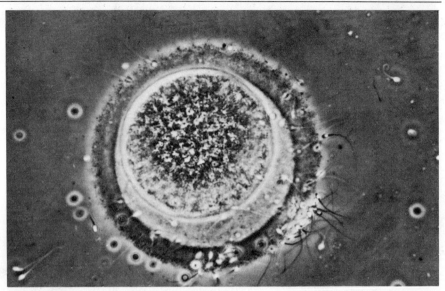

Figure 3-1   A zygote at the moment of conception with several sperm near it. (*Courtesy of the American Museum of Natural History.*)

The zygote lives in an environment. Like us it quickly would die if removed to an alien one. Like our own, the zygote's behavior consists of interactions with its environment. We must look at both the zygote and its surroundings to understand what it does.

The zygote lives as a parasite, depending entirely on mother's body for food, shelter, and appropriate conditions for life. But there is no suggestion that the zygote reacts to its mother as a person. We think a test tube with equivalent physical-chemical conditions would serve as well. Because it responds to the stimuli from mother as physical, rather than as distinctively social, the zygote can be considered asocial.

While small and single-celled, the zygote has specialized parts that do different jobs. The cell wall serves as a container that keeps it all together and influences what materials flow back and forth between zygote and environment. The genetic material inside contains the code, or plan, that directs growth. As the zygote grows, it keeps dividing so as to form more and more new cells from the old. At each step a coordinated sequence must take place. The genetic material divides and then a wall grows between its corresponding parts so that each new cell contains a duplicate copy of the original plan. From the start, then, we see self-maintenance, differentiation, and integration in the workings of the zygote. These features will continue through the life of the child.

BIRTH AND THE NEWBORN

Birth presents a dramatic change in environments. New problems and novel experiences result. Oxygen and food no longer are supplied automatically. Breathing and eating suddenly become necessary. Outside temperatures fluctuate, posing new problems of temperature regulation. Varied stimulation now reaches eyes, ears, skin, nose, and tongue.

Because the newborn, or *neonate* (the child during about the first month after birth), is a little person, we can review developmental areas. A distinction between physical and psychological development is basic.

Physical development

The neonate looks like a person because it has all the right parts put together in the right places. Many physical details have distinctive human qualities, but the newborn looks different from older people (see Figure 3–2). The head is large for the body; the forehead and cheeks stick out; and the face has a pushed-in look.

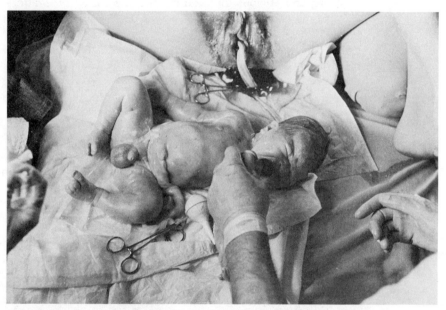

Figure 3–2   The newborn looks human but different from older people.

More careful examination shows that many parts of the newborn's brain and its workings contrast with ours. The insulating wrapping around nerves is not yet all present. Nerve impulses travel slowly. Brain waves are different. The upper part of the brain differs from ours. This *cerebral cortex* is more closely tied to such voluntary activities as walking and talking and to such functions as thinking and planning in adults. The lower brain, coordinating involuntary actions such as breathing and digesting, works more like ours.

Psychological development

We can survey the neonate's psychological development in terms of three main headings: perceptual-motor, cognitive-linguistic, and social-emotional.

Perceptual-motor development

Newborns live in the same environment as we do, but what they experience of it depends on their perceptual skills. Only if babies hear does it matter what sounds reach them. Only if different sights can be differentiated can they acquire varied meanings.

The main sensory channels all work at birth. Newborns see, hear, smell, taste, and feel sensations on the skin. With some kinds of information, they can discriminate between different stimuli, rather than just noting the difference between something and nothing. But skill at birth is less than it will be later.

The actions we observe in other people, such as smiling, talking, eating, and walking, involve movements of body parts. These movements result from the contractions of muscles inside. They are what we call *motor function*.

The newborn moves differently from us (Pratt, 1954). The contrast is so big and obvious that you get the impression of a different kind of behavior. Some complain that little babies don't do anything. That's not true, but the

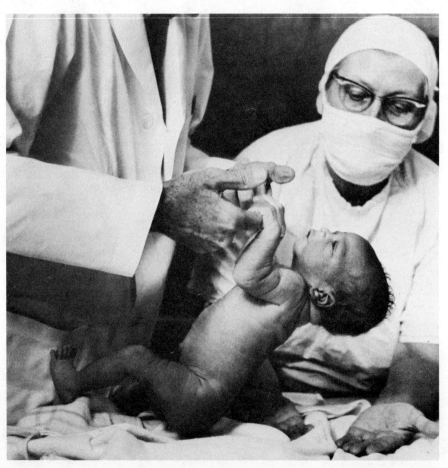

Reflexive actions such as grasping are prominent in the movements of newborns.

complaint shows that we cannot describe the neonate's actions with the concepts we use in talking about older people. We need different categories.

Reflex is a more useful term in talking about newborn behavior. A reflex is an inborn reaction to stimulus. Little babies have many reflexes (Pratt, 1954; Self & Horowitz, 1979). Reflexive actions are more prominent in their movements. A number of movements that are not reflexive for us are parts of reflexes at birth. For example, if we stroke the baby's cheek, the head often turns toward the side stroked (rooting reflex). If we stroke the baby's lips, the mouth often opens (mouth-opening reflex). If we insert a nipple between the lips, rhythmic sucking movements usually start (sucking reflex). These three reflexes help get milk into the mouth.

A second category is *general activity* (Pratt, 1954). Neonates tend to move everything at once. If the left arm moves, so does the right. Both legs move at the same time. When the arms move vigorously, the legs probably do, too. These movements look clumsy and uncoordinated and don't take the baby anywhere or involve interaction with objects. They do not seem to have any goal that we can figure out. The amount of movement is more meaningful than the kind.

Babies are prisoners of gravity. They lack most of the motor skills we use in dealing with the world. Newborns cannot stand, sit, or even roll over. They stay where they are put, able only to raise their head briefly and for an inch or so. They reflexively grasp small objects placed in their hands, but they neither reach out for them nor manipulate them.

Cognitive-linguistic development

Cognition is a general term for knowing, for mental processes such as thinking, reasoning, and remembering. The newborn's mind is hard to study, making it easy to take one of two positions. At one extreme you might think of the neonate as simpleminded, with a mind like a blank slate or as totally confused. At the other you could assume that the newborn thinks and knows the world exactly as we do and lacks only our store of memories and our ability to communicate our thoughts. Today both these positions seem wrong.

Instead we see the neonate's cognition as orderly, or *organized,* but different from our own. The order is clear when we look at reflexes. For example, when triangular targets are placed where newborns can look at them, we see a pattern in how the babies look at them. They focus mostly on corners and edges (Salapatek & Kessen, 1966).

Little babies don't act as if they think of the world as consisting of permanent objects existing in three-dimensional space. They don't look at what they touch. If we cover a rattle while baby (at about 6 months) reaches for it, we see a surprising reaction. The baby stops reaching. Attention turns elsewhere. The baby doesn't try to remove the cover or even stare at it. Some think newborns live in a world of separate and momentary pictures (Piaget, 1947/1960). They act as if objects are real only when they are interacting with them.

Language in the newborn is a mystery. No speech sounds are heard, only crying. But a newborn is more likely to cry after hearing the cries of other newborns (Simner, 1971). Moreover, human voices produce distinctive reactions (Eisenberg, 1976), suggesting that the roots of communication and language are already present.

Social-emotional development

Arousal refers to how "stirred up" you are. Deep sleep is at one extreme of arousal; extreme excitement is at the other. A calm, awake state is in between. By thinking of one dimension of arousal that ranges from sleep to excitement, we can put varied states, including those of emotional arousal, in one framework.

Arousal is conspicuous in newborns (Berg & Berg, 1979). Often they are quiet, almost motionless, with regular breathing and eyes closed. At other times they cry, become red faced, and thrash arms and legs in a peak of general activity. They also are at intermediate levels, sometimes quiet and alert, other times half asleep.

Arousal *cycles* are evident from right after birth, but they are much shorter than ours. The baby falls into a deep sleep, goes through intermediate states, and reaches a peak of excitement every three or four hours. Most of what the baby does fluctuates with level of arousal—for example, heart rate, breathing, reactions to tones, and reflex strength.

Environment influences arousal. Two of the best ways of quieting a crying newborn are to rock it or give it something to suck. Feeding the hungry baby and changing the wet one sometimes produce a more lasting calm.

Sudden and intense stimuli are most likely to produce crying and high arousal. Pin pricks, cold water, odors we call unpleasant, and other painful stimuli are among them. Along with the dramatic response to such stimuli as diaper pins come smaller increases in arousal when novel stimuli are present. Because most stimuli are novel to neonates, frequent slight increases in arousal are common.

Evidence of unpleasant emotion is present from the first birth cry. Crying accompanied by facial expressions that strike us as unhappy is common during states of excitement. In contrast, there is no clear evidence of pleasant emotion during the first weeks of postnatal life. The newborn does not laugh, coo, or gurgle. We do not see broad smiles or smiles linked to positive situations.

On the reflex level we see approach to positive stimulation and withdrawal from negative. When the newborn sucks a nipple, the behavior increases contact with the source of stimulation. If a piece of cellophane is placed over the baby's nostrils, there are movements that suggest an attempt to get away (withdrawal).

But there is no sign of the integrated sequences we call *goal-directed.* We don't see acts that look like means to an end, as when an older child reaches out, picks up a cup, and then drinks from it.

Newborns have a powerful influence on their social environments. Adults disrupt their own routines to wait on them. They get their way by crying (Murray, 1979). The care givers spring into action. Only when the cries stop can they get back to what they were doing. Even inexperienced adults soon become skilled in preventing long bouts of crying.

The newborn's cry is particularly dramatic in keeping care givers close and attentive. Other built-in responses such as sucking, grasping, and looking help create and maintain a two-way bond of attachment that simultaneously binds parents to baby and provides the foundation for the baby's love for particular individuals.

At first the newborn's attachment behaviors are all reflexive. Rocking and feeding by the mother quiet an aroused baby. But a mechanical cradle and a rubber nipple produce the same result. The baby grasps at mother's breast or finger, but grasps in the same automatic way when given the handle of a rattle.

Specimen box 3–1   Childhood in other cultures

How universal are the patterns of child development that we observe in North American children today? In what ways are the children we observe now like those of other times and places? We gain perspective on such questions by looking at descriptions of children growing up in societies that contrast greatly with our own.

Here are some excerpts from accounts written by anthropologists who studied children in so-called preliterate societies, cultures little influenced by modern trends such as schooling, science, and the growth of cities. Read them and consider what they suggest about the universal and the particular in child development. In what ways are children and childhood today probably typical? In what respects are modern children different? The question is discussed in Chapter 17.

> The child before he is five or six is said to be *durung djawa,* which literally means "not yet Javanese." The same phrase is applied to mentally unbalanced persons and to adults who are not properly respectful to their elders, . . . It implies a person who is not yet civilized, not yet able to control emotions in an adult manner, not yet able to speak with the proper respectful circumlocutions appropriate to different occasions. He is also said to be *durung ngerti,* "does not yet understand," and therefore it is thought that there is no point in forcing him to be what he is not or punishing him for incomprehensible faults [Geertz, 1961, p. 105].
>
> A perennial amusement among Ngoni boys of five to seven was playing at law courts. They sat around in traditional style with a "chief" and his elders facing the court, the plaintiffs and defendants presenting their case, and the counsellors conducting proceedings and cross-examining witnesses. In their high squeaky voices the little boys imitated their fathers whom they had seen in the courts, and they gave judgements, imposing heavy penalties, and keeping order in the court with ferocious severity [Read, 1960, p. 84].
>
> As the child grows older, it comes to participate more and more in the routine work of the household. Girls, from the age of about six or seven, are made to help in fetching water, firewood, earth, and ornamental clay, stamping corn, and cleaning the huts and courtyards. They start by imitating these activities in their play, and are gradually drawn into actual service [Schapera, 1941, p. 248].

There is no suggestion that the baby cries to get human attention or responds to rocking or cuddling because the stimulation comes from a particular person. Like the zygote, the newborn seems asocial.

The newborn's helplessness in getting food, avoiding danger, and even moving around makes other people crucial for both survival and everyday comforts. Newborns' control over their parents was emphasized because that fact often is lost in the face of the obvious influence that adults have on children in the early days.

A more accurate summary of the neonate's behavior gives a more balanced picture: incompetent in moving around, but competent in picking up information from the world; helpless in manipulating objects, but powerful in influencing people; uncoordinated in voluntary actions such as limb movement, but coordinated in terms of the internal activities that maintain a steady body temperature and match food intake to bodily needs.

AGE 2 YEARS

At 2, we see the distinctive behaviors that characterize human beings and that played a special role in our evolution. Two-year-olds walk on two legs, manipulate objects with their hands, communicate in words, and laugh. At birth we saw a child whose physical appearance was decidedly human, though different. Now we see behavior generally typical of our species, though different from our own.

Physical development

Two-year-olds are so short that we tend to bend down to talk to them, but at this age the typical child has reached almost half of his or her mature height. The brain is about 60% of its mature weight. Body proportions are more like ours than those of the newborn (see Figure 3–3).

Figure 3–3   Two-year-olds are at about half of their mature height.

Perceptual-motor development

The 2-year-old's movements, like ours, involve mostly patterned reactions by specific muscle systems. Usually we see walking, lifting, climbing, and so on, not general activity. Reflexes no longer are conspicuous. Actions such as grasping, crying, and looking, which started out on a reflexive basis, are now voluntary.

The basic skills needed to move around the world and deal with objects now have been mastered. At 2, children easily stand upright and walk. At about this age standing on one foot and jumping with both feet off the ground become possible. Gravity has been conquered. Children can use both hands, either separately or together, in handling objects. They can pick up things, hold them, drop them, and throw them.

Two-year-olds' skill in moving makes it possible to see their perceptual accomplishments. When they reach out and pick up apples, we can tell that they judge their size and distance with reasonable accuracy. When they stop, smile, and turn on hearing familiar voices, we know that they not only hear them, but recognize them and locate them in space.

These perceptual skills all require some ability to pay attention to what is crucial while ignoring irrelevant information, but attention skills are limited. When 2-year-olds look for a lost ball or inspect a complicated picture, we do not see systematic and efficient scanning patterns. When they watch "Sesame Street," they look away from the screen more frequently than older children do.

Cognitive-linguistic development

Two-year-olds show the dawnings of a distinctively human intelligence. Language and pretending provide striking examples.

Both talking and understanding others' language are noteworthy. The typical 2-year-old uses about 250 words. Terms such as *dog* and *spoon* apply to whole categories of animals, objects, and pictures. New examples are easily recognized and labeled, sometimes amusingly, as when a horse seen for the first time is called "doggie." Often the child seems to have caught on to the idea that objects have names. "Whasat?" often is heard as a demand for the name of a new object. One- and two-word utterances are most common. These short statements seem like genuine sentences because they express complete thoughts and show grammatical regularities. "Milk!" means "I want milk!" Sentences such as "Mommy go" and "Bye-bye car" reveal regular word orders and a tendency to use words that carry the most important information. But understanding has come even further. Two-year-olds can understand many words and sentences they do not yet say.

"Pretending" shows a use of inner symbols, or representations. When a child slowly and deliberately takes an empty spoon, goes through the motions of eating from it, looks at us, and smiles, we are confident that she is pretending to eat, not trying to eat from an empty spoon. Her smile indicates that she knows she is pretending and sees both the similarity and the difference between real eating and pretend eating. Both the pretending and the knowing require a way of representing, or symbolizing, events to herself.

There is little sign of planning, foresight, or reasoning. Even so simple a task as putting wooden animal cutouts each in their own places in a puzzle reveals a failure to look ahead or quickly modify an action that doesn't work. The 2-year-old often ignores what is crucial, as when he or she persists in trying to put a large piece in a small hole.

Social-emotional development

We see a broad range of emotional reactions. Happy smiling, delighted laughing, and dramatic temper tantrums all are common. Fears of noises and of strange objects, situations, and persons are most common, but decrease with age. Fears of animals, imaginary creatures, and the dark are less common, but increase with age. Laughter most commonly comes with big-muscle actions, as in splashing water, rolling down a slope, or going down a slide.

Arousal cycles are similar to our own. A basic day-night cycle has been established. Parents rarely are wakened in the middle of the night, but signs of the old, short cycles remain in the need for naps.

Extremes of arousal influence a host of ongoing activities, often disruptively. The child who misses a nap or is excited about a party cannot go through a normal routine.

There is goal direction. Objects are used as tools. A series of varied movements ties together in the accomplishment of one outcome, such as getting all the blocks into the wagon. But there is little sign of sustained pursuit of goals, as in collecting stamps or drawing a whole scene.

Exploration is common. Sand and water are examined, touched, and tasted. Closets and cabinets are opened and entered. Frequently parents comment that their child is into everything.

New skills also are explored. A newly learned word is often practiced over and over. Skills such as pulling pull-toys, jumping, stair climbing, and carrying large objects are exercised seemingly just for the fun of it.

People count as people. Human stimuli get different reactions than nonhuman ones. Being with people is pleasurable, and special people matter. The world now is genuinely social. Attachments to special people play a big role in emotional reactions. Just as being left at home with a baby-sitter can spark distress, a reunion with a loved one causes delight.

At 2, the child already has mastered basic social skills. Interchange can take place smoothly with familiar people. Words and gestures communicate wants and reactions. Parents' remarks, facial expressions, and gestures are often understood and responded to appropriately in many routine exchanges involving play, eating, bedtime, and so on.

Understanding of the social world is limited to concrete and immediate matters. Perhaps the question "Are you a little girl or a little boy?" can be answered correctly, but there is little sign of knowledge of society's contrasting expectations for the two sexes. Two-year-olds show no sign of understanding right and wrong except in terms of specific, previously labeled actions.

The 2-year-old's skills and limitations make for a special social situation. Capacities for understanding and self-control still are too limited to deal with all the problems posed by the ability to move around and by exploratory interests; so supervision is needed and friction is common. Children often tackle problems that are dangerous or too much for them and older people have to step in and forbid behaviors. Play with a sympathetic adult can go on happily for long periods of time, but when two 2-year-olds try to play together, the picture is more stormy. Real cooperation is absent. When it comes to give and take, each is stronger on take. Things go best when older children or adults are nearby, ready to step in. New symbolic skills foster self-assertion: "No!" and "I'll do it myself."

At 2, then, children present striking contrasts. We can see awesome achievements, but there is an equally impressive road to social maturity before them. There is competence in most areas, polish in few. There is genuine sociability with little sign of reciprocity. We see a striking ability to communicate that works only with a narrow audience. There is mobility in getting around the world accompanied by little tendency to anticipate what lies around the corner.

AGE 6 YEARS

Typical 6-year-olds cope successfully with the everyday world. In familiar situations they avoid danger and stay out of trouble. Because they are good at taking care of themselves, they often are allowed to go about without supervision.

Most cultures mark the self-control of 6-year-olds by giving them new freedom and greater responsibility (Rogoff, Sellers, Pirrotta, Fox, & White, 1976). Formal schooling begins at about this age in most complicated societies. In simpler ones there often are parallel trends: children are allowed to range farther from home on their own, often are put to work, and sometimes are given the job of taking care of younger children or animals. In most cultures children move from a more family-centered world to a broader one in which they must deal with more people.

Physical development

Much growth now has taken place. The trunk is about 60% of its mature size, but bodily proportions still are immature (see Figure 3–4). Boys and girls have similar shapes, with proportions that contrast with those of the sexually mature.

The brain is almost mature. It is nearly full sized and works more maturely. There is better coordination between brain areas, and the "higher centers" (basic to inhibition, or not doing) now are working.

Perceptual-motor development

The 6-year-old has the strength and endurance for sustained action. However, work such as carrying heavy loads separates the women from the girls and the men from the boys.

Figure 3–4 A six-year-old child-nurse illustrates the important responsibilities
often given to children at this age.

Six-year-olds have adequate small-muscle skill for many motor tasks. They
can master writing, buttoning, eating with a fork, turning on a television set,
or working a washing machine.

Cognitive-linguistic development

The child now knows and uses hundreds of concepts: big, smelly, nice,
bad, teacher, yellow, and so on. People, objects, and situations are classified
and labeled so readily that the child, like us, deals with the world largely in
terms of these symbols.

The child's concepts tend to be concrete. More often they relate to what
can be seen and touched—for example, *prison* rather than *justice*. When the
child is asked what a bicycle is, responses such as "you ride on it" or "it has
two wheels" are more common than "a means of transportation."

By 6, children usually can focus their attention and keep both external
demands and their own goals in mind. They can produce complex drawings,
construct buildings with blocks, and follow familiar routes between home and
school without mishap.

Six-year-olds readily drop an approach to a problem that doesn't work.
When playing Twenty Questions, they try a new question after being told "No,
it isn't an elephant," but their attempts show little sign of system or strategy.
In playing checkers, they don't look several moves ahead.

In many ways the child now seems to be at the threshold of the kind of
organized thinking needed in games with rules, mathematics, and systematic
reasoning. Six-year-olds have many concepts and are beginning to relate them,

as in classifying by size and color simultaneously. But their best thinking requires concrete and familiar situations, as in counting and adding pennies.

Six-year-olds have mastered their native language. They usually articulate all but a few sounds perfectly, have a vocabulary of thousands of words that is sufficient for everyday purposes, and spin grammatical sentences with ease. They can use language to communicate with anyone, not just members of their own circle. There are limitations, but we would be delighted to speak and understand Chinese or Spanish as skillfully as the average child aged 6 who grew up with it.

Social-emotional development

Emotions are complicated and sophisticated. Private feelings, physiological reactions, behaviors such as running and hitting, and verbal statements about feelings do not always run in parallel. Private feelings can be hidden or denied. Dramatic displays can be held in, though crying and red-faced shouting still are common.

When you ask a 6-year-old girl what she enjoys or wants, answers such as playing dolls, playing jumprope, wanting a new Barbie, and wanting to be a mommy predominate. If you ask the same questions of a boy, you are likely to get equally "appropriate" replies. Most commonly he says he is interested in games and sports involving action. Often he picks activities where winning and dominance are important. He is unlikely to mention goals involving taking care of others. Both the boy and the girl state personal feelings and goals that are appropriate for their sex in their society. Because they state these feelings as their own, rather than saying "I'm supposed to like Barbie dolls" or "They want me to enjoy playing cowboys," we say that external pushes now have become *internalized*.

Adults more often base approval on good performance now and children's own concerns are similar. They put a premium on doing things well. They want to be "a good boy" or "a good girl." They work at learning to read or ride a bicycle.

Understanding of the social world is broad, but superficial. Children know what is expected of girls and boys and what is called good or bad in general terms. They know what concrete actions are labeled "being brave" or "stealing," but often they are unclear about why actions are considered right or wrong.

The child's skills, goals, and understandings all contribute to the smooth social interaction with adults and peers that now is possible. Children fit in more easily because their wants are socially appropriate and because they are adept in figuring out what is called for in a particular situation. Inappropriate reactions, such as pointing at someone with a missing leg or being silly when other children want to be grown-up, quickly decline.

About half of the child's social interactions are with peers (Barker & Wright, 1955). Basic skills such as taking turns, sharing, following the rules, and saying you're sorry make it possible to interact without having adults step in to smooth out the rough spots. Cooperation is now possible. Elaborate play involving several children, varied toys, and long time periods is common.

Girls' and boys' different interests help produce a separation when they play, the amount of which varies with the materials and children present. Activities such as swimming are attractive to both sexes and bring them together, but first-grade recess often results in marked separation.

Friendships with particular children are important (Hartup, 1970). Often they follow same-sex and same-age lines and reflect both who is available and who has similar interests.

Differences among children are as striking as similarities. Free play reveals obvious sex differences. Classrooms show dramatic contrasts in aptitude for reading. The self-control so common among 6-year-olds is hardly universal. The "typical 6-year-old," like the "typical newborn" or "typical 20-year-old," is but a convenient fiction.

AGE 13 YEARS

When we turn to 13-year-olds, we must start with an important fact: much of our description of children at this age is not universal. At 13, even seemingly basic facts of biology and physical development vary with the time and place. The summary that follows is more a description of "our children" and less one of "children" than the earlier ones.

The behavior of 13-year-olds differs from culture to culture and is determined by social-historical contexts.

Physical development

In industrialized countries today the 13th birthday typically comes near the landmark called puberty. The average girl reaches *menarche* (the beginning of her cycle of monthly periods) a little before her 13th birthday (Zacharias,

Rand, & Wurtman, 1976). The typical boy reaches a comparable stage of sexual maturity a little after his (Tanner, 1970).

The average age of puberty has changed over the last few generations, and children are growing up earlier in a physical sense. The clearest evidence is on age of menarche in girls because investigators in different countries and decades have used the same definition. In places as varied as Norway, Japan, England, Poland, and the United States a similar trend is evident. In better-off groups living in countries with modern medical and nutritional conditions, the trend apparently has leveled off; so 13 most likely will remain as about the average (Garn, 1980).

The sexual maturity that comes with puberty is closely linked to widespread changes in physical development (Tanner, 1970). There is a rapid growth spurt around the time of puberty that includes marked bone growth, muscle development, and changes in body hair as well as the growth of the sexual organs. The modern children who reach puberty earlier, then, also show these changes earlier. The typical teenager now is more adultlike than earlier ones in size, shape, and bodily chemistry.

But a visit to a junior high school will show that the "typical 13" is even less typical physically than the average 6- or 16-year-old in the same community. The children whose growth spurt started at 11 contrast sharply with those whose growth spurt has not yet started. Among the more mature the contrasts between the sexes are greater than among the less mature. Taken together the variation related to age of puberty and to sex adds up to an unusually striking range of sizes and shapes (see Figure 3–5).

Figure 3–5   Thirteen-year-olds vary greatly in size and shape.

A few generalizations about the average child at 13 are useful if taken with caution. The body has reached about two-thirds size, but head and brain now are full size. Muscles are relatively larger than before. The ratio of hip width to shoulder width is moving toward adult proportions. The girls are broadening more rapidly around their hips and the boys are broadening more at the shoulders.

Perceptual-motor development

Strength is a major frontier at 13. Increased levels of sex hormones in the blood trigger changes that result in bigger muscles with a potential for much greater strength (Tanner, 1970). Under normal conditions the possibility of greater strength becomes a reality. With exercise the amount of weight that can be lifted increases greatly.

Specific perceptual-motor skills, such as ability to read rapidly, throw a ball far, or play a clarinet with skill, depend largely on the individual's personal history. A child who started playing basketball, swimming, or piano playing at age 8 and who practiced for 5 hours a week now has accumulated a total of 1300 hours of practice at that skill. Because practice and specific training make so much difference on perceptual-motor skills, we are not surprised to find many 13-year-olds who are superior to most adults in swimming or at playing the piano. But where sheer strength is crucial, as in lifting weights, the average adult is still superior to the average child.

Cognitive-linguistic development

The average child now can think in an organized manner. When faced with a problem he or she is capable of considering the situation as a whole, weighing alternatives mentally, and coming out with a response. We see strategy in the approach to problems and games, as when a series of questions is used to arrive at the answer in Twenty Questions: "Is it large?" "Does it live on land?" "Does it have four legs?"

The systematic quality of thinking makes it possible to learn abstract subjects such as mathematics in a formal and logical way. Geometry can be handled in terms of postulates and proofs, rather than as a collection of concrete facts about triangles and parallel lines. The rules of the game can now be used in a more flexible and general way, whether the game is geometry, chess, or social interchange.

With the abilities to consider the situation as a whole and to look ahead comes a new view of present reality. The way things are is more readily seen as but one possible alternative. Parents' rules about bedtime, dress, and chores now are understood as but one solution to problems that might be solved differently. School rules also are seen as arbitrary, rather than inevitable. Alternatives can be considered and often are.

A more abstract perspective makes it easier to look at the present in relation to the future. Planning makes it easier to deal with such short-term problems as getting homework done while still having fun on a weekend. Similarly, it is easier to imagine a future vocation, such as being a teacher or lawyer, and to relate it to present schoolwork and leisure activity.

Language development shows an enlarged vocabulary containing more abstract words and a command of more complicated grammatical forms. Considerations such as vocabulary level and sentence length are most important in determining what books or lectures a 13-year-old can understand.

Social-emotional development

The social world of today's 13-year-olds is so special in human history that particular caution is needed in deciding which features of 13-year-old social-emotional development are but a sign of the times, rather than something more universal.

Our 13-year-olds are in school, not at work. They are grouped together, not mixed with people of varied ages. They are given little responsibility, either for their own lives or for those of others. These and other new social facts of life combine with earlier sexual maturity to produce a unique situation.

Two features of 13-year-olds that probably are linked to the current scene are the importance of peers and of leisure. A desire for popularity with age-mates is one of the most common and strongest goals at 13 today. Conformity to peer pressures typically is higher than either earlier or later (Hartup, 1970). Because the peer world is a leisure world, the clearest signs of peer importance turn up in leisure activities. Fashion in music, clothes, and slang are examples. Watching the right television programs, following sports, and admiring the right heroes and heroines are not trivial matters. The use of such drugs as alcohol, tobacco, and marijuana in company with friends is common.

Age-old concerns related to growing up and looking toward the future remain. The child's rapidly changing body and new thinking capacities combine with social pressures ("And what are you going to be when you grow up?"). Questions of occupation and adult sex role become more important. In some the questions of "Who am I?" and "Where am I going?" loom large. Interest in the opposite sex grows, whether or not the child has started to turn from the same-sex friendships of childhood to close relations with the opposite sex. Usually the family becomes steadily less important as peer relations and the world outside the home grow in meaning.

At 13, understanding of people usually has moved below the surface. There is concern with feelings, goals, and moods—in oneself and in others. Children are more aware of their own emotions and spend more time thinking about them. A growing interest in listening to music often ties in with this concern. Thirteen-year-olds understand that others have feelings and opinions that can differ from their own; so sharing feelings with friends becomes more important. Wondering how others view them becomes common.

Often the deeper understanding of people is accompanied by new ways of thinking about right and wrong. By now the child usually has some understanding of why actions such as stealing and hitting are considered wrong. A common 13-year-old explanation of why you shouldn't lie or break laws would emphasize the importance of conforming to rules to support the government and preserve social values.

SUMMARY: OVERALL TRENDS

It is a long path from the zygote to the teenager. In trying to remember and understand what happens, we should start with the general pattern and worry about specific details only when we can fit them in. Four overall trends are basic parts of the pattern as a whole. They are but briefly described to encourage you to fill in the details as a review of what you have just read.

First, *the tempo of change is rapid at the start and then tends to slow down*. The intervals between the early reference points are smaller than between later ones because in the early months and years dramatic changes are much more common. One way of keeping the picture in mind is to think about a few basic questions concerning the mature human being and try to remember when each aspect of maturity is reached. Table 3–1 includes a set of questions that serves to summarize many of the details presented about the child at each reference age.

TABLE 3–1 Reference ages and steps toward maturity

Step	Zygote	Newborn	Reference Age 2 Years	6 Years	13 Years
Physical Appearance Does the child look like a human being?	no	*yes*	yes	yes	yes
Species-characteristic Behavior Patterns Does the child exhibit the activity patterns that are unique to mature human beings?	no	no	*yes*	yes	yes
Self-control Can the child take care of herself or himself in normal and familiar settings?	no	no	no	*yes*	yes
Adult Roles Can the child carry out adult social roles for sustained periods of time?	no	no	no	no	?

Second, *dramatic changes in different developmental areas take place at different times*. Varied landmarks, such as the body taking on recognizable form, the conquest of gravity, and the acquisition of language, are reached at different ages. One of the main gains from starting with the reference ages is to get a first picture of the sequence of major accomplishments and to see what frontiers are being explored when.

Third, *the reference points can be used to set off four developmental periods with contrasting environmental conditions and distinctive areas of accomplishment*. Because children's actions are always adaptive interactions with their environments, developmental changes result both from changes in the child and changes in the environment to which the child adapts. Table 3–2 sums up some of the universal and near-universal changes in the physical and social environments that the child enters with each key age. Table 3–3 shows how the reference ages can be seen as the borderlines between four major periods of childhood with characteristic accomplishments. When you look at the two tables together, you can see the close fit between children's accomplishments and what is expected of them.

TABLE 3-2 The changing environment

Reference Age	Characteristic and New Features of the Typical Environment

Zygote	physical: water
	  relatively constant
	  life-support substances supplied automatically
	social: asocial

Newborn	physical: air and land
	  varied stimulation
	social: asocial
	  indulgent
	  others crucial in life support
	  others crucial in moving through space and making contact with objects

2 Years	physical: stimulation more dependent on own actions
	social: others demand more self-help
	  others important in permitting and allowing movement and contact with objects
	  others ask for more conformity

6 Years	physical: minute-to-minute stimulation largely dependent on own actions
	social: others demand self-control and give responsibility for self-help in many areas
	  varied social pressures from outside family as well as in peer world prominent
	  others allow independent action in range of everyday settings

13 Years	physical: minute-to-minute stimulation largely dependent on own actions social: others expect and demand future-oriented actions aimed toward independent adulthood peer world more prominent and important than family on a day-to-day basis

Fourth, *as the child grows up, two forms of adaptive change can be distinguished: (1) New kinds of action such as walking and conversing appear and are refined and elaborated. (2) Children's minute-to-minute actions come to fit in more smoothly and appropriately in the life settings in which adults of their society live.* Maturity means both being able to do what is required and actually doing it appropriately at the right time and place. The more obvious kinds of psychological development involve the appearance and improvement of skills that are absent at first, as in learning to walk or talk. But it is just as

TABLE 3–3 Major developmental periods and dramatic accomplishments

Reference Point	Period	Physical Development	Psychological Development
Conception			
	Prenatal Period	human form emerges enormous growth in size	activity begins reflexes develop
Birth			
	Infancy	rapid growth to about 50% of height	basic perceptual-motor skills conquest of space and gravity beginnings of symbolic action and language varied emotions goal-directed activity attachment to familiar people basic social skills
2 Years			
	Early Childhood	continued brain growth	refinement of perceptual-motor skills language mastery growth of symbols and concepts internalization of social expectations growth of self-control growth of social skills social conformity increases
6 Years			
	Childhood (often divided into "middle" and "later")	brain growth completed	specific perceptual-motor skills organized and systematic thought develops cooperation peer friendships (usually same sex) social understanding increases moral development
13 Years			
	Adolescence	growth spurt begins	

important to adapt actions to the demands of the present situation. Two-year-olds can be hard to live with because of what they do, rather than what they can't do. Talking inappropriately, refusing to stop running, and putting the wrong objects in their mouths are as important signs of immaturity as not being able to talk fluently or control a pencil. Doing the right thing at the appropriate time and not doing the wrong thing are as much part of growing up as being able to do something new.

POSTSCRIPT: THE AGE-BOUND APPROACH

Child psychology starts from the everyday observation that as children grow older, their behavior changes. In approaching the field by summarizing typical actions of children at certain ages, we have a starting place that is simple and concrete. It yields a clear gain in predictive accuracy and the comfortable feeling that something solid has been learned. All this makes an age-bound approach that relates development to age a good starting point.

But this book, unlike many, is not organized in terms of ages and puts little emphasis on precise ages because the age approach has important limitations that turn up once you get past the starting point.

Two limitations already have been mentioned: (1) Children of the same age in any society vary. (2) Children of the same age in varied cultures and historical periods act in different ways. The age approach helps in predicting what is typical today in children around us, but it fails to deal with the variety that is as much part of child psychology as the commonality.

Other limitations are apparent as soon as you talk to people who look at children primarily in terms of an age frame of reference. All too easily they start bringing in ideas of what is "good" or "normal." A common idea is that children who aren't typical must have something wrong with them, particularly if the contrast is a delay in showing some behavior as compared with "the average." As you will see, this way of thinking often has been inaccurate and frequently has done more harm than good.

Another tendency that comes easily with an age-bound approach is to ignore environmental factors and assume that what is age related reflects only biological change. As stated, the age approach makes sense only when you keep both environmental shifts and changes in the child in mind. But because the child is in center stage with this viewpoint, the error is hard to avoid.

Finally, we have the most basic problem with an age approach: *it doesn't explain anything.* Knowing that language is acquired mostly between age 2 and age 6 doesn't tell us how language is acquired and doesn't explain which contributions come from brain development and which from the way people deal with young children. A universal trend toward a deeper understanding of people at 13 leaves us with similar mysteries. Because most children live in environments that demand more social skill later in childhood than earlier, the gains here might come in any of a number of ways. If we treat the age approach, as is done here, as a beginning, we can use it as a source of questions. We have to make sure we don't let it become a cover for ignorance or a way of smuggling in answers that really aren't there.

The remainder of this book is organized around such topics as language development, sex differences, and the child and the outside environment, rather than in terms of ages. This approach is used because the modern field of child psychology and the dominant theories are organized this way. As you deal with later chapters, you should find it helpful to relate them to the reference points provided here.

PART **II**
Basic Processes

Accomplishments such as those summarized in Chapter 3 are the products of development. Behavioral landmarks, such as beginning to stand up or to reason, result from the operation of processes of change. Thousands of small changes gradually add up to the big ones that are so obvious when we compare children at varied ages. When you live with a child, even a young one, these everyday changes take place so gradually that you hardly notice them. But these little changes and the often hidden processes that produce them are crucial if you are to understand development.

The summary of reference ages was like a movie run much faster than life so that you could quickly gain perspective on what takes years to happen. Now I take a contrasting approach: I start looking at events in real time and in slow motion in order to provide a better picture of the underlying processes that produce change.

First I look at physical development, the growth of the child's body. After a summary of growth trends, I focus on underlying change processes, such as nerve growth and hormone action. Next I examine learning, how children's actions are modified as a result of experience. Here the emphasis is entirely on change processes, the varied forms of learning and how they operate. Both chapters in this section, then, are process oriented. Together they form a basis for looking at both similarities and differences in children as they grow up.

CHAPTER 4

Physical Development

Psychological development depends on physical development. The zygote's lack of sensory systems, muscles, and a brain limits what it can do. The construction of a newborn's body makes it capable of hearing a bell, but not of crawling toward it. As the child's body grows, the actions she or he is capable of performing change. This chapter deals with the development of the body as it relates to its psychological potentials. First the main trends are summarized and the great changes before birth are described. Next the regularities of growth after birth are presented. Then attention turns to the processes that underlie the visible developments.

PRENATAL PHYSICAL GROWTH

The biggest changes in the human body take place before birth. Hidden in the mother's womb there is continuous action. The single-celled zygote becomes a multicelled newborn through a regular and predictable set of revolutionary transformations.

In the early weeks the body changes so radically that experts use different names for the same developing individual. The *zygote,* or *fertilized ovum,* becomes an *embryo* and then a *fetus* before it emerges as a *neonate.* The pictures in Figures 4–1 through 4–5 show the marked differences in external appearance that lead to the use of these different labels. Prenatal growth involves much more than growth in size.

The names *zygote*, *embryo*, and *fetus* are used during the three main periods of prenatal development: the germinal period, the period of the embryo, and the period of the fetus. It is useful to think of prenatal growth in terms of what happens during these three periods. There are developments both in the growing individual and in the relation of the individual to its environment.

Germinal period

Two important beginnings are accomplished in the first two weeks after conception. Cell specialization begins, forming the basis for later development of different body parts. The tiny zygote becomes connected with its host-mother, building a foundation for nutrition and protection during the rest of the prenatal period.

Immediately after the mother's egg and the father's sperm unite, the fertilized egg, or zygote, starts to change. There is a process of repeated cell division, or *mitosis,* so that the original single cell soon becomes two, then four, then eight cells, and so on. At first these cells are all similar and form a small clump. Then the clump becomes a hollow ball, at which point cell specialization begins. The hollow ball includes three layers made up of different kinds of cells. Later each layer will turn into a different set of body parts.

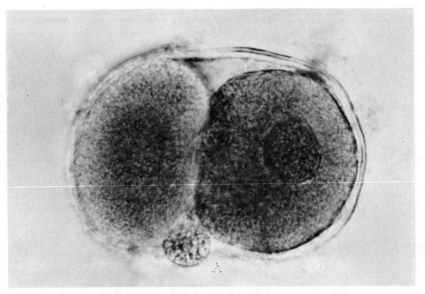

Figure 4-1 Zygote after first cell division. *(Courtesy of Carnegie Institution of Washington, Department of Embryology.)*

When the egg and sperm meet and join, both are on the move, floating through a tube in the mother's body (the Fallopian tube). The zygote formed by this merger stays on the move for several days while it changes. Then it becomes attached, or *implanted,* to the wall of the mother's uterus. Implantation follows the beginning of cell specialization.

Embryonic period

Two weeks after conception, when body parts begin to form from the specialized cells, the individual gets a new name: embryo. It is called an embryo from the third week until about the end of the eighth week, when the main parts of the body all have been completed. As you can see in Figure 4-2, during the embryonic period the individual takes on the appearance of a human.

The obvious changes during the embryonic period are in size and shape. Length increases 100-fold as the number of cells soars into the thousands. The larger body parts, such as head and limbs, take form first, followed by the finer details, such as ears, toes, and fingers. Figure 4-3 shows how the hand becomes progressively differentiated, illustrating the general trend.

Fundamental internal changes accompany the rapid transformations of external appearance. The vital organs, such as heart and liver, take form.

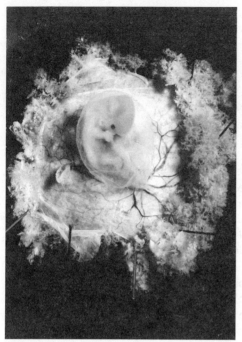

Figure 4–2 Embryo about 48 days after conception. *(Courtesy of Carnegie Institution of Washington, Department of Embryology.)*

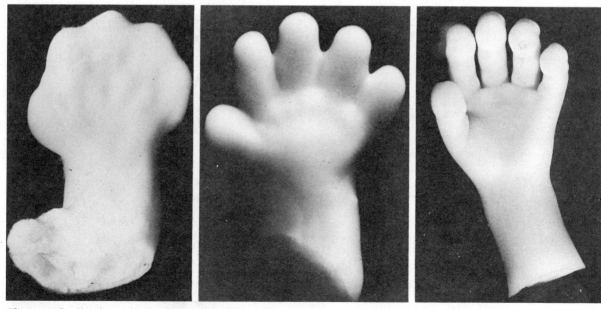

Figure 4–3 Hand growth illustrates progressive differentiation.

Typically, these organs begin to work, or function, soon after they are constructed. By the end of the fourth week, the heart is beating. The liver starts producing red blood cells at about nine weeks. Some of the biological processes that will be crucial for independent life later start while the embryo still is connected to its mother.

During the embryonic period the structures relating the embryo to its maternal environment develop in ways that parallel the changes in the individual itself. The connections involved in the original implantation become elaborated. The life-support system is built. A protective sac filled with fluid develops around the embryo. The sac reduces the amount of jostling when mother moves and helps to keep temperature constant.

Another structure, the *umbilical cord*, serves as a lifeline. It makes possible constant chemical interchange between the embryo's system and the mother's. Blood from the embryo and blood from the mother pass close to each other on different sides of the wall of cells, the *placental barrier*. The barrier works like a sieve. Large particles, including blood cells, cannot go through it. The two bloodstreams do not actually mix, but small particles can go through. Nutrients from the mother, such as sugars, fats, and proteins, get into the embryo's bloodstream. At the same time waste products from the embryo go into the mother's bloodstream. The sac surrounding the embryo and the umbilical cord protect and nourish it until birth puts the new individual on its own in the outer environment.

Fetal period

The fetal period is by far the longest prenatal stage, lasting from about the 9th week until birth at about the 38th week. It is a time for finishing

Figure 4-4 Fetus about 14 weeks after conception. (© *Joe Baker-Medical World News.*)

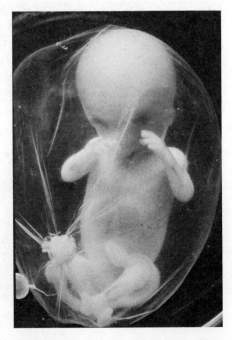

touches. The main body parts are constructed in basic form during the embryonic period. The details are worked out during the fetal period.

Bodily systems basic to postnatal behavior make much progress during the fetal period. The muscles are well developed by the end of 12 weeks and start to work soon afterwards. By 16 weeks the movements produced by muscle contractions are vigorous enough so that the mother can feel them. The nervous system continues to develop throughout the fetal period and remains unfinished at birth. By the end of 16 weeks, the sense organs have a mature appearance.

Behaviors typically can be carried out soon after the necessary structures are formed. Movement in response to touch can be observed in embryos. More specific reflexes, such as sucking and grasping, appear later, but even they are evident weeks before birth. By 28 weeks (about six and a half months) development has gone far enough so that a prematurely born fetus can survive if given the special help now possible. In other words basic functions such as breathing, sucking, and swallowing are far enough advanced that the fetus can do without the special support systems of being connected with the mother. However, at this point survival rate is closely linked to birth weight, with smaller babies more at risk.

The three periods as developmental stages

Prenatal growth is continuous. The embryonic period blends into the germinal period at one end and the fetal period at the other. Nevertheless, it is useful to think of these three periods as separate developmental stages.

Stage thinking provides an orderly way of summing up certain features of the complex changes that are lost if development is regarded as simply "more of the same." The three stages result from a focus on structure, function, and sensitive periods.

The original basis for creating the stages was *structure.* As cells multiply and grow, new parts, or structures, appear. The form of the body, its shape and composition, becomes different. With new parts there are new relations, or organizations, of parts. All these aspects of body growth are ignored when we say that growth is continuous. The stage concept emphasizes the fact that there is one period, the embryonic period, during which all the main parts are formed. No body parts are evident before it. Change afterwards involves finishing up, rather than adding new parts.

A second basis for the stages is *function.* The changes in what parts are present are paralleled by changes in function, in how the body works. Commonly, parts start to work, or function, soon after they are built. Thus, during the period of the embryo, the establishment of a link with the mother's system by means of the umbilical cord and the construction of body parts usher in important changes in functioning. Important internal organs such as the pituitary gland function in ways that influence other growth processes. For example, the pituitary gland (located just below the brain) produces a chemical known as growth hormone that stimulates other tissues to grow. Later during the fetal period, functional changes take place that make the crucial difference in whether life outside the womb is possible. Zygotes, embryos, and fetuses act differently.

The environmental agents that can disrupt prenatal development, such as X rays, certain drugs, and maternal diseases, have different influences at different times. This important fact led to the concept of *sensitive periods.* In general, one of these harmful agents, or *teratogens,* does the most damage to the parts of the body that are being formed when it acts. Exposure to X rays in the first two weeks of a pregnancy is likely to kill the developing individual. Exposure to the same dose of X rays a few weeks later when the legs are being formed is likely to produce an individual with malformed legs. If the same exposure comes still a few weeks later, the legs will develop normally but there might be minor defects in the heart or other aspects of the body not yet fully formed. Each body part, then, has a particular period when it is most vulnerable, or sensitive, to harm. The most obvious abnormalities in physical development are likely to be the result of problems during the embryonic period because this is when all the major body parts are forming.

Teratogens of the prenatal period include the following:

1. Diseases of the mother, such as rubella (German measles), chicken pox, hepatitis, and syphilis
2. Drugs taken by the mother, such as alcohol, nicotine, thalidomide, and stilbestrol (DES)
3. Diet of the mother, particularly protein deficiency
4. Exposure to X rays

Special hazards of the perinatal period include the following:

1. Rh problems resulting from incompatibility of a factor in the blood of mother and baby
2. Anoxia (lack of oxygen) resulting from birth complications
3. Low birth weight
4. Prematurity (being born early)

The existence of sensitive periods provides a third source of evidence supporting the value of thinking about prenatal development as consisting of three major stages. Some of the key facts defining the stages are summarized in Table 4-1.

BIRTH

The normal process

Birth normally occurs about 40 weeks after conception, the result of a complex set of reactions that apparently are triggered when a chemical message is released from the baby's brain (Macfarlane, 1977). The clear sign that the process has begun comes when the mother starts to feel the regular contractions that open the *cervix,* the entrance to the birth canal. These contractions signal the beginning of the first of three stages of labor. When the cervix is fully open, the baby's head can enter the birth canal. Now delivery, the second stage of labor, begins. The baby enters the birth canal, moves

TABLE 4-1 Stages in prenatal physical development

Stage	Begins	Initial Length	Main Body Parts	Common Teratogen Influence
Ovum	conception	0.01 cm	not present	death
Embryo	3rd week	0.03 cm	begin to form	major abnormalities
Fetus	8th week	3.0 cm	present	minor abnormalities
Birth				
Neonate	38th week	50.0 cm	present	——

through it, and comes out of the mother's body into the outside world. Finally, in the third stage of labor, the placenta is pushed out by additional contractions.

Delivery and the severing of the umbilical cord immediately force the baby to face new survival problems, such as getting oxygen and keeping body temperature constant. Newborns who have trouble in dealing with these problems must be identified and helped at once if they are to survive.

The Apgar Scale, developed by Virginia Apgar (1953), provides a quick and simple way of summing up the new baby's status, indicating which babies need immediate help and predicting which are most in danger of not surviving.

The Apgar score is based on an examination made one minute after birth. The newborn is rated on five objective signs:

1. Heart rate (the most important sign)—Is it normal or too slow or fast?
2. Respiratory effort—Is the breathing deep and regular?
3. Reflex irritability—Are reflexes such as coughing, sneezing, and crying present and strong?
4. Muscle tone—Is muscle tone good with activity level high? Or is the baby limp and inactive?
5. Color (the least revealing sign)—Is the baby all pink or blue?

The observer follows standard instructions and rates each sign 0, 1, or 2. The total score thus can range from 0 to 10. If the score is extremely low, say 3 or lower, expert attention is needed immediately. If the score is high, 7 or higher, there is no danger.

Special issues

Advances in our ability to influence the birth process have produced heated controversies about whether we should do it so often (Macfarlane, 1977). Often the disputes reflect inherent conflicts. For example, in guarding against important but unusual dangers, we may make routine deliveries more stressful than they have to be. Here are some of the issues of current concern.

Obstetric medication

Since 1847, medication to reduce the pain mothers experience during labor has become a common part of the birth process. But the use of medication varies tremendously among countries with good medical services, illustrating wide differences of opinion. In England and the United States obstetric medication is particularly common and apparently occurs for over 80% of all deliveries (Brackbill, 1979, p. 90). In sharp contrast, pain medicine is given for only 12% of the deliveries in Sweden and 5% in Holland (Macfarlane, 1977, p. 40).

In the United States concern about the impact of obstetric medication on the baby has grown and become a hot issue (Boston Women's Health Book Collective, 1976; Brackbill, 1979; Kolata, 1979; Macfarlane, 1977). Yvonne Brackbill (1979) is a leading critic of the practice of using medication to ease labor pains. She argues that the newborn is particularly vulnerable at birth to the impact of drugs, both because the nervous system is still developing and because the organs most involved in clearing drugs from the body (liver and kidneys) are poorly developed. She interprets the available evidence as showing that obstetric drugs have a negative influence on the baby's behavior later.

Brackbill's (1979) review of over 30 studies concludes that drugs given to mothers during labor and delivery can have an influence on infants that shows itself as much as one year later, and perhaps longer. The mothers who get the most medication and the more powerful drugs are more likely to have babies who show behavioral changes. The behavioral impact is negative, seems greatest in cognitive functioning and motor development, and is more likely to be found when the behavior test involves stress, as in requiring more exertion or sustained attention.

Not all experts agree with these dramatic claims about the dangers of obstetric medication. For example, one of Brackbill's own studies was sharply attacked by medical experts and statisticians (Kolata, 1979). A crucial interpretive question arises from the fact that Brackbill's studies, like most, are correlational. Brackbill and those who share her views think that with proper methodological controls mothers who get varying degrees of medication can be assumed equal in other important respects. But critics argue that mothers who are more tense and/or have more difficult deliveries are more likely to get medication and stronger medication (Federman & Yang, 1976; Kolata, 1979; Yang, Zweig, Douthitt, & Federman, 1976). Thus, they question whether the baby differences supposedly resulting from medication might instead relate to those nondrug variables. Critics also question whether short-term behavior changes associated with medication have any long-range importance (Kolata, 1979).

Induction and Caesarean section delivery

Today the normal process of labor can be started early, shortened, and even avoided. Labor can be induced, or started, by drugs or through surgical procedures (Macfarlane, 1977). The baby can be surgically removed through the mother's abdomen (Caesarean section, or C-section, delivery) so that it never passes through the birth canal. There are clear cases where induction and Caesarean section deliveries can save lives or reduce the dangers of major complications. However, the frequency of both procedures has increased greatly in recent years. Some question the wisdom of what they see as almost routine use of these procedures, arguing that they can have negative side effects.

Natural childbirth

Concern about possible negative influences of obstetric medication has helped stimulate an interest in alternatives, particularly natural childbirth (Macfarlane, 1977).

The basic idea of the natural childbirth approach is to help the mother prepare herself for delivery, physically and psychologically. Knowledge of what is to come, exercises to strengthen muscles, the presence of a familiar partner (usually the father), and a general sense of being in control all apparently can help the mother deal with birth with a minimum of anxiety and medication. Typically, the approach involves classes started a few weeks before delivery is expected, with the father attending the classes and later being present at the delivery.

Although some of the claims for the natural childbirth approach have not been fully evaluated, it often seems to work and is becoming more popular (Macfarlane, 1977). In the United States a growing trend is toward more classes preparing both parents for delivery, more participation by the father in the delivery process, and the provision of more homelike rooms and procedures within hospitals.

An argument for "birth without violence" also has gotten attention. Leboyer (1975) argues that standard hospital procedures are unnecessarily stressful on the new baby. He thinks that a gentler approach (including softer lights and immersion in warm water) would have lasting beneficial effects. But others have questioned how much discomfort the baby actually experiences and whether such brief experiences can have a lasting impact (Macfarlane, 1977).

Hospital versus home delivery

In the United States hospital delivery is the rule. In many states home delivery actually is illegal. Yet in Holland the majority of babies are born at home and the rate of infant mortality there is lower than in the United States (Macfarlane, 1977). Accordingly, some advocates of natural methods argue for home delivery as a preferred procedure, with hospitals used only when complications are likely.

Medical advances have become so familiar that we look at them in a more balanced way now. What is new and possible no longer is automatically assumed to be better. The years ahead should see a more careful evaluation of both the pros and cons of using the new techniques of delivery.

Complications

Complications occur in an important minority of births. Actually, birth complications often reflect problems that started early in the pregnancy; so it is a mistake to think of them in isolation (Kopp & Parmelee, 1979).

A broad view also is indicated by the fact that newborns suffering similar perinatal (around birth) problems can end up with tremendously varied outcomes (Kopp & Parmelee, 1979). In part this reflects the fact that a condition such as low birth weight can stem from tremendously varied factors, but it also reflects that what happens later is important. For example, premature babies born to middle-class families are much more likely to be psychologically normal six years later than those from poverty homes (Sameroff & Chandler, 1975).

No simple relations between birth complications and later outcomes have been found (Kopp & Parmelee, 1979), and none is likely to be found. The baby is born with tremendous capacities for growth and self-healing. Parents and society can and often do make special efforts to help children overcome the impact of potential handicaps (Sameroff & Chandler, 1975). Perinatal problems may put a child at risk for later trouble—that is, make difficulties more likely. But often the risk does not materialize.

Small babies illustrate the more general picture of what we are learning about the complications of birth. Babies born less than 37 weeks after conception are considered *premature.* Typically, they are small. But newborns can be small for their age since conception, regardless of whether they are born early or on time. For many purposes it is important to distinguish between these two sources of small size (being born early and being small for age) because they tend to stem from different factors (Kopp & Parmelee, 1979).

Dramatic strides have been made in saving small babies (Kopp & Parmelee, 1979; Tooley, 1981). Decade by decade the percentage that lives has risen and ideas about how small a baby can be saved have had to be revised. Now special neonatal units exist in which a tiny baby can be maintained, continuously monitored, and helped from a few minutes after birth.

Although more small newborns than normal-sized babies have problems later, there has been progress on this front as well. Most of the little babies who survive grow up normally, with a lower percentage having later difficulties than in the past (Tooley, 1981). In general both the chances for survival and the chances for normal development are related to size at birth, with smaller babies being more at risk.

A current frontier in helping small babies relates to their immediate environment: does the kind of stimulation to which the tiny baby is exposed make a difference? Apparently it does (Masi, 1979). A number of studies indicate that the baby does better physically and psychologically if extra stimulation is added to the relatively constant environment of the isolette (the special chamber in which the baby is kept). For example, measures such as weight gain and motor development tend to be higher for newborns given extra rocking or handling during the early weeks. Although research in this area is still in its earliest stages, the results so far are exciting.

Another frontier relates to the broader environment. Small and/or premature babies are more likely to be born to mothers in poor health before and during pregnancy, mothers with inadequate diets during pregnancy, and mothers who take drugs such as alcohol during pregnancy (Kopp & Parmelee, 1979; Robertson, 1979). Low-income mothers are much more likely to have small babies, as well as to have the low-birth-weight babies who develop problems later. Accordingly, one of the most important ways of reducing the number of babies born at risk is to provide better prenatal and postnatal care to all mothers.

POSTNATAL PHYSICAL GROWTH

The newborn's body shows the results of nine months of momentous change and provides a baseline for what follows. The newborn's form and proportions are much more like ours than those of the 8-week-old fetus. But at birth the head is still relatively large for the body and the legs are still relatively short.

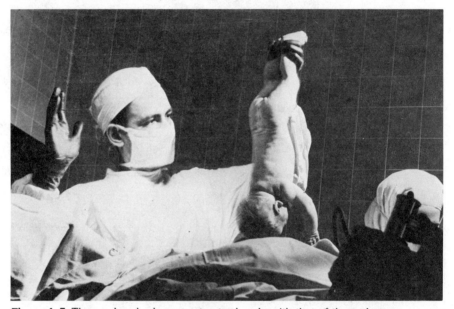

Figure 4–5 The newborn's shape contrasts sharply with that of the embryo.

Height

Children focus on height as an index of physical maturity. "Taller" means "bigger" to them. "Bigger" means "more grown-up." Their approach is a good one, though incomplete, for height is a good starting point in understanding postnatal growth.

Height growth is seen best when we repeatedly measure the same child as she or he grows up (Tanner, 1970). Such longitudinal studies reveal developmental regularities common to all children. When we look at height *gains,* how much the child adds each year, we see that height growth is at a maximum right after birth and at about 13 years (Figure 4–6). At other times growth is slower and more constant.

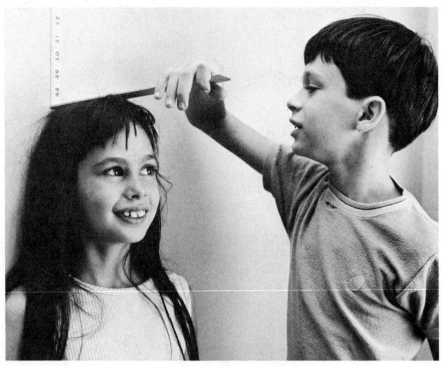

Children focus on height as an index of physical maturity.

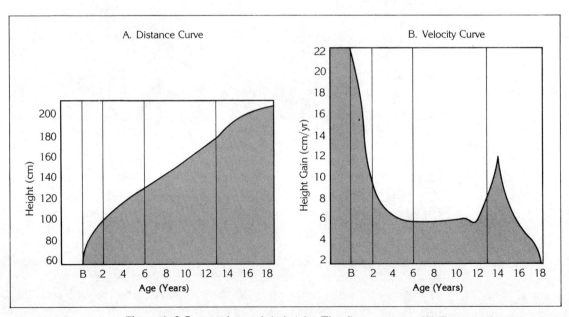

Figure 4–6 Postnatal growth in height. The distance curve (A) illustrates how a typical child's total height increases. The velocity curve (B) presents the same information in terms of yearly gains.

Special features

Height growth illustrates that there are two periods of postnatal growth that deserve special attention: during infancy and at puberty. The growth during infancy is a continuation and windup of the rapid growth of the prenatal period. An important feature of this early period is that the still unfinished brain is growing rapidly after birth. The growth spurt at puberty, in contrast, involves a new process: the secretion of sex hormones. Puberty is largely the story of these chemical messages and how they act.

Brain

The growth of the brain after birth is unique. After unusually great size increases during infancy, brain growth slows down, tapering off after age 6 and finishing at about age 13, when most parts of the body are just beginning a period of rapid growth (see Figure 4–7).

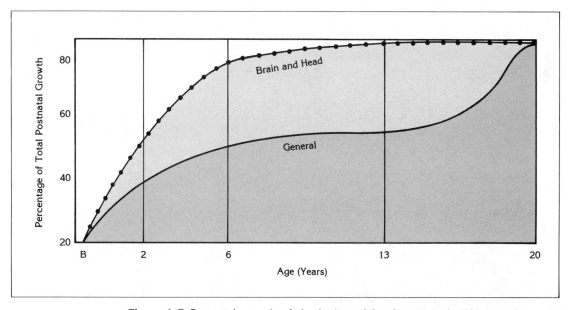

Figure 4–7 Postnatal growth of the brain and head compared with general growth. (*Adapted from "The Measurement of the Body in Childhood," by R. E. Scammon. In J. A. Harris, C. M. Jackson, D. G. Paterson, and R. E. Scammon (Eds.),* The Measurement of Man. *Copyright © 1930 by University of Minnesota Press. Reprinted by permission.*)

At birth the child's brain contains 10 billion neurons, or nerve cells. It never gets any more. If some are lost through injury or disease, they are not replaced, as are cells in other parts of the body. Further growth involves changes in the cells present at birth and the growth of new cells next to the nerve cells.

Two important changes take place in the brain cells during the months following birth: (1) an insulating sheath of myelin develops around them (*myelinization*) and (2) the branches (*dendrites*) at the end grow like branches on a tree, with new "twigs" developing (*arborization of dendrites*). You can see both the myelin sheath and the dendrites in the neuron sketched in Figure 4–8. In Figure 4–9 you can see corresponding portions of the top (*cortical*) layers of the brain at different ages. As the dendrites develop more and more branches, connections between nerve cells become more and more numerous.

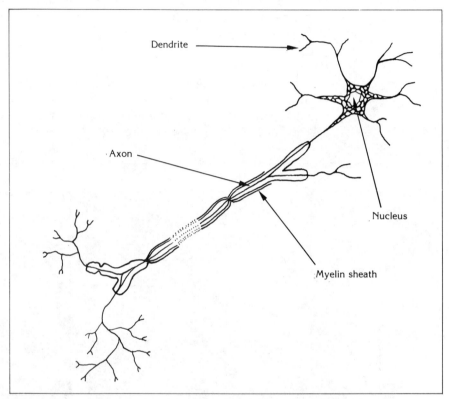

Figure 4–8 A neuron with an insulating sheath of myelin and dendrites.

Myelinization is not completed until after the first birthday (Reese & Lipsitt, 1970). The development of branching in the dendrites continues for several years and is not complete until about age 6. These structural changes seem to relate to important developments in the brain's function. Myelinization enables nerve cells to carry electrical messages more quickly. Arborization makes it easier for communication between brain cells. Most likely both the development of mature brain wave patterns and some changes in behavior are paced by these changes in the nerve cells (Reese & Lipsitt, 1970).

Both the physical maturation of the brain and changes in the electrical functioning of the brain follow an orderly pattern after birth. Myelinization occurs in certain areas before others, as does dendritization. Spontaneous brain waves and electrical responses to stimulation change in typical ways at certain ages (Reese & Lipsitt, 1970). These maturational patterns may have much to

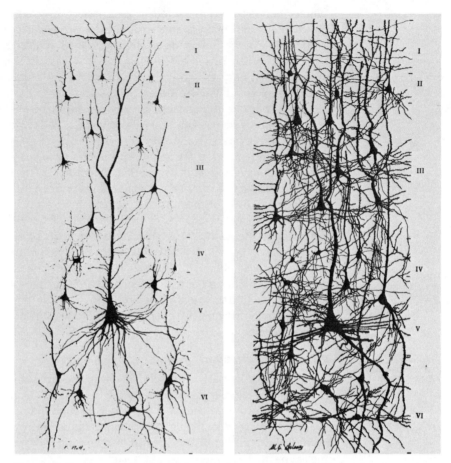

Figure 4–9   The growth of dendrites provides more connections between neurons.

do with some of the sequences seen in behavioral development, particularly during infancy.

Lower brain centers closely associated with more automatic actions such as breathing are more mature at birth. They soon work as they will later. In contrast, the upper part of the brain (cerebral cortex), more important in voluntary actions such as talking, coordinating information from different sensory channels, and waiting and planning, is less mature at birth. It takes on mature characteristics gradually. The shift from the reflexive action of early infancy to more goal-directed and complexly patterned behavior could be maturational in origin (Bronson, 1965; McGraw, 1943; Salapatek, 1975). Similarly, the shift to more self-controlled behavior at about age 5 to 7 may rest on maturational changes that make it easier to inhibit impulsive actions (White, 1965). But we still don't know.

We do know that the normal pattern of physical development in brain and nerves depends in part on a normal environment. The clearest evidence comes from isolation experiments with laboratory animals (Riesen, 1975).

When chimpanzees are reared in darkness, the volume of the nerve cells between eye and brain is smaller and there are fewer cells in the retina (the part of the eye that responds electrically to light and sends nerve impulses to the brain). When rats are reared in bare cages, the weights and chemical proportions in parts of the brain are different than if they grew up in a more complicated world. Austin Riesen (1975) emphasizes environmental demands for use as basic to the usual pattern of development. Without such demands organizations of nerves can be lost or changed. With an unusual environment physical development is unusual.

The long period of formation for the brain suggests that it might have a correspondingly long sensitive period. Accordingly, there has been concern about the impact of starvation on brain development (Kaplan, 1972). Children who die as a result of malnutrition typically have small brains, often as much as 30 or 40% smaller. Studies of experimental animals and malnourished children suggest that early starvation can result in fewer brain cells and inadequate myelinization, both irreversible changes. Later malnutrition apparently can produce smaller brain cells, probably a reversible condition. The relation between these brain problems and behavioral development is still unclear, but starvation in the six months before birth and for months after birth may produce both irreversible changes and accompanying mental retardation (Kaplan, 1972).

Puberty growth spurt

The growth spurt at puberty involves widespread changes in the body (Tanner, 1970). Puberty is started by the brain, which signals the master gland right below it to send chemical messages through the bloodstream to the sex glands. They send out their own chemicals, or hormones. The increase of hormonal output stimulates growth in many other systems. Bones complete their growth. The muscles become bigger and more efficient in function. The sex organs enlarge and take their mature form. The amount of body hair increases. Hair grows around the sex organs.

PROCESSES UNDERLYING PHYSICAL DEVELOPMENT

The regular changes that typify physical development provoke questions. Why does the human zygote turn into a person rather than a kitten or monkey? How does one cell "know" enough to become skin while another becomes bone? Why do the fingers always get formed before the brain is completed? What accounts for the changes in the growth rate at puberty? These questions all relate to the problem of *process*, the series of changes that produce the outcomes we observe more directly. Knowing when the arms are formed does not explain why or how they are formed.

The developmental changes within one developing child are best understood when related to a broader picture. The evolutionary processes that made us what we are, the hereditary processes involved when parent characteristics are passed on to their children, and the developmental processes that turn the zygote into a child all are part of the same story.

Evolutionary background

The human body emerged through evolutionary processes that took place over millions of years. We think it reflects the survival of what worked in past environments through the adaptive process of variation, selection, and preservation.

Human bodies combine characteristics evolved long before there were creatures resembling people and more recent features unique to *hominoid* (humanlike) forms. Lungs and hearts and the lower brain centers that regulate their workings are old in evolutionary terms. A thumb suited for precise grasping and the brain centers most closely related to its use are new.

Recent fossil evidence suggests that a crucial step toward humanhood came when a monkeylike creature changed environments (Campbell, 1974; Lancaster, 1978; Pilbeam, 1978). An early *primate* (the family including monkeys, apes, and people) left the forest and moved into the open plains. In this new world with different foods, a new set of body parts and behavior patterns evolved. Standing on two legs and moving about on them most likely was the earliest and most crucial change. The upright posture made it possible to use the hands and arms in new ways. Food could be gathered, collected, and carried back to a home base, where it was shared. Modifications in the thumb made possible a new precision that fostered tool use.

The changes related to the move from the forest apparently all took place before the evolution of a large brain. Seemingly, the big brain evolved in response to new selection pressures later. Perhaps the demands of cooperative hunting and of surviving during the ice ages put a premium on new ways of communicating, thinking, and remembering (Washburn, 1960).

Our bodies and culture (our shared ways of acting) evolved together. It's not that our bodies and animal nature were constructed first and then were followed by the invention of "higher" and special ways of acting, such as language and religion. Instead, we must see the emergence of unique physical features and new ways of acting as two sides of the same process (Geertz, 1973).

The new infancy

The evolutionary story puts human infancy in a special light. Perhaps it was a necessary compromise (Washburn, 1960). When standing upright and moving efficiently in this evolved position, the pelvis changed dramatically. As a result the opening through which babies are born became smaller. But the evolution of a large brain would have demanded a larger opening if nothing else had changed; so there had to be a compromise between the needs for walking erect and for having a large brain.

Human babies are unique. They are born with softer brains, softer skulls, and incompletely joined bones in the skull. These special features make it possible for them to squeeze through a tightly fitting birth passage without ill effects. Seemingly as a result, our infancy involves more helplessness than that of our closest relatives. This kind of infancy, in turn, ties in closely with the special social world that evolved at about the same time.

The new infancy put more demands on mothers, but other developments made it easier for mothers to meet them (Lancaster, 1978). Walking erect and new hand skills made it easier to carry babies. New social patterns such as food sharing among adults and a home base to which adults returned after searching for food made it easier for mothers to get help during the baby-tending period. The coevolution of a new kind of baby and a new environment for babies made a new form of childhood possible.

The human baby's inability to move independently or feed itself for many months makes a long period of close contact with adults necessary. As a result there is more time for social learning, as in mastering language and in watching adults. So the baby's helplessness is hardly a problem to be solved as quickly as possible. Our special infancy is intimately tied up with special features of a human way of life.

Parent to child

Generations of parents passed on a biological heritage that changed gradually. The modern human body and its psychological possibilities took form through that slow process of preadaptation. Now let's look at the quicker process by which parents today pass on this heritage to their children.

Chemicals in the mother's egg and the father's sperm combine at conception when the zygote is formed. These chemicals contain the information, or plan, that will guide the process of building a human body with human potentialities.

Genotype and phenotype

Genotype refers to the genetic information present in the zygote. *Phenotype* refers to the characteristics of the person later. The relation between such mature (phenotypic) characteristics as height and eye color and the (genotypic) information in the zygote is complicated and indirect.

The phenotype reflects both genotype and environment. Children will be short if they grow up under starvation conditions, even if their genotype includes information that would lead to tall stature under normal conditions. Similar appearance does not necessarily mean the same genotype: two children with brown eyes can have different genetic patterns related to eye color. (Some of the complex relations between genotypes and phenotypes of psychological importance will be discussed in later chapters on sex differences and intellectual differences.)

Chromosomes and genes

The genetic information from the parents is carried in packages known as *chromosomes*. Each chromosome includes a long string of *genes*, chemicals thought of as the unit characteristics of heredity. Genes are particular bits of information that relate to the phenotypic characteristics we observe.

The genetic material from each parent is contained in 23 chromosomes in each sperm and in each unfertilized egg (*ovum*). These chromosomes result from a special process of cell division (called *meiosis*) that takes place only in sex cells. At conception the two sets of 23 chromosomes come together. Each

Height and other phenotypic characteristics reflect both the genotype and the environment's influence on it.

zygote gets 23 pairs of chromosomes, one member of each pair from each parent. Each time that cell division takes place between conception and birth, the 23 pairs of chromosomes are reduplicated.

Thus, each cell in the newborn's body contains all the genetic information from each parent, and half of each child's genes come from each parent. *Meiosis* in the parents results in each egg or sperm being somewhat similar and somewhat different from other sex cells from the same parent. Thus any two siblings (children of the same parents) have half their genes in common (except for identical twins).

Now we turn to the question of how the chemical information in genes and chromosomes (known as DNA) guides physical development. In Chapter 14 I will consider how genes and chromosomes relate to sex differences and in Chapter 15 how they tie in with intellectual differences.

DNA—the central plan

DNA (an abbreviation for deoxyribonucleic acid) is a long chemical molecule present in every living cell. It works as a chemical blueprint that guides physical development. It starts, continues, and stops the chemical reactions basic to growth. Thus, it paces and coordinates the observable changes I have described.

Although DNA in all children (and all living creatures) is similar, each child has a unique form (except for identical twins). Every child's DNA is unique and also is like everyone else's DNA because all DNA is made of the same few basic chemicals combined somewhat differently in different individuals and in different species. Often an analogy is made between the chemicals in DNA and the letters in the alphabet. Just as the same 26 letters can be used to make thousands of different words and millions of different sentences, the four basic chemicals making up the genetic information in DNA get combined differently in different children.

Body part construction.   The information in DNA results in the production of diverse kinds of tissue, such as muscle, nerve, blood, and bone, and of specialized body parts, such as arms, legs, and livers. All the different kinds of tissues are forms of *protein*. DNA controls the production of proteins. Different parts of the DNA molecule regulate the manufacture of different proteins.

Feedback influences.   Physical development involves an enormous number of reactions happening in time. Without coordination there would be chaos. Some reactions, such as the construction of heart tissue, are started early and ended early. Other processes, such as the development of some of the sexual apparatus, wait until years later. DNA is responsible for both the messages that start construction processes and those that turn them off. DNA guides early physical development, as in building arms, and later events, such as growing pubic hair. The successful coordination of all these processes in normal development shows that in some sense the DNA "knows what time it is." Otherwise the right thing wouldn't happen at the proper time.

A *feedback system* operates; messages get back to the DNA to control what it does next. There is two-way control, with *hormones* and other chemicals providing the feedback. Information about how far development has gone comes back and helps determine what instructions go out next.

Other feedback processes

Chemical messages that feed back the information that regulates the action of DNA illustrate a more general theme: delicate coordination of growth processes is basic to biological development; this coordination depends on a variety of feedback processes.

Hormones play a role both in the development of body parts and in the regulation of bodily processes (Doering, 1980). These chemical messages from endocrine glands such as the pituitary, the thyroid, and the sex glands are important at varied ages. About ten weeks after conception the pituitary gland has developed and starts producing hormones known as *growth hormones* because of their central role in growth processes. The action of these growth hormones triggers the dramatic peak in growth rate during the fetal period. About 13 years after birth other hormones from the pituitary play a crucial role in the adolescent growth spurt and in the development of mature sexual organs.

Homeorhesis

Feedback processes make it possible for systems to maintain constancies in the face of disruptive influences. Temperature regulation is a good example. Despite changes in the temperature around the child, the body tends to maintain an internal temperature close to 98.6°F (37°C). Temperature regulation is achieved through the operation of processes such as sweating when it is hot (which speeds up the loss of heat from the body) and having less blood at the surface of the body when it is cold (which reduces heat loss). These opposite processes are controlled through the nervous system, which uses information from the skin and internal organs to "know" whether heat loss is to be sped up or slowed down. They illustrate *homeostasis*, the process by which our bodies maintain a steady state.

Waddington (1957) has argued that although we find homeostasis through-out life, during development we also find *homeorhesis* (the process of main-taining a constant developmental direction in the face of disturbing forces).

Tanner (1970) has presented an intriguing illustration of homeorhesis in human physical development: catch-up growth. Children growing up in occu-pied Europe during the Nazi occupation typically grew at a slower rate than would have been predicted from their growth curves prior to starvation. Then, after the war, when they returned to normal opportunities, they grew at a faster rate than would have been expected from their original growth curves, gradually slowing down toward their expected rate as they got closer to ex-pected size. A similar pattern occurs when a glandular tumor results in lower growth rate. Removal of the tumor is followed by a catch-up pattern. It is as if the growing body had a target toward which it was aiming, say a height of 65 inches (165.1 cm). When unexpected circumstances lower the growth curve, there is compensation, an apparent effort to get back on target.

Expected environment

Physical development is complex and time-consuming. Billions of separate events take place during millions of minutes before we get from the zygote to puberty. The similarity of outcome and the regularity of sequence in all children make us look for universal factors that operate in each case to produce the standard outcome.

DNA plays a central role in producing the regular sequences in physical development. All children's physical development is similar in part because they share similar chemical blueprints. But DNA does not do the whole job. We must look further if we are to understand why physical development is so regular. Think about size growth. At birth the child's weight is millions of times greater than the weight of the original zygote. The weight that was gained all came from outside the zygote. The blueprint in the DNA was only a construc-tion plan. The raw material for a child had to be supplied.

The environment supplies the raw materials for physical development. Crucial ingredients such as energy and amino acids must be present if DNA is to guide the construction of protein and tissues. The building process takes thousands of days. The supplies have to keep coming or the blueprint will never become an actuality.

But the environment must do much more. Normal development requires normal, or standard or expected, environmental conditions. Many of these crucial environmental conditions are so constant that they are easily taken for granted. They are conditions that have endured for our species for centuries and afford us the basis for life and behavior as we know it (Gibson, 1979). For example, for thousands of years radiation of the kind produced by X-ray machines and atomic bombs was at low levels wherever a human being was able to go. Now the picture has changed. Pregnant women are exposed to X rays and atomic blasts. The unexpected happens. Developing children are exposed to high levels of radiation while in the womb. Development goes wrong. The plan in the DNA produces a different and often tragic result: death, deformity, or bodily malfunction results instead of the expected, normal child. Only when DNA can operate in the kind of standard environment in which human beings evolved can we see the familiar regularities in physical development.

Homeorhesis shows the individual's ability to compensate for some fluctuations in the environment. But there are limits in the ability to stay on target. Radiation is one item on a growing list. Other departures from the normal teach us more about the crucial role of the environment in human physical development. A worldwide epidemic of rubella (German measles) left us with thousands of handicapped children whose mothers contracted the disease while pregnant. A new medication (Thalidomide) produced another group of children whose development was abnormal because the environment supplied the unexpected. These examples show how unusual physical-chemical conditions in the child's environment can influence development. More usual factors also are known to play a role (see Box 4–1). Maternal alcohol consumption and cigarette smoking during pregnancy may result in a smaller baby at birth. Starvation of the pregnant mother or the young infant apparently influences the size of the brain and some details of brain structure. Modern dietary and health conditions seemingly produce children who reach puberty earlier and grow larger.

Physical development results from a continuous interaction of the child and its environment. The pattern of changes in the developing hand or brain are not in the DNA any more than the hand or the brain themselves were in the zygote. The regularities show what happens when the DNA of our species interacts with the kind of environment in which our species evolved. In the years to come, changes both in the DNA and in the environment may possibly occur. When and if they do, there will be different patterns of physical development.

Applications box 4–1   Fetal alcohol syndrome

Alcohol is a familiar and socially acceptable drug. Advertisements portray drinking as sophisticated. On many campuses it is the "in" drug; so it is not surprising that as women are becoming more liberated, their drinking rates are increasing toward those of men.

But like some new and less popular drugs, alcohol is a teratogen, or "monster maker." Drinking by pregnant women can result in a fetal alcohol syndrome (FAS), accompanied by both physical malformations and behavior problems (Abel, 1980; Rosett & Sander, 1979). Babies of mothers who drink heavily show a pattern of abnormalities that is so distinctive that some think a look at the newborn makes it possible to diagnose the mother as alcoholic. The distinctive bodily pattern includes growth deficiencies resulting in small size, a small head, small eye openings, and abnormalities in joints, limbs, and heart. The most serious psychological problem is mental retardation, which may be the most sensitive indicator of FAS because it can occur in the absence of the physical pattern. Some consider alcohol to be the most frequent teratogenic cause of mental retardation in the Western world. Other psychological problems sometimes associated with FAS include withdrawal symptoms shortly after birth, such as hyperactivity, prolonged twitching, and more lasting problems such as distractibility, impulsiveness, and learning difficulties.

The syndrome occurs in at least partial form in about 1 in 200 babies born in the United States and is expected to become more common as female drinking rates increase. Like maternal smoking and exposure to X rays, drinking by pregnant women represents one of the most important and controllable hazards to the fetus.

The mechanisms by which alcohol influences development seem relatively clear. Once the placenta develops, alcohol passes from mother to fetus and distributes itself throughout the body in proportion to the water content of the tissues. Alcohol typically becomes more concentrated in the gray matter of the fetus's brain than in the white matter, because the gray matter has a higher water concentration. Presumably, the brain is most vulnerable between the 12th and 18th weeks, when nerve cells are multiplying, and again during the last three months, when dendrites are growing and connections between nerve cells are being established.

However, as Abel (1980) points out, it is not yet clear to what extent the mental retardation associated with FAS is a direct result of alcohol and to what extent it is produced by related factors. For example, genetic susceptibility to the syndrome seems to vary. Factors such as heavy smoking and poor nutrition, which are often associated with drinking during pregnancy, may contribute in some way.

What about the practical implications? Is there a "safe" level of drinking during pregnancy? The answer is yes only if you assume there are no important results of drinking when the obvious signs of the FAS are absent. In other words, at a level of a few drinks a week, drinking is highly unlikely to produce a baby with severe retardation and obvious physical abnormalities. Such dramatic symptoms become common only at drinking levels more like a drink or two a day. But we don't know yet whether subtler physical and psychological problems are increased by low levels of consumption; so wisdom suggests that pregnant women should not drink at all.

SUMMARY

The story of physical development is long, detailed, and yet incomplete. It is relevant to psychological development in two ways. It gives us both facts to try to relate to psychological development and also ideas, or metaphors, to apply when we think about the development of behavior.

Early growth, during the prenatal period and infancy, emerges as more dramatic and more complicated than the later physical growing up emphasized in daily conversation. The fetus and baby grow faster than the teenager in the midst of a growth spurt. The major changes in body form take place during a few short weeks, in contrast to the increases in size and the minor shifts in shape that stretch out for years after birth.

Perhaps the most amazing fact about physical growth is that it normally is so orderly and predictable, despite the fact that billions of separate events are involved. In looking for an explanation of the order and the regularity that is basic to physical development, attention turned to two basic patterns: the chemical code in DNA through which heredity is passed on and the stable, or expected, features of the environment that existed when our species evolved and that still exist today. Normal physical development, then, emerged as the result of a complex and continuing interaction between the two.

CHAPTER 5

Learning

Learning is a basic fact of child life. Children learn to walk, to talk, and to operate a television set. They learn when to be quiet and where not to crayon. They learn to recognize the letter *J* and how to tell the difference between a boy and a girl. Children learn to love some of the people around them and to hate others. Often they acquire fears. Most of the time they learn how to handle them "maturely." If we compare 13-year-old Nancy's actions with what she did the day she was born, we see that thousands of learning experiences played a key role in the change. If you take a nurture, or environmentalist, position, you try to explain more of the change in terms of learning. If you emphasize nature, you give learning less credit. But either way you cannot ignore it. If you want to understand children, you have to learn about learning.

Psychologists use *learning* as a broad term for all changes in activity that result from experience and cannot be explained by physical maturation or by temporary variables such as fatigue or drugs (Hilgard & Bower, 1966). In other words, learning includes much more than what goes on in school. It includes "hot" topics such as learning to love and hate along with "cool" ones such as learning the alphabet. Changes in attitudes, emotions, and personality can involve learning just as much as improvements in writing or arithmetic skills. The question is whether we see a change in behavior reflecting the role of experience, not what the change was or in what setting it took place.

Because learning is a vast and central topic, I shall approach it in several ways. I'll first discuss some basic processes. Then I'll examine biological constraints on learning and alternative conceptions of learning.

SENSORIMOTOR LEARNING PROCESSES

The most widespread forms of learning are those that do not require elaborate mental processes, such as reasoning. Little babies, like dogs and pigeons, profit from experience, even though their learning seems different from that of the older child mastering long division. It is convenient to label these earlier and more universal kinds of learning *sensorimotor* because they rest more directly on what can be sensed physically (*stimuli* such as the taste of milk or the sound of a bell) and often involve motor, or muscular, *responses* such as sucking, reaching, or turning the head.

In sensorimotor learning there is no process of representation, such as a child imagining that he is eating ice cream or thinking to himself about the spoon he sees. When we assume that symbolism or representation is involved in a child's learning, we must go beyond sensorimotor learning to explain it. I discuss symbolic learning later in this chapter.

First I'll examine three forms of sensorimotor learning: habituation, classical conditioning, and instrumental conditioning.

Habituation

Habituation is perhaps the simplest and the earliest form of learning we can observe. We see it when the same stimulus is repeatedly presented within a relatively short time, as when a tone is sounded over and over. The resulting change is a reduction in response. For example, a startled change in breathing at the first loud sound becomes less marked by the sixth time the sound is repeated.

It's useful to think about habituation in relation to the idea of orienting responses. A novel stimulus usually produces changes in arousal measures, such as heart rate. The reaction can be thought of as an *orienting response* that alerts the child and makes him or her more receptive to stimulation (Sokolov, 1963). When Pavlov observed the orienting reaction in dogs (including the familiar perking up of the ears), he called it the "what-is-it? reflex." With repeated presentations of the same "new" stimulus, "What is it?" turns into "Oh, that again." Habituation can be thought of as a process in which response to novelty disappears as the new becomes familiar.

Habituation is prominent in infant research (Berg & Berg, 1979; Horowitz, 1974; Jeffrey & Cohen, 1971). Its prominence makes sense when you realize that the newborn lives in a world in which most stimuli are new. A study by Trygg Engen and Lewis Lipsitt (1965) illustrates an important research function of habituation: we can use it to explore the new baby's picture of the world.

Engen and Lipsitt (1965) studied how newborns react to odors. A swab that had been dipped in a mixture of two smelly chemicals was placed in front of the baby's nose repeatedly, about once a minute. Usually the baby responded to the first stimulus presentation with a lot of wiggling and a marked change in breathing patterns. But by the 10th time the same mixture was presented such reactions were rare. On the 11th and 12th trials the stimulus was changed for half the babies. Now they were presented with one of the original two odors alone. This group responded to the new smell vigorously, giving as many strong reactions as they originally had to the mixture. The other half of the babies simply had two more trials with the mixture and continued to show little response to it. This confirmed that the infants who reacted strongly to the change in odors had smelled the difference and reacted to it. Thus, the experiment demonstrated habituation and simultaneously showed that even babies in the first days after birth can tell the difference between a mixture of two odors and one presented alone.

But what about life outside the laboratory? How might habituation contribute to normal development in the everyday world? Apparently it plays two roles, intellectual and emotional. Habituation probably makes it possible to focus attention on one task and not be distracted by every stimulus that comes along. Effective problem solving requires that you tune out all the familiar sights and sounds that are irrelevant to the task at hand. The emotional role of habituation is suggested by experiments on animals raised in isolation.

When a monkey is raised alone in a bare cage without exposure to varied sights and sounds, it often acts unusual when taken out and put in a normal environment. It seems upset and engages in repetitive actions, such as rocking. It has trouble learning from experience. Often these unusual behaviors disappear after a few weeks of living in a normal, complex world. Current explanations of these observations often focus on habituation (Fuller, 1967; Mason, 1968).

In the normal world there is constant novelty, but the baby can get used to it in small doses. There is probably a steady series of small arousal changes, or emotional reactions, as the baby gradually habituates to the environment. In contrast, the baby monkey who grows up in a simple and constant world and then moves to a normal one faces an enormous dose of novelty all at once. Apparently, behaviors such as rocking and the early learning deficits are reactions to a high level of excitement produced by all the novelty. Isolation experiments give us a concrete picture of what might happen if novelty and habituation were not common in early life.

Classical or respondent conditioning

Classical conditioning is always based on an inborn, or unconditional, reflex, such as the newborn's sucking of a nipple placed between the lips or showing a heart rate change when pricked with a pin. The term *respondent* emphasizes that in reflexes the child's action is passive, responding to the environment.

Classical conditioning probably relates to more aspects of behavior in the newborn than in older children because reflexive activity becomes less prominent during infancy. But it can help us understand the learning and unlearning of emotional associations at any age, as when Helen develops a stomachache the morning a spelling test is scheduled and Dan's palms start sweating when the teacher calls on him.

Baby Alex demonstrates a familiar example of classical conditioning. He cries at the sight of a person in a white coat. How did such a basically neutral stimulus come to produce such a reaction? By association. A doctor in a white coat gave Alex a series of injections; so the sight of a white coat took on a new meaning: injection is coming. I'll summarize this example in technical terms to illustrate the principles of respondent conditioning in general.

The original reflexive reaction in this situation was crying in response to the needle in the arm. We think of it as *unconditioned* because it always occurs, regardless of past experience. In all normal babies the needle in the arm, or unconditioned stimulus (US), produces the crying, or unconditioned response (UR), regardless.

    a. US → UR   (biologically based connection)

The neutral stimulus (person in the white coat) gets its connection with crying *conditionally*. The association depends on experience. (Before the first injection, the person in the white coat did not produce crying.) The person in the white coat in this example is called a *conditioned stimulus* (CS). The crucial condition that made for learning through experience was the repeated connection of the CS and the US in time. They occurred together. The CS came before and with the US (conditioning would not have occurred if the white coat had only appeared after the injection was over). There was thus a correlation, or association, of CS and US in time (as indicated by the broken circle connecting them in formula b):

b. US ↦ UR
   CS

As a result of the CS-US pairing, the CS got the power to produce a *conditioned response* (CR) similar to the reflexive, unconditioned, response:

c. US → UR
   CS --→ CR

The broken line connecting CS and CR in formula c, then, represents a learned connection, paralleling the inborn connection between US and UR represented by a solid line.

Because the association between CS and CR depended on special conditions, the connection can be broken when conditions change. For example, if Alex kept meeting people in white coats without getting any more injections, the crying at the sight of a person in a white coat would diminish and eventually disappear. *Extinction* is the term for this process, the disappearance of the CR as a result of repeated presentations of the CS without the US.

Stimulus generalization is universal in conditioning. Even if a single CS is paired with the US, as when only one coat plus person was paired with the injection, similar stimuli (such as other people in white coats) also gain new meaning.

Stimulus discrimination is the opposite of generalization. It follows generalization and depends on both extinction and conditioning. Alex might generalize his conditioned response and shriek in fear the first time he sees the ice-cream man in a white coat. But if he keeps meeting the ice-cream man and no injections follow, then the generalized reaction will extinguish. If, meanwhile, he were to keep getting injections from the doctor, he would end up with a discriminating pattern of reaction—fear of the doctor and no fear of the ice-cream man.

Instrumental or operant conditioning

Instrumental or operant conditioning focuses on learning involving muscular motor responses other than reflexes. Only through such motor responses can the child act upon the world. Pushing doors, lifting spoons, and walking are motor responses subject to the principles of operant conditioning, as are saying please and writing C-A-T. All these actions operate on the world, physical and social, and change it.

Operant learning gets the child something from the world. Some call it instrumental learning because the behavior serves as a means toward an end. The term for what operant behavior gets the child is *reinforcement* (similar in meaning to reward). Conventionally, reinforcement is thought of as a form of stimulation, such as food or praise, from the outside world. In operant conditioning the basic principles thus relate to responses (R) and to special kinds of stimuli (reinforcing stimuli, S^R) that sometimes follow them.

The basic principle, or law, of operant conditioning states that responses followed by reinforcement become more probable, or frequent. This principle, known as the *law of effect,* says that the actions that fit in with the environment survive. The behaviors that don't produce the right results become extinct. Operant conditioning and operant extinction, then, depend on whether a motor response is followed by reinforcement. The two types of conditioning are contrasted in Table 5–1.

Generalization and discrimination phenomena also are found in operant conditioning. A reinforced response such as putting a pea in the mouth is likely to be spontaneously generalized to stimuli such as pieces of dirt. However, when the pieces of dirt are chewed, the consequences are less rewarding. Discrimination in operant conditioning, as in respondent, results from the working of conditioning and extinction. Putting peas in the mouth is rewarded; putting dirt in the mouth is not. The originally generalized response becomes

TABLE 5–1 Two forms of conditioning contrasted

	Type 1	Type 2
Names	Classical Conditioning Respondent Conditioning	Instrumental Conditioning Operant Conditioning
Pioneer Investigators	Ivan Pavlov	Edward L. Thorndike B. F. Skinner
Adaptive Significance	Originally neutral stimuli that signal innately meaningful events to follow become meaningful signals themselves.	Responses that produce useful changes in the environment survive.
Basic Conditioning Procedure	Present a neutral stimulus (CS) in contiguity with an unconditioned stimulus (US)	Present a reinforcing stimulus (S^R) following a response (R)
Outcome of Conditioning	The neutral stimulus acquires meaning similar to that of the unconditioned stimulus.	The response becomes more probable.
Key Association	Between stimuli (CS·US)	Between a response and a stimulus (R·S^R)
Examples	Sight of bottle (CS) comes to elicit sucking	Sight of pea followed by picking it up
	Sight of person in white coat comes to elicit heart rate changes	Sound of little brother crying comes to be followed by giving him a piece of candy
Everyday Parallel	Involuntary	Voluntary

more discriminative. Responses such as using the pincer grip on peas are naturally reinforced because they produce immediate results from the physical environment. Responses such as saying please require the actions of other people for reinforcement.

Performance

Mrs. Taylor dreaded the arrival of her in-laws. They were sticklers for good manners, but Mrs. Taylor's son, Donald, seemed unable to learn how to hold his fork, to say please, or to sit properly at the table, despite her daily effort to teach him "decent" behavior. Then the crucial test came. Donald's performance amazed and delighted her. He sat properly, used his utensils with grace, and said please and thank you at all the appropriate times.

The learning/performance distinction

Donald's behavior illustrates the *learning/performance* distinction, an important one. On the day his relatives came Donald performed in a way that showed he had learned just what his mother had tried to teach him, even though his performance up until that day suggested he had not. In other words, learning and performance are not the same. *Learning* refers to the internal changes that take place. *Performance* refers to the behavior we can observe. A child can learn without necessarily showing it in performance. Now we will examine two important variables that influence performance, reinforcement and punishment. Then we will consider the implications of our knowledge.

Reinforcement and performance

B. F. Skinner (1953) played the major role in advancing our understanding of how reinforcement influences performance. He demonstrated how reinforcement processes work and inspired the development of a whole way of looking at behavior and thinking about it based on reinforcement principles. Three general ideas based on his work are presented here.

First, the child's activity tells us what is reinforcing. Reinforcement is defined in terms of what children do. If presentation of X makes Ron's behaviors more frequent, X is a reinforcer for Ron. Our picture of what's reinforcing Ron, then, must square with evidence on what actually influences his patterns of action. Ideas such as children seek approval provide a starting point, but only when we find that the actions the teacher praises go up in frequency can we conclude that Mr. Azrin's praise is a reinforcer for Ron.

Often careful analysis contradicts commonsense judgments. Many supposedly approval-seeking children who repeatedly get in trouble don't repeat what gets approved. Instead, it is attention and control over others that keeps problem behavior going. The actions that stop what is going on, rather than those that win praise, appear to be the ones that are strengthened. In these cases a reinforcement analysis results in a conclusion that attention, but not approval, is a reinforcer. Similarly, children described as lazy and not motivated to learn usually are ready to work when appropriate reinforcers are used. Often such children are not motivated to earn the reinforcers teachers use but are sensitive to the reinforcements their friends dispense.

A second idea based on Skinner's work is that the details of interaction and consequences often clarify puzzling activity patterns. Adults may be puzzled when certain behavior patterns persist in children. A nursery-school teacher looks for help when a child keeps standing near the grown-ups instead of joining in the fun with other children. Parents are perplexed when their child becomes more and more demanding, despite their willingness to give in to reasonable requests. Systematic observation often shows that the adults are reinforcing the very behavior patterns that puzzle and concern them.

Without realizing it teachers can easily fall into a pattern of paying attention to a child's misbehavior, while ignoring appropriate behavior. In a busy preschool the teacher's attention is caught when a child hits someone else or fails to join in group play. Smooth social interaction does not demand attention; it can be easily ignored. Sometimes a regular pattern can emerge. Tim stands alone with a sad face. The teacher comes over, talks to him, and suggests he join others on the jungle-gym. If he goes over to the jungle-gym, the teacher's attention turns to another child. If he remains near the teacher, he continues to get attention. Experiments (Hall & Broden, 1967) have shown that when teachers reverse this pattern of reinforcing the behavior they don't want and ignoring the actions they want, dramatic changes often result. Withdrawn children engage in more active play and peer interchange when teachers focus on desired behavior and ignore the withdrawn behavior. Similarly, aggressive children often become less aggressive when teachers praise their positive interactions, rather than focusing on the negative.

Parents, like teachers, apparently reinforce many children's actions that they don't like and don't want. Shopping centers are good places to see a common example. Sandy asks her father to buy her a toy or candy. Her father refuses. If Sandy persists and makes a big enough fuss, her father gives in. Notice that in this kind of sequence the parent can easily end up rewarding the child for persistent begging and loud fussing while never rewarding a single request made quietly and politely. The law of effect implies that in such a case the child would learn to ignore parental refusals and to keep escalating demands, which often seems to be what happens. Puzzling behavior can be understood in terms of the same principles that are more obvious in other cases.

The third general idea to be discussed is that the persistence of actions relates to the pattern, or schedule, of reinforcing consequence. Consider a typical experiment. Five-year-old Melanie comes into a psychologist's playroom to play a game. She is invited to turn a crank to earn plastic trinkets. She is told that sometimes cranking will produce trinkets, sometimes not. She is told that she may continue playing the game as long as she likes and keep any trinkets she earns.

For ten minutes the game is set up so that cranks earn trinkets. Then, without telling Melanie, the experimenter changes the system: cranks no longer produce trinkets. What will she do when the previously reinforced activity is no longer reinforced (during extinction)?

As you might expect, the typical child works for a while after the rewards stop coming, though with signs of increased emotion arousal. The amount of persistence after reinforcement stops depends largely on the pattern of previous consequences. If every crank produced a trinket during the first ten minutes, the child is likely to stop sooner when reward is discontinued than if only some of the cranks were reinforced. Partial, or intermittent, reinforcement results in more persistent activity later than 100%, or continuous, reinforcement. Any predictable pattern of reinforcement (such as a trinket after every five cranks) results in quicker cessation than a comparable, unpredictable pattern (such as a trinket sometimes after every crank, sometimes following four cranks, sometimes following ten cranks, and so on, with an average of one trinket every five cranks). These influences of reinforcement pattern on later persistence are easy to demonstrate and dramatic in nature.

Findings on persistence and reinforcement have broad implications. Working steadily and giving up, persisting and quitting, are important features of children's everyday behavior. Common sense and traditional theories often explain such matters in terms of such ideas as motivation, laziness, attention span, and frustration tolerance. Reinforcement schedule often provides a better explanation.

The same reinforcement can have dramatically different impact on a child's actions, depending on how it is scheduled. The common finding that individual tutoring has little carryover value to a child's classroom work habits illustrates the point. If Johnny does an addition problem and gets praised, does another, gets more praise, and so on, his math or arithmetic is maintained on a regular schedule of reinforcement with almost continuous feedback. When he is given the task of working alone in his workbook, the consequences are far different. Praise immediately after doing a problem is rare. Johnny is likely to turn to more immediately rewarding behaviors, such as looking out the window, drawing a picture, or talking to a neighbor.

More persistence could be produced if Johnny's tutor started by praising him for completing one arithmetic problem and then gradually shifted the reinforcement schedule so that praise came unpredictably and after more and more problems. A child who quits after one or two problems often can be gotten to complete several workbook pages at a time without stopping if the percentage of rewards is gradually reduced.

Punishment and performance

Psychologists define punishment as the presentation of an aversive, or unpleasant, stimulus following a response. Often this procedure makes the performance of the response less likely, as when Nancy stops saying *hell* in front of her father after she says it and he spanks her in three separate episodes. However, we must not confuse this kind of suppression of response with forgetting. Nancy's performance of the response in front of her father changes, but there is no reason to suspect that she can no longer say it.

One useful way of thinking about what happens when punishment has this kind of impact is in terms of classical conditioning, anxiety, and avoidance. Because Nancy can hear herself and feel herself saying *hell,* the word is a stimulus for her (as well as a response by her). In the punishment episodes there is a pairing of this stimulus word with spanking; so there is an opportunity for *classical conditioning* to take place. A neutral stimulus (the word) is paired with the unpleasant stimulus (the spanking). The taboo word can take on the unpleasant meaning of the spanking and arouse negative emotional reactions (*anxiety*) similar to those aroused by the spanking itself.

Once the word *hell* acquires this new power to arouse anxiety, *not* saying hell is reinforced by the reduction or avoiding of anxiety. We can think of the impact of the punishment as a complex one in which not emitting the punished response is an *avoidance* response that enables the child to avoid experiencing the unpleasant punishing stimulus.

Research on punishment indicates that it is more likely to suppress the punished responses if it comes soon after the response is emitted, is intense rather than mild, and is consistent rather than inconsistent. There also is evidence to indicate that the context in which the punishment occurs is important, with more suppression resulting if the punishment comes from someone with whom the child has a warm relationship and if the punishment is accompanied by an explanation, or rationale (Berkowitz, 1973; Hetherington & Parke, 1979).

Implications

The fact that we know how to use reinforcement and punishment to influence children's behavior is important. It helps explain why children act as they do and how adults influence them, but it hardly tells us what we *should* do. As with drugs that influence children's behavior, we must ask about negative side effects before we can start to make informed decisions about action.

Negative side effects of punishment.   Psychologists have been aware of negative side effects associated with punishment for a long time and traditionally have advised against the use of punishment because of them.

One of the more obvious problems in using punishment is that the adult who punishes provides a model of aggressive behavior. As we would expect from our general picture, one often unintended consequence of punishment is to teach the child to use aggression in dealing with others.

Another kind of problem associated with punishment follows from the idea that classical conditioning can take place. Any cue associated with the punishing stimuli can acquire its negative meaning, not just cues associated with the punished response. If father punishes, he can become a source of anxiety. If punishment takes place in school, it can become a source of anxiety. Because classical conditioning is determined by the closeness of CS and US in time, rather than by the logical connection between the two, these negative outcomes seem inevitable.

Another possible side effect of punishment is child abuse. In the United States physical punishment is an approved and widely used child-rearing technique. In China, Taiwan, and Tahiti, physical punishment is far less common, as is child abuse. Some think that by making physical punishment acceptable as a normal disciplinary method, we might foster its abuse (Parke & Collmer, 1975).

Negative side effects of reinforcement. The new sophistication about reinforcement has made it possible to formulate and communicate principles of behavior modification that anyone can use to control children (Kazdin, 1975, 1981). Not surprisingly, parents and teachers have been quick to learn and use these ideas. Although obvious benefits have resulted from this trend (Box 5–1), caution is indicated here, too (Deci, 1975; Farnham-Diggory, 1981; Lepper & Greene, 1978).

Applications box 5–1 Behavioral coaching

Conditioning principles have now been successfully applied in a tremendous range of situations, including the training of the handicapped and running factories. One of the least explored areas has been athletic coaching. A recent study done at Georgia State University indicates that here, too, are advantages to be gained by systematically applying learning principles.

Mary Allison and Teodoro Ayllon (1980) developed a standard behavioral-coaching technique that they taught to a football coach and a gymnastic coach. The coaches used it with their own students, concentrating on second-team members who were judged to have not yet mastered fundamental skills but who seemed ready to learn them. In football the experiment focused on five boys, 11 and 12 years old. They were coached in blocking. In gymnastics the subjects were six girls, aged 13 and 14, who were coached on backward walkovers, front hand springs, and reverse kips.

In all cases the behavioral coaching involved a standard series of steps:

1. *Executing the play.* The coach verbally instructed the athlete in what was to be done and what the consequences were to be. For example, "When I blow this whistle, I want you to block Myron. If you screw up, I'm going to yell 'freeze,'—stop exactly in the position you're in and do not move until I tell you. I'm going to try to tell you what you're doing wrong so I can help you learn to block better. If you do it right, I'll let you know and you don't have to freeze. O.K.?"
2. *Judging correct execution.* Next the coach watched the play and decided whether it was correct, saying "great," "right," and so on when it was, blowing the whistle for freeze when it was not. If the movements were correct, the player was asked to do it again. If they weren't, the coach moved to steps 3, 4, and 5.
3. *Describing the incorrect position.* When the athlete was asked to freeze, the coach told him or her in specific terms what was being done wrong.
4. *Modeling the correct position.* Then the coach assumed the correct position and asked the athlete to stay frozen and look at it. The coach described the correct position while the athlete looked at it.
5. *Imitating the correct position.* Then the coach had the athlete assume the correct position, with the coach describing it as the athlete held it.

Overall, the coaching procedure took about a minute each time that the coach had to go through the five steps.

An observer kept systematic records while the coaches tried out the behavioral system as part of their regular routine. The results revealed dramatic progress in each case. Typically, the athletes started at rates of 10% or less correct and quickly moved up toward 50% or higher success. In some cases a reversal technique was used in which the coach went back to standard coaching after seeing progress with the new technique. In each case the reversal resulted in a rapid decline in performance, showing both that the behavioral coaching (rather than just more practice) was responsible for the improvement and that the performance gains still depended on external feedback.

As has been so common, this research showed that the systematic application of learning principles can result in dramatic improvement over standard techniques used by "experts," even though it is common for many to call these new approaches common sense or what they've been doing all along.

An obvious problem is that behavior modification can be used against children as well as for them. For example, a school for scoundrels could use behavior modification to produce better thieves and liars.

A less obvious problem deserves more attention. The use of *extrinsic* reinforcers, including praise, prizes, and grades, may undermine *intrinsic* motivations such as curiosity, exploration, and a desire to become more competent. Studies conducted at Stanford University illustrate the problem. David Greene and Mark Lepper investigated the influence of a prize (a good-player award) on an activity that preschoolers commonly pursue for its own sake (intrinsic motivation)—drawing with magic markers (felt pencils of different colors).

In the first study the magic markers were initially provided as a regular nursery-school activity in order to get a picture of the baseline amount of play (Lepper, Greene, & Nisbett, 1973). Then some of the children were introduced to an adult who promised a good-player award for making good pictures. These children drew pictures for the experimenter and were given the extrinsic reward. Then after one or two weeks had passed by, the magic markers were again made available as a regular option in the nursery school. The results showed that children who drew to win a prize did less spontaneous drawing later when compared to both their baseline performance and to a control group not exposed to the extrinsic reward for drawing.

A second study produced a similar result (Lepper & Greene, 1975). Where intrinsic interest in an activity is high, the use of extrinsic rewards can lower it (Deci, 1975; Lepper & Greene, 1978).

Apparently play can be turned into work. The findings are of special interest because children seem so full of curiosity before they get to school and so often seem less interested in learning later. Many have argued that the use of grades, prizes, and other good-player awards has the long-run effect of undermining curiosity and love of many activities for their own sakes. Now we must pay attention to their argument.

The facts are not all in (Morgan, 1981), but even better facts will not settle questions about what we should do. We have to relate the evidence to our ethical standards. Like the researchers who study punishment and reinforcement, those who apply them must put children's welfare first.

SYMBOLIC LEARNING PROCESSES

When older children learn, symbolic processes are prominent. Words, pictures, and numbers are symbols—they stand for something else. If Bill learns the differences between African and Indian elephants from a book, the stimuli are symbols (words and pictures) rather than real elephants. Carmen "walks like an elephant" the day after a trip to the zoo and uses some kind of private symbols, perhaps mental pictures, to guide her performance. When Judy figures out that six elephants weighing a ton each would weigh 12,000 pounds all together, she uses numerical symbols in several stages of a complex process.

Today psychologists look at symbolic learning in varied ways. The most popular approach is to look at it in terms of information processing. That approach will be presented in Chapter 8 as part of a consideration of memory. In this section the focus is on two models of learning that grew out of traditional learning theory: Albert Bandura's social-learning model and Robert Gagné's hierarchical model.

Social-learning model

Bandura (1977) emphasizes the social nature of much symbolic learning. He focuses on learning through social processes, as when Todd watches Tim eat a berry and then copies the action. He also highlights the learning of social behaviors, such as hitting others and helping them. The theory is social in two ways, then.

Symbolic learning can be thought of as involving indirect, rather than direct, experience. In conditioning, the child experiences physical stimuli and responds to them directly, as when Karen reaches out, touches a hot stove, feels pain, and withdraws her hand. Bandura emphasizes that if Jenny watches the sequence, she can learn from the events without moving and without feeling the pain. Jenny's observational learning would be based on indirect experience. Similarly, if Jenny tells Heidi about what she saw, Heidi, too, can learn indirectly on the basis of words. Both learning by imitation and learning based on language are symbolic and indirect. Both usually depend on other people. According to Bandura, indirect forms of learning are the most important ones when children learn new ways of acting.

Bandura still uses conditioning principles. Conditioning can take place on the basis of observation. A child who watches a dog bite her friend can acquire an emotional response to dogs through a process resembling respondent conditioning. A child who watches a TV character hit others and get rewarded can learn to hit through a process similar to operant conditioning. How events are associated in time is important, even when the events are symbolic.

Bandura also uses conditioning principles to help explain performance when and if children actually carry out the behaviors they learn through indirect experience. Lois might learn how to say please in a polite tone of voice by imitation, but Bandura thinks direct experience in saying please and in being rewarded for it in some situations and not in others has a big influence on where and when Lois says it.

Observational learning, imitation, or *modeling* (the terms are used interchangeably) are the most important kinds of indirect learning, the key processes in understanding child development for Bandura (1977) and his followers (Rosenthal & Zimmerman, 1978).

Imitation involves four main subprocesses. Any particular instance, as when 4-year-old Molly says to her little brother, "Dear, I'm sick and tired of your nagging!" in a tone similar to their mother's, depends on a complex set of factors. Variables found to make observational learning more or less likely, such as the relationship between the child and the model, are explained in terms of the subprocesses. As illustrated in Figure 5–1, these ingredients of modeling are termed *attentional subprocesses, retention subprocesses, motor reproduction subprocesses,* and *motivational subprocesses.*

Attentional subprocesses are crucial while the model is performing. Actions that are ignored won't be imitated later, no matter how often they are performed in front of the child. As "Sesame Street" demonstrates, if you can command children's attention, you can produce observational learning (Lesser, 1974).

What influences attention, then, can influence learning by imitation. Characteristics of the models, their actions, and those of the observing child that relate to attention relate to what is learned. Models whom children see as attractive and powerful are more likely to be noticed, watched, and listened to. Actions that are interesting are more likely to command attention. Adults who trip and fall, hammer a nail, or wiggle their ears will capture a child's attention ahead of someone who just stands and talks. With the right sequence of action, novelty, and surprise, you can keep even young children attentive

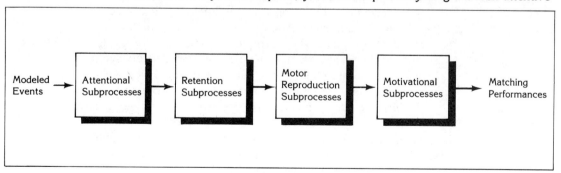

Figure 5–1   Subprocesses in the social learning view of observational learning. (*From Albert Bandura,* Social Learning Theory, © *1977, p. 23. Reprinted by permission of Prentice-Hall, Inc., Englewood Cliffs, New Jersey.*)

Observational learning involves paying attention to the model while the model is performing and then imitating the model's actions.

for many minutes. That's part of the secret of "Sesame Street." There is action, a quick pace of transition, and unpredictable repetition. Factors in the child also influence what gets attention. A sleepy child has trouble paying attention to anything. A frightened child might look away when a friend pats a big dog. Past experience influences what is novel and what is interesting. The modeling stimuli, the child, and their interrelation all influence attention.

Retention of what is observed is important if a model's actions are to have a lasting influence. Attention is important only while the original demonstration takes place. Three types of activities help the child store information so that the demonstration can be remembered later: symbolic coding, rehearsal, and organization. These activities relate to what children can do with the information they get from the model so as to store it better for future use.

Symbolic coding involves putting what is observed into words or other symbols. Children who talk to themselves about what they are watching remember more. They retain a higher proportion of the actions encoded into words (Bandura, Grusec, & Menlove, 1966). *Rehearsal* can be either motor or imaginal. Both the child who actually swings the imaginary bat after his hero hits a home run and the child who closes her eyes and pictures herself doing it are more likely to remember the details of the action. *Organization* involves creating some organized scheme for relating different aspects of the behavior modeled. Students would probably retain the sequence of *m*ultiplying, *d*ividing, *a*dding, and *s*ubtracting better if teachers related it to the sequence *My Dear Aunt Sally*.

These retention activities sound like methods that would help a child remember anything, not just the actions of a model. Bandura's picture of memory, and also of attention, in observational learning ties in nicely with a broader picture of cognitive processes (Chapter 8).

Motor reproduction subprocesses come into play when actions that were attended to and remembered are acted out by the observer. If the model's performance included only movements previously mastered, these motor processes go off smoothly and are hardly noticed. For example, an 8-year-old would have no trouble imitating a model who walked across a room and sat down on a chair. Often, however, the child lacks the motor skill to do what a model does, even though the child might have learned what correct performance looks or sounds like. A child who says *fumb* may hear and remember *thumb* without being able to reproduce the necessary muscle patterns. Similarly, a child may make a series of scribbles to imitate writing because of an inability to control precise finger movements, rather than through an inability to discriminate *A* from *B* visually. Problems related to motor reproduction, then, are more likely to turn up in skill areas such as walking, talking, and playing tennis than in the mastery of concepts or in playing house.

Motivational subprocesses relate more to performance than to actual learning. Incentives and rewards have a lot to do with whether a child who has learned to recognize the letter *J* from "Sesame Street" will show off her competence. They have less to do with whether she learns about the letter *J* in the first place. However, motivational factors can influence what the child attends to and thus play some role in the original learning. Praise and a desire to read, along with the catchy TV presentation, contribute to acquisition. But Bandura sees the more crucial contribution of motivation as explaining which prior learning is exhibited in a particular situation.

Hierarchical model

Robert Gagné (1968, 1977) developed a hierarchical model of learning that is valuable in helping us see the continuous nature of learning in everyday life. He shows how the complex *rule learning* involved in such processes as learning algebra rests on the prior learning of *concepts,* such as *number,* which in turn depend on sensorimotor *discrimination learning.* He directs our attention to key processes that are central in complex forms of learning: overlearning, transfer, and cumulative learning.

Overlearning

Abby grew up in Maine and learned to ice-skate long before she entered school. When she was 6, she moved to Florida and didn't get a chance to skate again until she was 16. To her surprise she soon was whizzing across the ice with skill, despite the ten-year gap in her experience. *Overlearning* helps us

Continued practice after skills are first mastered results in overlearning and long retention of those skills.

understand this example and other cases of learning that endures for months and years. It also relates to other important aspects of the learning process.

Overlearning is defined in terms of practice past the point of original mastery. A common criterion of whether Frank has learned what $2 + 3$ equals is to present him with the problem repeatedly until he is correct on five or ten consecutive presentations. At this point psychologists would say that he has learned. Continued practice afterwards would be overlearning.

Overlearning has predictable consequences (Gagné, 1977; Hilgard & Bower, 1966; Travers, 1977). One result is longer retention of the learning; another is that the learned performance often becomes better coordinated and less subject to interference from similar activities. We see this when motor skills such as printing the letter Y or playing the piano are practiced over and over. With these changes there often are gains in the child's ability to perform what has been learned in varied situations and at varying levels of arousal. A child who has just learned to ride a bike will have more trouble riding a friend's bike, riding a bike on the grass, or riding when excited or sleepy than a child who has practiced bike riding for hours and hours.

After a skill has been thoroughly overlearned, we see additional changes, often related to *automatization* (Case, 1980; Fowler, 1980; Kimble & Perlmutter, 1970). Children who have just learned to give the correct answer to $2 + 3 = ?$ or to ride a bike have to pay attention to what they are doing while doing it. With overlearning it becomes possible to perform without thinking about it. Once performance is automatic, the child's attention seemingly is freer to focus on other matters. At this stage of learning, the original capability seems to be more available as a component, or subroutine, to be used as a part in more complicated tasks (Connolly, 1973). For example, once the child can do 2 + 3 automatically, it becomes easier to do problems like 12 + 13 = ?, in which skill in adding 2 and 3 is a component. Trick riding on a bicycle, as when Dan rides with one hand while playing a harmonica with the other, becomes much easier after bike riding is automatic.

Cumulative learning

By elementary school most learning builds on past learning. Even when Sarah approaches a new subject such as reading or arithmetic, we find that she is building on past learning (for example, language learning and learning to recognize objects). Only by seeing this morning's learning as part of a constantly growing set of accomplishments can we make sense out of it.

Transfer

Most significant learning involves *transfer* (using what was learned in one situation in another that is at least partly different). Bike riding or baseball wouldn't be fun if you always rode around the same block or swung at a pitch delivered at the same place. Language learning would be a far different task if you mostly responded to familiar sentences with stereotyped replies, as in "How are you today?" "Fine, thanks.", rather than having to deal primarily in unique sentences. In the child's world there are constant demands to use old learnings in new situations and combinations.

Overlearning is important in transfer. When something is thoroughly learned, it is more likely to be useful in new situations or in building more complex skills. Another important factor in transfer is experience with a broad variety of examples, or situations, during the original learning. A child who has practiced counting with 20 kinds of objects is more likely to be able to count correctly when faced with a new kind.

When transfer is the goal, another important factor is *understanding*. With rote-learning approaches a child can learn to respond quickly and perfectly to the stimulus 2 + 3 = ? and not be able to solve 3 + 2 = ? Approaches that emphasize concepts like addition and number group can result in broader transfer.

Executive control processes

Older children monitor their own learning performance and adjust it to meet the needs of the situation (Brown, 1977), as when they say to themselves, "Nope, that's not working. Guess I'd better try something else." In other words they sometimes "take charge" of their own learning. This aspect of symbolic learning was ignored in traditional formulations. In his recent work Gagné (1977) pays attention to it, writing about *executive control processes* that plan and direct action.

Executive control processes are illustrated in some fascinating experiments on thinking skills. A productive thinking program was developed, consisting of 16 cartoon booklets that each involved a mystery story (Olton & Crutchfield, 1969). In each story Jim and Lila solve problems, such as figuring out why a container of water disappeared. Fifth- and sixth-graders can work through the program on their own and learn from Jim and Lila's experiences. The booklets teach strategies in problem solving. The emphasis is on strategies that can transfer, such as listing all possible solutions to a mystery rather than jumping to a conclusion without exploring alternatives.

The training program worked. It improved the children's strategies, as reflected in the number of puzzling facts they noted and the number of available elements they used in their solutions. Most important, the gains transferred. There were signs of increasing ability as they worked on more mysteries. The investigators concluded, "It seems likely that the program showed the student how to make far more effective *use* of the cognitive capacities he already had." They quoted the remark of a student, "Now I see that I'm not dumb; I just didn't know how to use my mind" (Olton & Crutchfield, 1969, p. 84).

BIOLOGICAL CONSTRAINTS ON LEARNING

Why do most children learn concepts like dog and car before they learn concepts like brown or tall (Nelson, 1973, 1977a)? Perhaps it's because of the way the young learner looks at the world. Objects that move and change attract their attention. Qualities like brownness and tallness don't seem as obvious and interesting, even though they, too, are common and concrete.

This explanation of concept learning illustrates the idea that there seem to be *constraints,* or inherent limitations, in what children learn. Not all learning is equally easy. This notion has become more and more influential in theories of animal learning (Hinde & Stevenson-Hinde, 1973; Tarpy, 1982); now it is becoming prominent in child psychology (Reese & Porges, 1976). A number of studies of early learning have supported it. For example, it has proven much easier to condition newborns by using prepared (inborn) responses like sucking and headturning than by selecting arbitrary ones like kicking (Sameroff, 1972; Sameroff & Cavanaugh, 1979). Later in infancy classical conditioning is far easier with certain combinations of stimuli and responses. For example, time cues are easier to associate with change in eye pupil size, and sounds are more easily connected to eye blinks (Fitzgerald & Brackbill, 1976).

Frank Keil (1981) used the constraint idea in an important explanation of why knowledge grows so rapidly and extensively in early childhood. He argued that if children had to engage in real trial and error in learning about the world, the process would go far more slowly. For example, learning that the word *dog* refers to a particular set of animals might require such constraints, or biases, as a tendency to notice similarity in dogs of varied sizes, colors, and breeds, rather than seeing each dog as unique, or thinking of black dogs and white dogs as unrelated groups.

Putting it differently, Keil (1981) rejects a "blank slate" approach that assumes the child starts acquiring knowledge from a neutral starting point in which a great variety of early concepts would be equally likely.

Keil draws on varied evidence to argue that the constraints on conceptual learning are highly elaborated. He thinks that children come to the learning task with a far more complicated preparedness than, say, a tendency to see

Spot as the same dog whether he is wet or dry, awake or asleep. He also thinks that some important constraints are *domain specific,* applying only to particular areas of learning, such as language, number concepts, or map reading. These ideas add up to a sharp contrast with stage theories, such as Piaget's, that imply that at any age a child has one approach to learning that shows itself in varied domains (Chapter 7). They also conflict with a notion popular among learning theorists: that there is a small number of basic learning processes, such as operant conditioning, that operate similarly in varied domains at all ages.

Keil's views tie in closely with a growing tendency to emphasize what young children *can* learn, rather than what they can't (Chapter 7). For example, when Rochel Gelman (Gelman & Gallistel, 1978) looked at the number concepts formed by 3- and 4-year-olds, she found them to be surprisingly sophisticated—as long as small numbers of objects (one to three) were involved. Keil's orientation implies that such early competencies show that the young child and the adult share constraints, so that within the same domain (such as number or language) the basic approaches of the two are similar.

Whether or not Keil's radical views are supported, it does seem likely that the general idea of thinking about biological constraints on learning will become more prominent, for this approach gives us a far more useful way of dealing with an old issue than before. You can think about the constraint idea as a replacement for the old idea that behavior was either learned or unlearned. As illustrated in Figure 5–2 and Table 5–2, today we recognize that many behav-

TABLE 5–2 Contrasts between maximally constrained and minimally constrained behaviors

	Maximally Constrained Behaviors	Minimally Constrained Behaviors
Old Terms	Innate, instinctive	Learned
New Terms	Constrained, biased, prepared, environmentally stable, species characteristic	Unconstrained, nonprepared, environmentally labile
Examples	Walking, dropping objects, concept of two	Skating, typing, concept of oxygen
Distribution	Nearly universal in biologically normal children	Learned only by particular individuals
Nature of Teaching	Largely self-taught	Major contributions by teachers and models
Environmental Factors	Expected environment or environment of evolutionary adaptedness is all that is crucial.	Specific environmental factors beyond those defining the expected environment are crucial.

Based largely on Bowlby, 1969; Hebb, 1949; Keil, 1981.

The Old View

All human behavior was seen as either entirely learned or entirely unlearned. So there were two separate categories, thought of as sharply contrasting with no middle ground.

Category 1
Unlearned Behavior

Category 2
Learned Behavior

The New View

All human behavior is seen as reflecting both learning and biological constraints. Accordingly, a continuum, or gradation, is hypothesized, rather than separate categories. There are no clear separations since all differences are thought of as a matter of degree.

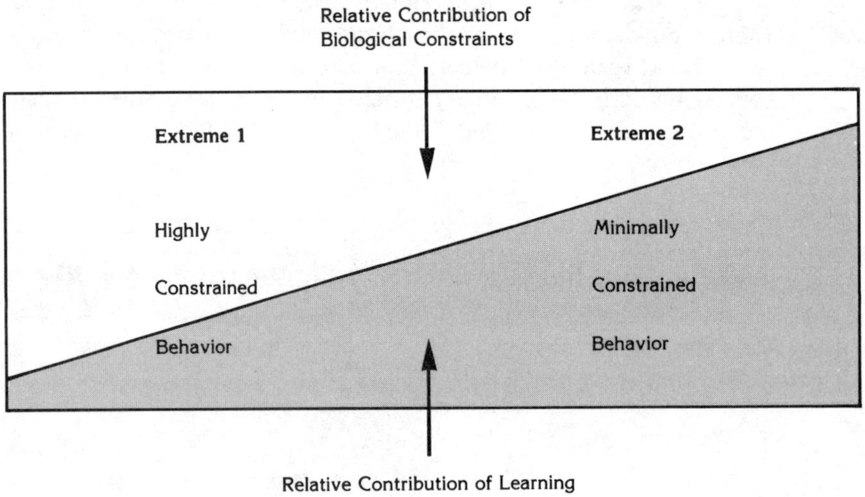

Relative Contribution of
Biological Constraints

Extreme 1

Highly

Constrained

Behavior

Extreme 2

Minimally

Constrained

Behavior

Relative Contribution of Learning

Figure 5–2 A shift in thinking about biological constraints and learning

iors are influenced both by biological constraints and by learning. We need a way of talking about a child who is neither a blank slate for whom all learnings are equally easy nor an insectlike creature with little capacity for learning. The constraint view, along with such concepts as bias and preparedness, is needed in dealing with present evidence. It will turn up again and again in the chapters that follow.

ALTERNATIVE CONCEPTIONS OF THE LEARNER

Now that you have learned about specific aspects of children's learning, we can turn to the broader question of how psychologists think about learning in general. The central issue apparently is whether to take a *mechanistic* or an *organismic* view of the child more generally (Chapter 2). In other words, contrasting ideas about learning seem to reduce to disagreements about the nature of the learner.

Mechanistic view

For theorists who take a mechanistic view, learning is seen as the key to understanding child development more generally. For them, learning is the crucial mechanism by which psychological development takes place. Why does the older child think more logically and act in a more conventional way than the younger child? Because she has so learned. How is development to be understood? By seeing it as a result of learning. For Bandura (1977) the process of observational learning is basic to understanding how the asocial newborn becomes a socialized member of society. For Gagné (1968) the processes of cumulative learning and transfer explain how thousands of brief learning experiences add up to a dramatic transformation in how the child thinks.

The mechanistic model of the child as learner also is distinctive. It emphasizes the child as a neutral quality whose characteristics result from interactions with the environment. In an old metaphor the child's mind was a blank slate. Today the notion of the environment shaping the child is popular, suggesting a claylike child. In this conception what the child learns depends on the actions of parents and other adults. They are models and control the discriminative stimuli and reinforcers that the child encounters. What is learned depends basically on what they teach.

Learning processes such as conditioning and observational learning fit in closely with the mechanistic orientation. Not surprisingly, they are emphasized the most by psychologists who take this view.

Organismic view

The organismic approach reverses the relation between learning and development. Organismic theorists, such as Piaget, see how and what the child learns as a *result* of development more than as a cause of it. The analogy of the new learnings of the bird who has just left the nest and started to fly is apt here. The dramatic shift from nest-bound baby to flying juvenile makes it possible for the bird to learn in new ways, as when it learns to land on a branch, to catch flying insects, or to find its way home. The developmental shift (based on both maturation and learning) provides the starting point in explaining the new learning, rather than vice versa.

The organismic position emphasizes constraints on learning and thus contrasts with the blank slate view. Actually, the move toward emphasizing constraints in learning has been part of a decline in the influence of mechanistic theories and a rise in importance of organismic ones.

In the organismic view the child is an active learner who takes a central role in selecting stimuli and constructing the learning environment. Children who play, explore, ask questions, and thus control their own learning fit in with this perspective. This picture makes the child more a self-teacher whose curiosity plays as big a part in determining what is learned as do the pushes from the outside environment. Concepts like attention and executive control process that emphasize the self-directive aspect of learning fit in with this approach.

Trends

We are passing out of a period where mechanistic views were dominant to one in which organismic thinking is much more popular (White, 1970). However, it is not clear where the future will take us. I emphasized Bandura's and Gagné's models because they illustrate how traditional mechanistic models have been expanded and enlivened so as to deal more successfully with the active nature of the child learner. Perhaps this kind of broadening and modification of the learning position will emerge as the dominant trend (see Rosenthal & Zimmerman, 1978).

Alternatively, as suggested in Keil's ideas about constraints, learning models may continue to decline in importance and give way to explanations of learning that incorporate specific kinds of learning in other frameworks. Further examples of how this might happen will become clearer in the chapters that follow.

Another possibility is that both traditions will flourish. To those interested primarily in problems of instructing children, as in school, learning theories might turn out to be more useful. To those trying to explain naturally occurring development, organismic models might be favored.

SUMMARY

This chapter focused on learning, a central topic in explaining how children acquire new ways of acting and how they manage to act adaptively in an ever-changing world. Learning was defined broadly as all changes in activity resulting from experience.

A variety of forms of learning were distinguished and detailed. A major distinction was between sensorimotor learning processes (involving physically defined stimuli and responses) and symbolic ones (involving representational processes). Three forms of sensorimotor learning were presented in detail: habituation, classical conditioning, and instrumental conditioning. Then the learning/performance distinction was introduced and two important influences on performance were summarized: punishment and reinforcement. Ideas about symbolic learning were introduced in relation to Bandura's social-learning model and Gagné's hierarchical model. With Bandura the main focus was on observational learning and on subprocesses related to it. Gagné's ideas about overlearning, cumulative learning, transfer, and executive control processes were presented.

After dealing with specific aspects of learning, I addressed two general topics: biological constraints on learning and alternative conceptions of the learner. The section on biological constraints emphasized that we have moved from the idea that behavior is either learned or unlearned to the notion that all learning is more or less constrained by biological factors. A variety of disagreements about learning and its role in development were related to whether theorists took a mechanistic or an organismic view of the learner.

PART III
Development of Competence

The next four chapters summarize the development of competence, one side of the story of universals in development. Part IV deals with the other side, regularities in social-emotional development.

The growth of competence, or skill, is the better understood part of the story. We have a detailed description of the typical sequences in development and a sense of what usually comes when. I'll emphasize the sequences most (rather than the when), with an effort to relate the changes we can see to what we know of underlying processes.

One important reason for the more predictable nature of change in perceptual-motor, cognitive, and language skills is that in each of these areas development usually is *cumulative.* In learning to walk, talk, or reason, a common rule usually prevails: keep what you had yesterday and add to it. Competence rarely is lost. If Paul could skate last week, it's safe to guess he still can skate and will be skating somewhat better now if he's had an opportunity to practice. Although it's hard to predict exactly where he'll be, knowledge of general trends will help.

Two trends are useful in thinking about progress in all areas of competence (and in other developmental areas as well): *differentiation* and *hierarchic integration* (Werner, 1948). When Paul first learns to skate, he is likely to have only one skating style, or set of skating skills. But with further development the first skating movements will give way to more specific refinements, such as skating backwards and skating on one foot. With these more specific, or differentiated, forms of skating comes the ability to put them together in more elaborate combinations, as in playing hockey or performing a figure-skating routine (hierarchic integration). Thus, as with physical development, the cumulative progress is not just more of the same. Along with minor improvement and new pieces of skill come new organizations, or patterns. These two trends will turn up in varied guises in all four of the chapters in this part.

For convenience I approach the development of competence in terms of perceptual-motor development, cognitive development, memory development, and language development. But, as you will see, the lines drawn are somewhat arbitrary. Perceptual and motor development can be split as well as linked. Perceptual development shades into cognitive development. Language development includes perception, as in distinguishing speech sounds, motor development, as in learning to say *thumb* instead of *fumb,* and cognitive development, as in knowing what concepts go with words such as *red* or *love.* Accordingly, after you read the chapters separately, try to relate them as a review.

CHAPTER 6

Perceptual-Motor Development

Perceptual-motor skills are skills in doing. *Perception* is the interpretation of information from the eyes, ears, nose, and so on. Perceptual development is involved when the child comes to recognize faces and discriminate between smells. Motor development is an increase in skill in using the muscles. Standing up for the first time and becoming able to catch a ball are landmarks in motor development.

Perceptual-motor skills are basic to all the child's interactions with the world. Eating a meal or learning to read requires that the child accurately interprets information from the outside and contracts the right muscles at the right time. The development of perceptual and motor skills provides the foundation for much of psychological development. All elaborate actions, such as holding a conversation or playing basketball, depend on this joint foundation.

Notice the difference between perceptual-motor development and physical development. Physical development involves changes in body parts. The eye changes in shape; nerves become better insulated; muscle action chemistry is influenced by hormones. Perceptual-motor development, in contrast, is a change in how the body parts work in dealing with the world.

In this chapter I emphasize perceptual-motor development as basic to children's adaptation to their environment. I focus on how children's skills tie in with everyday living. Vision and hearing get the most attention because they are more crucial to socially important events. I emphasize connections between vision and touch because eyes and hands must work together in such actions as eating or writing. I discuss children's ability to judge depth and distance in relation to their ability to move about successfully.

First I review perceptual development, then motor development and some of the important accomplishments that bring perception and movement together. The chapter ends with consideration of the nature/nurture question.

PERCEPTUAL DEVELOPMENT

Perception is distinguished from sensation and cognition, though it blends into both. Questions about sensation, such as whether a newborn can hear, are questions about what information from the outside world can be detected. Questions about perception, in contrast, refer to the interpretation of information, as when we ask if Frank can recognize his mother despite her new hairdo. Perception and cognition are often involved in the same action. When

Terry finds her way home from school, she both interprets what she sees now—for example, the sight of a store (perception)—and draws on what she previously learned about the neighborhood—for example, that the store is around the corner from her building (cognition).

The overlap between sensation and perception is greatest at birth, when past experience and knowledge are minimal. As experience, knowledge, and thinking skills grow, the tie between perception and cognition becomes stronger and stronger. Thus, a recent book was entitled *Infant Perception: From Sensation to Cognition* (Cohen & Salapatek, 1975).

In looking at perceptual development, we first will consider two important theoretical positions. Then we will examine early perceptual skills and preferences. Finally, I'll summarize three general trends in perceptual development.

Two theoretical positions

Current thinking about perceptual development is dominated by two contrasting approaches: differentiation theory and constructionist theory. Each focuses on a different part of the story; so they complement each other.

Differentiation theory

Eleanor Gibson (1969) offers a general answer to the question "What is gained in perceptual development?" She says that there always is an increase in the ability to get information from the environment. When Nancy recognizes a face that she could not recognize yesterday, she gets more information from the same situation. When Chip goes from treating a blue block and a green one as if they were the same to discriminating between them, he uses color cues he did not use at first. A wine taster who distinguishes between wines that all taste the same to you or a teenager who reacts in varied ways to records that all sound like a lot of noise to her parents shows the same kind of gain. The experienced perceiver gets more information out of the world than the novice.

The approach is a *differentiation theory* because it pictures perceptual development as a process of finding new differences among similar stimuli. At first only a few distinctions are noticed. Broad categories of stimuli are treated as if they were the same, as in hearing the difference only between high and low notes when piano keys are struck. With perceptual development you find more and more distinctions, splitting the world into finer and finer categories, as in hearing which of any two notes is higher (Figure 6–1).

The detection of distinctive features is central in the differentiation process. Cartoonists concentrate on the more distinctive features of a person's face, such as a politician's smile or a singer's hairdo, exaggerate them, and draw sketches that easily can be recognized. A similar process of paying attention to important contrasts is basic to all perceptual differentiation. When you read letters such as *h, b,* and *d,* you must use the features open-closed and left-right. In hearing language it's crucial to pay attention to features that distinguish *bit* and *pit* and *set* and *sat.* The features that distinguish men's from women's voices, in contrast, are irrelevant in distinguishing words. In any

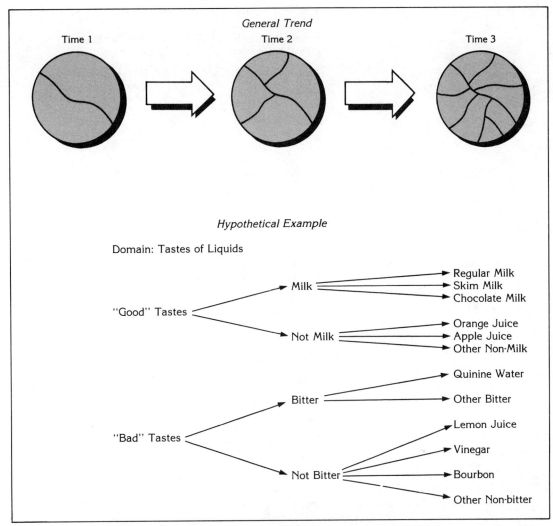

Figure 6-1 Perceptual differentiation. More and more distinctions are made within a perceptual domain; so initially broad categories are split into smaller and smaller ones.

perceptual domain the problem is to find which features are distinctive and crucial and which are irrelevant.

Constructionist theories

Constructionist theories of perceptual development present an alternative to Gibson's (Gratch, 1975). Differentiation theory emphasizes the information that is perceived; constructionist theories emphasize what's in the perceiver's head. They assume that perceptual development involves the creation of *schemas,* images that serve as internal maps of outside reality. When Sarah comes to recognize cats and distinguish them from dogs, Gibson emphasizes that

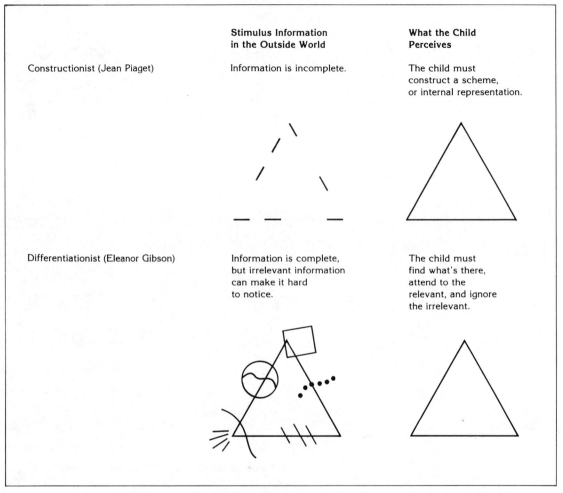

Figure 6-2 Contrasting views of perception: Seeing a triangle as explained by a constructionist and a differentiationist

Sarah must ignore color and focus instead on features such as head shape. In contrast, a constructionist would say that Sarah must build up an image of cat in her head and relate new examples to that image (see Figure 6-2).

Piaget and other constructionists can be thought of as enrichment theorists because they think of perceptual development as getting more—adding mental schemas. Their view is also useful, even though it sounds like the opposite of Gibson's. Actually, both get at part of the story. Taken together they give us a fuller picture. Differentiation theory helps us remember that we are flooded with information from the outside world and that skill lies in picking out what is crucial. The constructionists emphasize that experience builds up a lasting picture of the world.

Early perceptual skills and preferences

At birth babies react to some of the information around them. With maturation and learning their skills grow and become easier to observe. Because it is so hard to get little babies to tell us what they perceive, we often are left with a mystery. Is what looks like a new skill really new? Or is it just that we now can observe clearly an ability that might have been present earlier? As investigators get smarter about how to study perception, we keep finding more perceptual ability in young babies. As a result we have become extremely cautious in drawing conclusions about what babies can't perceive. It is much safer to focus on what they can.

From birth on babies show marked preferences, or biases, toward certain kinds of stimulation. They universally stare at certain kinds of targets more than at others, seek out certain tastes, and prefer to listen to certain sounds. These preferences are useful in showing what can be discriminated, for a baby who prefers stimulus A to stimulus B must be able to tell the difference between the two. But early preferences are more important in showing how perceptual development is constrained by the baby's own activities. I'll talk more about this important point after a review of early vision, hearing, and taste.

Early vision

Newborns show a strong preference for looking at edges and at movement. When shown a uniformly gray surface, they move their gaze around it. But if a pattern is placed on it, they stare at the target. If it moves slowly, their gaze follows. At this age vision seems suited for answering the questions "Is something present or nothing?" and "Where is it?" The kind of detailed analysis needed to answer "What is it?" apparently develops later (Salapatek, 1975).

By age 3 months we see visual skills more suited to answering the "What is it?" question (Salapatek, 1975). There is the beginning of a preference for novel over familiar sights, showing that babies' own experiences now contribute to their visual reactions (Pick, Frankel, & Hess, 1975). At about the same time the baby begins to look at details inside a pattern, as in looking at facial features like eyes or at small squares inside a bigger circle (Salapatek, 1975). Colors are distinguished more. Faces are recognized even when seen with varied expressions and from varied perspectives.

The visual maturity at 3 months is impressive (Cohen, DeLoache, & Strauss, 1979). It ties in closely with social-emotional developments at about the same age, as when babies begin to look at other people's eyes and smile at their faces (Chapters 12 and 13).

Current research on vision after 3 months focuses on such topics as color, configuration, and constancy. In each area there is evident progress and the lurking question of what has really changed.

Recent findings by Marc Bornstein (1979) seem to settle an old issue about color vision. Adults see the color categories blue, green, yellow, and red as qualitatively different, even though physicists portray the light spectrum as continuous, with no breaks in it and nothing more special about red and yellow than about blue-green or greenish yellow. One possibility is that something about our visual system makes us see color in this way. An alternative view is that our language categories influence the way we see (Whorf, 1956). Perhaps our use of such concepts as red and yellow makes them look more real and distinct. Bornstein's research shows that at 4 months infants divide the color spectrum the same way adults do. He also finds that the focal hues, or wave lengths, hold the babies' attention longer. Bornstein's findings strongly support the view that we are biologically constrained to see color the way we do. Our language practices are more likely the result than the cause of our special way of seeing colors.

Frontiers box 6–1 Can babies put together information?

Mark Strauss (1979) conducted an ingenious study that provides support for the idea that 10-month-old babies can abstract information from a series of related stimuli and form a prototype, or schema, based on the average values of varying dimensions of the series.

He showed a series of 14 faces made with an Identikit like those police use to help witnesses construct a picture of someone they have seen. With the kit it was possible to make a series of pictures of similar faces with four dimensions systematically varied: length of face, length of nose, width of nose, and amount of separation of eyes. This made it possible to show a baby a series of faces that were similar and for which average values could be constructed for any dimension, such as length of face. This way a baby could see faces that had lengths of 2 and 4. In such a series the average length would be 3, but the baby never would have seen a face of length 3.

The research question was whether babies would act as if they had put together the information from the series as a whole so as to construct a mental average (say of length 3, nose length 4, nose width 2, eye separation 3). And, of course, a key question was how to get babies to tell us what they had done.

Strauss's answer was to use a preference test. Considerable evidence indicates that 10-month-old babies prefer novelty: when given a familiar picture and a new one, other things being equal, they look longer at the novel picture.

Strauss's experiment focused on a simple question: how would babies react to a genuinely novel picture that included the average values for a series of pictures that they had seen? If they had mentally averaged the pictures seen, the picture with average values would look familiar, even though they never had seen it before. By pairing the new, average picture with a familiar one, he could answer the question.

The babies' performances were striking. They treated the novel picture of an average face as if it were familiar. Thus, they seemed to have constructed an internal prototype, or schema, supporting the constructionist approach to perception advocated by Piaget.

Current research aims at clarifying the nature of early pattern vision, seeing configurations or relations among elements. Work with complicated, natural patterns such as faces makes it clear that babies discriminate between complex patterns by 5 months but leaves it unclear when they see the parts as an organized whole. A study by Bertenthal, Campos, and Haith (1980) suggests there is no simple answer to the question. Five-month-olds showed pattern perception, but only after extensive experience with the patterns. In contrast, 7-month-olds were sensitive to the configurations after only brief experience.

Somewhat after 3 months the child clearly demonstrates the visual constancies basic to our kind of vision. We see a car as the same-sized object as it drives away from us, even though its image on our eye becomes smaller (size constancy). We see a plate as round even when it is turned so that our eyes do not get a round image of it (shape constancy). In order to perceive this way, we have to put varied cues together. For example, we use the differences between what the two eyes see in judging depth and the color and shading of objects in judging distance. Apparently, perceptual constancies based on these kinds of cues emerge at about 7 to 13 months (Cohen, De-Loache, & Strauss, 1979). However, with better research methods we might find that they are present earlier.

Early hearing

Early hearing apparently is constrained toward sounds of social significance. Little babies are more skilled in dealing with complicated, natural sounds, such as speech sounds, than with pure tones (Berg & Berg, 1979; Eisenberg, 1976). They hear contrasts basic to language, such as that between *ba* and *pa* (Eimas, 1975), and discriminate voices soon after birth (DeCasper & Fifer, 1980). Apparently, some of the ways that adults talk to babies reflect the babies' sound preferences. For example, Fernald (1981) demonstrated that 4-month-olds worked harder (turned their heads more) to hear recordings of adults talking to infants than for recordings of adult-directed speech. Seemingly, it is the expanded pitch range that people use in talking to babies that is attractive, for when artificial sounds were created with pitch contours similar to those of infant-directed speech, babies preferred them even to actual infant-directed speech (Fernald & Kuhl, 1981).

Early taste

The limited evidence on early taste also shows the pattern of early skill and preference of apparent adaptive value (Cowart, 1981). Newborns can discriminate the fundamental taste stimuli: sweet, sour, salt, and bitter. But even prior to any experience in eating they show signs of differential preferences: sometimes the sweet taste associated in nature with beneficial foods evokes smiles; the sour and bitter tastes more often associated in nature with harmful foods produce negative facial expressions (Cowart, 1981; Steiner, 1979).

Early preferences and self-teaching

Now that you have a concrete picture of some of the infants' early perceptual preferences, you can appreciate how they contribute to early learning and help constrain it. Babies' biases prepare them to notice and thereby learn about the more important parts of their environment. For example, people, dogs, and other moving, noise-making animals get far more attention than blank walls or sky. And it is just these living creatures that afford some of the richest opportunities for perceptual learning (Gibson, 1979).

A more general preference for perceptual activity also is obvious (Gibson, 1969; Woodworth, 1958). Actually, that preference is at the core of many research techniques. Just show babies something to look at and they'll look. Make a sound and they will listen. When awake, babies use their perceptual abilities constantly, often looking and listening just for the sake of seeing and hearing.

Even young infants are self-teachers. In spontaneously using their perceptual skills to attend to what is around them, they start an active process of learning about the world months before they become able to walk around in it, weeks before they can explore it with their hands.

Trends in perceptual development

Perceptual development after the early months has been summed up in terms of three main trends: (1) increased differentiation, (2) more optimal attention, and (3) increased economy in picking up information (Gibson, 1969). Progress typically is smooth and gradual.

Increased differentiation

Experiments with pictures of scribbles illustrate the general trend. Children were shown one scribble and then shown similar ones. They were asked if each scribble was the same as the original. Younger children (6 to 8 years) were much more likely than older children (8½ to 11 years) or adults to say that the differing stimuli were the same. When the items were presented repeatedly, adults quickly learned to be completely accurate in saying when they were seeing the original and when they were looking at a different one. The older children mastered the discrimination, but took much longer. Most of the younger children never reached perfect performance. Perceptual development involves a growing ability to make fine discriminations among stimuli (Gibson, 1969; Shepp, 1978).

More optimal attention

Children in a playroom looking at pictures or listening to a conversation do not take in all the information around them. Instead, like us, they tune in only to some. They look at a face more than a shoe. When interesting topics come up, they listen more carefully. They notice the words people say more than the sounds of airplanes and cars in the background. There is continual *filtering*. The environment they actually notice and react to is more limited than the total set of events they might have noticed. Their own selective activities play a role in determining what they experience. *Attention* is the technical term for this selective process. Although everyone attends, there is important progress as the child grows older. Three kinds of advances make attention more optimal (Gibson, 1969).

1. *Attention becomes more voluntary and exploratory.* The young infant seems to be caught by stimuli such as patterns on a screen. Only later in the first year do we observe a picking and choosing of what to look at that seems voluntary (Bond, 1972).

2. *Search strategies become more systematic and task-relevant.* When children are blindfolded and given toy animals to identify by touch, the method of examining the toy changes with age. A 7-year-old is more likely to run her fingers all over the toy and spend the most time touching the places that give the most information, such as the head. A child of 3 or 4 typically doesn't touch as much of the animal or use a method that provides so much information in the same time (Zaporozhets, 1965).

3. *Pickup of information becomes more selective.* The ability to tune in on the wanted information while tuning out what is not wanted grows with age (Gibson, 1969). In one study children heard a recording of a man's voice saying words through one loudspeaker at the same time that a woman's voice said words on another (Maccoby & Konrad, 1966). The children were asked to pay attention to one voice or the other and to report the words they heard. Between kindergarten and fourth grade there was a steady increase in their ability to report what the target voice said and to avoid reporting what the other said.

Increased economy of information pickup

Along with skill in attending to the wanted information and finding it efficiently comes progress in wanting the right information (Gibson, 1969). If you start to learn a new language, say Japanese, your early efforts are frustrated by not knowing what sound contrasts are crucial. If you hear a word and then hear several more, you have trouble telling if the original word was repeated. Your progress in pronouncing new sounds is limited by the fact that you cannot hear the difference between correct and incorrect pronunciations. For the young child each realm of experience poses this problem of not knowing what information should get attention and what should not.

We laugh when the child reaches out to touch the bright, full moon. But just what do you look at and what do you ignore in figuring out whether you are looking at a basket-ball-sized moon nearby or an enormous one thousands of miles away? The child's problem with the moon is similar to our own when we are fooled by a painting designed to look three-dimensional or think that a ball of clay squashed flat into a pancake looks smaller even though we know it contains the same amount of clay.

Our ability to judge the size and distance of a ball and to recognize familiar people when they are transformed by new clothes and new hair styles rests on the development of perceptual abilities that grow from birth onward. Knowing our eyes can fool us helps us. The line between perception and cognition (knowing) is not firm.

Progress in perception forms a basis for much of early cognitive development. The child's perceptual progress feeds into such advances as recognizing that the squashed ball does not change in volume though it looks smaller. But cognitive development also helps perceptual development. The strategy shown by blindfolded older children in touching a toy reflects their mental capacities in general, not something specific to perception.

MOTOR DEVELOPMENT

Motor development is more obvious and dramatic than perceptual development. The progress between birth and 2 years transforms the helpless newborn, whose movements we have trouble categorizing, into a child who moves in easily recognizable ways that result in solutions to such basic problems as moving about, getting food into the mouth, and putting blocks in a pail. The toddler's clumsy movements gradually give way to more precise and well-coordinated actions like our own. Before turning to the trends that sum up that transformation, consider the question of biases in motor development.

Motor biases

Like perceptual development, the emergence of motor activities is constrained in varied ways. The construction of the human body biases us toward certain movement patterns rather than others. Grasping is a natural behavior for the human hand, not for the dog's paw. Less obviously, basic movements such as the rhythms of walking may be coordinated by inherited timing mechanisms common to a variety of species (Thelen, 1981). But regardless of how it happens, the striking fact is that early movements take similar form in babies growing up in tremendously varied societies (Kopp, 1979).

Babies show a strong bias toward practicing the newest movements they can make. Just watch babies learning how to crawl or pull themselves to an upright posture. It's as if they give themselves homework assignments: "Work on crawling." "Practice standing, now." "Now it's time to stop crawling and work on walking." Often the pattern is so pronounced that it can be a nuisance. Eight-month-old babies who have just learned how to pull themselves up typically don't know how to get down. The following sequence is common: They eagerly pull themselves up. They cry. Parents sit them down and go back about their business. They get up. They cry. Parents come back. And so on.

Often babies not quite ready to walk on their own get others to hold them while they walk. Despite all the praise for this assisted walking, they usually abandon it emphatically as soon as they don't need the assistance. Although adult help and encouragement may play some role in developing such skills as walking, the situation is far different than when they teach ballet or baseball. When a child masters a universal skill, such as grasping or standing up, the adult is more a teaching assistant than a coach. The baby's own self-teaching activities seem to set the agenda (Bruner, 1973).

Trends in motor development

Motor development makes it particularly easy to see two trends that Heinz Werner (1948/1961) argued were typical of all development: differentiation and hierarchic integration.

Differentiation

In the newborn everything moves at once (a phenomenon known as *mass action* or *general activity*). In the months and years that follow we see a steady trend: the child becomes capable of ever more specific muscle movements. Early differentiation is seen when babies first become capable of moving their arms without moving their legs, later of moving their left arm without moving the right. The same trend is evident when children become able to turn a door knob without tensing their whole body or press a piano key with one finger without tightening the neighboring ones. Motor differentiation involves breaking down action into smaller and smaller pieces, just as perceptual differentiation involves analyzing stimuli into ever smaller categories.

Hierarchic integration

When several differentiated movement patterns are coordinated into an overall pattern, we see hierarchic integration. When a sixth-grader dribbles a ball down a basketball court and successfully goes around opposing players, his or her whole body is in action. But, unlike the general activity of the

When a number of differentiated movement patterns are brought together and coordinated into an overall pattern, we see hierarchic integration.

newborn, the activity includes a number of separate skills brought together to achieve one goal, getting the ball to the basket. One hand keeps bouncing the ball while the other reaches out to ward off and confuse the other team. The legs and feet make walking and running movements. The trunk is tilted at varied angles that relate to the dribbling, the moving, and the faking. All the movements tie together (see Figure 6–3). The coordination, or integration, is called *hierarchic* because a higher, or controlling, influence brings the differentiated parts into a pattern.

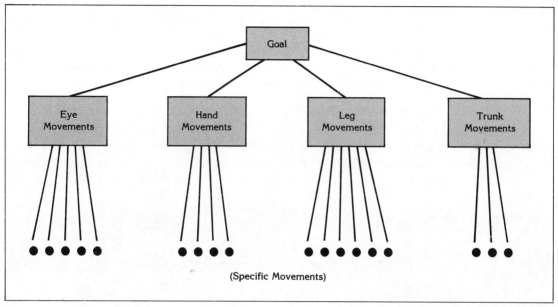

(Specific Movements)

Figure 6–3 Hierarchic Integration in movement patterns. A number of separate motor skills are coordinated or integrated into one complex pattern with a central goal, as in riding a bicycle, playing a melody on the piano, playing tennis, or putting on a coat. For example, here the goal is getting a basketball down the court to the basket without committing a foul.

Sequences

The sequences in early motor development follow such a regular and predictable schedule during infancy that it has been possible to scale them in surprising detail. For example, Bayley (1969) uses six items just dealing with sitting on a hard surface. At an average age of 3.8 months the child sits with the support of a pillow or hand. At about 6.0 months the child can sit without support for at least 30 seconds. By 6.6 months we observe sitting for sustained periods of time. At 6.9 months the typical child can manipulate toys and turn while sitting.

Although motor development after infancy is much less predictable, children within our culture follow similar paths on up through the elementary years. Table 6–1 gives some examples.

TWO IMPORTANT PERCEPTUAL-MOTOR ACCOMPLISHMENTS

Now that perceptual and motor development have been viewed separately, we can put them together. I focus on two perceptual-motor accomplishments that reflect uniquely human evolution and play a central role in our lives. First we

TABLE 6-1 Typical ages for mastery of selected motor skills

Age	Behavior
3	Can hop from two to three steps, on preferred foot
4	Running with good form, leg-arm coordination apparent
5	Can catch large playground ball bounced to him or her
6	Skipping
7	One-footed balancing without vision
8	Rhythmical hopping in 2-2, 2-3, or 3-3 pattern

Based on Cratty, 1970.

consider the conquest of space, the process by which children start immobile, come to stand erect and move about the world on two legs, and finally manage to navigate independently around town without getting lost. Next we examine the exploitation of objects, the process by which the eye and hand are brought together in a partnership that makes it possible to deal skillfully with objects, including such varied items of daily life as the fork, the pencil, the basketball, the clarinet, and the automobile. Although each of these developmental stories is important in itself, both also will be used to illustrate more general points.

Conquest of space

The conquest of space involves a series of accomplishments. There are obvious gains in the ability to move around when crawling, standing, and walking first become possible. These accomplishments call our attention to less obvious ones. Crawling and walking must be coordinated with seeing or the child will bang into walls and fall down stairs. Once vision and movement are coordinated well enough for efficient movement around the house and yard, we become aware of a third frontier. For children to travel safely and efficiently through spaces that cannot all be viewed at once, they must have some kind of internal map to guide them. In tracing the conquest of space, we will look at each of these varied yet related accomplishments in turn.

Babies start as prisoners of gravity, unable either to lift their bodies vertically or to move in a horizontal plane. Try a simple experiment to get the feel of what babies experience and so see how vertical and horizontal progress tie together in the early months. Lie down flat on the floor on your stomach. Keep your chin, your hands, your feet, your arms, and your legs on the floor. Now look around the room and try to move toward a wall without lifting any part of your body off the ground. Notice two facts: first, this posture sharply limits what you can see, even of a small room, and, second, in order to move along the floor, you must move something up.

Now try another experiment. Lie down on the floor as before and notice what happens to your opportunities to look around the room, to use your hands, and to move to different parts of the room as you take the following postures in sequence: (1) chin up with everything else still flat on the floor (including your chest), (2) chest up, (3) sit, (4) stand.

These experiments simulate the baby's progress in coping with gravity, in developing the muscular skill and balance required to stand erect without help. They illustrate that progress toward the upright posture opens the way for new kinds of movement through space (locomotion) and for new opportunities to explore the world with the eyes and the hands.

Figure 6–4 shows the relation between the exercises you performed and the typical baby's developmental progress. The picture is based on some pioneer research by Mary Shirley (1931).

Figure 6–4 Postural-locomotor development. (*Adapted from M. M. Shirley,* The First Two Years—A Study of Twenty-five Babies (*Vol. 2,* Intellectual Development). *Minneapolis: University of Minnesota Press, 1933. Copyright © 1933 by University of Minnesota Press. Reprinted by permission.*)

Two trends are involved in the progress toward standing and walking. There is a *cephalocaudal,* or head-to-tail, trend (Gesell, 1954). Progress comes first at the head end and last at the bottom. Achievements involving the head end, such as chin up and chest up, come before those involving the upper trunk and arms. Use of the legs for support comes last. The second trend, *proximodistal* progress, is less obvious in the pictures. Muscles proximal (closer) to the center of the body are controlled before those more distal (farther) from it (Gesell & Amatruda, 1947). The shoulders can be moved before the hands. The knees can be raised before the baby can use the feet for pushing.

This motor progress is better thought of as perceptual-motor because successful movements always require coordination with information from the senses. Walking around a room involves at least three different perceptual systems. Visual perception (including accurate judgments of distance, depths, and directions) is needed to avoid obstacles and follow a reasonable route. Information from sense organs in the semicircular canals inside the head is needed to maintain balance. Coordinated movements of the two legs require information from inside the muscles.

The visual cliff

Experiments on the visual cliff illustrate the more general problem of how visual space and locomotor space are integrated. The visual cliff situation itself provides a safe and easily controlled way of studying how babies of any species react to depth (Gibson & Walk, 1960). A baby is put on a board in the center of a table made of heavy plate glass (see Figure 6–5). On one side (the shallow side) a sheet of checkered linoleum is directly under the glass. On the other (the deep side) a similar piece of linoleum is 40 inches below the glass. In other words, the deep side *looks like* a 40-inch cliff to anyone who can see depth. This way, while their reactions show whether they avoid "going over" the deep side, subjects are equally safe from falling no matter where they go.

The extensive findings have been consistent. Babies go to the shallow side much more frequently than to the deeper one. The ability to see depth develops before the ability to move around on the table top in baby rats, goats, chickens, monkeys, and humans (Gibson & Walk, 1960). This finding illustrates a general pattern in perceptual-motor development: visual capacities typically emerge before the motor skills that call them into play.

Overall, the evidence implies that depth perception is innate but improves with experience (Walk, 1978). Thus, a common finding is that although young babies discriminate depth, older ones do it more accurately. This mixing of nature and nurture in perceptual-motor development is common, as you will see.

Another outcome of research on the visual cliff is the discovery that the relation between seeing depth and avoiding cliffs is by no means simple. For example, Campos, Langer, and Krowitz (1970) showed that babies discriminate depth months before they can crawl by recording heart rate as babies were lowered over the two sides. The fact that heart rate changed when the babies were lowered over the deep side but not when lowered over the shallow clearly indicated that they saw the difference. But the heart rate changes were not

Figure 6–5   A baby at the edge of a visual cliff.

the kind that go with fear reactions. Heart rate and other changes suggesting fear, such as "freezing" and not crawling, don't predominate until near 12 months (Walk, 1978).

Rader, Bausano, and Richards (1980) tried to clarify what experience in moving contributed to reactions on the visual cliff by studying babies who had had extensive experience with commercial walkers, which make it possible for the babies to move themselves around the house before they can crawl. The main finding was that when tested in a walker, those babies "walked off" the cliff! Even those who avoided the deep side while crawling failed to avoid it when in the walker. It is thus important to distinguish between seeing depth and reacting to it with caution. Babies see depth months before they show fear of the deep side or develop crawling ability. Walkers provide early mobility but certainly don't foster caution about cliffs.

Cognitive maps

Older children deal with spatial problems that call for cognitive skills along with perceptual-motor ones. For example, Helene figured out the best route to take in riding her bike from school to the grocery store the first time that she had to make the trip. She drew on her earlier experiences in going back and forth from home to school and from home to the store in doing it. It was as if she had a mental, or cognitive, map of the neighborhood in her head.

Cognitive maps, or mental representations of space, seem basic to the kind of flexible and efficient navigation characteristic of the person who goes freely about a complex environment without getting lost. We are beginning to understand how they develop. A sequence involving first the use of landmarks, then routes, and finally survey maps seems central (Siegel, Kirasic, & Kail, 1978).

The use of landmarks as navigational aids seems important at all ages from about age 1 year, when infants are near the transition from crawling to walking. Recent experiments support Piaget's idea that babies start with an egocentric system of orienting in terms of their own body. The reliance on external, or objective, landmarks apparently emerges later (Siegel, Kirasic, & Kail, 1978). This conclusion comes out of an ingenious series of studies by Linda Acredolo in which babies learned to look consistently either to their right or left to see a pleasant adult appear in one of two windows (Acredolo, 1978; Acredolo & Evans, 1980). Then the babies' position relative to the windows was reversed in order to see if they used the external landmark (the window) to orient or instead oriented egocentrically (for example, continued to turn left even though this now pointed them at the wrong window). At 6 months orientation was primarily egocentric. By 16 months most babies used the external landmark.

The importance of landmarks in children's orientation in space has been supported in several studies. Acredolo, Pick, and Olsen (1975) took children on walks through specially set-up environments and "accidentally" dropped keys at predetermined places. The children were asked to pick up the keys immediately and later were tested to see if they could remember where the keys had been dropped. In a differentiated environment containing dissimilar landmarks the 3- and 4-year-olds did better than in one without landmarks.

After children use single landmarks as aids in getting about, they begin to show knowledge of routes, or paths made up of connected landmarks (Siegel, Kirasic, & Kail, 1978). This kind of route knowledge probably grows out of active experience in going from one landmark to another. At first it can be quite specific and rigid in nature, suggesting that nothing like a mental map is involved. For example, consider 6-year-old Fred's system for getting from his house to his grandmother's. When he walks out his door, he looks for the big pine tree. He goes to the pine tree and from there spots the white fence. Once he gets to the white fence, he can see the yellow house. He goes to the yellow house, walks around it, and then sees his grandmother's house. Although Fred's system gets him to grandmother's, it can't get him home again. What's more, if the yellow house were repainted red between trips, he would be lost, unable either to find grandmother's or to get back home. With more experience he might be able to reverse his route, but he would still lack a functional map (see Figure 6–6).

Fred's situation is probably familiar to many adults because many of us also use landmarks and fixed routes, particularly when we are first learning our way around a new environment. However, there apparently are developmental differences in the extent to which landmarks are needed, even at first. Cohen and Schuepfer (1980) studied this problem systematically. They had second-graders, sixth-graders, and college students learn the same new routes with landmarks present. Then the landmarks were taken away. The second-graders' performance was impaired much more, suggesting that they had depended more on the landmark cues and had not integrated the information into a mental representation, as had the older learners.

As implied in these findings, it probably is toward the end of the elementary-school years that we start finding genuine cognitive maps, sometimes called *survey maps,* that coordinate information about specific landmarks and routes into one coherent representation (Siegel, Kirasic, & Kail, 1978). Their development probably reflects a more general advance in the ability to manipulate spatial information mentally, as in imagining how a route would look when reversed or what you would see from a landmark you are not at (Hardwick, McIntyre, & Pick, 1976). The final developments in the conquest of space seem to be neither perceptual nor motor, but basically cognitive in nature.

Exploitation of objects

The objects around us afford a tremendous range of opportunities for exploration, entertainment, and use (Gibson, 1979). Whether the object is a fork, a ball, an electronic game, or a simple piece of string, coordinated use of eyes and hands is needed in order to take advantage of the opportunities. Only through the development of a working partnership between these two contrasting bodily systems can the child exploit the world of objects. First I summarize the early progress that culminates in using the eyes in grasping objects. Then I consider some later refinements and elaborations.

Early progress

The 1-year-old grasps a pea on her plate much as we do. Her hand goes straight out to the pea. Thumb and index finger open before they reach it and then close with a suitable, delicate pressure. This simple sequence culminates a series of changes going back for more than a year (Halverson, 1931).

In the fetus, grasping is a two-phase reflex. When the palm is touched, the fingers close around the stimulating object. If the object is pulled against the fingers, there is a clinging response. At birth there is similar reflexive grasping involving the whole hand. "Palming" (object in palm with all fingers around it) is the method for holding small objects for about six months after birth. Then "pincer" grasping, involving thumb and index finger, emerges. At first too much pressure is used in holding small objects. By 1 year of age, the baby starts with the right pressure in picking up objects previously grasped.

Think of the square below as a map of a neighborhood with landmarks, such as buildings and billboards, in it (the letters).

Map

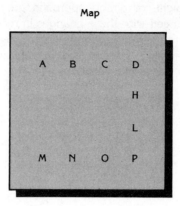

Now suppose that Harry learns one route to get from his house (H) to that of his friend Alice (A) and another route from his house to Mike's house (M) as illustrated in the two diagrams below:

Route to Alice's House

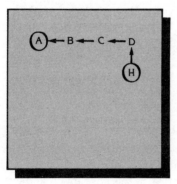

Route to Mike's House

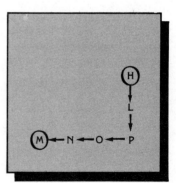

Suppose that all of his spatial knowledge were route knowledge and that he had gotten to the point where he knew each route both ways, but had not integrated the knowledge into a cognitive map. His only way of getting from A to M would be to go through H. But if he had built up an internal representation similar to the map above he would know how to get from A to M directly, as well as knowing how to get from B to N, C to O, and so on.

Figure 6–6 Routes and Cognitive Maps

Only later are novel objects picked up for the first time with suitable pressure (Halverson, 1931).

The reaching movement that gets the hand to the pea at 1 year also develops gradually (Halverson, 1931). At 16 weeks, babies use sweeping movements that do not get the hand any closer to the target. By 30 weeks, a straight, or direct, approach predominates. The relation of arm and hand changed with these changes in reaching. At first the arm carried the hand so that it moved passively. Later it seemed to be the hand that directed the arm. There is a *proximodistal* trend: skill moves from arm to hand, with the finger tips becoming skilled last.

The ability to coordinate information from two modalities—touch and vision—develops rapidly between the ages of 3 and 8.

Later developments

Developments between 3 and 12 years are interesting in illustrating intersensory development, the development of the ability to coordinate information from two modalities, in this case touch and vision. For example, a child might be shown a wooden circle and asked to feel several blocks underneath a screen and pick out the one that matches. Here the child starts with visual information and must match it to corresponding information from touch. Alternatively, the child might be asked to touch a single hidden stimulus and decide which of several choices it looks like. This kind of coordination of information from different channels is a special accomplishment of more "advanced" animals like ourselves (Birch & Lefford, 1967).

There are dramatic gains in intersensory coordination between age 3 and age 8, with continuing, though more gradual, progress thereafter (Abravanel,

1968; Birch & Lefford, 1967). Developments after about age 5 or 6 stem largely from more systematic exploration of the standard to be matched.

During the elementary-school years important progress comes in putting together spatial and eye/hand skills under time pressure, as in catching fly balls or returning serves. A study by Williams shows the trend (Cratty, 1970). A ball-throwing machine was used. The children were positioned so they could see the ball for only a brief period after it left the machine. Their task was to run to where they thought the ball would land, mimicking the problem faced by outfielders in baseball, who must start running soon after a ball is hit if they are to be at the right spot to catch it. Six- to 8-year-olds tended to react quickly and inaccurately. They seemed excited, with no clear idea where the ball would land. By 9, there were slower and more accurate reactions, suggesting that children now saw the difficulty of the task. But only at about 10 to 12 years was the combination of quick starts and accurate judgments common.

When the Little League player runs in and catches a fly ball, the accomplishment only looks simple and routine. Instead, we should think of this skill as the integration of two complex lines of perceptual-motor development, spatial and eye/hand skills, that have been developing since before birth.

NATURE/NURTURE ARGUMENT

Now that you have a concrete picture of what happens in perceptual-motor development, we can turn to the question of why it happens as it does. The old-fashioned way of putting the question was to ask about the contributions of nature and nurture and to expect that one or the other was the answer. In more modern terms the question becomes: How is perceptual-motor development constrained by heredity and maturation? How do experience and learning contribute? In other words, as already suggested, we see development as including both inborn biases, or constraints, and learning from experience and try to see how they come together (Anastasi, 1958).

Readiness

The regularity of perceptual-motor development with its timetable of accomplishments has led some to emphasize the concept of readiness. One use of the term is to predict, as in saying that children who stand alone are likely to take their first independent steps soon or that children who can discriminate the letter *b* from *p* can more easily be taught to tell the difference between *b* and *d* than those who can't. Employed this way, the readiness idea is useful. It can reduce the frustrations that are almost inevitable if you try to teach 2-year-olds to tie their own shoes or 3-year-olds to catch a forward pass.

But some go further with the readiness concept. They assume that the typical ages and sequences in which perceptual-motor skills appear are inevitable and the results of unchangeable patterns of physical development. It is at this point that disputes begin.

Obviously, physical development paces perceptual-motor development in a general sense. Eyes, ears, and muscles must be built before they can function.

Coordinations involved in walking or using a pencil require a nervous system that works. Behavioral accomplishments always require the prior development and functioning of relevant body parts. No one in psychology argues with this basic idea.

The questions arise from more specific formulations. Some argue that maturational changes, such as myelinization and the growth of dendrites, play the main, or exclusive, role in the sequence of behavioral changes we see after birth (Gesell, 1954; Kopp, 1979). This claim raises controversy. Before I review the main evidence relevant to the controversy, consider what an evolutionary perspective might make us expect.

Evolutionary hypothesis

Current ideas about constraints on learning (Chapter 5) suggest a particular pattern of findings. Universal human behaviors of obvious value in any environment, such as accurate judgments of where objects are and the ability to pick them up, ought to be highly constrained and easily learned (strongly influenced by maturation and not dependent on special kinds of environmental conditions) (Fishbein, 1976). At the same time, our adaptability to varied environments suggests that specific experience ought to play a major role (and maturation a minor one) in other aspects of perceptual-motor development. A jungle calls for efficient reactions to cues different from those of a desert or a suburb. Using a spear, a hammer, a violin, and a typewriter each calls for a distinctive set of skills. Learning should be the dominant factor in these environment-specific adaptations. Now consider the main findings. They seem to fit in with these expectancies.

Relevant findings

The evidence can be organized around five main themes: the universality of developmental schedules, the irrelevance of special training, the existence of maturational pacing, the importance of practice and encouragement, and the utility of teaching certain skills.

Universal schedules

Developmental schedules for early perceptual and motor development are universal across a wide variety of natural environments. The sequence of developments in such areas as eye/hand coordination, sitting up, and learning to walk is similar in all human cultures that have been examined (Kopp, 1979). The typical timetable for most of these accomplishments also is about the same in diverse environments, though sequences tend to be more predictable than average ages (Scarr-Salapatek, 1976).

The finding of behavioral regularity in the face of cultural diversity suggests that two factors contribute to the developmental process, as in physical development (Chapter 4). One contribution comes from universal bodily changes that follow a genetically controlled maturational schedule. The other factor is the expected environment, the features that are constant in all natural human environments despite their diversity. These features have been constant throughout human evolution and afford distinctive opportunities for perceptual-motor behaviors (Gibson, 1979). For example, constant gravity and life on land (rather than in water) provide a similar setting for the conquest of space whether a child grows up in Iceland or Mexico. The presence of objects that can be seen and grasped is universal in all homes, as are human care givers who model and encourage perceptual-motor competence.

Variations in experience often don't matter

Specific variations in perceptual-motor experience and training often make little or no difference in the developmental process. Studies of both other animals and children support this generalization. We now have extensive evidence from deprivation studies in which animals have been subjected to a variety of unnatural rearing conditions that limit opportunities for perceptual experience and motor practice (Ganz, 1975). Animals have been reared within dark and soundproof cages. Others have been immobilized in chairs and casts while growing up. These deprivation studies indicate that in rats, cats, and monkeys such abilities as avoiding seen objects, reaching in the right general direction for objects, and avoiding deep cliffs rest on maturation and do not require relevant experience (Ganz, 1975). A scattering of nonexperimental studies of children have given similar results. Comparisons of traditional Hopi Indian babies raised on cradle boards with Hopi babies raised without them revealed no basic difference in age of walking, despite great differences in opportunities for exercise (Dennis & Dennis, 1940). Similarly, Lenneberg (1967) claimed that children whose legs are immobilized by casts (for correcting inborn hip deformations) develop normal gait and walking without practice. Studies of babies born without the higher portions of the brain (Monnier, 1973) have shown that their motor behavior is similar to that of normal babies, supporting the idea that those portions of the brain are not involved in the normal neonate's motor functioning. Finally, in some famous studies done at Yale in the 1930s, special training was given to one of a pair of twins on such tasks as stair climbing. The training did not make a difference (Gesell & Thompson, 1929).

Maturational pacing

There are known parallels between maturational and behavioral schedules of development after birth that suggest maturational pacing. Both the general finding that higher brain centers reach mature functioning later than lower ones and more specific gradients of myelin and dendrite development make it plausible that certain perceptual-motor developments come later than others because the required "wiring" is not yet complete. Shifts in visual functioning in the early months suggest that newborn vision rests mainly on brain systems that evolved early and the more refined pattern vision and interest in interior details of targets like the face don't appear until about 2 or 3 months because that's when the higher and newer (in evolutionary terms) centers first become operative (Salapatek, 1975).

"Unexpected" environment and its impact

"Unexpected" or "unnatural" environments can have a big impact on some aspects of perceptual-motor development. Some of the most extensive evidence here is on the development of binocular (two-eyed) vision (Allik & Valsiner, 1980; Aslin & Dumais, 1980; Walk & Pick, 1978). Both deprivation studies with animals and studies of children with eye problems indicate that the normal development of binocular depth perception requires normal experience in seeing with both eyes. In humans, experience during infancy seems crucial if normal fusion of the images from the two eyes is to develop and if the two eyes are to work together normally in fixating targets and perceiving depth (Aslin & Dumais, 1980). Interestingly, current evidence suggests that the mechanisms for binocular vision are present at birth but are kept from operating by other behavioral tendencies. Normal development involves the reduction of these restraining factors as a result of experience. Without normal experience the constraints remain (Aslin & Dumais, 1980).

There also is evidence that the lack of normal learning opportunities can dramatically impede postural and locomotor development. When Wayne Dennis studied babies growing up in Iranian orphanages, he found that even accomplishments like sitting alone and walking could be delayed tremendously (Dennis, 1960; Dennis & Najarian, 1957). In one orphanage in which the children spent most of their time lying in cribs on their backs with minimal social interaction and no toys or other props, only 42% of the children between 1 and 2 years could sit alone and none could walk alone. Of the children between 2 and 3 years, almost all could sit alone (95%), but only 8% could walk alone. Contrasting data from another orphanage suggested that this tremendous lag could not be explained either in terms of malnutrition or general characteristics of Iranian children. Opportunities for practice and encouragement apparently make a big difference in how rapidly human motor development takes place.

Importance of skill training

Some training programs can make a big difference. Demonstrations that a particular training program fails to influence one aspect of perceptual-motor development leave open the question of what a different training program might achieve. No one can prove that training makes no difference because a new approach devised tomorrow might succeed where all others have failed. We must remain open-minded.

Singing.   An intriguing set of training studies has produced dramatic results. Arthur Jersild (1932) conducted an important study in 1930–1931. He set out to see if training could influence the extent to which 3-year-olds could sing new musical tones and intervals. In a remarkably careful and thorough study he trained 19 children for a total of 400 minutes each (in 10-minute sessions spread out over about six months). They worked on singing songs that included notes both within and outside the child's initial pitch range. Periodic tests required that they match notes sung and played on instruments such as a pitch pipe and xylophone.

The children enjoyed the training and made dramatic progress, both when compared with their own baseline and with a control group who received no training. For example, on a test of the ability to sing 11 notes ascending from middle C to F, they started with an average of 4.2 notes correct in December. By May the score was up to 10.7. After a four-month period without any more training, they were retested and did almost as well (10.3).

In some cases children who started as monotones or who had unusually high or low voices made dramatic progress, suggesting that what looked like a lack of musical ability or a naturally different voice was little more than a habitual pattern that might have become more permanent if training had not started early. Jersild's laboratory study, like more recent efforts to teach little children to play the violin, suggests that it is not so much maturational readiness as our ingenuity as teachers that limits what young children can accomplish musically.

Reading and writing.   O. K. Moore (1966) was successful when he tried to teach preschoolers how to read and write. His method involved the use of an electric typewriter and a teaching technique that emphasized the child's own curiosity and interest in learning. His movies of 3-year-olds cheerfully writing their own stories challenge traditional concepts of school readiness.

Swimming.   Perhaps the most dramatic of the training studies have dealt with accomplishments in early infancy. Myrtle McGraw's (1939) work on early swimming deserves special attention. When she placed babies in the water, she found that in the early weeks there were surprisingly well-coordinated swimming movements, presumably on a reflexive basis. As you can see in Figure 6–7, her film records show organized swimming movements totally inconsistent with our picture of the newborn out of water. She found that under normal conditions these early, organized movements become less common and disappear by about 7 months. Her work inspired others to teach babies to swim while the organized patterns were still present. Now we know that swimming can be learned in the first year (Kennedy, 1971).

Figure 6–7   Reflex swimming movements. (*From M. B. McGraw,* The Neuromuscular Maturation of the Human Infant. *New York: Columbia University Press, 1943, by permission of the publisher.*)

Walking. Findings on early walking parallel McGraw's work on swimming. Zelazo, Zelazo, and Kolb started with the stepping reflex present right after birth: when babies are held over a flat surface so the bottoms of their feet just touch, they often make stepping movements (Zelazo, 1976). The researchers gave babies regular stepping practice and found that by the end of a six-week training program (ending at the eighth week after birth), the experimental group averaged over 30 steps per minute and control groups averaged about 5.

The explanation of these surprising findings seems to relate to the idea that reflexive swimming and walking are under the control of lower brain centers and normally disappear as higher centers become operative. The child who does not have the reflexes exercised regularly loses them and presumably has to start from scratch in learning voluntary swimming and walking. In contrast, the practice groups in these studies apparently learned voluntary swimming and walking movements through instrumental learning from a stronger baseline because reflexive organizations were still present.

These findings on early swimming and walking once again raise questions about simple maturational explanations. They also show that perceptual-motor development is more complicated than it seems at first. The idea that progress *always* involves "start with a little and gain more" is too simple (see Bower, 1974, 1977).

Two-step formulation

Like physical development, perceptual-motor development arises from a continual interaction between forces originating in the DNA and the environment. It's beginning to look like we can go beyond this assertion of interaction and hypothesize a more specific formulation, supported both by some of our best animal research and by scattered findings on humans.

The developmental pattern often seems to be that (1) the *ingredients* of complicated perceptual-motor patterns appear regardless of environmental conditions and (2) the *coordination, precise elaboration*, and *efficient use* of these ingredients require the presence and support of an expected environment.

Research on song birds raised in isolation provides some of the clearest evidence for this pattern. When raised entirely in isolation, some species of birds will nevertheless sing notes and phrases characteristic of their species. But they will not put them together properly if they never hear the correct song from another bird (or tape recorder) (Thorpe, 1961). Austin Riesen (1975) interprets the findings from isolation studies more generally along the same lines.

The idea of an inborn behavioral baseline that requires interaction and learning for elaboration and use is supported by several lines of human research. At first deaf babies make noises like those of other babies. After a few months they typically become quiet (Lenneberg, 1967), which suggests that their failure to hear their own noises makes no difference at first, but does later. The babies in Iranian orphanages failed to put together the movement

TABLE 6–2 A two-step formulation of perceptual-motor development

	Step 1	Step 2
Basic Model[a]		
Basic formula	Component skills appear	Component skills are elaborated, coordinated, and put to efficient use
Genetic-maturational contribution	High	Low
Specific environmental conditions and practice	Unimportant	Important
Well-documented Example[b]		
The characteristic song of the male white-crowned sparrow	Basic notes are sounded	Notes are integrated into the complex song
Hypothesized Examples in Humans		
Vocalization	Simple sounds are made	Sounds are elaborated and coordinated into spoken language
Movement	Simple movements such as grasping and kicking are made	Movements are elaborated and coordinated into actions such as throwing objects and walking
Vision	Discrimination of movement, depth, color, simple forms	Discrimination and recognition of complex forms, binocular depth perception

[a]Based in part on Riesen, 1975.
[b]Konishi, 1978; Thorpe, 1961.

patterns needed for independent walking without a normal environment. But when Dennis and his collaborators provided the usual kinds of help and encouragement, progress came quickly (Dennis, 1960). Bruner's (1973) observations of how babies learn manual skills also fits this picture, as do recent interpretations of visual development (Allik & Valsiner, 1980; Aslin & Dumais, 1980).

The perceptual and motor biases described earlier provide a picture of the special human qualities that fit into the more general model suggested here. Original equipment, such as human hands and hearing apparatus, a general bias toward using what you have, and attentional preferences toward seeing edges and noticing speech/sound contrasts help fill out our picture of the specific ingredients that children bring to perceptual-motor learning and development.

Analyses of early motor development suggest that these ingredients are often put together through some familiar learning processes (Chapter 5) (Bruner, 1973; Connolly, 1973). First new skills are refined and made automatic by practice. Once they are automatic, attention is freed for other purposes and the early skills can be used as building blocks. The refined ingredients now can be put together in elaborate combinations and coordinated sequences. The two-step sequence is heavily weighted toward maturation in the first step and learning in the second. What gets learned is constrained by what the maturational schedule provides. But only when we supplement the concept of maturation with ideas about learning and the environment can we explain what happens.

SUMMARY

This chapter focused on the perceptual and motor skills basic to the child's interactions with the world. The focus was on how these skills tie in with daily living.

First perceptual development was reviewed. Two theoretical positions that supplement each other were presented: differentiation theory and constructionist thinking. Differentiation theory, with its emphasis on distinctive features, stresses perceptual development as a process of getting more information from the environment. Constructionist theories focus on what happens in the child's head; internal schemas are built up. Next early perceptual skills and preferences were described, with a major concern with vision and with the fact that the infant starts with biases and skills of adaptive value. Three trends in perceptual development after infancy were summarized: increased differentiation, more optimal attention, and increased economy of information pickup.

In describing motor development, the main concern was with motor biases and with trends. As with perception, motor development reveals both specific biases and a more general bias toward activity and self-teaching. The general developmental trend toward increased differentiation and greater hierarchic integration was particularly clear. The regularity and predictability of early motor development was emphasized, but later motor development was described as less regular and predictable.

Two important accomplishments that bring perceptual and motor progress were presented in detail, as in each case we see a uniquely human pattern of central importance in our way of life. The conquest of space was presented in terms of three subtopics: progress toward standing and walking, the visual cliff, and cognitive maps. In each area both specific accomplishments and their relation to more general points were described. Next the exploitation of objects was examined, with a focus both on the early progress in forming a partnership between eye and hand skills and on the later developments through which these relations are refined.

Finally, the nature/nurture argument was considered. The topic of readiness was used to put it in focus. Then the main findings were summarized in relation to an evolutionary hypothesis and to a two-step formulation that emphasized the maturationally constrained nature of basic behavioral components and the importance of learning in the process by which basic components become elaborated, coordinated, and put to practical use.

CHAPTER 7

Cognitive Development: Piaget's Viewpoint

Cognitive development takes many forms. It includes progress in recognizing what is familiar, learning from experience, forming concepts, solving problems, and reasoning. Common to these diverse improvements is a growing ability to deal with information from the outside world. We can think of cognitive development as progress in information processing or use older terms like mental development or intellectual development.

Cognitive development is central to all psychological functioning. When children become capable of reasoning, they become more reasonable people to deal with. Intellectual progress leads to a better understanding of right and wrong, along with insight into why one nickel is better than four pennies. Appreciation of jokes and riddles depends on comprehension of ordinary situations. Knowledge of future possibilities provides new sources of pleasure and of pain. Cognitive capacities are involved in everything children do and feel.

Today two orientations to cognitive development are prominent. Jean Piaget's is the most influential. I present it in this chapter. The information-processing approach is the other important viewpoint. I summarize it in the next chapter as part of a look at memory development.

Psychologists hail Piaget as a psychologist, which he was. But it helps in understanding his ideas when you realize that he preferred to describe himself as a biologist who turned to philosophy. His background in biology is reflected in his basic concepts. His philosophical interests defined his basic question: how do we come to understand reality as we do? (Flavell, 1963)

Piaget observed children in action. His curiosity about mental development was aroused when he was given what looked like a routine job: translating some new English tests of reasoning into suitable French form. Piaget became fascinated with the *wrong* answers some children gave. He invented a clinical method designed to find out what errors showed about how children's minds work. For example, if you show a child about 5 years old a set of toy animals including eight dogs and two cats and ask if there are more dogs or more animals, you are likely to get the answer "more dogs." Further questioning often makes it clear that the child knows that dogs and cats are animals and understands what "more" means. The young child's problem, instead, seems to tie in with a problem of simultaneously paying attention to the whole collection (animals) and to its parts (cats and dogs). Through interviews, tests, and observations of babies and children on their own, Piaget amassed an enormous collection of observations of how children of varied ages act when confronted with problems. His theory interprets these observations (Flavell, 1963).

FUNCTIONAL INVARIANTS: WORKING CHARACTERISTICS OF THE MIND

Piaget's idea about how the mind works and grows can be summed up in terms of eight key concepts: organization, scheme, assimilation, accommodation, adaptation, invariant sequence, stage, and equilibration. They apply to all of us: newborn, 6-year-old, or adult. They explain why all normal children in any natural environment show similar patterns of mental development (Flavell, 1963; Piaget, 1970).

Organization

Piaget saw organization as fundamental in living creatures, as reflected in terms like *organism* and *organ.* He thought that children's behavior, like their breathing and digestion, must be understood in terms of coordinated patterns.

If we want to understand how children change, Piaget thought we have to start with the organized patterns already present. His emphasis on the inborn reflexes as the beginnings of mental life thus is typical of his whole position. It contrasts with the idea that the newborn's mind is a blank slate, or *tabula rasa.* Cognitive development starts with something, not a disordered jumble or a vacuum. The built-in organizations, or reflexes, are the starting point. From there on progress always involves a change in some existing, organized pattern, not the creation of anything completely new.

Scheme

Schemes are the specific organizations for dealing with information, such as particular reflexes, symbols, or operations. Actions such as reflexively grasping a finger, putting blocks in a pail, using the concept cat, and adding 2 + 2 all are organized patterns of action that appear repeatedly, rather than being accidental and temporary. All, then, belong in the same category: scheme.

Diverse schemes work in parallel ways. There are important differences between such early schemes as grasping or banging a rattle and later schemes such as cat or adding. There are also universal features that apply to all schemes. The terms *assimilation, accommodation,* and *adaptation* sum up those common, working principles.

Assimilation

Assimilation is the tendency to try to fit new information into the schemes we already have. When newborns start sucking a nipple, the sensations in their mouth are assimilated into the sucking scheme. When you look at newborns and think they look like little monkeys, you are assimilating the sight of them into your scheme of little monkeys. Assimilation is a working characteristic of all schemes of all kinds.

Assimilation is a tendency to use "mental equipment" whenever something seems to fit it. Sam looks up to watch a bird and happens to notice an unusual cloud. He exclaims, "It looks like a turtle!" Diane picks a dandelion and ties the stem in a knot. Joe glances out the window and reads, "S-T-O-P, stop." In each case an accidental encounter with a new stimulus results in the use of a previously learned scheme that would not have been exercised if the suitable raw material had not come along.

Because both early schemes, such as looking at edges, and later ones, such as naming familiar objects, can be used in any setting, the tendency to assimilate implies a bias to be active. To be alive and awake means to be using some scheme at any moment. Piaget thought that assimilation is the most basic tendency of the mind. He made activity fundamental.

Piaget's emphasis on activity ties in closely with trends described in earlier chapters. The experimental finding that sensory experience is needed for the normal development of eye and brain (Chapter 4) echoes a slogan that Piaget proposed before modern studies of sensory deprivation: light is the food of the eyes.

Piaget thought that new schemes are particularly likely to be exercised in an assimilatory way. A child who has just learned how to throw is particularly likely to throw a new object. A child who has just learned to hammer is more likely to discover that much can be hammered. A child with a new word, such as *mama*, spontaneously applies it whenever someone like mother comes along. The child who is just mastering counting often counts and counts and counts, continuing long after the adults around her or him lose interest.

The hypothesis that the child spontaneously exercises new schemes leads to the general idea that children's play often reflects their developmental level. Sean has just learned that objects can be put in a pail and dumped out; so Sean is likely to spend lots of time playing with pails and objects. Rita is figuring out social roles and rules. She spends countless hours with her friends, enacting dramas that use her schemes of families and social interchange. An emphasis on assimilation as an inherent and basic part of the mind makes play and exploration central to mental development.

Accommodation

Accommodation is what happens to schemes as a result of experience: they change and come to fit outside reality better. The tendency for children to use new words spontaneously illustrates accommodation and how assimilation and accommodation work together. After learning to call the family collie dog goggie, Laura says goggie every time she sees a similar sight. She says goggie to the poodle next door, the picture of Snoopy on her shirt, and the sheepdog in the television commercial. These examples all show successful assimilation. But Laura also says goggie when she sees a live cat, a picture of a horse, and a seal at the zoo. Her family explains that those are *not* goggies and soon something changes. Her scheme, or concept, of goggie is revised. It accommodates so as to fit the facts better.

Accommodation depends on feedback. In the goggie story the feedback came from other people. Laura learned how her speech community defines goggie from others' reactions, but often the child gets the feedback directly from the physical environment. Doug treats a juice glass like a ball. He tries to bounce it and quickly learns that balls and glasses have different properties. Betsy counts her pennies. She rearranges them and counts them again. As a result she learns for herself that the number stays the same regardless of the arrangement. Accommodation always is accommodation to external reality, regardless of how the information about the world is gathered.

With this view of accommodation, Piaget postulated a truth-seeking ingredient as basic to the mind. Some theories emphasize the importance of feedback external to mental functioning, as when a child learns in order to get food or praise. Piaget agreed that accommodation often results from extrinsic factors, such as the social pressure in the goggie example. But he saw accommodation to information about the nature of reality as even more fundamental. Accommodation, like assimilation, is a biological given.

Both assimilation and accommodation are crucial in making sense out of the world. It is handy to interpret new experiences in light of the ideas (schemes) that have worked in the past, as long as we are ready to alter or discard those that do not work in new situations. Intelligent interaction with the environment depends on a good balance between assimilation and accommodation.

Adaptation

When assimilation and accommodation are in balance, Piaget called the result adaptation. A one-sided emphasis on assimilation can be fun, and even educational, as when a child pretends that sand is food or practices grown-up skills such as cutting and sharing. But such play cannot solve the immediate problem of getting enough to eat, for playful schemes must accommodate to reality. Similarly, almost complete accommodation to outside stimuli, as when the child flawlessly imitates a TV commercial over and over or carefully walks in exactly the same manner as daddy, does not result in problem solving either. Only when intellectual structures are used to blend assimilation and accommodation realistically is there realistic coping with the immediate situation.

Piaget's use of the term *adaptation* this way ties cognitive development in with the way biologists look at all life processes in all creatures. Biologists see each form of life as adapted to fit in with its environment—the clam for life under water, the cactus for desert conditions. Piaget saw mental development as the ancient process of adaptation now taking place on a new level.

Piaget's image of the developing child makes the child similar to the scientist (see Table 7–1). Both seekers after truth work from theories about the nature of reality. Both try to extend their theory so as to encompass new and diverse observations. Both revise a theory when it doesn't seem to fit the facts. In each case understanding of the world moves ahead without ever becoming perfect.

The assimilation-accommodation model provides an explanation of why children develop cognitively. Assimilation results in constant activity, practice of new schemes, and generalization from familiar to new situations. Accommodation ensures that the activity results in useful learning: the improvement of what is there at the beginning of an interchange with a new problem. In

TABLE 7-1 Parallels between the scientist and the child as seen by Piaget

	Scientist	Child
What do they start with in dealing with new information?	A *theory*: an organized conceptual scheme	A *scheme*: an organized mental structure such as a reflex, symbol, or operation
What happens to new information?	If it seems relevant, it is interpreted in terms of the theory.	If it seems relevant, it is *assimilated.*
What happens if the new information cannot successfully be dealt with in terms of the preexisting organization?	The theory is changed.	The scheme *accommodates.*

each encounter the fit between activity and environment becomes a little better. Children built along these lines gradually become more intelligent as long as they are given a chance to have thousands of encounters with natural environments.

Piaget went further than the claim that the mind is built to develop if given a reasonable chance. He had specific ideas about the nature of progress, which relate to the concepts of invariant sequence, stage, and equilibration. These ideas are more controversial than the assimilation-accommodation model.

Invariant sequences

Piaget hypothesized that all children follow the same path in developing cognitively. He thought they start at the same point and go through the same sequence of steps. They vary in how rapidly they move, but no one skips a step or follows a different path.

Tests of Piaget's ideas about invariant sequences typically have supported him, even when children in varied cultures (Dasen, 1977; Modgil & Modgil, 1976) and mentally retarded people (Weisz & Zigler, 1979) have been studied. Both the idea that there are invariant sequences and the more specific notion that Piaget has described seem generally sound, although there are exceptions.

Stage

The concept of stage as used by Piaget involves a hypothesis about how cognitive development takes place that is even more specific than the idea of invariant sequences. He portrayed stages as qualitatively different periods in which a particular mode of thinking is present, such as thinking in sensorimotor or symbolic terms. There is a variety of domains of mental growth you could observe in a child: number concepts, understandings shown in drawings, ideas about right and wrong, and so on. The idea of invariant sequence implies that within each domain there are universal paths. For example, all children might understand the concept of counting one by one before they realize you have the same number of objects in a row whether they are bunched together or spread out as long as none is added or taken away (number conservation). The stage concept goes further: it says that children perform similarly in all domains (Figure 7–1).

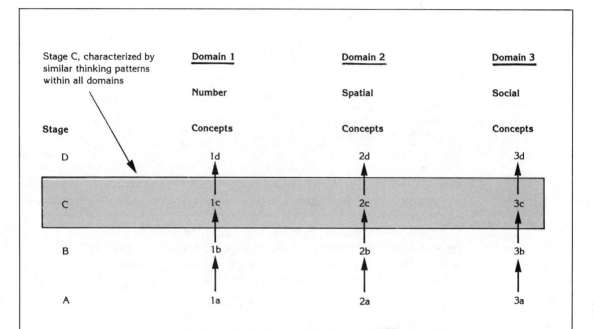

Invariant sequences: step-like progress within each domain, as in going from step 1a to 1b to 1c in understanding number concepts, or in going from 2a to 2b to 2c in understanding spatial concepts.
Stages: periods characterized by particular modes of function in all domains, as in showing similar ways of thinking about number concepts, spatial concepts, and social concepts, for example "C" thinking.
Equilibration: an explanation of why progress is similar in all domains that implies that the mind "pushes for internal consistency" so that 3c would fit better with 1c and 2c than 3d would.

Figure 7–1   Invariant sequences, stages, and equilibration

Similarity of thinking in varied domains is assumed to result from the fact that only one kind of thinking can be present at a particular point. A child who does not yet have symbols cannot imagine something to fear, look ahead to tomorrow, understand a concept such as more, or plan a drawing. The stage concept implies that if we know how the child's mind works in one area, we can do well in predicting all others.

The stage concept can be used in either a tight or a loose sense. Piaget used it in a tight way. He thought that there are close connections between performance in varied areas and believed that much more of childhood is spent during periods of unified functioning than in transition times (when the child is passing from one stage to another and shows characteristics from both). This tight concept of stages has not held up well in more recent research. It seems to make the child's mind more unified than it actually is and to imply more abrupt transitions than we usually find (Fischer, 1980; Gelman, 1978).

A looser use of the stage concept seems much more defensible. You can accept Piaget's idea that there are distinctive modes of thought that follow in succession without expecting either abrupt transitions or close connections between thinking in varied areas. This looser version of Piaget's theory is the one that I and many other American psychologists favor. Accordingly, I use the term *period* rather than *stage* when summarizing cognitive development and reserve the term *stage* for Piaget's careful and tight concept (Selman, 1980).

Equilibration

Piaget explained the existence of tight, or unified, stages in terms of another concept: *equilibration* (Appel & Goldberg, 1977). The scientist metaphor is helpful in understanding it. Scientists try to construct theories that are internally consistent. Explanations of different sets of events are not supposed to be contradictory. Better scientific theories, such as those relating physical development to DNA, are regarded as better because they extend the range of evidence that can be explained in terms of a small number of central ideas. Piaget thought that the mind has natural tendencies similar to scientists' deliberate efforts to produce internal consistency. He thought that mental structures move toward greater equilibrium, or internal balance. This is the equilibration tendency that is hypothesized as responsible for stages. Because Piaget claimed that inconsistent mental structures cannot exist side by side, he thought transition periods are relatively short and training children in forms of thinking beyond their stage cannot produce durable results.

Equilibration, then, refers to a hypothesized tendency for self-regulation in cognitive development. Piaget (1971) saw an intimate connection between self-balancing forces in cognitive development and in physical development. He saw his concept of equilibration as related to Waddington's concept of homeorhesis (Chapter 4) and, like it, necessary in explaining how thousands of separate changes add up to a pattern of coordinated change in a predictable direction. Because of central, unifying forces, the individual instances of assimilation and accommodation are seen as producing one general trend. Early and unstable forms of interaction give way to more and more balanced and permanent ones. Self-organizing tendencies coordinate varied schemes into stages. They take the child from less balanced and adaptive stages to better integrated ones.

Equilibration gets us back to organization. Schemes are particular forms of organization. Stages are organized, or equilibrated, sets of schemes. They involve the total workings of the mind at a particular time.

Because equilibration explains the existence of unified stages, the same evidence that casts doubt in tight stages raises questions about equilibration. As a result many doubt the validity of the equilibration concept. But we are short on findings that get to the heart of the issue.

MAJOR PERIODS OF COGNITIVE DEVELOPMENT

Piaget described cognitive development as including four main periods. Each begins at one of the turning points called a reference age in Chapter 3. As summed up in Table 7–2, he thought of each turning point as ushering in a new kind of interaction. I'll summarize each of the major periods, emphasizing the main forms of progress and the features that distinguish it from others.

TABLE 7–2 Piaget's major periods of cognitive development

Typical Age of Onset (Turning Point)	New Mode of Functioning	Major Period
Birth	Behavioral interaction	Sensorimotor period
2 Years	Symbolic interaction	Symbolic (or preoperational) period
6 Years	Logical interaction with the real world	Concrete operational period
13 Years	Logical interaction with the world of possibilities	Formal operational period

Sensorimotor period

The baby's intelligence is down to earth, similar to that of many animals at first. Problem solving starts from concrete situations, such as getting the fist to the mouth or watching a face go by. Efforts to cope with problems involve movements of the body rather than manipulations of ideas in the head. During the sensorimotor period (birth to about 2 years) progress starts on this physical level. A puppy tries to catch its own tail and eventually stops trying. A kitten learns to pounce toward where a ball is headed rather than at where the ball is at the beginning of the jump. The human baby makes similar discoveries during infancy.

The nature of progress

The specific accomplishments within the sensorimotor period are part of a coherent, general pattern. All progress has a common starting point: the organized reflexive actions present at birth, such as sucking, grasping, and looking. From this small set of starting schemes a large set of more useful ones grows. The first schemes become differentiated (as when early grasping gives way to precision and power grips), elaborated (as when reflexive looking at edges matures into more involved scanning of faces), and coordinated (as when looking and grasping start to work together in picking up objects). But progress is not just more of the same; there are dramatic shifts as well.

Piaget emphasized the transitions during the sensorimotor period by summarizing it in terms of six unified substages. But here, as elsewhere, his hypothesis of tightly organized stages has not held up (Fischer, 1980; Gratch, 1979; Hunt, 1977; Uzgiris & Hunt, 1975). Accordingly, they will not be discussed here. Instead, I'll sum up the progress during infancy in terms of lines of progress described by Piaget and confirmed in most relevant studies. These seem to give a picture that is still Piagetian, but more easily understood and more defensible.

Paths of progress.   This description of sensorimotor progress in terms of paths, or lines, of progress comes from the research of Ina Uzgiris and J. McV. Hunt (1975). They took Piaget's informal observation procedures and used them as a basis for constructing scales, or tests, that anyone could use in testing babies (Chapter 2). They developed seven scales. Each seems to be an *ordinal scale,* meaning there is a strong tendency for babies who pass one item on a scale to pass all items on the same scale that have lower numbers. For example, if we know that a baby passed item 9 on scale I, we can be reasonably confident that the baby also passed items 1 through 8. This technical matter ties in with the notion of invariant sequences previously discussed. The existence of ordinal scales based on Piaget's description supports his idea that there are universal sequences that all babies follow. The Uzgiris-Hunt work, then, is typical in supporting Piaget's ideas about specific sequences in development while challenging claims about stages.

The Uzgiris-Hunt scales can be thought of as separate paths that all emerge from a common starting point (the reflexes present at birth), as illustrated in Figure 7-2. The nature of each path is described in Table 7-3. The steps on each path are the actual test items used. An approximate age scale is presented to show that there are typical ages at which particular steps are reached, but those ages vary with environmental conditions (Hunt, 1977) and are less important and predictable than the sequences. The central points are that all children apparently go down the same paths and that these paths reflect the nature of cognitive development in infancy.

Object permanence.   Object permanence (scale I) is the best understood path (Gratch, 1979; Harris, 1975; Hunt, 1977). It consists of the following steps (Uzgiris & Hunt, 1975).

1. Following a slowly moving object through a 180° arc
2. Noting the disappearance of a slowly moving object
3. Finding a partially covered object
4. Finding a completely covered object
5. Finding an object completely covered in two places
6. Finding an object completely covered in two places alternately
7. Finding an object completely covered in three places
8. Finding an object after successive visible displacements
9. Finding an object under three superimposed screens
10. Finding an object following one invisible displacement
11. Finding an object following one invisible displacement with two screens
12. Finding an object following one invisible displacement with two screens alternated

13. Finding an object following one invisible displacement with three screens
14. Finding an object following a series of invisible displacements
15. Finding an object following a series of invisible displacements by searching in reverse of the order of hiding

It starts with the simple skill of watching, or visually pursuing, an attractive object such as a colored toy as it is moved slowly in front of the baby. Only at about 1 month is there smooth following throughout the entire arc as the object is moved from one side of the baby to the other (step 1). Attention turns next to how the baby reacts to the disappearance of the moving object, as when it is moved below the edge of the chair. At first babies seem to lose interest when the object disppears. Later their glance lingers at the point where it disappeared (step 2). This is the first hint that an object out of sight is not entirely out of mind. But infants still do not act as if they believe the object continues to exist when out of sight. That comes months later.

TABLE 7-3 Developments in the sensorimotor period

Paths of Progress	The Nature of Progress
I. Visual pursuit and the permanence of object	The baby comes to understand that objects are enduring and permanent.
II. Means for obtaining desired environmental events	Means and ends become differentiated; babies use objects to get what they want and show foresight in problem solving.
III. Development of vocal (IIIa) and gestural (IIIb) imitation	Babies become able to imitate first familiar and then unfamiliar sounds and gestures.
IV. Development of operational causality	Babies become able to make interesting sights last by their own actions and become able to make objects and people repeat interesting actions.
V. Construction of object relations in space	Babies become able to localize objects by sound, follow the path of rapidly moving objects, recognize the reverse side of objects, and appreciate the relation between objects in space (containers, detours, and so on).
VI. Development of schemes for relating to objects	Babies become able to act on objects through holding, mouthing, shaking, and so on. Such complex actions as sliding and throwing objects appear. Social actions such as drinking, hugging, and making objects walk develop, followed by showing and naming objects.

Uzgiris & Hunt, 1975.

Scale I.   Visual Pursuit and the Permanence of Objects
Scale II.   Means for Obtaining Desired Environmental Events
Scale IIIa.   Vocal Imitation
Scale IIIb.   Gestural Imitation
Scale IV.   Operational Causality
Scale V.   Localization of Objects in Space
Scale VI.   Schemes for Relating to Objects

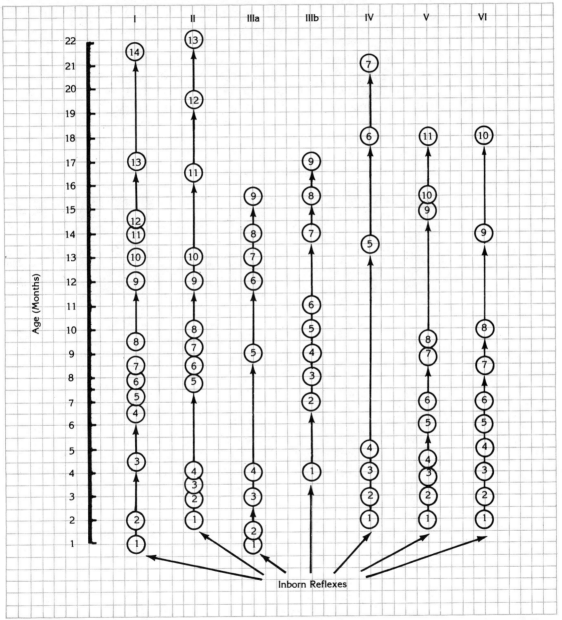

Figure 7–2   Seven lines of progress of sensorimotor intelligence (*after Uzgiris & Hunt, 1975*)

Step 4 is particularly dramatic. The baby's attention is engaged with an attractive object, such as a rattle. It is put down within reach. Then it is covered (such as with an uninteresting scarf) before the baby's hand gets to it. The younger infant loses interest in the object at this point, perhaps looking away and stopping the hand movement toward it, perhaps fingering the screen without acting as if it covered the object. Only at about 7 months do most babies reach the milestone of uncovering the object and picking it up (step 4).

Step 4 is but the beginning of a mental construction of the object as permanent. More complicated hiding games reveal the nature of further progress. At step 8, the object is hidden behind three screens in succession and left behind the third screen. The baby sees it reappear after going under the first two. The solution of looking for it under the third screen comes at about 9 to 10 months, but at this point understanding seemingly depends on the fact that the baby was allowed to see the object in the hand when it was not under the screens. If the object is hidden in the palm or a box throughout the process (invisible displacements), we do not yet see behavior implying a clear mental construction of what happened. This comes at about 20 to 22 months.

Figure 7–3 A baby without object permanence loses interest in a hidden object.

The development of object permanence is one of the central achievements of infancy, revealing a fundamental advance in the baby's understanding of reality. In later chapters, I'll relate this achievement to progress in language, social, and emotional development.

Taken together, the seven Uzgiris-Hunt scales add up to a dramatic journey. The reflexive newborn becomes a spontaneous problem solver. Actions bridging but a few seconds of time give way to longer sequences. Practical puzzles that at first are not even seen as puzzles become challenges that are met.

Sensorimotor play

Children's play develops in parallel with their thought. In infancy play is on a sensorimotor level. When babies splash water, drop all their toys out of the crib, pound a block on the table, or go "ba-ba-ba," the fun seems to be in the actions themselves and in the sights, sounds, and other sensations they produce. In other words the props and movements are treated only for what they are. There is no sign of symbolism, as in pretending to sleep or playing house.

Within the sensorimotor period, play changes as competence changes, supporting Piaget's idea that play is an assimilatory activity with special satisfactions coming from the exercise of new schemes. Thus, as competence grows, a particular game, such as simple peek-a-boo, first rises and then falls in prominence (Lobel, Miller, & Commons, 1981).

Challenges to Piaget

Piaget's picture of infant cognitive development is the best we have, but it may be inadequate, even when modified to deemphasize stages (Gratch, 1979). The biggest question comes from a few studies suggesting that the baby starts with far more competence than Piaget assumes.

A study by Andrew Meltzoff and Keith Moore (1977) illustrates the challenge. They studied gestural imitation in babies only 12–21 days in age. They videotaped the model and the baby separately so that judgments of the baby's actions could be made by judges who knew nothing at all about which gesture had just been modeled. The adult models presented a total of four different actions in a varying series: mouth opening, tongue protrusion, lip protrusion, and some finger movements. Note that three actions were facial gestures that the babies could not see themselves making. Past research implies that the actions cannot be imitated until about age 8–10 months. The judges scored the babies' actions during a 20-second period immediately following one in which the model repeated one action four times. The judges were asked to rate each response period on a multiple-choice basis: which of the four gestures do you think was most clearly observed? For all four gestures the ratings indicated that the babies made the just-modeled gesture more often than would have been expected from chance. The imitation did not occur all the time, but it apparently was there. This experiment is a major challenge both to Piaget's ideas about imitation and to his whole picture of development in infancy. However, Hayes and Watson (1981) were unable to replicate the results when they used more stringent controls.

Gerald Gratch (1979) sees two patterns of reaction beginning that he thinks will become more prominent if dramatic experiments like Meltzoff and Moore's and Hayes and Watson's can be replicated. One approach is for investigators to keep working from Piaget-inspired events in infancy to develop alternative formulations that fit both his and discrepant findings. The other is to resolve the issue in terms of a competence/performance distinction. Meltzoff and Moore argue that the baby has from birth the competence that Piaget thinks is gradually constructed. If they turn out to be right, we still are left with the fact that this competence takes a long time to become obvious. Puzzling actions such as the baby's reactions to object permanence games still have to be explained. Perhaps studies by Piaget and by Uzgiris and Hunt trace the way babies gradually become able to use their competence in everyday situations. But if so, why does the original competence take so long to be realized?

Symbolic or preoperational period

By about 18 to 24 months clear evidence of symbolic representation appears. Imitations of actions seen hours earlier show that the child has some-how stored and later used a mental picture of what happened. Sometimes the nature of the symbols used is relatively clear, as when a child pretends to give you an injection, holding a spoon like a hypodermic needle, or says "Mommy go" in a situation where the words clearly stand for an event that just took place. At other times all you can tell is that the child used internal represen-tation of some kind. For example, when a child watches you hide a toy under one of several boxes and minutes later goes directly to the correct box, you know there are no external cues guiding the behavior. But you cannot be sure whether the internal guidance comes from a mental image, words, or some other kind of symbol.

The evidence of representation becomes more and more widespread in the following months, and the symbolic or preoperational period lasts from about ages 2 to 6 years. Play shows what happens generally.

Symbolic play

Symbolic play reveals the growth of more general skills in representation (Nicolich, 1977; Piaget, 1962). We see it first in isolated acts, such as pretending to sleep, in which what is symbolized is close to what the child does in reality. But gradually the isolated symbols develop into complex combinations and the distance between the symbol and what is represented grows (Werner & Kaplan, 1963).

The distancing of representations from the activities they represent has been documented in several studies. An early developmental progression is from the child pretending to eat, to pretending to feed a doll, to pretending that the doll is feeding itself (Fenson & Ramsay, 1980; Watson & Fischer, 1977). A later one can be seen if you ask children to use an imagined object in an action sequence—for example, asking them to pretend to brush their teeth with a toothbrush or comb their hair. Younger children respond by using their fingers as representations of the brush or comb. Only later is the hand shaped around an imaginary brush or comb (Overton & Jackson, 1973). In each case we see first the use of the child's own body as the symbol and only later a more abstract form of representation.

The growth of complex combinations of symbols is obvious in many domains. Houses built of blocks get bigger and include more details such as windows. Pretend actions such as cooking or driving become embedded in longer and more complicated plots (Nicolich, 1977). By age 4 or 5, children can put together a diverse set of materials and actions in a coherent whole and show foresight while doing it.

Here is an example of the kind of complex, symbolic play seen at 4 or 5. A 5-year-old and her 2-year-old sister came to a laboratory playroom for the first time and were introduced to a 4-year-old girl, also there for the first time. Within a few seconds the trio became mother, big sister, and baby. Then while being this family and carrying on appropriate dialogue, they invented situations that made it possible to simultaneously try out the toys that had been left around the room. They announced suppertime and used the plastic dishes. Nighttime arrived. The blocks were turned into beds. Some of the dolls became additional family members to be put to sleep. After breakfast (the night passed quickly) it rained. The miniature parasols were raised as children paraded around the room in dress-up clothes. The story made up and enacted during the hour was a creative product composed of dozens of separate parts unified around a central theme.

The girls' pretend play, like the plays written by adult playwrights, involved a symbolic transformation of reality. The room, the physical props, time, and the actresses themselves all were turned into something else through the actions of the girls' minds.

Cute remarks

As language develops young children make many statements that adults find cute. A closer look at the cute remarks of children between 2 and 5 years old helps you appreciate both the power and the limitations of their symbolic thinking. Here are some examples collected in the Soviet Union by Kornei Chukovsky (1963, pp. 1–3, 21–23, 24). Many illustrate a creative ability to recognize and state analogies.

1. Once when we were taking a walk on the beach, Lialia saw, for the first time, a ship in the distance. "Mommie, Mommie, the ship is taking a bath," she cried with excitement and amazement.
2. "What is a knife—the fork's husband?"
3. "Can't you see? I'm barefoot all over."
4. "Mommy, turn off the sun."

Other examples show that the confident generalizations often reveal both a lack of logic and a failure to realize the lack.

5. "Our Granny killed the geese in the wintertime so that they would not catch cold."
6. "Mother, who was born first, you or I?"
7. "Mother, who gave birth to me? You? I knew it! If daddy had given birth to me I'd have a mustache."
8. Little Olia was feeding bits of cabbage leaves to the chickens. "Chickens don't eat cabbage," her mother informed her. "I'm giving it to them so that they may save it for after they become rabbits."

Chukovsky's examples show that the enormous number of new concepts learned during this period often emerge from an active search for meaning and understanding.

The quotes suggest that the children are like magicians who don't really understand the difference between magic and what is real. The line between what it is possible to imagine and what it is possible to do seems fuzzy at best. Olia's explanation of why she feeds cabbage leaves to the chickens resembles reasonable thinking, but it is based on a pseudologic rather than actual reasoning.

Limitations of preoperational thought

According to Piaget, this pseudologic of the preschool child arises from four qualities of early symbolic thought that limit its value for logical and realistic problem solving. It is centered, perceptually dominated, static, and irreversible.

Centration, or being centered, means a tendency to focus, or center, on only one aspect of a situation at the expense of seeing it in broader perspective. In a famous Piagetian demonstration the child watches as water is poured from a tall, thin glass into a much flatter one (see Figure 7–4). Younger children often think that there is less water as a result of this simple act of pouring. Seemingly, they first center on height and ignore the corresponding change in other dimensions. This failure to understand that the amount of water is conserved, or remains constant, relates to broader tendencies. In the water demonstration the children seemingly are tied to perceptual reality, the way things look, and have trouble understanding that the way things look is not always the way they are; that is, the children are perceptually dominated. In an amusing experiment DeVries (1969) demonstrated that when she put a realistic dog mask on a live cat, the children acted as if she had actually transformed the animal, even though its tail was visible when she put on the mask.

Centration on immediate perceptual factors is characteristic of younger children. The child who looks down at you from a chair and gleefully says "I'm bigger" seems to believe it.

Centration appears as *egocentrism,* the tendency for the child to have trouble seeing that there are alternative perspectives, that the world looks different to different people. If Joan and Mary are the only children in a family, Mary is likely to have trouble realizing that Joan has a sister.

Centration seems to underlie preschool children's tendency to be unconcerned about how they look and sound to other people, as long as people make no overtly negative response. Three- and 4-year-olds will talk to themselves out loud and play with no sign of inhibition even when in a demonstration playroom with 20 spectators. The confident pronouncements in the Chukovsky examples seemingly illustrate the common lack of awareness of how the audience is reacting.

The young child's thought is said to be *static* because of a focus on states and an inability to deal with changes. For example, the preschooler has trouble understanding that when a pencil drops from a table to the floor, there is a whole series of positions that it occupies on the way down. The idea that a child gradually turns into an adult is also hard to handle. The magical notion of a sudden transformation is easier. The idea that babies come from the union of eggs and sperms and a series of gradual transformations from zygote to newborn seemingly cannot be understood, even when there are explanations and books with pictures. Here is a transcript of a young child's interview with an experimenter exploring her understanding of how babies are made (Bernstein & Cowan, 1975, p. 87):

> (How would the lady get a baby to grow in her tummy?) Um, get a rabbit. 'Cause one day I saw a book about them, and . . . they just get a duck or goose and they get a little more growned . . . and then they turn into a baby.

(A rabbit will turn into a baby?) They give them some food, people food, and they grow like a baby.

A third characteristic of the thought of children between 2 and 6 is a lack of *reversibility.* Reversible operations such as adding and subtracting or pouring

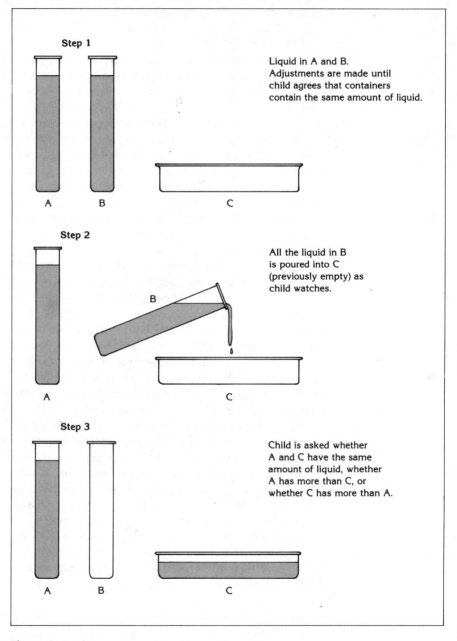

Figure 7–4   Conservation of liquid quantity problem

water from a tall glass to a short one and then pouring it back are basic in understanding which changes in the world are stable and which are transient. You can't turn a chicken into a rabbit. You can spread out a set of pennies and then put them close together again. The young child's failure on conservation problems relates to a lack of reversibility in thought, as well as to centration problems and a tendency to focus on the beginning and end states and to ignore the transformation itself.

Challenges to Piaget

There is growing dissatisfaction with Piaget's formulation of cognitive development between 2 and 6 years. His own observations typically have been replicated, but observations of other kinds and a new way of thinking have fostered discontent.

It has become clear that Piaget exaggerated the young child's limitations. For example, when simple and more familiar tasks are used, children are less egocentric than when tested on Piaget's tasks (Chapter 13). Similarly, some brief training programs make it possible for preschoolers to master problems that Piaget said were impossible for them (Brainerd, 1978; Gelman, 1978, 1979; Gelman & Gallistel, 1978).

More important, Piaget seems to have made a fundamental error in defining the thought of children below age 6 largely in terms of what it lacks, as in his label *pre*operational and his focus on the logical abilities that older children have and that they lack (Gelman & Gallistel, 1978). A more fruitful approach is to accept the fact that younger children think differently, but to look at what they can do (Flavell, 1977; Gelman & Gallistel, 1978; Keil, 1981).

Rochel Gelman's work on number concepts is perhaps the best example of the new look that seems likely to replace the traditional emphasis. She (Gelman & Gallistel, 1978) found that children as young as 2½ years already understand and regularly use several number principles, even though their performance on the number task of central interest to Piaget (number conservation) looks illogical. For example, when she looked at early counting, Gelman found that youngsters usually understand the idea of one counting term for each item counted (the one-to-one principle) and usually use a set of counting terms in a consistent and systematic way (the stable order principle).

But often the 2- and 3-year-olds made counting errors, despite their understanding of number principles. For example, at this age many count by saying, "A, B, C," "two, six, ten," or use some other nonstandard set of terms from the alphabet or number set. But children typically use their own terms in a regular way. For instance, the child who counts three objects "two, six, ten" is consistent when faced with two objects and counts, "two, six." Similarly, children who understand the one-to-one idea often get mixed up when starting and stopping to count a set of objects. Despite use of a systematic set of tags and of the one-to-one principle, errors are common, especially when more than three items are counted.

Gelman's strategy is to develop a detailed picture of how number abilities grow, starting with the component principles that are present remarkably early and building upward from there. Her approach has promise and is similar to that Piaget took in describing the other periods of cognitive development.

The most common strategy in studying children's humor has been to present humor stimuli, such as jokes and cartoons, to children in order to see how they react (McGhee, 1979). As a result we know much more about children's reactions to humor than about their own efforts to be funny.

Lori Moglia (1981) conducted one of the rare investigations of humor production as her undergraduate honors thesis. She observed 13 children, aged 15 to 45 months, during free-play time in a day-care center. She dictated her observations into a tape recorder, focusing on the humor, the situation, and on play cues (signals to others indicating "I'm joking now").

The typical child produced a joke about once every eight minutes, accompanying all jokes with looks, facial expressions, and giggles that made it clear to the audience that humor, not misunderstanding, was involved in the incongruous actions.

The humor was classified in terms of a developmental scheme proposed by Paul McGhee (1979) on the basis of Piaget's reports of his children's actions: first, incongruous actions toward objects; second, incongruous labeling of objects and events; and third, conceptual incongruity. Moglia's evidence suggested there was indeed a progression through these three stages. However, the connection between age and type of humor was weak, with even the younger children producing "sophisticated" jokes.

Examples of the jokes Moglia observed are listed below (Moglia, 1981, pp. 34, 35, 38, 40-43, 47, 49). Read them and consider how well they support the general idea that children's humor reflects their level of cognitive development.

Stage 1—incongruous action toward objects
1. Smiling, puts toy monkey in the "oven," closes door, looks up at me and giggles. (25 months)
2. Child and Rebecca are cleaning up together. They try to pass the powdered soap from one hand to the other. But it drops on the floor. Child begins to giggle and slide on it like a skater on ice. (26 months)
3. Picks up a doll, points it at Christopher like a gun and goes "Boom!" and then giggles. (32 months)

Stage 2—incongruous labeling of objects and events
1. Smiles at Pat, points at Morgan (a boy) and says, "He's a doggy," and laughs. (32 months)
2. Says "She goes up there, she goes up there" laughing and in a sing-

song voice about Kristen going *down* the slide, while giggling at me.
(35 months)

3. Says seriously, "There's nothing in my bag," which is clear plastic
through which a set of six little dolls can be seen. Then she giggles at
Pat and Shawn. (43 months)

Stage 3—conceptual incongruity

1. Child picks up a tobacco can, looks in it, and says, "All gone," then
tilts it at me where I can see something inside it, then he laughs. (32
months)

2. Child runs up to Ryan, taps him on the back smiling, holds up two
fingers, and says, "five," and giggles and giggles. (33 months)

3. Child says to Charlotte, "I have poison peanutbutter!" and then giggles.
(43 months)

Source: From unpublished honors thesis, Bucknell University, 1981.

Period of concrete operations

Signs of more systematic thinking appear at about 6 or 7 years, and the
period of concrete operations lasts until about age 13. During the symbolic
period there was a growing ability to put symbols together in combination, as
in the long sequences of pretend and statements such as "Our Granny killed
the geese in the wintertime so that they would not catch cold." Now the loose
sequences of ideas become genuinely logical in some spheres.

Part of the shift is in orientation (Flavell, 1977). Elementary-school children
seem to have a better sense of what a problem is and what a reasonable
solution might look like. They also take a more quantitative approach and are
more ready to use such tools as counting and measuring in solving problems.

Classification and ordering

Skills in classification and ordering are central in the emergence of systematic thinking. The preschooler can label big sticks and little sticks and
sometimes can take a collection of sticks such as those in Figure 7–5 and line
them up from smallest to largest on a trial-and-error basis. Older children, in
contrast, can perform such a problem in *ordering,* or *seriation,* systematically,
as when they start with the smallest, look for the next largest and move it,
then look for the next largest, and so on. Similarly, although children of 3
might be able to put all the black blocks from a mixed collection together,
they typically would fail a task such as that illustrated in Figure 7–6, which
requires classification in terms of two dimensions (size and color) simultaneously.

Operations

The word *operation* is used in naming this period because we now see
true operations: mental actions that can be reversed (such as adding and
subtracting). The term *concrete operations* is applied because during this period
there are only operations on concrete stimuli, such as pennies or dogs (no
operations on operations, as in algebra or logic).

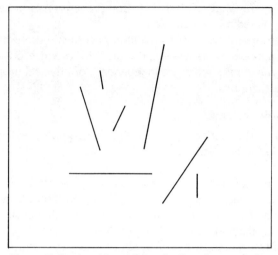

Figure 7–5   An older child typically solves seriation problems such as this one through a systematic approach.

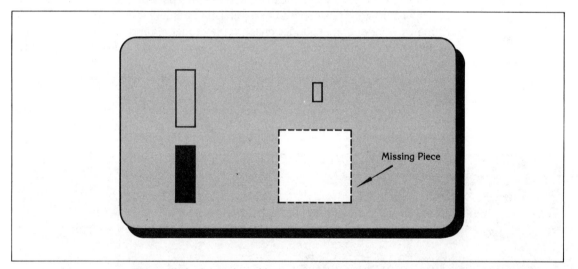

Figure 7–6   Logical problem requiring simultaneous consideration of two bases of classification

Elementary arithmetic gives some good and familiar examples of what is needed in concrete operational functioning. Simple statements of relations, such as six apples take away two apples equals four apples, involve work with a *system* of operations. Adding and subtracting must be seen as reversible. Adding always can get you back where you started from before you took away. To order sticks systematically or to deal with the number system, you must be able to consistently apply operational concepts such as more than, less than, and equal to. The child does best in grasping basic operations if they are tied to concrete experience in manipulating actual objects. Two apples plus two apples is easier to understand than two plus two. Two what? asks the concrete operational child at first. Comprehension is better when the objects are manipulated as well as seen.

As an operation such as addition becomes more practiced, the need for concrete aids becomes less important. With practice on varied materials the skill becomes more and more independent of physical props and easier to use in novel situations.

Play with rules

As in earlier periods, play provides a good perspective on what is new in thought during the elementary-school years. A central theme now is play with rules.

Cooperation is an important advance. When used carefully, the term *cooperation* means more than getting along with others. It means an ability to *operate* together, to share common agreements about rules and roles. If several children are playing school at the cooperative level (Parten, 1932), there is a shared and continuing agreement about who plays what role. A student cannot become a teacher without mutual agreement. Spanking either is against the rules or it isn't. Everyone must treat the same part of the playroom as the principal's office. These shared and persisting agreements provide a common framework for action. Younger children play together and often join in playing around a common theme, as with the three girls in the demonstration play-room. A close look shows that they usually do not make and keep strict agreements about what they are doing. It isn't always nighttime for everyone at the same time.

Genuine cooperation in free play is paralleled by the emergence of play involving games with rules. After age 6, games such as checkers, hopscotch,

Mastery of games with rules is characteristic of the concrete operational period.

and baseball can be understood. They become an important form of play for many children. Sticking to the rules often seems to be fun for its own sake, just as exercising new sensorimotor skills and pretending were earlier. At times strict rule following becomes a more important matter than it need be.

Accomplishments and limitations

The intellectual accomplishments of the concrete operational period span many areas. They involve the warm, social world as much as the cool world of calculations, as the following list of typical accomplishments involving progress in thinking ability shows.

1. Play: mastery of table games with rules, such as checkers; mastery of outdoor games with rules, such as baseball; spontaneous play involving different roles and shared understanding about who does what
2. Problem solving: plans ahead on familiar tasks such as drawing and building; abandons hypotheses when they are not confirmed; can explain what words such as *bicycle* mean; is less susceptible to perceptual illusions
3. Mathematics: can learn to add, subtract, multiply, and divide; understands equations, equalities, and inequalities
4. Comprehension of the physical world: distinguishes magic and pretend from what is real; understands that pouring water into a container of a different shape does not change the amount
5. Comprehension of the social world: uses kinship terms such as sister and uncle accurately; understands social rules, such as those governing marriage; emphasizes factors such as fairness in explaining right and wrong; shows increased ability to understand others' motives and intentions

Actually, developments in social understanding during this period are so important that they are described in detail as part of the summary of social development (Chapter 13).

These accomplishments relate to the fact that formal schooling is begun at about the beginning of this period, for real school, even more than pretend school, requires the ability to understand rules. Success both in curricular subjects such as arithmetic and in the hidden curriculum of rules and regulations governing conduct requires concrete operations (Chapter 19).

The limitations of concrete operational thought will become clearer after formal operational thinking is described, for to describe what is missing now is to summarize what is gained later. But for now a few remarks may be helpful.

According to Piaget, the elementary-school child is not yet capable of mastering academic subjects such as algebra and geometry even if they are presented in a systematic and logical manner. The concrete thinker can deal with concepts like triangle or equals, but not with logical propositions and formal proofs.

The concrete operational thinker also lacks the appropriate attitude, or orientation, for more abstract subjects such as formal mathematics and symbolic logic. Although there is a quantitative attitude, there is not yet a concern with "elegant" solutions, those that are the simplest and most general possible.

There is an inclination to think logically about what is real and concrete, but there is as yet little interest in thinking about the hypothetical or only possible.

Challenges to Piaget

Piaget's ideas about school-age children have met with less objection than his hypotheses about younger ones, but challenges now are emerging. Piaget's claim that children under about 12 cannot deal with logical propositions has been questioned (Ennis, 1978). I'll examine this issue after I describe formal operational thinking. Another challenge can be considered now. It relates to metacognition, executive control, and a shift in emphasis with important implications.

Metacognition is a term for knowledge about your own mind and thought processes, as when a child knows that it is easier to remember short grocery lists than long ones (an instance of a particular kind of metacognition known as metamemory, Chapter 8). A general finding is that metacognition grows dramatically after age 5 years. Piaget knew this. What is new is the view that metacognition is central in the advances in thinking skills that take place in the elementary-school years (and after).

One reason for the new emphasis on metacognition is that it apparently relates to the development of the *executive control processes* discussed in Chapter 5 (Brown & Campione, 1978; Flavell & Wellman, 1977). Children who deliberately use their mind more actively and systematically, as in stopping to see if they have considered all alternatives before reaching a conclusion, are engaged in executive control. Presumably, this important ability to use mental skills consciously and deliberately rests on knowledge of what these skills are and how they apply—metacognition.

Metacognition may be basic to the development of self-directed thought, which becomes more evident during the elementary-school years and which is central to what Piaget described as formal operational thinking. At minimum there seems to be a shift underway from thinking of operations as central in the growth of thought between age 5 and 13 to putting the main emphasis on metacognition and executive control processes.

A more radical possibility is that this new emphasis will lead to a broader reconceptualization of cognitive development. As illustrated in Chapter 8, concepts like metacognition and executive control are part of an approach to cognitive development that contrasts with Piaget's—the information-processing approach. As shown in a number of neo-Piagetian theories that have been proposed, it is possible that Piaget's insights about developmental changes in thinking will be retained, but cast in a new form. Like some recent work on sensorimotor intelligence and Gelman's ideas about number concepts, the growing emphasis on metacognition and executive control may mark the beginning of such a shift.

Period of formal operations

Both new thinking skills and a new approach to problems appear with adolescence at about age 13. The new skills involve thinking about *propositions*, such as all people are created equal or p cannot be both q and not q at the same time. With propositional thinking comes a more systematic approach to problem solving, one that deals with a wider range of possibilities.

During the period of formal operations, a systematic approach to problem solving appears.

Skill with formal operations

According to Piaget there are four basic formal operations: deduction, combination, permutation, and correlation (Inhelder & Piaget, 1958). Operations such as deduction (What voting laws are consistent with the proposition that all people are created equal?) are formal rather than concrete because they are not tied to particular evidence and need not even deal with factual truth. (A problem in deduction can start with an impossible, unlikely, or incorrect premise, as in the question "What consequences would follow logically if starting tomorrow every person who ever lived were to come back to life?")

Here is a *combination* problem. Suppose that Marlene, Sylvia, Deborah, and Linda wanted to have a checkers tournament in which each girl played against each other girl once and only once. How many checker games would there be in the tournament?

Suppose you have four dolls of four different colors (red, white, blue, and green). In how many different orders could the four dolls be lined up? This is a problem in *permutation*. You could solve it by manipulating actual objects or symbolic ones. You could use pencil and paper or do it in your head. If you've had the right math course, you might quickly apply a general formula (n!) and see that in this case it becomes $4 \times 3 \times 2 \times 1 = 24$. Piaget argued that children without formal operations cannot work out answers to novel specific questions of this kind through understanding by any method because they lack the prerequisite logical abilities.

The concept of *correlation* (which is needed in understanding later chapters of this book) is needed in reasoning about the relationship between two variables from evidence on their joint occurrence. For example, children might be presented with hypothetical evidence such as the following: (1) All patients with disease X have green germs in their blood. (2) No patients without disease X have green germs in their blood. (3) All patients who have green germs in their blood have disease X. (4) No patients who do not have green germs in their blood have disease X. Then they would be asked if green germs could be the cause of disease X. The ability to categorize the findings in a table such as Table 7-4 and to come up with a plausible conclusion (in this case green germs apparently could cause disease X, though the facts don't prove it) requires formal operational thought.

TABLE 7-4 Summary of the evidence about the relation between the presence of green germs and disease X

| | | Disease X | |
		Absent	Present
Green Germs	Present	No	Yes
	Absent	Yes	No

New approach to problems

During this period we see a new attitude toward problem solving and, with it, a more systematic approach. In the classic work by Barbel Inhelder and Piaget (1958), children were given the problem of figuring out what happens when you try to balance different sized weights on the two arms of a simple balance. The older children used more systematic procedures making observations, such as formulating general hypotheses and testing them, and were much better at tying their findings together in the form of a unified interpretation. Their methods resembled those of scientists, in contrast to the more hit-and-miss or piecemeal efforts of concrete operational children.

The formal thinker's approach can be thought of as more hypothetical because it deals with the possible rather than accepting the problem as given, as the concrete thinker does. With this orientation the problem solver takes a more active role and transforms the task presented to him or her, as illustrated in a study by Edith Neimark (1976). Children from 4th to 12th grade were given words printed on separate cards and told they would have five minutes to memorize them by any means that they wanted. Then the cards would be removed and their memory for the words would be tested. Rearranging the cards and self-testing became more and more common with increasing age. Strategies like alphabetizing the words or classifying them in terms of parts of speech were common at the 12th-grade level but rare at the 4th. The younger children tended to deal with the information supplied to them; the older children transformed it.

New intellectual horizons

Formal thought opens up new intellectual horizons, for the world of the possible is vast indeed. Speculation about other worlds becomes more meaningful, as in science fiction, political reform, and religious questioning. On the personal side, both the present and the future are seen more complexly. The new understanding that other people have thoughts of their own (Chapter 13) fosters endless wondering about "what they think of me" (Elkind, 1967). The creation of astounding life plans becomes common, with elaborate daydreams about all that will happen. Piaget (1964/1967) reported that a French teacher who inquired about the daydreams of his 15-year-old students found that many already had seen their statues in the squares of Paris. In a sense, then, the thinking, dreaming, and wondering of adolescence is a kind of intellectual play, the exploration of a new mode of thought.

Generality of formal thought

This final period of cognitive development is less universal than the earlier ones. Apparently, all normal children develop concrete operational thinking sooner or later, but formal operational thinking may be reached in only some societies (Inhelder & Piaget, 1958). Important fractions of high-school and college students in our society lack formal operations, posing major problems for teachers who present subjects like physics and biology in a formal and systematic manner (Cowan, 1978). Finally, there is question about whether normal adults typically use formal thinking in dealing with everyday problems. For example, Capon and Kuhn (1979) went to a supermarket to see if adult female shoppers used logical reasoning in deciding which of varied sized and priced containers of deodorant were the best buy. Only 32% of them used a logical strategy when the problem was simple. With a more complex ratio of sizes, only 20% approached the task logically. Formal thinking is hardly universal, even among normal adults in our own society.

Basic aspects of formal operational thinking probably emerge without specific schooling, but cultural inventions such as mathematics are crucial in developing systematic thought further. For Piaget (Inhelder & Piaget, 1958) this was an important illustration of the general idea that cognitive growth does not result from maturation alone, but from the interaction of biological potential and appropriate experience. The question of why not everyone attains and uses formal thinking in a society like our own is complex. Like other questions of individual differences, it was ignored by Piaget.

Challenges to Piaget

Piaget's ideas about formal operational thinking have gotten mixed support. Typically, formal operations do not appear until after age 11, as he claimed (Neimark, 1975). Neimark's (1975) longitudinal studies showed a transition to formal thinking that looked stagelike: it happens relatively abruptly with varied aspects of performance changing together. But Ennis (1976, 1978) cites evidence that younger children can deal with certain logical propositions and can deal with simpler logical problems. He questions the idea that children under 11 cannot deal with formal logic in general. Ennis argues that the difference between younger and older is one of degree, not a stagelike contrast.

Training studies by Robert Siegler (1978b) and his associates also raise questions about the contrast between concrete and formal operational thinkers.

Siegler, Liebert, and Liebert (1973) found that 10- and 11-year-olds failed to solve a pendulum problem spontaneously, as Inhelder and Piaget (1958) had found. But with a brief training program the children were able to do it. In another experiment it was found that the crucial factor in 10-year-olds' failure on another problem in scientific reasoning was their disinclination to keep written records of what happened (Siegler & Liebert, 1975). When instructions were used that promoted record keeping, they kept records and solved the problem. Findings like these imply that it is not that the younger children are incapable of formal thinking, as Piaget suggested, but that for varied reasons they don't do it spontaneously.

PIAGET'S POSITION TODAY

In the early 1960s, Piaget was said to have commented, "The Americans are assimilating my work. But they have yet to accommodate to it." Today considerable accommodation has taken place, for Piaget inspired fundamental changes in our thinking about the child, along with the specific ideas and findings more easily assimilated.

Now comes a somewhat speculative summary of where Piaget's ideas stand today within child psychology. It supplements the descriptions of specific challenges presented earlier.

Basic contributions

As reflected in this chapter (and throughout the book), one basic contribution has been the image of the child summed up in Piaget's assimilation-accommodation model. Piaget's picture of the child's mind as active and playing a central role in its own construction has replaced the image of a receptive blank slate that dominated earlier thinking. The scheme concept in its varied forms has captured not only child psychology, but neighboring fields as well (Abelson, 1981).

Piaget's description of how the mind works at different developmental periods is the fullest and most accurate ever presented. Although particular findings and the value of special concepts have been questioned, most of what is summarized here is accepted by most psychologists as an accurate and useful picture. As suggested in my specific "Challenges to Piaget" sections, current work focuses mostly on reinterpreting what Piaget observed, not in denying his observations.

When you think about Piaget's theory in terms of what makes a theory valuable (Chapter 2), it becomes clear that his has been one of the most useful, for it stimulated more research and more progress than any alternative. Our growing sense that we may now see cognitive development more clearly than Piaget did results directly from the fact that we started by looking at what he saw. Thus, although a number of Piaget's own concepts are beginning to seem less central and drop from circulation, almost everyone working on cognitive development now is a neo-Piagetian in one sense or another. We endorse some of the central ideas, but depart from a strictly Piagetian, or orthodox, point of view.

Basic criticisms

Most of the important criticisms of Piaget's position already have been made. His central concepts of tight stages and equilibration have been challenged and may well fade away. Piaget often underestimated young children's abilities in many cases because he used complex and unfamiliar tasks and language in testing them.

Other important criticisms relate to the limitations of his clinical method of observation, more suited to exploratory research than to the later stages of investigation (Chapter 2). His failure to deal with individual differences is another limitation, as was his tendency to explain why development moved ahead in untestable terms, for it appears there is no way of proving either the assimilation-accommodation model or the concept of equilibration false.

FUTURE ISSUES

Jean Piaget's death in 1980 makes us wonder about where future thinking will go; so now my focus shifts to issues and alternatives. This chapter concludes with a look at two central issues that divide current theorists. In the next chapter we turn to memory development and look at it from an information-processing orientation, the approach most popular among those studying the mind from a clearly non-Piagetian viewpoint.

Evenness-unevenness

The question of unity in the mind is a good starting point in considering alternative theories. Is mental development even or uneven when we look at such varied domains as number concepts, social understanding, and concepts of space?

Piaget's emphasis on tight stages and equilibration put him squarely in the unity, or evenness, camp. He thought that a child's level of mental development had to be similar in varied domains and emphasized domain-general ways of thinking, such as sensorimotor or concrete operational thought.

Now the evidence makes it clear that there is less unity across domains than Piaget implied. Performance, in fact, is characteristically uneven (Fischer, 1980). Now consider some responses to this finding.

The evenness camp

John Flavell's position has been particularly influential and interesting. In 1977, he was impressed with the evidence for inconsistency. "It is time to abandon the assumption (so prevalent till now) that everything is glued together; perhaps it is time instead to seriously entertain the hypothesis that nothing is glued together unless proven otherwise" (Flavell, 1977, p. 249).

But in 1981, in his presidential address to the Society for Research in Child Development, Flavell switched sides. He argued that although the facts clearly showed unevenness in performance to be the rule, we should not jump to the conclusion that the underlying competence was not unified. Instead, he proposed that competence may well be similar across domains, but that a variety of problems in studying cognitive skills contributes to a misleading picture of unevenness. An obvious example here is motivation. Children with different levels of interest in math and in drawing might look uneven when tested in the two areas simply because they paid more attention and tried harder when tested on the preferred area. Flavell catalogued a variety of less obvious factors that would operate similarly in exaggerating the degree of unevenness in the mind.

One important group on the evenness side call themselves neo-Piagetian. They accept Piaget's idea of stages but substitute a radically different explanation of them. Juan Pascual-Leone (1973) and Robbie Case (1978, 1980) explain unity in terms of information-processing concepts. They emphasize that younger children are much more limited in how much information they can deal with at one time. If you can think about only two things at once, rather than seven, this limitation will show up in diverse ways in varied domains. So mental space (M-space) and its growth becomes a basic alternative to equilibration in explaining the evenness we observe.

Interestingly, Kurt Fischer (1980) agreed with this notion of general processing limitations that produce similarities across domains, even as he presented a theory focused mostly on unevenness, domain-specific progress.

The unevenness camp

Theorists on the unevenness side include both those who put the main emphasis on environmental factors and those who focus on biological, domain-specific constraints.

In the United States a popular position has been to explain cognitive development primarily as a function of learning opportunities. With this approach it follows that the process of cumulative learning and transfer will move at varied rates in different areas, depending on opportunities to learn (Gagné, 1968). Advocates of this idea have commonly tried to demonstrate that specific training on cognitive skills can foster master development in that area. They have often been successful (Brainerd, 1978).

But unevenness can be explained from a contrasting position. Noam Chomsky (1965) argued that children are specifically prepared to learn language on a biological basis and, accordingly, advance much more rapidly in this domain than in others. Frank Keil (1981) presented a more general version of this idea, arguing that domain-specific constraints are the rule rather than the exception (Chapter 5).

The metaphor: Natural scientist or social dancer?

A second issue has emerged as a central source of difference among theorists: what kind of metaphor of cognitive development is most valuable? All the theorists mentioned so far, like Piaget, focus on the child as an individual who gradually comes to understanding reality better. Typically, the emphasis is on the child's understanding of the physical world, as in object permanence and number conservation. Like Piaget, most of the theorists would be content with an image of the child as a natural scientist, coolly learning about external affairs.

An alternative is to emphasize the child's coming to understand social reality by participating in it. As illustrated in Table 7–5, there are big differences between the two viewpoints. Thus, those who put more emphasis on the social side typically start from a metaphor that emphasizes the interactive and rule-bound nature of the social world. A social-dancer image applies because children are conceived as joining the dance before they understand it and learning the rules gradually through dancing with more experienced partners. In this kind of formulation the real-time aspect of events becomes much more important than for the child who sits alone on the beach playing with shells and discovering properties of numbers.

TABLE 7–5 Contrasts in the processes of developing understanding of the physical and social worlds

	Physical World	*Social World*
Typical degree of emotional involvement in what is to be understood	Low	High
Possibility of taking a detached attitude toward what is to be understood	High	Low
Clarity of lawful relations in the domain	High	Low
Demands for immediate action based on one's understandings	Low	High
Presence of a more sophisticated partner in the observation situation	Sometimes	Usually

Based in part on Block and Block (1980).

Theorists taking this approach have been particularly interested in areas such as communication and language, where cognitive and social matters meet and cross. I'll explain their ideas more fully in Chapter 9.

I highlight these two issues in this section because it seems likely that they will help shape future trends. As research and theory related to these questions move ahead, the outline of future thinking should become much clearer.

SUMMARY

This chapter took a broad view of mental development, focusing on Piaget's ideas and where they have taken us. The approach was to deal mostly with his more generally accepted ideas and to point out both specific and general challenges to his viewpoint.

First his picture of the universal, working principles of the mind (functional invariants) was presented. The concepts of organization, scheme, assimilation, accommodation, and adaptation added up to a picture of an active mind, built to move ahead as long as opportunities to interact with the environment are present. The concepts of invariant sequences, stage, and equilibration were described as both more specific and more controversial.

Next the four major periods of cognitive development were considered. Piaget's picture of sensorimotor development was described in terms of the Uzgiris-Hunt scales. These scales define seven paths of progress, starting from the reflexes present at birth and ending with practical skills that are used spontaneously. The best understood path, object permanence, was described in detail. Sensorimotor play was described as paralleling the development of sensorimotor intelligence. Challenges to Piaget's picture of infant intelligence were discussed, focusing on controversy related to apparent demonstrations of more competence in early months than Piaget thought was there.

In summarizing the symbolic, or preoperational, period, symbolic play was used to illustrate more general trends, such as the distancing of symbols and the rise of more elaborate combinations of symbols. Then a look at cute remarks was used as a springboard to a discussion of the limitations of pre-school thought as seen by Piaget: he saw it as centered, perceptually domi-nated, static, and irreversible. Discussion of this period ended with a description of the growing discontent with Piaget's negative formulation of this period and a look at the newer approach of focusing on what preschoolers can do.

The discussion of the period of concrete operations emphasized the rise of more systematic thinking, as shown in skills in classification and ordering and in thinking operationally about the real world. Play with rules was described as one of many areas in which the new accomplishments could be seen. Challenges to Piaget's view of this period were presented as arising from a growing emphasis on metacognition and executive control processes, sug-gesting that either a shift in emphasis or a more radical one might be underway.

The formal operational period was described as including both new skills in thinking (propositional thinking with the basic formal operations of deduc-tion, combination, permutation, and correlation) and a new approach to prob-lems. The new approach is a more hypothetical one that deals with possibilities, rather than just the real. With this orientation comes a more systematic prob-lem-solving method, similar to that used by scientists. With its emphasis on the possible, formal thought makes speculation about the future, other worlds, and the opinions of others relevant. Formal thought was described as less general than earlier forms, both in the sense that fewer people reach this level and because people don't necessarily use their formal thinking in everyday situations. Challenges to Piaget's ideas here focus on the question of whether a genuine stagelike shift takes place and whether concrete operational thinkers are incapable of thinking in formal terms or just don't do it spontaneously.

The chapter concluded with an overall assessment of Piaget's position and with a focus on two issues that divide current thinkers: the evenness-unevenness question and the question of what kind of central metaphor is most useful.

CHAPTER 8

Memory Development: An Information-Processing Perspective

All learning, thinking, and problem solving draws on memory of past experience. Starting soon after birth, everything the child does reflects past experience and what is remembered of it; so memory development is an important enough topic to deserve a chapter of its own. But the real reason for separating memory from chapters on learning and cognitive development is historical. Work on memory development has been dominated by the information-processing orientation rather than by learning theory or Piagetian thinking. As a result it is easier to understand current ideas about memory development when they are cast in terms of the concepts used in the information-processing tradition. To integrate the related topics of learning, memory, and cognitive development now would be to sacrifice something of the richness that resulted from the varied approaches.

INFORMATION-PROCESSING ORIENTATION

Information-processing models of cognitive development were influenced by the invention of computers. Once we had "thinking machines," it was natural to use them as analogies in trying to understand how people think (Klahr & Wallace, 1976; Simon, 1962).

Another influence was new knowledge about how the nervous system works. At first the brain could be studied only after a person or animal died, but now we can study the living nervous system in action. This research shows how electrical and chemical messages move through the body and relates information processing in the body to everyday action. Information-processing models often draw on this new knowledge. The goal is to have concepts explaining psychological activity that parallel what we know about how our bodies work.

MEMORY

As children get older, their performance on memory tasks improves. This fact is reflected in the old practice of using memory tasks in tests of intellectual development (Dempster, 1981). New research confirms this old finding and enriches it. Now two themes stand out: (1) Memory is not one thing. (2) Memory development does not take place in isolation, but in interaction with other cognitive skills (Kail & Hagen, 1977).

The idea that memory is not unitary rests on a central fact: memory tasks vary in how they link with age. On some tests of memory we find little difference between 3-year-olds and college students, but on others the contrasts are enormous. Today we have a detailed and differentiated picture of how varied memory performances relate to age. They fit together in a coherent model. Before I get to the model, consider two extremes, memory tasks showing the least and the most development change.

Frontiers box 8–1   Infant memory

When do babies start to form lasting memories? The problem of finding a suitable method of investigation is central. Recent work at Rutgers University uses a new method and indicates that the formation of durable memories begins at an early age.

Central to the approach is a simple but powerful means of capturing the attention of babies about 3 months of age. Carolyn Rovee-Collier originally developed it with her young son. She hung a mobile over the baby's crib and looped a ribbon attached to the mobile around one of the baby's ankles. This sets up a "conjugate reinforcement" situation in which the amount of mobile movement (the reinforcement) depends upon the amount of kicking. Numerous studies have shown that most babies kick vigorously in this situation and that the kicking depends on the mobile movement (rather than simple excitement) because kicking does not increase if there is no connection between the amount of kicking and the mobile movement (Rovee-Collier & Gekoski, 1979).

 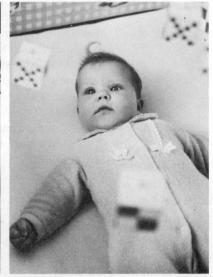

During reinforcement the baby's kicking makes the mobile move.   During reinstatement the baby sees the mobile move but cannot make it move.

In recent research the conjugate reinforcement system has been used to study memory. For example, sometimes a baby is exposed to two contrasting mobiles in turn in a discrimination situation. Kicking makes one move (the S+ mobile) and does not influence the other (the S− mobile). Under such circumstances babies quickly come to learn the difference and kick much more to the S+ mobile. If the babies have a few minutes of experience in the discrimination condition, they can be given an extinction test in which neither mobile moves. This test shows whether they kick more for the mobile formerly associated with reinforcement and thereby show memory of past experience.

With such a testing system the babies show memory for the discrimination if tested immediately but do not show memory over longer periods. Does that mean that they forget after a few minutes or hours? No.

More recent work has involved a special technique borrowed from research on young rats (Rovee-Collier, Sullivan, Enright, Lucas, & Fagan, 1980). A *reactivation,* or reinstatement, procedure is used in which the babies are given a reminder of which mobile is associated with reinforcement. Specifically, the S+ mobile is briefly hung over their crib and moved by the experimenter the day before testing, but without being connected. They see the "old" mobile moving for three minutes but don't get any more experience in moving it by kicking.

With such a reminder, testing the next day reveals striking retention. Babies remember the association between kicking and movement of the S+ mobile. For example, in a recent study by Fagan, Yengo, Rovee-Collier, and Enright (1981) babies 78 to 92 days at the time of original training showed that they remembered the discrimination 21 days after training. Interestingly, the accurate retention performance depended on reactivation by means of the S+ mobile. Experience with the S− mobile, like no reminder experience, was followed by chance performance. A study by Mary Enright (1981) further documented the specific importance of the S+ mobile. She exposed babies to a moving novel mobile (neither S+ nor S−) and found that it too had no impact.

Babies as young as 11 weeks in age can remember for as long as three weeks. With the new evidence of long-term memory, Rovee-Collier (1981) was moved to title a recent talk "Babies and Elephants: Do They Ever Forget?"

Contrasting memory tasks

Recognition memory is the simple ability to recognize what you have encountered before and what you haven't. Tests of recognition memory show perhaps the least developmental progress, which makes it interesting as a baseline and as a point of contrast in looking at what does change. When you realize you have met someone before, you are showing recognition memory, whether or not you remember more, such as the person's name and where you met.

From the day of birth the child sees a steady parade of scenes and people. A few weeks after birth the ability to recognize them as familiar over relatively long periods of time (days) emerges (Cohen & Gelber, 1975). Once the child is about 3 or 4 years old, we can study recognition memory through techniques similar to those we use with older children and adults. Experiments with children at this point demonstrate that their recognition memory is essentially equal to that of older children and adults. For example, Brown and Scott (1971) cut pictures from children's books and showed them to 3- to 5-year-olds one at a time. Some of the pictures were shown only once, others were repeated. On each of 100 trials the children were asked to say yes if they had been shown the picture before and no if they had not. Later the children were tested for long-term retention. Recognition memory was excellent. On the immediate retention tests they averaged 98% correct. For pictures they had seen twice during the first session their accuracy was over 90% a week later. The remarkable accuracy of their recognition memory was similar to that of college students run in similar experiments.

In contrast to studies showing similarities between age groups, Neimark's memory tasks (Chapter 7) are typical of those that show large age differences when younger children and adults are compared. Children were given a set of pictures or words and told that they would be tested for retention after a five-minute study period. The age groups varied both in their strategies for studying the material and in their actual retention performance. The study illustrates a clear trend: when an active memorization strategy can help retention, older children do better than younger children, with a general trend of improvement from the preschool period to adolescence.

Taken together, these tasks that show small and large age differences give us a starting point in formulating memory and memory development. *Multistore models of memory* help us in putting it all together.

Memory stores

The most popular models of memory today assume that information is placed in at least three "stores": a sensory store, a short-term store, and a long-term store. Processes such as recognizing and remembering are thought of in terms of these storage places and the ways information is gotten in and out of them. First I'll describe the varied parts of the memory system and summarize developmental findings related to them. Then I'll present overall implications.

Sensory store

When information from the outside world enters the child's eyes or ears, it apparently enters a *sensory store,* or register, that we don't notice in everyday life. The sensory information persists for a fraction of a second after the stimulus is gone. In the laboratory, stimuli are presented momentarily in quiet or dark rooms so that sensory storage can be studied in detail (Hoving, Spencer, Robb, & Schultz, 1978).

Sensory memory gives us a brief impression that fades without more lasting impact unless further processing takes place. The information in the sensory store must be encoded through some process of selective attention or it is lost. If it gets attention, the information is coded and transferred to a second store, the short-term store, where it can be held a little longer.

Developmental studies suggest that sensory memory changes little, if at all, with age (Hoving et al., 1978); so we must look to other aspects of memory for developmental change.

Short-term store

The *short-term store* and its properties are familiar. If I tell you the name of three kinds of memory store, you know you can easily remember them for a few seconds but may have forgotten them after a week. This phenomenon illustrates the contrast between the temporary nature of short-term memory and the more lasting quality of *long-term memory*. If I ask you to think of the first four letters of the alphabet, you quickly become aware of *A, B, C,* and *D.* You realize that there is a difference between having them "in mind" so that you can "work with them" (short-term storage) and knowing them in a more lasting sense (long-term storage).

If I say a list of grocery items once and ask you to remember them all, you know that the task is easy with only 3 items and extremely difficult with 20. In technical terms you are aware of a basic quality of short-term memory: it has limited capacity. The short-term store, then, is a working memory that can hold a limited amount of information for a brief period (a few seconds). When we pay attention to something in the sensory store, information from the outside enters short-term memory. Sometimes the information is lost at this point, as when we forget a name seconds after hearing it for the first time. But sometimes the information moves on to more lasting storage in long-term memory.

Short-term memory apparently increases with age, particularly during the preschool years. A 2-year-old can repeat about two words accurately after we say them. A 5-year-old can manage more, about four words. This increase may well reflect progress in *using* memory capacity rather than an actual change in capacity (Case, 1978), but the improvement is important. Only material that can be kept in mind in short-term memory can be worked on mentally. The difference between the two or three items that a young child can retain and work on and the "7 ± 2" items that an older child or adult can hold in working memory (Miller, 1956) probably contributes to a variety of thinking differences. If you tell a child that Margie is taller than Susan and Susan is taller than Fran and then ask who is the shortest of the three, the solution depends on keeping all the information in mind while reasoning about it. A child with limitations in short-term storage may fail this and many other "logical" problems simply because of capacity limitations. Similarly, 2-year-olds might speak in short sentences in part because of problems in keeping their ideas and the appropriate grammatical rules in mind all at once.

Long-term store

Some of the information that reaches the sensory and short-term stores is represented more permanently. Long-term store is the name for the part of memory that includes relatively permanent memories. Information there lasts for years.

The amount of material in long-term storage apparently grows steadily with age, throughout childhood and after. The fact that the 2-year-old knows about 250 words and the typical adult knows tens of thousands illustrates the enormous growth in what is remembered permanently.

There are also shifts in how the stored material is organized. A library with 2 million books would be less useful than one with a few thousand if the books were arranged in haphazard fashion. Knowledge is useful only when it can be retrieved and used. Organization is essential in order to be able to search efficiently and find what you want. Children's memories become organized differently and more systematically as they grow older (Lange, 1978; Moely, 1977). Younger children apparently encode and organize material in terms of more superficial and perceptual qualities, such as the way words sound and what objects are together in a particular situation. Older children, in contrast, work more in terms of abstract aspects of the stimuli, such as word meanings, categories such as furniture, and logical distinctions such as living and nonliving (Moely, 1977).

Memory processes

Now we can turn to the processes that influence how information moves from one store to another. First we will consider attention and memory strategies. Then I'll discuss metamemory and executive control processes.

Attention

Attention plays a critical role in determining what enters the short-term store (Kail & Siegel, 1977). Only some of the information that reaches the sensory store gets attention and moves on. The form that attention takes determines how the sensory information is encoded. The same visual image of a person might be encoded as big, Martha, lady with a red dress, or running, depending on what is noticed. It might be coded in words like *red* or in images. Because it is the coded information that moves on through the memory system, not the original picturelike image, the original selective attention limits and colors all that follows.

Developmental changes in attention (Chapter 6) turn up again when we look at developmental changes in memory. The older child's greater efficiency in paying attention to what is important makes a difference both in storing what is important and in retrieving it later. A more systematic inspection of the objects in a room results in storage of the information in a more coherent form. For example, information about where in the room each object was is more likely to be held in memory if the child paid attention to where each object was when looking at it. Later, when trying to remember what was present, a systematic mental search of the whole room would benefit recall.

Memory strategies

Memory strategies are voluntary, purposeful moves that a person decides to make in order to do better on a memory task (Flavell, 1977). They can be used both in storing the to-be-remembered material and in finding, or retrieving, it later. Changes in memory strategies during the elementary-school years are dramatic. They account for much of the improvement in memory performance that takes place (Flavell, 1977; Kail & Hagen, 1977; Ornstein, 1978).

The findings on rehearsal illustrate more general trends. If you present children of varied ages with a set of pictures, point at some, and ask them to try to remember which ones you pointed at, children 5 years and under rarely say the names of the objects over and over to themselves during the study period while waiting to be tested. By age 10, most do (Flavell, Beach, & Chinsky, 1966). There is a general trend for children to become more active in using strategies to try to remember during the elementary-school years. Other studies have shown a tendency for simple, rote strategies to give way to more complicated ones. Ornstein, Naus, and their collaborators have given children lists of words to be learned, presenting one word at a time and asking the children to rehearse out loud between words (Ornstein & Naus, 1978). When eighth-graders worked on lists of unrelated words such as *yard, cat, man,* and *desk,* a typical rehearsal pattern after hearing *desk* would be to rehearse all the words on the list, *yard, cat, man,* and *desk.* In contrast, a typical third-grade reaction would be to rehearse only the word just presented, *desk, desk, desk, desk.*

Studies of rehearsal show a developmental progression that probably holds for other memory strategies (Flavell, 1977). First, the child is unable to use a strategy such as simple rehearsal even when instructed in it. Next, the child uses the strategy if someone suggests it but does not use it spontaneously. Finally, the child spontaneously produces the strategy. This important sequence perhaps shows the contribution of repeated practice and overlearning in making a strategy useful.

Organization and *elaboration* are two other memory strategies used in storing information. I described organization in "Contrasting Memory Tasks" when summarizing how older children reacted to Neimark's task of memorizing 20 cards containing words. A good example of elaboration is when you are given two facts to be remembered together and make up a picture or story to tie them together, as in picturing Jean Piaget sitting in front of a computer as a way of linking two approaches to cognitive development. The findings on organization and elaboration generally fit those on rehearsal: big progress during the elementary-school years with more spontaneous and active approaches becoming more and more evident.

Strategies for retrieving information from memory develop similarly. Retrieval strategies, such as actively searching for information you can't remember immediately, become more common during the elementary-school years. There also is a progression toward a spontaneous use of strategies that originally cannot be used at all (Kobasigawa, 1977).

The research on memory strategies pinpoints the elementary-school years as the time of great advance. But the particular age at which a strategy appears or is produced spontaneously depends on the details: What task was presented? Exactly how was it presented (Flavell, 1977; Kobasigawa, 1977)? It thus seems fruitless either to look for "the" age at which a general advance occurs or to expect a tight stagelike progression.

There have been two important reactions to the evidence on strategy development. One is to think of memory as applied cognition, to see memory not as something separate from other parts of cognitive development, but as an area in which children use whatever cognitive resources they have (Flavell, 1977). Another reaction is to look at the developments that make spontaneous and efficient strategy use possible. Here attention turns to metamemory and executive control processes.

Metamemory

Metamemory means knowledge about memory. I drew on your meta-memory in talking about the short-term store by picking familiar examples that show the characteristics of short-term memory that we all know and use. The developmental question is how and when you learned so much about your memory and how it works. The question is important because your ability to use memory strategies efficiently depends on your understanding of how

Metamemory, or knowledge about memory, enables children to better use their memory because they understand how it works.

your memory works and of the task before you. For example, if you realize that rehearsal and organization are important in getting material into long-term storage, you might take notes on this chapter, go over them, and then put them together in a novel organization that makes sense to you. What you know about your own memory opens up possibilities for better memory performance. Of course, it doesn't guarantee you will use them.

Children's sophistication about memory increases steadily (Flavell & Wellman, 1977). A study by Kreutzer, Leonard, and Flavell (1975) illustrates the trend. They asked children what they would do or what would happen in hypothetical memory situations. "If you wanted to phone your friend and someone told you the phone number, would it make any difference if you called right away or if you got a drink of water first?" Kindergartners answered yes or no about equally. Older children knew they should phone immediately. Similar findings emerge when children are asked to predict their own performance on memory problems. Younger children often seem amazingly unrealistic, even after they have had a chance to see how well they do (Yussen & Levy, 1975).

Executive control processes

Executive control processes are master thinking methods that plan and direct action by influencing other processes (Chapter 5). They become more and more important during middle and later childhood.

The great gains in memory performance during the elementary-school years seem to stem from new abilities in selecting strategies that efficiently meet the problem facing the child. A consistent finding is that younger children often can use strategies such as rehearsal but don't do so spontaneously (Flavell, 1977). This implies that progress during the second half of childhood is largely growth in skills in using the mind, in figuring out how to match your own capacities to the particulars of the problem.

The gains in memory performance probably rest in part on gains in metamemory and in greater sensitivity to task characteristics, such as the amount to be remembered (Flavell, 1977). The trend for relevant knowledge and better performance to rise together supports this idea, but the connection is more assumed than demonstrated.

A more direct attack on the problem of how executive processes contribute has come from what has been called the instructional approach (Belmont & Butterfield, 1977). Researchers try to show that executive processes are responsible for performance differences between groups by training the groups assumed to lack them. If contrasts between normal adults and children (or retarded people) can be eliminated by teaching the "have-not" group to do what the "have" group does, a direct link between process contrasts and performance differences is documented.

In a growing list of studies, training in executive control processes has eliminated the differences between younger and older, or retarded and non-retarded, subjects (Belmont & Butterfield, 1977). We need more evidence, but this direct approach is an exciting one.

Applications box 8–2 Memory training

New insights about memory development give us fresh ideas about how we might help children improve their memory skills. Perhaps the performance of slow learners could be improved if they were taught the memory skills that develop naturally in normal older people.

Research on this issue has moved ahead rapidly, and excitement about practical possibilities is growing. We can look first at what has become clear and then turn to current frontiers. This review is based on an important summary by Ann L. Brown and Joseph C. Campione (1978), whose work at the University of Illinois has attracted wide interest.

Early efforts to apply recent findings on memory development focused on the teaching of strategies. Training was considered successful when three criteria were met: (1) Performance must *improve,* both becoming more accurate and showing that the strategies taught were actually used. (2) The improvement must be *durable,* lasting well after training was ended. (3) The progress must *generalize* beyond the particular task on which there was training to similar ones as well.

Direct training on a strategy, such as rehearsing or forming a mental picture of a word to be remembered, can easily be made successful in terms of the first two criteria, as long as the training is appropriate and thorough. Generalization is the biggest problem. In many studies younger or mentally retarded people have been taught to do as well as older or brighter controls on a particular memory task. But when generalization is tested by presenting similar but not identical tasks, the trained subjects often do not use what they might have learned and thus fail to show benefits from training.

In some cases limited generalization is not a serious, practical problem. For example, when a retarded person has to remember something in order to perform a particular industrial task, the concern is entirely with improvement and durability of improvement. Generalization is not needed. Thus, training in strategies has in some cases made a valuable contribution, making it possible for retarded people to carry out jobs previously regarded as impossible for them.

However, the broader goal of teaching children to use their minds in general is close to our concept of education (as distinguished from narrow training). The Illinois group now has taken up the challenge of producing generalized improvement.

Basic to their approach is the notion that a broad set of metacognitive skills in self-interrogation is useful on virtually any intellectual task. They try to teach them in the form of a stop-check-and-study routine. The children are taught to ask themselves a series of questions before proceeding with an intellectual problem:

1. Stop and think!

2. Do I know what to do (understand the instructions)?
3. Is there anything more I need to know before I can begin?
4. Is there anything I already know that will help me (is this problem in any way like one I have done before)?

Current efforts are centered on teaching educable retarded children to learn and use these self-interrogation techniques while performing meaningful activities, such as assembling toys or following cooking recipes. Soon we will know whether this promising approach bears fruit.

SUMMARY

The current picture of memory can be summarized in the spirit of the information-processing approach by a series of block diagrams. Figure 8–1(a) illustrates what many now call the basic hardware of the memory system, the parts of the system that are present and working in early infancy. A common hypothesis is that these components are closely linked to the construction of the nervous system and that any developmental changes in their workings are minor and depend largely on physical maturation (Flavell, 1977). In Figure 8–1(b), what often is called the software of the memory system is added, the parts that change more developmentally and are assumed to be much more closely linked to individual experience and learning. In Figure 8–1(c) the memory system is linked to an action system so that you can see how the elaborate collection of cognitive processes is assumed to link to performance, the behaviors we directly observe.

A more detailed summary of how memory develops in information-processing terms can be found in Table 8–1, in which current knowledge of individual components is presented.

Another way of summarizing how we look at memory and memory development is in terms of the concept *constructive* (Flavell, 1977; Paris & Lindauer, 1977). Everyday language makes the process of storing and retrieving information from memory similar to that of making and replaying a tape recording. But this commonsense impression contradicts most of what I've said here. Only in the sensory store do we find anything resembling the making and using of a recording or film. From there on processes of coding, elaborating, and organizing enter in. Storing material is a constructive process, more like writing a story about what was experienced than putting away a recording of it. Recalling information is *reconstruction* more than replay.

A final summary of memory development gets us back to the theme that it does not take place in isolation. Any modern picture of memory development must be an account of cognitive development more generally. Such key concepts as attention, strategy, and executive control processes refer as much to the mind in general as to memory. These concepts take us to the heart of what grows, as reflected in the notion of memory as applied cognition; so we can look at memory development in terms of cognitive development generally.

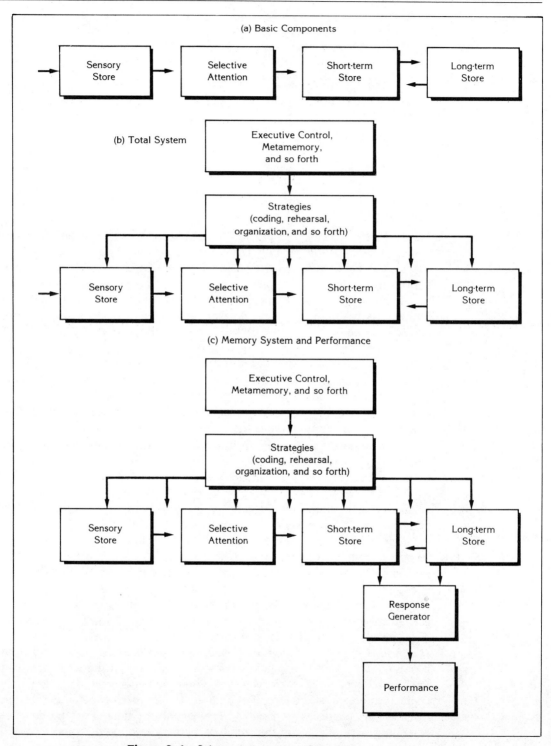

Figure 8–1   Schematic summary of the memory system

TABLE 8–1 Development of the memory system

Component	When Does Developmental Change Seem Most Dramatic?	What Kinds of Changes Are Evident?
Sensory Store	Early infancy	Little if any change after the first few months
Short-term Store	Early childhood	Effective capacity increases
Long-term Store	At all times	Contents grow Organization increases and changes
Attention	Infancy and early childhood	Attention becomes more optimal (Chapter 6)
Strategies for Storage and Retrieval	Middle and later childhood	Use starts Become more active, spontaneous, and organized
Metamemory	Middle and later childhood	Knowledge of self and sensitivity to tasks grows
Executive Control Processes	Middle and later childhood	More efficient selection, construction, and use of strategies that fit the situation and the child's goals

Based primarily on Flavell, 1977; Kail and Hagen, 1977; Ornstein, 1978; Siegler, 1978a.

CHAPTER 9

Language Development

The more we learn about language development, the more amazing we find it. Some basic facts about the task, the child who faces it, and the outcome of their interaction help show you why. The task of mastering a first language is enormous and complex. To communicate with other people children must learn the sounds, meanings, and grammatical rules of a language that is foreign to them, but they lack knowledge of a native language to help them. They have to figure out the language at the same time as they make sense out of the real world that is talked about. The challenge for the child makes the job you or I would face in learning Chinese seem simple.

Toddlers usually take up the challenge of serious language learning at about age 18 months. Although we find such tots charming, we often use terms like *short attention span, illogical, egocentric,* and *uncooperative* in describing them—hardly the qualities that seem likely to help in dealing with the job of learning a language.

Considering the task and the little learner together, you might well expect to find that language learning moves slowly and with great difficulty, but it doesn't. Remarkably, the child of 18 months completes the important aspects of language development within about two or three years.

SOLVING THE MYSTERY: AN INTERACTIONIST SOLUTION

Our efforts to unravel the mystery of how children learn language have produced a wealth of facts and some hot arguments about how to interpret them. Before getting to the details, I'll summarize what now is emerging as our general answer to the question of why language development goes so well. The modern perspective requires an *interactionist* answer, one that emphasizes the child, the social environment in which language is learned, and how the two come together.

The child: Preparedness

The child comes to language with special biological equipment (Lenneberg, 1967). The human brain, our mechanisms for hearing, and our apparatus for speaking all seem to have evolved in ways that preadapt the child for language learning in the same sense that baby birds are born prepared to learn to fly. There are disputes about how far this preadaptation takes the child and about what form it takes, but there clearly are biological constraints that make language learning far easier than it might be.

As psychologists, we can focus on the child's biases, or preparedness, in terms of how the child acts in relation to the language-learning task. When we do this, we see both general and specific operating characteristics that seem universal in children and that seem to foster language development.

Perhaps the most important general characteristic the child brings to language development is a desire to communicate (Glucksberg, Krauss, & Higgins, 1975). Children seem to want to communicate from early in infancy. They communicate through gestures and facial expressions before real language begins. Deaf children in institutions where sign language is forbidden in an effort to foster lip-reading and speech nevertheless use gestures to communicate in secret among themselves (Lenneberg, 1967). The desire to communicate appears to be a universal and powerful motive, one that helps make language learning worthwhile from the child's point of view.

The details of language development often reveal a close fit between universal features of human languages and the typical operating characteristics of children learning their first language. Three examples illustrate the point.

Sounds

All languages are made up of *phonemes*, elemental sounds such as the /m/ sound in ma, that are put together in varied combinations to form meaningful utterances. Basic to hearing and understanding any language is the ability to recognize and attend to these key sounds. Research on adults has shown that we hear these speech sounds in a special way (categorically) that is different from the way we hear most nonspeech sounds, such as bird songs or thunder (continuously). Now we know that young babies, too, hear speech sounds categorically months before they say their first word. Babies start off by hearing speech in a way that maximizes their opportunity to decode the sounds of the language around them.

Words

In all languages words are most commonly labels for categories, such as women or game, rather than names for unique beings or events, such as Lois Bloom or Superbowl XV. Young language learners around the world tend to treat words as if they were labels for categories, rather than assuming that the words apply only to a particular object or event. Hippolyte Taine (1877, p. 255), an early student of language development, thought this "aptitude for seizing analogies" was basic to language development. He described his young daughter's behavior:

> She was in the habit of seeing a little black dog belonging to the house which often barks, and it was to it that she first learnt to apply the word *oua-oua*. Very quickly and with very little help she applied it to dogs of all shapes and kinds that she saw in the streets and then, what is still more remarkable, to the bronze dogs near the staircase. Better still, the day before yesterday when she saw a goat a month old that bleated she said *oua-oua*.

Grammar

All languages have grammatical rules that must be mastered, such as our rules for forming the past tense: I talk, I talked; I pick, I picked. Children spontaneously engage in rule learning when they master grammar, as is shown dramatically when they make errors that demonstrate they even apply rules where the rules result in incorrect speech: I eated and I runned instead of I ate and I ran.

We find a fit between the child and language similar to that between a key and a lock (see Figure 9–1). Perhaps the child's characteristics and those

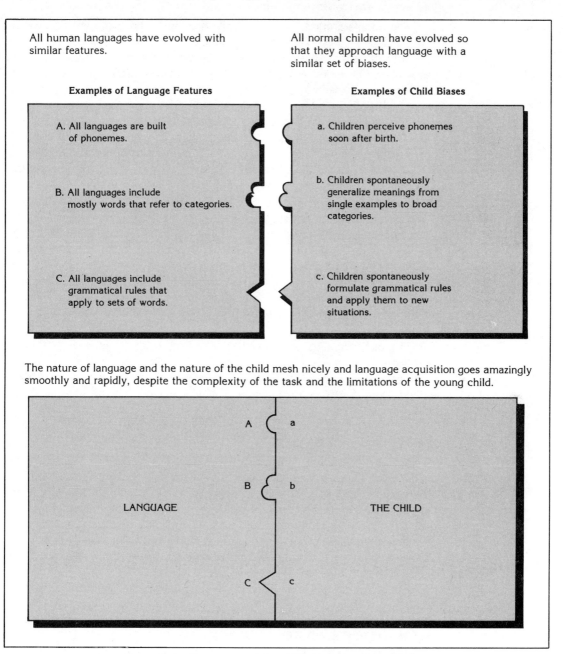

Figure 9–1   Language and the child: Made for each other?

of language evolved together. Language characteristics that were easy for children to master were more likely to survive. Children were thus better "prepared" to master language. Through coevolution, then, both language and the language learner may have become more complicated in compatible ways.

The social environment: Support

The people around the young child help make language learning easier than it might be. For example, adults talk to infants long before there is any reason to think the babies understand their words (Bretherton & Bates, 1979; Bullowa, 1979). Judith Adams (Rheingold & Adams, 1980) sat in a newborn nursery and recorded what the hospital staff said. She found that, starting right after the babies were born, most of the staff who came near them talked to them. Typically, the staff spoke to them often and in a meaningful and caring way. Comments like "Would you like me to hold you?", "I gave you 30cc, now I'm just quitting," and "Your mama's a little under the weather" were common. They illustrated a general tendency to engage the babies in conversation and to treat them as if they were listening and understanding.

Several studies of mothers interacting with young babies show that this tendency continues at home. More and more investigators argue that adults foster language development by treating babies as if they understood language and were actively trying to communicate (Kaye, 1979; Schaffer, 1979; Snow, DeBlauw, & Van Roosmalen, 1979). It appears that babies "learn how to mean" (Halliday, 1975). At first they communicate without meaning to, as in their first cries. But with help they soon reach a point where they can communicate intentionally (Bretherton & Bates, 1979).

A new picture of how the environment supports language development is emerging. It is more specific than past views and points in somewhat different directions. I'll sum it up later, but for now a central idea is that we should emphasize *dialogue,* or *conversation,* between language learners and those around them if we are to understand why language learning progresses so smoothly.

The interaction: Dialogue

There are two reasons for the new emphasis on dialogue. One is that children don't simply learn language; they learn how to converse with it. The difference is a big one, as many students of high school French learn when they walk into a French restaurant. Holding a conversation requires that you deal with the language in real time, with problems of time pressure and divided attention that don't occur while doing a homework assignment at leisure. Conversation requires mastery of social niceties, as in selecting the appropriate words for your audience.

The second reason for stressing dialogue is that dialogue develops ahead of language (Ziajka, 1981). Children learn to converse before they learn to talk, even though it might be more logical (and schoollike) if they did it the other way around (Bullowa, 1979).

How can this be? The answer, of course, is that dialogue does *not* have to involve spoken language. Facial expressions, hand gestures, and postures all serve to convey meaning. Children converse in these nonverbal ways months before they talk (Bretherton & Bates, 1979; Collis, 1979). Seemingly, children master the basic rules of a conversation before they have a spoken language with which to talk.

We can think of a conversation, or dialogue, as taking place as long as we have two people who follow some basic rules:

1. *Take turns.* Only one should perform at once (Kaye, 1979).
2. *Pay attention.* Focus on the other's performance.
3. *Assume meaning.* Act as if the other is trying to communicate meaning.
4. *Try to get meaning across.* Do whatever you can that is likely to work.

These rules result in a patterned interaction, or dialogue, that involves the two people interacting according to shared rules to share feelings and pursue shared goals.

PRAGMATICS: MASTERY OF COMMUNICATION SKILLS

The modern emphasis on communication makes it useful to begin our detailed examination of language development with a look at *pragmatics,* "the study of the use of language in context, by real speakers and hearers in real situations" (Bates, 1974, p. 277).

A central finding from such study is that the child starts a lifelong series of conversations in the days immediately after birth (Condon, 1979; Kaye, 1979). In the early days communication includes such transactions as babies molding their posture to the body of the adult who holds them and the adult responding to this molding with looking and cuddling (Brazelton, 1979). It also involves a dialogue in which nursing babies punctuate bursts of sucking with pauses during which mothers jiggle them (Kaye, 1979). As you can imagine, early communication is asymmetrical, with mothers showing more flexibility in accommodating their behavior to the babies. As babies develop new skills, the conversation becomes both more elaborate and more balanced.

This picture suggests a metaphor of language development as an ongoing dance in which the child gradually becomes more skilled, more accommodating, and capable of interacting with a wider and wider circle of partners (Halliday, 1979; Mead, 1934). A theoretical image of a solitary child figuring out language in a detached way like a scientist becomes less satisfactory (Chapter 7).

Early communication

Elizabeth Bates and her colleagues (Bates, 1979; Bretherton & Bates, 1979) emphasize the importance of gestural communication. They find that intentional communication through gestures appears at about 9 months, as when babies look at adults while opening and closing their hand when in front of an unreachable object instead of desperately straining for it. Their data suggest that the sophistication of a child's gestural communication is a good measure of early language development.

Studies of pointing show that gestures quickly become part of a flexible, two-way communication system. Before their first birthdays children point out airplanes, pictures, and other interesting objects (Rheingold, Hay, & West, 1976). By age 1 year they respond appropriately when others point, looking at what is pointed at rather than at the hand or face of the person doing the pointing (Lempers, Flavell, & Flavell, 1977).

By age 2 years there is surprising skill and success when toddlers communicate with familiar people in everyday situations (Wellman & Lempers, 1977). Toddlers usually are successful in getting the attention of others, partly because they try mostly when people are not busy. They also adapt their messages to the listener's demands and respond to feedback.

Marilyn Shatz and Rochel Gelman (1973) conducted an experiment that demonstrates the skill of 4-year-olds. They compared how the children talked about the same situation to adults and to younger children. Here are transcripts that illustrate the same 4-year-old explaining the same dump truck station first to an adult and then to a younger child (Shatz & Gelman, 1973, p. 13):

> You're supposed to put one of these persons in, see? Then one goes with the other little girl. And then the little boy. He's the little boy and he drives. And then they back up. And then the little girl has marbles. . . . And then the little girl falls out and then it goes backwards.
>
> Watch, Perry. Watch this. He's backing in here. Now he drives up. Look, Perry. Look here, Perry. Those are marbles, Perry. Put the men in here. Now I'll do it.

These recent studies contradict Piaget's claim that young children can neither understand another's viewpoint nor adapt to it. Clearly Piaget exaggerated the egocentrism of children under 6 (Chapter 7).

Part of the disagreement between Piaget and more recent researchers results from the use of contrasting ways to study communication. Apparently it is much easier for children to communicate about present objects than absent ones and to talk to people they can see rather than those who are not present (as on the telephone). When we observe children in naturalistic situations and when we set lower standards, we see communication skill even in babies and toddlers. When we use artificial situations and set higher standards, 5-year-olds show limited ability.

Later communication

Piaget (1926/1955) started the tradition of posing difficult communication tasks to children. For example, he told children a story and then asked them to retell it to other children who had been waiting outside. He explained how a water faucet worked and then asked the child to explain it to someone else. Studies of referential communication of this kind go beyond the question of whether the child can communicate. They push the limits of children's skill and reveal the kinds of problems often encountered when you ask a 5-year-old to explain what happened in last night's television program.

This kind of research shows that kindergartners do poorly at referential communication and that skill increases with age (Glucksberg et al., 1975). Older children are better at talking about the crucial features of what they see in a way that helps the listener who can't see it. Similarly, older children are better at taking the listener's situation into account, as in not saying "this one" when talking to someone who cannot see the object at which they point. Another intriguing difference is in how children respond to feedback. When 5-year-olds give an unclear message and are asked "tell me more," they are likely to repeat the original statement or say nothing. An older child, like an adult, is more likely to elaborate.

Registers

Varied language styles, or *registers*, are called for in different social situations. For example, we tend to pronounce the *ing* ending differently in formal and informal settings. In a relaxed atmosphere we more often say "workin'" and "doin'." In formal settings we say "working" and "doing." Children from varied social backgrounds learn these distinctions, but poor children get less experience with the formal register. They are thus at a disadvantage in school, where formal styles are more common (Labov, 1970). Linguists believe that poor children's thinking and language skills have been underestimated in many studies because they have been observed in settings where unfamiliar, formal registers predominate (Houston, 1970).

Language development context

As we turn from communication to language, a crucial fact must be highlighted: language is learned in the context of communication. Language can be learned through isolated language lessons, as second languages are in many schools, but that is not the way normal children learn a first language. They learn their language while communicating, as part of the process of exchanging messages and sharing activities rather than as something separate. This fact probably helps explain why first-language learning goes so well.

BASIC CHARACTERISTICS OF LANGUAGE

Three fundamental characteristics of language provide perspective on language development: creativity, system, and comprehension and production.

Creativity

Most sentences children utter and hear are unique. Aside from such remarks as "Hello" and "I'm sorry," children mostly compose sentences that they never said before. Similarly, most sentences that they hear are novel creations; so dealing with sentences is more like jazz improvisation than playing in a marching band. There are no fixed cues or unchanging responses to be memorized. Instead, you have to use what you know in new ways.

The endless variety in everyday sentences puts a special light on what is learned (Chomsky, 1967). Successful performance rests on symbolic learning involving concepts and rules, not on sensorimotor learning, as when a dog learns to respond to "Sit down" (Chapter 5).

System

Every natural language is a complex system made up of related subsystems. There are thousands of separate parts, but organization makes it possible for the parts to work smoothly.

If a language were not a system, language acquisition would go differently. If the thousands of words children hear could be learned only as a collection of disconnected items, children probably would master only a few dozen, rather than thousands. If there were no regular system for putting words together in sentences, we all would talk differently. Most likely our sentences would more closely resemble the communication of other animals, with only one or two elements in an utterance. System, then, is a key.

Every football game is a unique string of basic plays. Once we understand the rules that govern the plays, we can make sense out of any game. The systematic nature of language offers a child the same possibility. Mastering language depends on a genius for finding system in the jumble of sounds and sentences.

Production and comprehension

Language is a system for achieving something: communication. When children learn to master language, they learn how to play both sides of the communication game: *speaker* and *listener*. We pay more attention to the progress they make in talking. The changes are obvious, but advances in understanding language are just as basic.

Comprehension of language can be seen in nonverbal responses that children make, as in this "touch my nose" picture.

Language acquisition can go on even when nothing is being said. Babies might do important language learning before they produce their first word. Actually, linguists think that comprehension usually comes before production. For example, the typical child can distinguish between "fis" and "fish" when you say it when he or she still says "fis" for "fish." Focus on listening skills, as well as on talking, when thinking about language.

SIX ASPECTS OF PROGRESS

All languages are made up of three basic subsystems: *phonology,* a system of sounds; *syntax,* a system of rules for combining sounds and words; and *semantics,* a system of meanings that relate language to the rest of the world.

Children must master each subsystem both as speakers and as listeners. For example, they must use the word *dog* correctly in their own sentences and also understand what it means when others say it. As shown in Figure 9–2, we can think of language development as involving six main areas. Each of the three subsystems must be mastered in two different ways.

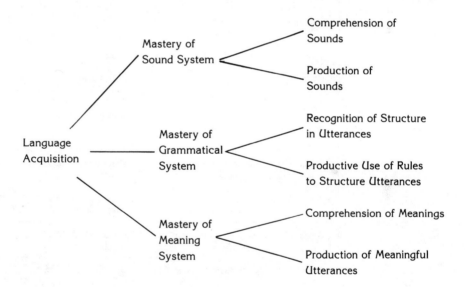

Figure 9–2   The major facets of language acquisition

This six-part picture of language development helps in thinking about both general trends and individuals. Helen isn't poor at "language" just because her pronunciation is unclear. Her comprehension of meanings and use of grammatical rules might be excellent.

Different developmental trends are evident for the subsystems of language. Mastery of sounds starts early and is completed during childhood. The learning of meanings for words and sentences probably starts later. In most cases knowledge of language meanings continues to grow through adulthood.

For example, your college education involves an increase in your vocabulary with little or no improvement in your pronunciation of your native language. Acquisition of syntax, or grammar, follows a still different progression. Mastery of grammar apparently is accomplished mostly between age 18 months and 5 years, though improvements continue through adolescence. A summary of landmarks in language development, as shown in Table 9–1, illustrates the contrasting schedules of progress.

TABLE 9–1 Landmarks in language development

Age	Sound	Meaning	Grammar
birth	cries		
2 months	vowellike coos hears phoneme features		
6 months	syllablelike babbling		
1 year	repeated syllables (da-da)	first word understands some words	
2 years	utterances intelligible to family	produces about 250 words	first two-word sentences
3 years	most utterances intelligible to strangers	produces about 1000 words understands most of what is said	adultlike short sentences
6 years	adultlike with minor exceptions	produces about 2500 words	adultlike in most respects

Based primarily on Bayley, 1969; Menyuk, 1971; Smith, 1926.

Mastery of the sound (phonological) system

Mastery of the sound system includes learning the sound elements and such features as intonation, pauses, and stresses. We know mostly about the mastery of the elements, or segments, of sound.

Phonemes

Each language uses a small set of basic sounds in varied combinations. The thousands of words the child hears and says are all combinations of the same basic sound elements, or *phonemes*. The English language includes 41 phonemes: 26 consonant sounds (such as the /m/ sound in ma and the /p/ sound in pa) and 15 vowel sounds (such as the /a/ sound in ma and the /u/ sound in tool).

Linguists think of the sounds of a language as *categories.* Many different physical examples are treated as if they were the same (as when speakers of different ages, sex, and hometowns say oh). The categories are defined by *distinctive features.*

The child's task in mastering the sound system is to learn to pay attention to some differences while ignoring others. In English the child must learn that the *voiced/voiceless* contrast, or distinctive feature, is crucial. It distinguishes the first sounds in pin and bin, in tin and din, and in kin and gin. The similarity of the first sounds in these pairs reflects the fact that they differ in respect to only one distinctive feature, the voiced/voiceless one. Highly dissimilar phonemes, such as the /p/ and the /a/ in pa, differ in terms of many features.

Distinctive features relate both to the sounds of language the child hears and to the physical processes that produce the sounds. It's the same parallel as when we relate the patterns in the noises made by a piano to the patterns of keys that are pressed. In language sounds the most basic distinction is between consonants and vowels. The consonant/vowel distinction the child hears rests on whether the stream of breath through the speaker's mouth is interrupted (consonants) or not (vowels). Among the vowels the differences relate largely to where the tongue arches up as they are produced (front, as with the /i/ in sit; middle, as with the /a/ in ask; or back, as with the /u/ in full). Consonants vary in respect to whether the vocal cords vibrate (voiced/voiceless) and how the tongue and lips are held when moved. Basic contrasts in muscle movements underlie the features in language sounds.

Mastery of the sound system rests on parallel processes of perceptual and motor learning. Children must learn to perceive the categories and the features in the sounds of others. They also must learn to control their muscles so that they produce similar sounds. Both kinds of mastery put special demands on the learner.

Speech production

Consider first what goes into normal speech production. Adults speak English at average rates of about 215 syllables, or about 500 phonemes, per minute. About 100 different muscles are involved in producing the sounds. In mature speech several hundred coordinated messages must go out to the muscles each second (Lenneberg, 1967). Normal speech, then, should be thought of as requiring coordinations of muscles similar to those needed in skilled piano or violin playing.

Speech perception

The perception of speech, like rapid reading, requires the child to follow and decode rapidly. When adults speak for even a few minutes, they usually produce more words than are contained in the typical first-grade primer.

Skills in producing and understanding normal speech pose demands comparable to those of learning to write and read swiftly. Toddlers seemingly handle the sound system with more rapid and universal success than children learning reading and writing at later ages. Studies of speech perception are beginning to show how the complex task is mastered so easily.

Adults hear speech sounds in a special way: *categorically*. A comparison between this *categorical perception* of speech and our usual *continuous perception* illustrates the point. If we use a machine to produce ten sounds that range from very soft to very loud and ask people to judge each sound for loudness, we find continuous perception. There is a middle range where sounds seem equally similar to loud and soft. The ten sounds seem to make a continuous range rather than being divided into loud and soft. But if we use a machine to produce ten sounds that go from a speech sound such as pa to a contrasting one such as ba, we get a different result. Even though we can produce a continuous range (as measured by instruments), it doesn't sound like one. Instead, we hear some of the in-between sounds as pa and the rest as ba, with little or no sense of uncertainty. We hear each sound as fitting definitely into one of the speech categories, even when the machine shows it to be borderline, or similar to both. This categorical perception makes it much easier to decode speech sounds.

Even little babies hear speech categorically (Eimas, 1975). Habituation techniques have been used to study how babies from 1 to 4 months old respond to such contrasts as ba-pa and ra-la. The finding has been consistent. Young babies respond categorically and in some ways go further than adults. One study used fragments of speech sounds that resemble chirp noises made by birds. Adults treated the series of chirplike noises as if they formed a continuous scale. Babies responded to the same series categorically. Babies respond categorically to speech contrasts that are not distinctive in their own language. Adults do not.

Perhaps *feature detectors* are part of the baby's biological equipment (Eimas, 1975). Experience might help turn off attention to features not used in the particular language the child hears. These interpretations are controversial (Diehl, 1981), but the capacity to discriminate between sound categories and to pay attention to the important distinctions between them apparently is built in.

Exciting findings on newborns suggest that we hear speech rhythms from the day of birth. William Condon and Louis Sander (1974) played tape recordings of adult speech to newborn babies and simultaneously made movies of them. They looked for coincidences, or shared rhythms, between the adult speech and the baby movements. The onset of baby movements, such as raising an arm, tended to coincide with the syllables of the recorded speech. However, Dowd (1981) was unable to replicate this finding.

Babies are born prepared to listen to speech in a special way. They start off by tuning in to the distinctive features and, perhaps, the rhythms that are basic in all languages. Later development, and perceptual learning, most likely is a matter of fine tuning rather than of building complex categories.

Mastery of the meaning (semantic) system

Languages encode hundreds of diverse meanings. As illustrated in the size of unabridged dictionaries, they include tens of thousands of different words. Mastering semantics, or meaning, is a far more extensive task than learning the sound system.

The smallest meaningful elements in a language are called *morphemes.* They include both elements that are meaningful when alone (cat) and those that occur only with others (the *s* in cats and the *ing* in crying). Morphemes include both words like *cat,* which lose or change meaning if subdivided, and nonwords like the *er* in louder and softer. River contains one morpheme; softer has two.

Every language is a code that relates sound patterns to meanings. The meaning code (or morpheme code or semantic system) is like the sound system in emphasizing categories. If someone speaking a strange language were to walk into your room and say wug, your best bet would be that wug means some category of events, not the name for a particular object or event.

A convenient way of seeing how far children have gone in mastering the semantic system is to measure their vocabulary. With young children this can be done by making lists of all of the words they utter. At all ages we can do it by testing comprehension of a standard list of words—for example, by showing the child several objects and saying "Show me the ball."

Studies of vocabulary growth show that there is a typical trend. As shown in Figure 9–3, the usual growth curve starts at 1 year with the first word and rises slowly during most of the second year. Then a tremendous spurt starts, usually toward the end of the second year. It peaks at about age 3 or 4, with

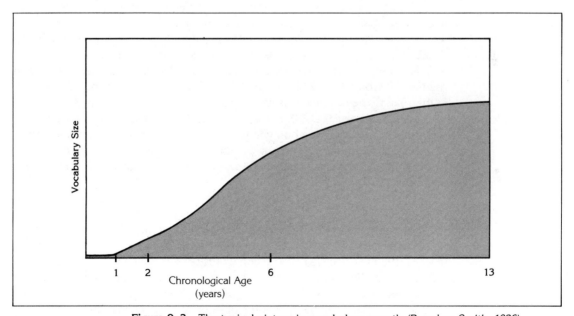

Figure 9–3 The typical picture in vocabulary growth *(Based on Smith, 1926)*

the average child learning new words at the rate of about two a day at this point. As a result of the cumulative progress, the typical child has mastered a few thousand words by the time she or he starts school. The child continues to pick up new ones throughout childhood (and after), though at a diminishing rate. Vocabulary size gives us but a crude picture of semantic development. It's more enlightening and interesting to look more closely.

Meanings in protolanguage

With the new emphasis on early communication comes the realization that children often understand and express meanings before they have words in the usual sense. Michael Halliday (1979) studied meanings in the *protolanguage* (prelanguage) developed by his son, Nigel. He found that between 9 and 12 months Nigel had three distinct ways of using sounds and gestures, each with its own separate possibilities of language meanings. Nigel used signs *instrumentally,* with an object-oriented focus, as in making a sound that meant "give me that." He also used them in a *regulatory* way with a person-oriented focus, as a sound that meant "do that (again)." A contrasting use was *interactional,* with sounds that meant "nice to see you" and "look." We don't know if all children develop protolanguages and don't know if all protolanguages resemble Nigel's. However, Nigel's protolanguage does tie in with an important idea that is widely held now: first words are best understood when related to earlier developments. The point becomes clearer when we consider studies of first words.

First words

Children's early words demonstrate strong and apparently universal biases about meanings. Children studied in the 18th and 19th centuries started with words similar to the first ones of children today (Bar-Adon & Leopold, 1971). Children hearing varied languages start with similar vocabularies.

A study by Katherine Nelson (1973) shows the usual trend. She studied the first 50 words learned by each of 18 children in New Haven, Connecticut, in the 1970s. The coincidences were striking. Sixteen of the 18 children learned *dog* as one of their first 50 words; 13 learned *ball*; and 13 learned *car.* The pattern becomes clearer when you think about everyday words that were not learned. For example, not one of the children learned *table* or *diaper* or *sun.* The common early words all related to objects that change, move, make noise, and so on.

The meanings of early words seemingly tie in closely with Piaget's picture of cognitive development at the time vocabulary expansion begins, about 18 to 24 months. Apparently the newly constructed picture of the world as made up of permanent objects provides the foundation for early words and meanings (Bloom, 1973; Nelson, 1973). The first words refer almost exclusively to objects and focus chiefly on those objects that act, disappear, and reappear.

Gail Roberts and Kathryn Black (1972) looked at the relation between the child's response to verbal labels for objects and the child's development on the Uzgiris-Hunt Scale of Object Permanence (Chapter 7). They presented pairs

Common early words such as *dog, ball,* and *car* reflect children's interest in objects that move, change, and make noise.

of toys to toddlers aged 18 to 22 months. In some pairs they selected one toy and named it in several sentences. For example, they said "Here is a *train,*" "You can pull the *train,*" and so on. In other pairs they talked about a toy without naming it. For example, they said, "Here is a *toy*" or "You can pull *it.*" Later the children were given a chance to play with each pair and their free choices were studied. Naming, or labeling, a toy substantially increased the child's tendency to look at it and manipulate it later.

However, the tendency for a child to be influenced by the verbal naming procedure was related to level of object permanence. Children at the lower levels of object permanence were not influenced by the verbal labeling procedure. Children at the highest level of object permanence were influenced more than those with intermediate understanding. There was direct support for the idea that cognitive development provides a necessary precondition for the meanings of language.

Heightened interest in early meanings has led to a number of theoretical controversies. For example, the Roberts and Black finding on a clear relation between object permanence and language meaning contrasts with findings from some other studies. Most likely the problem here is that contrasting definitions and measures yield contrasting results (Corrigan, 1979). Another issue centers on the sources of early word meanings. One group emphasizes the perceptual basis of language categories and argues that similar looking or sounding objects are likely to be grouped (Clark, 1973; Tomikawa & Dodd, 1980). This group emphasizes the well-known phenomenon of overgeneralization, as when a child calls all men daddy.

Another group thinks that perceptually based naming is but one of several sources of early meaning. They point to meanings based on feelings and object use as well and argue that the majority of early words are not overgeneralized (Nelson, Rescorla, Gruendel, & Benedict, 1978). This dispute results in part from the basic problem of figuring out what children actually mean when they say a word. For example, when little Eva Bowerman applied the word *moon* first to the real moon and later to such objects as a half grapefruit, mounted steer horns, and hangnails, one interpretation is that she was overgeneralizing, misnaming the other objects. Alternatively, she might have been pointing out the interesting fact that they looked like the moon, even though they were different from it (Nelson et al., 1978).

First sentences

Early two-word sentences, like first words, show strong biases. A large proportion of them express a small number of meanings—for example, nomination, recurrence, and nonexistence. In *nomination* the child simply names a present object, as in "Here mommy" and "That kitty." *Recurrence* involves pointing out the existence of another one of the same or the reappearance of something that was gone—for example, "Nother truck" or "More Daddy." *Nonexistence* is conveyed in such sentences as "Allgone egg" and "Dog away." These are matters of great interest to toddlers and make up a surprising amount of their spontaneous conversation. Notice that the words that supplement the object names are largely words such as *here, more, go,* and *allgone,* words needed in talking about the important things that happen to objects.

Later developments

The most important general trend in children's meanings is from the concrete and immediate to the abstract and absent. Little children talk mostly about what is in front of them, often saying nothing that someone else present could not have figured out for themselves, as in "Mommy go," "More Daddy," and "Allgone egg." Only later do such language functions as reporting what was seen yesterday or what is to be done tomorrow come in (Brown, 1973). The development of meanings continues to parallel the development of thought after the early stages.

Work on later stages of semantic development has not gone far. One intriguing finding can give you a start in seeing where we are. It comes from word-association studies, in which you say words and ask people to respond with the first word they think of. When children under 6 are asked to associate to words, their associations usually reflect common *sequences* in everyday sentences, as in responding to man with work and to blue with sky. In contrast, when children over 8 (and adults) associate, their responses most commonly come from the same grammatical class as the stimulus word, as in responding to man with woman and to blue with green (Nelson, 1977b). This shift (known as the *syntagmatic-paradigmatic shift*) seemingly reflects a more general shift. It illustrates that the question of how diverse meanings are organized and stored in memory is a central one in understanding later semantic development.

Adults' meanings are apparently organized in terms of a system of distinctive features. Seemingly, we categorize words in terms of a variety of features, including grammatical categories, such as part of speech, and semantic categories, such as living/nonliving and large/small. Semantic organization of this kind possibly enables us to remember meaningful material so efficiently. When suddenly asked, "What is the name of the small black and white animal that has the smelly spray?", our speed and accuracy make it clear that we are not forced to scan every entry in our mental dictionary to find "skunk." We have to learn how semantic organization develops.

Mastery of grammar (syntax)

An obvious sign of children's progress in mastering syntax is that they put words together in longer and longer utterances as they get older. Such early statements as "Mommy" and "Milk" occur at about the first birthday. Near the second, utterances such as "Mommy go" and "Milk all gone" are heard. Progressively longer sentences, such as "Where me sleep?" and "This not ice cream" follow.

The relation between sentence length and language maturity is close (McCarthy, 1954). It reflects the fact that most of the new grammatical rules children learn result in longer sentences, particularly if you measure sentence length in morphemes rather than words (Brown, 1973). Apparently, the child produces only rule-guided sentences, never scrambled ones such as "Two mommy milk feet allgone doggie." The length of children's longest sentences reflects the complexity of the grammar they can manage.

Rule learning

Even the 2-year-old engages in an active process of *rule learning* in mastering grammar, rather than simply imitating or responding to social pressure. For example, there is an apparently universal tendency for children to make such mistakes as "I goed" instead of "I went" or "two sheeps" instead of "two sheep." These kinds of mistakes are revealing because (1) they imply a tendency to use general rules even where they don't apply, (2) they don't sound like imitations because adults don't talk like that, and (3) when you try to correct them, your teaching usually has little lasting impact. Jean Berko (1958) made a more controlled test of the rule-learning idea in an ingenious study. She used nonsense words rather than real ones in order to remove the possibility that children were using specific learning in producing new forms. For example, she presented a picture of a nonsense animal and said "Here's a *wug*." Then she presented two of them and said "Now there are two _____." The children said wugs without any hesitation. She showed a picture of a man performing an unfamiliar action and said, "This man is *spowing*. This man *spows*. Today he *spows*. Yesterday he ____." The children said spowed. Her results made it clear that the children had mastered general rules for forming plurals, the past tense, and other forms and readily used these in new situations. Grammatical development is an active, constructive process, not one of imitation or conditioning.

Basic questions

The basic questions about syntactical development relate to (1) the similarity of the rule systems different children use, (2) the relation of the early grammars to the grammars of the children's native language, and (3) the progressive changes that transform the early rule systems into mature ones. Tentative answers to these questions are emerging.

The rule systems different 2-year-olds use are surprisingly similar. Children learning English in Cambridge, Massachusetts, Berkeley, California, and New York City utter two-word sentences with striking resemblances. Important evidence has been gathered by studying children learning languages other than English, such as Russian, Japanese, Hebrew, Mandarin, Garo (spoken in India), and Luo (spoken in Kenya). The cross-cultural studies are generally consistent with comparisons of English-speaking 2-year-olds. Early grammars around the world are similar (Brown, 1973).

The early grammars are similar both to one another and to the grammars of the parent languages. This, of course, can be true only because different languages share grammatical similarities. It is the more universal characteristics that appear in all grammars that also are likely to appear in the first production grammars. The distinction between subject and predicate is a good example of a universal distinction. "Mommy go," "Milk allgone," and many other early sentences combine a one-word subject with a one-word predicate. Distinctions more specific to our language, as in "the doggie," "white milk," and "is running," come later. Comparable trends appear in other languages (McNeil, 1970).

Progress from the first grammars to later ones involves a trend toward more and more grammatical distinctions that make sentences both longer and more complex. There is a process of progressive differentiation, as in phonetic development. Detailed analysis is underway to see how lawful and similar these trends are for different children and different languages. There are signs of regularity. For example, the order of acquisition of features such as *in* and *on*, plurals, and the articles *a* and *the* has been found to be similar for a number of children. Commonly, *in* is introduced and used correctly before plurals. Plural forms appear before the articles *a* and *the* are used (Brown, 1973). By putting together these kinds of findings, you can make specific guesses about how the "same" sentence would sound as the child's grammar develops: "Doggie run" to "Doggie runs" to "The doggie runs."

Roger Brown (1973) developed a convenient way to study grammatical development based on a measure of average sentence length, or *m*ean *l*ength of *u*tterance (MLU) in morphemes. Children with similar MLU scores have similar productive grammars, even when they vary in age. As a result Brown found it useful to distinguish stages of grammatical development based on MLU scores.

Looking at particular kinds of sentences, such as questions, will help you appreciate some of the trends in grammatical development. At first children form questions simply by using a rising inflection. Sentences such as "Ball go" or "I ride train" become "Ball go?" or "I ride train?" Later *wh* words, such as why and what, come in. When the *wh* words first appear, they usually are used at the beginning of otherwise typical sentences, as in "Where my mitten?" and "Who that?" Only later, when more elaborated nonquestions are used, do we start to hear changes in word order, as in "What did you doed?" Sentences like "Why me not sleeping?" illustrate early efforts to wrestle simultaneously with the question form and negative statements.

It is as if the child gets the idea of questioning early and masters a sequence of more and more complicated rules to do it. The first rule, use a rising inflection, soon is combined with the rule add a *wh* word to the beginning of the sentence. Later these rules are put together with more complicated ones related to word order in complex sentences. With questions, as with other features of early grammar, we find regular progress from one system to another (Klima & Bellugi-Klima, 1966).

Later developments

Although the essentials of grammar are usually mastered by age 5, there also is progress during the elementary-school years (Palermo & Molfese, 1972). Preschoolers misunderstand such sentences as "John promised Bill to leave." They think that Bill is the one who leaves because the words *Bill* and *leave* come closer together in the sentence. Similarly, when presented with the sentence "Mary asked Sue to give her the doll," younger children miss the point that Mary is the one who is supposed to get the doll. Mastery of these kinds of grammatical complexities comes after age 5.

There is a general parallel between the growth of logical abilities and the correct use of terms such as *because* and *therefore.* Younger children treat these terms as if they tell about the sequence of what happens rather than about causality. Meaning and grammar are intertwined in this example, illustrating a more general pattern. As children get older, it becomes harder and harder to separate the different subsystems of language from each other and from cognitive development generally (Palermo & Molfese, 1972).

Explorations of what young children know about grammar illustrate one of the ties between cognitive development and language development. Here is part of an interview between linguist Lila Gleitman (Gleitman, Gleitman, & Shipley, 1972, p. 150) and her 7-year-old daughter, Claire. Mother has been asking Claire for her opinion about a variety of sentences:

> Mother: How about this one: *I am knowing your sister.*
> Claire: No: *I know your sister.*
> Mother: Why not *I am knowing your sister*—you can say *I am eating your dinner.*
> Claire: It's different! (*shouting*) You say different sentences in different ways! Otherwise it wouldn't make sense!

Claire has "metalinguistic" knowledge. She not only speaks grammatically, but knows about how you are supposed to speak and why. Research suggests that although children speak grammatically from about age 2 and have adultlike grammars by about age 4, it is only at about 5 to 8 years that adultlike metalinguistic functioning is seen, even in talented children. Metalinguistic skills appear at about the same time as we see a rise in metamemory (Chapter 8) and other metacognitive functions (Gleitman, Gleitman, & Shipley, 1972).

PROCESSES UNDERLYING LANGUAGE DEVELOPMENT

Today there is broad agreement about the main features of the process of language development. The *interactionist view,* so widely held now, is a rejection of both the extreme environmentalist view common in psychological theories of the past (for example, Skinner, 1957) and the strongly biological position presented by Noam Chomsky (1965), the most influential linguist of recent times. What looked like a choice between an impossible theory (an account of language development entirely in terms of associations and conditioning) and a magical one (a theory that children were born with a knowledge of grammar) has given way to an alternative that seems more reasonable (Bruner, 1978).

Learning processes

I've mentioned current ideas about language learning throughout the chapter, including an image of an active learner whose approach to language is constrained by both perceptual and cognitive biases that influence which sound contrasts and meanings are learned more readily. The learning process is seen as one of cognitive learning, emphasizing categories and rules, rather than a conditioning process. With this view the importance of reinforcement and imitation are questioned.

Parental influence

The implications of the cognitive view of language learning become clearer when you consider how parents fit in with it. A traditional environmentalist approach gave parents prime responsibility for the child's progress. For example, reinforcement theories require that the parents must be near, must reward utterances, and must gradually shift their reward pattern so that such crude first statements as "Mamma" gradually are molded into statements such as "Mother may I please have a cookie?", with correct phonology, syntax, and meaning.

A variety of facts contradicts this kind of picture. Children say "two feets" and "me goed" at first and show little inclination to learn to say "two feet" and "I go" despite parental pressure. Tape recordings of home conversations indicate that parents commonly reward bad grammar when it comes as part of a true statement (Brown, 1973). For example, sentences such as "Me have two feets" typically get a positive reply from parents. In contrast, parents correct perfectly grammatical statements that are untrue, such as "I have two noses." Because parents "pay off" for truth rather than good grammar, reinforcement theories have trouble with the finding that grammar nevertheless improves at a rapid rate. Social-learning theories emphasizing imitation do better here, particularly when they emphasize rule learning and thus account for the creativity illustrated in such novel utterances as "I runned" (Rosenthal & Zimmerman, 1978).

The fact that children all around the world learn language at about the same time strains conventional ideas about parental coaching, as does the fact that toddlers learn about grammatical niceties that their parents don't know exist.

Some argued that the child's genius in mastering language reflects a biologically given talent, independent of what those around the child do. It was claimed that children were exposed to the full, confusing nature of adult speech and yet quickly got to the heart of it with no special help. But this view of the child as provided with a self-sufficient language-acquisition device (Chomsky, 1965) looks as inadequate as the picture of the child equipped only with a blank slate, for the child apparently gets important help from parents, though not necessarily the kind of help that behaviorist theories hypothesized.

Parents (and others) talk differently when they talk to little children in the early stages of language development (Newport, 1977). Mothers (and others) shift to "motherese." They speak more slowly and pause between sentences. They speak in shorter and simpler sentences with many fewer of the sentence fragments and irregular forms so common when adults speak to adults. Even 5-year-olds speak motherese when addressing 2-year-olds. Children normally do not have to deal with the same language that the rest of us do. They get a much more comprehensible set of sentences to figure out.

The fact of motherese becomes particularly significant when put together with a fact about comprehension. Shipley, Smith, and Gleitman (1969) found that children comprehend better when presented with language about one level above their own. Children in the two-word stage comprehend more if spoken to in language a little more complicated. Children a bit past the two-word stage do better when given normal adult speech. Perhaps the best language-teaching situation is when children hear language a little ahead of their own. Apparently that's how most people talk to little language learners. Most likely it helps.

When children are new to the language-learning game, their parents evidently speak to them in simpler terms and also make less stringent demands on them. Then, as children progress, the parents apparently keep raising the standard, using more and more complicated language in talking and simultaneously demanding more mature speech (Moerk, 1976). What the parents do is probably a reaction to their picture of the child's current ability. Although they don't seem to run the show in language development, and may not even set the pace, parents do seem to act like intelligent and helpful partners.

Individual differences

The dominant view in recent years has been that there is one path to language maturity and that we can make the best progress in understanding development if we focus on the similarities in how children go down it. As reflected in this chapter, the approach has been fruitful.

Now we are beginning to see the rise of an alternative view, one that looks at contrasts among children as a key to understanding development in general. Katherine Nelson (1981) pointed out similarities within several versions of the idea that we must look at differences in how children acquire language. She argued that this approach has much to teach us.

Nelson's own work illustrates this new orientation and its potential. When Nelson (1973) looked at the early vocabularies of 18 children growing up in similar environments, she was impressed that two contrasting strategies seemed to be used in constructing vocabularies. Some children took a primarily referential approach, exploiting the cognitive power of language by mastering mostly words with clear reference to objects around them, such as ball, shoes, and car. Other children focused more on the social-emotional functions of language and developed early vocabularies related more to them: hi, nite nite, stop it, and want it. Nelson thinks that these contrasts not only illustrate that there are important differences in how children advance, but also give us clues about how children view language. She argues that children don't approach language in terms of the distinctions so basic to linguists, such as phonology-semantics-syntax, but work in terms of contrasts such as referential-expressive, as in Nigel Halliday's protolanguage (see "Meanings in Protolanguage"). Her views suggest that the current climate of agreement about language development may soon give way to new arguments that take us toward deeper understanding.

The common finding that children who master language quickly have parents who talk to them differently proves nothing about the importance of parent teaching. Language skill runs in families, but as long as we study only children who are raised by their biological parents, the correlation can be used equally well to support hereditary and environmental positions (Chapter 15).

Experimental studies in which the ways parents deal with the child are systematically varied are more to the point. Well-controlled experiments of this kind are rare. However, the few we have suggest that parental actions may, indeed, make a big difference in the rate of language acquisition (Box 9–1).

Applications box 9–1 Accelerating early language development

Can language development be accelerated, made to move along more rapidly than is usual? We don't know. Good evidence is too scarce for us to be sure whether special approaches can make early language advance faster or to know how early acceleration might relate to later development.

Exciting work by William Fowler at the Ontario Institute for Studies in Education provides perhaps the best support for the idea that we can accelerate early development. His sophisticated and well-controlled experiments with Amy Swenson (Fowler & Swenson, 1979) have produced dramatic results. Babies trained by his approach reach early language milestones at surprisingly young ages. For example, one group of three babies each used seven words properly by 10 months (compared to a norm of 15 months), and all began to combine words at about 12 months (as compared to a norm of about 21 months).

Although training was stopped at about 12 months, follow-up studies showed that the gains were maintained. For example, this trio started referring to themselves as "I" and "me" at about 19 months (compared to a norm of about 28 months) and used some plurals starting by about 24 months (compared to a norm of about 34 months). If these findings of dramatic and maintained gains can be replicated, both the theoretical and the practical implications will be enormous.

Fowler's training program is of special interest here because it is based on the mainstream picture of normal language development that has emerged in recent years and is summarized in this chapter. The central idea is that language acquisition is a process of cognitive learning (rather than being primarily maturational or a result of conditioning). The child is assumed to learn a series of language rules gradually in a standard sequence as a result of interacting with others. With this orientation the focus is on helping the child learn language rules, working on rules that can be used either in understanding or producing speech (rather than training the child in speech behavior, as a conditioning theory would suggest).

Parents carry out the training program. They are provided with written guides describing what to do and also given guidance during weekly home visits. A great variety of teaching activities is used, including having the parents model certain words, engage in language play while carrying out daily routines, take the baby to explore, and look at books. In the basic study the infants were given an average of about 100 minutes per day of language stimulation starting at age 5.4 months and continuing to 12.3 months.

A special feature of the findings was their generality. Similar results were found with girls and boys, children of parents of varied educational backgrounds, and children learning three different languages (English, Italian, and Chinese). Evaluation tests were given by examiners who did not know what the study was about or which children had been trained and which were in the control group. The scores showed big gains in language resulting from the training program, both when the language of experimentals and controls was compared and when progress in language was compared with development in nonlanguage areas for the trained children.

An important finding was that training apparently had a major impact on the speed of language acquisition without changing the developmental sequence. Language development in the trained group showed the familiar landmarks and sequences, even though the babies progressed at a remarkable pace. Perhaps the nature of language and maturation define the path to be followed, but the kind of experiences encountered have the biggest role in influencing how rapidly the child moves down that path.

SUMMARY

This chapter dealt with language development. The central focus was on the question of how the young child is able to master such a difficult task so quickly and easily. An interactionist answer that emphasized the child's preparedness and the support of the social environment was offered. With this orientation the early mastery of communication skills was highlighted.

The child was pictured as engaged in dialogue from right after birth, learning how to communicate through gestures before learning language. Communication skills and the fact that language is learned in the context of communication were emphasized as contributing to the child's rapid progress with language.

Basic characteristics of language (creativity, system, and comprehension and production) were described to introduce a systematic look at language learning. Because there are three main language systems (phonological, semantic, and syntactic) to be mastered in two ways (receptively and productively), there are six general kinds of progress in language development.

In describing mastery of the sound system, I first described the nature of phonemes. Then I summarized progress in speech production and perception.

Mastery of the meaning system was introduced by looking at meanings in protolanguage. Then the common features of meanings in first words and first sentences were described. Finally, the complex question of later developments in the semantic system was summarized.

In discussing mastery of the grammatical system, I focused on rule learning because children master grammatical rules, as shown in such common errors as "I goed" and the ready application of grammatical rules to nonsense words. The basic question of universality in early grammars was tentatively answered by saying that the evidence available suggests there are important similarities in how children master grammar in diverse languages. In talking about later developments in mastering syntax, I highlighted the close connection between cognitive learning and language learning.

The chapter closed with a discussion of the processes underlying language learning. Ideas about language learning as a cognitive learning process were summarized. The question of parental influence was emphasized as a way of dealing with the question of what environment does and does not contribute. The current interactionist view was contrasted both with old blank-slate views that downplayed the child's own contribution and biological ideas that implied the environment made little or no difference. In closing, I suggested that the current climate of agreement about language acquisition is likely to end soon as investigators move on to new frontiers. The topic of individual differences in language learning was presented to illustrate a new and contrasting approach that questions the conventional wisdom of emphasizing universals in language acquisition.

PART IV
Social-Emotional Development

Now attention turns to happiness and unhappiness, love and hate, good behavior and bad, and related topics. Taken together these matters make up what is often called the social-emotional side of development. They are discussed in four interrelated chapters.

These chapters build on the previous ones. The child's ability to make sense out of the world and deal with it is an essential part of social-emotional development. The chapters in this section, then, include views of the growth of competence from new perspectives.

More than children's skills are important here. When Jill says "I hate you," when Ellen pushes Joe, and when Peter says "I can't do anything right!", their ability to form sentences or use their arms is only part of the story. In this section we consider both capacities and other variables.

With a focus on both competence and other aspects of children's actions, the developmental story becomes more complicated. The growth of capacities is essentially cumulative. But the older child cannot be described as happier, sadder, more or less interested in the world, or more or less loving than the baby at 1 year. Objects can gain emotional meaning, but they can also lose it. Eventually peek-a-boo loses its thrill. The boy who hates girls often changes his attitude. Getting mad and getting over it, losing a friend and getting a new one, dropping one worry and gaining a new one— these are common sequences. In the social-emotional area fluctuation is common.

CHAPTER 10

Emotional Development

Children's lives are punctuated by emotional episodes. The quiet activity of arithmetic period is interrupted by a roar of laughter when a dog enters the room. When Holly sees her mother arrive, she stops playing and smiles broadly. In each episode we have to consider both the situation that evokes the reaction and the emotional reaction itself. Both change developmentally. Newborns cry but don't laugh. They cry at a sudden, loud noise but are unmoved when told "You stink!" Six-year-olds might be startled and then laugh at the noise but cry at the insult.

In this chapter we look first at these two different sides of emotion and then put them together. First we consider developmental trends in emotional reactions. Next we look at the situations that produce emotional reactions. Finally, we consider emotional episodes as complex combinations of the two.

DEVELOPMENTAL TRENDS IN EMOTIONAL REACTIONS

Each emotional reaction has three parts. There is (1) physiological arousal (as in changes in brain waves, blood chemistry, and heart rate), (2) behavior (smiling, running, talking, and so on), and (3) cognition (understanding or interpreting the situation, as in thinking "This is great!").

The three parts of emotional reactions each develop at a different pace. Important changes in arousal come first, with the most dramatic changes occurring before age 1 year. Behavioral aspects of emotion parallel motor development: big changes during the first few years, mostly refinement and elaboration after age 6. The cognitive side of emotion, like understanding more generally, develops more slowly and continues changing throughout childhood; so it is useful to look at the three separately.

Arousal

Arousal is the most important aspect of emotion in the newborn. We can sum up the early picture largely in terms of it. Later emotion is more complex, but arousal remains central at all ages.

Excitement in the newborn

When new babies get "emotional" we see a dramatic pattern. Their skin turns red; their arms and legs thrash around; their heart rate speeds up; their breathing becomes irregular; and their brain waves and blood chemistry change. The internal changes are triggered by lower centers in the brain and influenced by chemical messages from the endocrine glands. The physiological reactions are similar to those seen in peaks of emotion throughout the life span.

Because the excitement pattern usually includes crying and unhappy facial expressions and sometimes follows negative events, it often is called *distress*. At birth and for several weeks afterward there is no "delighted" excitement.

Arousal level

Excitement can be thought of as one extreme of an arousal dimension, with sleepiness at the other. States of ordinary wakefulness are in the middle (see Figure 10-1). This approach puts emotional excitement in the same framework as the rest of life, rather than viewing it as something separate (Duffy, 1962).

At all ages physiological measures of arousal, such as brain waves, heart rate, and amount of sweat on the palms, tend to vary together (though not closely). Thus, we can think of a person's level of arousal as his or her overall degree of emotional arousal. Such everyday terms as being stirred up, uptight, calm, and loose refer to particular levels of arousal.

At all ages emotional reactions involve an increase in arousal level. The baby's distress, like extreme reactions in older children, shows dramatic physiological reactions. But if we look carefully, we see similar, though smaller, changes every day. Mild emotional reactions, as when a child laughs at a joke, tells a deliberate lie, or tenses up when criticized, include changes in heart rate, breathing, and palm sweating that parallel the large changes seen in extreme arousal.

Arousal level sums up the major patterns of internal activity. The brain, the heart, and other organs work constantly. The level of activity, or arousal, forms a backdrop, or baseline, for everything the child ever does.

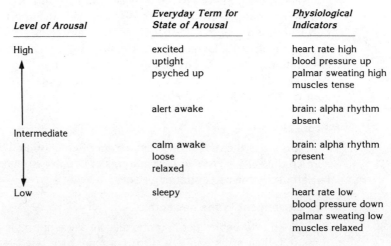

Level of Arousal	Everyday Term for State of Arousal	Physiological Indicators
High	excited uptight psyched up	heart rate high blood pressure up palmar sweating high muscles tense
	alert awake	brain: alpha rhythm absent
Intermediate		
	calm awake loose relaxed	brain: alpha rhythm present
Low	sleepy	heart rate low blood pressure down palmar sweating low muscles relaxed

Figure 10-1 Level of arousal

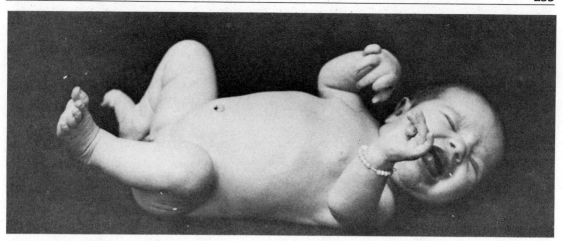

Arousal level influences both the physiological reactions and outward movements of newborns.

In the newborn the behaviors we see relate more closely to this baseline of internal activity than in older children. Diverse measures such as amount of movement and strength of the sucking reflex fluctuate with arousal level and with each other (Bell, 1960; Sameroff, 1972), perhaps because the lower brain centers regulating arousal mature first and because at birth little goes on except for basic biological activities. Later the baby becomes more wakeful and more attentive to the outside world. Then action becomes less directly tied to the arousal baseline. However, arousal level influences interactions with the outside world at all ages.

Development of the sleep-awake cycle

The biggest developmental change in arousal itself is the establishment of a sleep-awake cycle. Newborn babies have only brief periods of being asleep or awake. They relate neither to dark and light nor to the cycles of those around them.

The shift to longer and more conventional periods of being asleep and awake starts early. First the brief naps grow longer. By 16 weeks there are much longer sleep periods, occurring mostly at night (Parmelee, Wenner, & Schulz, 1964). Soon baby sleeps through the night. Long periods of wakefulness develop after long sleeps.

By age 1 year a regular cycle is common, usually including sleeping through the night and taking a nap each morning and each afternoon. The naps become shorter and usually disappear by age 5.

The dropping of daytime naps is part of a trend toward less sleep with increasing age. Newborns average about 16 hours of sleep a day, 2-year-olds about 12 hours, 13-year-olds about 9 hours.

The sleep-awake cycle and behavior

The fact that all children soon establish a regular 24-hour cycle is more important than the changing details of how long they sleep and when. Once arousal falls into a daily cycle, the child's psychology, like our own, depends in part on the time of day.

The child's attentiveness, efficiency, and emotional reactions vary with the 24-hour rhythm of arousal. The relation between emotional reactions and clock time was shown when Florence Goodenough (1931) had mothers keep daily records of their preschool children's outbursts. Angry displays were more likely when the children were tired or hungry. There was a dramatic peak before suppertime. Restless nights, sickness, and other factors that disrupted the daily routine also raised the frequency of anger outbursts. The daily cycle helps explain both the tantrums on normal days, when trouble comes at predictable clock times, and on special days, when trouble comes unexpectedly.

Arousal and the performance of organized behaviors

The observation that sleepy and excited children often are not at their best can be put in a broader framework. Five hypotheses help in predicting what happens to interactions with the outside world when arousal level shifts, whatever the reason (Duffy, 1962; Hebb, 1955; Yerkes & Dodson, 1908).

Hypothesis 1.   For each skill such as walking, reading, or riding a bicycle there is an optimal intermediate level of arousal. Any of these skills is performed best at its optimal level. When arousal gets higher or lower than this level, performance is poorer or impossible, perhaps because attention is impaired (Kahneman, 1973; Mandler, 1975). A child who is either sleepy or excited does not read or remember as well as when arousal is in the middle range. If the child becomes wildly excited, as in panic, most organized actions such as reading become impossible, just as in sleep.

Hypothesis 2.   The optimal level of arousal for a skill depends on the complexity of the skill and how much attention it requires (Kahneman, 1973). Varied skills work best at different degrees of excitement. Stage fright is more likely to interfere with the performance for John, who has to give a long speech, than for Henry, who simply walks across the stage. The excitement of a track meet may psych children up so that they run their fastest but get mixed up on the more complicated problem of passing the baton in a relay. Academic tasks such as reading and arithmetic are complicated; so they are done best when the child is wide awake, but not too tense and aroused.

Hypothesis 3.   With practice the optimal range of arousal for a skill becomes wider, as does the range of levels of arousal in which the capacity can be performed at all (Bindra, 1959). When a child has just learned how to read, even small shifts in arousal can produce noticeable changes in reading performance. Fatigue, anxiety, illness, and excitement are mirrored vividly in performance. The sophisticated teacher can tell if something unusual is going on in the child's life just by listening to her or him read. By sixth grade it takes a bigger change in arousal to disrupt reading. We become almost able to read in our sleep, just as we get to the point where we can drive a car smoothly in states of drowsiness and excitement that at first make performance impossible.

Fire drills and drills in athletics and water safety are sound methods of preparing children to perform appropriately when excited. A skill that is learned but not practiced over and over after it is first mastered is not likely to help a child when arousal gets high. With drill and overlearning, skills come to be performed automatically and seemingly take up less attention (Chapter 5). Most likely this is why they are interrupted less than newer skills when arousal becomes extreme.

Hypothesis 4. Shifts in arousal level are likely to disrupt more actions in younger children than in older ones. This hypothesis follows from hypothesis 3 and the fact that younger children have more limited attentional capacities than do older children (Chapter 6).

All of a baby's actions are new. Nothing has been practiced much. As children grow older, they master new skills. But many old ones, such as reaching, grasping, walking, and dressing, remain important. If you date a capacity from the time it is first mastered, you can see that the proportion of a child's skills that are a particular "age," say one month since mastery, keeps getting smaller as the child gets older. For a 6-year-old only a few skills out of hundreds are one month old. In contrast, much of what a 6-month-old baby does was mastered in the last month. When 6-month-olds get sleepy or excited, a much bigger percentage of their actions is likely to be disrupted.

This hypothesis implies that the same degree of sleepiness or excitement has a much bigger impact on the young child than on the older one. This impact might be part of the reason for the big decline in temper tantrums between 2 and 5 years of age (Goodenough, 1931).

Hypothesis 5. Shifts in arousal level disrupt children's new and less mature behaviors more than their older and more mature ones. Here again an implication of hypothesis 3 provides a fruitful way of thinking about an important observation. Roger Barker, Tamara Dembo, and Kurt Lewin (1941) conducted a famous experiment demonstrating that frustration leads to regression. When preschool children were allowed to see attractive toys that they could not play with, their play became less constructive.

This finding, along with everyday examples of children who behave less maturely when excited or sleepy, can be thought of in terms of arousal level. Mature behaviors typically are both more complicated and less practiced than earlier and less mature ones. Saying "I'm sorry" is more vulnerable to sleep and to emotion than the action of sticking a thumb in the mouth and looking down.

Emotional arousal plays an important and somewhat changing role in children's lives. It is of special importance when we try to understand how emotional reactions interact with the child's other activities.

Behavior

Emotional behaviors develop rapidly in the months after birth, along with other motor behaviors. By 4 months smiling and laughing have appeared. They occur as part of a "delighted" excitement reaction, often when an increase in arousal is followed by a return to a calm, awake baseline (Sroufe & Waters,

1976). By the first birthday a full set of basic facial expressions has appeared. They occur in situations that suggest that the basic emotions, including happiness, sadness, anger, surprise, fear, and disgust, are now present (Bridges, 1932; Charlesworth & Kreutzer, 1973; Ekman, 1972). The fundamental emotional behaviors appear early, although most are not observed at birth.

After the first year the main trends are elaboration and modification. Actions such as hitting and running away take form mostly in the second year. Verbal behaviors, such as saying "I'm scared" and "I'm happy," develop as part of the upsurge in language following the second birthday.

Most likely the appearance of these elaborate behaviors is much more variable from child to child and society to society than the developmental schedule for early facial expressions and vocalizations. Such behavior as hitting or saying "I'm scared" apparently can be modified as easily as others. We even have suggestions that smiling and crying in the early months can be influenced by reinforcement (Brackbill, 1958; Etzel & Gewirtz, 1967).

Both maturation and learning probably enter into the development of emotional behaviors. Universal facial expressions and vocalizations such as frowning, smiling, crying, and laughing are most likely linked to a genetic-maturational schedule. There is similarity across cultures and normal early development in babies born deaf and blind (Eibl-Eibesfeldt, 1972; Freedman, 1974). Babies exhibit these basic reactions in similar form and at about the same age despite variations in experience. Perhaps the development of the brain and of hormonal systems paces behavioral development (Bousfield & Orbison, 1952; Bronson, 1965). Experience certainly influences the form and frequency of even basic emotional reactions after they emerge (Ekman, 1972).

Frontiers box 10–1 Facial expression

A modern perspective suggests we look at infants to learn about the emergence of biologically based universals in emotional expression and study older children to gain insight on how and when emotions are hidden and disguised (Ekman, 1972; Izard, 1978, 1979). Research on both problems is moving ahead.

Muscular components of facial expressions

Harriet Oster and Paul Ekman have been taking an atomistic approach, looking at the early emergence of the muscle movements that are put together to form complex facial expressions later (Oster, 1978; Oster & Ekman, 1977). They use an anatomically based coding system (the Facial Action Coding System, or FACS), which classifies specific facial movements in terms of the muscles that produce them. For example, movement pattern AU 12 is based on contractions of a muscle called zygomaticus major. When it contracts, we see the upturned mouth characteristic of all smiles and elevation and expansion of the cheeks, deepening and straightening of the furrow below the eyelids, and raising and pouching of the lower lids. Another pattern, AU 4, involves knitting of the brows, or frowning. Videotapes of babies aged 4 to 12 months reveal cycles of AU 4 action followed by AU 12 contractions: frown, end frown, smile. There is no sign of distress connected with AU 4. Instead, the pattern suggests that early frowns might reflect a special form of attention, perhaps that accompanied by early efforts to figure out the face scheme.

Facial expressions: movement patterns

Other recent studies have focused on the familiar combinations of muscle movements that we recognize as joy, surprise, fear, and so on. Comparisons of judgments based on the FACS system with more global use of labels such as joy or fear show close agreement (Hiatt, Campos, & Emde, 1979). It is reasonable to think that our everyday use of such labels as surprise in judging faces does involve judgments based on use of the specific cues coded in the muscle-oriented FACS system. Using a similar system of coding, Izard, Huebner, Rissner, McGinnes, & Dougherty (1980) found that adults had high agreement in judging expressions produced by 1- to 9-month-old babies, whether slides or videotapes were used. Brief training helped.

Another important finding is that standard situations, such as a peek-a-boo game (Hiatt et al., 1979) or medical innoculations (Izard et al., 1980) tend to produce particular facial expressions, supporting the idea of innate and universal emotional reactions during the first year.

Later development: faking and hiding emotional expressions

The ability to fake an emotional expression apparently develops gradually (Ekman, Roper, & Hager, 1980). Improvement in imitating facial expressions was particularly great between 5 and 9 years, with expressions of fear, sadness, and anger being hard to imitate even for 13-year-olds. However, practice and the use of a mirror helped.

Further evidence that the elementary-school years are a period of great progress came from Carolyn Saarni's (1979) study of children's understanding of display rules. She showed comic strips to children. The strips were all of conflict situations and included photographs of real faces. She interviewed 6- to 10-year-olds about the stories. The 10-year-olds mentioned more rules for displaying emotion in their spontaneous comments and showed more complex social understanding generally, as in apt remarks, "You wouldn't want to hurt your aunt's feelings" and "If he shows he's scared, they'll beat him up for sure." Both the ability deliberately to control facial expressions and the social knowledge about when and how to do it grow during later childhood. (These findings tie in nicely with our overall picture of the growth of social understanding, Chapter 13).

Here is a plausible conclusion: Children need little or no specific experience either to exhibit basic facial expressions such as smiling or to cry, and they smile at appropriate times. Special forms of experience and learning probably are much more important in other aspects of emotion. Whether the child continues to smile and cry openly, what the child does and says in situations evoking laughing and crying, and what makes a child cry and laugh are the aspects of behavioral reactions that are more varied and probably more closely linked to the child's experiences and learning.

Cognition

Cognitive development paces emotional comprehension. If you know how a child interprets the environment generally, then you can guess what kind of situations will produce emotional reactions. At first, when the baby's interactions with the world are largely reflexive, most of the environment lacks emotional significance. The outside stimuli that do count are simple and physical: a loud sound, a sweet liquid. By 3 months the baby shows more sign of making sense of the world in terms of stimulus patterns and past experience. Cues such as the sight of a face or a bottle can trigger emotional reactions. As experience and comprehension move forward, objects, words, and concepts come to make a difference emotionally. The 4-year-old often has emotional ups and downs that hinge on small, symbolic cues—the difference between "you can go" and "you can't go" or a hand that beckons rather than threatens. Only later, when children's understanding of people and social interaction gets below the surface, can they be stung by subtle forms of rejection and amused by sophisticated jokes. Because this kind of deeper understanding develops largely after age 5, emotional understanding changes tremendously during middle childhood and adolescence.

The connection between comprehension and emotional reaction is so close that emotional reactions can be used to figure out what a child understands (Charlesworth, 1969). Babies who smile at faces, but not at certain faces more than others, show the limits of their social understanding. Children who are surprised to find that liquid mercury (quicksilver) acts as it does reveal their knowledge of "normal" metals.

Additional evidence of the close link between cognitive development and emotional reactions comes from studies of children with Down's syndrome, a genetic disorder typically accompanied by severe mental retardation. When stimuli used to evoke emotional reactions, such as the visual cliff and laughter stimuli, are presented to babies with Down's syndrome, their reactions can be predicted more accurately from their level of cognitive development than from their age (Cicchetti & Sroufe,1978). Within infancy, tests of emotional reaction could be used as "intelligence tests."

SITUATIONS THAT PRODUCE EMOTIONAL REACTIONS

It is useful to look both at basic properties of all emotional stimuli and at the varied ways in which situations can become emotionally meaningful.

Basic properties of emotional stimuli

The universal characteristics of emotionally significant stimuli can be summed up in terms of what they do to the child: they command attention, interrupt ongoing activity, and change arousal level (Mandler, 1975). Emotional episodes start when something catches the child's attention and thereby interrupts whatever the child was doing (Hebb, 1949; Simon, 1967). Normally, the shifts in attention and interruption are accompanied by at least a small change in arousal level. As illustrated in Table 10–1, we can see this common pattern in emotional episodes of diverse kinds.

TABLE 10–1 Examples of emotional episodes illustrating the interruption concept

Traditional label	Episode
surprise	As George sits down, Molly pulls his chair out from under him.
fear	As George walks across the street, Henry yells, "Here comes a car!"
anger	As George daydreams, Lucy says, "You stupid fool!"
delight	As George studies the spelling list, the bell for recess rings.
grief	When George walks into his room, he discovers that his pet hamster is missing.
disgust	When George lifts his milk glass to drink, he discovers a dead bug in it.

Paths to stimulus meaning

Stimuli apparently get their power to evoke emotional reactions through three contrasting paths: (1) biological preparedness, (2) associative learning, and (3) nonassociative learning.

Biological preparedness

A biological reason is needed to explain why certain stimuli can trigger distress in all newborns and why other stimuli can reduce it. As suggested in Table 10–2 it looks as if organized activity and interruption are central concepts in understanding what is built in at birth.

Universal stimulus meanings that appear after birth are harder to interpret. A fear reaction to the sight of a visual cliff is universal, but only appears at about 2 months (Chapter 6). Smiling at faces and similar stimuli shows a similar pattern. We still are not sure about the contributions of maturation and experience in these cases.

Fear apparently develops in the visual cliff situation regardless of a baby's previous falls, experience with glass surfaces, or level of object permanence. Given a minimum of experience, the maturation of hormonal systems might be the key factor (Scarr & Salapatek, 1970).

TABLE 10–2 Stimuli with the universal power to influence distress reactions in the newborn

Early Evokers of Distress	Early Inhibitors of Distress
Specific examples	
sudden, loud noises	soft, rhythmic music
being dropped	being rocked
foot in ice water	nipple in mouth
pin prick	swaddling (wrapping) in blanket
General stimuli	
intense and pain producing	(mild and attention getting)*
sudden and unexpected	repeated and expected
novel	(familiar)*
interruptive of ongoing organized behaviors	releasers for organized behaviors

*tentative—evidence lacking

The maturational hypothesis fits in with some animal evidence. Gene Sackett (1966) reared baby monkeys individually in isolation from birth with no opportunity to see other monkeys or their own reflections. He studied their reactions to a set of pictures projected on a screen. Special responses to pictures of monkeys appeared abruptly at about age 2 months. For example, pictures of adult monkeys with threatening faces produced more vocalization and signs of upset. Apparently the emotional meanings were prewired, though not observable at birth.

Associative learning

Words, objects, people, and places can acquire emotional meaning through association with stimuli that already have much meaning. The sight of the doctor's white coat can take on the emotional meaning of a painful injection. The word *book* can come to arouse joy or fear or remain neutral, depending on the child's experience with books.

The principles of classical conditioning are useful both in explaining and in modifying emotional associations (Chapter 5). Neutral stimuli can be given emotional meaning if they are paired with unconditioned stimuli. Acquired emotional associations, such as trembling and turning pale when confronted with the cues of swimming, horseback riding, or flying in an airplane, can be extinguished.

Symbolic learning also contributes (Chapter 5). Older children often acquire strong emotional reactions to people and events before they encounter them directly. For example, during World War II, children in the United States commonly learned strong negative associations to Germans and "Japs" without ever meeting them. Films, patriotic school assemblies, and the comments of others all fostered the learning.

Nonassociative learning

Past experience can give a stimulus emotional meaning even when there is no specific association between the stimulus and a prior emotional event. Fear of strangers at about 8 months provides a good example. Infants often start reacting fearfully when strangers approach at about this age. Usually the new fear rises quickly, but cannot be traced to a bad experience (Schaffer & Emerson, 1964a). Although maturational changes might increase fearfulness at this point (Emde, Gaensbauer, & Harmon, 1976), past experience determines who is feared. The learning apparently is perceptual—who is strange and who is familiar—not the association of particular people with negative events (Hebb, 1946).

It is possible that nonassociative learning processes contribute to a broad range of emotional reactions. For example, familiar people and places may have an important calming influence on children simply because they are familiar (Bowlby, 1973).

With such varied ways for stimuli to take on emotional significance, it is hard to tell why a particular situation happens to be an emotionally arousing one for a child. As you will see now, it is even harder to predict what happens in an emotional episode evoked by a particular situation.

EMOTIONAL EPISODES

Emotional episodes are complicated. When a child becomes afraid or otherwise aroused, you have to consider both the emotional reaction and the original ongoing activity that was interrupted by it. A second kind of complexity stems from the fact that the emotional episode itself has varied aspects.

Emotional episodes and ongoing activities

An everyday episode illustrates the varied parts of the picture. It is Betsy's turn to read. She recognizes the printed words *Jane ran* and says "Jane ran." Then she sees a new word, *rapidly,* and pauses. She stares at the book, wrinkles her brow, and twists her mouth. Her face turns a little red and she thinks to herself "I'll get it." After a few seconds she remembers, says "rapidly," smiles, and thinks "I knew I'd get it." Her face returns to its normal color. As illustrated in Figure 10–2, we can relate this episode to a general picture.

We must think of the action as unfolding over time. There are two different streams of action: the reading sequence (1-2-3-4-5) and the emotional sequence (A-B-C-D). The emotional sequence starts with an interruption of the reading. At the point where we first observe the emotional episode (A), we are interested both in it and in what happens to the reading sequence. The emotional sequence includes three kinds of components: the *physiological arousal* (as reflected in the red face), *behavioral reactions* (staring at the book, brow wrinkling, mouth twisting, smiling), and *cognitions* ("I'll get it." "I knew I'd get it."). The two different streams of activity interact in varied ways.

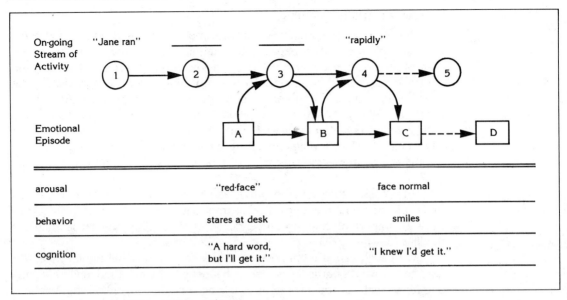

Figure 10-2 Episodes

Aspects of emotional episodes

We look at the varied components separately in order to see what each contributes. It has been particularly interesting to examine the contribution of cognitive elements, or understandings.

Cognition and emotional tone

The main finding has been that cognition has a big influence on what kind of emotion is experienced (*emotional tone*) (Mandler, 1975). A sudden ring of the phone can result in joy, fear, or anger—depending on what you were doing when it rang and what you expect when you answer it.

Recent work on children's emotion has focused on the role of cognition in determining when the emotional reaction is pleasant and when it is unpleasant. When do children smile and laugh? When do they cry and frown? Current theory provides a cognitive answer: Does the child think he or she can cope with the situation? When the answer is yes, we see a positive emotional reaction. When the answer is no, we see a negative one (Mandler, 1975; Rothbart, 1973).

The hypothesis follows from seeing emotion as involving interruption of the normal flow of activity. Now the interruption is seen as a *challenge*. When children think they can master the challenge, happiness results. If they think they cannot cope, the result is unhappiness.

Pleasant emotional episodes

The cognitive hypothesis has become popular in efforts to explain children's smiling and laughing (Harter, 1974; Rothbart, 1973; Sroufe & Waters, 1976). Piaget suggested the idea. He thought that the earliest smiles were

How children react to a situation depends on whether they think they can cope with or master the situation: a roller-coaster ride can be enjoyable for one child and terrifying for another.

smiles of recognition. Seemingly, babies smile first when they can relate what they see to past experience. Smiling seems to show pleasure resulting from being able to assimilate something into a scheme.

Thomas Shultz and Edward Zigler (1970) directly tested the idea. They hung a brightly colored toy clown in front of two babies between 8 and 18 weeks.

> A typical infant studied the stimulus very quietly and seriously for several minutes. Then his eyes brightened, his arms and legs began to move excitedly, and he began smiling and vocalizing to the stimulus. All this activity gradually peaked and then dropped off. As he quieted, the infant began to look away from the stimulus, usually toward the experimenter [p. 399].

The babies saw the clown under two conditions. Sometimes it was stationary, sometimes swinging. As predicted, when the harder to assimilate swinging clown was presented, smiling and laughing came after a longer period of study.

We can put the smile of recognition in broader perspective (Sroufe & Waters, 1976). Any stimulus can lose the power to produce smiling. With 3- and 4-month-olds there is less and less smiling at the human face when it is presented repeatedly. After this age a stationary face doesn't work at all. Older babies smile and laugh at more challenging situations.

Trends during the first year illustrate the changing nature of challenge. Mothers presented standard situations to their own babies in their own homes (Sroufe & Wunsch, 1972). One of the best items at 4 months was when mother said "I'm going to get you" and suddenly tickled her baby. By 12 months, laughter came mostly when the situation included incongruity—for example, when the mother walked like a penguin or sucked a baby bottle. There was a developing tendency for babies to laugh more when they took an active role in the situation. The 1-year-olds laughed at mother when she had a cloth in her mouth with the end hanging out, but they laughed hardest when they themselves stuffed the cloth back in after removing it.

More direct support for the hypothesis comes from evidence that the same stimuli that produce smiling and laughing in one setting evoke wariness and fear in another. Sroufe, Waters, and Matas (1974) studied how the same babies reacted to a mask under different conditions. It was a good fear stimulus when worn by a stranger. When mothers wore the mask in their homes, their babies smiled and laughed at the sight. When mothers put on the same mask in an unfamiliar laboratory setting, there were no positive reactions. Megan Gunnar-vonGnechten (1978) demonstrated a similar contrast with a toy mechanical monkey that loudly clapped cymbals. For 12-month-old babies who controlled the monkey's clapping, there was more smiling and laughing and less fussing and crying than for another group who witnessed the clapping but had no control over it.

Mary Rothbart (1973) showed how such concepts as mastery and safety could be used to make sense out of the picture. "I'm going to get you" illustrates the safety idea. When mother says "I'm going to get you" and suddenly tickles baby, the response is quite different than when a stranger does it. (Think about your own reaction to varied people saying "I'm going to get you" under varied conditions.) Apparently the child's understanding of the situation as safe or not determines the emotional coloring of the arousal. In older children reactions to a ghost story or a roller coaster ride probably vary in the same way.

The mastery idea is illustrated in Susan Harter's work with older children. She has studied children's smiles as they deal with puzzles and test items. Both 4- and 8-year-olds smiled more when giving correct responses on a vocabulary test than when giving incorrect ones, even though they were not informed whether their responses were correct (Harter, Shultz, & Blum, 1971). With fifth- and sixth-graders smiling and ratings of enjoyment were more common for anagram problems that were solved correctly than for those that were not (Harter, 1974). When the children did the correctly solved problems a second time, there was less smiling, further supporting the idea that the smiles related to challenge and mastery.

Children's reactions to jokes and cartoons also show developmental trends. Older and brighter children understand more challenging jokes and cartoons (McGhee, 1971; Shultz & Horibe, 1974).

Paul McGhee (1976) constructed jokes based on specific Piagetian landmarks. Here's a "conservation joke": "Mr. Jones went into a restaurant and ordered a whole pizza for dinner. When the waitress asked if he wanted it cut into six or eight pieces, Mr. Jones said 'Oh, you'd better make it six! I never could eat eight!'" (p. 422). Presumably, this kind of joke would not be funny to a child who did not yet understand conservation or to one who understood the conservation but took it for granted. Such jokes would only fit the challenge-mastery requirement for children just catching on to conservation or having recently caught on. Sure enough, fifth-graders rated the jokes lower on funniness than first- and second-graders with newly emerging or emerged conservation skills. The first-graders without conservation also found them less funny.

Diverse observations suggest that mastery, or coping with the world, is a basic source of happiness. They show that pleasure isn't so much in the stimulus as in the child's interpretation of it.

Unpleasant emotional episodes

Our evidence on unhappiness points to a parallel conclusion. Efforts to help children deal with failure, frustration, and fear have led to a more powerful set of helping methods. Workers in different decades often have reached a similar conclusion: fostering a coping approach helps.

Frustration and failure. Efforts to help children who react poorly when confronted with tasks that are hard to master have highlighted the importance of the child's expectations.

An early study by Mary Elizabeth Keister (1943) focused on 3- to 5-year-olds with undesirable reactions to failure. Children with such responses as crying and sulking, retreating from the task, repeatedly seeking help, and destructive behavior became the participants in a training program.

The program was based on doing a graded series of puzzles that started with easy ones and progressed to harder and harder ones. Keister encouraged the children to try. As they worked, she made comments such as, "That was fine. You are learning to try hard and not have anyone help you. You did that all by yourself." The children's reactions changed markedly. They persisted more after training. Their comments shifted from "I can't" to "Say, this is sure a hard game, but I can do it." Reactions such as sulking, crying, and destructive behavior disappeared.

More recently, Carol Dweck (1975) did a similar study as part of the current concern with learned helplessness, an attitude assumed by some to underlie depression and other forms of unhappiness (Seligman, 1975). Dweck worked with children age 8 to 13 who expected to fail and often did worse following failure. One group got training emphasizing the idea that failure was due to a lack of effort. Another group was given a more typical therapy involving repeated success experience. Dweck found that the emphasis on effort was superior. The learned helplessness was treated more successfully when the focus was on changing the child's way of thinking about coping.

Fear. Work with fearful children also seems to be moving toward a focus on changing their expectations about whether they can cope, though the trend is more clear in work on adult fears (Bandura, 1977).

Varied research indicates that there are two basic conditions that appear to be necessary and sufficient for getting rid of an unrealistic fear. The conditions are those that define extinction of classical conditioning: repeated presentation of the CS without the US (Chapter 5).

Putting it in terms of fear reduction, condition 1 is *fear reactions to a particular stimulus diminish if and only if the child has repeated contact with the stimulus.* A child who is afraid of snakes and never encounters them in any way is likely to keep the fear indefinitely. A shy child who successfully avoids talking in class will not get over the fear just through the passage of time. Fear of climbing on diving boards, trees, and other high places will diminish only through some kind of contact with high places. Active contact appears to be a crucial factor in getting over a fear.

Condition 2 is *during the repeated contact with the fear-producing stimulus, there should be no contact with an innately painful stimulus.* Repeated looking at a snake will not result in reduced fear if the snake repeatedly bites the child. Experience in walking on a diving board will not reduce fear of heights if children keep falling off and banging their heads. The active contact must be of a special kind: inherently painless.

The key conditions can be met in many ways and are present in all the varied methods of fear reduction clinicians use. Each method in the following list probably would help a fearful child if it were repeated often enough, but today many emphasize that coping with the situation producing the fear is more important than simply reducing the fear.

1. Direct extinction—Peter repeatedly looks at a real dog.
2. Live modeling—Peter watches Alice interact with a real dog.
3. Symbolic modeling—Peter watches a movie of Alice interacting with a dog.
4. Covert, or imaginal, desensitization—Peter closes his eyes and creates and watches mental pictures of himself interacting with a dog.
5. Covert modeling—Peter closes his eyes and creates and watches mental pictures of Alice interacting with a dog.

Applications box 10–2 Anxiety reduction through symbolic modeling

Symbolic modeling is an established method for reducing children's fears. When a child watches a film or television program in which someone encounters a fearful situation and comes through it safely, the child's own fear is reduced. For example, in a classic study by Bandura, Grusec, and Menlove (1967) children who watched a movie in which other children interacted nonanxiously with a dog were less fearful of real dogs afterwards.

A practical question is whether we can incorporate symbolic modeling into films and television programs that have a significant impact on real-life fears. A shortage of good evidence makes a general answer to this question impossible (Graziano, De Giovanni, & Garcia, 1979; Thelen, Fry, Fehrenbach, & Frautschi, 1979). But a careful study by Barbara Melamed and Lawrence Siegel (1975) is encouraging. It suggests that we already know enough to make good use of symbolic modeling in some important settings.

Melamed and Siegel concentrated on a situation well known for its power to scare children (and adults): hospitalization for surgery. They experimented to see if a carefully constructed film of a model could reduce both the immediate fear and the more lasting negative emotions often associated with surgery. Their positive findings are particularly encouraging because they compared the film with a standard, or control, procedure that many would regard as a psychologically sound one.

In the standard hospital procedure children were prepared for potentially frightening experiences in advance. A nurse explained what was going to happen and showed them pictures of the operating room before they went there. A member of the surgery team visited the children in their room to get acquainted in advance.

In the Melamed and Siegel study the question was whether adding a special film to the standard preparation would make an important difference. All children received the regular preparation and saw a film in addition. The 30 children assigned to the control group viewed a film about a boy on a nature trip in the country. It was designed to interest the children without providing anything relevant to their hospitalization. In contrast, the 30 children in the experimental group saw *Ethan has an Operation,* a specially constructed film about a 7-year-old hospitalized for a hernia operation. This 16-minute film included scenes of the events that characterize hospitalization for most children, from admission to discharge. The 15 scenes included having a blood test, separating from mother, and being in the operating and recovery rooms.

The experimental film was narrated by a child. It was based in part on earlier findings about coping models (Meichenbaum, 1971). These findings indicated that a coping model (one who felt some fear and apprehension but who successfully and nonanxiously coped) produced more fear reduction in viewers than a mastery model (a child who dealt with fearful situations with no sign of fear). In the sound track for the experimental film Ethan talked about his fears and concerns at each stage of hospitalization, indicating at each point that he had been nervous but had controlled his anxiety and that all had worked out well.

Melamed and Siegel found that the experimental film reduced anxiety in the children who saw it, both within the hospital and three to four weeks after discharge. The anxiety reduction showed up in varied ways—palms were less sweaty the night before the operation; the children rated themselves as less fearful; and observers rated them as calmer. In the weeks after discharge the parents of children in the experimental group reported fewer problems than the parents of children in the control group.

Principles of symbolic modeling can be incorporated in films and videotapes that can play an important role in helping children deal with stressful, real-life situations. It is intriguing to think about other situations in which one film might help thousands of viewers.

The focus on coping has two sources. In the everyday world we don't want a child simply to get over being fearful at the sight of dogs or panicking when approached by other children. We want the child to interact with dogs and children and enjoy it. The other reason for highlighting coping is that treatments that include success in active coping apparently are more effective in reducing fear than the less active ones in the previous list (Bandura, 1977). Interestingly, recent research supports what parents told Jersild and Holmes (1935) in the 1930s: the best way to help their children overcome fears was to get them into active interaction with what they feared, working gradually so that the children became more skilled in coping with the situation.

DEVELOPMENTAL PARALLELS

Children's emotions and their competence are linked in important ways. Emotional development involves the growth of perceptual-motor, cognitive, and linguistic capacities. A close-up look at emotional episodes reveals further connections. The interruption idea implies that emotion comes about when the regular exercise of capacities is somehow disrupted. The coping attitude evidence suggests that children's pictures of their own competence in dealing with the interruption is crucial. A self-confident child is likely to react to the disruption as a pleasant challenge. Children who doubt their ability to cope will respond negatively. The close connection between emotion and competence makes it fruitful to think about the two areas together.

The essential story in the development of capacities is that a relatively helpless child with few skills quickly turns into a competent individual. Passive, or reflexive, interaction is replaced by active manipulation of the world in the early months. By 2 years, basic perceptual-motor skills have been acquired. By 6 years, language and cognitive skills have reached a point where children can take care of themselves in a variety of situations.

Now think of some highlights in emotional development (see Table 10–3). The child starts out with lots of distressed arousal. Positive emotions appear only a few weeks later. By 6 years, prolonged displays of negative emotion are rare. The similarities in the two stories might not be coincidental; perhaps they reflect a basic connection.

SUMMARY

In examining emotional development we looked first at emotional reactions, next at the stimuli that produce them, and finally at emotional episodes.

Emotional reactions always include changes in arousal level, as when the heart beats faster. Arousal changes are particularly dramatic in the newborn and become less conspicuous with the development of a mature sleep-awake pattern and the emergence and mastery of more elaborate behavior patterns. An important aspect of arousal shifts is that they can influence ongoing behaviors such as walking or reading. A series of hypotheses related arousal changes to the performance of organized activities, starting with the idea that for each activity there is an optimal level of arousal.

TABLE 10–3 Coincidences in the development of competence and emotion

Age	The Development of Competence	The Development of Emotion
birth	few organized activities passive reactivity to events	much distressed arousal no pleasant emotions
3 months	more organized activities beginnings of active initiative	diminished distress clear pleasant emotions appear
18 months	onset of symbolic functioning	peak of temper outbursts
6 years	independent functioning in familiar environments	emotional outbursts less common

Emotional behaviors such as happy and angry facial expressions emerge during the first year. The basic emotions take form early. Further developments mostly involve elaboration, as when the acquisition of language makes more complex expressions of anger or happiness possible.

Cognitive development paces the development of emotional understanding. The child's level of understanding influences how emotional stimuli are interpreted. For example, a baby is more likely to react emotionally to the sensorimotor aspects of stimuli, as in becoming frightened at a loud sound, while an older child more often reacts emotionally to the symbolic meaning of stimuli, as in responding to the meaning of a word.

At any age emotionally important stimuli are those that command attention, interrupt ongoing activity, and change arousal level. Stimuli can acquire this power through three contrasting paths: biological preparedness, associative learning, and nonassociative learning.

Emotional episodes are complicated because they involve the interaction of several ingredients: the ongoing activity that is interrupted when the episode begins and the varied aspects of the emotional reaction itself.

Cognition is central in emotional episodes because it influences what kind of emotion is experienced. The same interruptive stimulus can produce varied emotions depending on how the child interprets it. A key question is whether the child thinks that he or she can master the situation. When children think that they can cope with an arousing situation, typically we observe positive emotional reactions. When they think that they can't, the reactions are negative. Thus, successful efforts to help children deal with failure, frustration, and fear often have involved the development of a coping approach.

CHAPTER 11

Motivation:
Direction in Activity

It's a sunny July morning. Virginia sits on the lawn reading a Nancy Drew mystery book. Jeannie rides up the drive on her bicycle. Virginia stops reading, gets on her own bike, and joins Jeannie. They talk as they ride off. When they get to Carrie's house, they get off their bikes. They join Carrie in playing with her new puppy.

Why did Virginia exhibit this sequence of activities rather than some other one? She might have continued reading, fallen asleep, gone in to watch TV, mowed the lawn, jumped rope with Jeannie, walked to Carrie's, ridden past Carrie's house without stopping, shouted insults at Carrie, and so on. A tremendous range of actions was within Virginia's capacities. Only one sequence of behaviors actually took place. The contrast between the many might have beens and the single actuality sets the basic problem for this chapter.

THE CENTRAL PROBLEM

Why Virginia did *that* is the central problem of motivation. I will consider ways of thinking about it and some answers.

The selection-direction question

Virginia had to do *something*. Children are always active. Looking and thinking go on when arms and legs are still. The brain keeps working during sleep; so *inactivity* and *doing nothing* are misleading terms. They make us wonder why children become active, but that's the wrong question. The question of motivation is really the question of selection, or direction (Hebb, 1955). Our real task is to explain which action comes out at a particular time, why the direction of a child's behavior shifts from one goal (such as reading) to another (such as bike riding).

Two interacting sources of direction

We answer the question of selection, or motivation, by looking at factors both in the child and in the situation. Virginia's reading reflected several facts about Virginia: her *ability* (she was skilled in reading), her *interests* (she liked reading well enough to do it without pressure from others), her *level of arousal* (she was in the right state—calm and alert, not too sleepy or excited), and her current *intention* (she wanted to finish the book). But factors in the situation also made a difference. A book was present; otherwise she would not have read at all. When situational factors shifted, so did her actions. Reading was the behavior Virginia selected when there was a book and no friends were present. When a friend turned up, she put reading aside and her behavior moved in other directions.

At all times the particular actions a child performs depend on the complex interaction of internal and external factors. In the episode involving Virginia, factors in her remained relatively constant; so shifts in activity depended largely on situational factors. At other times—for example, in emotional episodes (Chapter 10)—shifts in activity depend more on internal changes. Arousal level can change quickly and thus produce rapid changes in behavior. Abilities and interests change more slowly and relate to more gradual shifts in what a child does.

Goal direction

The concept of goal direction is a good starting point in analyzing motivation. We assume there is a direction in any activity we observe. Then we try to make sense out of the behavior in terms of possible reference points, or goals (Bindra, 1959).

There are two main alternatives in trying to figure out where a child is headed. For example, when Lynn gets out of her seat and starts to walk across the room, we can either ask her where she is headed or watch her behavior and try to figure out her goal from it. A verbal statement of a goal or intention, such as "I want to sharpen my pencil," or a series of actions with a clear focus, as in walking to the pencil sharpener, sharpening a pencil, walking back, and sitting down, can tell us what goal directs the behavior. The first approach emphasizes *cognitions*, what children know and say about their own behavior. The second is *behavioral;* we infer direction from the overall pattern of actions.

We get a somewhat different picture of a child's goals depending on whether we define them cognitively or behaviorally because the two do not entirely coincide. The approach taken in practice depends on your own goal and on your theoretical biases.

Because psychologists' aim in studying motivation is to predict which actions actually are selected, we all are interested in behavior and the observable events that influence it, regardless of our theoretical orientation. As a result experiments on reinforcement processes (Chapter 5) have produced findings of general interest.

THE NATURE OF CHILDREN'S GOALS

What kinds of goals direct children's actions? Studies of reinforcement help answer the question because by definition a positive reinforcer is something for which a child will work. The finding that praise from a peer is a reinforcer for Stuart tells us that some of Stuart's behavior is directed toward the goal of getting praise. More generally, evidence on the nature of reinforcers tells us about the nature of goals.

Reinforcers

Three important findings about reinforcers have influenced the way we think about motivation: variety, satiation, and relativity. First consider those findings; then you will be ready to appreciate a useful theoretical perspective.

Variety

Just about anything can work as a reinforcer. The list of reinforcers for children is long and varied. You can get children to work for tangible rewards, such as candy, pennies, or plastic trinkets. Children also are motivated by smiles, praise, and attention. They will work for the opportunity to play with toys, solve puzzles, or run. Most likely any consequence that can catch children's attention can direct their activity to some extent.

Satiation

Most reinforcers lose reinforcing power if presented repeatedly. Candy becomes less powerful when the child has just eaten five pieces. A new toy gradually becomes less interesting as it becomes more familiar. Praise, too, becomes less rewarding when you have just had a lot of it (Gewirtz, 1967).

A practical implication of satiation is evident in systems designed to manipulate children's actions over long periods of time. Psychologists usually turn to systems that give the child a chance to work for varied reinforcers rather than depending on any one to stay powerful. For example, token systems in which the child earns points, stamps, or money that can be exchanged for a variety of payoffs are often used. Or the child can work for free time that can be used in any of a number of ways.

Relativity

David Premack (1962) showed that the reinforcer relationship is relative and reversible. Rats will eat in order to run as well as run in order to eat. Under some conditions first-graders will eat in order to get an opportunity to use a pinball machine. Under others they work the machine in order to earn candy.

Premack explained these findings by emphasizing the *spontaneous rates of activities.* If when left alone individuals perform activity A at a high rate and activity B at a low rate, then Premack predicts that activity A can be used to reinforce activity B. This has become known as the Premack principle. For example, if Jack spends lots of his free time reading and little playing baseball, Premack predicts that you can get Jack to play baseball in order to earn a chance to read. If Jill plays baseball frequently and rarely reads, Premack predicts that you can get Jill to read in order to get a chance to play baseball. If the spontaneous rates of the two activities change over time for an individual, so will the reinforcer relationship.

Observation of what children do in their free time shows you what will reinforce them. The idea has been used in controlling children's behavior through reinforcement (Chapter 5). It also is familiar to many parents: "Drink your milk. Then you can go out and play."

The Premack principle raises basic problems for anyone who expects a list of fundamental drives or primary reinforcers, for Premack emphasizes activities such as drinking and running rather than external stimuli such as food and praise. His work implies that reinforcers can be as varied as actions. Because such activities as jumping and eating vary in frequency from time to time, he predicts that at times A can reinforce B but at other times B can reinforce A. He's right, but the Premack principle challenges conventional ideas.

The problem of explaining why reinforcers work is much tougher than that of describing how they work. But if we are to understand children's motivation, we must get past the circular idea that a reinforcer is what rein- forces. Here is an approach that seems to fit the facts better than traditional ones.

Two kinds of motivational goals

A useful first step is to assume that there are at least two contrasting sets of basic goals, or motives. If both these categories are seen as fundamental and as resting on biological preparedness, the evidence fits together better (White, 1959).

TABLE 11-1 Two contrasting kinds of motivation

	Traditional Drives	Interaction Motives
Common Labels	hunger, thirst, fear, pain, biological drives	curiosity, exploration play, competence motivation, intrinsic motivation
Basic to Maintaining	stable *inside* environment	interaction between child and *outside* environment
Common Goal-directed Activities	*reduce* arousal level	*increase* or *maintain* arousal level
	reduce amount of stimulation	*increase* or *maintain* amount of stimulation
Universal Early Manifestations	eating, drinking, withdrawing from pain, struggling for air	orienting toward stimulus patterns, manipulating objects, exercising schemas
Typical Working Characteristics	relate to *small* percentage of goal-directed sequences	relate to *large* percentage of goal-directed sequences
	intense and demanding quality when highly aroused	rarely intense or demanding

The first category can be called the traditional drives. Goal-seeking tend- encies such as hunger, thirst, and pain and the associated goals such as candy, milk, and escape are universal and obviously related to the child's biological makeup.

The second category looks just as universal and just as clearly tied to heredity and evolution. It includes the tendencies termed curiosity, exploration, play, assimilation, and so on. Activities such as spontaneously looking at novel patterns and exercising capacities just for the fun of it can be thought of as reflecting *interaction motives,* basic biases toward using capacities to deal with the world. Comparative studies suggest that these interaction motives evolved along with the complex brains and the importance of learning that are so distinctively human. Curiosity looks as basic to human and monkey nature as hunger, even though it is not as prominent in frogs and fish.

Table 11–1 illustrates that it is useful to think of these two motivational categories as distinct because they work so differently. Such drives as hunger, pain, and oxygen seeking are well thought of as emergency systems. Curiosity and exploration are less dramatic but more common in everyday activities (White, 1959). In the traditional drives we commonly see a highly aroused child seeking such goals as food or pain reduction, which lower the arousal level and relieve inside or outside stimulation.

The common use of starvation and electric shock as motivators in the animal laboratory supports a drive-reduction or arousal-reduction picture of motivation. But in normal life children spend much of their time in actions that increase the stimulation level and maintain or increase the arousal level. Looking at a face, watching television, inspecting a new toy, jumping rope, pretending, or playing tennis produce stimulation rather than reduce it. They keep arousal up or elevate it.

The traditional drives inspired early formulations of reinforcement. The starving rat working for food and the frightened dog trying to get away from intense electric shock provided models for general principles. When these ideas were tested against observations of animals and children in more normal motivational situations, the old concepts seemed inadequate. It is a nonstarving rat with free access to food who is likely to eat in order to get a chance to run in an activity wheel. A monkey in a cage without an electrified floor is likely to pull a lever just to look at interesting sights or work a mechanical puzzle for the fun of it. Similarly, the everyday child is likely to work for any novel change in the environment but is soon sated if pressing a button keeps producing the same old result. The facts that contradict old ideas often result from observations made when no emergency drives are operating (White, 1959).

By recognizing that fear and hunger are important motivational forces, but not the kind basic to most of the child's goal-directed activity, we can go further.

A global hypothesis about goals

It would be good if the contrasting kinds of motivation could be brought together in a common framework. Several theorists have tried to do it (Deci, 1975). Here is an important example of this kind of integrative thinking, a hypothesis about what is common to all goal-directed activity.

Children always seek an "optimal" level of arousal, normally an intermediate one. This idea applies to both groups of motives. When excitement is high, children tend to select actions that bring it down. Two-year-olds in a frightening situation are likely to cling to a parent, burying their face in the parent's lap if arousal is extreme. This behavior cuts out the cues from the upsetting situation and brings arousal down. Six-year-olds show a more sophisticated version of the same pattern when they hold their hands over their eyes or walk out of the room when the scary TV show reaches its climax. In these examples the common goal is to bring arousal down from high to medium. In more usual sequences children seek to raise low arousal or maintain medium levels. Children sitting in a boring classroom scan the scene for something interesting, create diversions by drawing pictures, making faces at their neighbors, and perfecting new skills in using their fingers. These diverse activities seem to have the common goal of increasing or maintaining arousal. (Perhaps you have used similar methods in staying awake during boring college classes.) As illustrated in Figure 11–1, both the drive-reducing movement away from arousing stimulation and the interaction motives are hypothesized to have the same target, or goal, of optimal arousal.

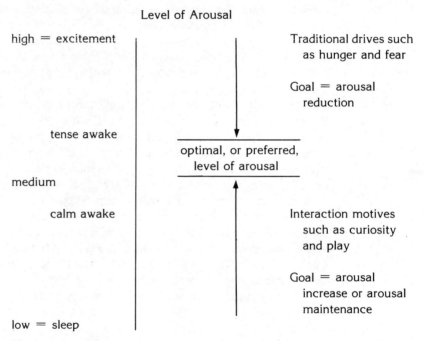

Figure 11–1 Optimal level of arousal as the hypothesized common goal of all motivational systems

Donald Fiske and Salvadore Maddi (1961) hypothesize that the preferred, or optimal, arousal level fluctuates with the daily sleep-wakefulness cycle (Chapter 10). Different degrees of excitement are sought, depending on where the child's baseline is at the time. When normally wide awake, say in the middle of the morning, a child is likely to favor such activities as climbing on a jungle gym, which involves some excitement and vigorous action. Near

Children prefer calming activities such as reading or listening to stories near bedtime when their arousal level is low.

bedtime, when arousal typically is lower, the same child would be expected to prefer calmer activities, such as reading and listening to stories.

We still don't have enough good evidence to know how useful these theories will be, for the idea of optimal arousal makes it easy to explain almost anything a child does after it happens. What we lack is a variety of careful studies in which what children do is predicted from measures of arousal.

The most encouraging evidence comes from a series of experiments on young chimpanzees by William Mason (1965). His studies are based on an unusual and valuable test situation. It gives young chimpanzees a clear choice between social interaction leading to arousal increase and social contact producing arousal decrease. Two research assistants dressed in contrasting costumes. Each played a different social role. They sat within squares marked on the floor that were placed so that a chimp could interact with only one of them at a time. In picking assistant A or assistant B the chimp selected one of two contrasting goals.

Whenever a chimp entered assistant A's square, A would play with it, vigorously—tickling, pushing, and pulling. Both physiological measures, such as heart-rate counts, and behavioral observations indicated that this playful interaction with assistant A increased arousal.

Assistant B wore a different colored mask and costume and interacted in a different way whenever a chimp entered his space. B responded to an approach by holding the chimp in a way that allowed clinging and cuddling. B's role was to produce a calming, or arousal-reducing, impact.

Each chimp was given a few sample sessions with each assistant alone so it could learn what to expect from A and B before encountering them together. In later sessions the chimps were given a simultaneous choice. The choices made it possible to measure the relative strength of arousal seeking and arousal reduction.

The experiments focused mostly on conditions that raised arousal. For example, amphetamine ("speed") was used to elevate arousal. Following a dose of amphetamine, the chimps showed a stronger tendency to seek assistant B and clinging. After exposure to loud noises the chimps showed a similar increase in clinging. Testing the chimps in different rooms showed that novelty increases arousal. In a novel room there was more clinging than when testing took place in a familiar room. With repeated testing in a novel room there was a shift. The initially stronger tendency to cling gave way to more and more playing as familiarity increased.

These experiments show that theories of optimal arousal can yield testable predictions. They further support the idea that children might act with the goal of keeping arousal in a middle range. As will be seen, they also fit an important development hypothesis.

Developmental trends in expected environments

Now we'll examine a hypothesis about contrasting developmental curves for the two motivational systems. Then we'll consider two processes common to different forms of motivation.

Mason's developmental picture

William Mason (1970) hypothesized that arousal-reducing actions and arousal-increasing ones follow contrasting age curves when the baby develops in a normal environment. As shown in Figure 11–2, he sees arousal reduction as predominant right after birth. But as the infant grows up, such arousal-reducing behaviors as clinging and cuddling become less and less prominent. Actions such as exploration and play, which increase arousal, are thought to follow an opposite trend. They are rare right after birth, becoming more common as the infant grows up. The two types of action reverse in prominence.

Mason based his ideas mostly on observations of chimpanzees and monkeys. For example, in his choice test the preference for keeper A and play becomes stronger as chimps grow up. But Mason thinks that the pattern applies to all primates, including humans. In Figure 11–2, I have taken his generalized picture of primate development and added ages that seem appropriate for normal children.

Child psychologists have paid little attention to Mason's theory, but Paul Weisberg conducted a direct test (1975). He set up a similar choice situation between a "tickler" and a "cuddler" and studied how children between 3 and

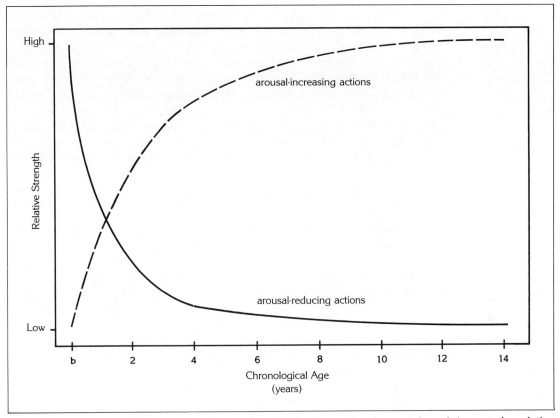

Figure 11–2 William Mason's hypothesized developmental trends in arousal-regulating activities (*From Mason, W. A. "Motivational Factors in Psychosocial Development." In W. J. Arnold and N. M. Page, eds., 1970 NEBRASKA SYMPOSIUM ON MOTIVATION. Copyright © 1971 by the University of Nebraska Press.*)

7 years responded when college students of both sexes played the two roles. The age trend supported Mason: play with the cuddler declined with age and the choice of the tickler rose. Both girls and boys showed the same trend (which was particularly clear when the experimenter combination included a college woman playing "cuddler" and a college man playing "tickler"). Weisberg pointed out that the findings also were consistent with John Bowlby's (1969) ideas about shifts in attachment behaviors (see Chapter 12).

Both this one direct test and other facts suggest that Mason's theory deserves more attention. Consider two of its major features: the infancy crossover and later developments.

Infancy crossover.   Mason's theory suggests that the most dramatic feature of motivational development is the switch in importance of the two main motivational systems during infancy. There are several lines of research on human babies that support this idea and suggest age 3 or 4 months as the crossover point.

J. McV. Hunt (1963) has expanded on some of Piaget's ideas to argue for a motivation shift early in the first year. Hunt emphasizes a shift from earlier preferences for the familiar to later ones for the novel. This idea has been supported (Chapter 6). Researchers at the University of Colorado have argued that the onset of the social smile at 3 months is accompanied by broad changes, including a big increase in stimulus-maintaining and stimulus-seeking activity (Emde et al., 1976). A similar trend could be involved in physiological response patterns (Graham & Jackson, 1970). Newborns mostly show a defensive reflex that tends to shut out stimulation. Babies a few months older are more likely to react to the same stimulation with the orienting reflex that involves taking it in.

Later developments.   Mason's approach also provides a fresh and useful way of thinking about later developments. His theory relates motivational and social development. He argues that babies' attachments to their parents normally are based on the arousal-reduction system. When arousal gets high, such actions as crying, clinging, and cuddling normally are directed at parents. In contrast, he thinks that attachment to peers is tied to the arousal-increase system. Interaction with peers and attachment to them is hypothesized as part of a broader set of interaction motives that lead to exploration and play.

The idea that peer attachments come out of a different motivational system than parental ones is new, but the available evidence fits (Chapter 12). Now consider two processes that are important features of all motivational development: channeling and fusion.

Channeling

Hunger, fear, and curiosity all reflect universal biases built into children before birth. But specific goals, such as a taste for hamburgers or a search for knowledge of dinosaurs, develop as a result of the child's interactions with the world after birth.

When Laura says "Hamburger, please!" her request reflects particular social learning, along with a universal biological drive for food. Similarly, when Bill buys an electronic game, his goal rests on both specific cultural conditioning and a universal tendency to play. Both the traditional drives and the interaction motives start from innate tendencies, but each motive system becomes socialized as the child grows up.

Channeling is a handy term for the process whereby universal drives such as hunger narrow down to an interest in only certain goals, such as hamburgers. Other examples of broad motivational tendencies becoming narrow preferences for certain goals are curiosity or novelty seeking becoming a preference for watching TV shows that are similar to past ones, but are not reruns; manipulation or control seeking becoming a preference for playing tennis with moderately skilled partners; and distress reduction through familiarity becoming a preference for one's own parents when one is upset.

The reality of channeling becomes clear as soon as you try to get older children (or adults) to change their eating patterns. The child raised on beef usually is not happy about switching to octopus. The child used to eating octopus may find the taste of beef unpleasant, the thought of eating cow meat revolting. Out of the dozens of foods eaten and enjoyed by children around the world, each child soon comes to prefer those from a narrow range, often disliking and rejecting other foods.

We know most about channeling with respect to social goals (see Chapter 12). The human baby soon develops a preference for certain individuals. A broad interest in social stimuli turns into the much narrower goal of being near particular people. In each normal baby the original, broad, universal motives become channeled into a few relationships.

Several theorists (Deci, 1975; Murphy, 1947; White, 1960) have argued that we should look at motives such as exploration and environmental manipulation in terms of such concepts as channeling.

All babies become interested in novelty. At first, curiosity in different children is similar enough so that certain events have universal appeal. Jingling keys, eyeglasses, and red blocks command attention and promote inspection around the world, but curiosity takes children down varied paths. Even among children with similar backgrounds we find a specialization of interests by elementary school. A horse, a subway train, and a new piano are not investigated with equal enthusiasm. Each child usually develops a somewhat narrower range of investigation. Books on horses, pictures of horses, toy horses, and real horses become a dominating interest for some. Others remain cool about horses but avidly seek knowledge about trains or baseball. With information, as with food and people, tastes come to narrow and to differ.

All children seem to get pleasure from using their skills and manipulating the world around them. Pleasure in being a cause and controlling the world looks like the goal of diverse actions. However, as with other motives, what has been called competence motivation becomes specialized. Just about all children gleefully exercise early perceptual-motor accomplishments, such as building a tower and knocking it over. But later singing, conversing, playing baseball, reading, and fixing motors take on different values for different children. A great variety of specific goals seemingly develops out of the same general tendencies. Goals as varied as a need for academic achievement, bossing other children around, and making pretty dresses can derive from similar roots.

No child lives long enough to pursue everything that might interest or attract him or her. Even the avid dog lover lacks the time to pat every pup and to read every book ever written about dogs. Appetites develop that are more finite and realistic than they might be.

Fusion

The narrow set of goals that frequently directs the child's actions usually ties in with varied motive systems. Leslie drinks her milk and thus pleases her mother and also earns a chance to play while reducing her thirst. The same goal, milk drinking, ties in with approval seeking, play, and thirst. Similarly, Joe's skill in hitting a ball with a tennis racket is a pleasing exercise of perceptual-motor competence, a source of status with his parents, and a way of

Applications box 11-1 Food preferences

How can children be helped to develop preferences for foods that are good for them? Until recently we had to rely on common sense; now we have studies of preschoolers with important practical implications. Most of them were conducted by Leann Lipps Birch and her associates at the University of Illinois.

Familiarity and sweetness seem to be important general factors in young children's preferences, with familiarity more important for children under 4 years of age and sweetness more important after (Birch, 1980). But other factors also can make a big difference.

The social-emotional context in which the children meet the food makes a difference over and above familiarity (Birch, Zimmerman, & Hind, 1980). For example, when snack foods such as raw carrots or vanilla wafers were used as rewards, preschoolers' preference for them increased. Similarly, when snacks were paired with attention from adults (Birch et al., 1980) or presented daily in a positive manner ("Hi George, have some cashews") (Birch, 1981), they become more attractive. In contrast, presenting snacks in a nonsocial context or simply having them present at snack time did not influence preference (Birch et al., 1980).

Modeling also helps. In one experiment target children were seated with three or four peers whose preference between two vegetables was opposite to their own. For three days in a row the vegetable pairs were presented at lunch. Each child was asked to pick which vegetable he or she wanted, with the target child picking last. The target children shifted and started picking their less-preferred vegetable. They not only picked it more but ate it more. In a classic study by Karl Duncker (1938) children heard stories about a hero with marked food preferences. The children's preferences for these foods went up. More recently, Harper and Sanders (1975a) found that adults were more successful in getting children to taste unfamiliar foods when they (the adults) tasted them than when they simply offered the foods. Mothers were more potent than friendly adult visitors in influencing tasting. But the visitors' example had an influence even when they were alone with the children.

There was an age trend in most of the modeling studies: younger children were easier to influence than older. Even a difference between age 3 and age 4 was found.

Instrumental use of a food can make it less attractive, in line with the evidence on undermining intrinsic motivation in other situations (Chapter 5). Children were asked to drink a fruit juice of average attractiveness to them in order to gain access to an activity—for example, "If you drink your orange juice, you can ride on the tricycle" (Birch & Birch, 1981). This instrumental treatment of a juice lowered its preference value.

> The evidence has striking implications. The general moral is to start early in introducing nutritious foods in a positive, social context, using important adult models to lead the way when possible. But other points also deserve emphasis.
>
> Parents in the United States commonly use candy and other sweets as rewards. The research indicates that this makes sweets more attractive, an unhappy outcome because expert opinion is that our children are eating twice as much sugar as they should (Birch et al., 1980). Similarly, the familiar line, "Eat your vegetables and then you can go out and play" reveals an instrumental use of nutritious food that apparently lowers children's preference for it. Seemingly, we would do better for children if we moved beyond common sense.

avoiding peer ridicule. Commonly, diverse motive systems are fused in the pursuit of everyday goals (see Figure 11–3).

The fusion process starts early. Eating and sociability go together from birth on. Having a snack is not a simple matter of satisfying hunger for the 4-year-old in nursery school or for a teenager at a favorite hamburger stand. The infant practices walking just for the fun of it, but walking also earns praise and gets the child to interesting places and away from scary noises. Reading good stories is fun in itself, but most people see skill in reading as a sign of status. Older children read; younger children don't. By the time the child gets to school, varied motives, intrinsic and extrinsic, have come together.

Fusion looks inevitable. Anything children do frequently is likely to become linked to varied motives. A skill first practiced for its own sake becomes more and more likely to win praise from others. Soon the social response becomes part of the goal. A symbol that is important to the people who are important to children is likely to become more important to the children. They might start out working for good grades, money, or good manners to please parents or teachers. But with success they come to value the tokens for themselves. Every time children seek a goal or reach one there is a new

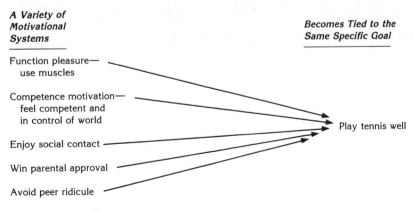

Figure 11–3 Fusion

opportunity for that goal to become linked to other motive systems. The more motives fuse together around a goal, the more likely that goal is to direct future activity. A circular process operates as the goals that fuse varied motives become preferred and more prominent.

Notice that once again the notions of differentiation and hierarchic integration appear to be useful in looking at development. In channeling, a differentiation process operates as a variety of goals relevant to a motivational system are distinguished and some come to be preferred. In fusion we see how originally separate motives, such as praise from others and the intrinsic pleasure of an activity, come to be linked in the pursuit of one goal.

A skill such as rowing a boat may be practiced for its own sake at the beginning, but it soon comes to be linked to other motives as fusion of diverse motive systems takes place.

The unexpected

Under normal conditions the developing child soon passes out of an early period in which motivational crises are common. Emergency motives such as hunger and pain fade into the background. Distress and arousal reduction remain real as motivators, but they operate rarely. For the typical child everyday activity and development tie much more closely to the interaction motives.

What about development under unusual, or unexpected, conditions? What happens when the emergencies remain prominent, when hunger or anxiety stay in the foreground as the child grows up? What happens when the interaction motives do not find support, when the environment is so restricted that curiosity and competence motives are not fed novelty and challenge in normal doses? Now we will consider these different versions of the unexpected.

Malnutrition

Malnutrition rarely is considered in relation to children's motivation, probably because hunger is of little importance in the lives of the children who have been studied most. But malnutrition is the norm for millions; we have to understand chronic hunger to understand children around the world.

In descriptions of malnourished children one word turns up again and again: *apathy*. Food deprivation probably increases interaction with the world at first. But when hunger continues day after day, decreased activity and less interaction result. When children remain hungry, their curiosity, exploration, play, and social interaction diminish (Levitsky, 1979).

Barry Lester (1975) used a heart-rate habituation technique (Chapter 5) to study this hypothesis about apathy. Malnourished babies did not show the characteristic orienting and habituation of normal controls. They neither responded strongly to the novel stimulus when it was first presented (orienting reflex) nor showed the typical decline in response when the stimulus was presented repeatedly (habituation). Lester's experiments documented a major deficit in attention as an apparent outgrowth of malnutrition.

When you think about the role of attention in both motivational and cognitive development, you can see the importance of Lester's findings. How can a baby who does not "tune in" on the environment learn from it? How can more sophisticated ways of dealing with information and more advanced forms of curiosity grow when the more basic assimilatory actions are not exercised?

Chronic anxiety

Anxiety can be an important motive. The realization that children's actions can have the goal of escaping or avoiding the cues that trigger anxiety has given us insights into many puzzling actions. Tom, who won't speak when spoken to, Sally, who tries to stay so super-neat and super-clean that she never has much fun, and Clara, who usually gives up without trying, each may be reducing anxiety through behavior sequences that usually backfire. When we see children repeating actions that seemingly don't work to produce obvious reinforcement, we consider the possibility that anxiety reduction is the goal (Dollard & Miller, 1950).

Some special aspects of anxiety as motivation make it possible for this emergency motive to become a big part of a child's daily life. Anxiety is easy to condition to neutral cues, through both direct conditioning and symbolic channels (Bandura, 1969a). The child who is beaten up once in the cloakroom can acquire a conditional response involving sweaty palms and a pounding heart at the sight of the room. The child who hears a teacher loudly threaten another child with being left behind can acquire a reaction including a dry mouth, tight throat, and lump in the stomach at the thought of failing a test.

Actions that get children away from anxiety-provoking stimuli are immediately reinforced by a decrease in arousal, regardless of what happens later. By not wearing a coat and not walking into the cloakroom, a child can avoid anxiety. By complaining of feeling sick, a child can stay home the day of a spelling test. Anxiety can be reduced or avoided in just about any environment.

Potentially, then, much of a child's behavior can come under the direction of anxiety reduction. When important settings, such as home or school, are frequent sites of punishing and frightening events, many cues associated with them can take on the power to raise anxiety. Unrealistic fear based on one or a few unpleasant events is likely to extinguish when the child repeatedly deals with the cues that produce it. But when realistic anxieties about what can happen at home, at school, or with peers are repeatedly strengthened, the situation is different. For some children reducing and avoiding anxiety is a goal that dominates much of every day.

Anxiety interferes with the interaction motives (White, 1959). The scared child, like the malnourished one, commonly shows less curiosity and seems less involved with skills mastery and with social interaction for its own sake. With even mild fear we see less of the relaxed and playful approach to life that is so common under normal conditions.

But, in contrast to starvation, chronic anxiety probably doesn't always impair development. In school an anxious child can find varied ways of relieving or avoiding anxiety: daydreaming or avoiding schoolwork by talking, doodling, working hard, and seeking social status. Similarly, anxiety at home or with peers can foster both appropriate and inappropriate actions. With excess anxiety developmental outcomes are varied.

Restricted environments

Animal experiments suggest that the normal development of the interaction motives depends on the usual opportunities for exploration and play. Thus, Mason (1970) does not think of the typical rise in prominence of these motives as entirely maturational. Instead, he thinks that it depends on a steady diet of appropriate experience.

Evidence on children growing up in environments such as overcrowded orphanages with limited opportunities for interaction with the world fits in with Mason's view. Hunt (1979) concluded that the data support the idea that experience in the first three years after birth is particularly important for the normal development of curiosity and initiative. In other words apathy apparently can result from a diet deficient in food for the eyes and hands as well as from one lacking in food for the stomach.

Research and thinking about the impact of limited environments has led several theorists to conclude that early experience in successfully controlling the world is crucial to the development of an active (and successful) problem-solving approach (Lewis & Goldberg, 1969; Watson, 1966; White, 1959). The idea is that only if trying is rewarded is it likely to develop, flourish, and foster new learning. Putting it negatively, a child whose early efforts to control the world are unsuccessful is likely to develop a feeling of helplessness and a passive approach to new learning situations (Seligman, 1975). A number of studies support this line of thinking and point to expectancies of successful outcomes as general outcomes of specific experiences in manipulating the world (Finkelstein & Ramey, 1977).

SUMMARY

"Why did she do that?" The question takes us to the problem of direction, or selection, because activity must be taken for granted. Actions always take place in a specific environment; so we have to look at factors in the child and in the environment. The concept of goal direction puts the focus on the child in relation to the environment.

Two main classes of goals direct children's actions: the traditional drives (such as hunger and fear) and the interaction motives (as in curiosity and play). Both seem rooted in biology. They work in contrasting ways, with the traditional drives looking more like emergency systems and the interaction motives seeming less dramatic but more basic to everyday life.

An integrating hypothesis is that both categories of motivation operate so as to take the child to a more optimal, intermediate arousal level, with the particular optimal level varying with the daily sleep-awake cycle.

There is support for Mason's developmental picture, with the traditional drives and arousal-reducing activities being more common at first and becoming less prominent and the interaction motives and arousal-increasing and -maintaining activities being rare at birth and growing in importance.

Both groups of motives show channeling, a tendency for broad tendencies to narrow down to particular goals, and fusion, a tendency for the same acts and objects to bring together varied motives.

Consideration of development in unexpected situations highlighted the fact that motivational development depends both on inborn tendencies and on the environment. When unexpected conditions prevail, as in chronic malnutrition, chronic anxiety, and restricted environments, we see unusual development, particularly for the interaction motives.

CHAPTER 12

Social Attachments
and Attitudes

Life is lived with people. Children grow up in a social world. Separation becomes possible at birth, but actual separations are brief. Awake children rarely are alone. When alone, they create social situations: they play with pretend people, read about people, and watch them on television. Social interaction is almost continuous.

Three sides of social development can be distinguished: affective (feelings), cognitive (understanding), and behavioral (actions). Each is important and relates to the others and to ideas I've presented earlier. I present the affective side of social development in this chapter. The next chapter focuses on social understandings and social behavior and relates them to the affective domain.

In looking at affective aspects of social development, I'll concentrate on love and liking for others, or attachment. First I'll examine the development of attachments; then I'll discuss the question of attitudes and how they relate to attachments.

SOCIAL ATTACHMENTS

Social attachment helps us understand why social development usually goes so well. Social living involves enormous demands for social learning. But when a child loves people, the learning comes "naturally."

A good hypothesis is that the early development of affection for other people makes successful social development almost inevitable. Children's loves cement them to their group. Because they are emotionally involved, they learn easily what they must in order to take their place in society.

New orientations to attachment

Our picture of attachment has changed since 1960. The shift resulted both from studies of other animals and from new evidence on human babies.

Animal research

Animal studies contradicted old assumptions. Freud and traditional learning theorists had assumed that hunger and similar drives were the basis of the attachment bond. A secondary reinforcement, or cupboard love, theory predominated (Bowlby, 1969). It rested on the idea that because mother always was there when food came and hunger was relieved, she became associated with the positive qualities of food (Mussen & Conger, 1963). Experiments on monkeys and other animals indicated that hunger was not the primary factor promoting attachments in other animals and seemed to have little or nothing to do with the process (Harlow, 1958; Sluckin, 1973).

A more positive result of animal research was a tremendous growth of knowledge (Alloway, Pliner, & Krames, 1977; Scott, 1968; Sluckin, 1973). Along with specific findings came a clearer overview. We see parallels in how baby animals of varied kinds relate to fellow species members. We have learned that even similar species, such as two different kinds of monkeys, can show important contrasts. We have discovered that early research findings often are misinterpreted.

The same action or stimulus frequently varies in importance in different species (Box 12-1). For example, in rhesus monkeys clinging and contact comfort seem to play an important role in the attachment process. A rhesus reared away from its mother usually develops a strong attachment to its blanket or to a surrogate mother of terry cloth if one is provided (Harlow, 1958). Zoo keepers have noted a similar tendency in chimpanzees and orangutans (Lang, 1963). But when the first gorilla baby (Goma) was raised successfully in a Swiss zoo, the keepers were surprised to find little tendency to cling (Lang, 1963). Apparently, clinging and contact comfort are not equally important for all primates.

Similarities between species are easier to find when you look at behaviors that seem to perform similar functions. For example, tail wagging in puppies and smiling in human infants seem similar in what they do for the baby and in how they fit in with the total picture. Both seem to communicate pleasure and encourage interaction from fellow species members. Neither behavior is present at birth. Both appear when the development of attachment to particular individuals seems to be beginning. Both are indiscriminate at first and later link more closely to special loved ones (Scott, 1968).

A look back at interpretations of animal research reveals a common tendency to misinterpret them (Box 12-1). An early example of this pattern involves research on the impact of handling baby rats and mice. Studies seemingly indicate that babies reared in isolation did better if they were briefly handled each day. At first this was hailed as a demonstration of the importance of love, but later studies indicated that periods of electric shock or being placed in a refrigerator produce the same benefits as handling. Soon it became clear that stimulation, not handling, had been the crucial factor in the first experiment (Levine, 1962).

Parallel trends emerge from studies of baby rhesus monkeys reared in isolation. Rhesus monkeys who grew up alone developed unusual behaviors: repeated rocking, excessive fearfulness, and inadequate social behavior (Mason, 1968). Early explanations often emphasized the lack of mothering, but further research suggested that here again nonsocial factors were important. William Mason (1968) showed that baby monkeys separated from their mothers and reared with moving robots (swinging devices that moved irregularly about the cage and could be ridden) did not develop stereotyped rocking. Those reared with stationary robots did. Similarly, he and others have shown that signs of panic and freezing in isolation-reared monkeys relate to overall level of stimulation during isolation rather than to mother absence.

Animal research does show that social experience has specific importance. Konrad Lorenz's (1937) work on imprinting in birds showed that a little early social experience had a long-term impact under normal conditions. Baby geese who start following mother goose in the first days of life continue to socialize with geese for the rest of their lives. Baby geese who instead start by following Lorenz, or another person, remain attached to people.

Early social experience plays an important role in influencing what happens later, but early attachments can be reversed. In both cases of geese the baby continues in a social environment that makes it easy to continue along the original path. In more recent experiments attached animals have been forced to live away from their original "love" and provided with potential substitutes.

The experiments that force contact with unfamiliar animals show that attachment formation is flexible (Cairns, 1977). The immediate negative reactions soon pass. Given an opportunity to form a new relationship with an initially upsetting stranger, animals usually do so. For example, Mason and Kenny (1974) raised baby monkeys in isolation and then penned them up with tame dogs. Despite initial fearful behavior, five of the eight monkeys approached the dogs within half an hour. All did so within six hours. The monkey babies developed attachment for their dog "mothers" even though the usual period for attachment formation had passed.

Human research

Direct observation of how attachment develops in human babies came recently. Rudolph Schaffer and Peggy Emerson (1964a) did a landmark longitudinal study in Scotland. They repeatedly visited a group of babies in their homes to see how reactions to people changed during the early months. Their results, supported by subsequent research, contradicted many traditional ideas. For example, they found that attachment to mother was neither as universal nor as exclusive as many had assumed. Even though their sample lived in traditional families, only 65% showed exclusive attachment to their mothers when they first formed a specific attachment. The others either simultaneously became attached to mother and others (particularly fathers) or were exclusively attached to someone other than mother (father or grandparent). Within six months after attachment started only 17% of the babies were attached only to their mothers. When Schaffer and Emerson tried to explain differences in the intensity of attachment to mothers, they found that measures related to feeding and toilet training (emphasized by psychoanalytically oriented theorists) contributed nothing to understanding.

Current theories

The new research has resulted in new theoretical models that draw on both animal and human research. Two elements are common to all the important new theories: (1) a picture of the interactions basic to attachment as

Frontiers box 12–1 Second thoughts

A pattern of second thoughts is more common in the area of attachment research than in most. A research study is published. Soon it becomes famous as an illustration of an important theoretical point. But later, after more evidence accumulates, there are second thoughts. The original study no longer is seen as having demonstrated what it was claimed to have shown.

Studies of monkeys reared in social isolation illustrate the trend. The early research used rhesus macaque monkeys, an easily available species. When rhesus were raised in isolation, they typically exhibited a number of unusual behaviors afterwards: (1) self-directed stereotyped behaviors such as rocking and clasping themselves, (2) deficits in positive social behavior when put with other monkeys, and (3) diminished exploration of the environment. The finding was interpreted as showing the importance of early social interaction for normal development. Some saw it as providing a useful model of how abnormal behavior may develop in humans. Dozens of psychology textbooks exposed thousands of students both to the finding and to its supposed implications for human development.

Now the second thoughts are beginning. Gene Sackett and his associates (Sackett, Ruppenthal, Fahrenbruch, & Greenough, 1981) extended the usual experiment. They looked at the impact of isolation on two macaque species closely related to rhesus macaques, as well as studying rhesus. Their basic finding was that isolation influenced different species in contrasting ways. What was thought to be an integrated pattern of outcomes was not. For example, after isolation, pigtailed macaques showed little positive social behavior (like rhesus), but showed little self-directed stereotyped behavior and were highly exploratory (unlike rhesus). Crab-eating macaques subjected to social isolation showed still a third pattern. They exhibited normal, positive social behavior, a moderate amount of self-directed stereotyped behavior, and were highly exploratory.

Genetic background, then, makes a tremendous difference in how much monkeys respond to isolation. The rhesus behavior that had been interpreted as one reaction pattern now seems to be made up of components that vary independently. Because the reaction of rhesus to social isolation is a poor predictor of how even closely related monkeys react to the same conditions, the notion of using the rhesus experiments as a model for human development becomes questionable.

It is not unusual to have our interpretations of pioneering research change as more is learned. It happens in all areas. What seems special about the attachment area is that so many people are so ready to draw sweeping conclusions from such limited evidence, perhaps because the questions here are so important to so many of us. Because they find an interested audience, preliminary results get much wider circulation than is usual. And because so many believe that love is the key to normal development, a study that seems to prove it gets a particularly sympathetic reception.

two-way (or reciprocal or dyadic) and (2) a view of both baby and adult as prepared, or preadapted, for the interaction through evolution (Cairns, 1977).

The new emphasis on two-way interaction is a sharp contrast with older views that highlighted the baby's helplessness and dependency. A change in terminology reflects the shift. Older theories talk about dependency. Modern ones say attachment and picture the baby as active and influencing others as well as needing and responding to them.

Modern ideas about preparedness for attachment fit an evolutionary perspective that sees sociability as an ancient and crucial part of the human heritage (Lancaster, 1975). Rather than picturing the baby as essentially individualistic and becoming social only as a result of social pressure, they make a bias toward the sociability part of basic human nature. Similarly, care-giving responses by adults are seen as resulting in part from built-in tendencies. Attachments are learned particularly easily.

Our list of signs of social preadaptation in the human baby grows steadily. Facelike stimuli are preferred as something to look at from the early weeks (Fantz, 1961). Human voices and speechlike sounds seem particularly interesting to babies and are interpreted through special systems (DeCasper & Fifer, 1980) (Chapter 9). There are signs of synchronized social interaction (Chapter 13) and of social imitation (Chapter 7) from the first days of life. With these built-in tendencies the need to explain attachment as externally, or extrinsically, motivated disappears. Attachment seems to stem from interaction motives (Chapter 11).

A common, though not universal, trend in modern theories is to consider cognitive development in looking at the development of attachment. For example, a goal such as being near a parent is assumed to show itself in new ways as object permanence develops. For a baby with little object permanence a parent in another room is gone. A little later the more sophisticated infant finds the sounds of dishes being washed from another room as reassuring as the sight of the person washing them.

Despite these shared theoretical ideas, we still find important contrasts. The biggest theoretical differences seem to be between *ethological* and *social-learning* theorists (see Table 12–1).

John Bowlby (1969) formulated the ethological position. He kept some important ideas from psychoanalysis and dropped others and replaced them with concepts from animal ethology and elsewhere. As illustrated in Table 12–1, ethological theorists often see attachment as centered on one person (object), as a broader organization of behaviors, and as relatively irreversible.

TABLE 12-1 Two contrasting orientations toward attachment

Ethological Orientation	*Social-learning Orientation*
Common Ideas	
two-way interaction biological preparedness cognitive factors	
Distinctive Roots	
psychoanalytic theory ethological theory (European)	learning theory (United States)
Contrasting Ideas	
attachment to one central figure crucial	attachment can be to one or more objects
attachment a broad organization of diverse behaviors	specific attachment behaviors relatively independent
early attachment irreversible	early attachment reversible
early attachment determines nature of later social-emotional development	early attachment important but no more crucial than later events
infancy a critical period for the development of trust	trusting relations with others usually start in infancy but can start later
early differences in attachment predict later social-emotional development	early differences in attachment predict later social-emotional development only if early variations in environmental conditions continue
Theorists	
John Bowlby Mary Ainsworth Alan Sroufe Robert Emde	Robert Cairns Harriet Rheingold Jacob Gewirtz William Mason Eleanor Maccoby

Often they see attachment to the mother as crucial in determining later social-emotional development because it reflects a crucial fit between the child and the social environment. Accordingly, they emphasize the development of trust as a crucial step in early attachment and think that individual differences in early attachment behavior are important as indicators of the future (Ainsworth, Blehar, Walters, & Wall, 1978; Sroufe, 1979). Research findings supporting some of their specific claims include a demonstration that an overall rating of how securely a baby is attached at 12 months predicts corresponding measures as much as 18 months later (Ainsworth et al., 1978). A support for their emphasis on the development of trust comes from the finding that mothers who respond more quickly to their babies when they cry have babies who cry less at the end of the first year (Bell & Ainsworth, 1972).

The social-learning group sees attachment more as a matter of specific behavioral elements, as more varied with respect to how many objects there may be, and as more reversible. Because they see attachment processes as reversible, social-learning theorists do not emphasize ideas about critical periods, basic trust, or the future implications of early variations in attachment (Cairns, 1977; Gewirtz & Boyd, 1977; Mason & Kenny, 1974; Rheingold & Eckerman, 1975). One finding supporting their specific ideas is that varied indicators of attachment (such as crying in response to separation and smiling at the sight of mother) are not closely related (Cohen, 1974; Masters & Wellman, 1974). Similarly, when Etzel and Gewirtz (1967) looked closely at crying behavior in two babies who acted like tyrants, they found that a reinforcement explanation was powerful. Apparently the babies had become tyrants because crying was rewarded by attention from hospital staff. When crying was ignored and positive reactions, such as smiling, were given attention, the picture changed quickly and dramatically.

It is too early to tell how the theoretical differences should be resolved. Often the two camps emphasize different parts of the story, suggesting that they might be brought together in a broader synthesis. The pattern of findings tends to parallel one pointed out by Kohlberg (1969) in other areas: short-run and close looks at social development often support social-learning concepts; broader and longer-term studies suggest they are less adequate.

The belief that early social experiences have an important and irreversible impact on later social-emotional development has been so strong and so popular that few have questioned it. But questioning has begun. Animal findings suggest that reversibility is the rule in nonhuman species. Clear evidence on human babies is limited, but follow-ups of adopted children and others exposed to radical changes in their social environments have led some to talk about "the myth of early experience" (Clarke & Clarke, 1976). There are suggestions that children, like monkeys, can endure shifts in love objects and also can grow up normally despite terrible early conditions.

Attachment systems

Both human and animal research started with mother-infant relations. It was often assumed that the baby's attachment to its mother was fundamental to all later social attachments, a key to love relations in general. But a less mother-centered view has become more prominent. The social world of the young child is rich and complex (Hartup, 1979; Lamb, 1976; Lewis & Rosenblum, 1975). Fathers and peers are more important than was thought—even in conventional families. As new family patterns emerge, it is vital that we construct a broader and more realistic picture of early attachments.

For now William Mason's two-track hypothesis (Mason, 1970) provides a useful framework. It works well in summarizing the evidence on monkeys and seems more useful than others in looking at children.

Mason's central idea is that attachments to parents and attachments to peers form two contrasting systems that parallel the two motivational systems (Chapter 11). Although the child's attachment to other children comes later than love of mother, peer attachment is not derived from parent attachment and is not of secondary importance. Attachment to parents is seen as crucial to distress reduction and as of decreasing importance after infancy as the child becomes more competent in dealing with the world. Attachment to peers is seen as linked to exploration, play, and the exercise of competence. Peer attachment becomes more and more prominent as the child moves out into the world.

This two-track view exaggerates the difference between the child's relation to parents and friends. Certainly parents can and do play with their children as well as comfort them (Chapter 18), and peers can play comforting roles from an early age (Hoffman, 1975). But the approach points up crucial questions: When does the child seek out different people? Do the same situations promote contact with care givers and with peers? The evidence on children fits Mason's theory. Let's look now at these contrasting attachment systems.

Attachment to care givers

The development of love for parents apparently follows a regular developmental schedule under normal conditions. There are four main phases. The following list, based primarily on Schaffer and Emerson (1964a) and Ainsworth (1973), shows the typical developmental sequence in attachment to care givers.

1. Birth to 3 months—asocial interest
2. 3 months to 6 months—indiscriminate social attachment
3. 6 months—indiscriminate social attachment
4. 2 years—detachment

Asocial interest

From birth to about 3 months the baby shows interest in social stimuli, but not to people as such. The baby is as content to watch a mobile as a face, to be rocked by a cradle as by a person. There are many signs of social interest arising from biological preparedness, but there are no special reactions when people come or go as long as suitable stimulation of other kinds is available.

Indiscriminate social attachment

At about 3 months the picture changes dramatically, seemingly as part of the broad shift that also results in more mature visual perception (Chapter 6) and the appearance of positive emotional reactions (Chapter 10) (Emde et al., 1976). Now *people* count. Human faces produce broad smiles. Soon pleasure coos and laughs become part of the reaction. The baby seems to want to be picked up, held, smiled at, and played with by people. Protest at being put down or left alone is perhaps the best index that this all reflects attachment. Logically, the best way of seeing if there is attachment to something is to see what happens when that something is removed (Schaffer & Emerson, 1964a).

When you look at what produces protest at separation from about 3 to 6 months, you see that at this age social attachment is real, but indiscriminate. If mother puts baby down and walks away, baby is likely to cry. However, if mother hands baby to a stranger and walks away, baby typically won't cry. People count, but not particular individuals.

It's not that the baby cannot tell the difference between individuals. Many babies show recognition of familiar and special people at about 4 months, and babies as young as 1 month apparently can tell the difference between their mother's face and that of a stranger (Maurer & Salapatek, 1976). The development of attachment for special individuals comes several months after the ability to tell people apart.

Something more than the ability to discriminate must underlie the shift to special love for certain people. One popular idea has been that the development of object permanence is crucial. However, the connection between the development of object permanence and specific attachment is not close enough to support the hypothesis (Flavell, 1977). Another possibility is that physiological changes make new kinds of emotional reactions possible at this point (Emde et al., 1976), but we remain unsure.

Discriminative social attachment

Usually the baby is about 6 to 9 months old when we first see clear signs of attachment to particular people (Schaffer & Emerson, 1964a). Reactions to separation show the new pattern clearly. A parent can no longer hand the baby to a friendly stranger and walk away in peace and quiet. Now this action produces protest. The baby's face sobers; the baby often cries. Not only being held or talked to counts now; the person matters.

Another sign of the baby's new differentiation between people often appears when strange adults approach the baby. Even friendly smiles and greetings from an unfamiliar adult can provoke frowns from a baby 8 months or older. When a friendly stranger "swoops in" to pick up the child, the reaction often is to cry. This so-called "stranger anxiety" presently is a matter of dispute. Rheingold and Eckerman (1973) reviewed the evidence and questioned whether it is universal, as some have claimed. However, Sroufe (1979) has argued that most babies react negatively to intruding strangers and that ethical concerns about upsetting babies have resulted in research procedures that minimize the reactions seen. In any case, negative reactions to intruding strangers are more common than not once a baby is 6 months old; so approach slowly.

Protest when loved ones leave and a negative reaction when strange adults approach define the main outlines of the older baby's discriminating love. Other reactions fill out the picture. Babies show affection for special people in many ways. They invite play and respond with smiles and laughs when parents start a game with them. When they find something new and interesting, they bring it to a parent and share it. As in all the friendships that will come later, doing things together and sharing experiences are important for their own sakes.

Although attached babies seek and enjoy contact with their care givers, they are not their only interests. There is a sharp rise in exploration and play that takes babies away from care givers starting at about the same time as the development of specific attachments. Moving out into a world of things develops in parallel with the special affections.

Consideration of when the baby is more likely to seek close contact with loved ones helps clarify the picture. Pain, illness, and being tired all promote clinging. The end of a period of absence, bedtime, or an unfamiliar environment make contact seeking more likely. Distress is the common denominator in the situations where we see the strongest and most frequent efforts to be close (Maccoby & Masters, 1970).

A parent, then, seems to serve as a secure base for exploration of the rest of the world (Ainsworth, 1973). When all goes well and parental contact can be taken for granted, the baby is calm and interacts with varied parts of the world. Exploration of interesting places, toys, and people is prominent. Play has a high priority. But when anything upsets the baby, closeness to the attachment figure takes on a higher priority. Contact with the loved one has a special power to reduce distress and arousal to a level where motives such as curiosity and mastery can operate. Parents, of course, can be partners in play and sources of stimulation and excitement. However, their unique contribution as attachment figures seems to be to maintain an emotional climate that allows the baby to interact with the rest of the world.

Somewhat paradoxically, a special contribution of early attachment is to pave the way for detachment. Growing up eventually means moving away from parents, both emotionally and geographically. Apparently detachment, cutting the tie to parents, starts early and develops gradually.

Detachment

Voluntary separations from loved ones become more and more obvious between age 1 and 5 years. At home baby becomes more likely to crawl or walk out of the room where father or mother is working. Trips back to check up on the parent become less common. Similarly, the child becomes more and more likely to stay with peers or toys when parents leave the room. Harriet Rheingold and Carol Eckerman (1970) did a pioneering study of the same trend in an unfamiliar environment. Mothers were seated in a chair in an unfamiliar yard and their children were allowed to do what they wanted. The mothers were instructed to behave naturally, but to remain in the chair. Observers recorded how far each child traveled away from mother during the 15-minute period. The farthest distance traveled for 1-year-olds was only 6.9 meters. The maximum separation increased steadily with age so that the 4-year-olds reached an average maximum distance of 20.6 meters and the 5-year-olds went even farther. Most likely a variety of measures would show a similar trend. Later cultural landmarks, such as entering elementary school and establishing one's own home, are but more advanced steps in a detachment process that traces back to middle infancy.

The process of physical detachment normally is accompanied by the rise of more abstract forms of attachment (Marvin, 1977). For the school-age child shared attitudes and plans provide emotional bonds to parents that are more sophisticated versions of being close. Learning to read or play baseball well can be as much an effort to be close as climbing on a lap.

Attachment to peers

If you met an 18-year-old who always preferred to spend time with parents rather than peers, you would consider her or him strange or immature. Somewhere between birth and age 18, peer attachments become as vital to the individual as the earlier ones to parents.

Peer play and friendship are important in all cultures after age 3. What happens earlier varies with the society. Our society downplays peer interaction during infancy (Lewis & Rosenblum, 1975); others make more of it.

Roots of early peer attraction

Attraction to peers starts early and apparently is stronger than attraction to adults when the two are equally unfamiliar. For example, when two unfamiliar mother-baby pairs are put in a playroom, the babies pay more attention to the other baby than to the novel lady. They also smile and react more positively to the other baby (Eckerman, Whatley, & Kutz, 1975; Lewis & Rosenblum, 1975). Similarly, babies show a positive reaction when approached by an unfamiliar 4-year-old in a situation where approach by unfamiliar adults produces negative reactions (Lewis & Brooks, 1975). Such findings contradict the one-track idea that peer attachment is generalized from attachment to parents.

Why are other children so special so early? Two possibilities are curiosity and similarity. Perhaps babies are attracted to other children because peers act in ways that are more comprehensible and thus more interesting than adults do. Certainly children soon look away from adults talking about politics but pay more attention to those digging holes in the ground or standing on their heads. The fascinating things that other children do might make them more attractive. Alternatively, peers could be attractive because they are seen as "like me." Maybe the special response to other children is an early expression of the more general tendency for the child to like what is similar to the self (Kohlberg, 1969; Lewis & Rosenblum, 1975). The mystery deserves attention.

Friendships: Later peer attachments

We know more about child-child relations after infancy, but much of what we know is based on studies done in preschools. They lead to the conclusion that peer interaction doesn't get moving until about age 3 years. Studies in homes and backyards where little children meet in smaller groups in the presence of their parents yield different results (Mueller & Lucas, 1975). In more comfortable and familiar settings interaction starts much earlier.

Children in preschools are discriminating in when they seek peer contact and when they go to adults (Maccoby & Masters, 1970). A 3-year-old playing happily with other 3-year-olds is likely to turn to adults when distressed. When falls, bruises, and quarrels upset children, they often seek comfort. Parent-like people suddenly become important. When all is calm, peers are more attractive.

This discriminating pattern fits in neatly with Mason's picture of motivational development (Chapter 11). Playing with friends seems to have the same motivational roots as playing with blocks, climbing on swings, and splashing water.

The early friendships between children of 3 and 4 differ from those that come later (Hartup, 1970).

1. They aren't as stable. If you ask children who their best friends are (or watch their spontaneous choices) and then come back in a few weeks, the younger the child, the more likely there will have been a shift.
2. At first quarrels and conflicts are more common with friends than with others. This is part of a more general trend for all forms of social interaction to go together during early childhood (Chapter 13).
3. A child's descriptions of his or her friendships can give a different picture than direct observations. John describes Amos as his best friend, but it might turn out that they almost never play together.

These characteristics of early friendship make sense when we consider the limitations of social understanding in early childhood and realize that the major patterns of interpersonal relations are just being learned (Chapter 13).

Early friendships do share some important features with those that come later. For example, the factors of propinquity, sex, and age help in predicting who makes friends with whom at all ages (Hartup, 1970).

The simple matter of whom we happen to have contact with is a major factor in determining whom we come to like and love. Friendships might be made in heaven, but somehow the girl next door, the boy in our class, and others we meet frequently are more likely to become our friends. *Propinquity* is the technical term for this nearness in time and place. Propinquity does much to explain why Helen and Rachel end up being friends. If they live near each other, ride on the bus together, are in the same class, both belong to Girl

Most children's friendships reflect similarity in age and sex, a pattern found after age 3 in all cultures.

Scouts, and are members of families who socialize together, the chance of their becoming friends is much greater.

Most children's friendships reflect similarity in age and sex (Hartup, 1970). At all ages and in all cultures boys are more likely to be friends with other boys, girls with other girls. The trend is particularly strong during the elementary-school years, but it exists as early as age 3 and continues into adolescence, when cross-sex friendships become important as well. The tendency for friendships to be mostly with children of a similar age also is a broad one, occurring at all ages after infancy and in varied societies.

Most likely the importance of similarity in age and sex reflects commonality of interests. Shared interests are an important basis for friendships, and interests vary with both sex and age. Girls and boys typically develop contrasting interest patterns (Chapter 14), and interests change as children grow up. What's fun for a 3-year-old often is not fun at 6. Eight-year-olds have much in common with 10-year-olds, little with teenagers.

The scientific findings support the wisdom of the child who sees a moving van stop to unload in front of a vacant house down the block. She runs to the driver with three questions: Do they have any children? Are they boys or girls? How old are they? Nearness in space, sex, and age are crucial in children's friendships. It's fortunate that children are so prone to like children who are available and similar to themselves. The factors that produce peer friendships result in a social world that is friendlier than it might be.

ATTITUDES

As symbolic powers grow, symbolic likes and dislikes emerge. We call them *attitudes.* Children acquire feelings toward whole groups: Baptists, ballplayers, and ballet dancers. They develop strong feelings for individuals they never meet: Abraham Lincoln, Madame Curie, and Lassie. At this point our observations of liking and disliking no longer are limited to concrete matters such as a child tagging after an older sister or crying when a stranger approaches. Attitudes can be inferred from such statements as "I love school," "Communists are bad," or "The Irish are the greatest!"

We can define an attitude as a learned predisposition to respond in a consistently favorable or unfavorable manner with respect to a given object (Fishbein & Ajzen, 1975).

The concept of attitude became central in psychology because it is vital in dealing with one of the most basic facts of social development: children come to conform willingly to the demands placed upon them by society (Sherif, 1980). Through a process of *internalization* their most private likes and dislikes develop so as to resemble those of their society. As a result there is social conformity in attitudes, not just in behavior. This internal, attitudinal conformity contributes to self-regulation. Normal children end up monitoring their own behavior and doing what is right even when no one is watching.

I'll focus here on two principles that help explain why internalization takes place and why similarity plays such an important role in friendships. A balance principle sums up how children's attachments influence their attitudes, a key

As children's symbolic powers grow, they can develop strong feelings for characters in stories.

question in explaining internalization. A similarity principle rounds out the picture by telling how attitudes influence the formation of new attachments, or friendships. Taken together, these two principles show how personal relationships and social attitudes influence each other. The interaction of attachments and attitudes proceeds in four steps:

1. The child becomes attached to a small circle of individuals with whom she or he has personal contact.
2. The child internalizes group members' attitudes (balance principle), resulting in a set of early attitudes similar to those of the people to whom the child is attached.
3. The early attitudes bias the child toward forming later attachments to people who have similar attitudes (similarity principle).
4. Later attachments, in turn, constrain the development of new attitudes so that they tend to be consistent with those of the new friends (balance principle).

Notice that this model implies (1) a process that typically is conservative and likely to result in the maintenance of early attitudes and (2) that forced exposure to new groups with contrasting attitudes might be an important way for an individual's attitudes and attachments to take new directions.

Balance principle

The balance idea is that children acquire attitudes that result in more balance, or harmony, between them and those to whom they are attached (Heider, 1958). If their loved ones and friends like X, then they too are likely to come to like it. Imagine a child growing up in Los Angeles who happened to dislike the Los Angeles Dodgers. In a typical Los Angeles family, neighborhood, or classroom there would be friction, conflict, and strain because everyone around the child probably likes the Dodgers. This kind of imbalance rarely lasts. When it occurs, something usually changes to make the situation more balanced, less conflicted. The balance idea applies to any attitudes. It says:

1. Tell me whom the child loves.
2. Tell me what those people love and hate.
3. Then I'll predict what the child will come to love and hate.

The hypothesis is new in child psychology, although it is prominent in social psychology. Seemingly, balance thinking has been neglected in considering child development because of the popularity of the concept of identification.

Following Freud, many child psychologists have explained the tendency for children to take over attitudes from their parents by hypothesizing a unique process: *identification*. Through a desire to be like the same-sex parent, the child supposedly takes over that parent's values, attitudes, and behaviors. The distinct feature of the identification concept is the idea that the relationship with the same-sex parent (which also relates to feelings toward the opposite-sex parent) provides a unique basis for predicting what attitudes and behaviors the child will acquire.

Today there is a great variety of findings that contradict the hypothesis that children's attitudes are particularly similar to those of their same-sex parent (Mischel, 1970). The balance hypothesis explains the frequent finding that children take over their parents' attitudes and does not lead to the incorrect prediction about unique similarity with the same-sex parent. The balance principle also helps us deal with the common finding that children's attitudes can be influenced by everyone with whom they have a positive relationship: mother, father, sister, brother, teacher, or friend.

Similarity principle

Once a child has formed a set of likes and dislikes, these attitudes play a key role in forming new friendships, or attachments. Their influence can be summed up through the similarity principle: children come to evaluate positively what they see as similar to themselves (Kohlberg, 1966; Newcomb, 1956). I've already presented some evidence consistent with this idea. Babies prefer unfamiliar babies to unfamiliar grown-ups, perhaps because they see other babies as more like themselves. Same sex and same age are important predictors of friendship in older children at all ages, perhaps the strongest and clearest support for the hypothesis.

Numerous studies of college students support the similarity-attraction idea (Byrne, 1969), but direct tests of the hypothesis with children have been rare. In one study Byrne and Griffitt (1966) measured children's liking and disliking for such items as poetry, sports, comic books, boys, and girls. Then they gave the children descriptions of other (target) children. The target child's likes and dislikes on the same items were summarized. The children were asked to tell how much they thought they would like the child whose attitudes were summarized. Sure enough, on the average the more similar the attitudes of the target child to the one doing the rating, the stronger the attraction.

An important question that has not been answered is what determines whether a child sees someone else as similar. For example, if Betty is White and Henry is White, she could see him as similar because they both are White or different because he is of the opposite sex. Until we know more about what governs perceived similarity, it is hard to apply the similarity principle.

Gottfried and Katz (1977) looked at the relative importance of a model's belief on an important issue (Should there be school in the summer?) and his or her sex and race as aspects of similarity. They found that similarity in belief predicted the model's influence better than similarity in race or sex. Research of this kind is needed to clarify what cues are important to children in determining whom they see as similar to themselves.

Applications box 12–2 Modifying racial attitudes

Could teachers do more to promote positive racial attitudes in elementary-school children? Phyllis Katz and Sue Zalk (1978) think so. Their research shows that when based on the research evidence (Katz, 1976), even brief efforts can have lasting impact. They worked in desegregated schools, focusing on White children who had negative attitudes toward Black children.

The prejudiced children were assigned randomly either to one of four contrasting experimental groups or to control groups. Each experimental group received an intervention based on earlier research. Each intervention was designed to be quick and easy to use in a school setting and required only 15 minutes.

Despite their brevity, all four methods had positive impacts that could be detected two weeks later. Two approaches resulted in bigger changes and had an influence that still could be seen four to six months later. The study showed that the racial attitudes of highly prejudiced children are malleable (in contrast to those of prejudiced adults) and suggested that the schools could be doing much more to combat prejudice.

Descriptions of the two approaches that worked best illustrate how little it takes to modify children's racial attitudes. A *vicarious identification* method, based on earlier research, on school texts, and on "Sesame

Street," suggested that media exposure to people in the other group can be a potent source of attitude shift. In the study by Katz and Zalk groups of three children listened to a tape-recorded story illustrated by slides of Black people. The story involved a child (same sex as the listeners) who found his or her way home from school and, in the face of difficulties, helped to get his or her sick grandmother to the hospital.

A perceptual predifferentiation approach was inspired by earlier work showing that faces of people from other races appear more similar to children than faces of members of their own race and that this increased similarity is linked to ease in maintaining prejudice. The impression that they all look alike seems to make it easier to dislike them all. Katz and Zalk used two procedures aimed at helping children see differences in faces. The children either were asked to look at Black faces and count them or to look at faces varying in color and other characteristics and learn names for them. Like the vicarious identification method, this perceptual predifferentiation approach produced relatively large and lasting attitude changes.

Interestingly, one of the approaches that produced smaller attitude shifts might have worked better if the children had not been given room to change it. It was a group interaction technique, based on the idea that working in an interracial group that jointly earned rewards would influence attitudes positively. Two Black and two White children of the same sex were put together in a puzzle-working group. Each child was given pieces from a common puzzle, and they were encouraged to assemble the whole puzzle and earn a reward. During the brief sessions the children typically segregated themselves by race; so despite the plan, there actually was little interracial contact. Thus, a more prolonged version of this technique might have turned out to be more powerful.

A variety of methods based on these concepts could be invented and combined to produce a year-long series of classroom experiences. The evidence suggests that such an approach might produce dramatic and lasting reductions in prejudice.

SUMMARY

The feeling, or affective, side of social development was described in this chapter, focusing on attachments and attitudes.

New theoretical orientations to attachment were summarized. Both common elements, such as two-way processes and preparedness, and divergences between ethological and social-learning positions were detailed. Then the development of attachments was summarized as a two-track process that pictures attachments to parents or care givers and attachment to peers as following different developmental paths. Attachment to care givers was summarized in terms of a four-step developmental sequence: (1) asocial interest, (2) indiscrim-

inate social attachments, (3) discriminative social attachments, and (4) detachment. Attachment to peers was described as starting earlier and as being more
important and distinct than is often thought. Developmental changes, such as
a shift to more stable and consistent friendship patterns, and developmental
constancies, such as the continuing importance of propinquity, sex, and age,
were summarized.

Attitudes, or evaluative reactions to objects, were discussed mostly in
terms of their relation to attachments, emphasizing two central hypotheses. A
balance hypothesis describes how existing attachments influence attitudes:
children tend to acquire attitudes that result in more harmony with those to
whom they are attached. A similarity hypothesis summarizes how already
existing attitudes influence the formation of new friendships: children tend to
like people whom they see as similar to themselves.

CHAPTER 13

Social Behavior and Social Understanding

This chapter completes the picture of social development begun in the previous one. First I examine the growth of social behavior, focusing on the early years when it takes form. Then I consider social understanding, emphasizing the elementary-school years because they are when we see dramatic advances in social sophistication. Finally, I bring together the varied sides of social development in a consideration of prosocial and antisocial behavior that relates behavior, feelings, and understandings.

DEVELOPMENT OF SOCIAL BEHAVIOR

Social behavior begins at birth. In the ceaseless activity of the newborn there are reactions to such social stimuli as human voices and body movements. Babies' actions, in turn, serve as signals. Their cries and wiggles direct the actions of others. Babies interact with people before they love them or understand them. When there is social interaction, we call behavior social.

Birth starts a social dance in which the child is never entirely leader or follower, but always some of each. From the start social interaction is a conversation, not a series of commands followed by compliance (Chapter 9). Newborns are naive, although not passive; untutored, but not unbiased. Their sleeping schedule will accommodate to that of their parents. However, parents also will adjust to newborns. Babies learn to step in time with parents, but only as they pay attention to the newborn's rhythms. Adults can turn a little barbarian into a child with civilized behavior, and a baby can teach ordinary adults to act like parents (Rheingold, 1969).

Because social behavior involves back and forth relations, the development of social behavior is not so much in children as in their interactions. Social skills, such as settling an argument or picking teams to play baseball, cannot be observed when the child is alone. We must look at children in interaction (Lewis & Rosenblum, 1974).

General features

Consider three general features of the development of social behavior first: its relation to other areas, its discriminating character, and the special role of peer interaction in its development.

Relation to other areas

The growth of social interaction patterns is inseparable from other aspects of development. In early years the growth of social behavior and the development of communication are tightly linked, for dialogue and language are the medium of social exchange. Between birth and age 4, the rapid growth of skills in language and communication pace the rise of social behavior and tell much of its story. For example, the shift from gestures and hard-to-comprehend speech to clearer speech dramatically changes the possibilities for peer interaction. Less obviously, communication skills such as looking at the speaker while listening apparently foster the rapid increase in verbal interaction between peers during the third year (Mueller, Bleier, Krakow, Hegedus, & Cournoyer, 1977). From age 5 through 13, advances in social behavior tie closely to progress in social understanding. During this period comprehension of others moves from the level of overt actions, such as smiling and hitting, to a focus on feelings and intentions. With this shift, maturity and success in social interaction become a matter not only of acting nicely, but of acting sensitively, judging others' motives, anticipating their reactions, and so on.

Discrimination

From early in infancy children learn how to fit their behavior to the social situation. They learn that different approaches work with different individuals. Mother and father respond differently when you cry or make a request. Children develop contrasting ways of interaction with individuals, with males and females, children and adults, and so on. They also learn how to read more variable cues, such as facial expressions and tones of voice, and to use these in determining what to do next.

This discriminating aspect of social interaction is important in seeing why two vital theoretical approaches have become so useful in understanding it. Social-learning theory (Chapter 2) helps us analyze how particular discriminations arise and operate in terms of situational factors and learning concepts (Chapter 5). Cognitive-developmental approaches (Chapter 2) show how social comprehension grows and thus clarify what kinds of discriminations are likely to be made at a particular age.

Peer interaction

Peer interaction plays a special role in the development of social behavior. Interaction with peers increases steadily and becomes the most common kind by about age 6 (Barker & Wright, 1955). Peer interaction also appears to offer unique and important opportunities.

In the peer world the child operates more as an equal than in the world of adults. Seemingly, this equalitarian aspect of peer interaction makes it more crucial to the growth of mature social behavior (Piaget, 1932/1965; Rubin, 1980; Sullivan, 1953). Relations with adults are more one-sided. Sometimes adults play a directive role, as in setting rules and enforcing them; at other times they are especially accommodating, as when they patiently try to figure out what a youngster is saying or sacrifice their own preferences to play a game the child enjoys. With peers the give and take is more equal and more similar to what is required in adult living.

Now we turn to some of the details of how social behavior develops. First we examine developments in the early years when it takes form. Then we consider two kinds of social interaction of special interest, prosocial and anti-social behavior.

Children's interaction with peers increases steadily with age and are more characteristic of social relationships at maturity than of current relations with adults.

Early interactions with care givers

A big advance in social interaction occurs early. At first most baby-other contacts are dominated by crisis management, efforts to relieve distress. Within a few weeks relations take on a more relaxed and pleasant quality. Social behavior for its own sake emerges.

At birth babies' cries are their key social behavior. They set the pace of interaction. When Byron cries, his care giver springs into action, picking Byron up, feeding him, changing him, or looking for other ways of quieting him, such as rocking. The social exchange often ends once the emergency is over, as signaled by the termination of crying.

The shift from this early pattern apparently results mostly from developmental changes in the baby during the early weeks. Babies sleep and cry less and less. The awake/alert state suitable for sociability becomes more common and more sustained. By about 3 months social smiling and cooing have started, along with more advanced visual behavior.

The apparent impact of these universal changes in the baby was shown in a study by Howard Moss (1967). He watched mother-baby pairs in their homes when baby was 3 weeks old and then again when baby was 13 weeks.

Once the babies were older and more alert, the mothers spent more time with them. They held them less but spent more time in face-to-face contact: talking to them, imitating them, and being affectionate.

This three-month pattern of face-to-face interchange looks like the "first draft" of mature sociability (Stern, 1974). Babies' eye movements now are functionally mature (Chapter 6). They can direct and maintain their gaze with skill, even though they cannot yet sit. In looking at people and looking away from them they have an important channel of social approach, or positive communication, under control. They now look at eyes and smile, making eye contact possible and more pleasurable.

Daniel Stern (1974, 1977) has recorded early mother-infant "conversations" on videotape and analyzed them in detail. He found that these early social interactions are gamelike. Baby and mother each play somewhat standard roles. Mother's role is different from her normal one. She uses behavior patterns she rarely, if ever, uses in other social situations. For example:

> The facial expressions made by mothers for their babies during play are also quite extraordinary, especially in their degree of exaggeration, slowed tempo of formation, and long duration. The often seen "mock surprise" expression of mothers is a good example. The eyebrows go way up, the eyes open very wide, the mouth opens and purses and usually emits a long "Ooooooooo," and the head comes up and forward sometimes within inches of the baby's face. This expression may take many seconds to slowly come to a full bloom and then may be held for an unusually long time. Such an expression directed toward an adult would be experienced as quite bizarre. Mothers also violate adult cultural norms of interpersonal space utilized by frequently bringing their faces very close to the infants' during interaction [Stern, 1974, p. 192].

Babies thus get mothers both to imitate them and to engage in some pretty weird activity—quite a contrast with the notion that parents mold babies into conventional behavior.

Both partners play active roles. Mother more commonly starts a sequence of face-to-face gazing, often looking at baby's face until baby looks back. Once eye-to-eye contact starts, the baby typically looks away, looks back, and so on while mother keeps looking (Stern, 1974; Trevarthen, 1977, 1980).

The initiation of gaze-to-gaze behavior parallels other social interaction (Bell, 1974). Babies start about half their interactions with adults. They are "movers" as often as they are "moved."

Early interactions with peers

When given a chance, babies and toddlers interact and show developmental progress in their interactions. Probably the most advanced peer behavior can be seen when small groups get a chance to meet regularly in comfortable situations. Mueller and Lucas (1975) observed in this kind of situation. They studied triplets and pairs who played together weekly.

There were signs of progression through three stages. At first the peer interaction was *object-centered.* For example, when one child shook a rattle, others watched the rattle and listened to it, relating to the rattle and its action rather than to the first child. Only later was real interaction observed. At first it came in the form of *contingency interchange,* as when Bernie said "da" and looked at Larry. Larry laughed. Bernie said "da" again. This interchange was repeated 12 times! Each boy rewarded the other's action in much the same way as a rattle rewards you for shaking it. The third stage, *complimentary interchanges,* involved real reciprocity. The children did different yet coordinated things: one child threw a ball and the other caught it; one played the role of chaser and the other, the one being chased.

These stages should not be thought of as universal. Several studies (Jacobson, 1981; Vandell, Wilson, & Buchanan, 1980) suggest that simple interactions such as mutual smiling and touching develop before or in parallel with object-centered play. The nature of the situation and other variables probably influence what happens (Mueller & Brenner, 1977). Knowledge in this area is too limited for strong conclusions.

For example, we still don't even know what conditions bring about the most social interaction among babies. Many would argue that peer familiarity fosters social interplay, but a recent study calls even this obvious idea into question. When Jacobson (1981) compared what happened when the same babies met with both familiar and unfamiliar peers, he was surprised to find that longer social interactions were more frequent with unfamiliar peers.

Experimental studies such as Jacobson's are beginning to take us out of a purely descriptive approach to what happens when infants come together. For example, an experiment by Mueller and Brenner (1977) examined the specific contributions of experience with peers. They did a longitudinal study in which one group of boys started playing together when they were 12 months old, another group when they were 16½ months old. The findings indicated that neither maturation nor social experience with adults could explain the increased complexity of play with peers that appeared in the group that started playing together at 12 months. The group with extended experience in playing with peers showed more extended and complicated peer interaction at 16–17 months than the group that had just begun to play together. When we have additional experimental evidence of this kind, we should be better able to resolve apparent discrepancies and get a clearer picture of how varied factors contribute to the early growth of social skills.

Interaction in preschools and day-care centers

Most of our knowledge of early social behavior comes from looking at children in preschools and day-care centers. As more and more children spend time in such centers, this knowledge takes on broader relevance. However, we remain unclear about the similarities and differences between what happens in centers and in contrasting settings, such as homes.

Within centers the amount of interaction with peers increases rapidly with age in the early years (Finkelstein, Dent, Gallacher, & Ramey, 1978; Holmberg, 1980). In contrast, the amount of interaction with adults stays constant (Holmberg, 1980) or declines (Finkelstein et al., 1978). Typically, the amount of interaction with peers and adults becomes equal at about age 3 or 4 years.

A closer look suggests that the rise in peer interaction relates to the growing capacity to engage in reciprocal social behavior (as in Mueller and Lucas's second two stages) and in the growth of verbal skills that make elaborated social exchange easier (Finkelstein et al., 1978; Holmberg, 1980).

Holmberg's (1980) findings suggest that with 1-year-olds adult accommodation to the child, as in naming what the child points at, keeps interchanges going. At younger ages adult-child interactions are more complicated than child-child ones. By 42 months, when the children have more complex social responses available, child-child and child-adult interactions are similar.

Perhaps the most intriguing finding from studies of children in group settings is just how much social interaction goes on. In day-care centers with teacher-child ratios of about 1:3, infants and toddlers are found to spend about 30 to 48% of their total time engaged in social behavior (including both peer-peer and peer-adult interaction) (Finkelstein et al., 1978).

The sheer amount of social interaction in centers suggests how important this side of life is, for better or for worse. An old bias was that social interaction with the other children in a center was "good," more solitary play "unhealthy." Recent studies contradict that idea (Moore, Evertson, & Brophy, 1974; Rubin, 1981; Rubin, Watson, & Jambor, 1978). When observed carefully, solitary play most commonly seems to reflect maturity and independence. Children playing alone typically are observed in active, goal-directed behavior such as working puzzles, building with blocks, and looking at books, not sulking and pouting. Similarly, a more sophisticated view shows that social play includes both positive and negative episodes.

Our task is not so much to push for more or less social interaction in young children as to understand its present and potential role. Studies of prosocial and antisocial behavior help us do that.

Prosocial and antisocial behavior

Child psychologists have been particularly interested in "good" and "bad" behavior, actions that hurt and help others. Both kinds take clear form during the second year and become more sophisticated as the child's social skills grow. Although antisocial actions attract more attention, positive behaviors are more common than negative ones. Consider first what happens during the second year, then the developments later.

Age 2 years

Sharing is one of the prosocial behaviors that becomes prominent during the second year. Rheingold et al. (1976) studied it in a laboratory. They seated a parent in one playroom and gave his or her 18-month-old baby freedom to go back and forth from that room into adjoining playrooms with toys in them. They focused on showing (as in pointing at a toy or holding it up to someone), giving (putting an object in a person's lap or hand), and partner play (manipulating an object previously given to someone while they still have it). Sharing was common; all 111 toddlers did it. They shared both novel and familiar toys, whether or not parents "begged" for the toys or were enthusiastic about getting them. They shared with unfamiliar adults, not only with parents.

"Comforting" also is observed in the second year (Hoffman, 1978; Yarrow & Waxler, 1975). By 1 year many children react to people who are crying by patting, hugging, or giving them objects. More sophisticated efforts, such as getting a bandage for a wound or fetching mother to help someone else, soon follow. Seemingly, these helping actions stem from an early emerging reaction of empathetic distress, responding to distress in others by becoming distressed (Hoffman, 1978).

On the antisocial side the second year is marked by the growth of defiance, negativism, and aggression (Goodenough, 1931; Sroufe, 1979). At 1 year we observe some slapping, pushing, and hitting when the child is provoked. By 2, unprovoked aggression, such as pinching mother, has appeared. Actually, a naturalistic study (Schoggen, 1963) indicated that much of mothers' time with toddlers is spent in trying to be left alone, trying to get them to stop pestering and attaching.

Age 3 and over

Studies in preschools show that quarrels and conflicts are a common form of interaction between ages 2 and 5 (Freedman, Loring, & Martin, 1967). Typically, they are brief, rarely lasting for as long as 30 seconds. At 2 years they often stem from a focus on objects—for example, grabbing for toys. As children grow older, conflicts more often stem from differences of opinion, as in quarrels about how to play. The young children start more quarrels, but those of the older children typically are more aggressive in nature.

Researchers in Oregon (Patterson, Littman, & Bricker, 1967) showed how initially nonaggressive preschoolers can acquire aggressive behavior patterns through peer interaction. Over a year of observation in two nursery schools, they recorded the following sequence in most of the children who did not exhibit aggression at the beginning of the year.

1. Nonaggressive Bill is the victim of the aggressions of others, who take toys from him, push him, and so on.

2. Bill retaliates, fights back, or stands up for his rights, as we often put it. The retaliation is likely to be immediately and differentially reinforced. He gets to keep the toy when he fights for it; he loses it when he doesn't. Retaliation, then, becomes a more frequent response to attack.

3. Such aggressive behaviors as fighting, which worked when attacked, now are generalized. Fighting—for example, pulling on toys held by others—starts to occur in new settings, when no one else is attacking. Bill has learned to be an attacker.

Usually we see progress from the storm-ridden peer interactions of the early preschool years to smoother ones. Quarrels become less common and less physical. Sarcasm and verbal threats replace most actual fights. Telling teacher and getting even by indirect methods come to replace the more direct approach (Freedman et al., 1967; Hartup, 1974). Even when at their stormiest, peer relations are more positive than negative. Praising, helping, and sharing are prominent after age 2. The quarrels, physical or verbal, typically occur as brief interruptions of positive, joint activities.

Friendship

Friendship has become one of the most popular topics in current research on peer relations (Asher & Gottman, 1981; Gottman & Parkhurst, 1980; Rubin, 1980). Seemingly, the trend reflects the growing respect for peer relations in the child's world and the realization that positive and negative behavior are often better understood when viewed in the context of relationships.

The new studies highlight the complex and often subtle skills required in friendships. Rubin (1980) points out the need for skills in gaining entry into activities, in being supportive of others, and in managing conflicts with sensitivity and tact.

The development of such skills apparently explains a seeming paradox emerging from a comparison of friendships at varied ages between 3 and 6 years. Gottman and Parkhurst (1980) found that within this period friendships between younger children were marked by more compliance when the friend tried to control and more efforts to explain and avoid disagreement. In contrast to the general trend toward smoother peer relations, the friendship of the older children involved more conflicts. Putting all their observations together, Gottman and Parkhurst came up with an intriguing hypothesis. The younger children apparently tried to create and maintain a climate of agreement, seemingly because they were less able to keep squabbles from escalating once they started. The older children's greater social skill seemed to make it possible for them to live with conflict rather than being forced to try to avoid it entirely.

DEVELOPMENT OF SOCIAL UNDERSTANDING

Now we turn to the third main strand of social development, social understanding. I first review general trends; then I examine the development of moral judgment.

General trends

A hypothetical conversation illustrates developmental progress in social comprehension:

> Mr. O'Neill: What happened, Charlie?
> Charlie: Brian hit me.
> Mr. O'Neill: What happened, Brian?
> Brian: First I pushed him by accident. He got mad because he thought I meant it. So he hit me. That made me mad so I hit him back.

Charlie and Brian's statements illustrate the contrasting ways younger and older children talk about social interactions (Damon, 1978; Flavell, 1977; Selman, 1980; Shantz, 1975). Charlie's answer illustrates what we can expect from the typical 5-year-old. Brian's answer would be expected at about age 13. Three general trends are illustrated: simplicity to organized complexity, surface to interior, and egocentrism to objectivity.

Simplicity to organized complexity

Charlie's single sentence tells only part of what happened. Brian includes much more. Moreover, Brian tells an organized story rather than giving a hit-or-miss collection of details. He emphasizes the sequence in what happened and implies cause-and-effect relations.

Once more we find a familiar theme in development: there is movement toward greater differentiation (more different parts in his description) accompanied by new forms of integration (the parts are related to form an organized whole).

Surface to interior

Charlie restricts himself to the concrete and directly observable. He reports action with no reference to thoughts, feelings, or intentions. Brian, in contrast, implies intentions, thoughts, and feelings. During the elementary-school years there is a shift from observed actions and physical appearances to psychological inferences about what goes on inside people.

Egocentrism to objectivity

Charlie's answer is one-sided. We call it *egocentric* because the side on which he focuses, or centers, is his own. Brian's story is two-sided. He presents his own viewpoint and also puts himself in Charlie's shoes. His account is more objective because it is similar to what a neutral bystander, or third person, might have given.

Progress from egocentrism to objectivity is often described as growth in *role-taking* or *perspective-taking* skills. Older children are more accurate in taking others' roles in a variety of ways (Flavell, 1977; Selman, 1980). They do better in guessing games where you have to take into account what's going on in the other person. They are more accurate at figuring out another's feelings when the cues are not obvious.

There is some evidence of invariant sequences in the development of social cognition (Flavell, 1977; Selman, 1980; Selman & Byrne, 1974). Robert Selman (1980) has formulated a stage theory that describes the growth of interpersonal understanding in terms of how people and their relations are seen. His framework ties the previously described trends together and relates them to age. For example, consider his level 2. It characterizes children about 7 to 12. At level 2, children have gone beyond simply differentiating people's physical and psychological characteristics (level 1) and now understand that people's actions don't necessarily reveal their inner thoughts and feelings. But they are far from the point (level 4) where they think about people as having organized personalities that develop through time. They have a new ability to put themselves mentally in others' shoes and realize that others can do the same, but they cannot yet take a third-person perspective in which they can consider everyone's viewpoints simultaneously (level 3).

Despite its stagelike qualities, social understanding varies with the task (Forbes, 1978; Ford, 1979; Shantz, 1975). Children do better when the task is familiar. They can guess another child's emotions in front of a birthday cake more easily than those of an adult in front of a boss. How the question is put to them also matters. If you present a complicated story and then ask a child to give you a verbal explanation, the child is more likely to seem egocentric. If you simplify matters by using cartoon pictures and ask children to put them in a meaningful sequence, they show more sign of seeing alternative perspectives. You can get more or less social understanding, depending on how you look for it. We can be confident about the nature of progress as the child gains social wisdom, but it is hard to predict how much we will see in a particular situation.

There is a great increase in social comprehension between ages 4 and 14. It shows advances that go beyond mere gains in language skill. Research on object permanence and conservation taught us to think of children as amateur physicists who spontaneously learn about the physical world around them. Now we see that the child also is an amateur psychologist (Johnson, 1981; Mass, Marecek, & Travers, 1978), gaining a much deeper understanding of people and their actions during the elementary-school years (Flapan, 1967; Selman, 1980; Shantz, 1975).

Moral development: Understanding right and wrong

If your roommate accidentally hit you with a book, you'd judge her differently than if she did it on purpose. In a court of law a person who kills without provocation is punished more harshly than someone who kills in self-defense. We think that hitting and killing are wrong, but in a mature discussion of the morality of hitting or killing, we consider the actor's intentions and the situation along with the overt actions. For grown-ups, judgments of right and wrong often must reflect complicated reasoning.

A newborn baby is not ready to enter into discussions of the morality of killing in self-defense or of premarital intercourse. When does a child become morally mature, or able to understand the difference between right and wrong? The answer depends on our concept of maturity or understanding. Babies, like puppies, soon learn what actions are punished. They may even say no to themselves if they start a forbidden action. The 4-year-old can learn to say hitting is bad, but the baby's resistance to temptation and the 4-year-old's preachments don't show moral insight. Understanding of good and bad, like comprehension of other concepts and principles, is shown in other ways. We test comprehension of concepts and principles by asking the child to apply them in new situations or by getting the child to explain them in her own words.

Stage theory

Jean Piaget (1932/1965) pioneered in the study of children's ideas of right and wrong. He played marbles with children, asked them to teach him the rules, and then posed questions such as whether the rules could be changed. He gave them examples of wrongdoing and asked for explanations: "Why was that naughty?" "Is it worse to lie to another child or to an adult?" He concluded that moral understanding developed in a standard way, putting the main em-

Jean Piaget interviewed children about the rules of marble games as a way of learning about their ideas of right and wrong.

phasis on a shift from an early morality based on constraint, or respect for authority (*heteronomy*,) to a later mode of moral thinking in which cooperation and mutual respect were central (*autonomy*). Interestingly, he thought that the shift in moral thinking reflected in part the move from primarily child-adult relations to greater experience with the more equalitarian world of child-child relations.

Piaget's ideas about moral judgment have been both supported and contradicted. Moral thinking does seem to develop in the general way he described, although he does not seem to have been correct on all the details. Accordingly, current work on moral judgment focuses more on the specific ideas advanced by Lawrence Kohlberg, a follower of Piaget.

Kohlberg (1963, 1964, 1969) kept what seemed to be Piaget's most valid ideas and wove them into a new formulation. He proposed a stage theory in which moral judgment advances through three general levels: the premoral, the conventional, and the principled. There are two stages at each level, for a total of six stages in the development of moral reasoning (Table 13–1).

Longitudinal research supports Kohlberg's picture of the general trend. When children aged 5 to 8 were pretested and reexamined a year later, they typically had advanced along the lines he describes (Kuhn, 1976). Studies of teenagers indicate comparable movement if they are looked at over periods of two to three years (Rest, Davison, & Robbins, 1978). After the completion of schooling, and during adulthood generally, there seems to be more of a

TABLE 13-1 Kohlberg's six stages of moral judgment

Content of Stage

Level and Stage	What is Right	Reasons for Doing Right	Social Perspective of Stage
LEVEL 1— PRECONVENTIONAL, or PREMORAL Stage 1—Heteronomous Morality	To avoid breaking rules backed by punishment, obedience for its own sake, and avoiding physical damage to persons and property.	Avoidance of punishment, and the superior power of authorities.	*Egocentric point of view.* Doesn't consider the interests of others or recognize that they differ from the actor's; doesn't relate two points of view. Actions are considered physically rather than in terms of psychological interests of others. Confusion of authority's perspective with one's own.
Stage 2—Individualism, Instrumental Purpose, and Exchange	Following rules only when it is to someone's immediate interest, acting to meet one's own interests and needs and letting others do the same. Right is also what's fair, what's an equal exchange, a deal, an agreement.	To serve one's own needs or interests in a world where you have to recognize that other people have their interests, too.	*Concrete individualistic perspective.* Aware that everybody has his own interest to pursue and these conflict, so that right is relative (in the concrete individualistic sense).
LEVEL II— CONVENTIONAL Stage 3—Mutual Interpersonal Expectations, Relationships, and Interpersonal Conformity	Living up to what is expected by people close to you or what people generally expect of people in your role as son, brother, friend, etc. "Being good" is important and means having good motives, showing concern about others. It also means keeping mutual relationships, such as trust, loyalty, respect and gratitude.	The need to be a good person in your own eyes and those of others. Your caring for others. Belief in the Golden Rule. Desire to maintain rules and authority which support stereotypical good behavior.	*Perspective of the individual in relationships with other individuals.* Aware of shared feelings, agreements, and expectations which take primacy over individual interests. Relates points of view through the concrete Golden Rule, putting yourself in the other guy's shoes. Does not yet consider generalized system perspective.
Stage 4—Social System and Conscience	Fulfilling the actual duties to which you have agreed. Laws are to be upheld except in extreme cases where they conflict with other fixed social duties. Right is also contributing to society, the group, or institution.	To keep the institution going as a whole, to avoid the breakdown in the system "if everyone did it," or the imperative of conscience to meet one's defined obligations. (Easily confused with Stage 3 belief in rules and authority.)	*Differentiates societal point of view from interpersonal agreement or motives.* Takes the point of view of the system that defines roles and rules. Considers individual relations in terms of place in the system.

Content of Stage

Level and Stage	What is Right	Reasons for Doing Right	Social Perspective of Stage
LEVEL III—POST-CONVENTIONAL, or PRINCIPLED Stage 5—Social Contract or Utility and Individual Rights	Being aware that people hold a variety of values and opinions, that most values and rules are relative to your group. These relative rules should usually be upheld, however, in the interest of impartiality and because they are the social contract. Some nonrelative values and rights like *life* and *liberty*, however, must be upheld in any society and regardless of majority opinion.	A sense of obligation to law because of one's social contract to make and abide by laws for the welfare of all and for the protection of all people's rights. A feeling of contractual commitment, freely entered upon, to family, friendship, trust, and work obligations. Concern that laws and duties be based on rational calculation of overall utility, "the greatest good for the greatest number."	*Prior-to-society perspective.* Perspective of a rational individual aware of values and rights prior to social attachments and contracts. Integrates perspectives by formal mechanisms of agreement, contract, objective impartiality, and due process. Considers moral and legal points of view; recognizes that they sometimes conflict and finds it difficult to integrate them.
Stage 6—Universal Ethical Principles	Following self-chosen ethical principles. Particular laws or social agreements are usually valid because they rest on such principles. When laws violate these principles, one acts in accordance with the principle. Principles are universal principles of justice: the equality of human rights and respect for the dignity of human beings as individual persons.	The belief as a rational person in the validity of universal moral principles, and a sense of personal commitment to them.	*Perspective of a moral point of view* from which social arrangements derive. Perspective is that of any rational individual recognizing the nature of morality or the fact that persons are ends in themselves and must be treated as such.

From *Moral Development and Behavior: Theory, Research and Social Issue,* edited by Thomas Lickona. Copyright © 1976 by Holt, Rinehart & Winston. Reprinted by permission of Holt, Rinehart and Winston.

plateau, with most adults operating primarily at Kohlberg's fourth stage (Rest et al., 1978). Because Kohlberg's third stage typically is reached in our society at about age 13 (Kohlberg, 1969), moral judgment during childhood generally involves the first three stages.

Kohlberg thinks that cognitive development paces moral judgment. Children have to have reached a particular level of thinking before they can apply it to judgments about good and bad (Kohlberg, 1973). A child not yet able to think in terms of rules can't use such rules as "be nice so that others will be nice to you." Being able to think logically does not mean that logical principles will always be used in moral judgment. Delinquents often show lower levels of moral thinking than nonmoral thinking (Chandler, 1973).

Other findings on juvenile delinquents also support Kohlberg's ideas. There is not a simple correlation between level of moral judgment and juvenile delinquency (Blasi, 1980; Jurkovic, 1980). But among juvenile delinquents it is those who show the so-called "sociopathic" pattern, often termed "asocial" and "without a conscience," who are more likely to score at the premoral level on Kohlberg's measures (Jurkovic, 1980).

Kohlberg's theory has resulted in efforts to stimulate moral development. The basic idea is to stretch children's moral understanding by exposing them to arguments that involve a level of moral thinking slightly higher than their own. For example, children who think about right and wrong primarily in terms of living up to parental expectations (stage 3) are exposed to arguments between actors in which the broader question of doing what keeps society going harmoniously is raised (stage 4). Several studies support this idea. Apparently, moral education works best when the child is exposed to conflicts that require thinking one level above where the child is (Blatt & Kohlberg, 1973; Turiel, 1969). Two experiments have shown that this method works only when the children exposed to it already have developed the cognitive skills needed at the next level of moral thinking (Walker, 1980; Walker & Richards, 1979). The research on moral education simultaneously supports Kohlberg's theoretical position and offers some practical ideas.

There have been important challenges to Kohlberg's position (Aron, 1977; Gibbs, 1977; Kurtines & Grief, 1974; Rosenthal & Zimmerman, 1978). The adequacy of his research tools has been questioned. The claims that stages are unified and that sequences are universal remain in doubt. And now even Kohlberg (1978) has changed his mind on some points (see Box 13–1); so the situation is still unsettled. Nevertheless, knowledge of moral judgment has grown tremendously and supports the general value of the Piaget-Kohlberg approach.

Frontiers box 13–1 Moral development

The interplay between theory and evidence so central to scientific progress (Chapter 2) is illustrated in work on moral development. Lawrence Kohlberg's doctoral thesis in 1958 grew out of Piaget's theory and the research it inspired. Kohlberg developed both a new theory and a new method of collecting data. They stimulated both new studies and practical efforts in moral education. It is interesting to see what has happened to Kohlberg's methods and ideas as a result.

Kohlberg's method was to present people with moral dilemmas— for example, the story of Heinz. Heinz's wife was dying of cancer. Heinz was faced with a druggist who had a powerful new cancer cure that he would sell only for an exorbitant price. Respondents were asked what Heinz should do. For example, would it be right for him to steal the drug? Then they were interviewed to bring out the reasoning behind their answers. Finally, a complex scoring system was used to categorize the responses and determine what stage they indicated.

James Rest, one of Kohlberg's students, became dissatisfied with this system; so he developed a system in which subjects responded to statements about issues bearing upon moral dilemmas rather than constructing their own explanations. For example, for Heinz's dilemma the subjects were asked to consider whether or not a community's laws are going to be upheld and whether it is only natural for a loving husband to care so much for his wife that he'd steal. Next they were asked to rate how important each issue was in determining what was to be done. With Rest's method the investigator defined the issues and the respondent only had to judge them. This approach makes it far quicker and simpler to collect and analyze data (Rest, 1976; Rest, Cooper, Coder, Masanz, & Anderson, 1974; Rest et al., 1978).

Meanwhile Kohlberg and his associates have periodically changed the elaborate scoring system needed with his method (Colby, 1978). Simultaneously, they have shifted their working definition of moral judgment. For example, in a recent shift they came to the important decision that stage 6 was not really a separate stage (Kohlberg, 1978). Now it is considered a part of stage 5.

The results of practical efforts in moral education have also led to important revisions in Kohlberg's thinking. In early writings (1970, 1973) he argued that the moral educator should never indoctrinate—that is, advocate specific values such as the idea that stealing and aggression are wrong. Instead he thought that the adult's role should be value free and focused entirely on the task of stimulating more mature forms of moral thought.

Now Kohlberg (1978) sees it differently. Because children engage in stealing, cheating, and aggression before they are old enough to make "principled" decisions, he thinks that moral behavior has to be dealt with more directly. As long as the adult is democratic and recognizes children's rights, Kohlberg thinks that both indoctrination and efforts to facilitate development should be part of moral education. Another change is from an individual- to a group-centered approach to moral education (Kohlberg, 1978). Rather than focusing on individuals directly, current work is aimed toward helping groups in schools and prisons run their own "just communities" in which fair decisions are made (Power & Reimer, 1978). This shift, too, came out of research evidence, including both experiments in schools and prisons in the United States and observation of a similar, successful system in Israeli kibbutzim.

Two important distinctions

A sound hypothesis is that moral judgment advances slowly and in parallel with other aspects of social comprehension. When you think about it, the idea is obvious. After all, both custom and the legal system start from the idea that children don't understand right and wrong as adults do. There is broad agreement that children should not be held morally responsible in the same way as adults, but many have missed this obvious point.

One problem has been a failure to distinguish between moral *judgment,* or understanding, and *behavioral conformity.* People are often preoccupied with the question of conformity—does the child hit, steal, share, and lie? But the issue of moral understanding, although related, is fundamentally different. A child can refrain from hitting with little comprehension of why hitting is called bad. Another child might show more insight into why hitting is wrong, yet do it frequently. The connection between understanding and behavior is not direct.

A second source of confusion is less obvious. It relates to a distinction between the *structure* and the *content* of moral thought. Suppose you ask the same question of two children from different backgrounds: "Is it wrong to steal candy at the supermarket?" Amy says yes; Carol says no. The disagreement about what is called good or bad is one of content. Children vary widely in what actions they call right and wrong.

Now suppose you inquire further. After each child gives her answer you ask "Why?" Amy answers "Because my teacher said so." Carol replies "That's what my daddy says." Here the responses are essentially the same. Both children quote authority to justify their answers. Neither cites a rule or principle (for example, "Nobody will like you if you steal" or "Stealing is just getting even with the stores for cheating the customers"). The similarity in the way the girls justify their answers is called a similarity of structure. Piaget, Kohlberg, and others concerned with moral judgment focus on how children explain what makes actions good or bad (the structure of their moral thinking), not on what actions they support or condemn (the content of their morality).

The regularity in the development of moral judgment is regularity in structure, not content. What children call bad or good varies from group to group and child to child. Content shows little if any consistent trend, but the structure of moral judgment does look similar in children with different backgrounds. There are universal trends.

One trend is toward greater *intentionality* (Kohlberg, 1964; Piaget, 1932/ 1965). Older children are more likely to emphasize a person's intentions in deciding whether to call their actions good or bad (an emphasis on the interior). Younger children put more emphasis on the outcome or consequences of an action (the surface). One of Piaget's original judgment problems illustrates the shift and provides a starting point in seeing where recent research has been moving.

Piaget presented children with the following pair of stories and then asked, "Are these children equally guilty?" and "Which of the two is naughtiest and why?"

> John . . . goes into the dining room. But behind the door there was a chair, and on the chair there was a tray with fifteen cups on it. John couldn't have known that there was all this behind the door. He goes in, the door knocks against the tray, bang go the fifteen cups and they all get broken!

> One day when [Henry's] mother was out he tried to get some jam out of the cupboard. He climbed up on a chair and stretched out his arm. But the jam was too high up and he couldn't reach it and have any. But while he was trying to get it he knocked over a cup. The cup fell down and broke [Piaget, 1932/1965, p. 122].

Piaget found that younger children typically said John was guiltier and naughtier because he broke more cups. They were most influenced by the *consequences* of the actions in the two stories. Older children were more likely to say that Henry was guiltier and naughtier because he broke the single cup as a result of bad *intentions.*

Now we can put Piaget's finding in better perspective. The picture is complicated, as he suspected (Rybash & Roodin, 1978). We must consider the details of how children respond, the stimulus to which they respond, and specific training.

Children use the intentionality principle in judging actions before they actually verbalize the idea (Bresnitz & Kugelmass, 1967). A child may say that Jean was not bad when she accidentally knocked Mimi down, yet never use the concept of intention in talking about how she judges good and bad. Thus, it's hard to say when a particular child has intentionality; it depends on what criterion you use.

Another complication stems from the fact that the way of presenting a story influences the results. Piaget and others who presented the stories in verbal form found that children emphasize consequences until age 8 or 9, but even first-graders react quite differently when someone hits them on purpose or by accident. Michael Chandler and his associates did a study to see if they could explain the contrast (Chandler, Greenspan, & Barenboim, 1973). They made videotapes using child actors to portray the classic stories about John, Henry, and their misdeeds. Then 7-year-olds were asked to judge the same stories twice—once with verbal stimuli and once with the videotapes showing John and Henry in action. There was a reversal of findings. With the conventional stimuli the 7-year-olds judged mostly on the basis of consequences, but when they saw the stories acted out, they judged mostly on the basis of intentions.

A final example illustrates that moral judgments can be influenced by training. Albert Bandura and Frederick McDonald (1963) used a set of stories similar to Piaget's, but they tried to reverse children's judgments. A model who made moral choices opposite to the child's own and got reinforced for it influenced the child. Children originally high on intentionality switched to consequences; children high on consequences could be moved to intentionality. Although there has been debate on the durability of such changes, the finding that training has at least an immediate impact seems clear (Bandura, 1969b; Cowan, Langer, Heavenrich, & Nathanson, 1969).

Intentionality, like egocentricity, is a useful abstraction pointing at a broad developmental shift. We must look at the details of a situation before predicting a child's judgments. Current explanations of moral judgment include elements both from Piaget's view and from learning theory.

PUTTING IT ALL TOGETHER

Taken together, this chapter and the previous one gave you a three-sided view of social development. The growth of social *feelings* (attachments and attitudes), social *behavior,* and social *understanding* was considered in isolation. Now we turn to the question of how they fit together, using the question of what explains and influences the occurrence of prosocial and antisocial actions as a focus.

The general answer is that these social behaviors, like all others, can be understood if we look both at factors in the child and in the situation. Behavioral principles help in analyzing the role of situational factors. Ideas about social feelings and social comprehension are particularly important in seeing how factors in the child contribute.

Situational factors

Social learning concepts provide a powerful start in explaining when actions such as helping and hitting occur. The concepts of modeling and reinforcement (Chapter 5) are particularly useful.

Reinforcement principles help explain why aggression is common under some conditions and disappears under others. Consequences make a big difference, and, unfortunately, aggressive acts often are immediately reinforced.

But positive actions like smiling at others, taking turns, and playing by the rules also often have positive consequences. Actually, once a child starts to engage in prosocial behaviors, most social environments will provide reinforcement for them and keep them going. The question of how to get positive behaviors started is crucial.

Modeling is important here (Bandura, 1977; Mussen & Eisenberg-Berg, 1977). Laboratory studies make it clear that what adults model has a potent impact on whether children help or share. Adult experimenters who donate to charity or share candy promote similar actions in the children who see them do it. Television programs with prosocial content have a similar influence (Chapter 19). David Rosenhan (1969) became interested in prosocial models as a result of collecting case histories of adults who exhibited dramatic prosocial behavior. He found a clear pattern in interviews with some of the freedom riders of the 1960s who repeatedly broke segregation laws in the southern United States at great personal risk in order to achieve integration. Those who repeatedly went on freedom rides commonly came from families where prosocial action was a way of life—for example, in religion, social service, or politics. Findings from diverse sources point to a common conclusion: if you want children to act nicely, demonstrate what you want through your own behavior.

Modeling, like reinforcement, influences both positive and negative behaviors. What children do today on the playground reflects their history of watching models and being reinforced in similar situations.

Experiments on children's moods suggest that anything that puts children in a good mood is likely to make them more generous (Mussen & Eisenberg-Berg, 1977). Children instructed to recall happy events later donate more money to charity than controls. Similarly, children who just have been successful are more generous than either unsuccessful or neutral controls. The findings do not give us a clear picture of the impact of a bad mood, but the evidence on good moods suggests that any situational factor that increases happiness is also likely to foster generosity.

Situational factors such as consequences, models, and events that produce happiness help predict sharing or hitting, but they leave us with uncertainty. Even children exposed to the same situations vary in what they do.

Child characteristics

Both the child's level of social comprehension and his or her pattern of social attachments are relevant when we want to go beyond situational factors in explaining behavior.

Social cognition

Children's comprehension of social reality influences how situational factors act on them. A subtle act of charity will not make children more generous if they do not realize that generosity was involved. Their understanding of what others feel and intend influences their interpretation and recall of what actually happened.

When 3-year-old Lynn snatches a toy from Jo, she doesn't think about how Jo feels. Lynn's attention is centered on what Lynn wants. Similarly, when Jo bangs into Lynn, Lynn is impressed that it hurts. She's poorly equipped to see that Jo didn't mean it. At 3, then, friendly and unfriendly actions have a different meaning than they will later when children become more skilled in reading others' motives and are better able to decenter from their own viewpoint. Not surprisingly, several studies show that children with more advanced role-taking skills act more prosocially (Mussen & Eisenberg-Berg, 1977).

A study by Daniel Bar-Tal and his associates (Bar-Tal, Raviv, & Leiser, 1980) illustrates how the development of social sophistication can influence social behavior. They first played a guessing game with pairs of children of different ages. One child within each pair (the "winner") was "lucky" and got seven pieces of candy. The other child (the "loser") got none. Then they examined how the act of sharing the candy varied as a function of developmental level and situational factors by exposing the children to a series of situations in which the external push for sharing became ever stronger. First they simply left the winner and the loser alone together to allow for entirely spontaneous sharing. If none occurred, the children were read a story that happened to be about a child who got some candy at a party and later shared it with a friend. Children who had not shared at this point were promised an important role in a play if they shared. At the final step children who still had not shared were directly asked to share. The experimenters kept track of how many candies were shared and later interviewed the children about why they shared.

It was found that all the children shared, under one condition or another, and that the amount of candy given to the loser was not related to age. But the point at which sharing occurred and the verbal reasons for sharing related

closely to age. The fourth-graders were much more likely to share spontaneously and to share for altruistic reasons: "I like to share, to give others
satisfaction," "Candy should be shared to make the other child happy." Kindergartners were more likely to share only if promised a prize and to explain
their sharing in terms of external factors, "You promised me a prize," "You
told me to." The same sharing behavior reflected different internal factors at
different ages.

Aggressive behavior also relates to cognitive development. Willard Hartup
(1974) found an important contrast in the aggression of preschool and older
children. In the younger children aggression was almost entirely instrumental.
Four-year-olds typically hit, push, or grab someone's toy in order to achieve
a goal, such as getting a turn on the swing or keeping a toy. Hitting in order
to hurt is rare in the preoperational child, as you would expect from their focus
on the surface level of social interaction. In older children, who are more aware
of inner feelings, aggression involving a deliberate effort to make someone
unhappy is all too common.

During the elementary-school years the basic social skills developed earlier
fuse with the new skills in social cognition to produce far more sophisticated
forms of helping and hurting.

Applications box 13–2 Social problem solving

A new set of methods for helping children who have trouble getting along
with others and controlling their impulses is emerging. It reflects a cognitive approach that focuses on teaching skills in dealing with problems
of social living (Hobbs, Moguin, Tyroler, & Lahey, 1980; Urbain & Kendall,
1980). These methods contrast both with traditional psycho-
therapies oriented toward changing inner feelings and with behavioral
approaches aimed entirely at influencing overt action. Instead, in these
new interventions the emphasis is on changing the way children use their
minds in social situations.

Despite the varied names that have been applied to them, the new
training programs are similar in practice (Urbain & Kendall, 1980). They
typically combine some of a small set of core methods:

1. Direct verbal instruction about how to act
2. Modeling of the desired behavior
3. Reinforcement of some kind when the child produces the right action
4. Role play and rehearsal, or using the skills in lifelike practice sessions
5. Self-instruction training, as in teaching children to say to themselves,
   "Wait a minute. Let's see what I should do next"
6. Self-reinforcement, as when children say to themselves, "Good! I searched
   and found the right answer instead of giving up"
7. Feedback and group discussion, with either the adult or other children
   helping children see what they did and what the result was.

Notice that the use of such techniques as modeling and reinforcement illustrate that these cognitive approaches often actually combine cognitive and behavioral methods.

One of the better-validated approaches was developed by a Philadelphia group (Shure & Spivack, 1978; Spivack & Shure, 1974). Their approach centers on teaching children to think of alternative solutions to any interpersonal problem, to foresee the consequences of their actions, and to plan a series of specific actions for reaching a particular goal. They have developed a series of short training scripts that can be used in preschools, and they have taught teachers how to use them with demonstrated success in follow-ups a year later.

A contrasting approach developed by Chandler and his associates at the University of Rochester focuses on role playing (Chandler, 1973; Chandler, Greenspan, & Barenboim, 1974). In this approach older children write and videotape skits about people their own age. Each skit is redone until each child has played each role. Then the videotapes are reviewed and discussed. These efforts have been shown both to increase role-taking skill and to reduce rearrest rates of delinquents.

Present findings suggest that these techniques are valuable in helping children get along with others and manage their own behavior, although the evidence is less than adequate (Hobbs et al., 1980; Urbain & Kendall, 1980). We can be more confident that they work with relatively normal children than with those with severe problems because most of the controlled studies have focused on relatively normal children. Similarly, they more clearly have an immediate impact on behavior in current settings than on future behavior in novel places. However, part of their appeal is that they seem more likely to produce transfer than the simple behavioral techniques used in the past, for in the social problem-solving approach there is more focus on what's in children rather than simply changing how a particular setting reacts to them.

Social feelings

Feelings round out the picture. Attachments influence which reinforcers count and which models are more meaningful (Chapter 12). By considering these affective factors, along with cognitive ones, we can do better in predicting varied reactions to the same situation.

Social-learning principles explain how reinforcers influence social behavior, but why are some social stimuli reinforcing and others not? A child completes an arithmetic assignment and hears "good work, Jimmy!" Does working on arithmetic become more probable in the future? It depends in part on who said "good work." Praise from a teacher the child loves works as a reinforcer. If it comes from a hated teacher, the result would be different.

Many assume that the child's feelings about the models influence whether or not the child learns from them. The overall pattern of findings here has been inconsistent, but an important study by Marion Yarrow and her associates supports the idea. Because the models in this study played a much more enduring and lifelike role in the children's lives than in other experiments, it seems more relevant to questions about parents and teachers than the usual, brief experiment (Mussen & Eisenberg-Berg, 1977).

In the Yarrow, Scott, and Waxler (1973) study adults spent five days getting acquainted with preschoolers before serving as models. With half the children each adult always was nurturant, praising, helping, and as friendly as possible while working with them in a nursery school. With the others the models consistently were nonnurturant, being cool, aloof, and distant as much as possible. The modeling situations all involved altruism, being helpful to people and animals when you had no external reward to gain from it. There were a series of symbolic situations (pictures and little stages set) and realistic ones (involving people and animals). For all children the adult modeled being helpful, as in speaking in a comforting way to a child in a picture who saw another child fall off a swing or in helping a real mouse in a cage who was unable to reach the food.

Tests of transfer from the modeling situation to real life in nursery school showed that the relationship with the model made a big difference. Children exposed earlier to nurturant modeling increased their level of helping and expressing sympathy for others in real-life test situations, such as giving toys that had fallen out of a crib back to a baby when no adult was present or trying to comfort adults who accidentally hurt themselves. This careful study indicates that the kind of feeling relationship a child develops with an adult has a big influence on whether the child learns altruistic behavior from that model.

A common pattern

You better appreciate the complexity of social behavior when you simultaneously relate it to social cognition and to feelings. An example of a common pattern helps. Four-year-old Al is energetic. He moves through his social world rapidly. He likes other children, but his vigorous play often results in his hurting them. He loves Barney, the dog, but pesters him to play whether or not Barney feels like it. He is attached to his sister, but insists on wrestling with her when she would rather not. In sum, Al is warm, egocentric, and aggressive. At 4, he keeps hurting those he loves (a seeming contradiction of the balance principle, Chapter 12) because he is usually too centered on his own wants to think about those of others.

When he is 8, Al acts differently. His annoying behavior has disappeared. Now he can understand how others feel and use this understanding to anticipate the impact of his own actions; so he is much less likely to hurt those he loves. The balance principle operates and his antisocial behavior disappears. He is still energetic and loves wrestling, but now the discrimination between approved roughness and hurtful behavior comes easily.

As in this example, social behavior usually makes the most sense when we look at it in developmental terms, considering behavioral, cognitive, and emotional factors together.

SUMMARY

The story of social development was rounded out in this chapter. The growth of social behavior and of social understanding was described, the two were related to each other, and they were tied in with attachments to complete the three-sided picture of social development begun in the previous chapter.

The development of social behavior was described by first looking at three of its general features (relations with other areas, discrimination, and the importance of peer interactions) and then looking at several specifics. Early interactions with care givers and peers were described. Then the rise of prosocial and antisocial behavior was summarized. Both kinds of behavior become obvious in the second year and become more complicated and common in the years that follow. Then they were related to friendships because both positive and negative behaviors often occur in the context of friendship.

In looking at the development of social understanding, I first summarized three general trends: simplicity to organized complexity, surface to interior, and egocentrism to objectivity. Progress between ages 4 and 14 was emphasized, for social comprehension seems to make its most dramatic advances within these years.

Next attention turned to moral judgment, an important aspect of social understanding. The Piaget-Kohlberg position was highlighted because it has been the most important approach to the development of moral judgment. Piaget's focus on a transition from heteronomy to autonomy was followed by Kohlberg's idea of three general levels of moral judgment: the premoral, the conventional, and the principled. Both findings supporting Kohlberg's ideas and criticisms of his approach were described. Two important distinctions were emphasized: between the development of moral judgment and the development of conforming behavior and between the structure and the content of moral thought. Keeping these distinctions in mind, a simple generalization seemed sound: moral judgment develops similarly, even in children with varied backgrounds. One developmental trend is toward more emphasis on people's intentions in judging their actions. However, the details of the situation, how the child is asked to respond, and training all influence whether a child will focus on intentions in making a particular moral judgment.

Finally, the three facets of social development were brought together in a consideration of when prosocial and antisocial actions occur. Situational factors, such as modeling, reinforcement, and events that produce happy moods, provide a partial explanation of when and where we are likely to see helpful and hurtful actions. A fuller picture is possible by looking at internal factors in the child that change developmentally. When both social cognition and social feelings and their development are considered, we can do better in predicting.

PART V
Developmental Differences

Individual differences in behavior are evident at birth. Newborns vary in how much they cry, how vigorously they move, and how attentive they are to a moving red ring.

As new forms of activity emerge, we find new signs of individuality. When babies start smiling, we notice contrasts in how much they smile. The onset of walking reveals that some are early walkers.

Whenever we put children of the same age in the same situation, we observe varied reactions. For example, the first day of school produces striking contrasts. Some children are "tight," too scared to talk; others race around noisily, laughing and shouting.

How does this endless variety fit in with our search for patterns? Must we construct millions of child psychologies, a different psychology for each child? No. The differences in children that are not related to age pose exactly the same problem as those that are. In each case we start with a bewildering variety of observations and search for concepts and principles that put order in what we observe.

My daughter Kate's first sentence was "Puppy bite!"—a personal statement about an unsettling episode. It also was a textbook example of an early sentence: two words long, a concrete noun combined with a verb in correct order, an emotionally expressive utterance, and a comment on a here-and-now event. It illustrated universal trends.

It also illustrated textbook generalizations about differences among children of the same age. The average child starts putting words together in sentences at about the second birthday. "Puppy bite!" came months before Kate was 2; so she was different from the norm. But this contrast with her peers was predictable. Kate is a firstborn girl, and advanced language development is more common in this group. Her parents are college graduates; such children often are ahead in language.

Developmental contrasts such as early language interest child psychologists because they are part of a broad pattern. There is consistency from situation to situation, as when the child who constructs longer sentences in talking to parents also understands more of the words heard on television. There is also a consistency over time, as when the child who puts words together earlier turns out to be a better than average reader.

Many other differences do not help us find order. A few children can wiggle their ears. Some can make their eyes cross. So far no one has shown that these tricks relate to wider aspects of individuality. Thus, they are not important in child psychology.

We focus on forms of individuality that can be linked to a network of findings. These are the concern in the next three chapters. First we consider sex differences, then intellectual differences, and finally personality, or social-emotional contrasts.

CHAPTER 14

Sex Differences

Children come in two basic forms: girls and boys. This *sexual dimorphism* (two formism) is obvious when we look at their bodies. Even 3-year-olds get interested in who has what when they bathe together. A full description of child development must include some concern with the physical differences between the sexes.

Society treats girls and boys differently from the moment of birth. "It's a boy!" and "It's a girl!" are messages with contrasting meanings. Gender categories make a big difference to those around children long before children know or care what they are. Society pressures girls and boys to walk down contrasting developmental paths toward varied goals. Only by considering the differences in these paths can we appreciate what it means to grow up female or male.

Both biological and sociological facts of life must be considered in relation to sex differences. In this chapter I consider these areas first. Then I focus attention on psychological differences between girls and boys. Finally, I consider hypotheses about the origins of sex differences in behavior.

BIOLOGICAL FACTS OF LIFE: PHYSICAL DIMORPHISM

Origins

Sexual dimorphism starts at the moment of conception. There are characteristic variations in the genetic blueprints of female and male zygotes.

The mother's egg (*ovum*) contains 23 "packages" of genetic material (DNA) called *chromosomes*. Among the 23 there normally is one *X chromosome*. The father's sperm also each contains 23 chromosomes. About half the sperm include an X chromosome, but the others have one called a *Y chromosome* instead. The kind of sperm that unites with the egg, X or Y, determines whether the zygote is female or male. A zygote that gets an X chromosome from each parent (an *XX zygote*) normally is destined to become a girl baby. A zygote that gets a Y chromosome from its father (an *XY zygote*) typically ends up as a boy baby. The sperm from the father is the variable factor determining whether the genetic blueprint is female or male.

Every cell in the body is descended from the zygote. Each cell contains the same XX or XY "sex signature" as the original zygote. Girls and boys differ in every cell of their bodies.

It used to be thought there is a direct connection between the contrasts in the genetic blueprints and the kind of body form that followed. Now we know that the story is more complicated—we must consider *sex hormones* as well.

Sex hormones are chemicals produced by the sex glands. Either male sex glands (*testes* or *testicles*) are formed about six weeks after conception or female ones (*ovaries*) develop about a week later. The newly made glands start to produce a male or a female pattern of chemicals as soon as they are formed. These chemicals feed back into the developmental process and influence much that happens later.

The first research on sex hormones linked their action to physical changes and functions at puberty and after. More recent work has shown that sex hormones play an even more dramatic role in early development. Discoveries of how sex hormones influence prenatal development have resulted in a newer, more complicated, and rather startling picture of how female and male bodies come to differ. Two propositions sum up the current view:

> 1.   All people (and other mammals) are basically female. That is, all zygotes (XX and XY) will become newborns with normal female bodies if they are not exposed to any sex hormones during the prenatal period (or are exposed only to female sex hormones).
> 2.   Male bodies develop in people (and other mammals) if and only if there is sufficient exposure to male sex hormones during certain periods between conception and birth. In other words, all zygotes (XX and XY) will develop into newborns with normal male bodies if they are exposed to enough male sex hormones during certain parts of the prenatal period.

There is no need to go into all the details supporting these extraordinary conclusions here. They come from a variety of studies. Laboratory animals have been exposed to surgery and chemistry that stops normal hormone action or supplied artificial hormones. Some pregnant human mothers have taken artificial hormones—for example, in birth-control pills and in medicines designed to prevent miscarriage. A few babies have abnormalities that result in failures to produce sex hormones or to react to them normally. The evidence all ties together (Hutt, 1972; Money & Ehrhardt, 1972).

The new picture portrays the path to a mature female or male body as one with a series of choice points. At each choice point either a female or a male turn can be taken. If little or no male hormone is circulating in the body at the crucial point, the basic female choice is made. If sufficient male sex hormone is present, the body takes a masculine direction. Body form is not a decision made once and for all in the zygote (Money & Ehrhardt, 1972).

The construction of testes at six weeks is the crucial element in the XY zygote's strategy for becoming a boy in spite of the female tendencies within it. Once the testes are built, their production of male sex hormone usually ensures a male path from there on. For example, soon after the internal sex glands are formed, the individual faces the choice of forming a vagina or a penis. Years later puberty involves either a feminine turn toward breasts, relatively wide hips, and so on or a masculine line of development featured by beard, relatively wide shoulders, and the rest. Under normal circumstances the XY individual's own sex hormones will bias each of these choices in a male direction and the absence of male hormone in the XX person will mean staying on the female path.

Under unusual conditions a child can start down one path and get switched to the other at later points. These children can combine early developing features of a male body with later developing characteristics of a female body, or vice versa. For example, an XX zygote can develop ovaries rather than testes but be "masculinized" later if the pregnant mother is given drugs containing male sex hormones. An XY zygote can develop testes but fail to develop a normal penis if something goes wrong in the production of male sex hormones or in the body's response to them. In cases like these the internal glands (ovaries or testes) are often a better clue to gender development than the more obvious external organs (vaginal opening or penis). Sometimes a child known as a girl or boy is given corrective surgery and a new sex label so that mature capacities such as sperm and egg production will fit in with the person's label and appearance. Children with such mixed development have helped us understand the nature of physical dimorphism. They also are helping researchers see how biological and social factors interact in determining psychological development (Ehrhardt & Baker, 1974; Kohlberg, 1966; Maccoby, 1975; Maccoby & Jacklin, 1974).

All the obvious differences between girls' and boys' bodies show how sex hormones did or didn't enter into the construction process. The sex glands, the sex organs, and secondary features such as breasts and beards all reflect both past and present hormone levels in the blood.

But sex hormones influence nonsexual body parts and functions as well. Hormone-linked variations exist in such systems as muscles and brain—body parts basic to behavior. This fact makes the possibility of biological biases toward different activity patterns more plausible. I'll examine this question of whether hormones influence human behavior in more detail later. Now let's round out the picture of biological factors by considering sex contrasts in physical development.

General differences in physical development

Two overall contrasts in physical growth are relevant to child psychology: growth rate and vulnerability to problems.

Girls tend to be ahead. This general rule often applies in physical development. At birth girls are ahead in bone development by an average of about four weeks. Girls get permanent teeth first and reach puberty first. Boys don't catch up until they are adults (Tanner, 1970).

Males are more vulnerable to biological problems throughout most of the life span. The larger number of older women in most societies results from higher male casualty rates that begin before birth. A smaller percentage of XY zygotes than XX zygotes survives until birth. Among the survivors the boys have relatively more troubles. Boy babies are more prone to such birth complications as lack of oxygen; they suffer from more recessive gene problems, such as color blindness; and they typically don't live as long. The list of disorders such as cerebral palsy, ulcers, and heart disease that plague males more than females is longer than the corresponding list of female problems (Hutt, 1972).

Should you want to pick a weaker sex on the basis of the overall pattern of biological development, don't pick females.

Individuality in physical development

The contrast between girls and boys with respect to physical development means that a child's growth is better understood when we look at the individual in terms of her or his own sex. Tina and Tim can be seen in clearer terms if we compare them with norms, or averages, for girls and for boys than if we simply compare them with all children their age (Tanner, 1970).

Height growth provides a good illustration. All children show the same human pattern (Chapter 4), but there are predictable variations related to sex. The tendency for girls to be ahead of boys in bone development shows up clearly here. Girls usually reach their mature height at an earlier age. At any age from birth on they are closer to their mature height. Accordingly, if Tina and Tim are the same height at the same age during childhood, we can bet that Tim will be taller at age 18. He probably has more growing left to do.

SOCIAL FACTS OF LIFE

Sex roles: Comparative perspective

Comparisons of diverse cultures help us see what is universal in human groups and what is specific to our own. As we notice others' costumes and customs, we have a chance to realize that our own concept of what is "natural" reflects where and when we grew up.

The promise of an entirely objective perspective, unbiased by our own stereotypes, has not been fulfilled (Rosenblatt & Cunningham, 1976), but cross-cultural studies of so-called "primitive" peoples have revealed some noteworthy trends. All societies have *systems of social roles.* There are contrasting parts to be played by different actors on the social scene: producing food, providing entertainment, caring for children, settling arguments, and so on. The varying parts must fit together or the group's problems won't get solved. A school band made up of ten drummers and a violinist will not find appropriate music to play as easily as one with a conventional balance of players. Enduring groups have to work out a smoothly running system of roles.

All known societies have used biological sex as an important distinction in their social system. Adult role assignments everywhere depend on whether the actor is female or male (Bem, 1981; D'Andrade, 1966). Many social roles and categories vary with time and place. Only some cultures use such social labels as lawyer or wigmaker, but sex, or gender, roles are universal.

When roles require special preparation, success in having the right balance of role players at the crucial time requires anticipation. Music teachers start worrying about the combination of instruments needed in the 1985 sixth-grade band when they meet with first-graders in 1980. It takes months and years before a child can fill the role of tuba player adequately. Both the desire to master the tuba and lots of tuba lessons are useful preconditions if a child is to become a skilled tuba player. An adult role casts a long shadow before it in time. Children must stand in that shadow and let it color their thoughts, wishes, and actions if they are to be ready for the role. Societies that endure over generations prepare their children for adult roles and responsibilities long before they must face them. Our schools are but a special case of a more general pattern: *socialization is anticipatory.*

Socialization is anticipatory: children in most cultures are prepared for adult roles and responsibilities long before they are ready to face them.

Childhood everywhere involves contrasting developmental paths to varying goals for girls and boys. When you look at a 10-year-old, it's hard to know whether you are facing a future banker, teacher, or violinist. But you can tell what sex role children will play 25 years later just by looking at them at birth. Gender categories are more permanent and predictable than most. As long as adult sex roles continue, we are likely to find that girls and boys undergo different socialization patterns from the earliest months of life.

Sex stereotypes

Shared ideas about people in a particular role or social category are called *stereotypes.* There are *sex stereotypes,* as well as stereotypes of Poles and presidents. Stereotypes are concepts. They include generalizations that highlight the features seen as crucial in the people thought about, just as political cartoons emphasize elements in the actions and appearance of those pictured. Stereotypes can be mostly accurate, as in our image of lawyers as good with words, or mostly wrong, as in the idea that men are physically superior to women. By definition stereotypes are pictures in the heads of some people. Accurate or inaccurate, they reflect the way people think and influence how they act.

Cross-cultural findings

In turning to sex stereotypes we can get past particular sex-role responsibilities, such as babysitting or delivering papers, and look for broader patterns. They help us see what is common in diverse and often culture-specific sex-role assignments.

Three cross-cultural findings stand out. The first is that *sex stereotypes vary among human groups.* There are societies where men always do the cooking, where women always build the houses, where after marriage sons live with their parents, where after marriage daughters live with their parents (D'Andrade, 1966; Mead, 1935; Rosenblatt & Cunningham, 1976). Whatever the sex-role pattern, each group sees what is done as natural. Their stereotype of female or male nature varies with the contrasts in behavior that they expect.

Sex roles and stereotypes are universal, but their content is not. If a new culture is "discovered" in the Amazon jungle next year, they surely will have contrasting ways of raising girls and boys and parallel variations in their ideas about them. It's much riskier to bet on what the contrast will be.

Second, *societies vary greatly in how much they make of sex differences.* Some treat girls and boys quite similarly in most areas of life. In other groups the gulf between the male and the female world is large and ever-present. In looking at socialization patterns, a good first question is whether the sex stereotypes maximize or minimize contrasts (Barry, Bacon, & Child, 1957).

The third cross-cultural finding is that *groups that maximize sex contrasts in their thinking and living tend to do it in similar ways* (D'Andrade, 1966; Rosenblatt & Cunningham, 1976). If you are told that a culture emphasizes sex differences, you can probably guess how it does it. The traditional stereotypes of our own society turn up all over the world. Sexist thinking takes similar form in a variety of cultures. A classic study by Herbert Barry, Margaret Bacon, and Irvin Child (1957) shows the pattern as it relates to child rearing. They looked at reports on dozens of societies to see if girls and boys were pressured similarly or differently toward nurturance, obedience, responsibility (dutifulness in performing chores), and self-reliance. The strongest trends were for nurturance and self-reliance. For nurturance (being helpful to younger siblings and other dependent people) 82% of the groups were rated as pushing girls to show more; 18% pushed the sexes equally; and none pushed the boys to be more nurturant. On self-reliance 85% of the groups were rated as pushing the boys more; 15% did not differentiate; and none pushed the girls to be more self-reliant. On the other variables the trends also fit our stereotypes, but there were some reversals and more groups that did not differentiate. For example,

35% of the groups pushed girls to be more obedient; 3% pressured boys toward more obedience; and 62% were judged as pushing them the same amount in this direction.

The predominant stereotype in child rearing cross-culturally, then, was to push for boys who are more self-reliant and achievement oriented and girls who are more nurturant, obedient, and dutiful. Because socialization is anticipatory, it is not surprising that cross-cultural examination of political and economic systems has revealed parallel trends in the world of adults.

Political systems are more often organized around the male than the female role in preliterature cultures. The trend is for men to have higher *public* status (head of the house, political leader, religious leader). Family names, property, and titles more often are passed along on male lines (D'Andrade, 1966; Rosenblatt & Cunningham, 1976). In economic systems certain kinds of work turn up as almost consistently male or female. Making war, pursuing sea mammals, making weapons, trapping, working metal, and building boats are overwhelmingly male specialties around the world. Cooking, carrying water, making pottery, and repairing clothes are women's work in a high percentage of cultures (D'Andrade, 1966).

These cross-cultural trends raise two questions: (1) What determines whether a society emphasizes sex differences or plays them down? (2) Why do similar stereotypes emerge repeatedly in the diverse groups that emphasize sex differences?

Sources of stereotypes

Anthropologists have sought answers to these questions by looking at what culture characteristics go with variation in stereotyping. The findings here have led to three intriguing hypotheses about the sources of stereotyped socialization pressures.

Barry, Bacon, and Child (1957) found two trends more common among groups that treated girls and boys differently than among those that minimized socialization differences: (1) The more the group made its living by a system in which sheer strength and big-muscle skill was important, the more likely it was to treat girls and boys differently. (2) Girls and boys were more likely to be raised in a contrasting manner when they grew up in a large family unit with lots of cooperative interaction. Perhaps in a large living group you can afford to have stricter ideas about who does what because someone of the "right" sex for the job will always be around when the job has to be done. In a small family, in contrast, a rule that only women can cook or only men can light fires could become a major problem whenever one adult was away or sick.

Paul Rosenblatt and Michael Cunningham (1976) present an alternative hypothesis. Like most researchers, they focus on *work roles,* but the clearest pattern they find relates to whether the work requires going away from home or is carried out in or near it. They think that the mobility variable became a central aspect of female-male job assignment because of some basic facts of life in a prescientific world. In our own past and in current prescientific societies (1) women breast-feed babies until the babies are about 2 years old, (2) the typical woman has an average of about four babies who survive until the age of weaning (2 years), and therefore (3) the typical woman is immobilized for about eight years of her adult life because of nursing responsibilities. Eight years was a much bigger part of adult life in the old days. Puberty came later; death often came much earlier. Women were tied down with nursing for a big fraction of their working years. The mobility hypothesis is that this biologically linked contrast between the sexes generated varying role assignments. Men got the traveling jobs; women got those where they could combine other work with nursing and child tending.

The mobility hypothesis relates to an *inside/outside distinction* that turns up in our own stereotypes and in children's behavior. For example, Lawrence Harper and Karen Sanders (1975) recently studied preschoolers' use of space. Boys play outside more and use more space in their play despite the staff's equalitarian attitudes. Older studies reveal strong trends in book preferences. Girls prefer books about families and boys select more adventure stories (Terman & Tyler, 1954). Mothers seem more concerned with close-to-home daily affairs; fathers apparently worry more about what will happen to children when they get older and move out of the house (Chapter 18). We cannot tell if the mobility factor is crucial in the emergence of contrasting sex roles, but it certainly points up a common pattern that exists today.

PSYCHOLOGICAL DIFFERENCES

The biological and social realities both suggest that we should find contrasts in the psychology of girls and of boys, and so we do. First I'll describe the variations; then I'll deal with the more complicated question of tracing their origin.

The biggest and most significant contrasts between girls and boys turn up in social-emotional areas (Terman & Tyler, 1954). Girls and boys differ most on such measures as what they do with their free time, what they enjoy, and what they want for the future. Where we see contrasting behavior patterns, as in aggression and peer relations, the variations relate more obviously to motive than to skill.

The differences in the social-emotional area relate closely to our stereotypes of what it means to be female or male. The psychological content of these stereotypes thus makes a good starting point in examining psychological contrasts between the sexes more generally.

Psychological aspects of sex-role stereotypes

Once children realize that gender is permanent and related to their place in society, the cultural view begins to play a personal role. A social stereotype then becomes part of children's concepts of who they are and what they should become (Kohlberg, 1966).

Society's picture of a good girl becomes part of Rosa's image of what she should be like. If nice girls don't fight, then Rosa's evaluation of herself and her behavior comes to reflect the general stereotype. If big boys don't cry, then Mike's stereotype of boys colors Mike's picture of himself. The shared features of our sex stereotypes become part of children's pictures of themselves as well as of others, part of both internal and external psychological realities.

The common denominator that we each carry around in us and help communicate to children can be summed up in two points:

1. There are two psychological dimensions in sex stereotypes.
2. The psychological evaluation of females, males, and their qualities is not the same in our culture.

Two dimensions in sex stereotypes

The concepts of expressiveness and instrumentality sum up many features of the way we think about females and males. They help us see psychological similarities in a variety of symbols, roles, and actions. They even clarify the important differences between our stereotypes and the real world.

Females are expressive. Males are instrumental. That's what we think. The terms are technical (Parsons & Bales, 1955), but the concepts are familiar. A child who says girls play house and boys run races is getting at the same idea. We see it in the contrasting enrollments in college majors in engineering and in elementary education. Systematic studies get at the stereotypes through such methods as asking adults to indicate what descriptive adjectives go with which sex (see Bem, 1974; Broverman, Vogel, Broverman, Clarkson, & Rosenkrantz, 1972) or telling children stories and asking whether the characters more likely were female or male (Best, Williams, Cloud, Davis, Robertson, Edwards, Giles, & Fowles, 1978).

Expressiveness.   Expressiveness refers to such qualities as warmth, gentleness, sensitivity, and understanding (see Table 14–1). Expressiveness requires an orientation to other people because it is defined in terms of positive relations with others. You cannot be expressive in isolation from others. Table 14–1 shows that you can think of expressiveness as having a positive end (E+), defined by qualities such as warmth, and a negative extreme (E−), where their opposites prevail (qualities such as hostility, coldness, and insensitivity). These ends, or poles, are genuine opposites because you must leave one as you approach the other. In our culture the female role/stereotype is defined in terms of the positive end of the expressiveness dimension.

Instrumentality.   Instrumentality involves competence in dealing with the world, in getting the job done, in being strong, realistic, active, and rational (see Table 14–1). The focus is on tasks and, accordingly, often on things. People are important only as they relate to task orientation. Thus, competition and leadership are important social qualities related to instrumentality, but expressive social qualities such as sensitivity and warmth are not. As with expressiveness, instrumentality is a dimension with two opposite poles (I+ and I−). Helplessness, weakness, and passivity make up the I− pole because they are direct opposites of the competence qualities at I+. In our society the

TABLE 14–1 Expressiveness and instrumentality

	Expressiveness	*Instrumentality*	
(E+)	warm	competent	(I+)
	attractive	strong	
	emotional	rational	
	sensitive	realistic	
	nurturant	competitive	
	understanding	independent	
		active	
(E−)	hostile	incompetent	(I−)
	cold	weak	
	insensitive	helpless	
	rejecting	unrealistic	
	unfeeling	dependent	
		passive	
Orient toward	people	tasks	
Fulfillment through	family	career	
Related careers	nurse	astronaut	
	teacher	carpenter	

Based on Bem, 1974; Broverman et al., 1972

male role/stereotype is defined in terms of the positive end of the instrumentality dimension.

Independence of the two dimensions.   A point too often missed is that in real people expressiveness and instrumentality are independent dimensions, not opposites (Bem, 1974; Broverman et al., 1972; Constantinople, 1973). They are like the compass directions north and east (see Figure 14–1). You can go north without going west, east without going south. Similarly, we find warm competent people (E+, I+) and cold weak ones (E−, I−). We also find warm incompetent people (E+, I−), hostile skillful ones (E−, I+), and many people with combinations involving intermediate positions on both dimensions. Knowing where persons are on expressiveness cannot help us predict where they are on instrumentality any more than their position north or south in the United States can tell us how far east or west they are. We must chart actual psychological qualities in these two-dimensional terms if we are to portray everyone.

The world of conventional sex stereotypes is one-dimensional, however, unlike the real world. It leaves out possibilities. It distorts the actual picture. The stereotyped view is that expressiveness (E+) and incompetence (I−) must go together. Here the image is of "true femininity" as reflected in the picture of the typical woman as sweet and idiotic. At the opposite end a "real

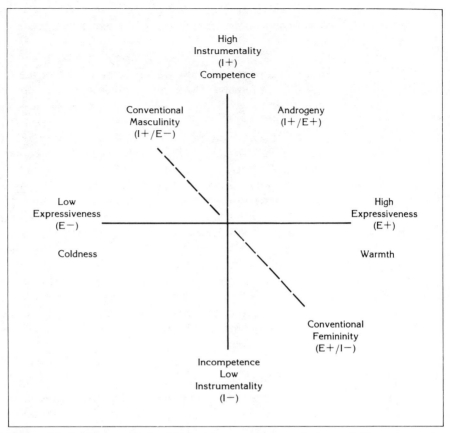

High
Instrumentality
(I+)
Competence

Conventional
Masculinity
(I+/E−)

Androgeny
(I+/E+)

Low
Expressiveness
(E−)

High
Expressiveness
(E+)

Coldness

Warmth

Conventional
Femininity
(E+/I−)

Incompetence
Low
Instrumentality
(I−)

Figure 14–1 Framework for looking at expressiveness, instrumentality and sex-role stereotypes

man" is portrayed as necessarily combining instrumentality (I+) with a hostile and insensitive approach to others (E−). The gunman of old western movies and the football coach who holds "kill rallies" show this view.

Androgyny. The conventional stereotypes of masculinity and femininity pose them as opposites. As illustrated in Figure 14–1, they thus leave out the attractive possibility of combining the positive aspects of both expressiveness and instrumentality (E+, I+). Instead, the conventional, or one-dimensional, view implies that a woman who becomes competent and independent loses her femininity and a man who expresses tenderness betrays his masculinity. Much more than a dry, technical issue is involved in the choice between two-dimensional and one-dimensional conceptions.

Sandra Bem (1974) popularized the term *androgyny* for the mix of two kinds of positive qualities that can and does occur in some females and some males. She has criticized psychologists appropriately on two grounds. The masculinity-femininity scales psychologists first developed incorrectly incorporated one-dimensional thinking and helped popularize the error of thinking that feminine and masculine are opposites psychologically. Psychologists have too often promoted conformity to traditional stereotypes as the path to mental health.

With a growing number of women taking jobs outside the home and pursuing careers seriously, we are confronted with the fact of greater instrumentality in females. Does this emphasis on competence and independence undermine the traditional female value, expressiveness, as a one-dimensional picture implies?

A growing body of evidence contradicts the prediction from traditional thinking. Sandra Tangri (1972) compared college women preparing for non-sex-typical careers (law, medicine, physics, and so on) with those with traditional plans (teaching, nursing, social work, and so on). The women in such fields as prelaw were more instrumentally oriented than those in the traditional fields, but there was no difference between the groups when their romances and friendships with men were compared. Comparisons of children of mothers working outside the home with children of homemakers have produced parallel findings (Broverman et al., 1972). The children of mothers who work outside the home see female expressiveness in terms similar to those whose mothers are homemakers, but children with career mothers are less likely to see females as incompetent. In the world of career women, as in the laboratory, we see both an independence of instrumentality and expressiveness and the possibility of greater androgyny.

Asymmetry

Separate but equal is how textbooks in child psychology have usually described the sex roles for girls and boys. Unfortunately, that's not the way our culture sees it. Like many cultures, we have a "second sex." "It's a girl" is not proclaimed with the same enthusiasm as "It's a boy!" Our culture teaches children that girls and boys are different and unequal in countless ways. What we really teach them is that boys are better.

Few adults today come out and give the basic message directly, "Sorry Jill, you're nice, but you're only second best." But the point gets through nevertheless. If you open your eyes and ears, it is easy to see how it happens. Start by looking inside yourself. Here are some simple questions. Answer them and get some of your friends to do the same; then read on.

1. Have you ever wished that you were a member of the opposite sex?
2. If you could have only one child, which sex would you want it to be?
3. If you could have two and only two children, what sex would you want the first one to be? The second?
4. How would you feel about getting to be friendly with a student your age who is a female who usually wears slacks?
5. How would you feel about getting to be friendly with a student your age who is a male who usually wears skirts?
6. Would you want a child of yours to be a "daddy's girl"?
7. Would you want a child of yours to be a "mommy's boy"?
8. How would you react if your 9-year-old nephew played mostly with girls?
9. How would you react if your 9-year-old niece played mostly with boys?

When typical American adults answer questions such as these, they show that the concept of male superiority is deeply ingrained, both in males and females (Brown, 1958). Many more female than male college students report having wished they were the opposite sex. Most men and a majority of women would rather have a boy if they could have only one child. With two children the preference for the male-female sequence is overwhelming, probably reflecting the notion that it is normal for the male to be bigger-stronger-older-wiser that is so prominent in our dating and marriage patterns (Westoff & Rindfuss, 1974).

Answers to questions about males who wear skirts and boys who play with girls reveal an important fact: most members of our society find it acceptable for girls to borrow from the male role and inappropriate for boys to borrow from the female role (Brown, 1958; Maccoby, 1975). This unbalanced view of role conformity turns up again and again. "Tomboy" doesn't even have a real counterpart. Certainly "sissy" is much more negative. "Momma's boy" is hardly equivalent to "daddy's girl." Often girls' first names are basically masculine. Roberta, Carla, Georgene, Bobbie, Billie, and Jo can walk among us with little discomfort, but Francis usually becomes Frank.

Boys are expected to walk a narrower path, and by the time they enter first grade, they typically do (Brown, 1958). The contrast links to the idea of male superiority. If male is better, we understand and tolerate a little girl who does "boy things." It is "only natural" that she wants what is "best." We are patient with her because her deviance helps confirm the general view of masculine superiority. As part of our unbalanced world, we expect females and males to share, but in a male-centered way. A girl who learns about baseball can make life pleasanter for boyfriends and sons later. But if a boy does "girl things," he's not just behaving inappropriately; he's challenging the social order. A boy who wears girls' clothing or plays girls' games hits at the deep-seated belief that male is better. The culture hits back.

Society, then, simultaneously gives two messages: (1) Girls are inferior. (2) Girls may borrow more freely from the male role society sees as number one. With their superior status, boys (like kings) are given a narrower set of alternatives and probably get a more negative response when they stray from their path (Brown, 1958).

Psychological contrasts in social-emotional areas

The concepts of expressiveness, instrumentality, and asymmetry give us a start at looking at sex differences in the social-emotional area. Most differences fit in with them, but shared social images of the psychology of girls and boys create a problem. Stereotypes do not always mirror reality. They often exaggerate minor matters and sometimes they are just plain wrong (Maccoby & Jacklin, 1974). Our stereotypes make it easy to see what isn't there. In the sections that follow I take a cautious approach, focusing on the areas where the evidence on sex differences seems relatively strong and leaving out a number of disputed or inadequately explored areas. Three topics stand out: interests, aggression, and peer relations.

Interests

The evidence on varying interests is clear and consistent starting at about age 5 years. When you know a child's sex, you can predict what the child will like, prefer, seek, and value. Some of the findings are summarized in Table 14–2. Notice that both the expressiveness-instrumental distinction and the related contrast of inside-outside relate to diverse findings about interests.

TABLE 14–2 Contrasting interests of girls and boys

	Stronger Interest By	
Category	Girls	Boys
Toy preferences	cosmetic set bracelet	trucks hammer
Reading preferences	family	adventure
Movie preferences	romance	western
Game preferences	sedentary activity	strenuous activity
Wishes	social and family relations	personal achievement

Based on Cobb, 1954; DeLucia, 1963; Fein, Johnson, Kosson, Stork, & Wasserman, 1975; Terman & Tyler, 1954.

Children's interests color what they do both in front of others and when alone (Terman & Tyler, 1954). When an 8-year-old pursues her interest in tree climbing outside, others see what is happening and react. Because everyone agrees on what girls and boys are supposed to like, it is not surprising that public signs of children's interests conform to stereotypes. Sex differences in outdoor play might be a simple and superficial matter of conformity, but more private forms of behavior show the same kinds of sex differences. The books children pick to read and even their wishes show a sex-typed coloration (see Table 14–2). Sex differences in children's interests cannot be dismissed as mere conformity; they reflect matters of personal importance.

The implications of sex-typed interest patterns become clear when you think about how interests relate to learning. Children's interests influence how they spend their free time. They create a whole curriculum of learning opportunities. If Heather is interested in baseball, she gives herself "homework assignments": play ball, read about it, watch games on TV, talk about baseball with parents and friends. Tom's interest in horses results in a different set of assignments. Sex differences in interests result in the acquisition of contrasting knowledge and varied skills.

We still don't know when the interests of girls and boys first begin to diverge. A conservative view is that big contrasts don't appear until 5 years. Some argue the patterns start early in infancy (Hutt, 1972).

Aggression

Aggression is a male specialty. Psychologists usually define aggression as behavior whose goal is the delivery of injury. No matter what your definition, the evidence is likely to show that boys do more of it. They fight more, try to injure more, tell stories with more aggression in them, watch more aggressive television, and report more dreams about hurting and killing. In fantasy and reality, in action and in intention we find this sex difference. Often the differences are large. The evidence is consistent across diverse studies in varied societies (Maccoby & Jacklin, 1974, 1980).

Notice how sex differences in aggression tie in with sex-typed interests. Early aggressive actions often involve responses such as hitting and pushing, which suggests a tie between male aggression and boys' greater preference for vigorous activity. Competitive activities require that there be losers. A preference for competitive fields in which you can win is simultaneously an interest in beating others and a way of delivering injury. Similarly, when adventure involves violence (as in reading about crime or playing war), contrasts in interests parallel sex differences in aggression.

The aggression difference emerges early. Children's aggression is seen first in peer interaction at about age 2 or 3 years. As soon as the behavior can be seen, the frequency is higher for boys than for girls (Maccoby, 1975). It is as easy to find when you watch 4-year-olds as 10-year-olds (Maccoby & Jacklin, 1974). The trend differs from the overall picture of interests, where the contrasts emerge gradually and become dramatic only during middle childhood.

There is a popular idea that girls are as aggressive as boys but show it differently. The claim is that girls are more verbally aggressive and catty rather than inclined to more direct fights. Eleanor Maccoby and Carol Jacklin gave this idea close attention in their important review (1974). They found that it did not hold up. It seems more accurate to say that the differences between girls and boys are less dramatic when we turn from physical to verbal aggression, but the trend is for boys to be more aggressive, regardless of the measure.

Boys usually aggress against boys. Girls typically are neither victims nor attackers in aggressive episodes (Maccoby & Jacklin, 1974). This pattern emerges at about the same age as that for attackers. Not aggressing against girls has been found at age 2½ (Maccoby, 1975) and continues from there on. Sex differences in aggression relate to broader contrasts in patterns of peer interaction.

Peer relations

When children play outdoors, the boys more often are in relatively large groups and the girls more commonly spend their free time with one or two friends. This tendency for boys to "run in packs" is cross-cultural (Maccoby & Jacklin, 1974). The evidence on adolescence suggests that even then the gang is a male matter, not a female one (Douvan & Adelson, 1966).

The contrast in group size becomes clear at about age 6 and ties in with varied findings about children's groups from there on. During the elementary-school years, children's groups tend to be girl groups or boy groups, another cross-cultural trend (Hartup, 1970).

Comparisons of girls' and boys' groups show that the contrast in aggression is part of a broader one. Boys' groups are more likely to emphasize dominance, competition, and power relations: Who is boss? Who is best? A boy's status in his group often relates to how tough he is and whether he can beat others. For girls, issues such as dominance and relative power are less important (Maccoby & Jacklin, 1974).

Fights can break out when children play house or play with Barbie and Ken dolls, but they are not the intention, as they are when children play war or wrestle. Boys' groups seem rich in opportunities for building instrumental competence, including skills in aggressive give and take. The more intimate peer relations between girls seem to make it easier for expressive skills to grow.

Psychological contrasts in areas of competence

Differences in ability between girls and boys are less common than social-emotional contrasts. They are usually smaller, but the question of sex differences in ability has been prominent. The doctrine of male superiority is basic to our cultural stereotype and to the discriminatory practices so common in our history. Sex discrimination in the workplace and in education has often been justified in terms of claims about differential ability. Claims and counterclaims have helped foster research in this area. Here is a summary of the main findings.

Perceptual-motor skills

Comparisons of the sexes on measures of strength indicate a small edge for the average boy until about 13 years. Then the difference becomes more substantial as the typical boy makes much bigger gains in strength during adolescence than the typical girl. For example, in one study of strength of arm pull at 11 years, the boys were stronger by an average of about 3 kilograms. At age 17, the average difference was over 20 kilograms (Tanner, 1970).

In contrast, the evidence on skills involving balance, rhythm, and accuracy of movement often shows female superiority (Cratty, 1970). For example, girls tend to start to walk earlier, do better at early hopping and skipping, and in the elementary-school years do better on such tasks as finger opposition (rapidly touching each finger to the thumb in order) and keeping their balance while walking on a beam.

Perceptual-motor skills are often specific. A child can be strong in one area while being poor in others. Because of this and because the sexes show lots of overlap, even where their averages differ, these findings provide little basis for predicting performance in areas involving complex perceptual-motor skills such as piano playing or baseball. On the average a 6-year-old boy is likely to be able to throw a ball better than a girl, but a girl is more likely to be able to catch it. Such trends provide little basis for practical decisions.

Intellectual skills

Intellectual skills have been the main focus in research on sex differences in ability. Tests of general intelligence normally are deliberately rigged so as not to show sex differences (questions that produce big sex differences are taken out and replaced with ones that don't). Thus, the work on sex differences emphasizes performance on more specialized tests emphasizing particular types of content (verbal, numerical, or spatial) or distinct processes (such as reasoning or memory).

The trend has been to find a few fairly consistent sex differences on tests of specific mental abilities. Girls often turn up with better average scores on measures of verbal ability, particularly before age 3 and after age 11 (Maccoby & Jacklin, 1974). Boys on the average do better on tests of visual-spatial ability, for example, in finding a picture of a diamond that is embedded in a complicated design or in visualizing what a pile of blocks would look like if it were turned around. This superiority emerges in early childhood and grows with age. Mathematical ability shows a trend similar to visual-spatial ability; on the average girls do as well as boys in elementary school and then fall behind (Maccoby & Jacklin, 1974).

Another trend in intellectual skills parallels the picture of male vulnerability found in physical development. Boys are more likely to be mentally retarded and to have special problems in such areas as reading and language development.

The differences in ability previously summarized fit common beliefs, but it is important to note that a number of other claims about sex differences in ability do not hold up. Girls don't generally do better on simple, repetitive tasks. Boys don't do better than girls on tasks requiring reasoning and high-level analysis unless the comparison is biased by measuring reasoning and analysis through quantitative and visual-spatial problems (as often was done in early studies) (McGee, 1979; Sherman, 1967). The evidence reveals somewhat contrasting patterns of abilities in girls and boys and contradicts claims about male superiority.

Differential patterning of psychological variables

Everyday observation suggests that the same actions and skills can have different meanings for girls and for boys. Pleasing the teacher, winning a race, getting into a fight, and writing a poem don't fit into female and male lives in the same way. Similarly, the same event, such as puberty, the first date, or getting a driver's license, is awaited and experienced in contrasting terms for the two sexes. A technical term for this idea that the same variable can play a different role in girls' and boys' lives is *differential patterning*.

So far the summary of psychological sex differences has focused on the question of how boys and girls differ on the average in how much they exhibit of a particular behavior, such as aggression or verbal ability. Now we turn to the more complicated question of differential patterning. The emphasis shifts from single variables to relations between variables.

Consider one of the better established patterning differences: the relation between intelligence-test scores and measures of social-emotional aspects of personality. The main finding is that within a group of girls intelligence correlates differently with measures of variables such as impulsivity, aggressiveness, and competitiveness than it does within a group of boys. Within a group of boys the relationship between intelligence and aggression (or impulsivity or competitiveness) is likely to be negative. Brighter boys are less likely to be relatively aggressive, impulsive, or competitive. With girls we don't find these relationships. Sometimes we find opposite ones (brighter girls turning out as more likely to be aggressive, impulsive, or competitive). Intelligence comes in a different psychological package for girls and boys (Maccoby, 1966).

Similar contrasts turn up when other sorts of patterning are examined. For example, in one sample, childhood aggressiveness was a relatively good predictor of similar adult qualities for boys, but not for girls (Kagan & Moss, 1962). Academic performances show other contrasts that are lost when only one variable is examined at a time. Girls tend to get higher grades than boys even in subjects such as math, while the boys do better on standard achievement tests (Maccoby, 1966). The relation between tested achievement and grades varies with sex.

If, as is likely, girls and boys differ most in goals and feelings, then we won't understand the contrasts in their psychology until we have much more information on patterning (Block, 1976; Terman & Tyler, 1954).

EXPLANATIONS

Why do girls and boys differ in their actions? Can we sort out the contributions stemming from biological dimorphism and from sex roles in any clear way? Certainly we lack a full answer. Our evidence is too limited; the story is too complicated. But we can begin to see the form that a satisfactory answer must take. First consider some general ideas relevant to any adequate explanation of psychological sex differences; then we'll turn to some plausible alternatives of contrasting kinds.

General points

Much of the everyday argument about why girls and boys contrast somewhat in their actions fails to take some basic ideas into account. There is less room for argument than many think. The basic alternatives are somewhat different from what you might at first suppose. The following points provide a useful foundation that helps reduce argument to reasonable alternatives.

Contrasting explanations

There is no logical reason to expect that all sex differences in behavior develop in the same way (Maccoby & Jacklin, 1974). Rather than looking for one answer to the question of why boys and girls differ in their actions, we must look at specific evidence in each area and be ready to construct contrasting explanations. Early appearing differences, as in aggressiveness, presumably result from causative factors that operate early. Differences in verbal ability emerge gradually and more likely reflect influences that continue throughout childhood. Why assume that the same explanations will work for varied patterns of development?

Relativity of differences

Psychological differences between girls and boys all are relative rather than absolute. Our task always is to explain why one sex shows more or less of some behavior, never to explain a unique psychological quality in one sex. There are girls who fight, boys who are skilled with words, girls who love adventure. An explanation of sex differences is reasonable only if it doesn't explain "too much."

Our typical finding is that even when boys and girls differ on the average, there is much overlap. The average girl surpasses the average boy on a number of tests of verbal ability, but many boys do better than the average girl. Many girls do worse than the average boy.

In most areas the average difference between sexes is smaller than that within sexes. For example, if you measure visual-spatial ability in a sixth-grade class, the difference between the best boy and the worst boy on your test will probably be bigger than the difference between the average boy and the average girl.

Plausible explanations of sex differences must explain the absence of contrasts in many areas and the typically small differences we find in others.

Role of learning

Psychological differences between girls and boys all occur in behavioral domains where learning plays a large role. Actions such as knocking down a peer, picking up a heavy rock, reading about horses, or playing chess all rest on extensive backgrounds of experience and prior learning. Plausible explanations of contrasts in these behaviors in girls and boys must somehow relate to the relevant learning processes.

Acknowledging the role of learning does not rule out biological theories. Even a horse raised in a literary environment is unlikely to learn to read about horses. Biological factors can limit and bias learning opportunities, but biological explanations of why girls and boys act somewhat differently become much more reasonable if they can link biology to differential learning.

Contemporary environmental explanations

For many psychologists the facts point to an entirely environmental explanation of girls' and boys' contrasting actions. The differences to be explained can be seen as relatively few in number and small in nature. The fact of differential socialization pressures is real. It is easy to argue that biology is irrelevant to the psychological contrasts that have been demonstrated.

Within psychology, then, arguments about the origins of sex differences relate more to alternative formulations of learning and psychological development than to disputes about the contribution of biology. As elsewhere, the most important disputes today tend to be between those emphasizing social-learning theory and the adherents of cognitive-developmental positions (see Kohlberg, 1966; Mischel, 1966).

Social-learning theory

Social-learning theory emphasizes concepts such as differential reinforcement and modeling. It implies that (1) psychological contrasts between girls and boys should be directly related to contrasts in the environmental pressures on them and (2) contrasts in how parents treat boys and girls are sources rather than outcomes of girl-boy differences in behavior.

As in other areas the social-learning theory explains much of the evidence while leaving room for argument. Certainly the cross-cultural evidence on the varied nature of female and male behavior and the fact that sex differences are much smaller in some cultures than others fit nicely with a social-learning position. The evidence suggests that as children grow older, the pressures on girls and boys become less similar (Maccoby, 1975). Thus, the finding that psychological contrasts between the sexes tend to become more prominent with age can also be seen as supporting a social-learning position. In other words, the broad trends relating sex typing in children to the way the environment treats them give a reasonable fit with the main contentions of a theory emphasizing reinforcement and modeling.

Cognitive-developmental theory

It is when we take a closer look at the evidence that some of the weaknesses in the social-learning position turn up. In some cases cognitive-developmental theory as formulated by Lawrence Kohlberg (1966) seems to provide a better explanation of the developmental process. At other points biological hypotheses become plausible. First consider some of the problems for social-learning theory that seem to point to a cognitive-developmental analysis.

A close look at early sex-role learning suggests that it isn't as other directed as social-learning theory implies. Younger children often develop narrower and more rigid sex-role stereotypes than the people around them (Kohlberg, 1966). A 4-year-old may surprise his parents by proclaiming that boys play only with boys. One little girl told me and a group of students that girls can't be doctors, to the embarrassment of her feminist mother, who pointed out that the child at times had been taken care of by female physicians. Sex-role stereotypes typically become less rigid during the elementary-school years (Garrett, Ein, & Tremaine, 1977; Marantz & Mansfield, 1977; Meyer, 1980). There is no question that a learning process goes on; the problem is how to account for it.

Cognitive-developmental theory puts more emphasis on the child as a self-teacher in explaining sex-role learning. Kohlberg (1966) argues that once the child sees herself or himself as girl or boy, the tendency to like what is "like me" comes into play (Chapter 12). He pictures the 4-year-old as actively selecting same-sex activities and models as a result, regardless of pressures from the outside. The younger child's limited understanding results in a more absolute, concrete, and perceptually dominated kind of sex typing than comes later. Such matters as dress, hairstyle, and superficial conformity thus can be more important to children than to parents.

Kohlberg's view reverses a basic sequence hypothesized by Freud (1924/1950) and kept by social-learning theorists (for example, Lynn, 1959; Sears,

Rau, & Alpert, 1965). They assume that attachment to the same-sex parent comes first. Modeling of sex-appropriate behavior and a view of oneself as female or male is thought to grow out of this attachment. In contrast, Kohlberg (1966) claims that the first step is for children to realize that they are female or male. He thinks this understanding of reality produces a tendency to adopt sex-typed behaviors and later to become especially attached to the same-sex parent. For Freud and social-learning theorists sex typing grows out of a special attachment to the same-sex parent; for Kohlberg it's the other way around.

Kohlberg's approach to sex-role development links it to cognitive development more generally. The emphasis on the child as self-teacher, or self-socializer, reflects Piaget's general idea that assimilation and intrinsic motivation are as basic to development as is accommodation to external reality. The idea that understanding of sex roles reflects cognitive development implies that if you know a child's general level of cognitive development, you should be able to predict how far that child's comprehension of sex-role concepts has come. The evidence supports this view (Kohlberg & Zigler, 1967). For example, a child's performance on tests of conservation of amount predict whether the child has caught on to the fact that gender cannot be changed through such procedures as changing clothing and hairstyle (Marcus & Overton, 1978).

Thus, an adequate psychological theory of sex-role learning must somehow integrate elements from the social-learning and cognitive-developmental approaches. One way of doing this is to recognize that both external influences, such as modeling and reinforcement, and internal ones, such as self-socialization, operate, with children using observations of what others do as the raw material in constructing their own understanding of sex roles (Kuhn, Nash, & Brucken, 1978; Maccoby & Jacklin, 1974).

Contemporary biological explanations

Plausible biological approaches to the contrasts between girls and boys emphasize both chromosomal and hormonal factors. Like cognitive-developmental theory, they become more interesting at the points where social-learning theory falls down.

Chromosome differences

Corinne Hutt (1972) presented one of the broadest and most intriguing formulations of how biological dimorphism might relate to psychological matters. She took the difference between the female XX chromosome pattern and the male XY pattern and showed how it might provide a source of male vulnerability in both physical and psychological development. She highlighted a fact psychologists often ignore and one not easily reconciled with most psychological theories: boys are more vulnerable than girls to a number of important behavior disorders, including mental retardation of varied forms, reading problems, language disorders, psychosis, and delinquency. She explained this fact, along with other forms of male vulnerability, in terms of chromosome differences:

1. Because males have only one X chromosome, they are more vulnerable to diseases that appear when an appropriate gene carried on the X chromosomes is missing.
2. Because males have more genetic information (both X and Y chromosomes rather than only X), they show more traits, including negative ones.
3. Because males develop more slowly (a chromosome-linked difference), the period during which they are at risk for many developmental problems is extended.

Thus, Hutt drew on biological research to construct an integrated explanation of diverse evidence, including some on psychological development.

Hormonal influence

Other biological hypotheses tend to be narrower. For example, a number of psychologists have tried to link sex differences in visual-spatial skills to biological factors. At present the most intriguing ideas here relate sex differences, timing of puberty, and the development of specialized abilities in the two sides of the brain (McGee, 1979; Waber, 1976). But the evidence is far too limited for firm conclusions.

Animal studies. Hormonal factors influence sex-typed behaviors in a variety of animals (Leshner, 1978). Male hormone level often has been shown to influence activity level and aggressive behaviors. Recent evidence on prenatal hormones has done the most to stimulate hypotheses about how hormones might bias psychological development in boys and girls.

Children have relatively low levels of sex hormones circulating in their bodies. Sex-typed behavior patterns emerge well before the rise in sex hormone levels associated with puberty. In the past these facts made it seem unlikely that there might be an important connection between sex hormones and psychological sex differences before puberty. But when we learned that prenatal hormones influence physical development, including brain development, the picture changed.

An experiment on rhesus monkeys by Young, Goy, and Phoenix (1964) showed how early hormones could bias later behavioral development. They focused on behaviors that are sex linked in monkeys. Male monkeys had been shown to engage in more rough-and-tumble play and to make threatening responses more than female monkeys. The researchers gave testosterone (male hormone) to pregnant monkeys and later studied their daughters. The daughters showed the expected masculinized pattern of physical development—their genitals had a somewhat male appearance. More important, their actions also were masculinized by the early hormones. Their play was more like that of normal male monkeys. Rough-and-tumble play and threats were prominent. The behavioral masculinization was still evident at age 3 (Hamburg & Lunde, 1966).

Research on children. Although we lack definitive evidence on whether prenatal sex hormones play a similar role in children, there is some research supporting the possibility. Anke Ehrhardt and Susan Baker (1974) studied a sample of androgenized girls—human girls whose pregnant mothers had taken hormones with masculinizing influences (the effects had not been known at the time). An important feature of this study was the use of a much better control group than usually is used in such clinical studies. The girls were compared to their own sisters and mothers. Interviews with the children and mothers focused on activities in areas where sex differences have been established among normal children. The androgenized girls were found to have more of a preference for high-energy-expending play, to play more with boys, to have less interest in dolls and in babysitting, to have fewer wedding and marriage themes in their play, and to have less interest in jewelry and makeup. More than half the androgenized girls were seen by themselves and others as tomboys throughout their childhood.

The tomboy concept seems useful in making sense out of the overall findings of this study. These girls did not seem abnormal. The few who had reached adolescence had typically begun to become romantically interested in boys. There was no suggestion of developing homosexuality. Seemingly, the prenatal exposure to male hormones had influenced their behavior more than their physical structure and had produced an impact primarily in the area of play interests, what they liked and preferred doing.

If the Ehrhardt and Baker study could be accepted at face value, it would be a dramatic support for a biological interpretation of varied sex differences in the social-emotional area. But it cannot. As Eleanor Maccoby (1975) has pointed out, this study, like most of the natural experiments on hormone-related patterns of unusual development, is far from adequately controlled and is open to varied interpretations. The girls' external genitals looked abnormal at birth and surgery took place in infancy to correct the problem. Perhaps their family's reactions to these events, rather than the prenatal hormones, were crucial to the development of tomboy patterns later. Maybe having a child who looked less feminine and had a corrective operation resulted in child rearing that put less emphasis on behavioral femininity. Ehrhardt and Baker explored this possibility and concluded that it was unlikely. But because their research was based on indirect evidence from interviews, we cannot be sure (Quadagno, Briscoe, & Quadagno, 1977). We must look at this study as one of a number giving plausibility to the hypothesis that prenatal hormones bias sex-role development without proving it.

There are a number of facts about normal child development that also fit in with hormonal and other biological interpretations of social-emotional differences. Sex differences in aggression occur so early and in such varied cultural contexts that it is hard to attribute them entirely to differential socialization pressures. The details of child-parent interaction often are as consistent with the idea that parent behavior is a reaction to child differences as with the environmentalist notion that parent behaviors produce child differences. For example, detailed looks at why boys get more punishment than girls suggest that parents may be reacting to the fact that boys don't stop as readily as girls when milder techniques are used (Maccoby, 1975).

IMPLICATIONS

Developmental differences, like developmental regularities, take us into complicated areas where single-minded approaches are inadequate. Both biological and sociological factors enter into explanations of the differences we find between girls and boys, just as they did when the focus was on similarities.

Our ability to describe contrasts in psychological development is far ahead of our insight into why these contrasts emerge. This, of course, is but another side of the developmental story. Our descriptions of common features in children's language or social development are similarly ahead of our ability to explain why two-word sentences or role-taking capacities appear when they do. But sex differences, like intellectual differences, are emotionally loaded, the focus of great social concern and controversy.

So far I have concentrated on the academic story, trying to give a balanced and objective summary. You have to decide for yourself how it relates to questions about how we should raise children and run our schools. I want to point out some of the links that I find between this chapter and the issues of our times.

The main implication for me is that the concept of masculine superiority is a myth without foundation. Whether you read the evidence to conclude that girls and boys mostly are similar (as I do) or see it in an opposite way, there is no basis for seeing it as showing that boys are better.

Another clear message is that even where sex differences exist, it is wrong to make absolutist conclusions, such as saying that females should be kept out of engineering because of their limited visual-spatial ability or males should be kept from holding power because of their aggressive tendencies. We will do far better if we focus on the match between the individual and the position than if we use sex as our criterion.

The question of whether we should have sex roles and socialize girls and boys differently takes us beyond the scope of this chapter. The universality of sex roles suggests that they had survival value in the past. Cross-cultural comparisons suggest that it is appropriate for our society to move from greater to lesser sex typing as physical strength and breast feeding become less relevant in our economy. It seems inevitable that the way we treat children will parallel the adult world. We will either rear children who can carry on our society or see an end to it. The question of abolishing sex roles, in contrast to making distinctions smaller and less rigid, takes us into sociological issues and enormous unknowns.

A final point relates recent trends to asymmetry. Girls are joining Little League. Female scientists have become more prominent in children's readers. These kinds of changes are relatively easy for society; we are used to opening up instrumental possibilities to girls. A deeper question is whether we will make it easier for boys to be expressive, for that would be a more fundamental change.

As more opportunities open up for girls and women in our society and the boundaries of traditional sex roles become less distinct, will it be easier for boys to be expressive?

SUMMARY

Sex differences were examined from varied points of view: biological, sociological, and psychological. The new view of physical dimorphism was presented, with an emphasis on both chromosomal and hormonal factors and a picture of the developmental path as involving a series of choice points. Sex roles and stereotypes were presented as cultural universals, along with a description of cultural variability and variables related to them. Psychological differences first were introduced in terms of the concepts of expressiveness, instrumentality, and asymmetry. Then evidence on psychological contrasts was reviewed. The relatively big differences in such social-emotional areas as interests, aggression, and peer relations were examined first. Then the much discussed but smaller and less significant contrasts in competence were summarized.

Contrasting explanations of sex differences were examined, focusing on the more plausible ideas and on the broad outlines that any reasonable theory must follow. Finally, some of the implications of current knowledge and ignorance were considered.

CHAPTER 15

Intellectual Differences

Differences in intelligence are easy to find; they are harder to interpret. Discussing them in a calm and reasonable way is hardest of all. Nevertheless, this chapter discusses them, focusing both on the facts and on the problems of interpretation.

The easy part is finding the differences. All you have to do to observe intellectual contrasts is to give a group of children who are the same age a set of tasks that taps their understanding of the world, or level of cognitive development (Chapter 7). You might ask them to explain why we have schools, to put together a jigsaw puzzle, to figure out which picture best completes a cartoon sequence, or to predict whether a ball of clay will weigh the same before and after you flatten it into a pancake. Use standard instructions in testing the children. Encourage them all to do their best. Praise them for trying. Having held the children's age, the mental tasks, and the observation conditions constant, you will find that some children do better than others. This finding—varied performance on problems tapping cognitive skills—is the fact that's so easy to observe.

Now consider four points central to the problem of making sense out of what we see. First, concepts such as intelligence, brightness, and dullness refer to competence, not performance. In going from what we see to these concepts, we must go beyond what is objective and make inferences, which is where all the trouble begins. Facts cannot be denied, but they can be viewed in varied ways.

Second, we can't do the impossible. No one can measure children's "innate intelligence" any more than their "inborn running speed." A modern picture of development makes statements about inborn intelligence as useless as those about innate leg length or innate brain weight. As a zygote Anne had neither legs nor brain. Only after millions of interactions between a zygote and specific environmental stimuli was newborn Anne constructed. At birth Anne's legs and brain are much different than those of a 13-year-old. Newborn Anne can neither run nor reason; those accomplishments will require millions of additional interactions with a further sequence of environmental situations. There is no way of measuring newborn Anne's innate height, brain weight, running speed, or intelligence. Each of these grows out of a unique life history, based on a unique zygote's interactions with a unique set of situations. All we can study is the result of the total set of events and where it has taken Anne at the point we observe her.

Children's present competence results from the continual interaction of their genetic blueprint and their life experiences. It's impossible to untangle the two, whether we want to know their innate running speed or their innate intelligence. Thus, modern psychologists reject the goal of their predecessors. Today we settle for the difficult job of trying to estimate current mental functioning from observable performance. It's hard enough. Why try the impossible?

Third, when a child performs successfully, we usually can be confident that the skill in question is present. But unsuccessful performance leaves us with questions. If John does poorly compared to others his age, his failure might be the result of fatigue, inattention, lack of motivation, or a problem in understanding the instructions. Only a series of observations ruling out other explanations can make it safe to go to the inference of limited ability.

Modern psychologists hold back from drawing conclusions about incompetence when our evidence is inadequate. We hesitate to call Richard retarded when other explanations of his poor performance are feasible. We don't conclude that one group of children is less competent than another just because their test scores are lower.

Fourth, unfortunately, psychologists have not always been cautious (Kamin, 1974; Sarason & Doris, 1969). When intelligence testing was new, extreme claims were common. Distinguished psychologists announced that the new tests measured innate intelligence. They jumped to conclusions about the political implications of their findings rather than emphasizing the interpretative problems. The pronouncements of these important gentlemen helped to get laws passed—laws promoting the sterilization of people with low test scores, laws to keep out immigrants from certain countries.

Psychology's heritage here is both sad and stormy. The English-speaking psychologists who first translated and popularized Alfred Binet's tests enlisted them in political battles. This move produced the inevitable reaction and claim led to counterclaim. Advocates of intelligence testing made too much of their evidence, which created an atmosphere where others found it easy to ignore everything they said. The history of extreme words and strong feelings is what makes it so hard to discuss this area.

NATURE OF INTELLECTUAL DIFFERENCES

Intelligence can be defined as what intelligence tests measure. Some laugh and call this a useless and circular definition and it could be. If anything could be called an intelligence test, this definition would take us nowhere. But if we have a reasonable system for deciding what we will permit to be called an intelligence test, the definition has some real advantages.

We know much about what intelligence tests measure. We have thousands of studies based on millions of people. If we define intelligence in terms of test scores, we can draw on this evidence.

Defining intelligence in terms of test scores reduces fruitless argument. By emphasizing the test-bound nature of our concept, we make it easier to avoid such traps as thinking of intelligence as innate potential or human good-ness. By making our concept narrow, we stand more chance of progress than if we let it mean anything to anyone.

In this chapter intelligence will be defined as what is measured by valid intelligence tests. This definition makes central the question of what a valid intelligence test is.

Two criteria

Only two rules are needed to define intelligence in terms of test scores reasonably and powerfully. The first anchors our concept to traditional usage. The second ties it to the basic fact of cognitive development. Think of these rules as criteria. A test will be called an intelligence test if and only if it meets them.

The first criterion is that intelligence tests are tests of information pro-cessing. The term *intelligence* has long related to cognitive matters. Dictionary definitions use terms such as *understanding, reasoning, acquiring* and *retaining information,* and *solving problems* in explaining what it is. In the army, as in the Central Intelligence Agency, the word refers to the gathering of information. The first criterion demands that intelligence tests most clearly be measures of cognitive functioning. Tests of running speed, finger dexterity, social poise, or emotional warmth do not meet this criterion. Tests of memory, concept knowl-edge, reasoning, and problem solving do. Not all valued qualities fit in with the traditional meaning of intelligence.

It is not enough simply to decide that you want a test of skill in dealing with information, for psychologists have discovered that you can't be sure what a test measures until you try it out. An apparent test of reasoning may turn out to be mostly a measure of familiarity with the examples used or of ability to work under pressure. Some way of finding out which apparent tests of cognitive functioning actually tap intelligence was needed.

The second criterion is that intelligence is something that grows during childhood. Alfred Binet invented a useful method for selecting among tests that looked like intelligence tests. He used a simple but powerful check on his hunches, a developmental criterion. He would devise a test item, such as asking a child to point at her nose or define "kindness." Then he would try it out on children of varied ages. Only if older children did better on it than younger children would the item be kept (as these two examples were). Directly or indirectly, all modern intelligence tests have passed Binet's developmental criterion.

Valid intelligence tests for children must be measures of cognitive (crite-rion 1) development (criterion 2). All yet-to-be-invented intelligence tests will probably produce evidence supporting the generalizations that follow in this chapter as long as they, too, are measures of cognitive development.

Recent work with Piaget's tasks illustrates what is likely to happen (Tyler, 1976). Some are using Piagetian measures of object permanence, logical mul-tiplication, and conservation of volume to look at individual differences. Studies including both Piagetian tasks (the designs test in Table 15–1 is an example) and conventional, Binet-tradition tests (such as the vocabulary test in Table 15–1) show that, despite the contrasts in test items, the same children tend to come out as relatively high or relatively low on Piagetian and on Binet-type measures. The statements that follow, then, are likely to hold up as long as intelligence is defined in terms of tests that pass our two criteria.

TABLE 15–1 Two intelligence tests

Test	Stimulus Situation	Response Requirements	Comments
Vocabulary Test	a) Ask child, "Show me the . . ." and present set of pictures or objects to pick from.	a) Point at appropriate object or picture.	Vocabulary items are the most common and most important contents of the intelligence tests used in schools. They are central to tests in the Binet tradition.
	b) Ask child, "What is a . . .?"	b) Verbally explain word meaning.	
Designs Test (Raven's Progressive Matrices)	Child is shown a design resembling a repetitive wallpaper pattern. A segment is missing. Six similarly shaped alternative pieces are shown below it. Child is asked to pick the piece that correctly completes the design. Instructions and guided practice ensure that the child understands the task before going on.	Point at one of six pieces.	Designs is typical of nonverbal intellectual-functioning tests used in cross-cultural studies. Tests of this kind are often good measures of such Piagetian concepts as logical multiplication, as in completing the pattern below:

0	00	000
X	XX	?

Consistency—the central problem

How useful is it to go from a child's performance on a particular intelligence test on a particular day to an inference about the child's intelligence? This is a key question. Our answer depends entirely on the *consistency* of what is measured.

Lisa did better than any of the other 8-year-olds in figuring out my puzzles today. Is she bright or intelligent? To answer this question, we must make assumptions about consistency. We'd like to know how she does on other tests and on other days before deciding. Lisa might do average or worse if I gave another set of puzzles to the same children tomorrow. If I wait two years and give my original problems over again to the whole group, Lisa's position might slip. Terms such as *high, low,* or *average intelligence* are useful only if performance is consistent. We need evidence on consistency of two kinds: (1) consistency from task to task (puzzle A to puzzle B, puzzles to conservation problems, and so on) and (2) consistency from time to time.

Our evidence shows that consistency is moderate. The degree of consistency depends on the age of the child and the tasks we examine. Thus, you make a big mistake if you think of a child's score on any test at any time as telling you everything about the child's level of intellectual functioning. This is the error of thinking of intellectual level as perfectly consistent. But you also err if you assume that a test score tells you nothing about performance in other situations and at other times. Here the error is in thinking of mental ability as entirely inconsistent.

Measuring the consistency of intellectual differences

Because consistency is a matter of degree, it's important to understand how we measure it. First we consider what kinds of studies are done. Then we focus on how the findings are boiled down into measures of consistency.

The basic ingredients of any study follow logically from our key terms. By *intellectual differences* we mean differences among children of the same age. To study intellectual differences, then, we need a group (two or more children) of similar age. *Consistency* implies that something is related to something else. In a study of intellectual differences the two somethings must be measures of mental skill. All studies of relevance are studies in which a group, or sample, of children is measured twice. A set of scores such as those in Table 15–2 always is needed.

TABLE 15–2 Test scores for a set of hypothetical 6-year-olds

Child	Vocabulary Score	Designs Score
Amy	33	17
Bill	27	10
Carl	32	15
Diane	37	13
Fred	26	12
George	31	9
Helen	23	6
Iris	30	11
Joe	40	14
Ken	34	16
Lily	29	7
Mike	25	8

Table 15–2 illustrates how a hypothetical group of 6-year-olds performed on two important and contrasting kinds of intelligence tests, a vocabulary test and a designs test (described in Table 15–1). Each child has earned a score on each test such that a higher score means better performance, defining more words accurately (vocabulary score) or completing more of the unfinished designs correctly (designs score).

After we have scores like those in Table 15–2, we need a way of summing them up that tells us how well we can predict from one test to the other. We use a *correlation coefficient,* a single number that results from putting all our information into a formula.

When there is perfect agreement, or consistency, between scores on the two tests, the correlation coefficient always comes out to be $+1.0$. If there is no consistent pattern, the correlation comes out to be 0.0. When there is a complete inverse, or negative, relationship between the two tests, the correlation coefficient is -1.0.

Correlation coefficients range from -1.0 to $+1.0$ and can take any intermediate value. This is crucial; it lets us handle the "more-or-less" cases that, in fact, are common. For example, the correlation for the scores shown in Table 15–2 is $+.69$.

In figuring out how good a correlation coefficient is, a simple rule helps: the square of a correlation coefficient is our best estimate of the amount of consistency. Suppose a vocabulary test correlates .2 with spelling grades and .4 with reading grades. If we square the correlation coefficients (multiply each by itself), we get .04 and .16. These figures tell us that there is something like four times as much consistency between vocabulary and reading as between vocabulary and spelling. Because both correlations squared yield numbers much closer to 0.00 than to $+1.00$, we can go even further. We can say that both correlations are low, indicating little predictability or consistency.

By looking at the size of correlations from many studies of children of varied ages and backgrounds, we can find trends. The general finding of intermediate consistency can be translated into more specific and useful statements about particular kinds of patterns. That's what happens in the sections that follow.

Consistency across situations

General intelligence has become a central concept. Charles Spearman introduced the idea in 1904. He claimed that intelligence was one thing, not a set of unrelated abilities such as memory, reasoning, or being good with words. He thought that there was only one way of being smart—having a lot of general intelligence (his name for this hypothetical single ability). Spearman argued that all mental tests measure general intelligence, although they vary in how well they measure it.

Spearman's theory led to a prediction upheld over and over: if you give a representative cross-section of children (or adults) any set of tests of mental functioning, you will find positive correlations between the tasks, no matter how diverse and seemingly different they look. The concept of general intelligence predicts that, in a representative sample, measures of skill with numbers will correlate positively with measures of verbal ability, memory tests with reasoning tests, intelligence tests with chess-playing ability, and so on. This prediction is upheld as long as your sample is representative. (A sample only of children with extremely high vocabulary scores would not be representative and would not be an appropriate group to study to test this prediction.)

The repeated finding of positive correlations among diverse cognitive tasks is one of the main supports for the use of such terms as *bright* and *dull*. The positive correlations mean that a child with a high rank on one mental task is more likely than not to be good at the next. A child with a low standing on the first measure is more likely than not to be low on the second. The tasks, or tests, that give the highest correlations with the most varied other tasks are our best measures of general intelligence. Vocabulary and designs are examples. They give us a basis for predicting a child's performance in a host of other situations and of thinking of the child as relatively bright or dull.

We can't always predict accurately. The correlations usually will be positive, showing some consistency, but they often will be closer to 0.0 than to +1.0, showing that the degree of consistency is low.

Spearman called general intelligence *g*. The symbol *g*, like *x* in algebra, reminds us that general intelligence is an unknown. It is not a thing, but a hypothesis. We use measures of performance to learn more about its nature, but there is room for alternative ideas about what *g* is.

Not all of Spearman's theory has been supported. There are special mental abilities as well as *g*. Two tests of reasoning are likely to correlate more closely than a test of reasoning and a test of memory. Children's ability to reason with words is a better predictor of their memory for words than is a test of reasoning with numbers. The size of the positive correlations between cognitive measures varies in a way that Spearman did not predict. Similar tests yield higher positive correlations than do less similar ones. A modern picture of mental abilities includes both *g* and more specialized talents (Brody & Brody, 1976).

The existence of special mental abilities means that, depending on your intelligence test, a somewhat different set of children will come out at the top or at the bottom. Both vocabulary and designs are good measures of *g*, but there are many real children like Diane and Fred who would earn average scores on one and more extreme scores on the other. Suppose you define bright, or gifted, as the top 10%. Three contrasting ways of identifying the brightest 10% of the fifth-graders in Middletown would result in different children being in Middletown's program for the gifted: (1) give only the vocabulary test, (2) give only the designs test, and (3) give both tests and average the results. The typical school psychologist uses a method like the third to decide who is gifted or retarded. Several tests with varied content are given and the scores are averaged. A program for identifying mathematically talented children, in contrast, is more likely to use a procedure like the second. Because there are varied ways of being smart or dumb, there is no best way to classify an individual.

Consistency over time

How much does a child's relative standing at one age tell us about where the child will be later? Is a "smart" newborn typically a better talker at 2 years? Is a 2-year-old with a relatively small store of concepts headed for trouble in the first grade? These questions all raise the issue of consistency of intellectual level over time.

Our evidence here is based mostly on the typical situation where children live in relatively constant environments. As a result it probably shows more consistency than in situations such as late adoption, where environmental inconsistency is large. The findings can be summed up in two statements relating what happens when we predict from an earlier age (age 1) to a later one (age 2) (Wohlwill, 1980).

The first statement is that age 1 is the most important variable in prediction. The older a child at age 1, the more accurately intellectual performance at this point predicts later level of functioning. This statement takes on more specific meaning when it is related to consistency at our reference ages.

Birth. Mental tests administered to newborns have near 0.0 correlation with measures of mature intellectual status. The results of tests given at birth have no predictive power (except with some severely retarded children). Newborns who grow up to be severely retarded do tend to perform poorly on tests from birth on, but many other babies who do poorly on early tests do not turn out to be retarded. High or average status does not help at all in guessing later rank (Honzik, 1976).

Two years. Intelligence tests given to 2-year-olds have a low positive correlation (about .40) with cognitive level at maturity (Honzik, 1976; H. E. Jones, 1954). The correlation, however, is too low for practical purposes. Big changes in relative rank still will be common.

Six years. By age 6, intelligence tests have moderate predictive power (they correlate about .70 with tests given at age 18) (H. E. Jones, 1954). We can do well in identifying children at the extremes. Children who rank in the top of their group at 6 are likely to stay above average from here on. Most adolescents and adults with high levels of intellectual talent already will be ahead by the time they enter first grade. Children in the bottom of their age group at 6 are real risks for having trouble mastering reading and other academic skills. Adults who are severely retarded almost always did poorly on intelligence tests given at 6 years. There will be many shifts in relative position after age 6, but large changes, such as going from the bottom quarter to the top, will be rare.

Thirteen years. Intelligence tests given at age 13 are good predictors of later measures of cognitive functioning (correlation about .85 with tests given at age 18) (H. E. Jones, 1954). Few big changes will take place. Rank at age 13 is a good predictor of rank at age 30 or 60.

The second statement is that predictive accuracy varies with the interval between age 1 and age 2 when age 1 is held constant. The second statement helps in remembering what we know about baby tests: they predict well over short periods even though they are useless for longer periods. A baby who does relatively well at 6 months is likely to be ahead at 9 months. Baby tests clearly measure something real, despite the fact that it is not the *g* that later tests measure (Honzik, 1976). The second statement also is important at later ages. A 6-year-old's standing on intelligence tests is a far better predictor of performance in first grade than in sixth. All we can measure is current status. At all ages some change is likely in the future. The longer the future we consider, the more likely the change.

Constant intelligence is a myth, but from middle childhood on relative standing is fairly stable. Our evidence on consistency over time contradicts notions of intelligence as fixed at birth. It calls for some other kind of explanation of the pattern of increasing stability we find.

One explanation of the consistency evidence relates it to growth curves for individual children (Bayley, 1955; Bloom, 1964; H. E. Jones, 1954). If all children start at about the same level, gain mental ability rapidly during the early years, and gradually slow down, we would have a picture like that in Figure 15–1. Being ahead or behind at birth would be unimportant because what is left to grow is so large relative to what has already been gained. Gradually the picture would change so that by 13 years few would shift much in overall rank.

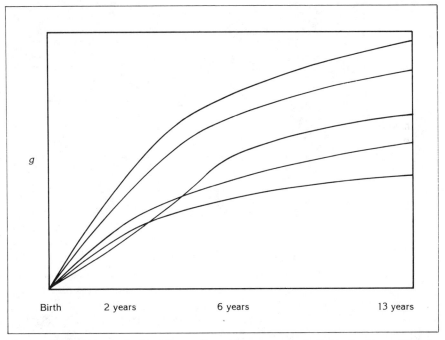

Figure 15–1 Hypothetical intellectual growth curves for individuals (From *"On the Growth of Intelligence,"* by N. Bayley, *American Psychologist,* 1955, 10, 805–818. Copyright 1955 by the American Psychological Association. Reprinted by permission of the author.)

Classification difficulties

Terms such as *bright* and *less intelligent* imply that children perform consistently. The evidence, thus, shows a limited value in these labels. They're not at all useful in talking about babies, and they pose problems even for talking about school-age children. We must be cautious.

A technical fact illustrates one of our next problems. When we give any intelligence test to a large group of same-age children, their test scores usually distribute themselves in a manner illustrated in Figure 15–2. Most children earn scores in the middle. As we move from the average score toward either end, we find some children at each level. There are no gaps in the series of scores.

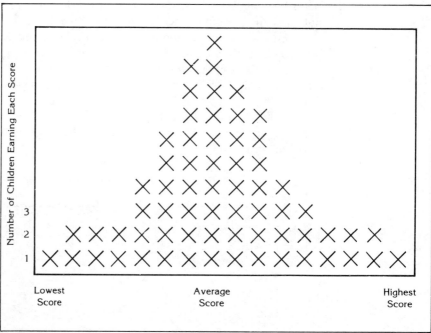

Figure 15–2 Typical Distribution of Intelligence–Test Scores in a Large Group of Children

We have to think of intellectual differences as a matter of degree. A "genius" or a "mentally retarded child" has "more" or "less" of what average children have, not something different. When we classify children as boy or girl, there are few cases that are hard to fit into one category or the other, but categories of intellectual level are different. Many children are hard to classify because such labels as brighter, average, and duller require that we take a smooth series and talk as if there were gaps in it.

Now you can see that grown-ups create "bright" and "dull" children through two arbitrary procedures:

1. We pick a particular set of tests and thereby determine the set of children who perform relatively well or relatively poorly.
2. We pick particular cut-off points to divide average from the extremes and thereby create some bright and dull children who would be average with contrasting boundaries.

Some are stingy with such terms as *retarded* and *gifted* and apply them to only 1% or 2% of each extreme. Others give the labels more freely and create 10% or even 25%. Were you known as a gifted child in high school? It depended on which system was used. Tom may or may not be retarded, depending on who is picking the test and the cutoff point.

There's an important distinction, then, between *academic* and *practical* questions. For academic purposes, *brighter* and *less intelligent* are useful terms when talking about trends in groups. Studies based on varied combinations of

Frontiers box 15–1 Cognitive style

Children differ in their style of approaching intellectual tasks (Kagan & Kogan, 1970; Kogan, 1976). Some are careful, working slowly and making few errors (*reflective style*). Others respond more quickly and make more careless mistakes (*impulsive style*). Another contrast in cognitive style is known as *field independent* versus *field dependent.* Field independent children are less influenced by the context, or field, a stimulus is in. For instance, they are better able to find a hidden figure, such as a triangle embedded in a complicated diagram or a drawing of a face hidden in the branches of a tree.

Psychologists interested in cognitive styles argue that these approaches to tasks are stable contrasts. Reflective and field-independent children are thought to show similar approaches to varied tasks. Cognitive styles are considered important in understanding the process of problem solving and in relating intellectual functioning to more general aspects of personality.

There is evidence to support the interest in cognitive styles (Kogan, 1976; Messer, 1976). Cognitive style relates to school performance (reflectives do better). Clinical groups such as hyperactive children and children with brain damage can be better understood when their ways of tackling problems are examined. For example, the finding that school difficulties are often associated with an impulsive style has resulted in some success in devising ways of training children to approach problems less impulsively (Messer, 1976) (see Box 13–2).

However, there are questions about the value of the cognitive styles approach. One concern is that cognitive styles are not as stable and as general as the term implies. The focus here is on the size of the correlations between alternative measures of the same style. Another criticism is that measures of cognitive style correlate with traditional measures of intelligence, raising the possibility that cognitive style measures are simply indirect tests of what conventional intelligence tests tap.

Such criticisms of the cognitive style concept have led to new sophistication in research and in efforts to document claims more adequately (Kogan, 1976; Messer, 1976; Messer & Brodzinsky, 1981). These newer efforts suggest that cognitive styles are real and do add something to our picture of individual differences in intellectual functioning.

tests and on different cutoff points take us to similar conclusions. But putting labels on individual children, such as Tom, is different. The particular definitions we pick influence their lives. The problem of whether we should use intelligence tests to label individuals must be separated from the academic abstractions.

Less intelligent children

When education became compulsory in Paris, France, many children failed to make satisfactory progress. The Ministry of Education asked Alfred Binet to help them develop a system for deciding which children were having trouble due to intellectual limitations (rather than because of other factors). Modern intelligence tests resulted from Binet's response to this request.

The Paris story illustrates a broader trend (Tyler, 1976). Each country that has made formal education a universal requirement has discovered that some children have special problems in coping with academic demands. Concern with less intelligent children results from laws that make education compulsory.

Compulsory education creates the problem because there are no known methods that make it possible for all children to achieve the academic goals set up for them in modern educational systems. Some children make unsatisfactory progress no matter how they and their teachers struggle.

School is a unique problem in the lives of most so-called duller, or retarded, children (Brody & Brody, 1976; Edgerton, 1979). Most of these children are "invisible," both before they enter school and after they leave it. Most children placed in special classes blend into the community once they get out of school. They take care of themselves, hold jobs, marry, raise children, and stay out of jail. Even in modern society limited g rarely has to be a bar to a normal life.

Less intelligent children often are slower in reaching developmental landmarks, such as talking in sentences or understanding numbers. Often their judgment is poorer and they cannot be trusted near danger as early as others. But these facts must be put in perspective. Most duller children master language adequately, learn enough about numbers to get along, and learn to stay away from dangers. Our schools and our society emphasize the development of cognitive skills at the "right" age, but for normal adult living the crucial question is whether you can cope, not when you learned how.

Severely retarded children

The majority of children who are called duller or retarded have problems that tend to be unique to school and to schoolish situations. A smaller group has more general limitations. They will be referred to here as severely retarded. They usually score in the lowest 1% on tests of mental ability. Among this minority we find some who make limited progress even in such areas of adaptive functioning as acquiring language and learning to feed and dress themselves. A look at these unusual children helps illuminate some general issues.

Even severely retarded children do not suffer from an inability to learn. They can learn much through sensorimotor, or conditioning, processes (Chapter 5). Exciting progress is being made in using behavior-modification techniques based on conditioning principles to teach these children to do more for themselves and to lead happier and more useful lives (Thompson & Grabowski, 1977). Many important skills mastered through language, logic, and observation can be learned through operant conditioning. For example, looking both ways before crossing the street and putting on a jacket are probably learned largely through verbal instruction and imitation by most children in our society. We can use conditioning methods to teach these skills to children who don't profit from indirect experience. As we discover more about the learning that severely retarded children can do, we keep extending their potential.

Severely retarded children thus help us see that intelligence is not the ability to learn. Operant learning tasks are poor intelligence tests (Stevenson, 1972), just as they are poor methods for distinguishing between the cognitive capacities of pigeons, monkeys, and humans (Skinner, 1958). Low intelligence-test scores predict poor performance in symbolic learning, as in mastering algebra. Learning to use a spoon, to say please, or to come in out of the rain has little to do with *g*.

Brighter children

Research on brighter children contradicts the common stereotype of more intelligent children as sickly, scrawny, unpopular, unable to deal with practical problems, unhappy, and doomed to early decline (Miles, 1954). A picture of the qualities actually associated with high test scores is summarized in Table 15–3. It nicely supports the concept of *g* as general intelligence because test-brightness turns out to correlate with many nontest situations.

TABLE 15–3 Contrasts between bright children and their peers

Bright Children Relatively High	Little or No Difference
School	
reading	drawing
arithmetic	handwriting
science	shop
composition	dexterity
	hand coordination
Psychological Traits	
common sense	fondness for large
originality	groups
desire to know	cheerfulness
self-confidence	freedom from vanity
sense of humor	
conscientiousness	
leadership	

Based on Miles, 1954.

In the social-emotional area brighter children typically are ahead where understanding and judgment are important—for example, in sense of humor and leadership. Where cognitive factors aren't obvious, we more commonly find no difference. Intellectually talented children don't tend to be more cheerful or less cheerful, fonder or less fond of big groups. The contrasts between high-scoring and average children go far beyond test performance and even beyond school performance, but brighter children don't have a monopoly on virtue.

Children with unusually high scores on cognitive tests often love reading, pursue scientific hobbies, and ask more than their share of intellectual questions. Such signs of intellectual curiosity are the basis of what Miles calls desire to know. The trend turns up both in biographies of children who later earn fame as adult "geniuses" (Cox, 1926) and in more direct observations of high-scoring children (Hollingworth, 1942).

Children with unusually high scores on cognitive tests often love reading and show other signs of intellectual curiosity.

Leta Hollingworth (1942) studied the highest scoring children she could find in the New York City area. She picked a dozen from among hundreds of thousands. Her findings suggest that the curiosity and intellectual play of high-scoring children is as unusual as their talent.

Child D, one of her cases, was particularly interesting. At 18 months he taught himself to read while sitting on his mother's lap in front of a typewriter. He learned to count at about the same time. A note in his mother's records said "counts all day long." At about 4 years of age he invented an imaginary country, Borningtown. For three years much of his play dealt with it. He made up a language for it (Bornish) and filled a dictionary with definitions of its made-up words. He spent hours mapping it and writing its history. At 7 years of age his play included holding a contest for the numbers under 100 to see which could be divided evenly by the most other numbers. Ninety-six won highest honors. He wrote music. He invented games such as three-handed checkers.

Classification was one of his chief interests. By the age of 10, this interest centered on science. D had "proper" scientific names for some species of birds that he regarded as improvements over those used by the American Ornithological Union. Children try to figure out the world around them, taking pleasure in playfully assimilating new experiences into their intellectual schemes. In child D, as in many distinguished scientists, we see how this desire to know can be a special passion accompanying unique intellectual power.

Unusual intellectual curiosity could be central to the story of bright children and to a more general one. Keith Hayes (1962) argued that the curiosity differences come first and produce the contrasts in ability that gradually emerge later. Other factors constant, a child who enjoys learning about language and a child who enjoys throwing sticks will teach themselves different skills. With our growing emphasis on the child's own activity as a factor in development, this hypothesis has broad implications.

USES AND ABUSES OF INTELLIGENCE TESTS

A movement to stop intelligence testing is gaining strength (Lerner, 1981). Two issues can be distinguished. One question is whether the popular tests used in schools should be called intelligence tests, whether we should continue with such terms as *intelligence quotient* and *IQ*. The other question is whether we should continue to use the tests that have been connected with these labels.

Naming tests and scores

The tests used on a large scale in our schools are best thought of as measures of scholastic aptitude, verbal ability, or vocabulary size. Although related to *g*, the popular tests rarely have been unbiased measures of it. Our schools emphasize verbal skills. Tests emphasizing verbal abilities best predict academic achievement. The intelligence tests used in schools fit their purpose better than their label. We will be better off if the trend toward more accurate labels, such as scholastic aptitude test, continues. Using the name intelligence test for these instruments creates misunderstandings and does more harm than good.

I have so far avoided the terms *intelligence quotient* and *IQ* because so much half-knowledge is associated with them. The heritage of false claims and misinformation is all too strong when they are introduced. So many "know" that the IQ is constant. So many textbooks in psychology still say that IQ scores are obtained by dividing mental age by chronological age. (They aren't. The limitations of this system were obvious by the 1930s. In 1960, it was dropped from the last important test [Cronbach, 1970].) But IQ scores still are routinely misinterpreted (Brody & Brody, 1976). Here again it would be progress to stop using misleading labels. (Neutral, technical terms such as *standard scores* are equivalent to modern IQs and don't cue in all the incorrect and emotional reactions [see Cronbach, 1970].)

Using tests

A test by any name should be evaluated in terms of the costs and benefits that come from using or not using it. A bad fit between a child and a curriculum can be painful. A good test can reduce the frustrations resulting from mismatching children and educational goals. In the past this benefit from sound testing was appreciated; today we also see the negative side. Labels such as retarded and not gifted can hurt, even when there is some truth in them. Because they are arbitrary and often inaccurate, labels can produce as much trouble as they reduce. Consideration of both costs and benefits in testing should result in using tests more carefully and less often (Brody & Brody, 1976).

One reason for using traditional intelligence tests less is that we now are more concerned with using tests to help determine how to teach. Traditional intelligence tests give few cues about what to do next or what to do differently in helping an individual. If Ernie is having trouble with first-grade reading, the information that his vocabulary is at the 20th percentile makes little difference. In contrast, information about his ability to discriminate among printed letters or his comprehension of terms used in first-grade workbooks (such as *same, all,* or *next to*) tells us what we might try teaching tomorrow.

As we focus more on teaching children with special problems, rather than just placing them, our emphasis shifts from intelligence tests to criterion-referenced tests (tests that relate the child's present skills to some educational criterion, such as first-grade reading or self-dressing) (see Baker, Brightman, Heifetz, & Murphy, 1977; Boehm, 1973; Levin, Henderson, Levin, & Hoffer, 1975).

The remaining area for intelligence tests is in making decisions about placement. Which children should be allowed in regular classrooms? Who should be placed in special rooms or in residential schools? If we have alternatives, decisions must be made. Intelligence tests have been popular in making placement decisions because they often reduce errors when compared with other systems.

Intelligence tests should not be blamed for the fact that placement decisions are often arbitrary and normally result in some mistakes. If a school system says regular class *or* special class, all one or all the other, it is the system that is arbitrary, not the tests. Any method of predicting children's future performance results in error; the question is how many errors of prediction result from tests relative to other systems.

The whole matter of selection and placement is being reexamined and with it the role of tests. Because intelligence tests are often our best single tool in reducing errors of predicting, it seems silly to drop them and turn to a less accurate system, but certainly they could be better used. Jane Mercer (1973) showed that the combined use of measures of social competency and intelligence tests often results in wiser special-education placements than the use of tests alone. Her idea is hardly new (Doll, 1953), but perhaps we are finally ready to put intelligence tests in their proper place—a more limited one than in the past.

SOURCES OF INTELLECTUAL DIFFERENCES

The search for the sources of intellectual differences has resulted in a complex picture, more complicated than anyone expected. I review our knowledge here by sampling selectively rather than pretending to cover everything. I've chosen areas and findings both to illustrate how our understanding is moving ahead and to show where we are going.

Family resemblance

Children's intellectual level correlates with that of their family. High, low, and average intelligence tend to run in families (Bouchard & McGue, 1981; McAskie & Clarke, 1976; Willerman, 1979). The finding is a good starting point.

If we give a newborn baby a test of cognitive functioning, it will not help us at all in predicting how well the baby will read at the end of first grade or do on an intelligence test administered 13 years later. But we can give intelligence tests right after a baby is born that will help in predicting the baby's later rank: we can test the baby's mother or father. Either score will enable us to do much better than chance in predicting the baby's later performance (though we will make many errors). If we test both parents and use the average of their two scores, we will do still better. Test scores for both parents better predict the child's future intellectual level than tests given to the child up until somewhere near age 6 (Brody & Brody, 1976; H. E. Jones, 1954).

If a baby has sisters and brothers of school age, we also can use their test scores to predict the baby's future level. For example, brighter third-graders are more likely to have siblings who also earn high scores. If the older children in a family get low scores and are in special education, a newborn baby in the same family is much more likely than others to be headed in the same direction.

This finding of family resemblance tells us that some of the factors that produce varied levels of mental ability run in families. If we want to know why children are brighter or duller, we can start with a crude answer: it's at least partly a result of characteristics of their family.

There are many family characteristics that might contribute. Three contrasting groups of variables vary with family membership: genetic blueprints, within-family environmental factors, and outside-family environmental factors. Red hair, membership in the Catholic Church, and tuberculosis run in families as a result of varying patterns of causation. Family resemblances in intelligence might result from any or all of these varying patterns.

Children get all their genetic material from their parents and thus share some with each parent and with each sibling (*genetic blueprints*). Parents do much that influences what their children experience. They serve as models and teachers, influence a child's diet and medical care, and play a role in determining their children's playmates and teachers *(within-family environmental factors)*. Family membership determines where a child lives and fits into society. Many environmental influences outside of parental control tend to have a similar influence on all family members. The community sees the Marstons as part of the same social group. It treats them all with the same respect or lack of it. It expects a similarly high or low level of intellectual performance from each of them. Factors such as diet, medical care, intellectual stimulation from the community, atomic radiation, and racial prejudice all operate similarly on different family members *(outside-family environmental factors).*

The fact that intelligence varies with family membership raises more questions than it answers. In many studies the goal has been to untangle the contributions of variables related to family status and see what each contributes. There have been two main strategies: quantification and the control and isolation of variables.

Quantification

Progress comes when we look at the relative size of several relationships. Through quantification we can see which trends look stronger and more central. For example, some argue that children's intelligence-test scores mostly are measures of their socioeconomic status, or social class background. This idea leads to the claim that the tendency for intellectual level to run in families is merely a reflection of social class biases in tests. But the correlation between child and parent test scores is higher than the correlation between child test scores and parental social class; so social class can hardly be the whole story of family resemblance. By using correlations and other quantitative methods, we can clarify which of several related variables deserves more attention.

Control and isolation of variables

The best way of seeing the causal contribution of a variable is to conduct an experiment: hold all other variables constant and systematically vary the one of interest. Ethical and practical considerations limit our possibilities. Breeding experiments in which we get adults of known intelligence levels to mate according to a systematic plan seem out of the question, as do studies in which we randomly assign newborns to environmental treatments expected to raise or lower mental ability.

Lacking opportunities for complete control and isolation of variables, we look to natural experiments as a substitute. Twins, adopted children, and efforts to help children with lagging intellectual development present important opportunities for sorting out variables that usually are tangled together.

Twins. Twins come in two varieties: *monozygotic* (one zygote originally) and *dizygotic* (two zygotes from the start). Dizygotic twins (often called *fraternal twins*) develop from two different eggs fertilized by two different sperm. Genetically, they are as similar as any other pair of siblings conceived by the same two parents (no more or no less similar), but from the start they grow up in an environment more similar than that of siblings born at different times (because both prenatal and postnatal conditions can change from year to year even in the same womb or home). Monozygotic twins, in contrast, originate when one zygote divides and becomes two individuals after a single egg and sperm have come together to create a unique genetic blueprint. Like cells of the same person, the cells of the two monozygotic twins share an identical genetic blueprint. Monozygotic twins (often called *identical twins*) are always the same sex and are genetically the same. As with dizygotic twins, monozygotic twins share an environment that is more similar than that of other siblings.

By looking at degree of similarity within such groups as same-sex siblings, same-sex dizygotic twins, and monozygotic twins, we have an opportunity to learn about the relative contributions of heredity and environment. When monozygotic twins are separated at birth and reared apart, the opportunity looks particularly good. Unfortunately, much of the evidence on twins is less clear and less dependable than many have assumed (Kamin, 1974). For now the best procedure seems to be to wait for more adequate twins studies. The finding that identical twins reared together are more similar intellectually than other same-sex siblings (including fraternal twins) is likely to stand, as is the finding that dizygotic twins are no more similar intellectually than other same-sex siblings. However, it looks as if we cannot trust the old finding that monozygotic twins reared apart are extremely similar intellectually, and we must be cautious in interpreting the other findings until we know more about the tendency for twins to be treated more similarly if they look alike (Brody & Brody, 1976).

Adopted children.   Children adopted soon after birth share genetic material with one family and postnatal experience with another. Like twins, they offer an opportunity to try to isolate the contributions of heredity to family resemblance.

Here again there is controversy. The early studies of adopted children seemed to show a major role for genetic factors. Such critics as Leon Kamin (1974) have raised important questions about these studies and their interpretation.

With adopted children we find modern studies that have passed the test of careful examination by such neutral critics as Erness and Nathan Brody (1976). In these technically more adequate investigations we find replication of an early finding: the intellectual level of adopted children is more highly correlated with that of their biological parents than with that of the parents who raise them (see Munsinger, 1975; Scarr & Weinberg, 1978).

This finding is one of the best supports for the argument that hereditary factors play an important role in determining intelligence level among children raised in "modern" environments. But don't draw any conclusions yet; as promised, the story is complicated.

Studies of adopted children also support the idea that environmental factors influence a child's intelligence level. A study by Sandra Scarr and Richard Weinberg (1978) illustrates the point. In their study the biological mothers of the adopted children apparently had an average level of intelligence on a national scale. The mothers and fathers who adopted the children soon after they were born averaged a much higher level. When the children reached late adolescence, their average intelligence level was between those of their natural and adopted parents. Seemingly, the above-average environments in which they were raised added to their intellectual level.

Do you have trouble seeing how two such findings are possible in the same study? You are not alone if you do. The crucial idea is that there are two different ways of examining the relation between intellectual level in parents and child: by correlating *relative ranks* within the groups and by comparing the *average levels* of the groups. The two measures can vary independently and did. Comparison of group averages indicated that the children typically earned higher scores than their mothers, but the mothers with relatively high scores (compared to other mothers) tended to have children with relatively high scores (compared to other children). We would get a similar result if we had a diet supplement that added 2 inches to the height of each child. The children would come out taller than their mothers on the average, but relatively tall mothers would have relatively tall children. The study by Scarr and Weinberg illustrates what has happened to that old argument about heredity *or* environment. It's over. Both operate.

Helping children who lag.   On the environment side one goal has been to go from crude definitions to more precise and psychologically meaningful ones. It's important to know that such parental characteristics as rich or poor, educated or uneducated help predict children's intellectual performance. Such distinctions don't tell what aspects of family environment make the difference or hint at how they work. We want to define home environment characteristics that can be concretely related to the child's learning experiences.

A pioneer study by Richard Wolf (reported in Bloom, 1964) helped make the shift to better definitions of family environment. He focused on 13 process variables that seemed important in fostering a child's mental development. They fell in three main areas:

1. Press for achievement motivation (for example, in the parents' intellectual expectations for the child)
2. Press for language development (for example, in emphasis on the use of language in a variety of situations)
3. Provision for general learning (for instance, in providing books and learning opportunities in the home)

Wolf interviewed mothers of fifth-graders and rated their reactions in terms of his 13 variables. Then he correlated the overall tendency to foster intellectual development in these ways with test scores. His process measures correlated .76 with intelligence test scores, and traditional measures of family environment, such as parental education, correlated .40 or less.

Robert Hess and Virginia Shipman (1967) did similar work aimed at defining why mental development lagged in many disadvantaged homes. They watched mother-child interaction rather than using interviews. They studied maternal teaching style by getting mothers to teach in front of them. First the researcher showed a mother how to do three simple tasks (such as classifying toys by shape and color). Then the mother was asked to teach her child how to do them.

Hess and Shipman found that characteristics of the mother's teaching style correlated both with the child's cognitive functioning at the time (age 4) and with reading readiness scores two years later. Maternal teaching style predicted better than traditional measures, including the mother's own intelligence-test scores. Maternal behaviors correlated with higher readiness scores later included anticipating the child's needs and giving necessary information and feedback related to task performance. R. D. Hess (1970) concluded that the most important variable is the type of appeal the mother uses in regulating the child's actions. Imperative commands, such as "Do this because I said so," predicted lower readiness scores. Higher readiness scores were predicted by such maternal statements as "How do you think your teacher will feel or you will feel if you don't know your lesson?"

Variables such as Wolf's process variables and maternal teaching style as defined by Hess and Shipman have emerged as the environmental character-istics most closely related to intellectual differences. They tie in with older measures, but these psychological aspects of the child's environment predict better than sociological indicators such as parent occupation (Bloom, 1964; Hess & Shipman, 1967).

Modern correlational studies have given us a far more exciting, useful, and specific set of hypotheses about environmental influences. However, they share a limitation that too often goes unnoticed (see Longstreth, Davis, Carter, Flint, Owen, Rickert, & Taylor, 1981; Scarr-Salapatek, 1975). The studies have looked at children growing up in the homes of their biological parents. As a result none of them can rule out genetics as a source of environment-child correlations. Perhaps maternal teaching style and child reading readiness cor-relations reflect two expressions of the same genetic pattern rather than the impact of mother's behavior on the child. Only when the adopted child method is combined with the new techniques for defining environment will we know. The findings we have let us predict from environment to child more accurately. They provide good hunches about how to foster intelligence, but they don't settle the question of *causation.*

Only experiments in which we manipulate some environmental conditions while holding genetics and other environmental factors constant can reduce our uncertainty about which variables actually produce higher or lower levels of mental functioning. At present the only studies that meet this careful de-finition of experiment fall under the category of education rather than child rearing. The notion that you can produce an Einstein by behaving like Einstein's mother remains untested.

Special troubles

Attempts to understand the origins of severe mental retardation take us in different directions than studies starting from the finding of family resem-blance. The reason is simple: severely retarded children often contradict the family resemblance trend. When we look at children in the bottom 1% intel-lectually, we find that they are born to parents of varied levels of intelligence and education (Edgerton, 1979). President Kennedy had a severely retarded sister; Vice-President Humphrey had a severely retarded granddaughter. In many college courses we meet bright students whose concern with the problem of retardation grew out of personal experience with severely retarded members of their own family.

Severe retardation often reflects the operation of different causative factors than those producing the variations in mental ability among children in general. The situation parallels that for height. The typical short child comes from a relatively short family. His or her height is best explained in terms of such factors as the genes and diet differences operating to produce the whole range of heights we see every day. But dwarfs are different. Their siblings and parents aren't particularly likely to be short. Their reduced stature typically results from special variables. In both cases a look at the child with special troubles helps illuminate the overall picture.

Studies of retarded children have shown that anything that can upset the complex and delicately coordinated process of brain development can result in a child with limited capacities. A problem in the genetic material, a biological mishap as the zygote is formed, a chemical problem a few weeks later as the brain first takes form, a brief shortage of oxygen resulting from a complication during the birth process, an extremely high fever during a disease in infancy, a diet of lead paint picked off the walls of an aging building during toddlerhood, a brain injury resulting from a car accident at any point in childhood—all these disruptive events can have a similar outcome: a slower rate of cognitive development and a failure ever to achieve the thinking capacities we consider normal.

Experiments with animals and studies of children exposed to natural experiments suggest that radical departures from an expected diet of learning opportunities can be as devastating as biological insults to brain development. Animals raised in isolation chambers and children raised in attics often come out with deficits in cognitive functioning. We still are unclear about the reversibility of such deficits (Clarke & Clarke, 1976). A tentative hypothesis seems reasonable: the more prolonged and intensive the reduction in opportunities for cognitive learning, the greater the likelihood of intellectual deficit.

Two of the best-understood forms of severe mental retardation illustrate how rare problems can illuminate the broader picture. Phenylketonuria (PKU) and Down's syndrome teach us much, even though neither is typical even of the 1% of children with major cognitive deficits.

PKU

In the 1930s, it was found that about 1% of severely retarded individuals (about 1 in 10,000 children) had an excess of a chemical (pyruvic acid) in their urine. This discovery was soon followed by dramatic breakthroughs. The source of the chemical peculiarity and its relation to the mental limitation became clear. With a fuller understanding of how the problem originated, great progress was made in helping the babies previously fated to become severely retarded (Kopp & Parmelee, 1979; Robinson & Robinson, 1965).

PKU starts in the genetic material itself. A zygote that gets a certain pair of genes—one from each parent—will under normal environmental conditions turn into a newborn whose brain contains an abnormal version of a chemical that helps in everyday brain processes. As a result, the process whereby food turns into certain substances in the brain does not work out as expected. As the body breaks the food down, certain chemicals come out in the urine instead of being broken down further. Others accumulate in the brain and interfere with its normal development. In a normal sequence of environments, the chemically unusual brain doesn't develop normally. Mental retardation accompanied by unusual urine are the common outcomes of this basically chemical problem.

If the chemically special brain is supplied with certain raw materials, it can do its job with normal results. If PKU babies are identified soon after birth and given special diets, their intellectual development is usually normal.

The story has two morals. First, it is not the genes or the environment that determine the course of development, but the interaction and match of the two. With a normal diet, the PKU genes produce an abnormal outcome. By adjusting the environment to fit the chemical situation resulting from the unique genes, we get a normal outcome. Second, the idea that a disorder with a genetic component is harder to treat is wrong. PKU illustrates that some hereditary problems can be corrected.

Down's syndrome

Down's syndrome occurs once in about 600 births and accounts for about 10% of severe mental retardation. Children with Down's syndrome show distinctive features of physical appearance, such as unusually shaped eyes and fingers. Western observers emphasized certain of these features, such as the eyes, by using the now discarded term *mongolism* for the disorder.

In 1959, the central problem underlying the disorder was identified. Children with Down's syndrome have extra genetic material. One common source of the problem is an error in cell division. This illustrates the most common situation in Down's syndrome: a problem originating in the genetic material, but one that is not inherited. The parents do not have distinctive genes, as in the case of PKU. The child's genetic blueprint is abnormal because something goes wrong at conception or soon after (Edgerton, 1979; Reed, 1975).

We know some factors that contribute. A mother exposed to X rays or an older mother has more chance of giving birth to a Down's syndrome baby. But we do not have biological techniques that alter the chance of retarded mental development, as with PKU.

We do have evidence that the Down's syndrome child's experience is important. Down's syndrome babies placed in residential institutions soon after birth typically end up with less mental ability than those raised by families (Edgerton, 1979). Work at the University of Washington suggests that educational intervention starting six weeks after birth can have dramatic results (Hayden & Haring, 1976). The Washington program is based on close cooperation with parents and combines home training with preschool classes. The first babies in the program reached kindergarten with psychological skills near the normal level. As illustrated in Figure 15–3, the program has resulted in reading skills ahead of the normal level for preschoolers.

It's still too early to tell how far we can go in eliminating the psychological handicaps traditionally seen in Down's syndrome children, but once again our evidence shows that it is wrong to think that biological factors fix a child's intellectual development and rule out environmental ones.

Figure 15–3 This girl with Down's syndrome is a better reader than most children
her age.

Risk factors

As we've learned more, there has been less talk about causes of lower
intelligence and more about risks. The child's future is uncertain, even when
unusually clear and specific factors operate, as in PKU and Down's syndrome.
It's better to think of certain variables as raising the risk of negative outcomes,
rather than as causing them.

Current thinking emphasizes the interaction of risk factors. Research on
low-birth-weight children illustrates the emerging picture. Children who are
unusually small at birth (below 2500 grams is a common definition) are at risk
for intellectual and educational problems later, but now we know that the risk
is small. Most children who are small at birth are intellectually normal at school
age. A closer look at which low-birth-weight children have problems later is
revealing.

A small baby born to a middle-class family rarely shows intellectual lag
at school entry. Similar babies born into poor homes are at much greater risk.
The combination of low birth weight and poverty predicts a big chance of later
intellectual lag. Again the evidence points to an interaction of factors in the
child and in the child's environment as more important than either taken alone
(Sameroff & Chandler, 1975). Now our attention is drawn to interaction of
different kinds of risks.

Focus on varied risk factors raises the question of their relative importance. The Kauai study helped answer it (Werner, Bierman, & French, 1971).
Kauai is a small island in the Hawaiian chain. Its size and isolation made it
possible to do a study there that included all live-born children born during a
three-year period. They were studied for ten years. With a large and full cross-

section of children it was possible to evaluate the relative contribution of many risk factors as they related to problems in school.

When varied factors were related to achievement, intellectual lag, and emotional problems at age 10, a dramatic finding emerged: "ten times more children had problems attributed to the effects of a poor environment than to the effects of serious perinatal (around birth) stress." Variables such as poverty, intellectual stimulation in the home, and emotional support from the family had more to do with behavioral problems than variables such as low birth weight and complications of pregnancy (Werner et al., 1971, p. 134).

Poverty and home environment stand out as the most crucial risk variables. When poverty and biological complications come together, we see a situation of double trouble, where the risk runs highest.

SUMMARY

A few trends stand out when you look at our present picture of intellectual differences among children. First, tools have paced our progress more clearly here than in many areas. Alfred Binet's success in creating valid intelligence tests resulted in a large growth of knowledge in a short time. The invention of correlation coefficients made it possible to put vast amounts of information into a convenient form and to see subtle patterns that were not immediately obvious. Methods such as longitudinal studies, twin studies, the examination of adopted children, and the description of home environments open up the possibility of going deeper and seeing more clearly. Our tools have limitations, however, as well as strengths. Weaknesses in our methods have continued and will continue to inhibit our progress. The continued reliance on correlational methods keeps us from the goal of isolating causative factors. Ethical considerations rule out many of the experiments that could help answer central questions.

Second, either-or concepts such as genius and all-or-none arguments about heredity and environment had to be abandoned once more precise, numerical evidence was available. As dependable knowledge accumulated, the dream of single answers to questions here disappeared. Cognitive development is a complex process resulting from the interaction of a host of variables. Not surprisingly, variations in cognitive development turn out to show the same multivaried situation.

Third, once there were naive physicists who thought that their discoveries inevitably would result in progress. This innocent dream disappeared in 1945 with the first atomic bomb. The field of intellectual differences should help cure naive psychologists and students of any similar illusions.

Alfred Binet created modern intelligence tests as part of his effort to help children. Decades later we must admit that intelligence tests and findings based on them have been used to hurt as well as to help. Findings about individuals and about groups have been used in injurious ways. Knowledge of intellectual measurement, like knowledge of atomic physics, is a two-edged sword.

If intellectual differences were not real and if we did not know how to measure them reasonably well, psychologists would be less powerful figures in the world of children. But our knowledge is real, although limited, and with it we become people to be taken more seriously. Intelligence testing, like behavior modification and modern drugs, calls for ethical and responsible actions by professionals because it works. We have to cooperate to make sure it is used in the best interests of children.

CHAPTER 16

Personality:
Social-Emotional Differences

When we talk about personality, we refer to social-emotional differences among children. We say that Ellen has a cheerful personality and actually mean that she is more cheerful than the average child. We call Hugh sociable because he spends more time with other children than most. Interestingly, then, Ellen's or Hugh's individuality is defined by contrasting each one with a group.

Personality is less consistent than many had thought (Mischel, 1973). A child more dependent than others at one age is often average when observed a few years later. A child who is honest in dealing with peers is often dishonest in talking to adults.

Children are discriminating in dealing with varied situations (Mischel, (1973). Henry is aggressive on the playground, but not in his reading group. Joan is nastier in the classroom than outside. To call either child aggressive misses the fact that their antisocial behavior comes out mostly under special conditions. Prediction from one situation to the other is poor. Similarly, a child who acts timidly in the early years may show a contrasting pattern when interaction shifts from home-related settings to peer-related ones.

The evidence of limited consistency for personality differences is influencing theory. Social-learning theory, with its emphasis on cues, models, and reinforcers, explains reversible and discriminative behavior nicely. As a result, a situational approach has become more popular in making sense out of social-emotional differences (Chapter 5).

Many find a social-learning explanation of personality incomplete. Consistency is part of the story in the social-emotional area, even though individual differences here are less stable than in intelligence. The individuality we do find is hard to reconcile with a one-sided approach that explains social-emotional differences entirely in terms of environment and learning. An interactionist view that assumes learning is important but opens the door to the possibility of biological predispositions seems sounder. It is the approach I take in this chapter. Accordingly, a key concept is *temperament.*

Frontiers box 16–1 Temperament

Child developmentalists are becoming more interested in temperament (Goldsmith & Gottesman, 1981; Yarrow, 1979), as evidenced by an upsurge in the amount and variety of research on temperament. For example, at the 1981 meetings of the Society for Research in Child Development the numerous papers on temperament included investigations of temperament in another culture (Banks, 1981), heart rate correlates of temperament (Garcia-Coll, 1981), early temperament as a predictor of later behavior problems (Bates, Pettit, & Bayles, 1981), and the validity of parental reports of infant temperament (Goldsmith & East, 1981).

There is a shift from arguments about whether temperament is important (more and more scholars agree that it is) to vigorous efforts to learn more about it. With more research comes more concern about how to coordinate findings, leading both to a renewed interest in theory (Buss & Plomin, 1975) and to more concern about the validity of particular research methods (Billman & McDevitt, 1980; Goldsmith & East, 1981; Rothbart, 1981).

Meanwhile, the steady accumulation of evidence gives us a clearer picture of temperament variables. Research on activity level illustrates what is happening. Two careful twin studies (Goldsmith & Gottesman, 1981; Matheny, 1980) indicate that identical twins are more similar in activity level than fraternal twins, providing stronger support for the idea that heredity contributes to activity level differences. A comparison of the range of activity levels of children in Malaya and New York shows them to be similar (Banks, 1981), suggesting that the activity level variable will turn out to be important within a variety of cultures.

Other studies give us a picture of how activity differences fit into the child's life and personality more generally. Buss, Block, and Block (1980) did an extensive study of activity level at the University of California at Berkeley as part of a broader, longitudinal study. They measured activity level with an *actometer,* a watchlike gadget worn on the wrist that records how much the wearer moves. Children wore it for two hours while in nursery school when 3 years old and again when 4. The actometer measures were related to personality descriptions made by teachers when the children were 3, 4, and 7. Thus, it was possible to relate activity level to personality variables over a four-year time span.

A consistent relation between actometer measures and personality descriptions was found. At all ages highly active children were seen by the adults as more energetic and restless, less inhibited, less obedient, less shy and reserved, more self-assertive and aggressive, more competitive, and more manipulative.

The Berkeley findings are particularly interesting because they show

> a relation between activity level and social behavior that has turned up in other studies. Thus, research on activity supports the notion that temperament links to both biological and social aspects of development.

TEMPERAMENT

Temperament is an old term, dating back to early Greek ideas about personality (Allport, 1961). Temperament refers to the how of reactions. Is the child relatively active or inactive, calm or excitable, restrained or impulsive, sociable or solitary, warm or cold, moody or not? With temperament the focus is on a child's style of action, not on skills or goals.

Temperamental variables are usually the social-emotional differences that show the most stability across situations and the most predictability over time (Bronson, 1972; Kohlberg et al., 1972; Scarr, 1969). That's the main reason for emphasizing them here. Outside the intellectual area the consistency we find is largely in individuality of temperament.

Studies by Wanda Bronson (1966, 1972) illustrate the usual pattern of findings. She wanted to find the aspects of personality that looked most central. She used several criteria. She wanted variables that worked both for girls and for boys during the whole period from 5 to 16 years. She looked for characteristics that were central both in relating to varied features of behavior in varying settings and in showing predictability over periods of several years. Two groups of characteristics, or dimensions, emerged as most central: reserved-somber-shy versus expressive-gay-socially easy and reactive-explosive-resistive versus calm-compliant. In other words, a 5-year-old who was strikingly quiet and calm in comparison to classmates was likely to show a similar style at home and in school and remain less explosive and outgoing than average when looked at a few years later. These are the kinds of temperamental variables that are most stable and predictable.

Biological foundations

Temperament is often linked to biological factors (Allport, 1961; Buss & Plomin, 1975). The hypothesis is that these stylistic aspects of how children act are rooted in their bodily characteristics *(constitution)*. Bodily constitution, in turn, is assumed to be influenced by heredity and perhaps by such experiences as brain injury.

The idea of biological foundations for temperament has gotten varied support (see Box 16-1). Babies contrast greatly in temperament even during the first year (Freedman, 1974; Fries & Woolf, 1953; Thomas & Chess, 1977). Longitudinal studies suggest a link between infant temperament and later personality (Kaffman & Elizur, 1977; Schaefer & Bayley, 1963; Thomas & Chess, 1977). Twin studies show that temperamental similarity is greater for monozygotic than dizygotic pairs (Buss & Plomin, 1975; Buss, Plomin, & Willerman, 1973; Scarr, 1969). Biological variation is probably part of the explanation for consistent individuality in temperament.

However, a calm reaction to a reading test or an explosive response to a frustrating shoelace undoubtedly reflects past experience, as does an easy, cheerful manner at a party or a more strained one. These and other indications of temperament, then, should not be thought of as a direct reflection of a child's bodily makeup. Temperamental contrasts must reflect a combination of influences.

Two lines of work illustrate how biological predispositions and life experiences come together in personality development. In each case they help us see how temperament can serve as a "bridge" between what is biological and the specific behavior patterns that emerge through experience and learning. One approach emphasizes conditioning concepts. The other looks more directly at social interaction.

Temperament and conditioning

Hans Eysenck (1957) thinks that inborn differences in children's nervous systems bias their learning experiences in two ways: ease of conditioning and physiological reactivity. An ease of conditioning difference makes children vary in how easily they are socialized. Suppose Jean's brain works in a way that results in unusually easy conditioning. Wouldn't she be more likely to be "tamed" quickly and to be prone to becoming overly inhibited even if her parents say "Don't!" only an average number of times? If Sally takes far more conditioning trials to acquire a response, isn't she likely to remain undersocialized even if reared in an average environment?

Eysenck hypothesizes a contrast in physiological reactivity as basic to a second personality difference. Emotional arousal includes physiological reactions such as heartbeat changes, sweaty palms, and more acid in the stomach (see Chapter 10). Even newborns vary in their heart rate reactions to mild stresses such as a puff of cold air on their stomachs (Richmond & Lipton, 1959). Physiological reactivity of this kind is more similar in identical twins than in fraternal pairs (Fuller & Thompson, 1978; Jost & Sontag, 1944). Eysenck thinks that contrasting arousal patterns make children vary in how prone they are to develop behavior problems. The same stress might produce an emotional problem in physiologically reactive Tony but not produce a problem in less reactive Joe. Eysenck's theory illustrates how learning concepts and ideas about biological individuality can be integrated.

Infant temperament and social interaction

Even little babies have varying personalities. Contrasts in how relaxed they are, how much they smile, and how actively they respond often do not seem to depend on prior experience. Later personality differences might result as much from the temperament that baby starts with as from the learnings parents foster. Observations of cuddlers and noncuddlers and of easy and difficult babies illustrate how this might be.

When Rudolph Schaffer and Peggy Emerson (1964b) watched the development of attachment in Scottish babies, they noticed differences in how babies reacted to being held and cuddled. Some (the cuddlers) seemed to enjoy close physical contact and tried to prolong it. Others tried to avoid being held and cuddled, even though they gave other signs of normal attachment. These noncuddlers enjoyed being swung or romped with, as long as their movements weren't restrained.

In the New York longitudinal study (Thomas & Chess, 1977; Thomas, Chess, & Birch, 1968) the main focus was on early temperament differences among 136 babies and their relation to what happened later. Babies were observed from the early weeks and on through the school years. The findings led to an interest in difficult and easy babies.

One group of 14 babies soon caught the attention of the researchers because they seemed particularly difficult to raise. Their biological rhythms in eating, sleeping, and eliminating were irregular. Their typical reactions to new foods, people, objects, or routines were negative. They cried more than other babies, smiled and laughed less. Their emotional reactions were more explosive and intense—shrieks, not whines, belly laughs, not smiles. As they grew, they were more likely than others to develop behavior problems in school, peer relations, and getting along with family members. They adapted to changes in their world, but it usually took longer and was harder on those around them. The research team found no difference in how the parents cared for these difficult babies. In some cases the parents had other children who were not difficult. Rather than finding an impact of special treatment on the babies, it looked as if these babies presented a special problem for parents. Some staff, in fact, called them mother killers.

Another group of babies was at the opposite extreme: the easy babies. Their rhythms were regular, their moods mostly positive, their reactions to new situations unusually positive. They developed fewer than average behavior problems as they grew up. Again, their reactions did not seem to reflect a special pattern of care or parental attitudes, and their impact on parents was often striking. They helped convince parents, especially new ones, that they were good parents. If you saw these happy babies with their confident parents only at the end of the first year, it would be easy to draw a false conclusion:

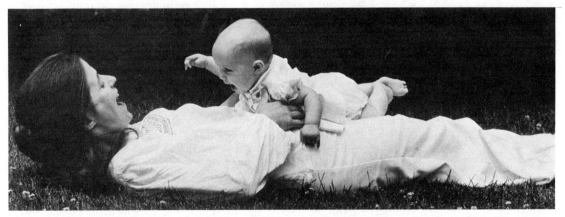

"Easy" babies are happy and have regular biological rhythms, positive moods, and unusually positive reactions to new situations, giving their parents much self-confidence in child rearing.

that the parents' self-confidence in dealing with them produced the babies' positive and secure manner.

These observations show how early temperament can influence parents' reactions and predict later personality. As with Eysenck's theory, they help us move toward a broader and more balanced view of social-emotional differences.

A two-dimensional framework

Now we focus on two important dimensions of temperament. Interest in them results from searches for central orientations or major dimensions of personality (Block & Block, 1980; Bronson, 1972; Eysenck, 1953; Jung, 1923; Kohn, 1977; Quay, 1972; Schaefer, 1959). Three findings have been supported again and again:

1. There are two broad dimensions of social-emotional individuality, analogous to *g* in the intellectual area (Chapter 15).
2. These two dimensions can be defined as extraversion-introversion and emotional stability-emotional instability.
3. The two dimensions are independent of each other, or correlated near 0.00.

Extraversion-introversion

Extraversion-introversion combines two related temperamental qualities: (1) *Sociability*—Does the child tend to make more sociable or more solitary choices? (2) *Restraint*—Does the child more commonly act in a cautious or careful manner or is she or he more impulsive and carefree? Extraverts are relatively sociable and impulsive; introverts are more solitary and restrained (Bronson, 1966; Eysenck, 1953).

A child's standing relative to others is our measure of extraversion-introversion. A child with a relatively high rate of happy-go-lucky and socially oriented behavior as compared with peers is what we mean by an extravert. An introverted child acts more cautiously and is more solitary than most. Most children are in the middle, showing both styles frequently. Only at the extremes do we find children who are more consistent from one day to the next and in varied situations.

Extraversion-introversion shows consistency from babyhood on, although the correlations are not high. The picture is complicated by the fact that behavior changes with age; so we must look at comparable, not identical, actions in babies and older children. Babies who are more active tend to become schoolchildren who are not shy and adolescents who are seen as bold (Schaefer & Bayley, 1963). The low positive correlations mean that we rarely see an active and rapidly moving toddler grow up to be an ultra shy 13-year-old, but many babies at the extremes shift into the average range and many average babies move out toward the extremes. Consistency is greater if we look at older children and predict over a shorter period of time (Bronson, 1972).

Several twin studies suggest that extraversion-introversion has a hereditary component (Scarr, 1969). Typically, pairs of identical twins are more similar to each other in this area than pairs of same-sex fraternal twins.

Studies of body build in relation to behavior suggest that a biological factor might be involved in the consistency of behavior here. For example, Richard Walker (1962) correlated measures of body build with ratings made by nursery-school teachers. The clearest connections were between extraverted behavior and a more muscular, or *mesomorphic*, build. For boys muscular build was associated with an active, assertive manner, as in such ratings as energetic, takes chances, easily angered, and attacks others. For girls meso-morphic build correlated with similar measures, but overall the mesomorphic girls had positive sociability as a more central feature of their activity, with less sign of hostility and sheer energy than the boys.

Introverted behavior patterns tend to correlate with a lean, or *ectomorphic*, body build. For both sexes the more slender and angular looking preschoolers usually got teacher ratings opposite in direction to the mesomorphs in Walker's (1962) study. With his rating scales this meant they often were summed up by "not": not self-assertive, not social in play, not inconsiderate, and so on. A picture of how they did act is suggested by ratings such as enjoys hand activities, slow tempo, conscientious, verbal interests, and daydreams.

It is intriguing that body build correlates more closely with temperamental variables than with other behaviors, but we cannot be sure how much to make of the link. We don't always find it, and some argue what we actually see are stereotypes that gradually influence children as they live with people who hold them. This argument is plausible, but two aspects of Walker's study contradict it. He did not find the fat-happy connection that so many think exists, sug-gesting that teachers were not simply seeing what they expected to see. What's more, he found body-behavior correlations to be as strong at age 2 as at age 4, contradicting the notion that the connection results from a gradual social-learning process.

Emotional stability-emotional instability

You have to understand our overall picture of behavior problems to see how individual differences fit in. Three findings are particularly important. If you watch a representative sample of normal children grow up, you will see that (1) psychological problems are common, (2) psychological troubles are usually transient (come and go), and (3) the nature of the behavioral difficulties changes with age (Anthony, 1970; Clarizio & McCoy, 1976; Graziano et al., 1979).

A changing picture

Psychological problems are common among "normal" children (Achen-bach & Edelbrock, 1981; Tuddenham, Brooks, & Milkovich, 1974). A study in Buffalo, New York (Lapouse & Monk, 1964), showed that in a large cross-section of children 6 to 12 years old, 43% had seven or more worries. The Buffalo mothers saw 30% of their children as restless and 49% as showing overactivity. The children were less likely to see themselves as restless, but the Buffalo children reported even more nightmares, fears, and teeth grinding than their mothers' descriptions of them indicated. No matter what the pathological behavior, it usually is common at some age. When a representative group was observed repeatedly (MacFarlane, Allen, & Honzik, 1954), a wide variety of symptoms was shown by at least one-third of the children at some age: lying, temper, excess reserve, disturbing dreams, oversensitiveness, and so on.

If you catalog behavior problems in all the children in an elementary school this year and then come back two years later, you'll find that most of the problems are gone. If you ask teachers to nominate disturbed children you'll get a similar finding. Most of the children seen as disturbed this year will not be so seen two years later. (In contrast, the small group of children classified as schizophrenic and typically unable to function in regular schools is more likely to show persisting problems [Gossett, Barnhart, Lewis, & Phillips, 1977; Kohlberg, LaCrosse, & Ricks, 1972].) The disappearance of problems has little or nothing to do with treatment. Similar patterns emerge whether you look at groups who get psychological help or those who don't (see Clarizio & McCoy, 1976). The reduction or disappearance of psychological troubles appears to be as basic a part of growing up as the acquisition of them.

The psychological problems that appear and disappear in children vary with age (MacFarlane et al., 1954). Bed-wetting and food finickiness are early problems that become less conspicuous. Lying is common mostly from 3½ to 5 years. Overactivity is most apparent between ages 3 and 9. A few problems peak at about 5 to 7 and again at the beginning of adolescence: disturbing dreams, demand for attention, and irritability. The average child suffers from a gradually changing series of psychological troubles as she or he changes and meets a series of contrasting developmental hurdles.

Because problems are normal and change developmentally, it's hard to define emotional stability-instability. The more practical systems often emphasize the number of problems relative to age peers. You start with a long list of specific difficulties such as temper tantrums and frequent nightmares. Someone who knows the child (usually parent or teacher) checks those that apply. Then you use the child's relative position to determine whether he or she is high, low, or average in emotional instability (Quay, 1972).

Regardless of the system for defining them, such terms as *problem children* or *emotionally disturbed children* are inherently misleading. Specific problems and disturbances usually fade with time. A child who is much more disturbed than average at one age commonly is average a few years later. With intellectual differences, big shifts in rank are rare after age 6; with social-emotional trouble, shifts are common at all ages.

We can do better than chance in predicting that a difficult baby will have more than his or her share of psychological problems later, but most difficult babies probably don't develop special problems. Many of those who do get over them within a few years. There are statistical consistencies of theoretical importance. For practical purposes the safest and most accurate prediction is that social-emotional troubles will disappear.

Ego development

We can define emotional stability in terms of positive qualities as well as by saying that emotionally stable children have fewer problems. A useful approach is to focus on ego development, the growth of the self. Qualities such as self-control follow a developmental sequence, with younger children giving in to temptation and distraction more easily than older children. At any age we can think of less stable children as being behind in ego development. Unusually stable children are ahead.

This approach builds on ideas formulated by Sigmund Freud and developed further by varied theorists (Loevinger, 1976). Freud thought that babies are dominated by the *pleasure principle* and that gradually the *reality principle* grows and becomes stronger. The pleasure principle is a tendency to seek immediate gratification regardless of the consequences, as when children take candy they have been told not to eat. The reality principle means acting in a way that brings more long-term satisfaction but involves sacrificing and resisting the impulse of the moment, as when a child agrees to wash the dishes in order to earn money to buy a bike. Because measures of self-control and resistance to temptation show developmental progress and some consistency across tasks and times, there is support for Freud's ideas (V. Jones, 1954; Kohlberg, 1964; Mischel, 1974).

Later ego development ties in closely with social development (Loevinger, 1976). Skills in role taking and in getting along with people are important parts of ego development during the elementary-school years. An ego-development interpretation of emotional stability relates emotional stability and social maturity in the older child.

There is some longitudinal consistency in self-control, or coping in the face of difficulties. For example, Halverson and Waldrop (1974) studied how toddlers coped with a barrier that was between them and toys. They looked at the relation between how children faced the task at 2½ years and how they coped with intellectual and social problems five years later. The children who stuck with the problem and tried to solve it at 2½ were more likely to be tackling problems in an effective way at 7½ years. Similar results came from a longitudinal study that followed children from day-care centers to elementary school (Kohn, 1977). Ratings of task orientation (dealing with problems realistically) in the preschool years predicted school learning.

We can think of level of ego-development, or ego strength, as a somewhat consistent part of the child's personality. An important part of the modern picture is the recognition that self-control and related variables vary with the situation as well as with the child. Walter Mischel's (1974) research clarifies how and why. In his laboratory 3- and 4-year-olds wait for a snack for as long as 15 minutes or as little as 1 minute, depending on what they do while waiting. (Waiting is brief when they think about the reward and how they will enjoy it. They wait much longer when they think about something else and occasionally remind themselves that the reward will come.)

What we need, then, is a picture of emotional stability as involving both qualities in the child and in the situation. The child's "ego" includes skills that grow with age. Cues and rewards in the situation have to do with whether these competencies are used. That's why children's performances are not highly consistent across situations (Mischel, 1974).

Extraverted and introverted problems

Neither an extravert nor an introvert has more psychological problems, but usually they have different kinds. A big gain from the two-dimensional framework is in seeing how children's difficulties often relate to their temperamental style.

A sociable, carefree child is more likely to hit and lie than to worry or become overly shy. With an outgoing, active manner problems more often result from interactions with others: quarrels with other children and a failure to comply with adults' rules and requests. Less restrained youngsters more often have difficulties involving too little inhibition for their age. Both bed-wetting at 4 and wandering around the classroom at 6 years can be thought of as a result of not showing age-appropriate self-control.

In contrast more cautious and solitary children are likely to develop worries that bother them at bedtime and make it hard to fall asleep. Introverted children's style more commonly results in excessive shyness in new situations and difficulty in letting themselves go and plunging in.

The picture of extraverted and introverted problems is similar whether we look at everyday difficulties or at the children who are brought to clinics and

Getting into fights with other children is more often a problem for extraverts because of their outgoing, active manners.

courts (Achenbach, 1974; Achenbach & Edelbrock, 1978; Kohn, 1977). Most troubles fall into either of two clusters. A child with one kind of problem is more likely to suffer from others in that cluster. We more rarely find children mixing the two. Table 16–1 illustrates the trend. It lists some of the psychological difficulties more commonly associated with each cluster and provides some of the names that have been given to each.

TABLE 16–1   Two clusters of social-emotional problems

	Cluster 1	Cluster 2
Characteristic Problems	phobia stomachache worrying withdrawal nausea shyness insomnia	disobedience stealing lying fighting cruelty temper tantrums showing off
Labels for the Cluster	internalizing symptoms	externalizing symptoms
	introverted problems	extraverted problems
	personality disorder	conduct disorder
	overcontrol	undercontrol

The characteristic problems list is based on Achenbach, 1974, pp. 554–562.

The importance of separating and contrasting the children with problems from the two clusters becomes more obvious as evidence accumulates. Sex and background differences, as well as extraversion-introversion, correlate with problem type. More important, the long-term prospects for children with severe problems vary, depending on which they are. Let's examine first the picture of children with introverted, or internalizing, problems and then go on to those with externalizing difficulties.

Children with introverted problems

Our picture of introverted problems in younger children is suggestive. In the Berkeley sample shyness between 10 and 36 months predicted shyness at 9 and 12 years (Schaefer & Bayley, 1963). In the New York longitudinal study a pattern called "slow to warm up" included both social reserve and other behaviors. The babies who were slow to warm up tended to have a lower activity level and less intense reactions, along with withdrawal tendencies in new situations. Often these babies grew into preschoolers who spent the early weeks of nursery school standing on the sidelines. In elementary school, again, they often reacted to new subject matter with "I don't like it" and nonparticipation (Thomas et al., 1968). Cautious and negative early response to social situations, then, often predicts similar behavior later.

At the elementary-school level our picture is much fuller. By elementary school, children with introverted problems tend to see themselves and their own actions as a problem (see Table 16–2). They are unhappy; their symptoms are on the inside: crying, worrying, and reacting in an overly sensitive way.

TABLE 16–2 Typical characteristics of children with introverted problems

Behavior Traits	Life History Characteristics
social withdrawal	seclusiveness
hypersensitivity	timidity
anxiety	worriedness
shyness	shyness

Questionnaire Responses

I don't think I'm quite as happy as others seem to be. TRUE
I often feel as though I have done something wrong or wicked. TRUE
I have more than my share of things to worry about. TRUE

Based on Quay, 1972.

Although introverted problems are common in both sexes, they are more common in girls. In the Buffalo study 36% of the boys and 50% of the girls were reported by their mothers as having seven or more fears.

We now have a consistent set of findings on the futures of the children with severe internalized problems (Clarizio & McCoy, 1976; Kohlberg et al., 1972; Robins, 1979). Usually the troubles are shortlived. Within two years most of the so-called "neurotic" children brought to clinics will improve, whether or not they are treated. Follow-up studies tracing clinic cases into adulthood show a normal set of lives. When compared to normal controls, clinic cases experience adult problems in marriage, career, community living, and so on about as commonly as nonclinic cases. There is no particular tendency for these children with more fearfulness and shyness than average to become psychiatric cases, whether we look for adult neurosis or adult schizophrenia.

With introverted problems, then, there is a consistent picture whether we look at average children or at children more disturbed than average. With time things get better.

Children with extraverted problems

Children with extraverted problems usually are boys (Anthony, 1970; Clarizio & McCoy, 1976; Eme, 1979; Kohn, 1977; Quay, 1972). From babyhood to adulthood the trend is clear and consistent. Early irritability and fussiness, temper tantrums and hyperactivity, attention getting and lying, stealing and disobedience—all are more often "boy" problems. The well-known link between boys and aggressive behavior (Chapter 14) is but part of a broader picture.

For outgoing problems the sex contrast often is large (unlike the picture for fears, where girls have more, but boys have many). Clinic populations often include at least twice as many boys as girls with conduct disorders (Anthony, 1970).

TABLE 16–3 Typical characteristics of children with extraverted problems

Behavior Traits	Life History Characteristics
disobedience	assaultiveness
disruptiveness	defiance of authority
fighting	inadequacy of guilt feelings
destructiveness	
impertinence	
attention seeking	

Questionnaire Responses

I do what I want to whether anybody likes it or not. TRUE
It's dumb to trust other people. TRUE
The only way to settle anything is to lick the guy. TRUE
If you don't have enough to live on, it's okay to steal. TRUE
I go out of my way to meet trouble rather than try to escape it. TRUE

Based on Quay, 1972.

A summary by Herbert Quay (1972) provides an overview emphasizing children with externalizing troubles of an antisocial kind. Table 16–3 illustrates the trend. It highlights the fact that these problems are external in two ways. Extraverted children have difficulties that put them in conflict with others, both adults and peers. Destructiveness and fighting, along with direct attention seeking, demand a response from others. Inadequate guilt feelings and such questionnaire responses as "It's dumb to trust other people" reveal another kind of externalizing. Children with extraverted problems typically do not see themselves as responsible; it's the other guy. Their complaints center on people in their environment, not on themselves.

Sin and guilt, then, are often negatively related. Little extraverts who yield to temptation and engage in forbidden behavior show few signs of self-blame or guilt. It is the sensitive and restrained children who are more likely to worry about their misdeeds and criticize their own past actions, even when their record is good.

Outgoing problems are not always antisocial. Hyperactivity and academic difficulties also are more common among extraverted children (Kohn, 1977). Extraverted children are more likely to show restlessness, distractability, and trouble in paying attention to what adults emphasize. Not surprisingly, such actions often go with poor academic achievement. What is called hyperactivity often is not an excess of movement in all situations; the contrast emerges when measures of attention and goal direction are used (Sroufe, 1975).

Concern with restless and inattentive behavior often reflects adult expectations. At age 2 years many children are into everything, always on the go. At this point adults don't demand sitting still and paying attention; such concerns arise at school entrance, when tolerance of restlessness decreases. The great stir about hyperactivity in 6-year-olds tells us more about the new environment than about the child. Typically, the same children were even more hyperactive earlier (Wender, 1971).

Most likely, inattention and poor self-control become less of a problem as children with special difficulties in these areas grow older, but we can't conclude that hyperactivity is a minor problem because children outgrow it. The big question is whether associated problems in school and in dealing with people continue. Some follow-up studies give a negative picture (Wender, 1971). At least one is more positive (Battle & Lacey, 1972).

We know more about longitudinal consistency in antisocial behavior. For boys (not for girls) there is almost as much consistency as there is for intelligence (Olweus, 1979, 1981). We can do better than chance in predicting who will be a relatively antisocial adult from an early age. By elementary school the correlations are high enough so that we can be quite safe in predicting that a child who has not developed an antisocial pattern of behavior will not do so later. But many boys who get into trouble through bullying, theft, and disobedience will not become problem adults.

The best clue in predicting which boys with antisocial problems will continue to have trouble comes from a landmark study by Lee Robins (1966). She traced the later histories of children seen in a St. Louis child-guidance clinic. Robins found that the best single predictor of adult troubles was a count of the number of areas in which a boy had antisocial difficulties. A variety of childhood problems in areas such as aggression, theft, truancy, sex, running away, and being unmanageable indicated a much higher risk for the future

Frontiers box 16–2 Attachment differences

The study of infant–care giver attachment (Chapter 12) stimulated important research on early personality differences. Mary Ainsworth and her associates (Ainsworth, 1973, 1979) observed contrasting patterns of attachment behavior among babies about 1 year old. These differences apparently reflect enduring personality patterns.

Attachment behaviors typically are observed and classified by means of a strange-situation test (Ainsworth et al., 1978). Such tests involve introducing baby and mother into an unfamiliar room, having them joined by a stranger, and then having mother briefly leave baby in the test room (either alone or with the stranger). The main interest is in how baby reacts to mother when she returns after a brief separation (the reunion situation).

Contrasting behavior patterns during the reunion are thought to reflect the nature of the babies' attachment. *Securely attached* babies are most common. They usually show heightened attachment behavior following separation, exploring less and sticking closer than usual to mother. Two forms of anxious, or insecure, attachment are observed. *Anxious/resistant* babies, too, show increased attachment at reunion, but they also show anger and resistance. *Anxious/avoidant* infants, in contrast, show a striking tendency to avoid their mother when she returns, either ignoring her or combining a tendency to approach with moving away or looking away from her.

A series of studies has shown that secure attachment behavior predicts more adequate coping as the child faces new challenges in the years that follow. Differences in attachment at 12 months predict how a baby reacts in the same situation at 18 months (Waters, 1978). More securely attached 15-month-olds are more likely to be self-directed and successful in dealing with peers later in the preschool (Waters, Wippman, & Sroufe, 1979). Attachment contrasts at 18 months predict how maturely children play and deal with problem situations at 2 years (Matas, Arend, & Sroufe, 1978) and how much curiosity and resiliency in dealing with problems they show at 4 and 5 years (Arend, Gove, & Sroufe, 1979).

A search for the sources of these contrasts in personality has supported the interactionist view of personality development, for both early temperament and environment apparently contribute to the development of anxious attachment and less mature patterns of coping later. Two studies suggest that babies at risk for developing insecure attachments can be identified soon after birth, months before the period in which attachments develop. Waters, Vaughn, and Egeland (1980) found that newborns with less mature behavior and less adequate physiological regulation were more likely to be anxious/resistant at 1 year. Susan Crockenberg (1981) related newborn irritability to insecure attachment later. Other findings indicate that mothers who are more sensitive and responsive to their infants during their first year are more likely to have babies who develop secure attachments (Ainsworth, 1979; Crockenberg, 1981; Egeland & Sroufe, 1981).

Susan Crockenberg (1981) has documented the complexity of the developmental picture by looking at the mother's social support in relation to both infant temperament and maternal responsiveness. When babies were 3 months old, she interviewed mothers about how much help and emotional support they got from fathers, older children, and others. She found that social support was the best predictor of attachment at 1 year, particularly for mothers with irritable babies. Thus, the present picture suggests that attachment differences reflect an interplay of factors. Difficult babies apparently are more likely to develop insecure attachments as well as problems in coping in other important situations later. But how a care giver deals with a baby also makes a big difference in what kind of attachment develops (as in other aspects of development). Care givers, in turn, are influenced by their own environments. Environmental stresses and the support a care giver gets in coping with them play a big role in how adequately the care-giving tasks are handled.

than problems in only one or two areas. Children with many antisocial problems were found to be at greater risk for a variety of adult difficulties, including criminal behavior, marital conflict, poor military records, alcoholism, vagrancy, unemployment, and schizophrenia (a psychiatric illness).

PREDICTING FUTURE TROUBLES

Interest in children with social-emotional problems was stimulated by the belief that there was a close connection between childhood and adult difficulties. Children who were fearful or who had trouble getting along with others were thought of as likely to develop into adult mental patients and criminals. It was believed that by treating a youngster's psychological problems we could prevent a more serious disorder later. This faith in our ability to spot early warning signs and to do something about them was a pillar of the mental health movement that created child-guidance clinics and popularized concepts of mental health (Kohlberg et al., 1972).

Now we must reconsider these beliefs and the practices they supported. The evidence has undermined them, showing that the experts were often wrong (Anthony, 1970; Eisenberg, 1969; Kohlberg et al., 1972; Robins, 1979). It's time to rethink what we are doing.

The biggest problem stems from the finding that unpredictability is the rule when you try to use current troubles as a basis for forecasting which children will grow up to be adults with serious problems. The result is the same whether you look at biological factors (such as birth injuries), the child's own actions (for example, bullying or withdrawing), or the child's home environment (as in looking at children in stressful homes). In each case you will incorrectly label many children as trouble prone in the process of correctly predicting the cases where early signs of troubles are actually followed by trouble later. When you try to forecast unusual outcomes, such as a child growing up to be a serious criminal or a mental patient, you almost always will be wrong more often than you are right (Meehl & Rosen, 1955).

Calling a child delinquency prone or likely to become mentally ill can be harmful; so predicting from trouble is dangerous, not just inaccurate. Therefore, more and more experts are arguing against efforts to identify children with social-emotional problems and to put them in special programs. They argue that it is sounder to strengthen programs for all children (Kohlberg et al., 1972).

SUMMARY

"Personality" refers to differences in social-emotional behaviors. Because they have been found to be less consistent than intellectual differences some have turned to social-learning concepts, focusing on the discriminating and reversible (inconsistent) aspects of personality. But an interactionist position was taken here instead.

The central idea was that there is some stable individuality in the social-emotional area. Because temperamental, or stylistic, features of children's personality are most enduring and consistent, temperament was emphasized.

First ideas about temperament as a bridge linking biological predisposi-tions to later personality were reviewed. Then a two-dimensional framework was presented based on two broad aspects of temperament: extraversion-introversion and emotional stability-emotional instability.

Extraversion-introversion involves two facets: how sociable or solitary and how impulsive or restrained the child is. Stability-instability was summed up both in positive and negative terms. The number of problems relative to peers has been a useful way of measuring instability. Stability can be defined in terms of ego development or self-control measures, such as the ability to focus attention and resist temptation.

The two-dimensional framework is particularly useful in approaching psy-chological problems in children because introverts and extraverts tend to have contrasting sorts of problems. Contrary to past opinion, modern research has shown that children with introverted problems such as worries and social withdrawal tend to get over them. When extraverted problems take the form of numerous and varied types of antisocial behavior, there is some tendency for childhood psychological problems to predict adult ones. But overall, child-hood trouble is a bad predictor. Psychological troubles are common and usually transient. Accordingly, to single out children with problems as at risk for adult difficulties inevitably results in much false labeling.

PART VI
The Child in the Environment

We shift perspective now. Children have been in the foreground and their environments have been in the background in previous chapters. Now the environment becomes central as we look at the relation between children and the worlds in which they live.

First I provide a framework. I describe a new and comprehensive way of looking at child-environment relations in the next chapter. It helps us look at child-environment interactions at three levels: in particular settings such as within families and classrooms, in terms of the child's whole world of immediate experience, and at the level of society as a whole. This framework makes it possible to look at a variety of questions in a systematic way, such as the interaction between children and parents, the family's position in the community as a factor

in child development, and how modern childhood and children compare with those of times gone by.

Families get a chapter to themselves. It is called "Families" rather than "The Family" to highlight the fact that families have taken many forms, are diverse today, and are likely to continue to change in the future. In it I examine both traditional questions such as discipline and contemporary issues such as divorce and day care.

In the final chapter we face up to the fact that maturity involves moving out of the family of origin and dealing more and more with the world outside of it. I examine the peer world, school, and television in detail because these are the main areas in which the modern child begins to meet and cope with the outside world.

CHAPTER 17

Child-Environment
Interactions

Our vision of the child in the environment must expand. We have to find room in our picture for active children who shape their environments at the same time as the environments shape the children (Baumrind, 1980; Bell, 1979). We must face such topics as television, poverty, and changing family structure, as well as old topics, such as the influence of mothers' discipline. We need an image that is both broader and better balanced than those of the past.

MODELS OF INFLUENCE

New ideas are emerging to meet this need. We are shifting to two-way models of influence and to a picture of the environment as more than mother. The new models emphasize such concepts as complexity, levels of analysis, settings, and systems.

Complexity

The new models are complicated. Figure 17–1 illustrates why. When you look at more people, the number of relationships goes up faster than the number of people. A family with four members has six relationships. If you look at each relationship as involving *bidirectional* (two-way) influence, a family with four members has 12 lines of influence. That's quite a jump from just thinking about how mother influences a child.

Levels of analysis

The more promising views of the child in the environment deal with complexity in terms of *levels of analysis*. We can think of the mother-child relationship both as a particular two-person relationship and in relation to the family as a whole. At one level we can watch how mother and child talk, smile, and influence each other. We also can look at these interactions at another level: as part of broader family matters. What happens to mother-Henry conversations when sister walks in? How do mother-father quarrels influence mother-Henry interactions? With this approach the two-person relation (Figure 17–1b) can be thought of as one level and the family pattern (Figure 17–1c) is viewed as another. A levels approach provides a systematic way of shifting from one part of the picture to another without forgetting the whole.

Settings and objects

Figure 17-1 deals only with people and their interactions, but concern with children's environments often takes us to such topics as playgrounds, toys, television, and physical safety. In life, as in the theater, the social action always takes place on a "set" with "props." We must consider the physical *settings* in which children live and the *objects* they encounter along with the people.

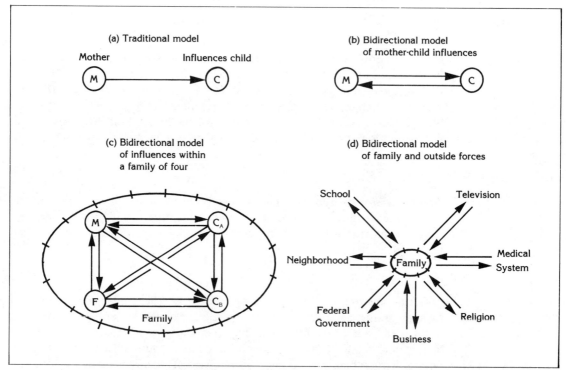

Figure 17-1   Contrasting models of influence

A child always is somewhere. Any hour, day, or year in a child's life can be described in terms of where the child spent his or her time. A catalog of the settings in which a child lives provides an objective and complete starting point in summing up that child's world.

Special people and activity patterns tend to go with each setting; so a focus on the child's environment as a collection of settings quickly gets to meaningful patterns of experience. The settings concept gives us a way of looking at the child's total environment in convenient terms while still orienting toward the more important patterns of social experience.

Systems

System, like level of analysis, is a key concept in dealing with complex situations. Language development becomes more orderly when considered as mastery of separate systems, such as the sound system and the grammatical system. Analysis of environments, too, is helped when put in systems terms.

NESTED SYSTEMS

Urie Bronfenbrenner (1977, 1979b) presents a broad way of looking at child-environment interactions. It combines the settings concept, a levels of analysis orientation, and *systems* thinking. I use his framework here.

Bronfenbrenner distinguishes three kinds of systems: microsystems, mesosystems, and exosystems. *Microsystems* include the activity patterns associated with particular settings, such as home or school. A child's whole world of experience takes place in the collection of microsystems in which she or he lives. That's what Bronfenbrenner terms the *mesosystem.* Everyone children meet, every object they encounter, and every place they go is in their mesosystem. The rest of society influences children, too. The president of the United States and other people they don't meet have an impact on their world; so we use the concept of *exosystem* to include these surrounding parts of the environment that must also be considered. As illustrated in Figure 17–2, these three systems are "nested" one inside the next. Each microsystem is inside the mesosystem; the mesosystem is within the exosystem.

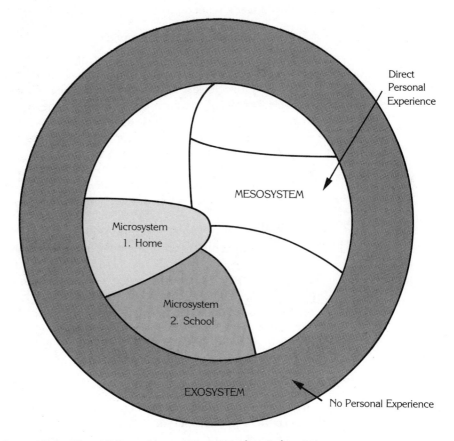

Figure 17–2   The child's environment as a set of nested systems

Everyday scenes of action: Microsystems

The bulk of children's time is spent in a few easily recognized settings (Barker & Wright, 1955). Many hours are spent in and around home and school; the remaining time also is concentrated. If we watch a child for a week, we soon discover a few places, such as the Tenth Street playground, Peterson's candy store, and Charlene's backyard, where many experiences take place.

Each of these regular physical settings usually has its own special cast of characters and activity patterns. Roger Barker and Herbert Wright (1955) called the persisting actions "standing patterns of behavior" to emphasize that they go on although individuals leave and enter the scene. A corner of a playground has a continuing jumprope session. School bus Q-23 has its own special customs for teasing the driver that get passed on to new children when they join the route. Thus, knowing where children are means knowing what is likely to be going on around them.

Almost every setting has its own appropriate and inappropriate behavior, its expectations and demands. That's why each of these little worlds can be called a microsystem. The child who arrives at the bus stop last and tries to board first calls out a predictable response from peers, just as predictable as the bus driver's reaction to someone who gets up while the bus is in motion.

Settings' influences on behavior

Children's behavior usually conforms to the expectations and demands of the situation they are in. This was a main conclusion of laboratory experiments in the social-learning tradition. A similar conclusion also came out of ecological research in which children were observed in their natural environments as they went about their daily routines.

Barker and Wright (1955) found that the best way of predicting what a child was doing was from the setting the child was in. As a child moved from bedroom to breakfast to schoolroom to playground, the stream of activity shifted dramatically with the setting. If you want to understand how children will act, get a detailed picture of the microsystems in which they will be acting.

Settings' demand for person power

A unique contribution of the ecological approach centers on the relation between the supply of actors in a setting and the demands of the setting's activity patterns. Any activity needs a minimum number of people to go well: playing ball, getting supper ready, playing house, or even holding a conversation. As a result, a setting can have a shortage of people or even a surplus. Ecological research indicates that person shortages tend to produce characteristic consequences (Gump, 1975; Schoggen & Barker, 1977).

A ballfield example illustrates more general trends. Imagine a group of children getting ready to play baseball on a playground. Now one more child arrives, Bob. It makes a big difference whether Bob is the 18th or the 28th to arrive. Varied social pressures will operate, depending on whether he is needed. His experiences in the setting will vary even though the setting, the props, the activity, and most of the cast are identical in the two conditions.

In a setting in which there is a shortage of people, boys and girls of varied ages will play together to satisfy the demands of the setting's activity patterns.

With a person shortage the following consequences are common:

1. Treat each individual as being more important (think of the greetings Bob would get in the two conditions)
2. Give the individual more responsibility (he'd be lucky to pinch hit if he was 28th)
3. Put more of a premium on a person's concrete accomplishments in the setting and less emphasis on general personal qualities (if he's 18th, the main question is will Bob play, not is he bright and charming)
4. Set lower standards (if he's 28th, his skill will matter more in getting to play)
5. Generate more insecurity (with a person shortage, he's on the spot and playing even if he's out of practice or out of his league)
6. Call on people to be more versatile (with 18 players he's more likely to be forced to play an unfamiliar position)
7. Get each person to work harder (with 18, Bob will play whether or not he's tired and have trouble leaving before the game is over)

These ideas about person shortages fit in with the fact that societies with smaller family groups downplay sex differences in their socialization practices (see Chapter 14). The need for versatility is greater with a smaller group and smaller groups have important implications for school size (see Chapter 19). The broad implications of this variable illustrate the advantage of thinking in ecological terms.

Physical aspects of settings

The environmental crisis has heightened our interest in the physical environment and its relation to children's behavior (Altman & Wohlwill, 1978). Research on preschools and on housing areas illustrates where we stand (Gump, 1975).

Because children in preschools often get time for free play, we have a good opportunity to see how physical factors influence what they do. There are reliable correlations between physical props and activity patterns that go beyond the obvious: block play generates more conflict than art; the amount of equipment has more impact on social behavior than does the amount of space; dramatic activities such as playing with blocks promote more peer reinforcement than such table activities as puzzles (Gump, 1975).

Research on housing has drawn attention to spaces outside apartments and to overall site design as perhaps more important than the interiors themselves. Many findings relate to safety and supervision. In low-rise projects mothers often let young children play on the landings and stairs while listening to what goes on through half-open doors. The monitoring by mothers increases the safety of these areas. In comparable high-rise projects doors more commonly are locked with the children inside. A general finding has been that the combination of high-rise buildings and welfare families results in disaster: wrecked buildings, children killed in ruined elevators, and so on. Older children and adolescents play a key role in the destruction. In contrast, when comparable families are in low-rise buildings, things go much better. The crime rate was only one-third as high in the low-rise apartments in one study. It is not surprising, then, that poor children in cities often learn contrasting codes of living: a helping-sharing system inside the home, a picture that might makes right outside (Gump, 1975).

Children's influence

The idea that children influence others is leading to a picture of how it happens. Children start about half their interactions with parents at all ages (Bell & Harper, 1977). Asking for what they want is frequent (Bell & Harper, 1977). They use reinforcement in controlling those around them, both peers (Charlesworth & Hartup, 1967) and adults (Patterson, Reid, Jones, & Conger, 1975). Children, then, shape the flow of interaction within their settings in much the same way as adults.

Control systems

We can think of the child's relationships as *control systems* in which each person's actions direct, or control, what the other does. The trick is to use concepts that make it easy to see that each action is both a response to what the other did and a stimulus guiding what the other does next. Richard Bell has presented concepts we can apply to any of the child's face-to-face interactions (Bell, 1968; Bell & Harper, 1977).

Bell's theory emphasizes *limits* and *controls*. Each member of the microsystem has limits for the actions of the other, ideas about when there is too much or too little of certain behaviors. Controls are efforts to keep the other's actions within limits. Controlling actions take two basic forms: upper- and lower-limit controls.

Upper-limit controls are like saying "Stop!" The goal is to decrease a behavior when there is too much of it (when it reaches the upper limit). Any action that states "I've had enough of that" is an upper-limit control, whether it comes from the child or the other.

Lower-limit controls always have the goal of getting more action of some kind out of the other person (when their behavior falls below the lower limit). These do-more actions also come from both children and their associates.

In this conception controlling behaviors are simultaneously seen as re-actions to what the other is doing and as attempts to influence. Linda's "Stop bossing me around!" tells us both about her partner's behavior and Linda's goals for her partner. When Tony says "Please play with me," we learn what his associate is not doing as well as learning what Tony wants. Bell's model is handy because his concepts build in two-way influence.

The control systems approach is useful in thinking about discipline, adult efforts to get children to "shape up" and act "properly." It shows how these actions fit in with others and emphasizes that it is the combination of what children do and how adults see it that determines when behavior is a problem and when control techniques are used.

What would you say about a mother who always was saying "No!" and "Stop!" to her child and gave many spankings? Traditional psychologists would say she was punitive or controlling. If her son were found to be hyper-active and aggressive, his behavior would be explained as a reaction to her discipline pattern. Bell points out that we could as easily see it the other way around. The mother's frequent use of upper-limit controls might be a reaction to her son's excess of extraverted problem behavior. Evidence for inborn temperamental differences makes this a reasonable hypothesis (Chapter 16).

Bell argues that parental controlling behaviors are organized in sets. When a child's behavior needs limiting, some reactions are more likely to come out first. "Please stop" is an earlier and more common parental reaction than spanking. Accordingly, extreme forms of parental control often may reflect the failure of the more common and gentler attempts at control that come first. This idea has gotten support in research on interaction patterns of the families of extremely aggressive boys.

Gerald Patterson and his associates at the University of Oregon (Patterson, 1980; Patterson et al., 1975) have been looking closely at families where hitting and other strong forms of social influence are common. They have concluded that boys who hit a lot often teach their family to respond with equally strong measures (see Box 17–1). Selective reinforcement seems to operate. Parents and siblings of these boys often find that mild control efforts don't get quick results, but hitting back does. Mothers and siblings thus are often shaped into a pattern of meeting attack with attack. (Fortunately, the researchers are making progress in teaching family members how to use effective control techniques based on positive reinforcement.)

These findings illustrate why we cannot draw cause-and-effect conclusions just because we see correlations in the actions of children and those around them. Attack generates attack and tends to produce a strained and conflicted microsystem regardless of how the pattern gets started. More positive control techniques tend to produce more positive reactions and a more harmonious interaction system. We should expect parallels in the behavior of children and those around them, but we cannot jump to quick conclusions about how and why those correlations originate.

Frontiers box 17–1 The victims

Gerald Patterson (1980) turns conventional thinking upside down. Observation of the families of aggressive boys has led him to the conclusion that the real and unacknowledged victims in these families are the mothers. Evidence on normal families gives a similar, though less extreme, picture.

When hours and hours of family interaction are observed and recorded, it turns out that mothering involves a lot of unpleasantness, being the target of disapproval, whining, negative commands, and so on. In "normal" families there are minor troubles about once every three minutes and "major" ones about three times an hour. In the families of aggressive boys mothers are subjected to trouble more than twice as often.

It doesn't surprise Patterson to find that the mothers of aggressive boys are an unhappy group, coming out as depressed and low in self-esteem on personality tests. He thinks that the unhappiness results from their being the victim of so many attacks and from typically being the crisis manager in the family, the one who is supposed to deal with the problem an aggressive boy poses.

Patterson's approach to solving the problems of families with aggressive boys is as unconventional as his definition of what's going on. He highlights the fact that in these families mothers usually lack skill in accurately seeing deviant behavior and in dealing with children. Others would downplay this skill problem or see it as a symptom of the mothers' depression and low self-esteem, but Patterson turns it around. He thinks that the mothers are psychologically disturbed because their inept approach to child management results in a constant diet of conflict and unhappiness.

How sound is his analysis? When Patterson teaches mothers to be more skillful in managing their sons, there are dramatic changes. The boys' behavior becomes less aggressive and the mothers' morale improves. Their depression fades and they become more normal looking on personality tests; so despite its unconventional nature, Patterson's argument deserves serious attention.

The immediate environment: The mesosystem

All the child's experience goes on in the mesosystem, the total set of settings and microsystems in which the child lives. Mesosystem, then, is roughly what we mean when we talk about the world of childhood or a child's immediate environment.

Mesosystem as a system

The parts of a child's world tie together (Bronfenbrenner, 1979a, 1979b); so the term *system* is apt here. What happens in the separate settings is connected and it has to be seen that way. Home and work place used to be the same place. For most of human history parents worked near where they ate and slept. When parents started working somewhere else, home and family became a new kind of microsystem (Chapter 18).

When home was a work place, children worked there, too. When specialized work places such as factories, mines, and offices were created, children often followed the work to them. In 18th-century England 7-year-olds often worked in coal mines and textile mills, but in many countries that situation soon changed.

School replaced work place in the modern mesosystem. As a result, to make sense out of modern schools we must relate them to what *isn't* happening: children aren't producing economically any more. And we have to relate school to other parts of modern childhood. The school-home relation is one of the best understood. We know that some children have schools and homes that fit together nicely and others don't. Teachers in schools in inner cities or in developing nations can tell you what happens when these two mesosystems clash: children suffer. We know that school and home often are connected by a school bus. School busing connects to social problems, to newspaper headlines.

The school-television connection is newer. At first it raised an obvious problem we now ignore. A child's day always contains 24 hours. Whenever a new setting takes up time in a child's life, something else has to give it up. In the 1950s, a hot question was where television time came from (Chapter 19): sleep, homework, reading? Television and school-related activities were seen as competing. Once television was taken for granted as occupying a large part of children's lives, the relation between TV content and the school curriculum became more central: what happens to kindergarten after children have learned their letters from "Sesame Street"? Now a broader and deeper concern is emerging: Is television changing the role of school and school learning in children's lives? What becomes of traditional schooling when we have television generations used to a richness of information, to attention-commanding programs, and to nonreading as a mode of going beyond personal experience (Coleman, 1971)?

These connections between settings turn up everywhere we look. Usually they are central to the problems and social issues that involve children. A question such as "Why can't Johnny read?" takes us beyond home, school, and even home-school relations. Day care is an issue because today large numbers of mothers work outside the home. Child abuse relates to the fact that fathers cannot find work. Such problems as teen smoking and teen drinking connect to the nature of the modern peer group, which, in turn, cannot be separated from the age grouping basic to modern schools. We cannot ignore the mesosystem if we are to recognize and reduce problems seen as in the child, family, school, or peer group (Bronfenbrenner, 1979a, 1979b).

Describing mesosystems

The assertion that everything is connected can be discouraging. We can't look at everything at once, but two features of children's overall environment seem central. They give us a concrete starting point: community organization-disorganization and socioeconomic status.

Community organization-disorganization.   Perhaps the most central question about a child's world is how well it hangs together. Do the separate settings and microsystems mesh well or clash? Sociologists have studied this question. Emile Durkheim (1893/1933) used the analogy of bodily organs. When the parts of the mesosystem work in harmony, he termed this an "organic solidarity," a parallel with healthy functioning in the body. When separate groups and microsystems fail to fit together well, he termed the situation *anomie* (pronounced an-o-me) and compared it to pathology on the physiological level.

We cannot equate social health with an absence of social conflict (Skolnick, 1973), but Durkheim's concept of anomie is useful in characterizing communities. Events such as high infant mortality rates, juvenile delinquency, unemployment, truancy, alcoholism, mental illness, and suicide tend to accompany each other and vary greatly across different parts of our society. By thinking of the child's world in terms of overall community organization and disorganization, you make a first step in understanding it as a whole.

During the 1960s, psychologists broadened their concerns. They started looking at individual problems more in relation to families and broader social settings, an approach often called *community psychology* (Golann & Eisdorfer, 1972). This kind of orientation to psychological problems soon led to an emphasis on *support systems,* the network of people and resources drawn on for help, or support, when problems arise. Support systems became important because it soon seemed clear that an individual's or family's ability to cope with life's hurdles often hinges on the question of whether they can turn to outside resources. Were a new baby, a handicapped child, major illness, unemployment, divorce, and death challenges that were overcome or stresses that produced negative outcomes? Often advice, emotional support, and money from others made the difference.

In an organized community, support systems are common and are easily used. A child's family, neighbors, and teachers easily turn to each other and to resources beyond when problems arise. Because difficulties such as premature birth have outcomes that vary with the type of family involved (Chapters 4 and 15), a concept such as support system provides an important key in relating child development to the child's community.

Socioeconomic status.   In complicated societies such as our own the concept of social class, or socioeconomic status, provides a second way of describing a child's community and seeing where and how the child fits into the community as a whole.

Socioeconomic status (SES) relates to people's prestige in the community as a whole. Those who are looked up to have higher status. The people looked down on have a lower status position. In the United States parental occupation, educational level, family income, and place of residence are the main criteria used in measuring social class. Professional and executive occupations (physician or bank president) have high status. Occupations such as secretary and electrician are further down. Unskilled occupations (dishwasher) are at the bottom (see Kohn, 1969; Mueller & Parcel, 1981; Williams, 1970).

Children's social class is determined by that of their parents. The newborn son of the president of the board lives in a different mesosystem than the new son of the man who cleans the executive washroom. If born in the same hospital, they move out of it to different worlds a few days later. They grow up in contrasting homes, neighborhoods, and schools. If they attend the same high school, they are likely to be in separate programs and to take different courses. In school halls and after school they mingle with contrasting crowds. Within a community, then, children's parents determine which of several environments is the one in which they actually grow up.

Social class relates to many parts of adult life: political preferences, church membership, death rates, illness rates, and sexual behavior. Both the most public and the most private aspects of parents' lives correlate with their socioeconomic status (Kohn, 1969).

Social class is just as important in the lives of children. Social class differences are common and often large (R. D. Hess, 1970). For example, SES contrasts in intellectual development are bigger and more consistently found than intellectual differences related to sex or to birth order (Brody & Brody, 1976).

Social class, then, like community organization-disorganization, gives us a good way of summing up important features of a child's overall environment. It orients us to environmental contrasts that predict varying experiences and variations in development.

Community organization and socioeconomic status tend to be related. Middle-class children more often live within organized communities and children whose families are at the bottom of the scale are more likely to live in anomie. But the correlation is far from perfect.

At present I live in rural Pennsylvania. Many of the children in my neighborhood are Old Order Amish and Mennonites. They grow up in a tradition that has not adopted the automobile and many other features of modern life. The children live in an amazingly well knit community of a few dozen farm families. Although they own land, these families are not high on the economic scale. In the wealthy suburb where I lived before, most of the children were from higher-status and higher-income families, but the community solidarity was lower. Parts of California, such as Beverly Hills and Marin County, have become famous for their combination of high incomes and high divorce rates.

Thus, we have to think of community solidarity and social class as separate variables, even though they often covary.

Among my Amish and Mennonite neighbors support systems are so strong and important that they get along without insurance or governmental Social Security. Juvenile delinquency and divorce almost never occur, but tragedy does strike in traditional forms: death, illness, and mental retardation. In facing these problems parents do not stand alone. The community provides both personal and economic help. A widowed mother gets help in raising children and making a living (Bryer, 1979). A family with a child who requires special attention is allotted special funds by the church group. Problems are less disruptive when they occur in this context of solidarity.

In our cities economic poverty and anomie often go together. The combination puts many children there at risk for developmental troubles. An uneducated mother trying to rear children alone in Detroit often lacks social support as well as cash. The special demands of rearing a handicapped child are more wearing when you have neither money for special help nor relatives to share the burden.

The world beyond: The exosystem

People whom children never meet impinge on their world of direct experience. The television programs and commercials that come into the family room are created by strangers in distant cities. Before the children were born, highway planners made decisions that influence how they get to school and how far their parents travel to work. Child labor and school attendance laws determine what they can and cannot do, but they don't meet the legislators, lobbyists, union leaders, and business executives who shape those laws. Children and their immediate environment are linked to a broader one, the exosystem, including places, people, and events outside the mesoenvironment.

The exosystem, the bigger outside world that encloses their own, includes both tangible and intangible influences. A constant stream of books, cars, medicine, and food comes out of it into the child's immediate settings, as do ideas and values. The Women's Movement and the Right to Life Movement influence our children as surely as their textbooks and the pollution in their air.

Concern with the exosystem takes us far beyond child psychology and forces us to think about history, economics, political science, and geography. Both academic thinkers trying to understand childhood and practical people trying to help children have turned to a much broader framework. The focus here is on a way of looking at macroenvironments as they influence the child's immediate world. The concepts of integration and complexity are central.

Integration

Once again the system concept is central. Societies are *integrated systems;* religion, economics, language, and a host of other elements relate. Families and the socialization process are central in all societies. Not surprisingly, then, we find connections between the society as a whole and the main features of childhood.

Child rearing varies with the kind of society. Contrasts in whether obedience to adults is stressed provide a good example. Nonliterate cultures whose economy is based on hunting and fishing emphasize self-reliance more than obedience in children; obedience is more important when the economy is based on agriculture (Barry, Child, & Bacon, 1959). Obedience was more central in Europe when agriculture was dominant before industrialization (Skolnick, 1973). Today we find that working-class parents value obedience more than middle-class parents (Kohn, 1969). Child rearing is but one element in a broader social system.

Complexity

In relating childhood to society it is particularly important to consider the *complexity* of the society. A host of specifics tie in with this central characteristic. For example, the emphasis placed on obedience varies with complexity. Obedience is a more central concern in societies that are intermediate in complexity; those that are simple and those that are extremely complicated pay less attention to it (Skolnick, 1973). Modern, complicated societies tend to create childhoods that are similar to each other and different both from childhoods past and from those in nonliterate societies today.

THE MODERN CHILD'S WORLD

Modern children live in a distinctive world. Their daily life is carried out in new kinds of settings. Their activities and routines contrast as much with those of their great-grandparents as do the objects around them. A visitor from centuries past would be astonished by the television sets, cars, telephones, magazines, and toys that surround modern children, but the way they live would be just as amazing. We must focus on the distinctive features of modern childhood if we are to understand modern children.

I've already mentioned a few elements of modern childhood. Here is a list that includes those and others, brought together to highlight the special combination of facts of life that are so basic to childhood today and so alien to human history.

1. *Separation of children from the world of work.* In modern societies children are not members of the labor force. They may do a few chores, but unlike children of the past, they spend few hours in economic production. The employed members of their families make their economic contribution outside the home. Children rarely enter factories or offices. Children, then, are separated from the world of work in varied ways.

2. *Growth of formal socialization.* In smaller and simpler groups children learn from everyone, everywhere, at any time. Socialization is an informal process carried out by amateurs, usually while they are doing something else. In a complex society socialization often is carried out by specialists, in specialized settings, and according to a preset schedule. Professionals with licenses make socialization a career.

3. *Age segregation.* Our children spend much of their time with children almost exactly their age and with adult socializers. Seven-year-olds rarely meet babies,

The leisure, wealth, and age-segregation tendencies of modern children are as distinctive to human history as the new toys they play with.

teenagers, or older people. They have little contact with children even two years older or younger.

4. *Loss of responsibility.* In traditional societies children not only worked, but took care of others. By age 7, responsibility for younger children and animals was common (Rogoff et al., 1976). Modern children have lost these responsibilities. They live in a world where they are not needed by others, older or younger.

5. *Consumer role.* Two hundred years ago dogs and horses were productive members of the farm family; they paid for their keep, pulling, hauling, and protecting. In our country today dogs and horses mostly are just pets. They are expensive luxuries and don't pay for their keep by any economic measure. They are nice to have if you like them and can afford them. The position of the child in the modern family has changed in parallel with that of the horse or dog.

Like the rest of us, the modern child is rich when compared with people in other societies. But without responsibilities for others, the child's economic role is narrower. Spending and being spent on is the modern child's contribution to the economy.

6. *Indirect experience.* The reading so prominent in elementary school and the television watching so conspicuous at home are parts of a broad trend. Today children's lives include much indirect experience—experience through symbols. There is less doing, less direct contact with people and things. There is more time with books, television, records, and the happenings of distant and imaginary people.

The communication media bring whales and war, moonwalks and murders into children's homes and classrooms. Ricardo shares such emergencies as floods with people he never meets and goes through adventures with fictional characters such as Wonder Woman and the Hulk, but he has never seen birth, human or animal. Experience with the marriages and deaths of people he knows is rare. Direct participation in community festivals is infrequent, but more and more often television brings him together with a national community, as in witnessing the funeral of a president or in enjoying a Superbowl game.

Modern children grow up in an information-rich world. The home, like the school or office, is now filled with symbols and opportunities for indirect experience (Coleman, 1971).

MODERN CHILDREN

Are modern children different? What about grandma's feeling that children today are spoiled brats? Does grandpa's claim that he was too busy earning a living when he was 19 to have an identity crisis have any validity? Or are these kinds of complaints about the younger generation meaningless reflections of the age-old tendency for each generation to see the world as going downhill when turned over to the newcomers?

The question is central. We need a perspective on modern children, both to understand them and to know how to look at child psychology. Perhaps we are studying history, the characteristics of children in our own time and place, not "the child." The child's world has changed and is changing, so why not the child?

Here is an overview of the trends that have emerged when children growing up in modern, complicated societies such as our own have been compared with those in more traditional environments.

Physical development

Modern children are bigger, healthier, and reach puberty earlier than those of earlier days and in nonmodern groups today (Roche, 1979; Tanner, 1970).

Frontiers box 17-2 Children outdoors

Contemporary child psychology is largely the psychology of children indoors. Tests, experiments, and even naturalistic studies usually have been carried out within the walls of buildings. Does this distort our picture? It is hard to tell, but both common sense and the evidence we have suggest that more attention to children outdoors would enrich our picture.

One reason for taking the outdoors more seriously in child psychology is that it has a special emotional significance for children (Hart, 1979; Moore & Young, 1978). When children are asked where they like to play or what they like about where they live, emphasis on the outdoors is common.

Interestingly, the accumulating evidence suggests that for modern children there is a contrast between the importance they assign to the outdoors and their actual use of it (Moore & Young, 1978). The outdoors seems to play a far bigger role in their minds and feelings than in their actual behavior.

Much of the evidence on what children do outside relates to the concept of range, which refers to how far children range from home. As you would expect, children are allowed to go farther and farther from home as they grow older (Moore & Young, 1978). A child's range is negotiated between child and parent; it is not determined by parent alone (Hart, 1979).

Sex differences in how range is defined and used illuminate contrasts. For example, Roger Hart (1979) found that parental range restrictions were much clearer for girls than for boys. In interviewing boys he found that they would often mention a boundary and later talk about going beyond it. Questioning older boys turned up responses such as, "Well, she knows that I go, but I'm not supposed to." Apparently, an attitude of boys will be boys prevailed. Mothers often ignored rule breaking by boys, as long as they did not get in trouble while doing it. Another sex contrast in Hart's study was that the boys ranged primarily in play, but girls more often went on errands and other trips that were part of their domestic routines.

Hart (1979) treated children and parents as "experts" who could teach him about their world. His approach resulted in important suggestions about why the outdoors is so meaningful to children. His findings on shortcuts are typical. Elementary-school children often have shortcuts for getting from one place to another, special routes that grown-ups don't use, often involving cutting through other people's yards. When looked at objectively, the shortcuts often turn out to be longer than conventional routes and save neither effort nor time. Why are they so common and so special? Apparently, children prize shortcuts because they discover them for themselves and make them part of their worlds. Like forts and play houses, they are part of a children's world that is special largely because it is their own, free of adult supervision and knowledge.

Some feelings about the outdoors are negative (Hart, 1979). For example, woods are often considered scary places, like abandoned houses. They are associated with bears, bats, dragons, and scary stories. At the same time they are attractive. Children's actions seem to reflect their conflicted feelings about woods. They tend to stay on the edge of a forest rather than going inside. When they go through them, few leave the path.

Stray facts about how children act in the woods make more sense when we relate them to the children's own feelings and to the broader culture's image as reflected in such stories as "Hansel and Gretel." Little pieces of knowledge about children outdoors are beginning to add up to a more coherent picture.

More children at all ages today survive and become adults. Until modern times most babies died before age 5 years. There still are countries where one in three children dies before this age. In contrast, over 95% of modern newborns reach age 5 and about half reach age 70 (Newson & Newson, 1974; Thomlinson, 1976, pp. 131 and 136).

Cognitive development

When we turn from physical to psychological development, comparisons become more difficult. Language differences complicate matters. Problems such as ensuring that the instructions, motivation to perform, and familiarity with the materials are comparable can never be solved fully, but two trends emerge from the best efforts to get past these difficulties.

The most general finding is that children who grow up in similar learning environments tend to develop similar patterns of cognitive skill. Children in modern and traditional societies often contrast in their performance on Piaget's conservation tasks. Children in traditional societies usually don't conserve until they are several years older. The Tiv of Nigeria are an exception; even though few Tiv children go to school, they perform similarly to Western children on conservation tasks. They achieve conservation at an earlier age and show a more active approach to the task than children from most traditional societies. But this exception actually supports the more general trend. Tiv society cultivates more independence and assertiveness in children than most traditional groups; both their child rearing and their children's conservation performance contrast with other nonmodern groups in similar ways (Munroe & Munroe, 1975).

A second trend is more specific: *decontextualized thought.* Children from our kind of society more often use thinking skills acquired in one setting when they face problems in another context. They will use a skill such as counting or measuring in new settings and with materials never counted or measured before. Children (and adults) in a traditional world take a more specific approach. Skills are more *embedded* in the context, or situation, in which they originally are learned. If grain is measured frequently and clay is not, conservation of amount of grain might be way ahead of conservation of amount of clay. A child who is a potter and works regularly with clay may conserve clay quantity but not apply the same principle to grain (Munroe & Munroe, 1975).

Because decontextualized, or generalized, thinking processes are somewhat specific to modern societies, it is possible that g (Chapter 15), or general intelligence (Goodnow, 1976), and formal operational thinking (Munroe & Munroe, 1975) are also much more prominent in them.

Social-motivational development

Modern children tend to develop a contrasting motivational, or personality, pattern. The findings in three areas tie together here: competitiveness, achievement motivation, and self-orientation (Munroe & Munroe, 1975).

Competitiveness

Experiments with games reveal dramatic contrasts in competitiveness (Kagan & Madsen, 1971; Shapira & Madsen, 1974). For example, a marble game is played by two children at a time. If they work together and take turns, each wins more marbles than if they compete, with both trying to get marbles for themselves. Mexican children cooperate much more than U.S. children on this task. The competitive approach is more common among U.S. children. Within several cultures more urban (modern) children compete more and those from rural-traditional groups show a less competitive, more cooperative approach (Munroe & Munroe, 1975).

Achievement motivation

Psychologists define *achievement motivation* as competition with a standard of excellence. Striving to do well, showing involvement with a goal of excellence over a long time period, and having a strong emotional reaction to the achievement or nonachievement of excellence are common criteria in deciding when achievement motivation is present (McClelland, Atkinson, Clark, & Lowell, 1953).

Achievement motivation tends to be more common in modern Western societies and in the traditional groups whose child rearing most resembles ours, such as the Ibo of Nigeria and the Manus of the South Pacific. These societies emphasize early independence and self-direction for children, rather than obedience (Munroe & Munroe, 1975).

Self-orientation

"As long as the child is not needed he will focus on himself" is how Robert and Ruth Munroe (1975, p. 147) integrate the findings. The modern child is *self-centered* in comparison with children in traditional societies. In the six cultures study (Whiting & Whiting, 1975) American children sought attention, help, and dominance far more commonly than children in less complicated societies. Cultural complexity correlated both with the work load on the mother and the number of tasks assigned to children. Groups with less differentiated societies, such as the Nyansongo of Kenya, Africa, and the Juxtlahuaca of Mexico, had mothers with more to do than in such complicated societies as Orchard Town, New England, and Khalapur, India. The simpler societies give children more responsibilities, such as preparing food and taking care of animals. These children showed more frequent nurturant-responsible behavior and less egotistic behavior of the "look at me," "help me," and "do what I want" varieties. Munroe and Munroe (1975, p. 145) formulated an overall picture: "cultural complexity breeds an efficiency that reduces the need for children to contribute to the family, and the result is an orientation away from the family and toward the self. In a word, the self is a luxury item that emerges in surplus economies."

When they hypothesize about self, Munroe and Munroe go far beyond childish behaviors of the "look at me" variety. They see concern with self-realization and self-development as distinctively modern as well. The search for self, like formal operational thinking, may be largely a product of the modern world (Munroe & Munroe, 1975).

IMPLICATIONS

This chapter should help you understand why much thinking about the child in the environment now appears to have been far too narrow. It also gives perspective on a pattern of negative findings in many studies of child rearing and education.

Because so many variables act on the child, it is unlikely that any particular ones make a great difference. Parents are influenced by children and by forces outside the family, so it is unlikely that an approach seeing parents only as causes can take us far. The negative findings, then, can be seen as documenting the complexity of child-environment relations (Bell, 1979; Bronfenbrenner, 1979a). They don't imply that environment doesn't matter.

Actually, we often find strong and easily replicated correlations between environment and behavior when we look at bigger and broader environmental variables. Investigators have subjected monkeys and dogs to far more restricted environments than we find in any natural settings. These extreme conditions often produce dramatic and lasting changes (see Moltz, 1971). Equally extreme environmental variation would probably produce dramatic results in children. Research in cultures where only some children go to school suggests that schooling as a whole has a big impact on children's thinking, even though we usually find that minor shifts in how we run a school doesn't (Bruner, 1965; Scribner & Cole, 1973). When children are adopted out of generally negative environments into more positive ones, we often see bigger shifts in behavior than when we compare particular child-rearing contrasts within relatively similar families (Clarke & Clarke, 1976). Within varied cultures social class usually correlates with a wide range of child behaviors. When the environmental contrasts are sharp, as in comparing children from disorganized poverty homes with those from "mainstream America," environmental variables loom large and overshadow biological ones (see Sameroff & Chandler, 1975).

The negative results of past research helped prepare us for the newer approaches. Now it is harder to believe that there is some little quirk in how we treat children that will have an enormous impact on their future. We no longer expect quick and easy answers to age-old questions, but we do expect that a more sophisticated orientation will gradually clarify child-environment relations and give us a better basis for making decisions about children. The next two chapters look more specifically at what we are learning.

SUMMARY

This chapter developed a framework for looking at child-environment interactions and then used it in describing childhood in modern societies. First we examined key concepts: complexity, levels of analysis, settings and objects, and systems. Then I used them to summarize children's worlds as nested systems.

Microsystems are the basic units of the child's environment. Each setting is a microsystem because it has its own cast of characters and patterns of activity. Children's behavior typically conforms to the demands of each microsystem. Since each setting needs some minimum number of people for its action pattern, settings with a person shortage exert special pressures. The physical aspects of settings also influence what happens. Children's relations with others make up control systems. Each person tries to keep the other's behavior within limits. Accordingly, correlations between child and parent behavior patterns do not necessarily show the influence of parents on children.

The child's immediate environment (mesosystem) includes all the varied microsystems in which the child spends time. Changes in one part of the mesosystem result in changes elsewhere. Two features of mesosystems are particularly important: community organization-disorganization and socioeconomic status.

The child's environment also includes the outside world (exosystem) because influences such as the federal government can have a big impact even when the child does not encounter them directly. Accordingly, child psychologists now emphasize broader social factors once ignored. Because societies are integrated wholes, their methods of raising children relate to other matters, such as their economic systems. Comparative studies show that the complexity of the society is particularly important in predicting what childhood is like within it.

Modern childhood in complex societies contrasts both with childhood in past ages and with contemporary childhoods in simpler societies. Distinctive features of modern childhood include separation of the child from work, the growth of formal socialization, age segregation, loss of responsibility, the consumer role, and indirect experience.

Apparently modern children are also different. Typically they are healthier, bigger, and reach puberty earlier than their historical counterparts. Their thinking seems less bound by the context. They appear more competitive, show more achievement motivation, and seem more self-oriented.

The new orientation to child-environment interactions presented here is far broader than traditional ones. It highlights the complexity of the area and helps explain why we usually find that correlations between child characteristics and specific environmental factors are not close.

CHAPTER 18

Families

Families are a universal in the story of children, but we must not confuse families as we see them today with "the family." Families vary. Within Western society the typical family has changed over the centuries and it is changing now.

What we see as the family is "the modern family," a creation of the last few centuries. Apparently, it emerged in parallel with the industrialized world (Goode, 1963; Shorter, 1976; Skolnick, 1973). As modernization spread around the world, it came to places with varied systems: families with one husband and several wives, families with one wife and several husbands, extended families where parents and their children are parts of a larger group and household. Whatever the family system before modern times, people in varied countries have moved toward a modern family similar to ours (Goode, 1963).

DISTINCTIVE FEATURES OF THE MODERN FAMILY

Our pattern is a *nuclear* one. A nuclear family includes two parents and their children. They form a distinct unit, rather than being part of a larger one. They make up a separate household not shared with relatives or other outsiders. By law and by custom they are "in it together," financially and psychologically, separate from kin and community.

The separateness of the modern nuclear family apparently is even greater than what existed for nuclear families in other times. When homes were work places, they were tied more closely to the stream of community affairs. Apprentices and other employees ate and slept in the home as well as working there. Cars, refrigerators, supermarkets, and television all make it easy for a family to cut itself off from its neighbors. Larger communities and frequent moves from place to place make it less likely that the family has close ties to its neighbors anyhow. Whether we call it privacy or isolation, our families have more of it (Ariès, 1960/1965; Shorter, 1976; Skolnick, 1973).

Families are smaller now, mostly because they have fewer children. A hundred years ago most children had six or more brothers and sisters. Children from one- or two-child families were rarities—less than 10% of all children. Now about half our children come from one- and two-child families and only a tiny minority grow up in families with more than seven children (Bane, 1976).

Family ties usually last longer now because people live longer at all ages. Grandparents, parents, and children lost each other often and earlier in the families of the past. Stepmothers and orphans are common in old books because they were common in everyday life. As recently as 1915, children born in the United States had about a 22% chance of losing a parent before they reached age 18. Children born in the 1970s probably will have less than half of that rate. Families broken by divorce have become more prevalent, but only recently has this kind of broken home become as common as homes broken by death used to be. Almost all children today live with at least one of their parents; fewer are raised by other relatives or grow up in orphanages (Bane, 1976).

Our smaller, more private, and more enduring families play a more specialized role in the lives of their members. Families have given up such responsibilities as economic production and vocational training. Care of the elderly is less often a family matter. The proportion of meals prepared and eaten at home is going down. What is left? What is the specialty of the modern family? Love!

Love helps us understand the modern family, see its place in the modern world, and trace its history. The family's key function is "the nurturant socialization of the newborn" (Reiss, 1971, p. 19). It provides close and lasting emotional ties for all its members, parents included (Reiss, 1971; Skolnick, 1973).

In the home you are accepted for who you are, no matter what you do. As schools, work places, and communities have gotten bigger and less personal, the contrast between the family's personal focus and the impersonal atmosphere elsewhere has become greater (Newson & Newson, 1976).

The love-family connection is new. When Edward Shorter (1976) traced the rise of the modern family in Europe, he emphasized "waves of sentiment," pointing at the increasing importance of love, first in mother-baby relations, later in wife-husband ones. Philippe Ariès (1960/1965) relates the rise of love for babies to the fact that only recently have parents been able to count on babies living beyond infancy.

Today in Third World areas where infant death is frequent there is little of the face-to-face emotional interchange with babies so common in our families (LeVine, 1974). We find it natural to see love as central to parent-child relations and to what makes a family a family, but what we find natural reflects our own times and our own culture.

Parent choices

Our family system is based on the choices of parents. Marriages are arranged by individuals, not by clans. Family privacy is so great that outsiders know little of what goes on and have trouble intervening even when children are abused (Skolnick, 1973). The choices parents make are a good starting point, then, in looking at our families.

When parents talk about their decisions, they emphasize the situational factors they face, the narrow limits in which they move (Stoltz, 1967). When Whiting and Whiting (1975) reviewed the evidence on parents in six varied cultures, their conclusion was similar: parents do what they have to do. Child-rearing patterns are natural consequences of such matters as what work has to be done by the family and who is in it. Such questions as whether Beth should milk the goat are answered largely in terms of whether you have a goat and whether anyone else is free. More and more experts seem to be taking the Whitings' position, looking at parents in relation to their own environment rather than presenting an image of mothers and fathers as freer than the rest of us (Advisory Committee on Child Development, 1976; Keniston & The Carnegie Council on Children, 1977).

In this chapter I present parents the way I presented children in earlier ones: pushed by forces outside themselves while doing their own share of pushing. Parents are neither puppets on a string nor puppeteers. It would not be progress to replace the image of children as helpless and passive with one of parents as clay, entirely molded by their surroundings.

Parent goals

All parents in all cultures want similar futures for their children, according to Robert LeVine (1974). He sums up their universal goals in three categories:

1. Physical survival and health
2. Behavioral capacities that children will need to get along economically when they grow up
3. Behavioral capacities for maximizing other values of the culture (morality, wealth, religion, personal satisfaction, self-realization)

LeVine thinks that these three groups form a hierarchy: higher-numbered goals emerge only when lower-numbered ones can be taken for granted. When health and survival are at risk, concerns in this area dominate. Parents do not worry about such goals as learning to talk or self-realization. When physical survival and sound health can be taken for granted, economic security and the behaviors that produce it become the goal. Only when both survival and economic security are the norm do we find parents emphasizing goals such as self-realization and religious fulfillment.

Observations of child rearing in tribes where many babies die before age 2 suggested these ideas. LeVine saw similar patterns in the tropics in Africa, South America, and Indonesia, despite cultural diversity. Babies and small children were kept near the parents 24 hours a day, often being carried. Crying was attended to quickly, commonly by nursing. Crying was rarer than in Western infants. LeVine argues that this pattern increases the chance of physical survival by reducing key dangers such as illness, dehydration accompanying illness, and crawling into the fire. Despite the physical closeness, the parents rarely chatted, smiled, or made eye contact with their babies. They also showed little interest in the babies' psychological development or futures.

LeVine's ideas also explain a contrast between blue-collar and white-collar parents. When asked what they think is important in child rearing, working-class parents put more emphasis on such values as obedience, neatness, and cleanliness. These values tie in with getting and keeping a blue-collar job (the second category of goals in the previous list). Middle-class parents put a higher value on happiness, curiosity, and self-control (the third goals category). This trend holds both in the United States and in Italy for parents of varied religious backgrounds and from contrasting ethnic groups (Kohn, 1969). LeVine's hierarchy has broad explanatory power.

Parents as learners

Modern parents have fewer opportunities to learn how to raise a child before they have one. Smaller families and age segregation reduce the chance that new parents have had parentlike experiences in advance. Today parents see much more in the job of raising a child because they look beyond concerns with physical survival to psychological goals; so a parent has much to learn.

The simple solution of doing what your parents did often is not attractive. Moderns have little faith in tradition. Parents do draw on what their own parents did in forming their own ideas, but they also use those observations as examples of what they don't want to do (Stoltz, 1967).

Parents, particularly mothers, turn to varied sources for help: physicians, psychology courses, books on parenting, advice columns, relatives, and friends. Younger and less experienced parents do more help seeking (Clarke-Stewart, 1978b; Stoltz, 1967). With help they learn on the job.

Mother and father roles

In the past females and males learned contrasting roles. Performing mother activities was as different from carrying out the father role as being wife rather than husband, or woman instead of man. Now we wonder. Parents' roles are being reexamined as part of the broader concern with sex roles. Divorce, single-parent homes, and communes raise further questions about the future of mother and father roles.

Parent roles definitely are changing. They are becoming more similar, with less rigid contrasts between what mother does and what father does. The real questions are about how much change has taken place and what will happen in the future.

Trends

The life cycle of the typical mother has been transformed (Bane, 1976; Glick, 1977; Hoffman, 1979; Van Dusen & Sheldon, 1976). Today a typical mother has two children spaced about three years apart. As a result she is a mother of preschool children for only about 8 years. She has children in her home for only about 20 years. The period of active mothering has become shorter, but the adult years have become longer. She is an adult for about 60 years. About 80% of her adult life is spent without preschool children. About two-thirds of her days as a grown-up are without any children at home. With shorter lives, more children, and more widely spaced children, mothers of the past could equate woman and mother. Today mothers cannot.

Children and family are becoming less dominant in women's lives. Careers count, too, now. The statistics tell a consistent story: more education, postponed marriage, postponed childbearing, more mothers in the labor force, and reduced family size. Many women now combine the mother role and the career role. These dual-career women fit in with the needs of industrial society (Goode,

1963). They have become an important part of modern family life (Van Dusen & Sheldon, 1976). How is the family accommodating to the new role of women? Alternative answers give contrasting images of parents in the future.

Apparently parent roles still are traditional in most two-parent families. Mother usually takes the main responsibility for children and spends more time with them, regardless of her career interests and outside employment status. You could argue that this pattern will continue to be the main one, with adjustments to make it work more smoothly: more day care, more help from father, more eating out, and so on. This is an image of family business as usual, with more equality in parent roles.

A more radical future also can be imagined. Now there are some two-career families in which child care and homemaking are shared equally. Mother's outside career influences family decisions as much as father's. Perhaps genuinely equal parent roles soon will become the norm. You also could predict more single-parent families because they are on the rise, and you might predict "no-parent" systems of institutional child rearing because preschool schooling is becoming more popular. These images of a sharper break with the past require only that you see currently small trends as the beginnings of broader ones.

We face a mixed scene. Varied parent roles are played within a variety of family patterns. No single image of mothers and fathers will work (Skolnick, 1973). But it is useful to look at traditional parental role contrasts. They help us see where we were. A look at the old system also illustrates some of the tasks all parents face.

Traditional parent-role contrasts

In traditional families the roles of mother and father were separate and unequal. The father was boss, or head of the house. By 1966, an expert thought we had moved from father as boss to a norm of equality in decision making in the United States (Clausen, 1966). But the old power, or status, contrast is still important.

Power and status.   Marriage laws and customs illustrate how male superiority is embedded in the traditional family system. A woman follows custom in marrying a man older and taller. It's more acceptable if he is richer, brighter, or better educated. Following religious tradition, her father "gives" her to her husband. She promises to "obey" her new husband and gives up her father's last name to take on his.

The image of male ownership and domination continues when "she bears him children," who also take on his name and social position. Like mother and community, they are supposed to see him as head of the house.

Many educated North Americans laugh at this old-fashioned pattern, but it still colors both law and custom. Watch dating patterns if you think that age and height are irrelevant in modern courtship. Talk to married women who have tried to retain their maiden names. In 1966, the ideal was equality in parent decision making, but it was assumed that father would get his way when equality didn't work (Clausen, 1966).

Inside/outside.   Tradition connects home and mother. Our stereotype makes day-to-day inside relations with children mother's specialty. Father is expected to work outside. He's supposed to worry more about their futures— when they go out into the world.

Expressive/instrumental.   Expressive ideals make children and family relations more central to mother's fulfillment than to father's (Chapter 14). Being a good mother is more important in her life than being a good father is in his. Such goals as being warm, nurturant, and sensitive require that a mother invest more of her self-esteem in her relations with her children. A father can be competent, strong, and independent no matter what happens to his. These psychological contrasts pose bigger questions for the future than for current customs.

It is easy to imagine a future in which both parents working is typical because this pattern already is common, but what about the inevitable conflicts: staying home with a sick child or going out to work, taking a less attractive job with more time for family or a more attractive job with less time at home? In the past mothers and fathers felt differently about these conflicts; only with genuine androgyny can we expect them to feel the same (Chapter 14). As illustrated by the fact that women continue to take the children in the majority of divorces, we still are a long way from equality here.

The expressive/instrumental contrast helps in thinking about the division of responsibilities in the traditional family. Think of the mother as the expressive leader of the family, with father the instrumental leader (Parsons, 1955). Use the contrast to guess how actions are divided when they are not equal.

Mother, as expressive leader, is supposed to be more sensitive to children's feelings. She is supposed to model and teach such qualities as love, trust, and reciprocity. Because these are basic to all human relations, this way of thinking implies that mother-child relations are more basic and more similar for girls and for boys than father-child relations (Johnson, 1963, 1975).

As instrumental leader, father is concerned with the future and with his children's place in adult society. He takes a less family-centered view of the socialization process than mother and puts more emphasis on education (Stoltz, 1967). Because sex role is basic to life outside the family, he is more concerned with the development of sex-appropriate behaviors for both girls and boys (Johnson, 1975).

These ideas fit in with evidence on children's picture of their parents as shown in their answers to such questions as who they'd ask for help with a heavy door, who kisses the most, who's more God-like, and so on. They don't fit as well when adolescents are interviewed (Lynn, 1974).

The idea that both father-son and father-daughter relations are central in the development of sex-typed behavior has gotten considerable support. It is one of the areas where this approach has done relatively well (Johnson, 1963; Lynn, 1974). The position also implies that father is the law-and-order parent and more tied up with moral development than mother, but here the evidence goes the other way (Lynn, 1974).

Evidence on what contemporary mothers and fathers do in child rearing is limited and often unsatisfactory. Most of what we have comes from such indirect methods as interviews and questionnaires; little comes from actual observation of parents in action. Because so much has changed, we are troubled when using evidence from even ten years ago as a guide to what is happening now.

Interaction with babies and young children.   We are safest in comparing how mothers and fathers interact with younger children. The main finding in this research has been that mothers and fathers have similar relations with babies and young children, but that mothers do much more. When parents are studied in their homes under typical conditions, mothers do more with babies even when fathers are home (Clarke-Stewart, 1978a). In the first few months father-baby interaction is perhaps even less common than old stereotypes suggest.

Freda Rebelsky and Cheryl Hanks (1971) put microphones on ten babies for 24-hour periods every two weeks from the time the babies were 2 weeks old until they reached 3 months. The average father rarely spoke to his baby. Fathers averaged 2.7 vocal interactions per day, lasting a total of only 37.7 seconds! Unlike the mothers, the fathers did not spend more time talking with baby as baby grew older during this period. Father-baby interaction most likely becomes more common and grows with baby's age during later infancy, when baby starts doing more (see Clarke-Stewart, 1978a).

Babies often become attached to both parents at an early age. They seek and get comforting and smiling from both. Usually mother is more prominent in this kind of interaction, but we typically do not find the unique and exclusive mother-baby bond older theories emphasized (Lamb, 1976; Schaffer & Emerson, 1964a). Father does not always look like "the second parent." In some settings and for certain behaviors we find father doing as much or more.

Newborn nurseries and laboratories are good places to build a case for father's importance. There you find as much interest and affection between fathers and babies as between mothers and babies. Alison Clarke-Stewart (1978a) suggests that we need a competence/performance distinction. Fathers are capable of showing as much interest and love for little children as mothers. When babies are new or fathers are "on display" in labs, the fathers show it, but under normal circumstances they don't do it as often.

Father is often a play specialist with children between 6 months and 3 years; more of his interaction is playful. (Mother spends relatively more time in feeding, washing, and other care-giving activities.) He does more rough-housing and physical play. Mother's play is about as common but more often is verbal and with toys (Clarke-Stewart, 1978a; Lamb, 1976). Father's kind of play may be more fun for older babies and toddlers. At 30 months children were averaging more play periods per day with father than with mother in one study (Clarke-Stewart, 1978a). Once children are old enough to enjoy being bounced around, playmate often becomes a special feature of father's role.

Interaction with older children.   We find the same trends when we look at parent interaction with older children: mother does more; both parents engage in about the same range of child-rearing activities; but the proportions vary. By the 1960s, it was clear that in the United States mother did more of the disciplining and instrumental activities, along with much more of the loving-expressive ones (Clausen, 1966). A recent English study suggests a similar picture of fathers' participation today: less than mothers' but proportionately more instrumental (Newson & Newson, 1976).

Interaction with older children is more sex typed. Fathers do more with boys (Clausen, 1966; Newson & Newson, 1976); mothers and fathers have more of a companion relationship with children of their own sex. With children of the opposite sex they tend to be warmer and more indulgent emotionally (Newson & Newson, 1976).

Father as an indirect influence.   Father plays a smaller role in daily interaction, but this might be misleading. He might contribute as much, but indirectly, through his influence on mother.

Father's economic support obviously makes it easier for mother-child relations to go on smoothly, and perhaps his emotional support is just as important. Like his paycheck, it is most obvious when it is gone. For example, mothers' ability to cope effectively right after divorce correlates with the amount of emotional support from fathers (Hetherington, Cox, & Cox, 1978).

Implications.   Two conclusions are suggested:

1. When you look at families today, you should expect to find both the outlines of traditional roles and much more parent similarity than old ideas imply.
2. There are two different sides of what parents have done and must do in any kind of family: the internal and the external. Relating children to the outside world is as much a part of being a parent as loving them and disciplining them in the home.

We'll look at both sides now.

CHILD REARING: INTERNAL AFFAIRS

Three aspects of the family's internal life are considered: the child-rearing climate, siblings, and alternative family arrangements.

Child-rearing climate

Child-rearing climate means the broader and more stable trends in how parents deal with their children. What social-emotional qualities are prominent? What kinds of discipline are common?

A two-dimensional model

We can think of the climate in the home in terms of two characteristics, or dimensions, that vary separately: *warmth-coldness* (or love-hostility) and *autonomy-control* (or permissiveness-restrictiveness) (Schaefer, 1959).

The warm-cold dimension refers to the relative number of warm actions (praising, smiling, encouraging, and accepting) and cold ones (criticizing, frowning, punishing, and discouraging) that occur. Most parents are warm at times and cold at others; so the focus is on a parent's standing when compared to others in similar situations.

Apparently, a mother's standing on the warmth-coldness dimension is stable over time. An interview before mothers' first babies were born predicted how often they fondled the baby in the early weeks (Moss, Robson, & Pederson, 1969). Warmth ratings based on repeated observations during the first three years correlated .68 with ratings made when the children were 9 to 14 in another study (Schaefer & Bayley, 1963).

The autonomy-control dimension refers to how much freedom the parents give. How tightly do they hold the reins? How much do they let the child decide? Because most parents give more and more freedom as their children get older, it is easy for parents' ranks relative to other parents to shift. Although there is consistency in rank over short periods, we do not find much over longer periods (Schaefer & Bayley, 1963).

Because the two dimensions are separate, all possible combinations of them occur. Table 18-1 sums up the main patterns.

TABLE 18-1 Four examples of child-rearing climates

Climate	Prominent Parental Actions
Warm-Control (indulgent, protective)	close supervision, interaction common and positive, rewards and acceptance for conformity and obedience
Warm-Autonomy (democratic, cooperative)	few limits, emphasis on joint rule setting, acceptance whether or not there is conformity
Cold-Control (authoritarian, demanding)	close supervision, parent-set rules, punishment for disobedience
Cold-Autonomy (indifferent, neglecting)	lax supervision, often threats without follow-through, interaction rare but mostly punitive

Child-rearing climate and social class

Comparisons of white-collar and blue-collar homes show that on the average the white-collar parents are more democratic (give more warmth and more autonomy) and the blue-collar parents are more authoritarian (cooler and more controlling), but overall the two groups are quite similar.

Because the difference is small and there is much overlap, it's a mistake to say middle-class parents are democratic and working-class parents are authoritarian. You can't take a small trend and treat it as if it were a large and absolute difference (R. D. Hess, 1970).

Child-rearing climate and child behavior

We want to know how child-rearing climate relates to child behavior. After all, our main interest in looking at contrasts in parents is to see how these differences relate to what their children do. The correlations between child-rearing patterns and child behavior are not high, and because child-parent interaction is a two-way street, we are not sure how to interpret tham.

Probably the most important finding is that parental coldness is correlated with child behavior problems. Both extraverted difficulties, such as antisocial behavior, and introverted problems, such as high anxiety, are more common in the children of parents who are relatively cool (Martin, 1975).

There are at least three possible explanations for this correlation, but we lack the evidence needed to evaluate these alternatives.

1. Such practices as punishment produce problems such as delinquency and un-happiness.
2. Parents with children who are difficult, irritable, unresponsive, and so on are forced to resort to sterner measures, such as spankings, and to dwell more on their children's shortcomings.
3. Both the child problems and the parental coolness reflect genetic rather than experiential factors.

A more specific association between child-rearing climate and aggressive and delinquent forms of child behavior has been found over and over. Parents who combine hostility and autonomy (are neglecting, lax, indifferent) more often have children who act antisocially: bullying, stealing, and so on. The source of this specific correlation also remains unclear.

These correlational patterns have implications for child rearing, even though they don't give us sure formulas for how to do it. If you want to raise happy children who get along well with others, *don't* treat them hostilely. Hostile child rearing more often goes with unhappiness and poor social relations in children; so it's unlikely that beatings and criticism contribute positively to emotional stability, although we cannot conclude that they produce instability. On the other hand, the evidence suggests that parental autonomy-control is not crucially related to child behavior disorders. We find emotional stability to be about equally likely in children from homes high, low, and average on freedom giving. Parental autonomy-control possibly has important influences on how children grow up, but the present data imply that these influences are not centrally related to emotional stability. The correlations do tell us something.

A series of studies by Diana Baumrind (1971) suggests that a closer and more detailed look at child-rearing patterns predicts better than a broader approach. She showed that it is important to contrast what she terms *author-itative* and *authoritarian* parents. Both groups are more controlling and de-manding than average, but the details show important differences. The authoritative pattern combines demands for appropriate behavior with a warm and rational encouragement of the child's independence. The parents take charge and act like authorities, but they reason with their children and en-courage them to think for themselves. In contrast the authoritarian pattern combines a high level of control with an emphasis on obedience for its own sake. The parents don't reason with their children or encourage them to think for themselves. Parents who show the authoritative pattern are more likely to have children high on self-control and self-reliance than those with any other child-rearing style (including a permissive one that gives lots of freedom). Parents who act in an authoritarian way do not have children high on self-control or self-reliance.

Siblings

Sibling status is a child's age and sex relative to other children in the family. This is a better term than *ordinal position* (rank among siblings) because it deals with such contrasts as first child of two rather than ten or younger brother of a sister rather than a brother (Sutton-Smith & Rosenberg, 1970).

Watch families with two or more children. You'll see younger brothers and sisters who want to join in the play of older ones. Older siblings will use that desire to foster their own goals. When the going gets rough, the smaller ones will threaten to "tell." Parents will face the problem of explaining matters to a 2- and a 5-year-old simultaneously. Suppertime will reflect the fact that older and younger children and girls and boys often react differently to the same topic of conversation. Such scenes are a vivid part of childhood. Sibling status influences what part a child plays in thousands of family dramas.

Frontiers box 18–1 Child abuse

About 1962, the problem of child abuse caught the public eye. New precision in X-ray technique had made it possible to pinpoint the causes of bone fractures that had healed and enabled physicians to identify children who had been physically abused by their parents. An article in a leading medical journal (Kempe, Silverman, Steele, Droegemueller, & Silver, 1962) defined a pattern called the battered child syndrome and stimulated action. Between 1962 and 1967, every state in the United States enacted a new law on child abuse (Rosenheim, 1973).

Heightened interest in child abuse led to more research and increased understanding. As evidence has accumulated, it has become clear that the problem is complex and reflects the operation of many factors, in contrast to the media picture that child abuse is one thing with one cause (Rosenheim, 1973).

Early notions that child abuse could be understood in terms of the personality of the abusing parent have given way to concepts that implicate child-environment interactions of varied types at different levels (Chapter 17). For example, the finding that certain babies and children are more likely to be abused than others in the same families illustrates the two-way nature of interaction here, as elsewhere (Parke & Collmer, 1975). Apparently, babies who cry a lot and have particularly irritating cries are more likely to be beaten. The nature of the child rearing also seems important; abusing parents show such similarities as being inconsistent and punitive in their typical discipline efforts. Several findings suggest that stresses on the family and the family's resources in dealing with them are part of the picture. For example, premature babies are more likely to be abused (Brown & Bakeman, 1980) and families with unemployed fathers are more likely to be abusive (Parke & Collmer, 1975). Typically, abusive families are more isolated from their community (Parke & Collmer, 1975) and thus seem to lack social support systems to help them cope with special problems. The high rate of child abuse in the United States has been related to the fact that physical punishment is seen as a more appropriate way of dealing with children here, increasing the chance that excessive punishment is used (Parke & Collmer, 1975).

New ideas about the factors contributing to child abuse have led to a varied set of ideas about how to deal with it. The new laws emphasize reporting, often requiring professionals to report any situation in which child abuse is suspected (Rosenheim, 1973). Hotlines and crisis nurseries have been established to help in emergency situations. Counseling for individual parents and groups has been offered. Television programs and courses have been offered to alert the public and to teach parents more effective means of dealing with their children.

Unfortunately, the absence of well-controlled evaluations makes it unclear how effective these new techniques are (Parke & Collmer, 1975). As is often the case, the rush to do something has rarely been accompanied by a willingness to conduct unbiased evaluations of how well the something works.

Other problems emerge from a careful examination of how the new laws work out in actuality (Rosenheim, 1973). The laws often define child abuse so as to include both physical abuse and psychological maltreatment, but both community leaders and professionals differentiate the two forms of abuse (Sweet & Resick, 1979). When there is physical abuse, there is a willingness to intervene and stop it, but when the abuse is emotional, there is reluctance. Even where there is repeated physical abuse, the community holds back from terminating parental legal rights and forcing parents to give their children up for adoption (Rosenheim, 1973).

Parents who abuse their children force us to confront a conflict in our tradition and values. We try to do well by children, but we also grant parents the right to rear and discipline their children as they please within wide limits. As a result, the new child abuse laws have not solved the problems that many of their advocates said they would solve (Rosenheim, 1973). There has been progress in recognizing the problem of child abuse and in coming to understand it better, but no solution is in sight.

Because sibling positions such as oldest girl and only child often seem to result in special patterns of experience, we expect sibling status to influence later behavior patterns, and apparently it does. When we look at groups of children and adults, we find trends. Usually they are too small for making safe predictions about individuals, but they help show how family experience influences development.

An older and a younger sister have distinctive patterns of learning experiences that influence later behavior.

Firstborns

Three of the more reliable findings on firstborns are that they are more likely to achieve fame, particularly in academic areas; firstborn girls are more likely to be responsible; and firstborn college students tend to be more sociable when dealing with adults under conditions promoting anxiety (Sutton-Smith & Rosenberg, 1970).

The observation that firstborns of the past achieved more eminence proves little because being firstborn used to open special doors, including those to college. When you look at special achievement in academically related areas, however, the trend continues. For example, firstborns are overrepresented among National Merit Scholars from all family sizes. Exam scores are not related to family position for the total group who take the exam, illustrating that the special connection here is with outstanding achievement. Similarly, all the first group of United States astronauts were firstborn or only children. We find a continuing connection between birth order and eminence even when law and custom no longer give the first child such special treatment (Sutton-Smith & Rosenberg, 1970).

The evidence that firstborn girls are particularly likely to be responsible gets us closer to everyday life. Older siblings often teach younger ones (Pepler, 1981). We are used to seeing girls with younger siblings taking care of them. In colleges we find that firstborn girls are overrepresented among those training to be teachers, suggesting that early experience in taking responsibility for others can carry over into adult activity patterns (Sutton-Smith & Rosenberg, 1970).

The finding that firstborns are more sociable comes out of research by social psychologists and is based largely on work with college students (Schacter, 1959). When faced with threatening psychology experiments, firstborn college students more often are upset. Given the opportunity to be with others, the firstborns are more likely to take it.

Brian Sutton-Smith and Ben Rosenberg (1970) have argued that these findings on firstborns reflect their special and continuing early relationship with their parents. The firstborn child starts in a more adult-oriented world and tends to continue a special relation with parents even after other children enter the picture. The pattern is often contradictory on both sides. The parents expect more of the firstborn. As a result, the firstborn child performs well but seeks help. The parents give help but are critical and expect a higher level of achievement. Thus, the firstborn shows both high achievement and a continuing need for guidance and reassurance.

Subsequent children

Two observations of children born later illustrate how their behavior is shaped by that of other children in the family. Studies of two-child families indicate that the sex of the older child tends to have a modeling impact on the younger. Whatever their own sex, second children tend to develop interests that show the influence of older brother or sister. Both the younger brothers and sisters of a first girl show more feminine interests than controls. Both the younger sisters and brothers of a first boy show more masculine ones. A more general finding is that younger sisters and brothers tend to be more gregarious (sociable) and peer oriented than firstborns. The experience of growing up with older brothers and sisters, not surprisingly, seems to bias children toward the group more than the experience of growing up in a more adult world (Sutton-Smith & Rosenberg, 1970).

Alternative family arrangements

Two-parent families are not the only kind. In 1975, about one child in six in the United States lived in a single-parent home (Advisory Committee on Child Development, 1976). About 40–50% of children born in the 1970s in the United States will spend some time living in single-parent homes (Hetherington, 1979). In Israel a pattern of communal child rearing has been common in rural *kibbutz* settlements.

Divorce

Divorce is the biggest reason for the rising proportion of children in single-parent homes. Divorce rates are climbing sharply, but remarriage rates for divorced women have not been increasing as rapidly; so divorce now results in more children who continue in single-parent homes. The average time spent in a single-parent home is six years (Hetherington, 1979).

Divorce rates vary. They are far more common among the early married, the less educated, and the poor. Young, poorly educated women living in poverty often head single-parent households resulting from divorce (Advisory Committee on Child Development, 1976; Bane, 1976).

Only recently have we begun to get a close look at what divorce does to children (Hetherington, 1979). Hetherington, Cox, and Cox (1978) looked at divorced and nondivorced families repeatedly over a two-year period. Their findings highlight the importance of changes during the first two years.

The first year following divorce commonly was a painful and disorganizing experience. Mothers (who typically had the children living with them) often became more restrictive and commanding. The children frequently responded by resisting or ignoring them. The now-absent fathers commonly wanted their contacts with the children to be happy. Frequently, fathers fell into an extremely permissive and indulgent "every day is Christmas" pattern. These reactions to the stress of divorce often diminished in the second year. Signs of stability became more common after people had a chance to live with the new arrangements. Mother-child relations were particularly likely to become more stable after the first year. Depending on when you look at a recently divorced family, you get varied impressions. Trouble often is followed by less trouble.

Children's adjustment to divorce has been shown to relate to a complex set of factors such as the child's own coping capacities, how the parents handle the situation, and the financial pressures on the family. Lawrence Kurdek (1981) argues that these varied influences can be put in perspective if divorce is seen in terms of Bronfenbrenner's ecological model (Chapter 17). Kurdek argues that we should focus on how strengths at one level of the system—for example, in the child or family—can compensate for problems elsewhere, rather than looking for particular factors of special importance.

Illegitimacy

Births to unwed mothers produce the second largest category of single-parent homes. Here again rates vary tremendously. Single mothers rearing illegitimate children are much more likely to be young, poor, and to live in an inner-city slum (Advisory Committee on Child Development, 1976).

Single-parent homes and fathers' absence

Considering all groups together, about 40% of children born in the United States around 1970 will live in single-parent homes for some period before they are 18 (Bane, 1976). We still lack a clear picture of what impact, if any, this will have on their long-term development.

The 10 million children growing up in homes without fathers have more than their share of troubles, but it is hard to tell if those problems should be thought of as resulting from the father's absence. Often it is as reasonable to explain the children's problems as an outgrowth of poverty and/or living in homes with special stresses and fewer support systems (Herzog & Sudia, 1973; Hetherington, 1979; Shinn, 1978). For example, a single mother is more likely to have a job that takes her out of the home, even though a job raises more child-care problems for her. If the father's absence puts children at risk, it most likely is because of reduced parent-child contact and greater financial hardship and anxiety (Shinn, 1978).

Communes

In communal settlements in Israel (*kibbutzim*—plural of *kibbutz*) children are raised by professional care givers. From birth on they sleep, eat, and play within a peer group rather than a family. They spend a few hours each day with their parents, but discipline and socialization come from the professional (Spiro, 1958; Talmon, 1972).

The kibbutz pattern has worked well for decades (Kaffman, 1972; Kaffman & Elizur, 1977). Kibbutz children grow up without any more problems than others. They rarely become delinquent. They fill more than their share of leadership positions.

The communes that became popular in the United States during the 1960s have not demonstrated clear success in raising children. They rarely have survived for a whole childhood, and some observe that they have not served the children in them particularly well. Children are rare in them and seem to threaten the "do your own thing" attitude that is so basic (Kinkade, 1973; Rossi, 1978; Skolnick, 1973).

The success of the kibbutz and some religious communes illustrates that communal child rearing, like communal living more broadly, can work when individualism and the self are not the central value (Roberts, 1971). The failure of recent communes seemingly illustrates what happens to a communal system when self-expression is put ahead of common goals (Skolnick, 1973).

Implications

Varied family patterns apparently can work if they are in reasonable harmony with the society around them and include methods for dealing with basic problems of child care. The problems of today's single-parent homes seem to stem from limited adult time and money, not from any inherent pathology. The transcience of our communes seems to reflect a bad fit between the requirements of close, communal living and the premium they put on self-expression. It is not that our kind of exclusiveness in child-parent relations is essential. Not all family arrangements work well. However, our options are varied.

CHILD REARING: EXTERNAL AFFAIRS

The new features of modern families complicate their relation to the outside world. As a specialized unit, the family no longer can prepare children for their lives as adult workers and community members. They go outside for education.

As a smaller and more isolated unit, the family provides fewer opportunities for contact with peers. The concepts of gate keeping and power help us think about how parents deal with such problems. They relate the area to social class.

Gate keeping

Parents open and close doors to experience for their children (Parke, 1978). They pick a place to live and thereby decide where their children will go to school and with whom they might play. Parent choices determine their children's diet and medical care. The books, toys, and records parents buy or don't buy influence how children spend their free time. All these parent actions can be thought of as *gate keeping,* letting "traffic" in and out (Lewin, 1951).

The modern world offers a tremendous range of opportunities for experience. Parental gate keeping is a big influence on which of these opportunities a child actually realizes; so it is important to see what influences gate keeping.

Parental gate keeping, of course, reflects parental values. Parents who like music are more likely to bring it into the house. But values apparently are a small part of the story. Liking music and hiring a talented piano teacher are not the same. Many parents emphasize religious values without having a picture of what to do about them in daily living (Stoltz, 1967). Studies usually show little correlation between parental values and child behavior (R. D. Hess, 1970). As suggested earlier, value contrasts seem to reflect how confident parents can be about meeting universal goals such as survival and economic security. It is thus more useful to relate parental gate keeping to power, the resources that parents have in meeting their common problems.

Social class and power

A family's power in gate keeping depends on its socioeconomic status, or social class. Both money and community respect "open doors." By looking at social class in terms of family differences in power and gate keeping, you can understand why we so often find that the family's socioeconomic status predicts the child's behavior.

A study of mothers of 7-year-olds in Nottingham, England, is illustrative (Newson & Newson, 1976). At all social levels mothers were concerned about undesirable friends, but social class groups varied both in what they could do about the problem and in how they felt. Middle-class families could more easily pick desirable neighborhoods. They found it easier to supervise peer interaction by making the home an attractive place to play. The working-class parents had less control over the situation. Their lack of power encouraged a fatalistic attitude: "if you stop them playing with one kiddy, they'll go out and find one that's even worse" (Newson & Newson, 1976, p. 217).

The question of who is in charge is basic in the eyes of poor parents (particularly fathers) (R. D. Hess, 1970). Living at the "bottom" makes doing what you are told crucial in getting and keeping jobs. When you have to follow orders, you see giving them as the way to have status. Not surprisingly, lower-class fathers often equate respect from their children with obedience.

Dorothea Lange's famous photo captures the concern of a mother who lacks the power to open doors for her children.

Children who grow up in this kind of power-oriented family system are being prepared for jobs where their role is to follow rather than to lead or make their own decisions. By doing what comes "naturally" to them, deprived parents often promote behavior patterns that keep their children in a similar position (Newson & Newson, 1976).

Parental feelings of power have become important in work with disadvantaged preschoolers. Early intervention programs with a parent emphasis (Madden, Levenstein, & Levenstein, 1976) sometimes produce more lasting results (Bronfenbrenner, 1974). Ideas about parents' feelings of responsibility and power help in making sense of the evidence. Apparently, teacher-centered programs produce the conclusion that "other people are preparing my child for school" and can discourage the parents' own efforts. In contrast, parent-centered programs that focus on helping parents help their children can produce more lasting gains.

We have two different systems for meeting the needs of young children and families. Families with sufficient money get food, clothing, shelter, medical care, recreation, and education in the market economy. The supplier satisfies them or they go elsewhere. Poor families more often go to government and private welfare to meet the same needs. They are less able to go from door to door. As a result, they have much less control. In the poverty system parental gate keeping plays a much smaller role (Robinson, Robinson, Wolins, Bronfenbrenner, & Richmond, 1973).

A final point involves the view at the top. Prominent families, such as the Rockefellers and Kennedys, seem more like old-fashioned clans than modern nuclear families. Parents seemingly do more with their parents and siblings: socially, economically, and politically. This is a typical pattern around the world. When industrialism comes, upper-class families keep more of the older, extended family system, probably because they still have the power to provide jobs for their children when ordinary families have lost it (Goode, 1963). At all levels children's experiences reflect parental power.

Implications

"Life is unfair." President Kennedy said it and President Carter quoted him in referring to poverty and its impact. When you look at what families do for children, this issue of fairness turns up over and over. Children of poverty encounter bad luck again and again. Because their luck stems from family matters, not individual ones, concern with helping children focuses more and more on helping families, particularly those who need the most help in helping themselves (Advisory Committee on Child Development, 1976; Keniston, 1977; Talbot, 1976).

DAY CARE

With the rapid increase of mothers in the labor force, day care has achieved new prominence. In 1975, 52% of married women with children 6–17 years old were working outside the home or looking for employment. For those with children under 6, the corresponding figure was 37% (Advisory Committee on Child Development, 1976, p. 1). More than a third of mothers who live with their husbands and have children under 3 years of age are employed (Hoffman, 1979, p. 859). The question of who is minding the children is harder to answer now. A good starting place is to look at our evidence on what parents do and prefer to do.

Most parents who make day-care arrangements don't use centers and prefer not to use them (Woolsey, 1978). When mothers of preschoolers work outside the home, the most common place for day care is in the mother's home. Next most common is in someone else's home. Group care centers accounted for only about 10% of all the little children getting day care in 1971 (Woolsey, 1978, p. 131). Father care was as common as care in group settings. Care by other relatives was more common. Studies of what kind of day care people prefer give a similar picture. Most parents prefer an informal arrangement in the home or in the neighborhood.

Suzanne Woolsey (1978) argues that we hear so much about centers because of what she calls "Pied Piper politics." There are some who want to use day care as a means of getting women off relief and into the labor market. Others are concerned about how to employ teachers as elementary-school enrollments decline. These people and their opponents put the focus on formal day care; the more prominent fact of informal day care often is ignored.

The upsurge of interest in day-care centers has resulted in a series of studies (Belsky & Steinberg, 1978; Etaugh, 1980; Kagan, Kearsley, & Zelazo, 1977). They suggest that, with an adequate staff and program, day-care centers do not have a negative impact, even on babies. This finding is consistent with older evidence on communal child rearing in the kibbutz. The idea that group care is inherently bad for children seems unsound, but child behavior varies with such factors as care-giver involvement (Anderson, Nagle, Roberts, & Smith, 1981), and our overall evidence still is sparse (Belsky & Steinberg, 1978).

The informal day-care arrangements that are so common are even more of a mystery. They vary tremendously. Often a relative or neighbor takes care of a child in a family setting, but sometimes informal day care means an overcrowded situation in which children are neglected by a stranger whose main concern is money (Keyserling, 1972). Good centers are better than bad informal arrangements (Kagan, Kearsley & Zelazo, 1977; Ricciuti, 1976).

Quality of care, then, is the real issue before us. There is no reason to expect centers, informal arrangements, or traditional care to be all good or all bad. With millions of mothers working outside the home, we face a new problem requiring new solutions. Because so many of these mothers are young, poor, and single, we cannot assume they will find it easy to make satisfactory informal arrangements. If we sit back and let each family work out its own solutions, we guarantee that thousands of children already in difficult surroundings will get miserable treatment.

Creating a system of formal centers integrated with the public schools is not our only alternative. There are more family-centered alternatives that emphasize flexibility and helping parents devise systems that work for them. For example, direct income support programs in which low-income parents get money to use as they see fit would give parents the power to choose. Some might elect to stay at home and take care of their own children. Others might pay for informal or formal day care. Still others might seek help in organizing their own system of cooperative day care. By giving the support to families (as in some state scholarship programs in higher education), rather than directly to centers (as in elementary education), we might create a better solution. This is the direction suggested by two committees of experts (Advisory Committee on Child Development, 1976; Keniston & the Carnegie Council on Children, 1977).

SUMMARY

Families were viewed in broad perspective. Distinctive features of the modern nuclear family were examined first: its small size, separateness, and the special importance of love. Parents were looked at in relation to their choices and goals and to the fact that they are learners. Traditional contrasts in mother and father roles served as a starting point in examining what families do for children. Both internal family affairs and external relations with the outer society were emphasized.

Child-rearing climates were presented as broad and stable patterns of dealing with children that endure over time and characterize varied specific areas. A two-dimensional model, including a warm-cold and an autonomy-control dimension, was described as a useful way of summarizing findings.

Sibling status was considered, with an emphasis on the idea that both parents and siblings influence child development, with first children showing more of the influence of parental actions and those born later tending to have characteristics reflecting the impact of other children in the family as well. Alternative family arrangements were examined next, considering divorce, illegitimacy, single-parent homes, and communes. The possible implications of the changing present scene were discussed.

The concepts of gate keeping, power, and social class were used to organize the discussion of the family's role in linking the child to the outside world. A central idea was that in modern society the family's role in dealing with the outside world in the child's behalf is just as crucial as what happens inside. The handicapping impact of poverty on children was related to the special problems faced by poor parents in this realm of external affairs.

Finally, day care was considered. It has come to prominence as a result of the rapid growth in the proportion of mothers working outside the home. A proper viewpoint requires that we think both of formal day care in centers and the more common and more commonly preferred informal day care that takes place in the homes of relatives and neighbors. The available evidence suggests that quality of care, rather than where it takes place, is the main issue.

CHAPTER 19

The Child and the Outside World

Children become independent persons in the world outside their family at about 6 years of age. They begin to go about without escorts and close supervision. They enter elementary school and must learn to make their own way there. Now they spend as much or more time with peers as with parents and have the main say in picking their friends. Their choices widen in other areas as well. Where they go, how they spend their money, what they watch on television, and what they bring back into their home now are more their decisions. Outside the family has become about as important in day-to-day life as inside and their place in the outside world has become central to further development.

Between 6 and 13 years of age children become more and more familiar with this second world that someday will become their first. The transition from early containment in the family to an ever freer back and forth from it may be abrupt or gradual, but the shift always takes place and marks what we call growing up.

I emphasize three settings in this chapter: the peer world, school, and television. Each contrasts with the family and with the other two. Together they make up most of modern children's nonfamily world and account for most of their waking hours.

DISTINCTIVE FEATURES OF NONFAMILY SETTINGS

Classroom, playground, camp, and store share similarities that set them off from the home.

Performance

What you do counts more than who you are away from home. Children's status with peers, teachers, and strangers depends on how they perform and what they achieve. Maureen is "our daughter" and "my little sister" at home; her family loves and accepts her even if she has a bad day, or even a bad month. In the classroom and on the playground it's different. Does she do her homework, act nicely, learn to read, behave like a good sport? Becoming a friend or a second-grader depends on how she acts. Keeping her status with peers and teachers requires continued performance.

Impartiality

Teachers and peers judge Doug's face, baseball skill, and arithmetic achievement by the same standards they use in judging everyone else. A face that only a mother could love is a disadvantage when you meet 30 first-graders. In the Little League your parents are partial when you are up, judging the pitches that sail past you in a special way. But a good umpire, like a good teacher, treats children impartially.

Impermanence

Adam loves his first-grade teacher and can't wait to get to school in the morning. Jane can't stand hers and hates school because of it. But the year finally ends. Both Adam and Jane learn that a new year brings a new teacher.

Teachers, friends, and others move in and out of children's lives today in rapid procession. With frequent home changes and the accompanying shifts in school and neighborhood, long relations with people outside the family have become rarer (Toffler, 1971).

Segmentation

Parents know and care about all parts of a child's life. They see both Gail's success in making a new friend and her failure to carry out her promises to straighten up her room. Their broad perspective on the many sides of Gail may help her see her own life as a whole. Who else knows Gail as a whole child in this same way? Gail has school friends and neighborhood friends, reading teacher and music teacher—people who know but part of her. These segmental relations are typical outside the family (Toffler, 1971).

PEERS

Children grow up with other children. We take it for granted and seldom stop to think about the importance of peer relations. Child psychologists are beginning to wonder if perhaps peers are as crucial to normal development as parents (Hartup, 1976; Lewis & Rosenblum, 1975).

Importance of peer relations

The growing interest in children's relations with children has been stimulated in part by research on monkeys. Normal social-emotional development in monkeys depends on opportunities for interaction with peers (Harlow, 1971; Mason, 1970). Seemingly, the give-and-take of play with others gives young monkeys a chance to perfect the social skills they need for mature life. The hypothesis has been supported by laboratory experiments. Baby monkeys have been raised with and without mothers, with and without peer interaction, and so on. The findings point to peer interaction as perhaps the most crucial factor in social-emotional growth. Without contact with peers monkeys grow

Applications box 19-1 Playgrounds

Playgrounds are a new feature of the child's world. They are created in order to provide children with safe and entertaining settings for play. Joe Frost and Barry Klein (1979) think that most playgrounds in the United States are dangerous and dull and that we could do a much better job than we are doing.

Playgrounds are the setting for thousands of accidents every year (Frost & Klein, 1979). Metal swings and jungle gyms planted in asphalt or concretelike dirt are particularly dangerous. They are popular because they are cheaper to maintain than the alternatives, but the evidence shows that we could make playgrounds safer by providing equipment of rubber, wood, and rope. If fall areas (around equipment) were furnished with sand or tanbark, injuries could be further reduced.

The type, variety, and arrangement of play equipment influence what children do on a playground (Frost & Klein, 1979). For example, traditional playgrounds with swings, seesaws, slides, and climbing bars foster much less dramatic play than creative playgrounds furnished with play houses, wheel vehicle areas, and sand and water areas. With more equipment and more complex equipment there is more motor play and less social play and social conflict. Loose parts such as planks, crates, and tires seem to foster more cooperative play and keep children playing for longer periods of time.

Safer and more interesting playgrounds need not be more expensive (Frost & Klein, 1979). For example, the use of recycled materials keeps cost down and opens up better play opportunities. Old tires turn out to be a great material. They are surprisingly safe and durable. They can be used to make permanent climbers, tunnels, and bridges or left loose so children can improvise their own uses for them. Telephone and electric companies get heavy wire cable on large spools that when empty become another standard for modern playgrounds. Old telephone poles and railroad ties can also be used.

Two frontiers in playground design are adventure playgrounds and playgrounds for handicapped children. Common in some European countries, adventure playgrounds provide opportunities for building, fire making, and caring for animals, along with the usual range of outdoor activities. Because they often require special supervision, they must grow out of a commitment to continuing support after they are built. Access is the key problem in designing a playground for handicapped children. Ramps and handrails must be provided so that all children can use the equipment.

Although systematic research is still limited, Frost and Klein make a strong case. We do seem to know enough to make our playgrounds safer, more educational, and more fun.

up to be adults who have trouble getting along with others. Even mating behavior is rare in the peer-deprived adult. Monkeys who grow up without mothers end up as relatively normal if they have peer contact.

We have one human study that echoes the finding that monkeys who grow up without mothers still come out all right if they have normal peer contact (Hartup, 1970). It is a famous study of six children who spent their early years in a Nazi concentration camp during World War II (Freud & Dann, 1951). By the time the children were 12 months old, all their parents had been exterminated. Then they were taken care of by a series of other adult inmates, but these grown-ups, too, were put to death and played but temporary roles in the children's lives. When the war ended and the children were rescued at about age 3, the children themselves were the only people who had played a continuing part in one another's lives. They then were brought to England, where Anna Freud and Sophia Dann worked with them. At first the children stuck together. They resisted adult efforts to separate them or socialize them. They were hard to handle, to say the least, but they were not deficient, delinquent, or psychotic. They quickly learned a new language and made the other adjustments necessary for a normal life in their new world. Their dramatic story contradicts the popular idea that children must start with a trusting relationship with an adult if they are to develop normally.

Further evidence for the importance of peers comes from the repeated finding that adequacy of peer relations in childhood is one of our better predictors of social-emotional normalcy in adulthood (Kohlberg, LaCrosse, & Ricks, 1972).

Modern peer world

Today children's groups include mostly children of about the same age. Six-year-olds rarely play with 12-year-olds. This much age segregation is new and perhaps is exaggerated in some descriptions (see Ellis, Rogoff, & Cromer, 1981). Through most of human history children mingled in groups of varying ages (Konner, 1975). The peer group as we see it arose mostly in the last century with the large school and the rise of larger towns and cities (Kett, 1974).

The new peer world takes more of a child's time and probably influences the child more. Seemingly, other children gain in importance when adults and tradition lose their hold. Peer influence is apparently least in traditional societies where people of all ages mingle, where the family is the unit of economic production, and where the world changes little from generation to generation (Campbell, 1964).

A world of groups

The peer world is an adult abstraction. Children encounter particular other children, usually within informal groups. Soon after children come together we see a *social structure* emerge (Hartup, 1970). Both informal groups (the kids on the block) and formal ones (scout troops) show similar features of social structure: solidarity, norms, and status differentiation (Brown, 1965). These structural features give us a way of looking at groups and at how individuals fit in them.

Solidarity

A collection of children has to have some sense of togetherness if it is to exist as a group. Thirty children sitting in the same fourth grade may be a real group or six separate groups or (at first) not have any groups at all. The strains of some birthday parties reflect the fact that children who don't feel like a group suddenly are thrown together and expected to have fun playing together without group feeling. The magic of many camp experiences is that a bunk full of strangers quickly develops common bonds and a strong sense of group loyalty. Your first problem in figuring out a group of children, then, is to find out just how much solidarity there is.

Sociometric techniques provide a convenient way of studying solidarity (Hallinan, 1981; Renshaw, 1981). You ask everyone in a group to answer such questions as "Which children would you like to have in your car when we go to the zoo?" or "When we change seating assignments, with whom would you like to sit?" Then you analyze the choices and use them as indicators of solidarity. For example, by looking at seating preferences among all the children in a classroom, you can find the cohesive subgroups. Figure 19–1 is a *sociogram*, a picture summarizing choices. It shows all the first choices made by the girls in a fifth grade when they were asked about seating preferences. It reveals that May, Nan, and Rae are a cohesive group because they make all their first choices within the trio. Val and Win clearly are not part of the May-Nan-Rae group. No choices go either way. Sociometric methods get at the basic question of we-ness, or solidarity: who wants to associate with whom? The more mutual choice you see, the more solidarity you can infer.

Norms

Norms are shared standards of behavior (Triandis, 1980). If you see children with enough solidarity to be a cohesive group, you can expect to find that their group has norms. Being part of one group might require that you wear braids, help the teacher, and love horses. In another sharing your candy, rooting for the Braves, and smoking cigarettes might be norms. Shared norms and solidarity go together in a group, just as similar attitudes and friendship do when we look at pairs of children (Chapter 12).

Status

An enduring group usually has a *status hierarchy*. The group looks up to certain members and others are at the bottom. A child's position in the hierarchy is somewhat predictable from day to day (Hartup, 1970).

Sociometric techniques help you see status hierarchies. Figure 19–1 illustrates the usual picture: children vary greatly in how many positive choices they get from their peers. Amy, Bea, and Cass get more choices than Dora, Nan and Rae. Val and Win get no first choices at all. From this pattern we can

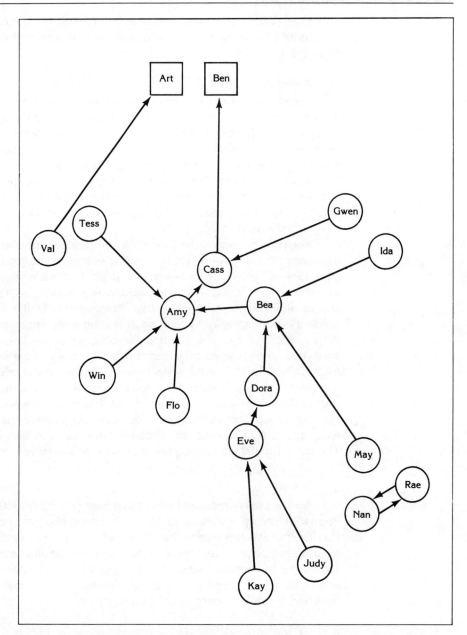

Figure 19–1   Sociogram

infer that Amy, Bea, and Cass have high status within the group and Val and Win are at the bottom of the status hierarchy.

Status hierarchies reflect the fact that the children in a group share norms and values (Brown, 1965). Because the children agree on what counts, they tend to agree on who has more of it.

Two kinds of status have been distinguished: *popularity* and *leadership*. Children's popularity is defined in terms of how much they are liked or accepted. It is measured best when the question is solidarity: whom do you want to be near? Leadership, in contrast, refers to a child's power in influencing others. You see it most clearly when the group faces a common task. Whose ideas, requests, and suggestions count most?

Popularity within a group is usually stable over periods of weeks or months. The older the children and the longer they have known each other, the more stable popularity is (Hartup, 1970). One reason for this stability is that it relates to enduring characteristics of individuals. The child who is popular in one group is more likely to be popular in other groups as well. The unpopular child may be unpopular even at home (Allen, 1981). The correlations between child characteristics and popularity are not large, but they turn up in varied groups (Hartup, 1970).

Measures of both social-emotional functioning and competence predict popularity. Friendlier and more sociable children tend to be more popular. At all ages and for both sexes the child who approaches others in a positive and friendly way is more likely to be accepted. Intelligence also predicts peer acceptance in more children's groups. Brighter children are more likely to be popular with their peers. Among boys size, strength, and athletic skill usually are positively correlated with popularity. Among teenage girls physical maturity tends to correlate with acceptance (Campbell, 1964; Hartup, 1970).

Social power, or leadership, within children's groups relates mostly to the same variables as popularity. A bright, sociable child is more likely to influence others, but there is an important exception. An assertive, aggressive child is more likely to be given power and looked to as a leader, particularly among boys, but this pushy pattern does not contribute to popularity (Hartup, 1970).

Leadership varies with the task facing a group. When children play baseball, they turn to somewhat different children for leadership than when they sit down to plan a party. Factors such as friendliness, intelligence, and assertiveness help in predicting who will play leadership roles. Specific factors, such as experience in playing baseball or planning parties, come to the fore with the particular task at hand. In children's groups, as in those of adults, leadership depends on how the individual fits in with the group's tasks and the needs of the day (Hartup, 1970).

The situational nature of leadership illustrates a broader point: what happens in groups of children often varies with the situation (Hartup, 1970). If you watch a group for a few weeks in a particular situation, such as morning recess, you can get an impression of stability. But if you observe for longer periods or look at the same children in a new setting, you see change. In putting on a class play, shifts in group structure and functioning can take place quickly.

Peer influences on the child

Peer relations may make fundamental contributions in such areas as personality development and interpersonal relations. Harry Stack Sullivan (1953) emphasized the importance of close relations with a chum as a vital step in personality development around age 9. Piaget (1932/1965) hypothesized that experiences in role taking within peer groups are basic in moral development. The give-and-take when children come together seems to provide opportunities for crucial social-emotional learning.

Our clearest evidence on peer influence relates to *conformity,* children's tendency to be influenced by their peers (Hartup, 1970). This evidence reveals a curvilinear pattern. Conformity to peer pressure rises to a peak at about age 11 to 14 and then declines. The peer group's power over the individual is maximum during the middle-school years.

Peers versus adults

Peer influence is often seen as opposite to adult influence. Supposedly, a fundamental conflict faces children among their peers: do they conform to peers or to adults (parents and teachers)? This viewpoint has gotten little support from careful studies.

Pressures from peers and adults usually don't conflict. Often there is harmony, with peers and parents pushing in the same direction (just what you would expect in light of the importance of the principles of balance and similarity in friendship choice, discussed in Chapter 12). When pressures from the two sources contrast, they usually involve different areas. For example, children's parents commonly have more impact in such areas as educational and career goals; their peers often are more important in companionship and recreational activities. Peer and adult influences, then, are better thought of as contrasting or supporting, rather than conflicting (Hartup, 1970).

Adult influences on peer interaction

In 1957, Robert Paul Smith wrote a book called "*Where did you go?*" "*Out.*" "*What did you do?*" "*Nothing.*" His title summarized what he remembered as the typical conversation when parents tried to find out what children did during his childhood. He lamented that the good old days were passing. Concerned adults were now succeeding in sticking their noses into children's free time.

Smith was probably pointing at a real shift. The baby boom, the growth of suburbs, the rise of TV, the increased educational level of parents, the growing age segregation of society, and the popularity of psychology all came together to reduce the independence of peer life from adult influence. Children used to learn games from older children in mixed-age peer groups. Apparently now they are more likely to learn them from adults—parents with more leisure, professional teachers and recreation directors, and television advertisers. Peer relations now are a larger part of childhood, but they take place more in settings where there is adult influence.

In socialist societies adults often try to use the peer group to achieve their own ends. Urie Bronfenbrenner (1970) describes how Soviet educators get children to maintain school discipline and promote educational goals. By using small groups and making them responsible for each member's actions, the teacher uses the peer group systematically, rather than seeing education entirely in teacher-pupil terms.

Adults today have a marked influence on the settings in which children come together, such as in organized activities like scouting.

Situational influences on groups

Muzafer and Carolyn Sherif (1956) showed how adults can influence children's groups. Their studies were conducted in isolated camp settings in Connecticut and Oklahoma. These outdoor environments provided special advantages. A total living situation provides many more opportunities for interaction within a few days. Camp life presents many ways in which children can formulate real goals connected to meaningful life problems.

The Sherifs thought that presenting children with the opportunity to work toward common goals would result in the formation of a structured group. Boys aged 11 or 12 who did not know each other were brought to camp and assigned to groups. The artificial groups were each presented with a series of problem situations and opportunities for group interaction. For example, hungry boys were given food in bulk form and allowed to work out the problem of eating together (with minimal adult participation). Building a fire, cutting up food, cooking it, serving it, and eating it all depended on the group's ability to get together, form a plan, and carry it out. After five days of presenting the group with common problems, the researchers presented them with sociometric techniques. The boys made their friendship choices overwhelmingly within their artificial groups. Other signs of group structure and solidarity were evident. The groups had taken on names like Red Devils, Bull Dogs, and Rattlers. They had nicknames for individuals, secret hideouts, and favorite songs. Status hierarchies had emerged. The demonstration suggests a clear guideline to promoting solidarity within a group of children: give them some common problems that they can solve together.

The Sherifs also tested ideas about what happens when two groups with solidarity (in-groups) come together. They hypothesized that when two in-groups meet in a series of situations where each is a source of frustration for the other, negative reactions will grow: each in-group will develop negative attitudes toward the other (the out-group). The Sherifs tested this hypothesis by putting on competitions, such as tug-of-war games, between pairs of groups. Because these competitive games always involved one winning team and one losing team, each group's goal attainment meant the other's frustration. The hypothesis was supported. Soon out-group members were sneaky and stinkers and fellow in-group members were brave and friendly. The boys sat separately at meals and raided each other.

The competition heightened in-group solidarity at the same time that it fostered antagonism between groups. This, of course, is the more positive side of competition usually emphasized by its supporters.

How do we reduce the negative feelings between groups of children? The Sherifs thought that if common, or superordinate, goals could be created for two hostile groups, tension could be reduced. They tested the hypothesis on the Rattlers and the Eagles, two groups who had developed strong negative feelings toward each other as a result of a series of competitive games. Having fostered a hostile situation, the experimenters now created emergencies that they thought would end it. A truck needed to get movies from town (that both groups wanted to see) wouldn't operate. Only the joint efforts of the two groups pulling together could get it turned around and going. The camp water system failed and everyone was needed to diagnose the problem and solve it. The strategy worked. As the groups worked together for the subordinate goals, tension between them gradually disappeared and solidarity replaced it. Name-calling discontinued and they started sitting together. At the end of the experimental camp both groups asked to leave together on one bus.

Helping unpopular children

We also have learned how grown-ups can help children with few friends and low peer acceptance do better in getting along with other children. One approach is to give less popular children special opportunities to perform new roles that win more acceptance—for example, by being leaders or helping others. This method often works in the short run, but typically does not produce gains that endure or carry over to other situations. In contrast when adults have coached less popular children in relevant friendship skills, more durable progress has been seen (Asher, Oden, & Gottman, 1977; Asher & Renshaw, 1981; Putallaz & Gottman, 1981).

A doctoral thesis by Sherri Oden is one of the most encouraging studies of coaching (Oden & Asher, 1977). Sociometric measures were used to identify third- and fourth-graders who were socially isolated. The isolated children were randomly assigned to experimental groups. The children who were coached were given a systematic training program involving several sessions over a period of about a month. First an adult instructed them individually on several concepts and skills important to friendship, such as participation, taking turns, smiling, and offering help. The instruction included getting children to think up their own examples of how to apply the concepts to a particular game situation. Then each child played that game with peers on six different occasions. After each play session the children had a session with the adult coach, who asked them to review what had happened, emphasizing the concepts originally presented. After the training period, sociometric instruments were administered again. The coached children made substantial gains in peer acceptance. A year later, when most of the children were in classrooms with new peers, the coached children had gained even further.

In another successful program Karen Bierman (1981) showed that the involvement of the peer group and the use of superordinate goals helped in maintaining the gains from coaching. Training programs built on current knowledge can help. We can influence peer acceptance and must consider both the gains and cost of doing so (Allen, 1981; Rubin, 1980).

SCHOOL

As work disappeared from modern childhood, school took its place. Now everyone goes to school, not just a rich minority. The school year has gotten longer and school years now stretch out into more of childhood. Thousands of hours in school are a standard and unique feature of a modern childhood; they provide the setting for much of the peer interaction I have discussed. Now we turn to school's influence, taking a broad look at two curricula.

The first curriculum: Academic learning

We think of school first as the place where children get the knowledge and skills taught in schoolbooks. We equate unschooled and illiterate. *Academic learning,* then, refers to a special kind of learning, one linked to books and words.

Our understanding of academic learning has been sharpened by looking at how it contrasts with the *informal education* that goes on in societies without schools. Jerome Bruner (1965) studied informal education partly by looking at thousands of feet of film taken of Kung children (members of a Bantu tribe in southern Africa). Everyday life for these children involved constant interaction with older people. Teaching-learning episodes often were part of the interaction. This informal education contrasts with formal schooling as we know it. Kung teaching almost always took place in the situation where the behavior was to be used, as when a child learned hunting while on the hunt or cooking while helping make a meal. The main method of teaching was showing (in many languages the words for teach and show are the same). Teaching by telling was rare, and drill came only in play, as when children practiced hunting or baby tending over and over on their own.

Comparisons of formal and informal education show that neither learning nor preparation for adult life is unique to schooling. Instead, learning out of context and what goes with that is central in formal education (see Table 19–1). School learning happens at a special time and place, not when and where it is needed. It takes place mostly through language rather than modeling and emphasizes general ideas instead of particulars. In school intellectual matters often are separated from episodes of social and emotional consequence,

TABLE 19–1 Contrasts between informal learning in everyday settings and formal learning in school settings

Feature of Contrast	Informal Setting	Formal Setting
Setting for learning	real life	specialized
Learning takes place	in context	out of context
Planning	mostly unplanned	mostly planned
Main focus	particulars	generalities
Common sequence	particular to general (inductive)	general to particular (deductive)
Dominant mode	observational learning	linguistic learning
Relation of cognitive and social-emotional elements	fused	separated

Based on Bruner, 1965, and Scribner & Cole, 1973.

as when a child takes out a workbook and does an arithmetic assignment because it is 10:30 A.M. In informal schooling cognitive and social-emotional meaning are more often fused, as for the village child who learns arithmetic while selling her family's harvest. Thus, when we remove children from the stream of everyday life and put them in school, we promote a particular kind of education.

The separation of cognitive and emotional matters so common in school learning produces both special opportunities and characteristic problems. It is hard to imagine teaching complex skills such as long division to children who are all "stirred up." The calm atmosphere of arithmetic time fits well with what is to be learned there. But an everyday word for what we often see during arithmetic class is boredom. The eagerness and curiosity so obvious in out-of-school activities is often missing in school.

The second curriculum: Nonacademic learning

The second, or nonacademic, curriculum evokes strong feelings and conflicts. Compulsory education in the United States arose in part from a concern about the immigrant children in our cities a century ago. Community leaders looked at these newcomers with alarm and promoted universal schooling as a way of making "better citizens" of them. They hoped that the public school would teach proper conduct to street urchins and wean them from idleness and delinquency (Boocock, 1976). Similar themes turn up today. The school is seen as a solution to such problems as drug abuse. Rising rates of VD and juvenile delinquency are cited as evidence that the schools are not doing their job. The nonacademic side of schooling is presented as education for good citizenship, but some put it less positively.

Social critics see the second curriculum negatively. They call it training in conformity and see "proper conduct" differently. Critics claim that in school children are taught to follow meaningless rules without questioning, to endure boredom silently, and to sacrifice their individuality as part of a mindless process of brainwashing (Averch, 1974).

Both those who want the schools to promote citizenship and those who complain about training in conformity agree that school presents our children with a curriculum of nonacademic learning. The arguments focus on what should be learned in it, but we still know little about what is learned here.

Robert Dreeben (1968) has given us a good lead in thinking about the nonacademic side of school. He relates it to the broader question of how children learn to live in modern society. Dreeben starts with the idea that the modern family does not prepare the child for life in a world of large organizations. He emphasizes the gap between the warm, personal atmosphere of the home and the world of impersonal rules and standards outside. He argues that the school is where the child learns how to get along in the settings and systems of the nonfamily world. The second curriculum is where children get their first opportunity to get along in a modern organization.

Our schools can be seen as miniature versions of the large organizations typical of business and government today. Our families cannot. Dreeben's view suggests that the second curriculum presents learning opportunities relevant to modern life—for better or worse. No wonder those content with our society criticize the school for not going further in making it run more smoothly and those unhappy with it criticize the school for going too far.

Studies of life in elementary schools and comparisons of students from large and small high schools fit in with Dreeben's idea and help us see the distinctive features of nonacademic life in modern schools.

Life in elementary schools

Philip Jackson (1968) collected minute-by-minute records of how teachers and children spend their time. They showed that teachers are busy, engaging in hundreds of separate social interchanges each day. Often they are managing social traffic, as in deciding who speaks next, handing out books, and making sure that activities begin and end promptly.

Classroom life has parallel features for children: delay, denial, and interruption. Much of their time is spent waiting. Their requests are often turned down. They are frequently stopped in the middle of what they are doing because it is time to do something else.

Jackson argues that children must learn strategies for dealing with the inevitable frustrations of classroom life. He thinks that patience is the central virtue needed in the second curriculum. He thinks that children often learn resignation and masquerade: they stop caring about what they really want to do, go along with the system instead, and fake their involvement while hiding their boredom.

According to Jackson, these unofficial learnings are as crucial as academic ones to success in school. You don't go to the principal's office for failing a spelling test.

Big school/small school

Jackson's picture of school life seems to reflect the size and organization of modern schools. Roger Barker and Paul Gump (1964) looked at the size question in a study of extracurricular experiences in high schools. Their findings fit the overall picture of how settings vary in their demand for people (Chapter 17).

In smaller schools the average student participated in more extracurricular activities. A comparison of a school with 794 juniors and one with 23 juniors illustrates what happened. Within the first three months of the junior year 98% of the small-school students played at least one performer role (such as playing in the band), but only 29% of the big-school students did. The small-school juniors averaged 8.6 performances, as compared to 3.5 for those in the big school.

When the students were asked what they got out of their participation in extracurricular activities, striking contrasts emerged. Students from smaller schools more often mentioned satisfaction from an increase in *competence* ("I learned how to get along with other people better"), from *challenge* ("It was a lot of work organizing the dance, but we all thought it was worth it"), and from being in an *action group* ("In the play our class worked together as a group"). The students from larger schools more often mentioned *secondary pleasure* ("I like to watch a good, suspenseful game") and *belonging to a crowd* ("Pep rallies give you a feeling of school spirit").

The contrasts between big and small schools were greatest for so-called marginal students, students who don't fit in well because of below average academic talent or disadvantaged homes. In a small school even marginal students participated a lot and felt pressure from others to perform, but in the larger schools marginal students were really out of it, particularly in respect to such performer roles as club leader or team player.

The big school/small school evidence fits in with Dreeben's thinking. Students from smaller schools reported being doers—their experiences and satisfactions seem like good preparation for an old-fashioned, small-town world with do-it-yourself recreation. In large schools the average student was more of an observer and belonger—seemingly an appropriate background for life in a world of large organizations and commercial recreation.

The second curriculum raises questions without easy answers. It is discouraging to think of school as good preparation for standing in line to get an automobile license or for faking a smile when the boss says, "Here's the way we do it." It also is sad to learn about schools that spend thousands of dollars repairing broken windows because they cannot get basic conformity.

Disadvantaged children and compensatory education

Children of poverty are at a disadvantage in both the first and the second curriculum. They have special problems with the verbal and out-of-context tasks of the academic curriculum, and their habits and motives fit badly with the system of the second. The school demands patience, but poor homes emphasize immediate gratification rather than waiting (R. D. Hess, 1970;

Silberman, 1970). No wonder that marginal students seem to suffer a special handicap in the larger high schools typical of our cities (Barker & Gump, 1964).

Since 1960, there have been many attempts at compensatory education, efforts to provide social experiences that would make up for the disadvantages of growing up in poverty (Averch, 1974; Bronfenbrenner, 1974; Horowitz & Paden, 1973). The outcomes did not support the unbridled optimism that was common at first, but they do not seem to imply the bleak pessimism that developed later. Instead, a cautious optimism seems indicated.

Before considering program outcomes, it is important to realize that children's achievement at the end of an educational program usually is highly related to child and family characteristics before the program begins. Brighter children and children with better educated and more concerned parents tend to end up at a higher level after any program. The trend holds up within poverty groups as well as in comparisons of poor and better-off children. As a result, program evaluation requires careful controls. Otherwise any new program will look misleadingly good because it will tend to attract children from the families most concerned about education.

School and curriculum characteristics, in contrast, rarely turn out to predict achievement once child and family characteristics are held constant. All kinds of factors, including student-teacher ratio, expenditure per pupil, and quality of buildings and equipment, have been related to pupil achievement. The results have been discouraging. They contradict the idea that such variables can be manipulated to reduce the educational problems of disadvantaged children (Averch, 1974). As a result, many have become skeptical.

The picture is brighter when we turn from large-scale comparisons of school systems and evaluations of national programs to more precisely defined experiments carried out on a smaller scale. A number of smaller experiments have shown promising outcomes (Averch, 1974).

A program of computer-assisted instruction (CAI) developed at Stanford University has boosted reading and arithmetic achievement at the elementary-school level (Atkinson, 1974). Disadvantaged third-graders who would have been expected to perform a year below national norms ended up slightly above grade level.

The most abundant and encouraging experimental work has been done on the preschool level. It points to an important set of conclusions:

1. Carefully defined and executed preschool programs can produce measurable gains in cognitive-linguistic and academic skills, often in short periods of time.
2. Follow-up studies now show that the gains from preschool programs can be lasting and important (Zigler & Valentine, 1979). A recent follow-up of 1599 children who had been studied as preschoolers is particularly exciting (Darlington, Royce, Snipper, Murray, & Lazar, 1980). Some of the children had participated in 11 of the pioneer preschool programs of the 1960s. The others had served as controls. They were restudied when they ranged in age from 9 to 19. The main question was whether the children had met basic requirements in school or whether they had ever been placed in special-education classes or left

behind. About 45% of the control children had not met the important criterion of fulfilling basic requirements in school. In contrast, only about 24% of those who had been in the preschool programs did not meet basic school requirements.

3. Certain kinds of programs are most likely to produce gains (Weikart, 1972). Usually a tutorial or semitutorial approach is present. For example, there often are daily sessions of one-to-one work for about 15 minutes and/or sessions with small groups. In the successful programs the main concern is usually to foster language and thinking. In contrast an entirely social-emotional or free-play approach has not been shown to help children intellectually. Finally, the more successful programs typically have been based on a systematic structure, or scheme, for thinking about what is to be accomplished, with a detailed sequence of goals and activities. Interestingly, a variety of structures (including Piagetian, operant conditioning, and linguistic) have produced similarly positive results. Perhaps the main benefit of a structured approach is in guiding the teacher, making it easier to focus on relevant activities without being distracted (Weikart & Lambie, 1970).

We may be able to do even better in the future. Longer programs that start earlier seem promising. Small experiments at the University of North Carolina (Robinson & Robinson, 1971) and University of Wisconsin (Garber & Heber, 1973; Heber, 1978) suggest that starting in the first year can produce more dramatic results.

Applications box 19–2 Critical TV viewing

Bad television is here to stay and will continue to be watched by many children; so some people are trying to equip children to be critical viewers. In the late 1970s, several critical viewing curricula were funded (Anderson, 1980), and researchers are now trying to evaluate their impact.

The general finding is that education in critical viewing can increase children's knowledge of how television works and make them more sophisticated and more skeptical about what they see (Dorr, Graves, & Phelps, 1980; Roberts, Cristenson, Gibson, Mooser, & Goldberg, 1980; Singer, Zuckerman, & Singer, 1980).

A group in Connecticut has developed materials for elementary-school children. They put together eight lessons on such topics as reality and fantasy on television, commercials and the television business, stereotypes on television, and how viewers can influence television. The lessons were made up of diverse ingredients, such as narrated videotapes, clips from current TV shows, and print materials.

An experiment with third-, fourth-, and firth-graders produced mixed results. The children found it interesting to learn about TV and particularly enjoyed seeing many of their favorite programs on the clips. The materials stimulated active class discussions, and test results showed that the experimental groups learned and remembered the content of the lessons. But the findings on attitudes were less encouraging. The children's attitudes seemed closely linked to those of their parents. The parents typically were uninterested in the project. They seemed to think that television was a problem for other children, not theirs; so the investigators remained skeptical about the impact of their curriculum.

In Texas a project has had a special focus on mediation, how others, such as teachers and parents, can influence what children learn from television (Corder-Bolz, 1980). It was found that comments by teacher aides such as "There is the 'ck' again" could significantly increase how much children learned from "The Electric Company." Another study showed that adult comments helped children get the antisexist message in a special episode of "All in the Family."

One of the most intriguing Texas studies raised the question of whether television could mediate itself. Special "spots" were videotaped and inserted where the commercials had gone in a "Batman" episode. In these spots adults spoke in a relaxed and authoritative way about "Batman." In the first they pointed out that although "Batman" was fun to watch, it was not real. In the second they explained that in the real world you could not do what "Batman" did (hurt people). In the final spot they explained that when someone presented a problem, children should not hit the person, but should get help from a parent or teacher. The spots reduced the amount of cynicism about people produced by the program. The children were surprised by the spots and argued among themselves about whether their content was true. Finally, they agreed that the message of the spots must have been true—because they were on TV.

Discouragement about changing television has led to a new focus on helping children cope with it. The early efforts raise a little hope.

TELEVISION

Television changed childhood. We look both at the broad picture and at a few specific areas of influence.

Overall impact

When television comes to a country, most children soon are watching it. They watch for many hours each week, with averages ranging from about 14 hours in Sweden to about twice that in the United States (vonFeilitzen, 1976). In the United States today the typical 18-year-old has watched about 15,000 hours of television (Lesser, 1974, p. 19). Television takes more of our children's time than any other single waking activity, more than school or play with peers.

Early studies answered the displacement question—the question of what activities give way to television when children start looking at it (Maccoby, 1964). The main trend was for television to win out in competition with relatively similar pastimes: movie going, radio listening, and comic reading. For example, in 1959, two similar communities in western Canada were compared. In Radiotown (no television yet) the sixth-graders were watching about five movies a month; those in Teletown (with television) were watching only one. In Radiotown 87% of the sixth-graders were reading ten or more comic books a month, but in Teletown only 34% were. In Radiotown the sixth-graders listened to the radio an average of over three hours a day. In Teletown the average was 57 minutes (Schramm, Lyle, & Parker, 1961, p. 18). Television did not seem to have a big impact on book reading, homework doing, or sleeping in North America or Britain. Here the findings varied from no impact to small impact.

An interesting contrast emerged when television's impact on organized and unorganized leisure activities was compared. Such organized activities as scouting typically did not lose time to television. Unorganized ones such as chatting with friends and daydreaming did. These findings help us keep perspective in the face of untrue statements that so frequently are made: Children used to spend much more time reading books before television came. Television results in a neglect of homework.

The developmental curve for television watching is similar in varied countries. Regular and prolonged watching starts at about 3 years and rises steadily to a peak at about 11 to 14 years (Comstock, Chaffee, Katzman, McCombs, & Roberts, 1978). Then it drops off. Children start by watching mostly children's programs, but the percentage of time watching adult programs grows steadily. By age 8, children look at programs for grown-ups about half the time (Brown, 1976).

TV viewing often is a family activity. However, experts argue about the value of this kind of togetherness.

Because school-age children watch lots of adult television, viewing is often a family activity. The question of what this kind of time together means in the lives of children is controversial. Bronfenbrenner (1970) thinks family viewing prevents more meaningful interaction. Others see it more as an extension of existing patterns (Brown & Linné, 1976). Research on "Sesame Street" shows that joint watching can be a way for parents to teach more effectively (Ball & Bogatz, 1970; Salomon, 1977). We need more evidence.

Impact on specific areas

Once television became an established part of children's lives, research turned from questions about its overall impact to more specific issues.

Aggressive behavior

Violence has been an outstanding feature of commercial television in the United States. Around 1970, about 30% of Saturday morning programs were considered saturated with violence. About 20 to 30 violent episodes per hour occurred in the cartoons directed at young children. About 80% of television plays included at least one incident of violence, with an average of about 8 violent episodes per hour. Concern about the impact of this diet of violence on children led to extensive research, more than on any other question of how television influenced children (Comstock et al., 1978; Stein & Friedrich, 1975).

The findings imply that the viewing of television violence often increases both aggressive behavior and positive attitudes toward violence. The pattern of findings has been similar across varied ages, for both sexes, and at all levels of socioeconomic status. The psychoanalytic notion of catharsis, that watching aggression on television drains off the child's aggressive tendencies, has not received support (Comstock et al., 1978; Stein & Friedrich, 1975).

Research suggests that violent television is most likely to stimulate aggressive behavior in children who already are relatively aggressive. There also is evidence suggesting that when children are angry or frustrated, they are more likely to pay attention to and imitate aggressive television models (Stein & Friedrich, 1975).

Defenders of commercial television often have argued that the impact of violence on television is minimal because children don't confuse cartoons and reality and because aggressive actions on television typically are punished. Neither of these claims has held up. Cartoons and more realistic programs seem to have a similar impact on children's later behavior. Violent actions that are followed by bad consequences (often much later in the show) produce about as much aggression in children as those that aren't. Actually, violent means are often rewarded on television, particularly when carried out by detectives and police heroes (Stein & Friedrich, 1975).

Stein and Friedrich (1975) concluded their review of the impact of television violence with two recommendations:

1. Parents should limit their children's early television viewing to avoid large-scale exposure to violence.
2. Television producers should reduce the heavy diet of aggression on commerical television.

Now that influential groups such as the Parent-Teacher Association, the American Medical Association, and Action for Children's Television have joined the campaign against TV violence, we are beginning to see important changes in program content.

Prosocial behavior

Pioneer studies of how television can influence cooperative and helping behaviors show that television can have a positive impact on children's social behavior. They imply that we already know enough to design programs that would work.

Lynette Friedrich and Aletha Stein have contributed the most here. In one study they created an experimental nursery school and included varied types of television for matched groups within it. They looked at the impact of the type of television on real-life nursery-school actions, both during and after the TV-watching period. One group of children looked at "Batman" and "Superman" cartoons. Their tendency to obey rules and tolerate delays went down. The group that looked at "Mister Rogers' Neighborhood" showed increases in such areas as following rules, tolerating delays, and persisting on tasks. For lower SES children cooperation behaviors also went up (Friedrich & Stein, 1973). A later study focused more on kindergartners' learning processes (Friedrich & Stein, 1975). This study once again demonstrated that watching "Mister Rogers" promoted positive behaviors, such as helping, that transferred to other situations. Additional training involving verbal labeling and role playing enhanced the impact of television. The message of the program was more often translated into action.

Stein and Friedrich (1975) argue that we now have clear guidelines for television producers who want to develop shows like "Mister Rogers," which foster prosocial behavior. They emphasize the importance of having varied models demonstrate the desired behaviors and of having positive consequences follow immediately.

Cognitive functioning

Traditional commercial television for children consisted of an unending parade of cartoons, as mindless as they were violent. Industry officials defended them with a standard claim: children did not enjoy educational programs and would not look at them. "Sesame Street" shattered this argument.

Gerald Lesser (1974), a psychologist who served as educational director for "Sesame Street," summarized the fascinating story of its origins. A few points stand out.

There were ample funds, $7 million from government and foundation sources. About 10% of the money went for research. Ideas came from a unique collaboration between psychologists, educators, and media experts. Preliminary hunches were checked against evidence: small groups of children were observed while watching sample programs. The research produced a number of useful insights. The rapid action typical of commercials and aggressive cartoons was a powerful way of catching and holding children's attention, but there was no need for either slapstick or aggression. The now-familiar commercials for letters and numbers on "Sesame Street" illustrate the attention-getting techniques that did emerge: fast action, surprise, and interesting content.

The first series of programs had not been fully tested when it went on the air in 1969. The basic questions remained: Would children look at them, enjoy them, and learn from them in their own homes? Would children in inner-city slums (the target audience for whom they were intended) look at them regularly?

The answers came quickly. "Sesame Street" was an immediate success. By the end of 1972, about 9 million children were watching, including over 90% of the potential audience in places such as Harlem and Chicago. What had looked like an expensive experiment turned out to be a bargain, costing only about a penny per child for each viewing. Educational television clearly could entertain children and hold their attention, and children learned from watching (Ball & Bogatz, 1970). The producers' goals, such as teaching children to recognize shapes, to name letters and numbers, and to learn such concepts as bigger, under, more, and today, were achieved.

Good educational television can educate children while entertaining them. "The Electric Company" and other programs for older children also have been shown to teach (Stein & Friedrich, 1975). "Feeling Free" fosters more positive attitudes toward handicapped people (Storey, 1981). Entertaining educational television is not scarce because children won't look at it; the problem is with adults.

Television commercials and children

The typical child in the United States is exposed to about 20,000 television commercials each year. About half of them are for candy, sugared cereal, and snack foods (Condry, 1978, p. 855). Complaints by dentists, nutritionists, and others concerned with children's health has moved us into an era of research on commercials.

Children's ideas about commercials change predictably with age and presumably with level of cognitive development. Kindergartners are less clear about the purpose of commercials than older children and discriminate program and commercials on the basis of perceptual cues. By second grade, children typically understand the purpose of commercials and have begun to mistrust them on the basis of concrete personal experience. A more general distrust grows with age (Ward, 1976; Ward, Wackman, & Wartella, 1977).

Children and television

Three misleading ideas have been common in thinking about children and television. First, many see television as mere entertainment. They ignore the possibility that it has lasting impact. The evidence contradicts this belief. Newton Minow's famous statement deserves renewed emphasis, "All television is educational television. The only question is what is it teaching?"

Second, people who do think that television can influence children often invoke the old image of the child as a blank slate. Instead, we find that children

Applications box 19-3 Peer tutoring

Today many children are teaching other children, meeting with them regularly for one-to-one helping sessions in such subjects as reading or arithmetic (Allen, 1976a; Ehly & Larsen, 1980). The tutoring usually involves an older child helping a younger one of the same sex, but other arrangements are also made. An intriguing fact about this new trend is that it is not new (Allen, 1976b). Peer tutoring involves a rediscovery of methods and outcomes that were popular in the early 1800s.

Both older and current writings on peer teaching emphasize the idea that tutoring often has a positive impact on the tutor. In 1803, Joseph Lancaster wrote "I have ever found, the surest way to cure a mischievous boy was to make him a monitor (tutor). I never knew anything to succeed much better, if as well" (Allen, 1976b, p. 114). More recent studies suggest a similar moral, as when a program in California used social-adjustment students who had been problems in their own classrooms as tutors for kindergartners. The kindergarten teachers didn't learn about the tutors' backgrounds until after they had watched them tutoring. The teachers were amazed, for they had been impressed with the older students' competence and maturity (Gartner, Kohler, & Riessman, 1971). In several studies tutors have been found to have made large academic gains, along with progress in social behavior, motivation, and self-concepts (Allen, 1976a).

Somewhat surprisingly, then, there are more questions about how to make sure that the tutees, the children who supposedly are getting help, also make progress. Simply creating a tutoring program does not guarantee success (Feldman, Devin-Sheehan, & Allen, 1976).

Training is an important ingredient of a successful program that helps both tutors and tutees (Lippitt, 1976). Progress is more likely when the tutor is given advance training both in the subject matter to be taught and in methods of working with younger children. Another promising approach is to prepare a structured method of tutoring, test it out to make sure it works, and then teach it to the tutors. For example, Grant Von Harrison (1976) has developed a system for teaching Mexican-American fifth- and sixth-graders how to help younger children with mathematics concepts. He found that the best approach included three phases. The tutors first read a description of what they were to do. Then they discussed it with a trainer. Finally, there were role-playing sessions in which each tutor took a turn at tutoring, with the trainer playing the part of the tutee. After using this system in three schools, Von Harrison concluded that most elementary-school children can be trained to use effective skills when tutoring.

Peer tutoring has emerged as an important way for children to take responsibility, feel useful, and be useful. Here is one way to remedy the modern child's loss of opportunities to be helpful.

here, as elsewhere, are active. They come to television to learn as well as to be entertained (Brown, 1976). They quickly learn to turn sets off and to select among alternatives. They become suspicious of commercials at a surprisingly early age. When their opportunities for alternative information are great, they do not readily form stereotypes from TV.

The third misleading idea is that the people who most commonly write about television often see only the negative side. There is ample reason to be concerned about many aspects of television, such as aggression and candy commercials, but the negative side is often overemphasized. "Sesame Street," "Mister Rogers," and other positive influences are as clearly documented. The potential for making television's impact more positive grows as we face a future of more diversified television (Kalba, 1975).

We must come to grips with the role that television plays in the world of the modern child. The modern child is cut off from opportunities to participate in and learn from the adult world. Television provides a window for a child who needs it (Noble, 1975).

It is easy to complain that television presents a distorted view of the real world. It stereotypes and presents fewer older citizens than there are; the male-superiority theme still comes through (Stein & Friedrich, 1975). But what about the world our children see when they look out of real windows? How many Blacks, factory workers, and older citizens does the child in a White middle-class suburb see walk by or enter through the front door? Television distorts, but how much of birth, death, courtship, and work can be learned in the usual third-grade or supper table conversation? Television is far from a perfect window on the world, but it may be one of the best that many children have.

SUMMARY

This chapter has focused on three worlds of experience outside the family. Together they take far more of the older child's time than interaction with family members. In each case they help fill the void created by the separation of the modern child from the world of everyday adult affairs.

In looking at these three areas we meet a similar problem in each case: a problem of balance. Traditionally, peers have been neglected in serious consideration of child development. Direct observation makes it clear that fears, fights, and friendships in the world of peers are intensely important to children. Indirect evidence makes us suspect that the basic social-emotional qualities that emerge from these interactions are at least as important as those that emerge from interactions with parents. With schools we find the opposite problem. The contribution of the school has been painted in such positive terms that a look at reality can be jarring. We looked to schools to solve all our problems, but they didn't. We justify compulsory schooling in terms of positive outcomes. When we see negative ones, it hurts to admit them. With television we often swing to both extremes. Sometimes we deny that the thousands of hours mean anything; at other times we claim that they mean everything.

Have we reached a lasting solution to the problem that was created when children were separated from the world of meaningful work and responsibility for others? Or is the well-known boredom of suburban children in modern countries (Popenoe, 1976) telling us something important? Perhaps the Sherifs' (1956) research has a broader moral. Maybe children can feel solidarity with their society and meaning in their lives only when they join in working toward common goals more exciting than we give them. Sarane Boocock (1976) has pointed out that those concerned with child development have said much of late about children's rights and little about their obligations. Urie Bronfenbrenner (1970) and James Coleman (1971) call for new ways of bringing children back into the common world of productive action in which they lived for most of human history. What do you think?

References

Abel, E. L. Fetal alcohol syndrome: Behavioral teratology. *Psychological Bulletin,* 1980, *87,* 29–50.

Abelson, R. P. Psychological status of the script concept. *American Psychologist,* 1981, *36,* 715–719.

Abravanel, E. The development of intersensory patterning with regard to selected spatial dimensions. *Monographs of the Society for Research in Child Development,* 1968, *33* (2, Serial No. 118).

Achenbach, T. M. *Developmental psychopathology.* New York: Ronald Press, 1974.

Achenbach, T. M. *Research in developmental psychology: Concepts, strategies, methods.* New York: Free Press, 1978.

Achenbach, T. M., & Edelbrock, C. S. The classification of child psychopathology: A review and analysis of empirical efforts. *Psychological Bulletin,* 1978, *85,* 1275–1301.

Achenbach, T. M., & Edelbrock, C. S. Behavioral problems and competencies reported by parents of normal and disturbed children aged four through sixteen. *Monographs of the Society for Research in Child Development,* 1981, *46* (1, Serial No. 188).

Acredolo, L. P. The development of spatial orientation in infancy. *Developmental Psychology,* 1978, *14,* 224–234.

Acredolo, L. P., & Evans, D. Developmental changes in the effects of landmarks on infant spatial behavior. *Developmental Psychology,* 1980, *16,* 312–318.

Acredolo, L. P., Pick, H. L., & Olsen, M. G. Environmental differentiation and familiarity as determinants of children's memory for spatial location. *Developmental Psychology,* 1975, *11,* 495–501.

Advisory Committee on Child Development. *Toward a national policy for children and families.* Washington, D.C.: National Academy of Sciences, 1976.

Ainsworth, M. D. S. The development of infant-mother attachment. In B. M. Caldwell & H. N. Ricciuti (Eds.), *Review of child development research* (Vol. 3). Chicago: University of Chicago Press, 1973.

Ainsworth, M. D. S. Infant-mother attachment. *American Psychologist,* 1979, *34,* 932–937.

Ainsworth, M. D. S., Blehar, M. C., Walters, E., & Wall, S. *Patterns of attachment.* Hillsdale, N.J.: Erlbaum, 1978.

Allen, V. L. (Ed.). *Children as teachers.* New York: Academic Press, 1976. (a)

Allen, V. L. The helping relationship and socialization of children: Some perspectives on tutoring. In V. L. Allen (Ed.), *Children as teachers.* New York: Academic Press, 1976. (b)

Allen, V. L. Self, social group, and social structure: Surmises about the study of children's friendships. In S. R. Asher & J. M. Gottman (Eds.), *The development of children's friendships.* Cambridge, England: Cambridge University Press, 1981.

Allik, J., & Valsiner, J. Visual development in ontogenesis: Some reevaluations. In H. W. Reese & L. P. Lipsitt (Eds.), *Advances in child development and behavior* (Vol. 15). New York: Academic Press, 1980.

Allison, M. G., & Ayllon, T. Behavioral coaching in the development of skills in football, gymnastics, and tennis. *Journal of Applied Behavior Analysis,* 1980, *13,* 297–314.

Alloway, T., Pliner, P., & Krames, L. (Eds.). *Attachment behavior.* New York: Plenum, 1977.

Allport, G. W. *Pattern and growth in personality.* New York: Holt, Rinehart & Winston, 1961.

Altman, I., & Wohlwill, J. F. (Eds.). *Children and the environment.* New York: Plenum, 1978.

Anastasi, A. Heredity, environment, and the question "how?" *Psychological Review,* 1958, *65,* 197–208.

Anderson, C. W., Nagle, R. J., Roberts, W. A., & Smith, J. W. Attachment to substitute caregivers as a function of center quality and caregiver involvement. *Child Development,* 1981, *52,* 53–61.

Anderson, J. A. The theoretical lineage of critical viewing curricula. *Journal of Communication,* 1980, *30,* 64–83.

Anthony, E. J. The behavior disorders of childhood. In P. H. Mussen (Ed.), *Carmichael's manual of child psychology* (3rd ed.). New York: Wiley, 1970.

Apgar, V. A proposal for a new method of evaluation of the newborn infant. *Current Researches in*

Anesthesia and Analgesia, 1953, *32,* 260–267.

Appel, M. H., & Goldberg, L. S. (Eds.). *Topics in cognitive development* (Vol. 1). *Equilibration: Theory, research and application.* New York: Plenum, 1977.

Arend, R., Gove, F., & Sroufe, L. A. Continuity of individual adaptation from infancy to kindergarten: A predictive study of ego-resiliency and curiosity in preschoolers. *Child Development,* 1979, *50,* 950–959.

Ariès, P. *Centuries of childhood.* New York: Vintage, 1965. (Originally published, 1960.)

Aron, I. E. Moral philosophy and moral education: A critique of Kohlberg's theory. *School Review,* 1977, *85,* 197–217.

Asher, S. R., & Gottman, J. M. (Eds.). *The development of children's friendships.* Cambridge, England: Cambridge University Press, 1981.

Asher, S. R., Oden, S. L., & Gottman, J. M. Children's friendships in school settings. In L. G. Katz (Ed.), *Current topics in early childhood education* (Vol. 1). Norwood, N.J.: Ablex, 1977.

Asher, S. R., & Renshaw, P. D. Children without friends: Social knowledge and social-skill training. In S. R. Asher & J. M. Gottman (Eds.), *The development of children's friendships.* Cambridge, England: Cambridge University Press, 1981.

Aslin, R. N., & Dumais, S. T. Binocular vision in infants: A review and a theoretical framework. In H. W. Reese & L. P. Lipsitt (Eds.), *Advances in child behavior and development* (Vol. 15). New York: Academic Press, 1980.

Atkinson, R. C. Teaching children to read using a computer. *American Psychologist,* 1974, *29,* 169–178.

Averch, H. A. *How effective is schooling?* Englewood Cliffs, N.J.: Educational Technology, 1974.

Baker, B. L., Brightman, A. J., Heifetz, L. J., & Murphy, D. M. *Steps to independence.* Champaign, Ill.: Research Press, 1977.

Baldwin, A. L. *Theories of child development* (2nd ed.). New York: Wiley, 1980.

Ball, S., & Bogatz, G. *The first year of Sesame Street: An evaluation.* Princeton, N.J.: Educational Testing Service, 1970.

Bandura, A. *Principles of behavior modification.* New York: Holt, Rinehart & Winston, 1969. (a)

Bandura, A. Social learning of moral judgments. *Journal of Personality and Social Psychology,* 1969, *11,* 275–279. (b)

Bandura, A. *Social learning theory.* Englewood Cliffs, N.J.: Prentice-Hall, 1977.

Bandura, A., Grusec, J., & Menlove, F. L. Observational learning as a function of symbolization and incentive set. *Child Development,* 1966, *37,* 499–506.

Bandura, A., Grusec, J. E., & Menlove, F. L. Vicarious extinction of avoidance behavior. *Journal of Personality and Social Psychology,* 1967, *5,* 16–23.

Bandura, A., & McDonald, F. J. Influence of social reinforcement and the behavior of models in shaping children's moral judgments. *Journal of Abnormal and Social Psychology,* 1963, *67,* 274–281.

Bandura, A., & Walters, R. W. *Social learning and personality development.* New York: Holt, Rinehart & Winston, 1963.

Bane, M. J. *Here to stay: American families in the twentieth century.* New York: Basic Books, 1976.

Banks, E. Malay childhood, temperament, and individuality. Paper presented at the Meeting of the Society for Research in Child Development, Boston, April 1981.

Bar-Adon, A., & Leopold, W. F. (Eds.). *Child language: A book of readings.* Englewood Cliffs, N.J.: Prentice-Hall, 1971.

Barker, R., Dembo, T., & Lewin, K. Frustration and regression: An experiment with young children. *University of Iowa Studies in Child Welfare,* 1941, *18*(386), 1–314.

Barker, R. G., & Gump, P. V. *Big school, small school.* Stanford, Calif.: Stanford University Press, 1964.

Barker, R. G., & Wright, H. F. *Midwest and its children; the psychological ecology of an American town.* Evanston, Ill.: Row, Peterson, 1955.

Barry, H., Bacon, M. K., & Child, I. L. A cross-cultural survey of some sex differences in socialization. *Journal of Abnormal and Social Psychology,* 1957, *55,* 327–332.

Barry, H., III, Child, I. L., & Bacon, M. K. Relation of child training to subsistence economy. *American Anthropologist,* 1959, *61,* 51–63.

Bar-Tal, D., Raviv, A., & Leiser, T. The development of altruistic behavior: Empirical evidence. *Developmental Psychology,* 1980, *16,* 516 524.

Bates, E. Acquisition of pragmatic competence. *Journal of Child Language,* 1974, *1,* 277–281.

Bates, E. *The emergence of symbols: Cognition and communication in infancy.* New York: Academic Press, 1979.

Bates, J. E., Pettit, G. S., & Bayles, K. Antecedents of behavior problems at age three years. Paper presented at the Meeting of the Society for Research in Child Development, Boston, April 1981.

Battle, E. S., & Lacey, B. A context for hyperactivity in children over time. *Child Development,* 1972, *43,* 757–773.

Baumrind, D. Current patterns of parental authority. *Developmental Psychology,* 1971, *4*(No. 4, Part 2).

Baumrind, D. New directions in socialization research. *American Psychologist,* 1980, *35,* 639–652.

Bayley, N. On the growth of intelligence. *American Psychologist,* 1955, *10,* 805–818.

Bayley, N. *Bayley scales of infant development.* New York: Psychological Corporation, 1969.

Bell, R. Q. Relations between behavior manifestations in the newborn. *Child Development,* 1960, *31,* 463–477.

Bell, R. Q. A reinterpretation of the direction of effects in studies of socialization. *Psychological Review,* 1968, *75,* 84–88.

Bell, R. Q. Contributions of human infants to caregiving and social interaction. In M. Lewis & L. A. Rosenblum (Eds.), *The effect of the infant on its caregiver.* New York: Wiley, 1974.

Bell, R. Q. Parent, child, and reciprocal influences. *American Psychologist,* 1979, *34,* 821–826.

Bell, R. Q., & Harper, L. V. *Child effects on adults.* Hillsdale, N.J.: Erlbaum, 1977.

Bell, S. M., & Ainsworth, M. D. S. Infant crying and maternal responsiveness. *Child Development,* 1972, *43,* 1171–1190.

Belmont, J. M., & Butterfield, E. C. The instructional approach to developmental and cognitive research. In R. V. Kail & J. M. Hagen (Eds.), *Perspectives on the development of memory and cognition.* Hillsdale, N.J.: Erlbaum, 1977.

Belsky, J., & Steinberg, L. D. The effects of day care: A critical review. *Child Development,* 1978, *49,* 929–949.

Bem, S. L. The measurement of psychological androgyny. *Journal of Consulting and Clinical Psychology,* 1974, *42,* 155–162.

Bem, S. L. Gender schema theory: A cognitive account of sex typing. *Psychological Review,* 1981, *88,* 354–364.

Berg, W. K., & Berg, K. M. Psychophysiological development in infancy: State, sensory function, and attention. In J. D. Osofsky (Ed.), *Handbook of infant development.* New York: Wiley, 1979.

Berko, J. The child's learning of English morphology. *Word,* 1958, *14,* 150–177.

Berko, J., & Brown, R. Psycholinguistic research methods. In P. H. Mussen (Ed.), *Handbook of research methods in child development.* New York: Wiley, 1960.

Berkowitz, L. Control of aggression. In B. M. Caldwell & H. N. Ricciuti (Eds.), *Review of child development research* (Vol. 3). Chicago: University of Chicago Press, 1973.

Bernstein, A. C., & Cowan, P. A. Children's concepts of how people get babies. *Child Development,* 1975, *46,* 77–91.

Bertenthal, B. I., Campos, J. J., & Haith, M. M. Development of visual organization: The perception of subjective contours. *Child Development,* 1980, *51,* 1072–1080.

Best, D. L., Williams, J. E., Cloud, J. M., Davis, S. W., Robertson, L. S., Edwards, J. R., Giles, H., & Fowles, J. Development of sex-trait stereotypes among young children in the United States, England, and Ireland. *Child Development,* 1978, *48,* 1375–1384.

Bierman, K. L. Enhancing the generalization of social skills training with peer involvement and superordinate goals. Paper presented at the Meeting of the Society for Research in Child Development, Boston, April 1981.

Billman, J., & McDevitt, S. C. Convergence of parent and observer ratings of temperament with observations of peer interaction in nursery school. *Child Development,* 1980, *51,* 395–400.

Bindra, D. *Motivation.* New York: Ronald Press, 1959.

Birch, H. G., & Lefford, A. Visual differentiation, intersensory integration, and voluntary motor control. *Monographs of the Society for Research in Child Development,* 1967, *32*(2, Serial No. 110).

Birch, L. L. Effect of peer model's food choices and eating behaviors on preschooler's food preferences. *Child Development,* 1980, *51,* 489–496.

Birch, L. L. Generalization of a modified food preference. *Child Development,* 1981, *52,* 755–758.

Birch, L. L., & Birch, D. "Eat your vegetables and then you can . . ." Effects of instrumental consumption on food preference. Paper presented at the Meeting of the Society for Research in Child Development, Boston, April 1981.

Birch, L. L., Zimmerman, S. I., & Hind, H. The influence of social-affective context on the formation of children's food preferences. *Child Development,* 1980, *51,* 856–861.

Blasi, A. Bridging moral cognition and moral action: A critical review of the literature. *Psychological Bulletin,* 1980, *88,* 1–45.

Blatt, M. M., & Kohlberg, L. The effects of classroom moral discussion upon children's level of moral judgment. In L. Kohlberg (Ed.), *Collected papers on moral development and moral education.* Cambridge, Mass.: Author, 1973.

Block, J. H. Assessing sex differences: Issues, problems, and pitfalls. *Merrill-Palmer Quarterly,* 1976, *22,* 282–308.

Block, J. H., & Block, J. The role of ego-control and ego-resiliency in the organization of behavior. In W. A. Collins (Ed.), *Minnesota Symposia on Child Psychology* (Vol. 13). Hillsdale, N.J.: Erlbaum, 1980.

Bloom, B. S. *Stability and change in human characteristics.* New York: Wiley, 1964.

Bloom, L. *Language development: Form and function in emerging grammars.* Cambridge, Mass.: MIT Press, 1970.

Bloom, L. *One word at a time: The use of single word utterances before syntax.* The Hague: Mouton, 1973.

Blurton Jones, N. (Ed.). *Ethological studies of child behaviour.* London: Cambridge University Press, 1972.

Boehm, A. E. Criterion-referenced assessment for the teacher. *Teachers College Record,* 1973, *75,* 117–126.

Bond, E. K. Perception of form by the human infant. *Psychological Bulletin,* 1972, *77,* 225–245.

Boocock, S. S. Children in contemporary society. In A. Skolnick (Ed.), *Rethinking childhood.* Boston: Little, Brown, 1976.

Bornstein, M. H. Perceptual development: Stability and change in feature perception. In M. H. Bornstein & W. Kessen (Eds.), *Psychological development from infancy: Image to intention.* Hillsdale, N.J.: Erlbaum, 1979.

Boston Women's Health Book Collective. *Our bodies, our selves* (2nd ed.). New York: Simon & Schuster, 1976.

Bouchard, T. J., Jr., & McGue, M. Familial studies of intelligence: A review. *Science,* 1981, *212,* 1055–1059.

Bousfield, W. I., & Orbison, W. D. Ontogenesis of emotional behavior. *Psychological Review,* 1952, *59,* 1–7.

Bower, T. G. R. *Development in infancy.* San Francisco: Freeman, 1974.

Bower, T. G. R. *A primer of infant development.* San Francisco: Freeman, 1977.

Bowlby, J. *Attachment and loss* (Vol. 1). *Attachment.* New York: Basic Books, 1969.

Bowlby, J. *Attachment and loss* (Vol. 2). *Separation.* New York: Basic Books, 1973.

Brackbill, Y. Extinction of the smiling response in infants as a function of reinforcement schedules. *Child Development,* 1958, *29,* 115–124.

Brackbill, Y. Obstetrical medication and infant behavior. In J. D. Osofsky (Ed.), *Handbook of infant development.* New York: Wiley, 1979.

Brainerd, C. J. Learning research and Piagetian theory. In L. L. Siegel & C. J. Brainerd (Eds.), *Alternatives to Piaget.* New York: Academic Press, 1978.

Brazelton, T. B. Evidence of communication in neonatal behavioral assessment. In M. Bullowa (Ed.), *Before speech.* London: Cambridge University Press, 1979.

Bresnitz, S., & Kugelmass, S. Intentionality in moral judgment: Developmental stages. *Child Development,* 1967, *38,* 469–479.

Bretherton, I., & Bates, E. The emergence of intentional communication. *New Directions for Child Development,* 1979 (No. 4), 81–100.

Bridges, K. M. B. Emotional development in early infancy. *Child Development,* 1932, *3,* 324–341.

Brody, E. B., & Brody, N. *Intelligence: Nature, determinants, and consequences.* New York: Academic Press, 1976.

Bronfenbrenner, U. Developmental theory in transition. In H. W. Stevenson (Ed.), *Child psychology.* Chicago: University of Chicago Press, 1963.

Bronfenbrenner, U. *Two worlds of childhood: U.S. and U.S.S.R.* New York: Russell Sage Foundation, 1970.

Bronfenbrenner, U. *Is early intervention effective? A report on longitudinal evaluations of preschool programs* (Vol. 2). Washington, D.C.: Department of Health, Education and Welfare, Office of Child Development, 1974.

Bronfenbrenner, U. Toward an experimental ecology of human development. *American Psychologist,* 1977, *32,* 513–531.

Bronfenbrenner, U. Contexts of child rearing: Problems and prospects. *American Psychologist,* 1979, *34,* 844–850. (a)

Bronfenbrenner, U. *The ecology of human development.* Cambridge, Mass.: Harvard University Press, 1979. (b)

Bronson, G. The hierarchical organization of the central nervous system: Implications for learning processes and critical periods in early development. *Behavioral Science,* 1965, *10,* 7–25.

Bronson, W. C. Central orientations: A study of behavior organization from childhood to adolescence. *Child Development,* 1966, *37,* 125–155.

Bronson, W. The role of enduring orientations to the environment in personality development. *Genetic Psychology Monographs,* 1972, *86,* 3–80.

Broverman, I. K., Vogel, S. R., Broverman, D. M., Clarkson, F. E., & Rosenkrantz, P. S. Sex-role stereotypes: A current appraisal. *Journal of Social Issues,* 1972, *28,* 59–78.

Brown, A. L. Development, schooling, and the acquisition of knowledge about knowledge: Comments on chapter 7 by Nelson. In R. C. Anderson, R. J. Spiro, & W. E. Montague (Eds.), *Schooling and the acquisition of knowledge.* Hillsdale, N.J.: Erlbaum, 1977.

Brown, A. L., & Campione, J. C. Memory strategies in learning: Training children to study strategically. In H. Pick, H. Liebowitz, J. Singer, & A. Sleinschneider (Eds.), *Application of basic research in psychology.* New York: Plenum, 1978.

Brown, A. L., & Scott, M. S. Recognition memory for pictures in preschool children. *Journal of Experimental Child Psychology,* 1971, *11,* 401–412.

Brown, D. G. Sex-role development in a changing culture. *Psychological Bulletin,* 1958, *54,* 232–242.

Brown, J. R., & Linné, O. The family as a mediator of television's effects. In J. R. Brown (Ed.), *Children and television.* Beverly Hills, Calif.: Sage, 1976.

Brown, J. R. (Ed.). *Children and television.* Beverly Hills, Calif.: Sage, 1976.

Brown, J. V., & Bakeman, R. Relationships of human mothers with their infants during the first year of life; effects of prematurity. In R. W. Bell & W. P. Smotherman (Eds.), *Maternal influences and early behavior.* New York: Spectrum, 1980.

Brown, R. *Social psychology.* New York: Free Press, 1965.

Brown, R. *A first language, the early stages.* Cambridge, Mass.: Harvard University Press, 1973.

Bruner, J. S. *The process of education.* Cambridge, Mass.: Harvard University Press, 1960.

Bruner, J. S. The growth of mind. *American Psychologist,* 1965, *20,* 1007–1017.

Bruner, J. S. Organization of early skilled action. *Child Development,* 1973, *44,* 1–11.

Bruner, J. Learning how to do things with words. In J. Bruner & A. Garton (Eds.), *Human growth and development.* Oxford, England: Oxford University Press, 1978.

Bryer, K. B. The Amish way of death. *American Psychologist,* 1979, *34,* 255–261.

Bullowa, M. *Before speech: The beginning of interpersonal communication.* Cambridge, England: Cambridge University Press, 1979.

Buros, O. K. *The eighth mental measurements yearbook.* Lincoln, Neb.: Gryphon Press, 1978.

Buss, A. H., & Plomin, R. *A temperament theory of personality.* New York: Wiley, 1975.

Buss, A. H., Plomin, R., & Willerman, L. The inheritance of temperament. *Journal of Personality,* 1973, *41,* 513–524.

Buss, D. M., Block, J. H., & Block, J. Preschool activity level: Personality correlates and developmental implications. *Child Development,* 1980, *51,* 401–408.

Byrne, D. Attitudes and attraction. In L. Berkowitz (Ed.), *Advances in experimental social psychology* (Vol. 4). New York: Academic Press, 1969.

Byrne, D., & Griffitt, W. B. A developmental investigation of the law of attraction. *Journal of Personality and Social Psychology,* 1966, *4,* 699–702.

Cairns, R. B. Beyond social attachment: The dynamics of interactional development. In T. Alloway, P. Pliner, & L. Krames (Eds.), *Attachment behavior.* New York: Plenum, 1977.

Campbell, B. *Human evolution* (2nd ed.). Chicago: Aldine, 1974.

Campbell, J. D. Peer relations in childhood. In M. L. Hoffman & L. W. Hoffman (Eds.), *Review of child development research* (Vol. 1). New York: Russell Sage Foundation, 1964.

Campos, J. J., Langer, A., & Krowitz, A. Cardiac responses on the visual cliff in prelocomotor infants. *Science,* 1970, *170,* 196–197.

Capon, N., & Kuhn, D. Logical reasoning in the supermarket: Adult females' use of a proportional reasoning strategy in an everyday context. *Developmental Psychology,* 1979, *15,* 450–452.

Carmichael, L. The onset and early development of behavior. In L. Carmichael (Ed.), *Manual of child psychology* (2nd ed.). New York: Wiley, 1954.

Case, R. Intellectual development from birth to adulthood: A neo-Piagetian interpretation. In R. S. Siegler (Ed.), *Children's thinking: What develops?* Hillsdale, N.J.: Erlbaum, 1978.

Case, R. The underlying mechanism of intellectual development. In J. R. Kirby & J. B. Biggs (Eds.), *Cognition, development, and instruction.* New York: Academic Press, 1980.

Chandler, M. J. Egocentrism and antisocial behavior: The assessment and training of social perspective-taking skills. *Developmental Psychology,* 1973, *9,* 326–332.

Chandler, M. J., Greenspan, S., & Barenboim, C. Judgments of intentionality in response to videotaped and verbally presented moral dilemmas: The me-

dium is the message. *Child Development,* 1973, *44,* 315–320.

Chandler, M., Greenspan, S., & Barenboim, C. Assessment and training of role-taking and referential communication skills in institutionalized emotionally disturbed children. *Developmental Psychology,* 1974, *10,* 546–553.

Charlesworth, R., & Hartup, W. W. Positive reinforcement in the nursery school peer group. *Child Development,* 1967, *38,* 993–1002.

Charlesworth, W. R. Surprise and cognitive development. In D. Elkind & J. H. Flavell (Eds.), *Studies in cognitive development.* New York: Oxford University Press, 1969.

Charlesworth, W. R., & Kreutzer, M. A. Facial expressions of infants and children. In P. Ekman (Ed.), *Darwin and facial expression.* New York: Academic Press, 1973.

Children's Television Workshop. *New Sesame Street study shows impact of deaf performers on viewers.* New York: Children's Television Workshop, 1979.

Chomsky, N. *Aspects of the theory of syntax.* Cambridge, Mass.: MIT Press, 1965.

Chomsky, N. The formal nature of language. In E. H. Lenneberg (Ed.), *Biological foundations of language.* New York: Wiley, 1967.

Chukovsky, K. *From two to five.* Berkeley: University of California Press, 1963.

Cicchetti, D., & Sroufe, L. A. An organizational view of affect: Illustration from the study of Down's syndrome infants. In M. Lewis & L. A. Rosenblum (Eds.), *The development of affect.* New York: Plenum, 1978.

Clarizio, H. F., & McCoy, G. F. *Behavior disorders in children* (2nd ed.). New York: Crowell, 1976.

Clark, E. V. What's in a word? On the child's acquisition of semantics in his first language. In T. E. Moore (Ed.), *Cognitive development and the acquisition of language.* New York: Academic Press, 1973.

Clarke, A. M., & Clarke, A. D. B. *Early experience: Myth and evidence.* New York: Free Press, 1976.

Clarke-Stewart, K. A. And daddy makes three: The father's impact on mother and young child. *Child Development,* 1978, *49,* 466–478. (a)

Clarke-Stewart, K. A. Popular primers for parents. *American Psychologist,* 1978, *33,* 359–369. (b)

Clausen, J. A. Family structure, socialization, and personality. In L. W. Hoffman & M. L. Hoffman (Eds.), *Review of child development research* (Vol. 2). New York: Russell Sage Foundation, 1966.

Cobb, H. V. Role wishes and general wishes of children and adolescents. *Child Development,* 1954, *25,* 161–171.

Cohen, L. B., DeLoache, J. S., & Strauss, M. L. Infant visual perception. In J. D. Osofsky (Ed.), *Handbook of infant development.* New York: Wiley, 1979.

Cohen, L. B., & Gelber, E. R. Infant visual memory. In L. B. Cohen & P. Salapatek (Eds.), *Infant perception: From sensation to cognition* (Vol. 1). New York: Academic Press, 1975.

Cohen, L. B., & Salapatek, P. (Eds.). *Infant perception: From sensation to cognition* (2 vols.). New York: Academic Press, 1975.

Cohen, L. J. The operational definition of human attachment. *Psychological Bulletin,* 1974, *81,* 207–217.

Cohen, R., & Schuepfer, T. The representation of landmarks and routes. *Child Development,* 1980, *51,* 1065–1071.

Colby, A. Evolution of a moral-developmental theory. *New Directions in Child Development,* 1978, *2,* 89–104.

Coleman, J. Children, schools, and the informational environment. In M. Greenberger (Ed.), *Computers, communications, and the public interest.* Baltimore: Johns Hopkins University Press, 1971.

Collis, G. Describing the structure of social interaction in infancy. In M. Bullowa (Ed.), *Before speech: The beginning of interpersonal communication.* Cambridge, England: Cambridge University Press, 1979.

Comstock, G., Chaffee, S., Katzman, N., McCombs, M., & Roberts, D. *Television and human behavior.* New York: Columbia University Press, 1978.

Condon, W. S. Neonatal entrainment and enculturation. In M. Bullowa (Ed.), *Before speech: The beginning of interpersonal communication.* Cambridge, England: Cambridge University Press, 1979.

Condon, W. S., & Sander, L. W. Neonate movement in synchronization with adult speech: Interactional participation and language acquisition. *Science,* 1974, *183,* 99–101.

Condry, J. Truth in advertising. *Contemporary Psychology,* 1978, *23,* 854–855.

Connolly, K. Factors influencing the learning of manual skills by young children. In R. A. Hinde & J. Stevenson-Hinde (Eds.), *Constraints on learning.* London: Academic Press, 1973.

Connolly, K. J., & Bruner, J. *The growth of competence.* London: Academic Press, 1974.

Constantinople, A. Masculinity-femininity: An exception to a famous dictim? *Psychological Bulletin,* 1973, *80,* 389–407.

Corder-Bolz, C. R. Mediation: The role of significant others. *Journal of Communication,* 1980, *30,* 106–118.

Corrigan, R. Cognitive correlates of language: Differential criteria yield differential results. *Child Development,* 1979, *50,* 617–631.

Cowan, P. A. *Piaget: With feeling.* New York: Holt, Rinehart & Winston, 1978.

Cowan, P. A., Langer, J., Heavenrich, J., & Nathanson, M. Social learning and Piaget's cognitive theory of moral development. *Journal of Personality and Social Psychology,* 1969, *11,* 261–274.

Cowart, B. J. Development of taste perception in humans: Sensitivity and preference throughout the life span. *Psychological Bulletin,* 1981, *90,* 43–73.

Cox, C. M. *Genetic studies of genius* (Vol. 2). *The early mental traits of three hundred geniuses.* Stanford, Calif.: Stanford University Press, 1926.

Cratty, B. J. *Perceptual and motor development in infants and children.* New York: Macmillan, 1970.

Crockenberg, S. B. Infant irritability, maternal responsiveness, and social support influences on the security of infant-mother attachment. *Child Development,* 1981, *52,* 857–865.

Cronbach, L. J. *Essentials of psychological testing* (3rd ed.). New York: Harper & Row, 1970.

Damon, W. *The social world of children.* San Francisco: Jossey-Bass, 1977.

Damon, W. (Ed.). Social cognition. *New Directions for Child Development,* 1978 (No. 1).

D'Andrade, R. G. Sex differences and cultural institutions. In E. E. Maccoby (Ed.), *The development of sex differences.* Stanford, Calif.: Stanford University Press, 1966.

Darlington, R. B., Royce, J. M., Snipper, A. S., Murray, H. W., & Lazar, I. Preschool programs and later school competence of children from low income families. *Science,* 1980, *208,* 202–204.

Darwin, C. A biographical sketch of an infant. *Mind,* 1877, *2,* 286–294.

Dasen, P. R. *Piagetian psychology: Cross-cultural contributions.* New York: Gardner Press, 1977.

DeCasper, A. J., & Fifer, W. P. Of human bonding: Newborns prefer their mothers' voices. *Science,* 1980, *208,* 1174–1176.

Deci, E. L. *Intrinsic motivation.* New York: Plenum, 1975.

DeLucia, L. A. *Stimulus preference and discrimination learning in children.* Unpublished doctoral dissertation, Brown University, 1963.

Dempster, F. N. Memory span: Sources of individual and developmental differences. *Psychological Bulletin,* 1981, *89,* 63–100.

Dennis, W. Causes of retardation among institutional children: Iran. *Journal of Genetic Psychology,* 1960, *96,* 47–59.

Dennis, W., & Dennis, M. G. The effect of cradling practice upon the onset of walking in Hopi children. *Journal of Genetic Psychology,* 1940, *56,* 77–86.

Dennis, W., & Najarian, P. Infant development under environmental handicap. *Psychological Monographs,* 1957, *71*(7, Whole No. 436).

DeVries, R. Constancy of genetic identity in the years three to six. *Monographs of the Society for Research in Child Development,* 1969, *34*(3, Serial No. 127).

Diehl, R. L. Feature detectors for speech: A critical reappraisal. *Psychological Bulletin,* 1981, *89,* 1–18.

Doering, C. H. The endocrine system. In O. G. Brim, Jr., & J. Kagan (Eds.), *Constancy and change in human development.* Cambridge, Mass.: Harvard University Press, 1980.

Doll, E. A. *The measurement of social competence: A manual for the Vineland Social Maturity Scale.* Minneapolis: Educational Testing Bureau, 1953.

Dollard, J., Doob, L. W., Miller, N. E., Mowrer, O. H., & Sears, R. R. *Frustration and aggression.* New Haven, Conn.: Yale University Press, 1939.

Dollard, J., & Miller, N. E. *Personality and psychotherapy.* New York: McGraw-Hill, 1950.

Dorr, A., Graves, S. B., & Phelps, E. Television literacy for young children. *Journal of Communication,* 1980, *30,* 71–83.

Douvan, E., & Adelson, J. *The adolescent experience.* New York: Wiley, 1966.

Dowd, J. M. *The temporal organization of limb movements in the human infant.* Unpublished doctoral dissertation, University of Massachusetts, 1981.

Dreeben, R. *On what is learned in school.* Reading, Mass.: Addison-Wesley, 1968.

Duffy, E. *Activation and behavior.* New York: Wiley, 1962.

Duncker, K. Experimental modification of children's food preferences through social suggestion. *Journal of Abnormal and Social Psychology,* 1938, *33,* 489–507.

Durkheim, E. *The division of labor in society.* Glencoe, Ill.: Free Press, 1933. (Originally published, 1893.)

Dweck, C. S. The role of expectations and attributions in the alleviation of learned helplessness. *Journal of Personality and Social Psychology,* 1975, *31,* 674–685.

Eckerman, C. O., Whatley, J. L., & Kutz, S. L. Growth of social play with peers during the second year of life. *Developmental Psychology,* 1975, *11,* 42–49.

Edgerton, R. B. *Mental retardation.* Cambridge, Mass.: Harvard University Press, 1979.

Egeland, B., & Sroufe, L. A. Attachment and early maltreatment. *Child Development,* 1981, *52,* 44–52.

Ehly, S. W., & Larsen, S. C. *Peer tutoring for individualized instruction.* Boston: Allyn & Bacon, 1980.

Ehrhardt, A. A., & Baker, S. W. Fetal androgens, human central nervous system differentiation, and behavioral sex differences. In R. Friedman, R. Richart, & R. Vande Wiele (Eds.), *Sex differences in behavior.* New York: Wiley, 1974.

Eibl-Eibesfeldt, I. *Love and hate.* New York: Holt, Rinehart & Winston, 1972.

Eimas, P. D. Speech perception in early infancy. In L. B. Cohen & P. Salapatek (Eds.), *Infant perception: From sensation to cognition* (Vol. 2). New York: Academic Press, 1975.

Eimas, P. D., Siqueland, E. P., Jusczyk, P., & Vigorito, J. Speech perception in infants. *Science,* 1971, *171,* 303–306.

Eisenberg, L. Child psychiatry: The past quarter century. *American Journal of Orthopsychiatry,* 1969, *39,* 389–401.

Eisenberg, R. B. *Auditory competence in early life.* Baltimore: University Park Press, 1976.

Ekman, P. Universals and cultural differences in facial expressions of emotion. In J. K. Cole (Ed.), *Nebraska Symposium on Motivation* (Vol. 19). Lincoln: University of Nebraska Press, 1972.

Ekman, P., Roper, G., & Hager, J. C. Deliberate facial movement. *Child Development,* 1980, *51,* 886–891.

Elkind, D. Egocentrism in adolescence. *Child Development,* 1967, *38,* 1025–1034.

Ellis, S., Rogoff, B., & Cromer, C. C. Age segregation in children's social interactions. *Developmental Psychology,* 1981, *17,* 399–407.

Emde, R. N., Gaensbauer, T. J., & Harmon, R. J. *Emotional expression in infancy.* New York: International Universities Press, 1976.

Eme, R. F. Sex differences in childhood psychopathology. *Psychological Bulletin,* 1979, *86,* 574–595.

Engen, T., & Lipsitt, L. P. Decrement and recovery of responses to olfactory stimuli in the human neonate. *Journal of Comparative and Physiological Psychology,* 1965, *59,* 312–316.

Ennis, R. H. An alternative to Piaget's conceptualization of logical competence. *Child Development,* 1976, *47,* 903–919.

Ennis, R. H. Conceptualization of children's logical competence: Piaget's proportional logic and an alternative proposal. In L. S. Siegel & C. J. Brainerd (Eds.), *Alternatives to Piaget.* New York: Academic Press, 1978.

Enright, M. K. The role of context similarity in memory reactivation and generalization in 3-month-old infants. Paper presented at the Meeting of the Society for Research in Child Development, Boston, April 1981.

Erikson, E. *Childhood and society* (2nd ed.). New York: Norton, 1963.

Eron, L. D., Lefkowitz, M. M., Huesmann, L. R., & Walder, L. O. Does television violence cause aggression? *American Psychologist,* 1972, *27,* 253–263.

Etaugh, C. Effects of nonmaternal care of children: Research evidence and popular views. *American Psychologist,* 1980, *35,* 309–319.

Etzel, B. C., & Gewirtz, J. L. Experimental modification of caretaker-maintained high rate operant crying in a 6- and a 20-week-old infant: Extinction of crying with reinforcement of eye contact and smiling. *Journal of Experimental Child Psychology,* 1967, *5,* 303–317.

Eysenck, H. J. *The structure of human personality.* London: Methuen, 1953.

Eysenck, H. J. *The dynamics of anxiety and hysteria.* New York: Praeger, 1957.

Fagen, J. W., Yengo, L. A., Rovee-Collier, C. K., & Enright, M. K. Reactivation of a visual discrimination in early infancy. *Developmental Psychology,* 1981, *17,* 266–274.

Fantz, R. L. The origin of form perception. *Scientific American,* 1961, *204,* 66–72.

Fantz, R. L., Fagan, J. F., III, & Miranda, S. B. Early visual selectivity. In L. B. Cohen & P. Salapatek (Eds.), *Infant perception: From sensation to cognition* (Vol. 1). New York: Academic Press, 1975.

Farnham-Diggory, S. But how do we shape vigorous behavioral analysis? *Developmental Review,* 1981, *1,* 58–60.

Federman, E. J., & Yang, R. K. A critique of obstetrical pain-reliever drugs as predictors of infant behavioral variability. *Child Development,* 1976, *47,* 294–296.

Fein, G., Johnson, D., Kosson, N., Stork, L., & Wasserman, L. Sex stereotypes and preferences in the toy choices of 20-month-old boys and girls. *Developmental Psychology,* 1975, *11,* 527–528.

Feldman, R. S., Devin-Sheehan, L., & Allen, V. L. Children tutoring children: A critical review of research. In V. L. Allen (Ed.), *Children as teachers.* New York: Academic Press, 1976.

Fenson, L., & Ramsay, D. S. Decentration and integration of the child's play in the second year. *Child Development,* 1980, *51,* 171–178.

Fernald, A. Four-month-olds prefer to listen to "motherese." Paper presented at the Meeting of the Society for Research in Child Development, Boston, April 1981.

Fernald, A., & Kuhl, P. Fundamental frequency as an acoustic determinant of infant preference for motherese. Paper presented at the Meeting of the Society for Research in Child Development, Boston, April 1981.

Finkelstein, N. W., Dent, C., Gallacher, K., & Ramey, C. T. Social behavior of infants and toddlers in a day-care environment. *Developmental Psychology,* 1978, *14,* 257–262.

Finkelstein, N. W., & Ramey, C. T. Learning to control the environment in infancy. *Child Development,* 1977, *48,* 806–819.

Fischer, K. W. A theory of cognitive development: The control and construction of hierarchies of skills. *Psychological Review,* 1980, *87,* 477–531.

Fishbein, H. D. *Evolution, development, and children's learning.* Pacific Palisades, Calif.: Goodyear, 1976.

Fishbein, M., & Ajzen, I. *Belief, attitude, intention and behavior: An introduction to theory and research.* Reading, Mass.: Addison-Wesley, 1975.

Fiske, D. W., & Maddi, S. R. *Functions of varied experience.* Homewood, Ill.: Dorsey, 1961.

Fitzgerald, H. E., & Brackbill, Y. Classical conditioning in infancy: Development and constraints. *Psychological Bulletin,* 1976, *83,* 353–373.

Flapan, D. *Children's understanding of social interaction.* New York: Teachers College Press, 1967.

Flavell, J. H. *The developmental psychology of Jean Piaget.* Princeton, N.J.: Van Nostrand, 1963.

Flavell, J. H. *Cognitive development.* Englewood Cliffs, N.J.: Prentice-Hall, 1977.

Flavell, J. H. On cognitive development. Paper presented at the Meeting of the Society for Research in Child Development, Boston, April 1981.

Flavell, J. H., Beach, D. R., & Chinsky, J. M. Spontaneous verbal rehearsal in a memory task as a function of age. *Child Development,* 1966, *37,* 283–299.

Flavell, J. H., & Wellman, H. M. Metamemory. In R. V. Kail & J. W. Hagen (Eds.), *Perspectives on the development of memory and cognition.* Hillsdale, N.J.: Erlbaum, 1977.

Forbes, D. Recent research on children's social cognition: A brief review. In W. Damon (Ed.), *New directions for child development,* 1978 (No. 1).

Ford, M. E. The construct validity of egocentrism. *Psychological Bulletin,* 1979, *86,* 1169–1188.

Forgays, D. G. (Ed.). *Primary prevention of psychopathology* (Vol. 2). *Environmental influences.* Hanover, N.H.: University Press of New England, 1978.

Fowler, W. Cognitive differentiation and developmental learning. In H. W. Reese & L. P. Lipsitt (Eds.), *Advances in behavior and development* (Vol. 15). New York: Academic Press, 1980.

Fowler, W., & Swenson, A. The influence of early language stimulation on development: Four studies. *Genetic Psychology Monographs,* 1979, *100,* 73–109.

Freedman, D. G. *Human infancy: An evolutionary perspective.* Hillsdale, N.J.: Erlbaum, 1974.

Freedman, D. G. The development of social hierarchies. In L. Levi (Ed.), *Society, stress and disease* (Vol. 2). *Childhood and adolescence.* London: Oxford University Press, 1975.

Freedman, D. G., Loring, C. B., & Martin, R. B. Emotional behavior and personality development. In Y. Brackbill (Ed.), *Infancy and early childhood.* New York: Free Press, 1967.

Freud, A., & Dann, S. An experiment in group upbringing. *The Psychoanalytic Study of the Child, 6,* 127–163.

Freud, S. The passing of the Oedipus complex. In S. Freud, *Collected papers* (Vol. 2). London: Hogarth, 1950. (Originally published, 1924.)

Freud, S. Formulations regarding the two principles in mental functioning. In S. Freud, *Collected papers* (Vol. 4). London: Hogarth, 1953. (Originally published, 1911.)

Freud, S. *An outline of psychoanalysis.* New York: Norton, 1963. (Originally published, 1940.)

Friedrich, L. K., & Stein, A. H. Aggressive and prosocial television programs and the natural behavior of preschool children. *Monographs of the Society for Research in Child Development,* 1973,

38 (4, Serial No. 151).

Friedrich, L. K., & Stein, A. Prosocial television and young children: The effects of verbal labeling and role playing on learning and behavior. *Child Development,* 1975, *46,* 27–38.

Fries, M., & Woolf, P. Some hypotheses on the role of the congenital activity type in personality development. *The Psychoanalytic Study of the Child,* 1953, *8,* 48–62.

Frost, J. L., & Klein, B. L. *Children's play and playgrounds.* Boston: Allyn & Bacon, 1979.

Fuller, J. L. Experiential deprivation and later behavior. *Science,* 1967, *158,* 1645–1652.

Fuller J. L., & Thompson, W. R. *Foundations of behavior genetics.* St. Louis: Mosby, 1978.

Gagné, R. M. Contributions of learning to human development. *Psychological Review,* 1968, *75,* 177–191.

Gagné, R. M. *The conditions of learning* (3rd ed.). New York: Holt, Rinehart & Winston, 1977.

Ganz, L. Orientation in visual space by neonates and its modification by visual deprivation. In A. H. Riesen (Ed.), *The developmental neuropsychology of sensory deprivation.* New York: Academic Press, 1975.

Garbarino, J. The impact of anticipated reward upon cross-age tutoring. *Journal of Personality and Social Psychology,* 1975, *32,* 421–428.

Garber, H., & Heber, R. *The Milwaukee Project: Early intervention as a technique to prevent mental retardation.* Storrs: University of Connecticut Technical Paper, 1973.

Garcia-Coll, C. T. Psychophysiological correlatives of a tendency toward inhibition in infants. Paper presented at the Meeting of the Society for Research in Child Development, Boston, April 1981.

Garn, S. M. Continuity and change in maturational timing. In O. G. Brim, Jr., & J. Kagan (Eds.), *Constancy and change in human development.* Cambridge, Mass.: Harvard University Press, 1980.

Garrett, C. S., Ein, P. L., & Tremaine, L. The development of gender stereotyping of adult occupations in elementary school children. *Child Development,* 1977, *48,* 507–512.

Gartner, A., Kohler, M. C., & Riessman, F. *Children teach children.* New York: Harper & Row, 1971.

Geertz, C. *The interpretation of culture.* New York: Basic Books, 1973.

Geertz, H. *The Javanese family.* New York: Free Press, 1961.

Gelman, R. Cognitive development. *Annual Review of Psychology,* 1978, *29,* 297–332.

Gelman, R. Preschool thought. *American Psychologist,* 1979, *34,* 900–905.

Gelman, R., & Gallistel, C. R. *The child's understanding of number.* Cambridge, Mass.: Harvard University Press, 1978.

Gelman, R., & Shatz, M. Appropriate speech adjustments: The operation of conversational constraints on talk to two-year-olds. In M. Lewis & L. A. Rosenblum (Eds.), *Interaction, conversation, and the development of language.* New York: Wiley, 1977.

Gesell, A. The ontogenesis of infant behavior. In L. Carmichael (Ed.), *Manual of child psychology* (2nd ed.). New York: Wiley, 1954.

Gesell, A., & Amatruda, C. S. *Developmental diagnosis* (2nd ed.). New York: Harper, 1947.

Gesell, A., & Thompson, H. Learning and growth in identical twin infants: An experimental study by the method of co-twin control. *Genetic Psychology Monographs,* 1929, *6,* 1–124.

Gewirtz, J. L. Deprivation and satiation of social stimuli as determinants of their reinforcing efficacy. In J. P. Hill (Ed.), *Minnesota Symposia on Child Psychology* (Vol. 1). Minneapolis: University of Minnesota Press, 1967.

Gewirtz, J. L., & Boyd, E. F. Experiments on mother-infant interaction underlying mutual attachment acquisition: The infant conditions the mother. In T. Alloway, P. Pliner, & L. Krames (Eds.), *Attachment behavior.* New York: Plenum, 1977.

Gibbs, J. Kohlberg's stages of moral judgment: A constructive critique. *Harvard Educational Review,* 1977, *47,* 42–61.

Gibson, E. J. *Principles of perceptual learning and development.* New York: Appleton-Century-Crofts, 1969.

Gibson, E. J., & Olum, V. Experimental methods of studying perception in children. In P. H. Mussen (Ed.), *Handbook of research methods in child development.* New York: Wiley, 1960.

Gibson, E. J., & Walk, R. D. The "visual cliff." *Scientific American,* 1960, *202,* 64–71.

Gibson, J. J. *An ecological approach to visual perception.* Boston: Houghton Mifflin, 1979.

Gleitman, L. R., Gleitman, H., & Shipley, E. F. The emergence of the child as grammarian. *Cognition,* 1972, *1,* 137–164.

Glick, P. C. Updating the life cycle of the family. *Journal of Marriage and the Family,* 1977, *39,* 5–13.

Glucksberg, S., Krauss, R., & Higgins, E. T. The development of referential communication skills. In F. D. Horowitz (Ed.), *Review of child development research* (Vol. 4). Chicago: University of Chicago Press, 1975.

Golann, S. E., & Eisdorfer, C. *Handbook of community mental health.* New York: Appleton-Century-Crofts, 1972.

Goldsmith, H. H., & East, P. L. Parental perception of infant temperament: Validity and genetics. Paper presented at the Meeting of the Society for Research in Child Development, Boston, April 1981.

Goldsmith, H. H., & Gottesman, I. I. Origins of variation in behavioral style: A longitudinal study of temperament in young twins. *Child Development,* 1981, *52,* 91–103.

Goode, W. J. *World revolution and family patterns.*

New York: Free Press, 1963.

Goodenough, F. L. *Anger in young children*. Minneapolis: University of Minnesota Press, 1931.

Goodnow, J. J. The nature of intelligent behavior: Questions raised by cross-cultural studies. In L. B. Resnick (Ed.), *The nature of intelligence*. Hillsdale, N.J.: Erlbaum, 1976.

Gossett, J. T., Barnhart, F. D., Lewis, J. M., & Phillips, V. A. Follow-up of adolescents treated in a psychiatric hospital: Predictors of outcome. *Archives of General Psychiatry*, 1977, *34*, 1037–1042.

Gottfried, A. E., & Katz, P. A. Influence of belief, race, and sex similarities between child observers and models on attitudes and observational learning. *Child Development*, 1977, *48*, 1395–1400.

Gottman, J. M., & Parkhurst, J. T. A developmental theory of friendship and acquaintanceship processes. In W. A. Collins (Ed.), *Minnesota Symposia on Child Psychology* (Vol. 13). Hillsdale, N.J.: Erlbaum, 1980.

Graham, F. K., & Jackson, J. C. Arousal systems and infant heart rate responses. In H. W. Reese & L. P. Lipsitt (Eds.), *Advances in child development and behavior* (Vol. 5). New York: Academic Press, 1970.

Gratch, G. Recent studies based on Piaget's view of object concept development. In L. B. Cohen & P. Salapatek (Eds.), *Infant perception: From sensation to cognition* (Vol. 2). New York: Academic Press, 1975.

Gratch, G. The development of thought and language in infancy. In J. D. Osofsky (Ed.), *Handbook of infant development*. New York: Wiley, 1979.

Graziano, A. M., De Giovanni, I. S., & Garcia, K. A. Behavioral treatment of children's fears: A review. *Psychological Bulletin*, 1979, *86*, 804–830.

Gump, P. V. Ecological psychology and children. In E. M. Hetherington (Ed.), *Review of child development research* (Vol. 5). Chicago: University of Chicago Press, 1975.

Gunnar-vonGnechten, M. R. Changing a frightening toy into a pleasant toy by allowing the infant to control its actions. *Developmental Psychology*, 1978, *14*, 157–162.

Hall, R. V., & Broden, M. Behavior changes in brain-injured children through social reinforcement. *Journal of Experimental Child Psychology*, 1967, *5*, 469–472.

Halliday, M. A. K. *Learning how to mean: Exploration in the development of language*. London: Arnold, 1975.

Halliday, M. A. K. One child's protolanguage. In M. Bullowa (Ed.), *Before speech: The beginning of interpersonal communication*. Cambridge, England: Cambridge University Press, 1979.

Hallinan, M. Recent advances in sociometry. In S. R. Asher & J. M. Gottman (Eds.), *The development of children's friendships*. Cambridge, England: Cambridge University Press, 1981.

Halverson, C. F., Jr., & Waldrop, M. F. Relations between preschool barrier behaviors and early school-age measures of coping, imagination, and verbal development. *Developmental Psychology*, 1974, *10*, 716–720.

Halverson, H. M. An experimental study of prehension by means of systematic cinema records. *Genetic Psychology Monographs*, 1931, *10* (No. 3–3), 110–286.

Hamburg, D. A., & Lunde, D. T. Sex hormones in the development of sex differences in human behavior. In E. E. Maccoby (Ed.), *The development of sex differences*. Stanford, Calif.: Stanford University Press, 1966.

Hardwick, D. A., McIntyre, C. W., & Pick, H. L., Jr. The content and manipulation of cognitive maps in children and adults. *Monographs of the Society for Research in Child Development*, 1976, *41* (3, Serial No. 166).

Harlow, H. F. The formation of learning sets. *Psychological Review*, 1949, *56*, 51–65.

Harlow, H. F. The nature of love. *American Psychologist*, 1958, *13*, 673–685.

Harlow, H. F. *Learning to love*. San Francisco: Albion, 1971.

Harper, L. V., & Sanders, K. M. The effect of adults' eating on young children's acceptance of unfamiliar foods. *Journal of Experimental Child Psychology*, 1975, *20*, 206–214. (a)

Harper, L. V., & Sanders, K. M. Preschool children's use of space: Sex differences in outdoor play. *Developmental Psychology*, 1975, *11*, 119. (b)

Harris, J. A., Jackson, C. M., Paterson, D. G., & Scammon, R. E. (Eds.). *The measurement of man*. Minneapolis: University of Minnesota Press, 1930.

Harris, P. H. Development of search and object permanence during infancy. *Psychological Bulletin*, 1975, *82*, 332–344.

Hart, R. *Children's experience of place*. New York: Irvington, 1979.

Harter, S. Pleasure derived by children from cognitive challenge and mastery. *Child Development*, 1974, *45*, 661–669.

Harter, S., Shultz, T. R., & Blum, B. Smiling in children as a function of their sense of mastery. *Journal of Experimental Child Psychology*, 1971, *12*, 396–404.

Hartup, W. W. Peer interaction and social organization. In P. H. Mussen (Ed.), *Carmichael's manual of child psychology* (3rd ed.). New York: Wiley, 1970.

Hartup, W. W. Aggression in childhood: Developmental perspectives. *American Psychologist*, 1974, *29*, 336–341.

Hartup, W. W. Peer interaction and the behavioral development of the individual child. In E. Schopler & R. J. Reichler (Eds.), *Child development, deviations, and treatment*. New York: Plenum, 1976.

Hartup, W. W. The social worlds of childhood. *American Psychologist*, 1979, *34*, 944–950.

Hayden, A. H., & Haring, G. Early intervention for high risk infants and young children: Programs for Down's syndrome children. In T. D. Tjossem (Ed.), *Intervention strategies for high risk infants and young children*. Baltimore: University Park Press, 1976.

Hayes, K. J. Genes, drives, and intellect. *Psychological Reports*, 1962, *10*, 299–342.

Hayes, L. A., & Watson, J. S. Neonatal imitation: Fact or artifact? *Developmental Psychology*, 1981, *17*, 655–660.

Hebb, D. O. On the nature of fear. *Psychological Review*, 1946, *53*, 259–276.

Hebb, D. O. *The organization of behavior*. New York: Wiley, 1949.

Hebb, D. O. Drives and the C.N.S. (conceptual nervous system). *Psychological Review*, 1955, *62*, 243–254.

Heber, F. R. Sociocultural mental retardation: A longitudinal study. In D. G. Forgays (Ed.), *Primary prevention of psychopathology* (Vol. 2). *Environmental influences*. Hanover, N.H.: University Press of New England, 1978.

Heider, F. *The psychology of interpersonal relations*. New York: Wiley, 1958.

Herzog, E., & Sudia, C. E. Children in fatherless families. In B. M. Caldwell & H. N. Ricciuti (Eds.), *Review of child development research* (Vol. 3). Chicago: University of Chicago Press, 1973.

Hess, E. H. Ethology and developmental psychology. In P. H. Mussen (Ed.), *Carmichael's manual of child psychology* (3rd ed.). New York: Wiley, 1970.

Hess, R. D. Social class and ethnic influences upon socialization. In P. H. Mussen (Ed.), *Carmichael's manual of child psychology* (3rd ed.). New York: Wiley, 1970.

Hess, R., & Shipman, V. Cognitive elements in maternal behavior. *Minnesota Symposia on Child Psychology* (Vol. 1). Minneapolis: University of Minnesota Press, 1967.

Hetherington, E. M. Divorce: A child's perspective. *American Psychologist*, 1979, *34*, 851–858.

Hetherington, E. M., Cox, M., & Cox, R. The aftermath of divorce. In J. H. Stevens & M. Mathews (Eds.), *Mother-child, father-child relations*. Washington, D.C.: National Association for the Education of Young Children, 1978.

Hetherington, E. M., & Parke, R. D. *Child psychology: A contemporary viewpoint* (2nd ed.). New York: McGraw-Hill, 1979.

Hiatt, S. W., Campos, J. J., & Emde, R. N. Facial patterning and infant emotional expression: Happiness, surprise, and fear. *Child Development*, 1979, *50*, 1020–1035.

Hilgard, E. R., & Bower, G. H. *Theories of learning* (3rd ed.). New York: Appleton-Century-Crofts, 1966.

Hinde, R. A., & Stevenson-Hinde, J. *Constraints on learning*. New York: Academic Press, 1973.

Hobbs, S. A., Moguin, L. E., Tyroler, M., & Lahey, B. B. Cognitive behavior therapy with children: Has clinical utility been demonstrated? *Psychological Bulletin*, 1980, *87*, 147–165.

Hoffman, L. W. Maternal employment: 1979. *American Psychologist*, 1979, *34*, 859–865.

Hoffman, M. L. Altruistic behavior and the parent-child relationship. *Journal of Personality and Social Psychology*, 1975, *31*, 937–943.

Hoffman, M. L. Toward a theory of empathetic arousal and development. In M. Lewis & L. A. Rosenblum (Eds.), *The development of affect*. New York: Plenum, 1978.

Hollingworth, L. *Children above 180 IQ*. New York: Harcourt, Brace & World, 1942.

Holmberg, M. C. The development of social interchange patterns from 12 to 42 months. *Child Development*, 1980, *51*, 448–456.

Honzik, M. P. Value and limitations of infant tests. In M. Lewis (Ed.), *Origins of intelligence*. New York: Plenum, 1976.

Horowitz, F. D. (Ed.). Visual attention, auditory stimulation, and language discrimination in young infants. *Monographs of the Society for Research in Child Development*, 1974, *39* (5, Serial No. 158).

Horowitz, F. D., & Paden, L. Y. The effectiveness of environmental programs. In B. M. Caldwell & H. N. Ricciuti (Eds.), *Review of child development research* (Vol. 3). Chicago: University of Chicago Press, 1973.

Houston, S. H. A re-examination of some assumptions about the language of the disadvantaged child. *Child Development*, 1970, *41*, 947–963.

Hoving, K. L., Spencer, T., Robb, K. Y., & Schultz, D. Developmental changes in visual information processing. In P. A. Ornstein (Ed.), *Memory development in children*. Hillsdale, N.J.: Erlbaum, 1978.

Humphrey, G. Introduction to *The wild boy of Aveyron*. New York: Appleton-Century-Crofts, 1962.

Hunt, J. McV. *Intelligence and experience*. New York: Ronald Press, 1961.

Hunt, J. McV. Piaget's observations as a source of hypotheses concerning motivation. *Merrill-Palmer Quarterly*, 1963, *9*, 263–275.

Hunt, J. McV. Sequential order and plasticity in early psychological development. In M. H. Appel & L. S. Goldberg (Eds.), *Topics in cognitive development* (Vol. 1). *Equilibration: Theory, research, and application*. New York: Plenum, 1977.

Hunt, J. McV. Psychological development: Early experience. *Annual Review of Psychology*, 1979, *30*, 103–143.

Hutt, C. *Males and females*. Baltimore: Penguin, 1972.

Inhelder, B., & Piaget, J. *The growth of logical thinking from childhood to adolescence*. New York: Basic Books, 1958.

Irwin, D. M., & Bushnell, M. M. *Observational strategies for child study.* New York: Holt, Rinehart & Winston, 1980.

Itard, J. M. P. *The wild boy of Aveyron.* New York: Appleton-Century-Crofts, 1962. (Originally published, 1806.)

Izard, C. E. On the development of emotions and emotion-cognition relationships in infancy. In M. Lewis & L. A. Rosenblum (Eds.), *The development of affect.* New York: Plenum, 1978.

Izard, C. E. Emotions as motivations: An evolutionary-developmental perspective. In R. A. Dienstbier (Ed.), *Nebraska Symposium on Motivation* (Vol. 26). Lincoln: University of Nebraska Press, 1979.

Izard, C. E., Huebner, R. R., Rissner, D., McGinnes, G. C., & Dougherty, L. M. The young infant's ability to produce discrete emotion expressions. *Developmental Psychology,* 1980, *16,* 132–140.

Jackson, P. W. *Life in classrooms.* New York: Holt, Rinehart & Winston, 1968.

Jacobson, J. L. The role of inanimate objects in early peer interaction. *Child Development,* 1981, *52,* 618–626.

Jeffrey, W. E., & Cohen, L. B. Habituation in the human infant. In H. W. Reese (Ed.), *Advances in child development and behavior* (Vol. 6). New York: Academic Press, 1971.

Jersild, A. T. *Training and growth in the development of children.* New York: Bureau of Publications, Teachers College, Columbia University, 1932.

Jersild, A. T., & Holmes, F. B. Children's fears. *Child Development Monographs,* 1935 (No. 20).

Johnson, C. N. Acquisition of mental verbs and the concept of mind. In S. Kuczaj (Ed.), *Language development: Syntax and semantics.* Hillsdale, N.J.: Erlbaum, 1981.

Johnson, M. M. Sex role learning in the nuclear family. *Child Development,* 1963, *34,* 319–333.

Johnson, M. M. Fathers, mothers and sex typing. *Sociological Inquiry,* 1975, *45,* 15–26.

Jones, H. E. The environment and mental development. In L. Carmichael (Ed.), *Manual of child psychology* (2nd ed.). New York: Wiley, 1954.

Jones, V. Character development in children—an objective approach. In L. Carmichael (Ed.), *Manual of child psychology* (2nd ed.). New York: Wiley, 1954.

Jost, H., & Sontag, L. W. The genetic factor in autonomic nervous system function. *Psychosomatic Medicine,* 1944, *6,* 308–310.

Jung, C. G. *Psychological types.* London: Routledge & Kegan Paul, 1923.

Jurkovic, G. J. The juvenile delinquent as a moral philosopher: A structural-developmental perspective. *Psychological Bulletin,* 1980, *88,* 709–727.

Kaffman, M. Characteristics of the emotional pathology of the kibbutz child. *American Journal of Orthopsychiatry,* 1972, *42,* 692–709.

Kaffman, M., & Elizur, E. Infants who became enuret-
ics: A longitudinal study of 161 kibbutz children. *Monographs of the Society for Research in Child Development,* 1977, *42*(2, Serial No. 170).

Kagan, J., Kearsley, R. B., & Zelazo, P. R. The effects of infant day care on psychological development. *Educational Quarterly,* 1977, *1,* 109–142.

Kagan, J., & Kogan, N. Individual variation in cognitive processes. In P. H. Mussen (Ed.), *Carmichael's manual of child psychology* (3rd ed.). New York: Wiley, 1970.

Kagan, J., & Moss, H. A. *Birth to maturity.* New York: Wiley, 1962.

Kagan, S., & Madsen, M. C. Cooperation and competition of Mexican, Mexican-American, and Anglo-American children of two ages under four instructional sets. *Developmental Psychology,* 1971, *5,* 32–39.

Kahneman, D. *Attention and effort.* Englewood Cliffs, N.J.: Prentice-Hall, 1973.

Kail, R. V., & Hagen, J. W. (Eds.). *Perspectives on the development of memory and cognition.* Hillsdale, N.J.: Erlbaum, 1977.

Kail, R. V., & Siegel, A. W. The development of mnemonic encoding in children: From perception to abstraction. In R. V. Kail & J. W. Hagen (Eds.), *Perspectives on the development of memory and cognition.* Hillsdale, N.J.: Erlbaum, 1977.

Kalba, K. The electronic community: A new environment for television viewers and critics. In D. Cater & R. Adler (Eds.), *Television as a social force.* New York: Praeger, 1975.

Kamin, L. *The science and politics of I.Q.* Potomac, Md.: Erlbaum, 1974.

Kaplan, B. J. Malnutrition and mental deficiency. *Psychological Bulletin,* 1972, *78,* 321–334.

Katz, P. A. (Ed.). *Toward the elimination of racism.* New York: Pergamon Press, 1976.

Katz, P. A., & Zalk, S. R. Modification of children's racial attitudes. *Developmental Psychology,* 1978, *14,* 447–461.

Kaye, K. Thickening thin data: The maternal role in developing communication and language. In M. Bullowa (Ed.), *Before speech: The beginning of interpersonal communication.* Cambridge, England: Cambridge University Press, 1979.

Kazdin, A. E. *Behavior modification in applied settings.* Homewood, Ill.: Dorsey Press, 1975.

Kazdin, A. E. Behavior modification in education: Contributions and limitations. *Developmental Review,* 1981, *1,* 34–57.

Keil, F. C. Constraints on knowledge and cognitive development. *Psychological Review,* 1981, *88,* 197–227.

Keister, M. E. The behavior of young children in failure. In R. G. Barker, J. S. Kounin, & H. F. Wright (Eds.), *Child development and behavior.* New York: McGraw-Hill, 1943.

Kempe, C. H., Silverman, F. N., Steele, B. F., Droegemueller, W., & Silver, H. K. The battered-child syndrome. *Journal of the American Medical Association,* 1962, *181,* 17–24.

Keniston, K., & the Carnegie Council on Children. *All our children: The American family under pressure.* New York: Harcourt Brace Jovanovich, 1977.

Kennedy, W. A. *Child psychology.* Englewood Cliffs, N.J.: Prentice-Hall, 1971.

Kessen, W. Research design in the study of developmental problems. In P. H. Mussen (Ed.), *Handbook of research methods in child development.* New York: Wiley, 1960.

Kessen, W. *The child.* New York: Wiley, 1965.

Kessen, W., Haith, M. M., & Salapatek, P. H. Infancy. In P. H. Mussen (Ed.), *Carmichael's manual of child psychology* (3rd ed.). New York: Wiley, 1970.

Kett, J. The history of age grouping in America. In J. Coleman et al. (Eds.), *Youth: Transition to adulthood.* Chicago: University of Chicago Press, 1974.

Keyserling, M. *Windows on day care.* New York: National Council of Jewish Women, 1972.

Kimble, G. A., & Perlmutter, L. C. The problem of volition. *Psychological Review,* 1970, *77,* 361–384.

Kinkade, K. *A Walden Two experiment: The first five years of Twin Oaks Community.* New York: Morrow, 1973.

Klahr, D., & Wallace, J. G. *Cognitive development: An information processing view.* Hillsdale, N.J.: Erlbaum, 1976.

Klima, E. S., & Bellugi-Klima, U. Syntactic regularities in the speech of children. In J. Lyons & R. J. Wales (Eds.), *Psycholinguistics papers.* Edinburgh: University of Edinburgh Press, 1966.

Kobasigawa, A. Retrieval strategies in the development of memory. In R. V. Kail & J. W. Hagen (Eds.), *Perspectives on the development of memory and cognition.* Hillsdale, N.J.: Erlbaum, 1977.

Kogan, N. *Cognitive styles in infancy and early childhood.* New York: Wiley, 1976.

Kohlberg, L. Moral development and identification. In H. W. Stevenson (Ed.), *Child psychology.* Chicago: University of Chicago Press, 1963.

Kohlberg, L. Development of moral character and moral ideology. In M. L. Hoffman & L. W. Hoffman (Eds.), *Review of child development research* (Vol. 1). New York: Russell Sage Foundation, 1964.

Kohlberg, L. A cognitive-developmental analysis of children's sex-role concepts and attitudes. In E. E. Maccoby (Ed.), *The development of sex differences.* Stanford, Calif.: Stanford University Press, 1966.

Kohlberg, L. Moral development. In D. L. Sills (Ed.), *International encyclopedia of the social sciences.* New York: Crowell, Collier and MacMillan, 1968.

Kohlberg, L. Stages and sequence: The developmental approach to socialization. In D. Goslin (Ed.), *Handbook of socialization theory and research.* Chicago: Rand McNally, 1969.

Kohlberg, L. Education for justice: A modern statement of the Platonic view. In T. Sizer (Ed.), *Moral education.* Cambridge, Mass.: Harvard University Press, 1970.

Kohlberg, L. *Collected papers on moral development and moral education.* Cambridge, Mass.: Lawrence Kohlberg, 1973.

Kohlberg, L. Moral stages and moralization. In T. Lickona (Ed.), *Moral development and behavior.* New York: Holt, Rinehart & Winston, 1976.

Kohlberg, L. Revisions in the theory and practice of moral development. *New Directions for Child Development,* 1978, *2,* 83–88.

Kohlberg, L., LaCrosse, J., & Ricks, D. The predictability of adult mental health from childhood behavior. In B. Wolman (Ed.), *Manual of child psychopathology.* New York: McGraw-Hill, 1972.

Kohlberg, L., & Zigler, E. The impact of cognitive maturity upon the development of sex-role attitudes in the years four to eight. *Genetic Psychology Monographs,* 1967, *75,* 84–165.

Kohn, M. *Social competence, symptoms and underachievement in childhood: A longitudinal perspective.* Washington, D.C.: V. H. Winston, 1977.

Kohn, M. L. *Class and conformity: A study of values.* Homewood, Ill.: Dorsey Press, 1969.

Kolata, G. B. Scientists attack reports that obstetrical medications endanger children. *Science,* 1979, *204,* 391–392.

Konishi, M. Auditory environment and vocal development in birds. In R. D. Walk & H. L. Pick, Jr. (Eds.), *Perception and experience.* New York: Plenum, 1978.

Konner, M. Relations among infants and juveniles in comparative perspective. In M. Lewis & L. A. Rosenblum (Eds.), *Friendship and peer relations.* New York: Wiley, 1975.

Kopp, C. B. Perspectives on infant motor system development. In M. H. Borsten & W. Kessen (Eds.), *Psychological development in infancy.* Hillsdale, N.J.: Erlbaum, 1979.

Kopp, C. B., & Parmelee, A. H. Prenatal and perinatal influences on infant behavior. In J. D. Osofsky (Ed.), *Handbook of infant development.* New York: Wiley, 1979.

Kreutzer, M. A., Leonard, C., & Flavell, J. H. An interview study of children's knowledge about memory. *Monographs of the Society for Research in Child Development,* 1975, *40* (1, Serial No. 159).

Kuhn, D. Inducing development experimentally: Comments on a research paradigm. *Developmental Psychology,* 1974, *10,* 590–600.

Kuhn, D. Short term longitudinal evidence for the sequentiality of Kohlberg's early stages of moral judgment. *Developmental Psychology,* 1976, *12,* 162–166.

Kuhn, D., Nash, S. C., & Brucken, L. Sex role concepts of two- and three-year-olds. *Child Development,* 1978, *49,* 445–451.

Kurdek, L. A. An integrative perspective on children's divorce adjustment. *American Psychologist,* 1981, *36,* 856–866.

Kurtines, W., & Grief, E. B. The development of moral thought: Review and evaluation of Kohlberg's approach. *Psychological Bulletin,* 1974, *81,* 453–470.

Labov, W. *The study of nonstandard English.* Urbana, Ill.: National Council of Teachers of English, 1970.

Lamb, M. E. *The role of the father in child development.* New York: Wiley, 1976.

Lancaster, J. B. *Primate behavior and the emergence of human culture.* New York: Holt, Rinehart & Winston, 1975.

Lancaster, J. B. Carrying and sharing in human evolution. *Human Nature,* 1978, *1* (2), 82–89.

Lang, E. M. *Goma, the gorilla baby.* New York: Doubleday, 1963.

Lange, G. Organization-related processes in children's recall. In P. A. Ornstein (Ed.), *Memory development in children.* Hillsdale, N.J.: Erlbaum, 1978.

Lapouse, R., & Monk, M. A. Behavior deviations in a representative sample of children—variation by sex, age, race, social class, and family size. *American Journal of Orthopsychiatry,* 1964, *34,* 436–446.

Leboyer, T. *Birth without violence.* New York: Knopf, 1975.

Lempers, J. D., Flavell, E. R., & Flavell, J. H. The development in very young children of tacit knowledge concerning visual perception. *Genetic Psychology Monographs,* 1977, *95,* 3–53.

Lenneberg, E. H. *Biological foundations of language.* New York: Wiley, 1967.

Lepper, M. R., & Greene, D. Turning play into work: Effects of adult surveillance and extrinsic rewards on children's intrinsic motivation. *Journal of Personality and Social Psychology,* 1975, *31,* 479–486.

Lepper, M. R., & Greene, D. Divergent approaches to the study of rewards. In M. R. Lepper & D. Greene (Eds.), *The hidden costs of rewards.* Hillsdale, N.J.: Erlbaum, 1978.

Lepper, M. R., Greene, D., & Nisbett, R. E. Undermining children's intrinsic interest with extrinsic rewards: A test of the overjustification hypothesis. *Journal of Personality and Social Psychology,* 1973, *28,* 129–137.

Lerner, B. Representative democracy, "Men of Zeal," and testing legislation. *American Psychologist,* 1981, *36,* 270–275.

Leshner, A. I. *An introduction to behavioral endocrinology.* New York: Oxford University Press, 1978.

Lesser, G. S. *Children and television.* New York: Random House, 1974.

Lester, B. M. Cardiac habituation of the orienting response to an auditory stimulus in infants of varying nutritional status. *Developmental Psychology,* 1975, *11,* 432–442.

Levin, G. R. *A self-directing guide to the study of child psychology.* Monterey, Calif.: Brooks/Cole, 1973.

Levin, G. R., Henderson, B., Levin, A. M., & Hoffer, G. L. Measuring knowledge of basic concepts by disadvantaged preschoolers. *Psychology in the Schools,* 1975, *12,* 132–139.

LeVine, R. A. *Culture, behavior and personality.* Chicago: Aldine, 1973.

LeVine, R. A. Parental goals: A cross-cultural view. *Teachers College Record,* 1974, *76,* 226–239.

Levine, S. The effects of infantile experience on adult behavior. In A. J. Bachrach (Ed.), *Experimental foundations of clinical psychology.* New York: Basic Books, 1962.

Levitsky, D. A. *Malnutrition, environment and intellectual development.* Ithaca, N.Y.: Cornell University Press, 1979.

Lewin, K. *Field theory in social science.* New York: Harper & Row, 1951.

Lewis, M., & Brooks, J. Infant social perception: A constructionist view. In L. B. Cohen & P. Salapatek (Eds.), *Infant perception: From sensation to cognition* (Vol. 2). New York: Academic Press, 1975.

Lewis, M., & Goldberg, S. Perceptual-cognitive development in infancy: A generalized expectancy model as a function of mother-infant interaction. *Merrill-Palmer Quarterly,* 1969, *15,* 81–100.

Lewis, M., & Rosenblum, L. A. (Eds.). *The effect of the child on its caregiver.* New York: Wiley, 1974.

Lewis, M., & Rosenblum, L. A. (Eds.). *Friendship and peer relations.* New York: Wiley, 1975.

Lewis, M., & Rosenblum, L. A. (Eds.). *Interaction, conversation and the development of language.* New York: Wiley, 1977.

Lippitt, P. Learning through cross-age helping: Why and how. In V. L. Allen (Ed.), *Children as teachers.* New York: Academic Press, 1976.

Lobel, M., Miller, P. M., & Commons, M. L. The development of infants' responses to peek-a-boo. Paper presented at the Meeting of the Society for Research in Child Development, Boston, April 1981.

Loevinger, J. *Ego development: Conceptions and theories.* San Francisco: Jossey-Bass, 1976.

Longstreth, L. E., Davis, B., Carter, L., Flint, D., Owen, J., Rickert, M., & Taylor, E. Separation of home intellectual environment and maternal IQ as determinants of child IQ. *Developmental Psychology,* 1981, *17,* 532–544.

Lorenz, K. The companion in the bird's world. *Auk,* 1937, *54,* 245–273.

Lynn, D. B. A note on sex differences in the development of masculine and feminine identification. *Psychological Review,* 1959, *66,* 126–135.

Lynn, D. B. *The father: His role in child development.* Monterey, Calif.: Brooks/Cole, 1974.

Maccoby, E. E. The effects of mass media. In M. L. Hoffman & L. W. Hoffman (Eds.), *Review of child development research* (Vol. 1). New York: Russell Sage Foundation, 1964.

Maccoby, E. E. (Ed.). *Development of sex differences.* Stanford, Calif.: Stanford University Press, 1966.

Maccoby, E. E. *Sex differentiation during child development.* Washington, D.C.: American Psychological Association, 1975.

Maccoby, E. E., & Jacklin, C. N. *The psychology of sex differences.* Stanford, Calif.: Stanford University Press, 1974.

Maccoby, E. E., & Jacklin, C. N. Sex differences in aggression: A rejoinder and reprise. *Child Development,* 1980, *51,* 964–980.

Maccoby, E. E., & Konrad, K. W. Age trends in selective listening. *Journal of Experimental Child Psychology,* 1966, *3,* 113–122.

Maccoby, E. E., & Masters, J. C. Attachment and dependency. In P. H. Mussen (Ed.), *Carmichael's manual of child psychology* (3rd ed.). New York: Wiley, 1970.

Macfarlane, A. *The psychology of childbirth.* Cambridge, Mass.: Harvard University Press, 1977.

MacFarlane, J., Allen, L., & Honzik, M. K. *A developmental study of the behavior problems of normal children between twenty-one months and fourteen years.* Berkeley: University of California Press, 1954.

Madden, J., Levenstein, P., & Levenstein, S. Longitudinal IQ outcomes of the mother-child home program. *Child Development,* 1976, *47,* 1015–1025.

Mandler, G. *Mind and emotion.* New York: Wiley, 1975.

Marantz, S. A., & Mansfield, A. F. Maternal employment and the development of sex-role stereotyping in five- to eleven-year-old girls. *Child Development,* 1977, *48,* 668–673.

Marcus, D. E., & Overton, W. F. The development of cognitive gender constancy and sex role preferences. *Child Development,* 1978, *49,* 434–444.

Martin, B. Parent-child relations. In F. D. Horowitz (Ed.), *Review of child development research* (Vol. 4). Chicago: University of Chicago Press, 1975.

Marvin, R. S. An ethological-cognitive model for the attenuation of mother-child attachment behavior. In T. Alloway, P. Pliner, & L. Krames (Eds.), *Attachment behavior.* New York: Plenum, 1977.

Masi, W. Supplemental stimulation of the premature infant. In T. M. Field, A. M. Sostek, S. Goldberg, & H. H. Shuman (Eds.), *Infants born at risk.* New York: Spectrum, 1979.

Mason, W. A. Determinants of social behavior in young chimpanzees. In A. M. Schreier, H. F. Harlow, & F. Stollnitz (Eds.), *Behavior in nonhuman primates* (Vol. 2). New York: Academic Press, 1965.

Mason, W. A. Early social deprivation in the nonhuman primate: Implications for human behavior. In D. C. Glass (Ed.), *Environmental influences.* New York: Rockefeller University Press, 1968.

Mason, W. A. Motivational factors in psychosocial development. In W. J. Arnold & N. M. Page (Eds.), *Nebraska Symposium on Motivation* (Vol. 18). Lincoln: University of Nebraska Press, 1970.

Mason, W. A., & Kenny, M. D. Redirection of filial attachments in rhesus monkeys: Dogs as mother surrogates. *Science,* 1974, *183,* 1209–1211.

Mass, E., Marecek, J., & Travers, J. R. Children's conceptions of disordered behavior. *Child Development,* 1978, *49,* 146–154.

Masters, J. C., & Wellman, H. M. The study of human infant attachment: A procedural critique. *Psychological Bulletin,* 1974, *81,* 218–237.

Matas, L., Arend, R. A., & Sroufe, L. A. Continuity in adaptation: Quality of attachment and later competence. *Child Development,* 1978, *49,* 547–556.

Matheny, A. P., Jr. Bayley's infant behavior record: Behavioral components and twin analyses. *Child Development,* 1980, *51,* 1157–1167.

Maurer, D., & Salapatek, P. Developmental stages in the scanning of faces by young infants. *Child Development,* 1976, *47,* 523–527.

McAskie, M., & Clarke, A. M. Parent-offspring resemblances in intelligence: Theories and evidence. *British Journal of Psychology,* 1976, *67,* 243–273.

McCarthy, D. Language development in children. In L. Carmichael (Ed.), *Manual of child psychology* (2nd ed.). New York: Wiley, 1954.

McClelland, D. C. Risk taking in children with high and low need for achievement. In J. W. Atkinson (Ed.), *Motives in fantasy, action, and society.* Princeton, N.J.: Van Nostrand, 1958. (a)

McClelland, D. C. The use of measures of human motivation in the study of society. In J. W. Atkinson (Ed.), *Motives in fantasy, action, and society.* Princeton, N.J.: Van Nostrand, 1958. (b)

McClelland, D. C., Atkinson, J. W., Clark, R. A., & Lowell, E. L. *The achievement motive.* New York: Appleton-Century-Crofts, 1953.

McGee, M. G. Human spatial abilities: Psychometric studies and environmental, genetic, hormonal, and neurological influences. *Psychological Bulletin,* 1979, *86,* 889–918.

McGhee, P. E. Development of the humour response: A review of the literature. *Psychological Bulletin,* 1971, *76,* 328–348.

McGhee, P. E. Children's appreciation of humor: A test of the cognitive congruency principle. *Child Development,* 1976, *47,* 420–426.

McGhee, P. E. *Humor: Its origin and development.* San Francisco: Freeman, 1979.

McGraw, M. B. Swimming behavior of the human infant. *Journal of Pediatrics,* 1939, *15,* 485–490.

McGraw, M. B. *The neuro-muscular maturation of the human infant.* New York: Columbia University

Press, 1943.

McNeil, D. The development of language. In P. H. Mussen (Ed.), *Carmichael's manual of child psychology* (3rd ed.). New York: Wiley, 1970.

Mead, G. H. *Mind, self, and society.* Chicago: University of Chicago Press, 1934.

Mead, M. *Sex and temperament in three primitive societies.* New York: Morrow, 1935.

Meehl, P. E., & Rosen, A. Antecedent probability and the efficiency of psychometric signs, patterns, or cutting scores. *Psychological Bulletin,* 1955, *52,* 194–216.

Meichenbaum, D. Examination of model characteristics in reducing avoidance behavior. *Journal of Personality and Social Psychology,* 1971, *17,* 298–307.

Melamed, B. G., & Siegel, L. J. Reduction of anxiety in children facing hospitalization and surgery by use of film modeling. *Journal of Consulting and Clinical Psychology,* 1975, *43,* 511–521.

Meltzoff, A. N., & Moore, M. K. Imitation of facial and manual gestures by human neonates. *Science,* 1977, *198,* 75–78.

Menyuk, P. *The acquisition and development of language.* Englewood Cliffs, N.J.: Prentice-Hall, 1971.

Mercer, J. R. *Labeling the mentally retarded.* Berkeley: University of California Press, 1973.

Messer, S. B. Reflection-impulsivity: A review. *Psychological Bulletin,* 1976, *83,* 1026–1052.

Messer, S. B., & Brodzinsky, D. M. Three-year stability of reflection-impulsivity in young adolescents. *Developmental Psychology,* 1981, *17,* 848–850.

Meyer, B. The development of girls' sex-role attitudes. *Child Development,* 1980, *51,* 508–514.

Miles, C. C. Gifted children. In L. Carmichael (Ed.), *Manual of child psychology* (2nd ed.). New York: Wiley, 1954.

Miller, G. A. The magic number seven, plus or minus two: Some limits on our capacity for processing information. *Psychological Review,* 1956, *63,* 81–97.

Miller, G. A. Psychology as a means of promoting human welfare. *American Psychologist,* 1969, *24,* 1063–1075.

Mischel, W. A social-learning view of sex differences in behavior. In E. E. Maccoby (Ed.), *Development of sex differences.* Stanford, Calif.: Stanford University Press, 1966.

Mischel, W. Sex-typing and socialization. In P. H. Mussen (Ed.), *Carmichael's manual of child psychology* (3rd ed.). New York: Wiley, 1970.

Mischel, W. Toward a cognitive social learning reconceptualization of personality. *Psychological Review,* 1973, *80,* 252–283.

Mischel, W. Processes in delay of gratification. In L. Berkowitz (Ed.), *Advances in experimental social psychology.* New York: Academic Press, 1974.

Modgil, S., & Modgil, C. *Piagetian research: Compilation and commentary* (Vol. 8). *Cross-cultural studies.* Atlantic Highlands, N.J.: National Foundation for Educational Research, 1976.

Moely, B. E. Organizational factors in the development of memory. In R. V. Kail, Jr., & J. W. Hagen (Eds.), *Perspectives on the development of memory and cognition.* Hillsdale, N.J.: Erlbaum, 1977.

Moerk, E. L. Processes of language teaching and language learning in the interaction of mother-child dyads. *Child Development,* 1976, *47,* 1064–1078.

Moglia, L. A. *Stage development of incongruity humor and the use of play cues in the play of preschool children.* Unpublished honors thesis, Bucknell University, 1981.

Moltz, H. *The ontogony of vertebrate behavior.* New York: Academic Press, 1971.

Money, J., & Ehrhardt, A. A. *Man and woman, boy and girl.* Baltimore: Johns Hopkins University Press, 1972.

Monnier, M. Response repertoire of the anencephalic infant. In S. J. Hutt & C. Hutt (Eds.), *Early human development.* London: Oxford University Press, 1973.

Moore, N. V., Evertson, C. M., & Brophy, J. E. Solitary play: Some functional considerations. *Developmental Psychology,* 1974, *10,* 830–834.

Moore, O. K. Autotelic responsive environments and exceptional children. In O. J. Harvey (Ed.), *Experience, structure and adaptability.* New York: Springer, 1966.

Moore, R., & Young, D. Childhood outdoors: Toward a social ecology of the landscape. In I. Altman & J. F. Wohlwill (Eds.), *Children and the environment.* New York: Plenum, 1978.

Morgan, M. The overjustification effect: A developmental test of self-perception interpretations. *Journal of Personality and Social Psychology,* 1981, *40,* 809–821.

Moss, H. A. Sex, age, and state as determinants of mother-infant interaction. *Merrill-Palmer Quarterly of Behavior & Development,* 1967, *13,* 19–36.

Moss, H. A., Robson, K. S., & Pedersen, F. Determinants of maternal stimulation of infants and consequences of treatment for later reactions to strangers. *Developmental Psychology,* 1969, *1,* 239–246.

Mueller, C. W., & Parcel, T. L. Measures of socioeconomic status: Alternatives and recommendations. *Child Development,* 1981, *52,* 13–30.

Mueller, E., Bleier, M., Krakow, J., Hegedus, K., & Cournoyer, P. The development of peer verbal interaction among two-year-old boys. *Child Development,* 1977, *48,* 284–287.

Mueller, E., & Brenner, J. The origins of social skills and interaction among playgroup toddlers. *Child Development,* 1977, *48,* 854–861.

Mueller, E., & Lucas, T. A developmental analysis of

peer interaction among toddlers. In M. Lewis & L. A. Rosenblum (Eds.), *Friendship and peer relations*. New York: Wiley, 1975.

Munroe, R. L., & Munroe, R. H. *Cross-cultural human development*. Monterey, Calif.: Brooks/Cole, 1975.

Munsinger, H. The adopted child's I.Q.: A critical review. *Psychological Bulletin*, 1975, *82*, 623–659.

Murphy, G. *Personality*. New York: Harper, 1947.

Murphy, L. B., & Frank, C. Prevention: The clinical psychologist. *Annual Review of Psychology*, 1979, *30*, 173–208.

Murray, A. D. Infant crying as an elicitor of parental behavior: An examination of two models. *Psychological Bulletin*, 1979, *86*, 191–215.

Mussen, P. H. (Ed.). *Handbook of research methods in child development*. New York: Wiley, 1960.

Mussen, P. H. (Ed.). *Carmichael's manual of child psychology* (3rd ed.). New York: Wiley, 1970.

Mussen, P. H., & Conger, J. J. *Child development and personality* (2nd ed.). New York: Harper & Row, 1963.

Mussen, P., & Eisenberg-Berg, N. *The roots of caring, sharing, and helping*. San Francisco: Freeman, 1977.

Neimark, E. D. Intellectual development during adolescence. In F. D. Horowitz (Ed.), *Review of child development research* (Vol. 4). Chicago: University of Chicago Press, 1975.

Neimark, E. D. The natural history of spontaneous mnemonic activities under conditions of minimal experimental constraint. In A. D. Pick (Ed.), *Minnesota Symposia on Child Psychology* (Vol. 10). Minneapolis: University of Minnesota Press, 1976.

Nelson, K. Structure and strategy in learning to talk. *Monographs of the Society for Research in Child Development*, 1973, *38*(1–2, Serial No. 149).

Nelson, K. Cognitive development and the acquisition of concepts. In R. C. Anderson, R. J. Spiro, & W. E. Montague (Eds.), *Schooling and the acquisition of knowledge*. Hillsdale, N.J.: Erlbaum, 1977. (a)

Nelson, K. The syntagmatic-paradigmatic shift revisited: A review of research and theory. *Psychological Bulletin*, 1977, *84*, 93–116. (b)

Nelson, K. Individual differences in language development: Implications for development and language. *Developmental Psychology*, 1981, *17*, 170–187.

Nelson, K., Rescorla, L., Gruendel, J., & Benedict, H. Early lexicons: What do they mean? *Child Development*, 1978, *49*, 960–968.

Newcomb, T. M. The prediction of interpersonal attraction. *American Psychologist*, 1956, *11*, 575–586.

Newport, E. L. Motherese: The speech of mothers to young children. In N. J. Castellan, Jr., S. B. Pisoni, & G. R. Potts (Eds.), *Cognitive theory* (Vol. 2). Hillsdale, N.J.: Erlbaum, 1977.

Newson, J., & Newson, E. Cultural aspects of child rearing in the English-speaking world. In M. P. M. Richards (Ed.), *The integration of a child into a social world*. London: Cambridge University Press, 1974.

Newson, J., & Newson, E. *Seven year olds in the home environment*. New York: Wiley, 1976.

Nicolich, L. Beyond sensorimotor intelligence: Assessment of symbolic maturity through analysis of pretend play. *Merrill-Palmer Quarterly*, 1977, *23*, 89–102.

Noble, G. *Children in front of the small screen*. Beverly Hills, Calif.: Sage, 1975.

Oden, S., & Asher, S. R. Coaching children in social skills for friendship making. *Child Development*, 1977, *48*, 495–506.

O'Donnell, J. M. The crisis of experimentalism in the 1920s: E. G. Boring and his uses of history. *American Psychologist*, 1979, *34*, 289–295.

Olton, R. M., & Crutchfield, R. S. Developing the skills of productive thinking. In P. H. Mussen, J. Langer, & M. Covington (Eds.), *Trends and issues in developmental psychology*. New York: Holt, Rinehart & Winston, 1969.

Olweus, D. Stability of aggressive reaction patterns in males: A review. *Psychological Bulletin*, 1979, *86*, 852–875.

Olweus, D. Continuity in aggressive and introverted, withdrawn behavior patterns. Paper presented at the Meeting of the Society for Research in Child Development, Boston, April 1981.

Ornstein, P. A. (Ed.). *Memory development in children*. Hillsdale, N.J.: Erlbaum, 1978.

Ornstein, P. A., & Naus, M. J. Rehearsal processes in children's memory. In P. A. Ornstein (Ed.), *Memory development in children*. Hillsdale, N.J.: Erlbaum, 1978.

Oster, H. Facial expression and affect development. In M. Lewis & L. A. Rosenblum (Eds.), *The development of affect*. New York: Plenum, 1978.

Oster, H., & Ekman, P. Facial behavior in child development. In A. Collins (Ed.), *Minnesota Symposia on Child Psychology* (Vol. 11). Hillsdale, N.J.: Erlbaum, 1977.

Overton, W. F., & Jackson, J. P. The representation of imagined objects in action sequences: A developmental study. *Child Development*, 1973, *44*, 309–314.

Overton, W. F., & Reese, H. W. Models of development: Methodological implications. In J. R. Nesselroade & H. W. Reese (Eds.), *Life-span developmental psychology: Methodological issues*. New York: Academic Press, 1973.

Palermo, D. S., & Molfese, D. L. Language acquisition from age five onward. *Psychological Bulletin*, 1972, *78*, 409–421.

Paris, S. G., & Lindauer, B. K. Constructive aspects of children's comprehension and memory. In R. V. Kail & J. W. Hagen (Eds.), *Perspectives on the development of memory and cognition*. Hillsdale,

N.J.: Erlbaum, 1977.

Parke, R. D. Children's home environments: Social and cognitive effects. In I. Altman & J. F. Wohlwill (Eds.), *Children and the environment.* New York: Plenum, 1978.

Parke, R. D., & Collmer, C. Child abuse: An interdisciplinary analysis. In E. M. Hetherington (Ed.), *Review of child development research* (Vol. 5). Chicago: University of Chicago Press, 1975.

Parmelee, A. H., Wenner, W. H., & Schulz, H. R. Infant sleep patterns from birth to 16 weeks of age. *Journal of Pediatrics,* 1964, *65,* 576–582.

Parsons, T. Family structure and the socialization of the child. In T. Parsons & R. Bales (Eds.), *Family socialization and interaction processes.* Glencoe, Ill.: Free Press, 1955.

Parsons, T., & Bales, R. F. (Eds.). *Family socialization and interaction processes.* Glencoe, Ill.: Free Press, 1955.

Parten, M. Social play among preschool children. *Journal of Abnormal and Social Psychology,* 1932, *27,* 243–269.

Pascual-Leone, J. *Cognitive development and cognitive style.* Lexington, Mass.: Heath, 1973.

Patterson, G. R. Mothers: The unacknowledged victims. *Monographs of the Society for Research in Child Development,* 1980, *45* (5, Serial No. 186).

Patterson, G. R., Littman, R. A., & Bricker, W. Assertive behavior in children: A step toward a theory of aggression. *Monographs of the Society for Research on Child Development,* 1967, *32* (5, Serial No. 113).

Patterson, G. R., Reid, J. B., Jones, R. R., & Conger, R. E. *A social learning approach to family intervention* (Vol. 1). *Families with aggressive children.* Eugene, Ore.: Castalia, 1975.

Pavlov, I. P. *Conditioned reflexes and psychiatry.* London: Lawrence & Wishart, 1941.

Pepler, D. J. Naturalistic observations of teaching and modeling between siblings. Paper presented at the Meeting of the Society for Research in Child Development, Boston, April 1981.

Pepper, S. C. *World hypotheses.* Berkeley: University of California Press, 1942.

Piaget, J. *The origins of intelligence in children.* New York: International Universities Press, 1952.

Piaget, J. *The construction of reality in the child.* New York: Basic Books, 1954.

Piaget, J. *The language and thought of the child.* New York: Meridian, 1955. (Originally published, 1926.)

Piaget, J. *Psychology of intelligence.* Paterson, N.J.: Littlefield, Adams, 1960. (Originally published, 1947.)

Piaget, J. *Play, dreams, and imitation in childhood.* New York: Norton, 1962.

Piaget, J. *The moral judgment of the child.* New York: Free Press, 1965. (Originally published, 1932.)

Piaget, J. *Six psychological studies.* New York: Random House, 1967. (Originally published, 1964.)

Piaget, J. Piaget's theory. In P. H. Mussen (Ed.), *Carmichael's manual of child psychology* (3rd ed.). New York: Wiley, 1970.

Piaget, J. *Biology and knowledge.* Chicago: University of Chicago Press, 1971.

Piaget, J. *The child and reality.* New York: Grossman, 1972.

Piaget, J., & Inhelder, B. *The psychology of the child.* New York: Basic Books, 1969.

Pick, A. D., Frankel, D. G., & Hess, V. L. Children's attention: The development of selectivity. In E. M. Hetherington (Ed.), *Review of child development research* (Vol. 5). Chicago: University of Chicago Press, 1975.

Pilbeam, D. Rearranging our family tree. *Human Nature,* 1978, *1*(6), 38–45.

Popenoe, D. *The suburban environment: Sweden and the United States.* Chicago: University of Chicago Press, 1976.

Power, C., & Reimer, J. Moral atmosphere: An educational bridge between moral judgment and action. *New Directions in Child Development,* 1978, *2,* 105–116.

Pratt, K. C. The neonate. In L. Carmichael (Ed.), *Manual of child psychology* (2nd ed.). New York: Wiley, 1954.

Premack, D. Reversibility of the reinforcement relation. *Science,* 1962, *136,* 255–257.

Putallaz, M., & Gottman, J. M. Social skills and group acceptance. In S. R. Asher & J. M. Gottman (Eds.), *The development of children's friendships.* Cambridge, England: Cambridge University Press, 1981.

Quadagno, D. M., Briscoe, R., & Quadagno, J. S. Effects of perinatal gonadal hormones on selected nonsexual behavior patterns: A critical assessment of the nonhuman and human literature. *Psychological Bulletin,* 1977, *84,* 62–80.

Quay, H. C. Patterns of aggression, withdrawal, and immaturity. In H. C. Quay & J. S. Werry (Eds.), *Psychopathological disorders of childhood.* New York: Wiley, 1972.

Rader, N., Bausano, M., & Richards, J. E. On the nature of the visual-cliff-avoidance response in human infants. *Child Development,* 1980, *51,* 61–68.

Read, M. *Children of the fathers: Growing up among the Nagoni of Nyasaland.* New Haven, Conn.: Yale University Press, 1960.

Rebelsky, F., & Hanks, C. Father verbal interaction with infants in the first three months of life. *Child Development,* 1971, *42,* 63–68.

Reed, E. Genetic anomalies in development. In F. D. Horowitz (Ed.), *Review of child development research* (Vol. 4). Chicago: University of Chicago Press, 1975.

Reese, H. W., & Lipsitt, L. P. (Eds.). *Experimental child psychology.* New York: Academic Press, 1970.

Reese, H. W., & Overton, H. F. Models of development and theories of development. In L. R. Goulet & P. B. Battes (Eds.), *Life-span development psychology: Research and theory.* New York: Academic Press, 1970.

Reese, H. W., & Porges, S. W. Development of learning processes. In V. Hamilton & M. D. Vernon (Eds.), *The development of cognitive processes.* London: Academic Press, 1976.

Reiss, I. L. *The family system in America.* New York: Holt, Rinehart & Winston, 1971.

Renshaw, P. D. The roots of peer interaction research: A historical analysis of the 1930s. In S. R. Asher & J. M. Gottman (Eds.), *The development of children's friendships.* Cambridge, England: Cambridge University Press, 1981.

Rest, J. New approaches in the assessment of moral judgment. In T. Lickona (Ed.), *Moral development and behavior.* New York: Holt, Rinehart & Winston, 1976.

Rest, J. R., Cooper, D., Coder, R., Masanz, J., & Anderson, D. Judging the important issues in moral dilemmas—an objective test of development. *Developmental Psychology,* 1974, *10,* 491–501.

Rest, J. R., Davison, M. L., & Robbins, S. Age trends in judging moral issues: A review of cross-sectional, longitudinal, and sequential studies of the Defining Issues Test. *Child Development,* 1978, *49,* 263–279.

Rheingold, H. L. The social and socializing infant. In D. A. Goslin (Ed.), *Handbook of socialization theory and research.* Chicago: Rand McNally, 1969.

Rheingold, H. L., & Adams, J. L. The significance of speech to newborns. *Developmental Psychology,* 1980, *16,* 397–403.

Rheingold, H. L., & Eckerman, C. O. The infant separates himself from his mother. *Science,* 1970, *168,* 78–83.

Rheingold, H. L., & Eckerman, C. O. Fear of the stranger: A critical examination. In H. W. Reese (Ed.), *Advances in child behavior and development* (Vol. 8). New York: Academic Press, 1973.

Rheingold, H. L., & Eckerman, C. O. Some proposals for unifying the study of social development. In M. Lewis & L. A. Rosenblum (Eds.), *Friendship and peer relations.* New York: Wiley, 1975.

Rheingold, H. L., Hay, D. F., & West, M. J. Sharing in the second year of life. *Child Development,* 1976, *47,* 1148–1158.

Rhodes, W. C., & Ensor, D. R. Community programming. In H. C. Quay & J. S. Werry (Eds.), *Psychopathological disorders of childhood* (2nd ed.). New York: Wiley, 1979.

Ricciuti, H. *Effects of day care experience on behavior and development. Research and implications for social policy.* Unpublished manuscript, Cornell University, 1976.

Ricciuti, H. Adverse social and biological influences on early development. In H. McGurk (Ed.), *Eco-*
logical factors in human development. Amsterdam: North-Holland, 1977.

Richmond, J. B., & Lipton, E. L. Some aspects of the neurophysiology of the newborn and their implications for child development. In L. Jessner & E. Pavenstedt (Eds.), *Dynamic psychopathology in childhood.* New York: Grune & Stratton, 1959.

Riesen, A. H. Interpretations and implications. In A. H. Riesen (Ed.), *The developmental neuropsychology of sensory deprivation.* New York: Academic Press, 1975.

Roberts, D. F., Cristenson, P., Gibson, W. A., Mooser, L., & Goldberg, M. E. Developing discriminating consumers. *Journal of Communication,* 1980, *30,* 94–105.

Roberts, G. C., & Black, K. N. The effect of naming and object permanence on toy preferences. *Child Development,* 1972, *43,* 858–868.

Roberts, R. E. *The new communes.* Englewood Cliffs, N.J.: Prentice-Hall, 1971.

Robertson, E. G. Prenatal factors contributing to high-risk offspring. In T. M. Field, A. M. Sostek, S. Goldberg, & H. H. Shuman (Eds.), *Infants born at risk.* New York: Spectrum, 1979.

Robins, L. N. *Deviant children grown up.* Baltimore: Williams & Wilkins, 1966.

Robins, L. N. Follow-up studies. In H. C. Quay & J. S. Werry (Eds.), *Psychopathological disorders of childhood* (2nd ed.). New York: Wiley, 1979.

Robinson, H. B., & Robinson, N. M. *The mentally retarded child.* New York: McGraw-Hill, 1965.

Robinson, H. B., & Robinson, N. M. Longitudinal development of very young children in a comprehensive day care program: The first two years. *Child Development,* 1971, *42,* 1673–1683.

Robinson, H. B., Robinson, N. M., Wolins, M., Bronfenbrenner, U., & Richmond, J. *Early child care in the United States of America.* London: Gordon & Breach, 1973.

Roche, A. F. (Ed.). Secular trends in human growth, maturation, and development. *Monographs of the Society for Research in Child Development,* 1979, *44* (3–4, Serial No. 179).

Rogoff, B., Sellers, M. J., Pirrotta, S., Fox, N., & White, S. H. Age of assignment of roles and responsibilities to children: A cross-cultural survey. *Human Development,* 1976, *18,* 353–369.

Rosenblatt, P. C., & Cunningham, M. R. Sex differences in cross-cultural perspective. In B. Lloyd & J. Archer (Eds.), *Exploring sex differences.* London: Academic Press, 1976.

Rosenhan, D. Some origins of concern for others. In P. H. Mussen, J. Langer, & M. Covington (Eds.), *Trends and issues in developmental psychology.* New York: Holt, Rinehart & Winston, 1969.

Rosenheim, M. K. The child and the law. In B. M. Caldwell & H. N. Ricciuti (Eds.), *Review of child development research* (Vol. 3). Chicago: University of Chicago Press, 1973.

Rosenthal, T. L., & Zimmerman, B. J. *Social learning and cognition.* New York: Academic Press, 1978.

Rosett, H. L., & Sander, L. W. Effects of maternal drinking on neonate morphology and state regulation. In J. D. Osofsky (Ed.), *Handbook of infant development.* New York: Wiley, 1979.

Rossi, A. The biosocial side of parenthood. *Human Nature,* 1978, *1*(6), 72–79.

Rothbart, M. K. Laughter in young children. *Psychological Bulletin,* 1973, *80,* 247–256.

Rothbart, M. K. Measurement of temperament in infancy. *Child Development,* 1981, *52,* 569–578.

Rovee-Collier, C. K. Infants and elephants: Do they ever forget? Paper presented at the Meeting of the Society for Research in Child Development, Boston, April 1981.

Rovee-Collier, C. K., & Gekoski, M. J. The economics of infancy: A review of conjugate reinforcement. In H. W. Reese & L. P. Lipsitt (Eds.), *Advances in child development and behavior* (Vol. 13). New York: Academic Press, 1979.

Rovee-Collier, C. K., Sullivan, M. W., Enright, M., Lucas, D., & Fagan, J. W. Reactivation of infant memory. *Science,* 1980, *208,* 1159–1161.

Rubin, K. H. Non-social play in early childhood: Necessarily evil? Paper presented at the Meeting of the Society for Research in Child Development, Boston, April 1981.

Rubin, K. H., Watson, K. S., & Jambor, T. W. Free-play behaviors in preschool and kindergarten children. *Child Development,* 1978, *49,* 534–536.

Rubin, Z. *Children's friendships.* Cambridge, Mass.: Harvard University Press, 1980.

Rugh, R., & Shettles, L. *From conception to birth: The drama of life's beginnings.* New York: Harper & Row, 1971.

Rybash, J. M., & Roodin, P. A. A reinterpretation of the effects of videotape and verbal presentation modes on children's moral judgments. *Child Development,* 1978, *49,* 228–230.

Saarni, C. Children's understanding of display rules for expressive behavior. *Developmental Psychology,* 1979, *15,* 424–429.

Sackett, G. P. Monkeys reared in isolation with pictures as visual input: Evidence for an innate releasing mechanism. *Science,* 1966, *154,* 1468–1473.

Sackett, G. P., Ruppenthal, G. C., Fahrenbruch, C. E., & Greenough, W. T. Social isolation effects in monkeys vary with genotype. *Developmental Psychology,* 1981, *17,* 313–318.

Salapatek, P. Pattern perception in early infancy. In L. B. Cohen & P. Salapatek (Eds.), *Infant perception: From sensation to cognition* (Vol. 1). New York: Academic Press, 1975.

Salapatek, P., & Kessen, W. Visual scanning of triangles by the human newborn. *Journal of Experimental Child Psychology,* 1966, *3,* 155–167.

Salomon, G. Effects of encouraging Israeli mothers to co-observe "Sesame Street" with their five-year-olds. *Child Development,* 1977, *48,* 1146–1151.

Sameroff, A. J. Learning and adaptation in infancy: A comparison of models. In H. Reese (Ed.), *Advances in child development and behavior* (Vol. 7). New York: Academic Press, 1972.

Sameroff, A. J., & Cavanaugh, P. J. Learning in infancy: A developmental perspective. In J. D. Osofsky (Ed.), *Handbook of infant development.* New York: Wiley, 1979.

Sameroff, A. J., & Chandler, M. J. Reproductive risk and the continuum of caretaking casualty. In F. D. Horowitz (Ed.), *Review of child development research* (Vol. 4). Chicago: University of Chicago Press, 1975.

Sarason, S. B., & Doris, J. *Psychological problems in mental deficiency* (4th ed.). New York: Harper & Row, 1969.

Scarr, S. Social introversion-extraversion as a heritable response. *Child Development,* 1969, *40,* 823–832.

Scarr, S., & Salapatek, P. Patterns of fear development during infancy. *Merrill-Palmer Quarterly,* 1970, *16,* 53–90.

Scarr, S., & Weinberg, R. A. Attitudes, interests, and I.Q. *Human Nature,* 1978, *1*(4), 29–37.

Scarr-Salapatek, S. Genetics and the development of intelligence. In F. D. Horowitz (Ed.), *Review of child development research* (Vol. 4). Chicago: University of Chicago Press, 1975.

Scarr-Salapatek, S. Genetic determinants of infant development: An overstated case. In L. P. Lipsitt (Ed.), *Developmental psychobiology: The significance of infancy.* Hillsdale, N.J.: Erlbaum, 1976.

Schacter, S. *The psychology of affiliation.* Stanford, Calif.: Stanford University Press, 1959.

Schaefer, E. S. A circumplex model for maternal behavior. *Journal of Abnormal and Social Psychology,* 1959, *59,* 226–235.

Schaefer, E. S., & Bayley, N. Maternal behavior, child behavior, and their intercorrelations from infancy through adolescence. *Monographs of the Society for Research in Child Development,* 1963, *28* (3, Serial No. 87).

Schaffer, H. R. *Mothering.* Cambridge, Mass.: Harvard University Press, 1977.

Schaffer, H. R. Acquiring the concept of dialogue. In M. H. Bornstein & W. Kessen (Eds.), *Psychological development in infancy.* Hillsdale, N.J.: Erlbaum, 1979.

Schaffer, H. R., & Emerson, P. E. The development of social attachments in infancy. *Monographs of the Society for Research in Child Development,* 1964, *29* (3, Serial No. 94). (a)

Schaffer, H. R., & Emerson, P. E. Patterns of response to physical contact in early human development. *Journal of Child Psychology and Psychiatry,* 1964, *5,* 1–13. (b)

Schapera, I. *Married life in an African tribe.* New York: Sheridan House, 1941.

Schoggen, P. Environmental forces in the everyday lives of children. In R. G. Barker (Ed.), *The stream of behavior.* New York: Appleton-Century-Crofts, 1963.

Schoggen, P., & Barker, R. Ecological factors in development in an American and English small town. In H. McGurk (Ed.), *Ecological factors in human development.* Amsterdam: North-Holland, 1977.

Schramm, W., Lyle, J., & Parker, E. B. *Television in the lives of our children.* Stanford, Calif.: Stanford University Press, 1961.

Scott, J. P. *Early experience and the organization of behavior.* Monterey, Calif.: Brooks/Cole, 1968.

Scribner, S., & Cole, M. Cognitive consequences of formal and informal education. *Science,* 1973, *182,* 553–559.

Sears, R. R. Your ancients revisited: A history of child development. In E. M. Hetherington (Ed.), *Review of child development research* (Vol. 5). Chicago: University of Chicago Press, 1975.

Sears, R. R., Rau, L., & Alpert, R. *Identification and child rearing.* Stanford, Calif.: Stanford University Press, 1965.

Self, P. A., & Horowitz, F. D. The behavioral assessment of the newborn: An overview. In J. D. Osofsky (Ed.), *Handbook of infant development.* New York: Wiley, 1979.

Seligman, M. E. P. *Helplessness.* San Francisco: Freeman, 1975.

Selman, R. L. *The growth of interpersonal understanding.* New York: Academic Press, 1980.

Selman, R. L., & Byrne, D. F. A structural-developmental analysis of levels of role taking in middle childhood. *Child Development,* 1974, *45,* 803–806.

Senn, M. J. E. Insights on the child development movement in the United States. *Monographs of the Society for Research in Child Development,* 1975, *40* (3–4, Serial No. 161).

Shantz, C. U. The development of social cognition. In E. M. Hetherington (Ed.), *Review of child development research* (Vol. 5). Chicago: University of Chicago Press, 1975.

Shapira, A., & Madsen, M. C. Between- and within-group cooperation and competition among kibbutz and nonkibbutz children. *Developmental Psychology,* 1974, *10,* 140–145.

Shatz, M., & Gelman, R. The development of communication skills: Modification in the speech of young children as a function of listener. *Monographs of the Society for Research in Child Development,* 1973, *38* (5, Serial No. 152).

Shepp, B. From perceived similarity to dimensional structure: A new hypothesis about perceptual development. In E. Rosch & B. B. Lloyd (Eds.), *Cognition and categorization.* Hillsdale, N.J.: Erlbaum, 1978.

Sherif, C. W. Social values, attitudes, and the involvement of the self. In M. M. Page (Ed.), *Nebraska Symposium on Motivation* (Vol. 27). Lincoln: University of Nebraska Press, 1980.

Sherif, M., & Sherif, C. W. *An outline of social psychology.* New York: Harper, 1956.

Sherman, J. Problem of sex differences in space perception and aspects of intellectual functioning. *Psychological Review,* 1967, *74,* 290–299.

Shinn, M. Father absence and children's cognitive development. *Psychological Bulletin,* 1978, *85,* 295–324.

Shipley, E. F., Smith, C. S., & Gleitman, L. R. A study in the acquisition of language. *Language,* 1969, *45,* 322–342.

Shirley, M. M. *The first two years: Postural and locomotor development.* Minneapolis: University of Minnesota Press, 1931.

Shorter, E. *The making of the modern family.* New York: Basic Books, 1976.

Shultz, T. R., & Horibe, F. Development of the appreciation of verbal jokes. *Developmental Psychology,* 1974, *10,* 13–20.

Shultz, T. R., & Zigler, E. Emotional concomitants of visual mastery in infants: The effects of stimulus movement on smiling and vocalizing. *Journal of Experimental Child Psychology,* 1970, *10,* 390–402.

Shure, M. B., & Spivack, G. *Problem solving techniques in childrearing.* San Francisco: Jossey-Bass, 1978.

Siegel, A. W., Kirasic, K. C., & Kail, R. V., Jr. Stalking the elusive cognitive map. In I. Altman & J. F. Wohlwill (Eds.), *Children and the environment.* New York: Plenum, 1978.

Siegler, R. S. *Children's thinking: What develops?* Hillsdale, N.J.: Erlbaum, 1978. (a)

Siegler, R. S. The origins of scientific reasoning. In R. S. Siegler (Ed.), *Children's thinking: What develops?* Hillsdale, N.J.: Erlbaum, 1978. (b)

Siegler, R. S., & Liebert, R. M. Acquisition of formal scientific reasoning by 10- and 13-year-olds: Designing a factorial experiment. *Developmental Psychology,* 1975, *11,* 401–402.

Siegler, R. S., Liebert, D. E., & Liebert, R. M. Inhelder's and Piaget's pendulum problem: Teaching preadolescents to act as scientists. *Developmental Psychology,* 1973, *9,* 97–101.

Silberman, C. E. *Crisis in the classroom: The remaking of American education.* New York: Random House, 1970.

Simner, M. L. Newborn's response to the cry of another infant. *Developmental Psychology,* 1971, *5,* 136–150.

Simon, H. A. An information processing theory of intellectual development. In W. Kessen & C. Kuhlman (Eds.), *Thought in the young child. Monographs of the Society for Research in Child Development,* 1962, *27* (2, Serial No. 83).

Simon, H. A. Motivational and emotional controls of

cognition. *Psychological Review*, 1967, *74*, 29–39.

Simpson, G. G. *The meaning of evolution*. New Haven, Conn.: Yale University Press, 1949.

Singer, D. G., Zuckerman, D. M., & Singer, J. L. How elementary school children learn about TV. *Journal of Communication*, 1980, *30*, 84–93.

Skinner, B. F. *Science and human behavior*. New York: Macmillan, 1953.

Skinner, B. F. The science of learning and the art of teaching. *Harvard Educational Review*, 1954, *24*, 86–97.

Skinner, B. F. *Verbal behavior*. New York: Appleton-Century-Crofts, 1957.

Skinner, B. F. *Cumulative record*. New York: Appleton-Century-Crofts, 1958.

Skolnick, A. *The intimate environment*. Boston: Little, Brown, 1973.

Slater, P. J. B. The relevance of ethology. In J. Sants (Ed.), *Developmental psychology and society*. New York: St. Martin's Press, 1980.

Sluckin, W. *Imprinting and early learning* (2nd ed.). Chicago: Aldine, 1973.

Smith, M. E. An investigation of the development of the sentence and the extent of vocabulary development in young children. *University of Iowa Studies in Child Welfare*, 1926, *3* (No. 5).

Smith, R. P. *"Where did you go?" "Out." "What did you do?" "Nothing."* New York: Norton, 1957.

Snow, C., DeBlauw, A., & Van Roosmalen, G. Talking and playing with babies: The role of ideologies of childrearing. In M. Bullowa (Ed.), *Before speech: The beginning of interpersonal communication*. Cambridge, England: Cambridge University Press, 1979.

Society for Research in Child Development. Ethical standards for research with children. *SRCD Newsletter*, Winter 1973, pp. 3–4.

Sokolov, Y. N. *Perception and the conditioned reflex*. New York: Pergamon Press, 1963.

Spiro, M. E. *Children of the kibbutz*. Cambridge, Mass.: Harvard University Press, 1958.

Spivack, G., & Shure, M. B. *Social adjustment of young children*. San Francisco: Jossey-Bass, 1974.

Sroufe, L. A. Drug treatment of children with behavior problems. In F. D. Horowitz (Ed.), *Review of child development research* (Vol. 4). Chicago: University of Chicago Press, 1975.

Sroufe, L. A. The ontogenesis of emotion. In J. Osofsky (Ed.), *Handbook of infancy*. New York: Wiley, 1979.

Sroufe, L. A., & Waters, E. The ontogenesis of smiling and laughing: A perspective on the organization of development in infancy. *Psychological Review*, 1976, *83*, 173–189.

Sroufe, L. A., Waters, E., & Matas, L. Contextual determinants of infant affective response. In M. Lewis & L. Rosenblum (Eds.), *The origins of behavior* (Vol. 2). *Fear*. New York: Wiley, 1974.

Sroufe, L. A., & Wunsch, J. P. The development of laughter in the first year of life. *Child Development*, 1972, *43*, 1326–1344.

Stein, A. H., & Friedrich, L. K. Impact of television on children and youth. In E. M. Hetherington (Ed.), *Review of child development research* (Vol. 5). Chicago: University of Chicago Press, 1975.

Steiner, J. F. Human facial expressions in response to taste and smell stimulation. *Advances in Child Behavior and Development*, 1979, *13*, 257–295.

Stern, D. Mother and infant at play: The dyadic interaction involving facial, vocal, and gaze behaviors. In M. Lewis & L. Rosenblum (Eds.), *The effect of the child on its caregiver*. New York: Wiley, 1974.

Stern, D. *The first relationship: Infant and mother*. Cambridge, Mass.: Harvard University Press, 1977.

Stevenson, H. W. *Children's learning*. New York: Appleton-Century-Crofts, 1972.

Stevenson, H. W., Lee, S., & Stigler, J. The reemergence of child development in the People's Republic of China. *Newsletter of the Society for Research in Child Development*, Summer 1981, pp. 1–5.

Stoltz, L. M. *Influences on parent behavior*. Stanford, Calif.: Stanford University Press, 1967.

Stone, I. *The origin*. New York: Doubleday, 1980.

Storey, K. S. Effects of the television series "Feeling Free" on children's attitudes toward handicapped people. Paper presented at the Meeting of the Society for Research in Child Development, Boston, April 1981.

Strauss, M. S. The abstraction of prototypical information by adults and 10-month-old infants. *Journal of Experimental Psychology—Human Learning and Memory*, 1979, *5*, 618–635.

Sullivan, H. S. *The interpersonal theory of psychiatry*. New York: Norton, 1953.

Sutton-Smith, B., & Rosenberg, B. G. *The sibling*. New York: Holt, Rinehart & Winston, 1970.

Sweet, J., & Resick, P. A. The maltreatment of children: A review of theories and research. *Journal of Social Issues*, 1979, *35*, 40–59.

Taine, H. Acquisition of language by children. *Mind*, 1877, *2*, 252–259.

Talbot, N. B. (Ed.). *Raising children in modern America: Problems and prospective solutions*. Boston: Little, Brown, 1976.

Talmon, Y. *Family and community in the kibbutz*. Cambridge, Mass.: Harvard University Press, 1972.

Tangri, S. S. Determinants of occupational role innovation among college women. *Journal of Social Issues*, 1972, *28*, 177–199.

Tanner, J. M. Physical growth. In P. H. Mussen (Ed.), *Carmichael's manual of child psychology* (3rd ed.). New York: Wiley, 1970.

Tarpy, R. *Principles of animal learning and motivation*. Glenview, Ill.: Scott Foresman, 1982.

Terman, L. M., & Tyler, L. E. Psychological sex differences. In L. Carmichael (Ed.), *Manual of child psychology* (2nd ed.). New York: Wiley, 1954.

Thelen, E. Rhythmical behavior in infants: An ethological perspective. *Developmental Psychology,* 1981, *17,* 237–257.

Thelen, M. H., Fry, R. A., Fehrenbach, P. A., & Frautschi, N. M. Therapeutic videotape and film modeling: A review. *Psychological Bulletin,* 1979, *86,* 701–720.

Thomas, A., & Chess, S. *Temperament and development.* New York: Brunner/Mazel, 1977.

Thomas, A., Chess, S., & Birch, H. G. *Temperament and behavior disorders in children.* New York: New York University Press, 1968.

Thomlinson, R. *Population dynamics.* New York: Random House, 1976.

Thompson, T., & Grabowski, J. (Eds.). *Behavior modification of the mentally retarded.* New York: Oxford University Press, 1977.

Thorndike, E. L. Animal intelligence: An experimental study of the associative processes in animals. *Psychological Review Monograph Supplements,* 1898, *2* (No. 8).

Thorpe, W. E. *Bird-song.* Cambridge, England: Cambridge University Press, 1961.

Tinbergen, N. *The study of instinct.* London: Oxford University Press, 1951.

Toffler, A. *Future shock.* New York: Bantam, 1971.

Tomikawa, S. A., & Dodd, D. H. Early word meanings: Perceptually or functionally based? *Child Development,* 1980, *51,* 1103–1109.

Tooley, W. Neonatology. Paper presented at the Meeting of the Society for Research in Child Development, Boston, April 1981.

Travers, R. M. W. *Essentials of learning* (4th ed.). New York: Macmillan, 1977.

Trevarthen, C. Descriptive analysis of infant communicative behavior. In H. R. Schaffer (Ed.), *Studies in mother-infant interaction.* New York: Academic Press, 1977.

Trevarthen, C. Neurological development and the growth of psychological functions. In J. Sants (Ed.), *Developmental psychology and society.* New York: St. Martin's Press, 1980.

Triandis, H. C. Values, attitudes, and interpersonal behavior. In M. M. Page (Ed.), *Nebraska Symposium on Motivation* (Vol. 27). Lincoln: University of Nebraska Press, 1980.

Tuchman, B. *A distant mirror.* New York: Knopf, 1978.

Tuddenham, R. D., Brooks, J., & Milkovich, L. Mother's reports of behavior of ten-year-olds: Relations with sex, ethnicity, and mother's education. *Developmental Psychology,* 1974, *10,* 959–995.

Turiel, E. Developmental processes in the child's moral thinking. In P. H. Mussen, J. Langer, & M. Covington (Eds.), *Trends and issues in developmental psychology.* New York: Holt, Rinehart &

Winston, 1969.

Tyler, L. E. The intelligence we test—An evolving concept. In L. B. Resnick (Ed.), *The nature of intelligence.* Hillsdale, N.J.: Erlbaum, 1976.

Urbain, E. S., & Kendall, P. C. Review of social-cognitive problem-solving interventions with children. *Psychological Bulletin,* 1980, *88,* 109–143.

Uzgiris, I. C., & Hunt, J. McV. *Assessment in infancy.* Urbana: University of Illinois Press, 1975.

Vandell, D. L., Wilson, K. S., & Buchanan, N. R. Peer interaction in the first year of life: An examination of its structure, content, and sensitivity to toys. *Child Development,* 1980, *51,* 481–488.

Van Dusen, R. A., & Sheldon, E. B. The changing status of American women: A life cycle perspective. *American Psychologist,* 1976, *31,* 106–116.

von Feilitzen, C. The functions served by the media: Report on a Swedish study. In R. Brown (Ed.), *Children and television.* Beverly Hills, Calif.: Sage, 1976.

Von Harrison, G. Structured tutoring: Antidote for low achievement. In V. L. Allen (Ed.), *Children as teachers.* New York: Academic Press, 1976.

Waber, D. P. Sex differences in cognition: A function of maturation rate. *Science,* 1976, *192,* 572–574.

Waddington, C. H. *The strategy of the genes.* London: George Allen & Unwin, 1957.

Walk, R. D. Depth perception and experience. In R. D. Walk & H. L. Pick, Jr. (Eds.), *Perception and experience.* New York: Plenum, 1978.

Walk, R. D., & Pick, H. L., Jr. (Eds.). *Perception and experience.* New York: Plenum, 1978.

Walker, L. J. Cognitive and perspective-taking prerequisites for moral development. *Child Development,* 1980, *51,* 131–139.

Walker, L. J., & Richards, B. S. Stimulating transitions in moral reasoning as a function of cognitive development. *Developmental Psychology,* 1979, *15,* 95–103.

Walker, R. N. Body build and behavior in young children: I. Body build and nursery school teachers' ratings. *Monographs of the Society for Research in Child Development,* 1962, *27* (3, Serial No. 84).

Ward, S. Effects of television advertising on children and adolescents. In J. R. Brown (Ed.), *Children and television.* Beverly Hills, Calif.: Sage, 1976.

Ward, S., Wackman, D., & Wartella, E. *How children learn to buy: The development of consumer information-processing skills.* Beverly Hills, Calif.: Sage, 1977.

Washburn, S. L. Tools and human evolution. *Scientific American,* 1960, *203* (3), 3–15.

Waters, E. The reliability and stability of individual differences in infant-mother attachment. *Child Development,* 1978, *49,* 483–494.

Waters, E., Vaughn, B. E., & Egeland, B. R. Individual differences in infant-mother attachment relationships at age one: Antecedents in neonatal behavior in an urban economically disadvantaged sample. *Child Development,* 1980, *51,* 208–216.

Waters, E., Wippman, J., & Sroufe, L. A. Attachment, positive affect, and competence in the peer group: Two studies in construct validation. *Child Development,* 1979, *50,* 821–829.

Watson, J. B. *Psychological care of infant and child.* New York: Norton, 1928.

Watson, J. S. The development and generalization of "contingency awareness" in early infancy. *Merrill-Palmer Quarterly,* 1966, *12,* 123–135.

Watson, M. W., & Fischer, K. W. A developmental sequence of agent use in late infancy. *Child Development,* 1977, *48,* 828–836.

Weikart, D. P. Relationship of curriculum, teaching, and learning in preschool education. In J. C. Stanley (Ed.), *Preschool programs for the disadvantaged.* Baltimore: Johns Hopkins University Press, 1972.

Weikart, D. P., & Lambie, D. Z. Early enrichment in infants. In V. H. Dennenberg (Ed.), *Education of the infant and young child.* New York: Academic Press, 1970.

Weisberg, P. Developmental differences in children's preferences for high- and low-arousing forms of contact stimulation. *Child Development,* 1975, *46,* 975–979.

Weisz, J. R., & Zigler, E. Cognitive development in retarded and nonretarded persons: Piagetian tests of the similar sequence hypothesis. *Psychological Bulletin,* 1979, *86,* 831–851.

Wellman, H. M., & Lempers, J. D. The naturalistic communicative abilities of two-year-olds. *Child Development,* 1977, *48,* 1052–1057.

Wender, P. H. *Minimal brain dysfunction in children.* New York: Wiley, 1971.

Werner, E. E. *Cross-cultural child development.* Monterey, Calif.: Brooks/Cole, 1979.

Werner, E. E., Bierman, J. M., & French, F. E. *The children of Kauai.* Honolulu: University of Hawaii Press, 1971.

Werner, H. *Comparative psychology of mental development.* New York: Science Editions, 1961. (Originally published, 1948.)

Werner, H., & Kaplan, B. *Symbol formation.* New York: Wiley, 1963.

Westoff, C. F., & Rindfuss, R. R. Sex preselection in the United States: Some implications. *Science,* 1974, *184,* 633–636.

White, R. W. Motivation reconsidered: The concept of competence. *Psychological Review,* 1959, *66,* 297–333.

White, R. W. Competence and the psychosexual stages of development. In M. R. Jones (Ed.), *Nebraska Symposium on Motivation* (Vol. 8). Lincoln: University of Nebraska Press, 1960.

White, S. H. Evidence for a hierarchical arrangement of learning processes. In L. P. Lipsitt & C. C. Spiker (Eds.), *Advances in child development and behavior* (Vol. 2). New York: Academic Press, 1965.

White, S. H. The learning theory tradition and child psychology. In P. H. Mussen (Ed.), *Carmichael's manual of child psychology* (3rd ed.). New York: Wiley, 1970.

White, S. H. The active organism in theoretical behaviorism. *Human Development,* 1976, *19,* 99–107.

Whiting, B. B., & Whiting, J. W. M., in collaboration with R. Longabaugh. *Children of six cultures: A psycho-cultural analysis.* Cambridge, Mass.: Harvard University Press, 1975.

Whorf, B. L. *Language, thought, and reality* (J. B. Carroll, Ed.). Cambridge, Mass.: MIT Press and New York: Wiley, 1956.

Willerman, L. Effects of families on intellectual development. *American Psychologist,* 1979, *34,* 923–929.

Williams, R. M. *American society: A sociological interpretation* (3rd ed.). New York: Knopf, 1970.

Wilson, E. O. *Sociobiology: The new synthesis.* Cambridge, Mass.: Harvard University Press, 1975.

Wilson, R. S. Twins: Early mental development. *Science,* 1972, *175,* 914–917.

Wohlwill, J. *The study of behavioral development.* New York: Academic Press, 1973.

Wohlwill, J. Cognitive development in childhood. In O. G. Brim, Jr., & J. Kagan (Eds.), *Constancy and change in human development.* Cambridge, Mass.: Harvard University Press, 1980.

Wolf, T. *Alfred Binet.* Chicago: University of Chicago Press, 1973.

Wolpe, J. *Psychotherapy by reciprocal inhibition.* Stanford, Calif.: Stanford University Press, 1958.

Woodworth, R. S. *Dynamics of behavior.* New York: Holt, 1958.

Woolsey, S. E. Pied Piper politics and the child-care debate. In A. S. Rossi, J. Kagan, & T. K. Hareven (Eds.), *The family.* New York: Norton, 1978.

Wright, H. F. Observational child study. In P. H. Mussen (Ed.), *Handbook of research methods in child development.* New York: Wiley, 1960.

Wrightsman, L. S. *Social psychology in the seventies.* Monterey, Calif.: Brooks/Cole, 1972.

Yang, R. K., Zweig, A. R., Douthitt, T. C., & Federman, E. J. Successive relationships between maternal attitudes during pregnancy, analgesic medication during labor and delivery, and newborn behavior. *Developmental Psychology,* 1976, *12,* 6–14.

Yarrow, L. J. Historical perspectives and future directions in infant development. In J. D. Osofsky (Ed.), *Handbook of infant development.* New York: Wiley, 1979.

Yarrow, M. R., Scott, P. M., & Waxler, C. Z. Learning concern for others. *Developmental Psychology,* 1973, *8,* 240–260.

Yarrow, M. R., & Waxler, C. Z. The emergence and functions of prosocial behaviors in young children. Paper presented at the Meeting of the Society for Research in Child Development, Denver, April 1975.

Yarrow, M. R., & Waxler, C. Z., in collaboration with D. Barrett, J. Darby, R. King, M. Pickett, & J. Smith. Dimensions and correlates of prosocial behavior in young children. *Child Development,* 1976, *47,* 118–125.

Yerkes, R. M., & Dodson, J. D. The relation of strength of stimulus to rapidity of habit formation. *Journal of Comparative Neurology and Psychology,* 1908, *18,* 458–482.

Young, W. C., Goy, R., & Phoenix, C. Hormones and sexual behavior. *Science,* 1964, *143,* 212–218.

Yussen, S. R., & Levy, V. M., Jr. Developmental changes in predicting one's own span of short-term memory. *Journal of Experimental Child Psychology,* 1975, *19,* 502–508.

Zacharias, L., Rand, W. M., & Wurtman, R. J. A prospective study of sexual development and growth in American girls: The statistics of menarche. *Obstetrical and Gynecological Survey,* 1976, *31,* 325–337.

Zaporozhets, A. V. The development of perception in the preschool child. *Monographs of the Society for Research in Child Development,* 1965, *30* (2, Serial No. 100).

Zelazo, P. R. From reflexive to instrumental behavior. In L. P. Lipsitt (Ed.), *Developmental psychobiology: The significance of infancy.* Hillsdale, N.J.: Erlbaum, 1976.

Ziajka, A. *Prelinguistic communication in infancy.* New York: Praeger, 1981.

Zigler, E., & Valentine, J. (Eds.). *Project Head Start: A legacy of the war on poverty.* New York: Free Press, 1979.

Author Index

Subject Index

Photo Credits